The First King of Hollywood

THE LIFE OF

Douglas Fairbanks

TRACEY GOESSEL

CHICAGO
REVIEW
PRESS

An A Cappella Book

Copyright © 2016 by Tracey Goessel
All rights reserved
Published by Chicago Review Press Incorporated
814 North Franklin Street
Chicago, Illinois 60610
ISBN 978-1-61373-404-9

Library of Congress Cataloging-in-Publication Data
Goessel, Tracey.
 The first king of Hollywood : the life of Douglas Fairbanks / Tracey Goessel.
  pages cm
 Summary: "The first truly definitive biography of Douglas Fairbanks, the greatest
leading man of the silent film era"— Provided by publisher.
 Includes bibliographical references and index.
 ISBN 978-1-61373-404-9 (hardback)
 1. Fairbanks, Douglas, 1883–1939. 2. Actors—United States—Biography.
3. Motion picture producer and directors—United States—Biography. I. Title.

PN2287.F3G84 2015
791.4302'8092—dc23
[B]

2015018526

All images are from the author's collection unless otherwise indicated
Interior design: Nord Compo

Printed in the United States of America
5 4 3 2 1

To Mom and Dad,
who bought me that first 8mm projector

Contents

Introduction

WRITERS HAVE STRUGGLED TO capture Douglas Fairbanks in words. To Michael Sragow, he was "Gatsby on a jungle gym." To Edward Wagenknecht he was "the Yankee Doodle Boy whom George M. Cohan had put on the stage when the eagle screamed more light-heartedly than he does today." To those of his generation, he was simply "Doug." This seemed to suffice.

To most people today, however, Douglas Fairbanks is not even a forgotten man—he was never known in the first place. Almost all who were alive when he was in his heyday are gone. Even among the cinephiles he is a neglected figure; Turner Classic Movies has never made him Star of the Month, or even of the Day. Although he preserved every film and turned multiple negatives over to the Museum of Modern Art before his death, a disgraceful number were allowed to deteriorate to powder. Yet he was the most popular male star of the silent era, recognized the world over. In 1924, a peasant in remote China or Soviet Russia might not have known of Abraham Lincoln, but he knew Douglas Fairbanks. His films crossed all language barriers. His sunny cheer and astonishing athletic prowess spoke to the virtues of America in an era when America had no self-doubts about possessing any.

But if the man is nearly forgotten today, why study him? He is, after all, only a movie star. Unless a star was a genius (think Chaplin or Keaton) or retains iconic status (Bogart, Wayne) or lived such a tremendous train wreck of a life as to be a juicy cautionary tale (insert your choice here), there seems to be little point.

But Fairbanks merits attention. He would have been the first to agree that he was no genius (although the skill and wit with which he handled the instrument of his body is akin to that of a virtuoso). He was an icon of his time, but time and memories fade. And for most of his life, he handled himself very intelligently. No train wrecks here.

He deserves our attention because although we do not recognize it, he is still here. When we settle in once a year to watch the Oscars, it is because he cofounded the Academy of Motion Picture Arts and Sciences. When we see the latest release from United Artists, it is because he formed the distribution company that gave independent producers a venue to sell their works. If we enjoy *The Wizard of Oz* or *Gone with the Wind*, we likely don't realize that the man who directed those films got his first chance as a director from Douglas Fairbanks. When we drink in the glories of Technicolor, we do so because his intervention saved the company. When we think of Beverly Hills as the place for the rich and famous, it is because he bought and remodeled a hunting lodge and moved into it when the area was nothing more than scrubby hills. When celebrities navigate the depths and shoals of fame with grace, it is because he and his equally famous wife established the pattern. When we try to get tan in the summertime, it is because he made being dark fashionable in an era when paleness was a virtue. When we see Superman put his knuckles on his hips and assume the hero's stance, it is because the young artist who first drew him based the character's bearing on that of *his* hero: Douglas Fairbanks. When Batman goes to the Bat Cave, it is because the creator of the comic strip drew his inspiration from Fairbanks's *The Mark of Zorro*. When we see Mickey Mouse (particularly in the early years), it is because his creator wanted a mix of Douglas Fairbanks and Doug's best friend, Charlie Chaplin. Walt Disney even stipulated that he wanted Prince Charming in *Snow White* to be modeled after Fairbanks, although it is hard to argue that his animators got very close. Prince Charming was bland. But there was nothing bland about Douglas Fairbanks. He made all the leading men of his era look sick.

He was the top male star of his generation for a reason. He was a lot of fun. He was engaging, creative, visually witty, and a force to be reckoned with. He shaped our idea of the hero to fit his own loopy mold, and it has never been the same since. He married the most famous woman of his generation, herself a powerhouse of formidable dimensions. Together they were called the King and Queen of Hollywood. This was hyperbole, of course, but only just. When his untimely death came, real kings and queens sent their condolences.

His story is also the story of the birth of an industry—the transition of the movie business from a nickel novelty to a worldwide phenomenon. He was not merely an actor in this scene; he was a producer, a distributor, a theater owner. His influence was prodigious.

And he did these things as the product of a bigamous marriage who was raised in a household deserted by its breadwinner when he was a mere five years old. He never finished high school. But he was the winner of the genetic lottery, having a healthy body that would respond to rigorous training; a handsome, amiable face; an intelligent determination; and an affable, good-humored, resilient nature. On top of it all, he had perhaps the most disarming smile in history.

1

The Father of the Man

I T IS A TALE TOLD in every history of Douglas Fairbanks, the all-purpose story to encapsulate the essence of the man in the activities of the child.

The setting was a middle-class section of Denver in the mid-1880s, the midst of the Gilded Age. A sturdy, nut-brown boy of three (some place the event on his birthday) had once again climbed onto the roof of an outbuilding on his parents' property. Up until now, his cheerful, *look-at-me* flips and graceful leaps had always served to extricate him from great heights. But this time, something went wrong. He fell.

He cut a gash that extended full across the left side of his forehead—an imposing, semi-lunar flap that would be visible in close-ups for the rest of his days. The human scalp is well vascularized, and children's heads are disproportionately large; the bleeding must have been impressive. The family version of the story included a brief loss of consciousness—with a twist. The boy, they claimed, had always been taciturn and unsmiling. But upon coming to, and being told what had happened ("You fell off the roof, darling!"), he did the unexpected. He laughed, joyously. He had fallen off the roof! How delightful!

It seemed to capture the nature of the man the world would come to know—or at least the construct he was to present: the dashing cavalier, enduring risks and injuries while performing his dazzling stunts, laughing at fate. "A smile at the right time has won many a battle in the prize ring and in the warfare of life," he once said. The anecdote is irresistible.

The reality, as recalled by the leaper in question almost forty years later, was a little more realistic. "I was three years old," he wrote:

> In company with my brother Robert, I was climbing along the edge of a roof that projected from a dug-out which was used as a sort of barn at our home in Colorado. Disaster overtook me and I fell from the dizzy height of possibly seven feet.
>
> I recall now the shrill cries of my nurse and the warm glow of satisfaction that mingled with my pain when I found myself the central figure of a thrilling drama. I think that occasion decided my future, for as soon as it became apparent that the eyes of the world, so to speak, were upon me for the moment, I began to act.
>
> Although I had a considerable gash on my forehead, the injury was not nearly so serious as it looked. Realizing, however, that this was my great moment, I set up a howl that kept me the center of attraction for quite a while. . . . I managed to put on such a dramatic performance that I all but sent my mother into hysterics.

This rings truer to human behavior. Children hit their heads; they cry.

But we want to see Douglas Fairbanks as he presented himself, or packaged himself, really: the man who, whatever tempests life (and a host of pesky villains) would throw at him, would come up smiling.

But the reality rarely matches the myth. The awful truth remains: while he often would arise, teeth and eyes glittering, showing a defiant smile and laugh to the world and its villains, there were other times when he simply cried. But even then—and this is characteristic of the man—he found a certain satisfaction in being the center of a great drama.

This same mythmaking challenges the examination of his family story. So shaded and decked in self-imposed myth are his forebears that we cannot even unearth some of them. But his paternal grandfather's story can be found. Lazarus Ulman was approximately twenty-five years old when he arrived through the port of Philadelphia in 1820 from

Baden, Germany. Little is known of him except that he was registered as a servant and was Jewish. He must have been a man of extraordinary initiative, intelligence, and luck. A mere ten years later he was the owner of 560 acres of land north of Harrisburg, Pennsylvania, and the head of a household that included wife Lydia, children, and servants. His occupation was listed variably on the national census as "merchant" and "butcher." The former seems more likely. Family history describes him as a major mill owner in the central part of Pennsylvania. The fourth of his nine children, Hezekiah Charles, was born in Berrysburg on September 15, 1833.

Williamsport, to the north, offered better schools, to Lazarus's mind, so he moved the family there. His oldest child, Joseph, became a merchant like his father. Edwin, older than Hezekiah Charles by two years, became a dentist. H. Charles, as the younger brother preferred to be called, began at fifteen as a clerk in his father's business, progressing at seventeen—at least according to his family—to a two-year stint founding and running a small publishing business in Philadelphia.* After this, he studied law in New York City under one James T. Brady.† Four years later, in 1856, he was admitted to the Pennsylvania bar. By 1860, H. Charles was approaching twenty-seven, living in Lycoming County, Pennsylvania, and married to twenty-one-year-old Lizzie. He was the father of two daughters, one-year-old Kate and newborn Alice. The household even had a servant. Lizzie was Christian, and H. Charles now was as well, having been baptized the same day he was married. But his five years of peaceful—and evidently lucrative—law practice were interrupted by the Civil War.

Demonstrating the sort of leadership that would later characterize his youngest son, H. Charles organized Company A of the Fifth Regiment of

---

* This may be apocryphal; he is not listed in Philadelphia City directories for these years.

† It has been written elsewhere that he went to law school. He did not. He "read law" under an attorney and took the written bar examination, a very common practice at the time. His youngest son, Douglas, would briefly attempt the same thing in the early 1900s but would only last a few weeks.

Pennsylvania Reserves and marched them 108 miles to Harrisburg, arriving in early May 1861. By the end of June he had been commissioned
as a captain, and within a matter of weeks the company was involved
in the occupation of Piedmont, Maryland. They were attached to the
Army of the Potomac in March 1862 and saw action at Manassas, the
Battle of Mechanicsville, and Bull Run. Had he not been mustered out
in December 1862 for a service-related injury, Ulman would have been
in the Battle of Gettysburg. This, of course, is presuming he would have
survived to see it; before the unit was disbanded, it had lost 14 officers
and 127 enlisted men to war wounds, and another 68 to disease. Disease
killed more than soldiers; he and his wife buried their nine-month-old
son, Jonathan, in March 1863.

But postwar H. Charles's fortunes improved, and by 1870 he was
living with his wife and two daughters in Middleton, an affluent community in the New York borough of Richmond, now known as Staten
Island. His estate was valued at $20,000—a highly respectable sum at
that time. The household was up to three servants now, and an 1873
passport application states that he was traveling to England for reasons
of health "and to join my family there." The document attests that he
was five feet seven and a half inches tall, with black hair and dark eyes.
Contemporary photographs suggest a figure of Byronic romanticism:
long, flowing locks of hair; steely eyes with an intelligent gaze over a
Roman nose; and—in later pictures—a hint of the double chin that
his son would sport for all his days. His leadership abilities were still
in play, and by 1876, he was the first president of the American Law
Association, the precursor to the American Bar Association.

Ulman's trajectory appeared to be headed in a comfortably upward
direction. No one could have reasonably predicted that within four
years he would have abandoned his family, his home, and his law firm
and be bigamously married to a beautiful young widow fifteen years his
junior. Her name was Ella Adelaide Marsh Fairbanks Wilcox (no small
story there), and she was very, very unlucky in love.

Of all the figures in Douglas Fairbanks's life, his mother is the hardest to pin down. She was probably born April 15, 1846, but she had

a feminine tendency to move the year forward with each subsequent census—and each marriage. Information concerning her parentage is vague. She claimed to have been born and raised in the South, but Douglas Fairbanks Jr. declared that she was born outside of New York City. Neither her mother nor father can be tracked down with any certainty. Family histories are silent on the subject, although all agree that she had a younger sister, Belle. Ella's story only comes into focus with her first marriage, to John Fairbanks III on May 6, 1867, in New York City. He reportedly was the holder of not-inconsiderable property in New Orleans, where they moved after their marriage and where their only child, John, was born in 1873. They lived at 494 Jackson Avenue, a block from the Mississippi River.

Their fortunes declined precipitously, however, when a partner cheated the elder John out of his portion of the business. Worse, he contracted tuberculosis. Appeals for help were made to Fairbanks's New York attorney, who happened to be H. Charles Ulman. He was evidently unable to do much. John Fairbanks's health declined along with his fortune.

Sister Belle, meanwhile, had married one Edward Rowe of the mercantile trade, and in 1871 the Rowes joined the wave of northern carpetbaggers and moved to Macon, Georgia. Thus, when in 1874 Ella decided she needed family support, she elected to take her ailing husband and their infant son to Macon, to join her sister. The locals, almost sixty years later, still remembered the pair as striking. "The most distinguished looking man I have ever seen," recalled one. "And a woman, petite, dainty . . . exceedingly." The kind attentions of the local church ladies were unable to save the day, however. Not only did Ella's husband die within a few months, but also Edward Rowe would end up dead that same year.*

The two widowed sisters were now alone with their children, John ("a beautiful blond boy") and his cousin Adelaide. But Ella was not to be alone for long. Enter thirty-four-year-old Edward Wilcox.

---

* Fairbanks evidently returned to New Orleans for his final days, as records indicate he died there on May 21, 1874.

Little is known of Edward A. Wilcox of Macon, Georgia, other than a local's recollection that he was a "fascinating personality, a successful man, and rather a dandy in dress." Some claim he was a judge, but evidence suggests he was a cotton broker with an estate valued in 1870 at $7,000. He was not a native Georgian, having been born in South Carolina. But one thing is certain: he was a fast mover. He and Ella exchanged vows in Bibb, Georgia, on January 4, 1875, less than eight months after John Fairbanks's death. If she married in haste, she had evident cause to repent at leisure. Mr. Wilcox, according to family whispers, drank. And when he drank, he "was probably abusive."

Ella gave birth to a son, Norris, on February 20, 1876. According to her family, it was shortly after the birth that she contacted the only attorney she knew: H. Charles Ulman. She was desperate to get a divorce—so desperate to get away that she willingly turned the newborn over to Wilcox's sister, Lottie Barker, and took little John to New York City. Norrie, as the baby was called, was supposed to be fetched by his mother once her situation stabilized. That day never came. In 1879 she was living with six-year-old John at 203 West Fifty-Second Street in Manhattan. The following year's census documents four-year-old Norrie still living with Lottie in the Georgia home of her cousin, Julia Jones. The intervening century (and the fire that destroyed most of the 1890 census) leaves the rest of Norris's youth a mystery, but it is of note that he eventually made it to Denver and forged some relationship with his jigsaw puzzle of a family.*

---

* By 1900 he was a twenty-four-year-old chemist (a term that translated to "pharmacist" in that era) who lived with his wife in Denver. Ten years later he was in the same occupation, but by 1918, he was an office manager at the New York offices of Famous Players–Lasky, the production company to which his half-brother Douglas was signed at the time. Clearly, the job had been provided at Douglas's behest; Norris went on to work for him at United Artists, living in Buenos Aires during much of the 1920s and overseeing the release of UA product in South America. Norris appears to have worked tirelessly and well for his half-brother (as did half-brother John and full brother Robert) but remained entirely off the public radar. Douglas was to leave a significant bequest to Norris of one-fortieth of his estate; full brother Robert was willed a two-fortieths share.

But before young Norris Wilcox could arrive in Denver to reunite with his mother, Ella herself had to get there, and her route was by way of her divorce attorney. Clearly, impulsiveness was one of her characteristics; having extricated herself from one bad marriage* she entered another. Most surviving photographs of Ella were taken later in her life, when she was as redoubtable a figure as Mary Pickford's Mama Charlotte, her counterpart in the stage-mother universe: stout, heavy browed, formidable. But a picture taken in her youth reveals a woman who was quite lovely, by the standards of both her era and today's. Her skin was flawless, her eyes wide spaced and clear, her mouth full, her nose classically perfect, her gaze direct. It is not hard to imagine that she would attract three spouses in her life and sire a matinee idol. Ulman, evidently, was besotted. In 1880 he abandoned his family and home and set up housekeeping with Ella and little John in Orangetown, New York. There was a slight hitch in the proceedings: there is no evidence Ulman obtained a divorce from his first wife.

After selling his interest in his Broadway-based law firm (Ulman & Remington), he decided to pull up stakes and move to Colorado. There was money to be made in the silver rush, certainly. But the fact that Ella was now pregnant, and that he was not in a position to divorce and remarry before this inconvenient fact would become evident to local society, might have contributed to the decision. It would be near impossible to take on a new wife in the state where he was already married. But the distant West? Anything was possible there. They would go to Denver.

They had no way of knowing, of course, but they could not have chosen a better town from which to launch Douglas Fairbanks. Denver in the 1880s possessed that mix of characteristics that its most famous citizen came to personify: a blend of the wild and the civilized. It was a town that still harbored old pioneers and wide-open spaces, a place where a boy could learn to rope and ride, to explore abandoned mines and to camp under the proverbial blanket of stars. But it was also a

---

* This is a presumption. Divorce records are not available.

town of mansions, of Molly Brown (later the "Unsinkable" of *Titanic* fame) and Horace Tabor, who built the city's opera house. It was a city with social pretensions. Their famous son was to carry with him these opposing characteristics, that of the city and that of the wilderness. This charming polarity was a significant contributor to his success in the following century.

Ella likely had no knowledge that her husband was still married when she exchanged her vows with him on September 7, 1881, in Boulder, Colorado. But then again, perhaps she suspected that something was wrong—they exchanged vows twice. Marriage records show that they were also married three weeks earlier, on August 14, 1881, in Nebraska. Robert was born in March 1882; Douglas Elton Thomas Ulman followed in 1883 on May 23.

The earliest claim about Douglas Fairbanks is that as an infant he was very dark skinned. The assertion came from one source: Fairbanks himself. "I was the blackest baby you ever saw," he told family members. "I was so dark even my mother was ashamed of me. When all the neighbors came around to look at the new baby, mother would say 'Oh, I don't want to disturb him now—he's asleep and I'd rather not.' She just hated to show such a dark baby."

This is, of course, stuff and nonsense. Not only did his mother and aunt vehemently deny this story (he delighted in teasing them with this tale), but also photographs reveal that there was no truth to the claim. Ella Ulman may have had to suffer straitened circumstances throughout her third marriage, but she never stinted on having her boys professionally photographed. Baby pictures—multiple baby pictures—exist of infant Douglas, documenting a round little head, a killer stare, and perfectly pale baby skin. He had the ability in adulthood to acquire a stunning coat of tan—to the point of appearing shellacked. But there was no evidence of this when he was an infant.

Still, it is possible that there was a grain of truth in his story. Infants are inefficient at breaking down bilirubin and can acquire a yellowish skin tone for the first few weeks of life ("yellow jaundice of the newborn"). In severe cases, the children can appear a darker, almost orange color. It is certainly possible that Ella might have had a certain level of embarrassment over a baby that, for a few weeks at least, resembled a ripe squash.

Why he made his claim has been grist for armchair psychologists ever since. It is one of the many challenges of undertaking the subject. Fairbanks would knead, stretch, and compress his story until it was crammed into the mold that he desired. "Almost anyone who begins to take up his past in a serious way, becomes, it seems, an inveterate liar," he acknowledged. "Or, to use more polite language, he becomes not a historian but a mythologist. . . . It is very much like asking a man to name his ten favorite books and expecting him to tell the truth." Fairbanks had an engaging tendency to understate his youthful accomplishments. But he had a corresponding habit of polishing the tales of his earliest years until they acquired a sheen of respectability that had never been there in the first place.

Case in point: his version of his childhood included a proper household with a mother and father. The father was never, ever identified as the Jewish H. Charles Ulman. No, *his* father was John Fairbanks—a lie he clung to until his death.* But he gave "Father" Fairbanks many of the traits that characterized his biological father: he was a lawyer, he claimed, and a great student of Shakespeare. Further, Dad had many, many friends in the theatrical line—fine, great names such as Edwin Booth and Frederick Warde. These men would come to the house whenever they were in town, Fairbanks asserted, and the young acolyte absorbed the words of the Bard by listening to their long parlor conversations. Ella had no problem propagating the family line. "Mr. Fairbanks was a splendid Shakespearean scholar, an intimate friend of Booth . . . and would have gone on the stage himself but for family objections," she declared in 1916, presumably with a straight face.

Mother, he claimed, had been a southern belle—sometimes from Virginia, sometimes from New Orleans. His home life was stable, of course. They lived at 61 South Fourteenth Street, he averred, but

---

* John Fairbanks was listed as his father on his 1939 death certificate.

Denver had grown, streets were renamed, and by the time he was famous, the address had changed to 1207 Bannock Street. Fan magazines were provided photographs of a two-story brick building with a sloped shingle roof and a gingerbread front porch on a leafy, tree-lined street. He had a nurse, certainly. Other servants were implied but never specified.

To be fair, there were authentic elements of respectability in his youth. They were, for example, a churchgoing family. The boys were baptized together in the Catholic Church; infant Douglas was a little over four months old and Robert was nineteen months. The external veneer was maintained; their loving mother routinely dressed them to the nines: dapper matching tam-o'-shanters, skirted woolen coats, flowing neck scarves, and high button shoes. They outdid Little Lord Fauntleroy, as young Patrick McGovern was to discover on the first day of classes at the Corona Grade School. Doug was inordinately proud of his modish and elegant dress—a weakness that was to remain with him for all his days—and could not abide the fact that Patrick's mother not only dressed him in the black velvet Fauntleroy suit with white lace collar but further adorned his head with the requisite Fauntleroy ringlets. A class photograph revealed little Patrick to be not so little at all, half a head taller than Douglas and brother Robert, and looking like he weighed more than the two of them put together. But this did not stop an indignantly jealous Doug from tugging at his curls, and earning a solid pop in the nose as payment. The photograph suggests that the battle was an ongoing one; McGovern sits between the two Ulman brothers, scowling miserably. Robert is leaning back, his head at an angle, the beginnings of a cocky grin on his face. Little Douglas is staring ahead fixedly.

Douglas and Robert were "even then as close as peas," according to Robert's daughter Letitia. "He was so taciturn that he rarely spoke to anyone. . . . Only with Robert would he bubble away and seem at ease. With anyone else he shut up like a tight little box." His father speculated that Douglas would likely grow up to be a judge, as "he had never known one yet to be born with a glimmer of humor."

Douglas may have shown little humor in his earliest years, but this stolid front was soon replaced by a well-developed sense of mischief. The principal of the Wyman School, one of many he attended as the family moved throughout the city, "had to walk home with Douglas nearly every night to carry a tale of wickedness to his mother," stated Letitia. While he was to claim his entire life that his interest in Shakespeare stemmed from the visits of his father's famous actor friends, his niece's version of events was more probable: teachers made him memorize Shakespeare passages as penance for his misdeeds. This punishment must have been administered often: "By the time he was nine, he was undoubtedly the youngest and peppiest Hamlet on record." Critic Burns Mantle, who lived nearby when young Fairbanks was a mere teenager, famously stated that he "would recite you as fine and florid an Antony's speech to the Romans as you ever heard. With gestures, too." Fairbanks was candid about his academic performance. "Schooling as such didn't appeal to me a bit," he admitted. "I wouldn't stop fooling."

His mischief was not confined to the classroom. Summers were spent—until H. Charles's desertion—out of the city, in various mining camps, the most remote (and primitive) of which was in Jamestown, forty-five miles northwest of Denver. "They were my first glimpses of the wild country that I love," he remembered. "We'd often spend two or three weeks at a camp; those were high times for me." One particularly beloved fixture of the camp was an old prospector nicknamed "Hardrock," who was particularly fond of children. He once damned up a local creek to create a pool for the brothers to swim in. Unfortunately, a local matron caught the boys splashing about in their birthday suits and gave Hardrock a piece of her mind for aiding and abetting such unholy activities on the Sabbath.

And here the troubles began. Hardrock, unthinking, commented, "That old biddy acts as if she had a heap of gold in her privy." Young Douglas took him at his word. Mrs. Jessup was hiding *gold!* In her *outhouse!* He and Robert initiated a stakeout in the latrine in question to await the good lady's arrival.

What followed was a scatological comic opera, complete with a half-undressed matron, lots of shrieking, and a thrashing that was stopped only when Hardrock brought his mule whip down on Mrs. Jessup's shoulders. The matron screamed in outrage; Ella, arriving late on the scene, fainted. Young Douglas possibly tucked the incident away for *Don Q, Son of Zorro* thirty-five years later. The boys' father, who had to discipline them for their misdeeds, might have welcomed the brouhaha as a distraction. He had learned just that morning that his last silver mine was worthless. Shortly thereafter, he left his second family as he had his first, ostensibly to become a hired speaker for the presidential candidacy of Benjamin Harrison. When Harrison was elected in November 1888, Ulman did not return. Letters and checks stopped arriving. Robert was six; Douglas was five.

The path of H. Charles Ulman after he deserted Ella and her sons was erratic. While the family claimed that he returned to Colorado on business only once in the subsequent years, the 1890 census documents that he was living in Denver as a lodger. Perhaps they were trying to spare the feelings of his youngest son. One morning, when Douglas was twelve years old, he encountered his father on the street. Ulman pulled his son into a nearby hotel bar for a reunion. Doug, evidently delighted to see him, drank sarsaparilla. Ulman drank whiskey. After he had fortified himself with enough liquid courage, he let his son bring him home to see Ella. The reunion, not surprisingly, did not go well. Ulman skulked out, never to darken their proverbial door again.*

Ella's outrage then turned to Douglas. She was not upset that he had brought his father home, but she was livid that he had spent the morning in a *saloon*. The sight of her husband, cuffs and collar frayed, alcohol on his breath while the sun was still high in the sky, inspired her to action. She took her youngest straight to the Woman's Christian

---

* He was to return to New York City by 1905 and live for a while with his now middle-aged daughters. By 1910, however, he had a third wife, forty years his junior, and was living in Brooklyn, suggesting that he was no ordinary bigamist but might actually have had *three* families. He died in 1915, evidently having no further contact with Ella or her children.

Temperance Union and had him sign the pledge of temperance. Surprisingly, it took hold. He was abstemious for most of his life. For the last ten years he might indulge in a mild cocktail but remained very modest in his intake.*

Poor Ella probably could have used a stiff drink now and again. Ulman's departure had put her and her children in a tight squeeze. The family claimed to have lived in only two places in Denver: the house where Fairbanks was born (Bannock Street) and the house that they were required to move to after Ulman departed (Franklin Street). This assertion hid a tale of peripatetic desperation. Even when Ulman was with the family, addresses were changeable things. In 1882 and 1883, the family lived at 333 Tremont Place. The city directory in 1884 places the family at 61 South Fourteenth Street, the house that managed to mysteriously change its address along the way to 1207 Bannock.

It must have been clear early on that Ulman would never return. Ella changed her and her sons' name to Fairbanks in 1889.† After this, the little family moved frequently: 1539 Arapahoe Street in '88 and '89; 634 Pearl Street in '90; 2119 Stout in '91 and '92 (when circumstances forced them to move in with older brother John, who was working as a traveling sales representative for the Morey Mercantile Company); 1333 Stout Street in 1893; then, for two years, the Glenarm Hotel; followed finally in 1896 by 1629 Franklin Street, where they remained for two years.

It is possible that Ella spent the years in the hotel while her sons were away at the Jarvis Hall Military Academy in Montclair. It has been speculated that her sister may have helped her with the tuition, but given Belle's widowed state, it is just as likely that hard-working, quiet older brother John was contributing. John moved out of the house and

---

* This made him virtually the only dry celebrity during the Roaring Twenties, with the possible exception of Baby Peggy and Rin Tin Tin.
† Neither name is listed in the Denver directories in 1885, 1886, or 1887. Not until 1888 does Ella Ulman appear listed, without Charles. All directory entries after 1888 list the name of Fairbanks for Ella and her two youngest sons.

boarded with the nearby grocer when he was a mere nine years old, so toxic were his relations with his step-father. He had worked for the company ever since, sacrificing his own education so his younger brothers could get theirs. It is unlikely that young Douglas understood his half-brother's sacrifice at the time, but he made certain to pay it back in adulthood. But no matter what largesse he tried to give to John and his family—and he shared generously—it could never equal the debt. John continued to provide his weight in gold in advice and management until his untimely death.

It is unlikely that young Douglas was encumbered by a sense of obligation in these early years. His only recollection from his time at Jarvis was that he enjoyed the uniforms. In the same vein, he enjoyed performing his duties as an altar boy, which, per his niece Letitia, he did "with customary—but dramatic—solemnity." Still, when the sacramental wine was spiked with vinegar and—more creative yet—the candles were doctored so that when fellow altar boy Robert tried to light them they fizzed out dramatically, good Father O'Ryan knew just where to look. But he did the unexpected and punished Robert, not Douglas, for the crimes.

This had the intended effect. Douglas could not bear to see Robert take the blame for his misdeeds, and he went to the priest to confess. "I knew you were the culprit," replied the Father. "Your penance, Douglas, is watching your brother absolve your blame." Doug's churchgoing decorum, recalled the family, "was remarkably spiritual from that day on." It was this same wise priest who was later to help Douglas foster his dreams of the stage.

The earliest evidence of this theatrical passion survives as a handwritten program, penned by Douglas himself in 1896. An amateur production was staged in the backyard of one Frank Hall—an all-male cast in *The Man from the Mountain*. D. Fairbanks was fifth billed, as "John Wilson—an old miner." Robert, who later was to find work as an electrician's apprentice, wired the stage with footlights and spotlights. History has not recorded the reception this masterpiece received, but clearly young Mr. Fairbanks felt encouraged to try for something on a larger scale.

He himself was to claim that his first appearance on the professional stage was unknown to his family. Steve Brody was a celebrity working his way through the American theater mill by virtue of his claim of having survived a leap from the Brooklyn Bridge. He toured the country with a play purporting to document this adventure: *On the Bowery.* The thirteen-year-old Fairbanks staked out the dressing room door until he could get an audience with the star. "I braced him and told him I could recite a piece in Italian dialect," he recalled. He got the job and for a week played a newsboy, saying his little speech nightly, just before Brody leaped off the stage bridge. Uncharacteristically, he did not let his family know of his debut until the show had left town.*

In the fall of 1896, he danced both a gavotte and a hornpipe with Miss Mary McCarron at a local production of *Kirmess* "under the direction of one Professor A.B. Mills." January 1897 saw him at the Masonic temple, providing humorous recitations shoehorned between speeches by the Eminent Commander and a soprano solo by a Mrs. Frederick C. Smutzer.

The family album contains a program for an 1898 Children's Matinee staged by the local public schools. Douglas, billed as a student of the Tabor School of Acting, gave a dramatic recitation. And, indeed, by the time he was fifteen, young Fairbanks was an enthusiastic pupil of tutor Margaret Fealy and her young daughter Maude. Margaret had been the leading lady for Sir Henry Irving in London and had appeared with William Gillette on the American stage—impressive credentials. Young Maude was also experiencing professional success. Their school, on the third floor of the Tabor Theater building, was to yield many renowned students. Fairbanks and Margaret Fealy remained close until his death, and financial records document him quietly sending her funds through the Depression. He answered each letter she sent.

Margaret's memories of him were both fond and loving, despite the exasperations of dealing with a teenage boy. Maude recalled a production

---

* Some of the productions that friends and family recalled for him cannot be confirmed. But *On the Bowery* indeed played in Denver for the week of November 2, 1896.

of *Virginius* in which young Douglas played Icilius, who was to give his lover's ashes in an urn to her father.* "Mother had a time getting Douglas to hold the urn up straight," Maude said. She had to remind him repeatedly that it was his lover's ashes he was toting, not a football. Years later she teased Fairbanks: "Don't you remember when your mother used to say, 'Douglas, Maude takes a bath all over every day. Why don't you at least let me wash your neck?'"

On another occasion Margaret found her hyperactive student bounding on a prized leather sofa in her office. "Get off that sofa!" she recalled shrieking. "You good-for-nothing, little black devil!"

This tickled him. "He seemed to like it," she wrote, "as he always joked on it and called himself that." Years later, he would send her a portrait of himself with his infant son and sign it "Yours, Lovingly, your good-for-nothing little black devil."

Young Doug made the society columns as well, entertaining at a private musicale at the home of Miss Maude Hunne. After the "dainty refreshments," the recitations of Master Fairbanks "brought forth much approval from the company, and he kept them in laughter for some time by his dialect recitations."† The *Denver Post* reports his March 1898 participation in an evening of "literary and musical entertainment" at the local YMCA involving "Professor Jones' Mandolin Club." Further, he played the not-insignificant supporting role of Martin that summer in the Tabor Grand School of Acting's production of *The Two Orphans* at Elitch's Gardens.

Elitch's Gardens was the summer setting for Denver theater, and major stars would travel to perform with the stock company there. "I had known him long," mused leading man Hobart Bosworth after Fairbanks's death: "Ever since the days of 1898 when he used to run

---

* There is no evidence of this production in Denver, although Frederick Warde had produced the play there in 1896. But urns of ashes were common in the theater of the day, and Maude may have simply confused productions. The anecdote rings true.

† History does not contemplate Douglas Fairbanks in terms of dance or mimicry, but evidently he was talented at both. His comic dialects stemmed from listening to the peddlers from the back alley of the house on Franklin Street.

to be the first to open the gates at Elitch's Gardens in Denver for me to ride my horse into the grounds."

The summer of 1898 found the fifteen-year-old participating with other members of the Tabor School in the Wolhurst Fete, an open-air fundraiser conducted on the grounds of the estate of Senator E. O. Wolcott. This was a major social event; ten thousand Coloradans arrived on special train cars from the Denver & Rio Grande and Santa Fe Railroads. Booths provided distractions ranging from palm readers to ice cream. There was a menagerie, a sham battle, a staged gypsy camp, a balloon ascension, and Robin Hood and his Merry Men. Bands and orchestras played, and a thousand Japanese lanterns lit the sky when evening came. Wolcott's barn was converted to a theater with Tabor School shows, including, on August 26, *The Happy Pair*, "a comedietta in one act, given by Douglas Fairbanks and Lydia Dixon."*

The show-in-the-barn got some special notice from the *Denver Sunday Post*:

> Mrs. Elitch's vaudeville show in the Wolcott barn was a grand card and the little fellow in the brown clothes who stood at the door and did the "barking" was a jewel beyond compare.
>
> "Oh, come on, come on, and see Corbett and Fitz! Corbett and Fitz! They will fight for blood—oh, come in and see the blood!"

A little over a month later he was to appear with Hobart Bosworth—the famous actor for whom he rushed to open the Elitch's gates—in a testimonial performance at the Manhattan Theatre. The one-act play was titled *A Duel in Wall Street*, and he was third billed, playing the office boy.

In October 1898 he was seen at Windsor Hall in a performance for the "Newsboy's Union Masquerade and Entertainment." He gave a

---

* If nothing else, this must have given the young man an opportunity to vigorously scrub his face, as earlier in the day he had been one of seventeen children giving a "fancy dress cakewalk and parade in blackface. All the children will be blacked," promised the *Denver Post* by way of inducement.

comic recitation and also appeared as "Gumpy" in a skit entitled "The Quiet Family: A Farce in One Act." This was an early foreshadowing of the sort of charitable theatrical event that would consume much of the recreational hours of Fairbanks's adulthood. The mayor delivered the opening address, and "newsboys and guests, including some of Denver's young society people, put on masks and entered the dance." A month later he was part of a program of special attractions at the Cathedral Fair, providing songs, and the following day he performed his comic dialect speeches at the Children's Matinee at the Broadway Theatre.

His school was beginning to draw national attention. The *New York Dramatic Mirror* devoted a column to the program in December 1898. "A remarkable thing about the entertainments given by the students of the Tabor Grand School of Acting is their freedom from amateurishness, a distinguishing feature which merits congratulation." The critic noted that Douglas Fairbanks was "a clever youth whose naturalness is particularly to be commended. He is a trifle self-conscious at times, however, and this detracts somewhat from his otherwise excellent work."

The *Denver Post* wrote that the Tabor students would be performing again on Thanksgiving Day: "Master Douglas Fairbanks has a part which fits him like a glove, and his friends will not be disappointed in him, as everything undertaken by him is well done. . . . Master Fairbanks had an interview with Mr. William Gillette last week and gave several dramatic readings for Mr. Gillette and his manager, who were enthusiastic in their praise. Mr. Gillette presented him with a card, on which was his permanent address, telling him when he wished to secure a professional engagement to write him, and he would place him, as his talent was worthy of it."

The tactic he employed with Gillette was adopted more than once. If a Great Man came through town on theatrical tour, Doug would make an appointment, secure an interview, and do some readings. In the end, the Great Man who would serve as his route to fame and fortune was not William Gillette but Frederick Warde. But even here,

Fairbanks's account of events was mercurial. One version was given in 1912, when, secure in his position as a young Broadway star, Fairbanks was conducting a rather tongue-in-cheek interview:

> One day happened to meet an actor man on the street whom I knew. Frederick Warde. He said to me:
>
> "Douggie—not doggie—what art thou about to do?" I said to him:
>
> "Go through school, as I should, fair sir," I answered. He said to me:
>
> "Wouldst not like to go on the stage?" And I, who all during my younger days had run crazy with my amateur theatricals, which I performed all over the place, leaped up in the air with a glad cry and grasped him warmly about the neck.

Equally unlikely is the family's telling of the event: stern doormen blocked the way to Frederick Warde's dressing room, and there was no way for a youthful actor to get an introduction. But an alley wall, a fire escape, and a window were described as "the simple hurdles in this case." Warde came into his dressing room to find it occupied by the charming, wheedling youngster—one so beguiling that Warde had to offer him a position with his touring company despite himself.

Neither account is true. But before understanding how a teenage Douglas Fairbanks got to Frederick Warde, it helps to understand Frederick Warde—and those of his stripe. To one scholar, he was "America's greatest forgotten tragedian," a man who trod America's stages bringing Shakespeare to the masses. He was not on the absolute top rung of the ladder of stage aristocracy, but he represented the first step down in the "legitimate" theater. He was, in the words of scholar Alan Woods, "the touring tragedian, a star actor providing connections between the 19th century tradition and the modern one . . . who kept alive the traditions of [Edwin] Forrest, [Edwin] Booth and [John Edward] McCullough." His ilk rarely, if ever, appeared in New York City or Chicago, where, if truth be told, they were subject to a bit of snobbish sneering. Instead they toured the rest of the country to great acclaim and respect.* When a Frederick Warde or William Gillette or Maurice Barrymore or Edwin Booth came to town, the folks knew that they were going to get ART, not only were going to *hear* Shakespeare's immortal lines rattling the rafters but also *see* the words acted out in the proper style of elocution.

Elocution is a topic unto itself. Here existed a near universe of gestures and positions of the arms and hands and face, each with a different meaning. The voice itself had a wealth of varying characteristics—modulation, quality ("pure or impure"), pitch, force, speed, emphasis ("radical, vanishing, median, compound"), and inflection ("rising, falling, circumflex, or monotone"). The great actor—the great *artiste*—would combine these elements with the text of a melodrama or the lines of Shakespeare and could move audiences to tears. Or, at least, to the satisfactory feeling that they had gotten their money's worth of culture. Besides, all that pinwheeling of the arms made for a dandy view even from the rear of the house—to say nothing of informing a mode of acting employed in the earliest silent films, a style that drives modern audiences to hysterics. But we are reacting with a twenty-first-century eye to a nineteenth-century tradition. These were not bad actors; these were actors engaging in a very formal style, a veritable Kabuki dance in comparison to the naturalistic one that supplanted it.

And the likes of Frederick Warde should not be made light of. To get to the second-highest rung of the theatrical ladder was no small accomplishment, and it was the Frederick Wardes of the world who were doing the heavy lifting: taking the long, weary, grinding tours for nine months of every twelve, bringing professional theater to the great majority of Americans who would never see New York City or Chicago. And he followed a model of civic duty as well—many of these city stops

---

* Even Washington, DC, was perhaps a little too cosmopolitan. The *Washington Post* wrote in May 1900: "Mr. Warde himself as Romeo acted well, even admirably, but he needs to practice repression." No other reviewer dared hint at such a thing, but it was likely wise that he and his troupe remained out of New York and Chicago and stuck with hick towns like Los Angeles.

were accompanied by lectures to local high schools or civic groups on such topics as "Shakespeare's Women" and "Eloquence as Illustrated by Shakespeare." It was one such lecture in the spring of 1899 at Denver East High School that provided the almost-sixteen-year-old Douglas his opportunity. Warde was to recall:

> While in Denver, Colorado, I made an address on the study of Shakespeare to the faculty and students of the High School. On the following day of [which] a very youthful student of the school called on me and expressed a desire to go upon the stage. Such applications were not uncommon, but this applicant, little more than a boy, had an assurance and persistence in spite of my discouragements, that attracted me. He replied frankly to all of my questions, realized the gravity of the step he desired to take, told me the conditions of his life and referred me to his mother for consultation.

Here was a move of near genius. Very few youngsters hoping to run away and join a theatrical troupe would have the wit to provide their *mother* for a reference. And few young men had such a redoubtable ally as Douglas did in Ella. She did not originally support his thespian ambitions. But here is where Father O'Ryan again enters the story. Young Douglas wanted desperately to go into theater, and he confessed as much to the priest. But his mother was doggedly opposed. What to do?

The good Father shrewdly posited another career. There were savages in remote Africa, he suggested, who needed converting. Of course, there would be adventures, wild beasts—much for an energetic young man to overcome in the course of saving those souls . . . Doug, reportedly, took the bait. "Within a few weeks," his niece Letitia wrote, "Douglas was wearing his most somber clothes and his face was a mask of studied benevolence. He began going to mass weekdays and from time to time dropped a word or two about the desperate plight of the unbaptized savages." Ella, bedeviled by visions of her darling baby skewered on a cannibal's spit, capitulated. The stage might be bad, but it could not have the dangers of darkest Africa. Accordingly, when her son asked, she visited Mr. Warde.

> The lady called on me the next day, indorsed all that her son had told me, approved of the boy's ambitions and the result was I engaged him for my company for the following season, to lead the supernumeraries and to play such small parts as his capacity and appearance would permit.
>
> The youth was of rather less than average height but of athletic build, with frank attractive features and his name was Douglas Fairbanks.

He was to start the following season, September 1899.* Which was just as well. Between the time of his Warde introduction and this heady day, he managed to get himself expelled from high school.

Here is another example of how he managed to manipulate his narrative. Douglas fully owned the mischief of his youth, and tales abound of his harmless hijinks. Water snakes were released in a streetcar; one boy threw a rock through a classroom window from the *inside*, while Fairbanks picked up a second rock from under his chair, proclaiming innocently, "Here it is, teacher!" He and a group of friends disconnected neighbors' electric doorbells, then charged them for budding electrician Robert to repair. His *how-I-was-expelled* story falls into this gentle category: it was Saint Patrick's Day, and as the student body entered the assembly hall, they were met by the customary busts of history's great men sporting green hats and ties. Young Fairbanks was found out as the culprit, and that was the end of his academic career.

Schools were strict in the 1890s, true, but this hardly constituted an expellable offense, even then. The truth was more damning. When the students filed in for that particular assemblage, one of the teachers struck a chord on the piano for the holiday march. The room resonated with

---

* Historians have routinely misstated this date, claiming that his professional debut was in September 1900. This is inexplicable, as countless newspaper articles document Fairbanks's involvement in the tour a year prior.

silence. Someone had cut the wires on the piano. There was a cluster of boys to whom the sight of the mute piano elicited undue hilarity, and it evidently did not take long to determine who was the guilty party in what was a very destructive and expensive prank.

Vandalism on this scale did not fit well into his gently mischievous story line, and Fairbanks managed to keep this particular misdeed covered up. He continued with temperate fibs about his educational history: his parents sent him for a while to the Colorado School of Mines (they did not); he took a short "special course" at Harvard after the two-year Warde tour (he did not). Occasionally he would throw in Princeton, for good measure. But this was rare.

The Colorado School of Mines yarn had deeper meaning. He readily admitted, of this fictional turn, that he was an academic failure, that he had no patience for the finer points of trigonometry and such. But the mere fact that he placed himself there (and later, in film roles, would cast himself as a mining engineer) may have stemmed from a high school crush. "His English teacher there was a young lady with blond hair, fair skin, and a happy disposition who measured up to all his ideals of feminine appeal," wrote his niece. "He spent hours every morning grooming himself before he dashed off to school." The teacher was taken with Lord Byron, so he grew his hair out accordingly, "carefully brushed and nurtured with olive oil from his mother's kitchen. . . . He rarely smiled and for hours on end sat brooding or verbally rebelling against 'conventions.'"

His dream was crushed, alas. The lovely young teacher became engaged to—of all things—an *engineer*. Somehow, he was just at that stage in his youthful development where this hit a psychological sweet spot. He would become one of the most famous men in the world, certainly among the most acclaimed and beloved. He would marry, in turn, three beautiful blondes. And yet he would always claim that he *almost* became a mining engineer. On behalf of mine safety, it is a fortunate thing that he was a good actor. Or at least good enough for Frederick Warde's touring company.

The offer to tour for a year with the troupe (it would ultimately stretch to two full seasons) was a tremendous opportunity for the sixteen-year-old. It served as a lesson in the realities of the professional actor, and what his future would be for the next sixteen years, as even Broadway stars would tour with their productions. The company consisted of twenty-five people, including Warde. Some of the actors additionally assumed administrative functions. In his second season, Fairbanks was the assistant stage manager. This was no small job: the production traveled with a sixty-foot baggage car for its scenery and costumes and performed a rotation of plays, both Shakespeare (*Richard III*, *Romeo and Juliet*, *The Merchant of Venice*, *Othello*) and those dramas suited to Warde's age and history (*The Lion's Mouth*, *The Duke's Jester*, *Virginius*). They were on tour every day from mid-September to early May, starting in the Mid-Atlantic and Southeast during the steamy late summers and autumns, moving up the West Coast of the country as the new year arrived, and spending the brutally cold winters in the upper West, Midwest, and Canada. Many nights were spent sleeping upright in trains as they moved between smaller towns for one- and two-night stands. For larger cities, where stays could be longer than a week, nights were spent in theatrical hotels or boardinghouses. He made thirty dollars a week, out of which he needed to pay his expenses.

Curiously, Fairbanks spent his entire career downplaying those two critical years. He was just a glorified extra, he would claim. "The school boy Douglas was no more," he said in 1912. "Instead there blossomed forth a youth with large hands and feet who carried spears in Shakespearian plays and thought he was the mainspring of each and every show." His favorite anecdote about that time was the *Hamlet*-in-Duluth story, which makes up for in charm what it lacks in veracity. His story went like this: He had been plugging along, the ultimate spear-toting supernumerary, when his Big Chance came. The actor who was to play Laertes in *Hamlet* ended up on the wrong side of a Minnesota jail cell. Doug stepped into the role and, "to make a long story short, I played the part so well that it only took about ten years more to become a star on Broadway." He never tired of quoting the purported theatrical review: "Mr. Warde's company was bad but worst of all was Douglas Fairbanks as Laertes."

This canard was debunked long ago. The troupe never played *Hamlet* in Duluth, and there were no bad reviews.* It was but a single thread in the tapestry he wove about those years. He made himself a comic figure of incompetence:

> I probably wore the most astonishing costumes ever beheld on the native stage, being fitted out by a well meaning but misguided costume mistress in odds and ends of ancient, modern and medieval garb. So effectively did my costumes succeed in breaking up the actors and actresses who happened to be on the stage whenever I made my entrance, that Mr. Warde released me without visible signs of pain.

Warde, in fact, appeared to grow fond of the boy, giving him progressively larger roles to play as the tour progressed. He recalled the teenager as having a "laughing face, a curly head of hair, and athletic figure, and the most prodigious amount of energy I ever encountered." One reporter in the 1920s quoted Warde as stating, "Douglas saved him much money for supernumeraries as he could be in so many places at the same time." He retained his affection even after his pupil's fame far exceeded his own. Warde visited him on the set of *The Three Musketeers*, and three years later said of Fairbanks, "He is one of the men whom fortune has not spoiled."

Another favorite Fairbanksian anecdote centered around the funeral scene in act 1, scene 2 of *Richard III*, which he claimed afforded him his first speaking line. In the scene, Gloucester is paying impolitic court to Lady Anne at the funeral procession of Henry VI. Fairbanks claimed that he headed up the funeral procession and had but a single line: "My lord, stand back and let the coffin pass." He was nervous about his first

---

* In fact, they did not perform *Hamlet* until November 1900, more than a year after Fairbanks started with the troupe.

line, he maintained, practicing it for days "with every inflection, every gesture possible; in the street, in restaurants, in railroad stations." But when the big night came? He boomed loud and clear, "Stand back, my lord, and let the parson cough."

This is likely as much an embroidering of the truth as his other yarns about those years. Eventually he repeated it often enough that even Warde used it as his go-to story when speaking in public of Fairbanks. But the old man was genuinely bewildered by Fairbanks's claim of having been so awful that Warde was relieved to see him go: "If he says it was so, it must be true," he said. "But I do not remember it so."

In fact, young Fairbanks was singled out for praise as his roles increased in size and importance. By November 1900, he was playing the juvenile romantic lead opposite Warde's daughter in *The Duke's Jester*. "Miss May Warde, as Benetta, and Douglas Fairbanks, as Florio, won the hearty applause of the audience by their capital rendition of a timid lover and a maiden who would wed," declared the critic of the *Fort Worth Morning Register*.

Warde was to have a tremendous influence on the youngster. His style of acting survives in a recovered print of 1912's *Richard III*. No sound, of course, is available. (By the end of the film, one is grateful for the fact.) Still, it informs us. Echoes of the old man's style can be seen in Fairbanks's performances in the 1920s. Was our hero thinking? An index finger planted on the side of his nose told us so. Did his heart ache? One fist balled into the other and clasped to the heart made it clear.

But Fairbanks studied more than his mentor's performance. Warde was a joiner, an active member of the Elks club who used this association to the advantage of his company. Many stops on the tour were accompanied by local Elks assemblies given in the actor's honor, and after-dinner speeches were quoted at loving length in the next day's papers. It was good business—the theater would then be filled with appreciative fellow clubmen and their wives. Further, Warde practiced public good citizenship. Every stop that was longer than a one-night stand was accompanied by the obligatory visit to the local high school, where the (presumably) starstruck youngsters would be sprung from algebra or history and get to sit in an auditorium and hear the Great Man hold forth on Shakespeare or how to succeed in life or some other grand topic.

Fairbanks, young as he was, watched and learned. Within a few years he would become an active member of the Lambs Club, and long before he became famous, his name would pop up in the newspapers in association with some club-related charitable function. And while he did not take up the education of America's young by way of the lecture circuit, he did publish a series of books directed at the youth market. And his work as a public citizen, through both the Red Cross and the Liberty Bond tours, was prodigious.

The two-year stint was educational in other ways. Warde urged him to learn swordsmanship skills. "Some actors draw a rapier," he said, "as if it were a toasting fork." He also urged all the youngsters under his tutelage to take acting seriously. "Some day they will stop lynching horse thieves and start in on bad actors, and nobody will say a word of protest."

Young Doug had many opportunities to see the hardships of theatrical life firsthand. In Kansas in 1900, the first act of *The Lion's Mouth* was interrupted by a sheriff's deputy crawling over his box and onto the stage to serve papers on a startled Warde. A disgruntled former actor was suing for $744 in back salary; the box office receipts for the day were attached. This incident may or may not have been related to another that occurred in Kansas, where a bout of fisticuffs became a local theatrical legend. "When I played at the old Willis Wood I got into a fight with a stage hand that was a pip," Doug admitted to local reporters thirty years later. When told that the man in question had acknowledged starting the fight without provocation and, what's more, that Fairbanks had won, Doug replied, "That's sporting of him to say that." Then, always gracious: "If he's still around, you might tell him that I met a little guy a couple of weeks later who took most of the fight out of me. I'm still trying to figure out how he did it."

Douglas, who had never been outside of Colorado, was able for the first time to scratch a lifelong itch for travel. The tour not only covered the country but also crossed the border into Canada. Newspaper articles about upcoming productions in places such as Winnipeg, Manitoba, touted: "Hockey scores will be given between acts."

Perhaps it was the small towns and the hockey scores between acts. Perhaps it was simply his supreme self-confidence. But after two years, young Fairbanks evidently decided that he had learned all he needed from the experience. He was always impatient, and he felt that it was time to move from the second-highest rung on the ladder to the highest. He was still a teenager, but he saw no need to wait until he reached the grand old age of twenty to begin his climb. He wanted to make it to the top.

It was time for Douglas Fairbanks to take a crack at Broadway.

2

The Heroine's Likable Younger Brother

T HE THEATRICAL UNIVERSE THAT the teenage Douglas Fairbanks
encountered was still in the throes of its Big Bang in 1901: large
and getting larger. More than forty "legitimate" theaters were in New
York City alone, in addition to six top vaudeville houses. Forty "Opera
and Extravaganza" companies competed with burlesque, vaudeville, and
four hundred dramatic and touring stock companies. It was not an unre-
alistic expectation for a young actor with two years' touring history in a
major company to believe he could break into Broadway. And he did,
with alacrity, being cast in July 1901 in *Her Lord and Master*. He was
paid forty dollars per week.

Her Lord and Master was a four-act "society comedy," and its New
York premiere was on February 24, 1902.* The play was the story of a
rich young heroine of the strong-willed, untamed variety who marries
a British viscount. She does tolerably well subduing her wild American
ways until the arrival in Britain of her family and childhood sweetheart
(Fairbanks) causes a crisis. She wants to join them at a hotel; her husband
wishes her to stay home, as nobility are not seen on Sunday nights at

---

* Not that the play had spared him the touring circuit. *Her Lord and Master* had been touring since September, hitting the hinterlands circuit of such cities as Vincennes, Indiana,
and Janesville, Wisconsin.

public restaurants. ("I am your guide, your adviser, your superior—in worldly knowledge.") She goes anyway and disobeys his injunction to return by midnight, and he locks her out of the house. Chastened, she realizes that she loves him as Her Lord and Master, and all is happy by curtain.

Fairbanks's role as the young American who fails to win the girl was small and not well written. "The most poorly drawn character in 'Her Lord and Master,'" wrote one critic "is that of Glen Masters, and the actor to whom is assigned this role is entitled to the sympathy of the audience. Douglas Fairbanks struggled manfully with it and did not seem to do it particularly well. But it is a question whether anyone could have done it much better." Most were kinder: he was "capital as an impulsive, unsophisticated and not very discreet youth," his "naturalness and refreshing spontaneity" were praised, as was his "boyish audacity."

As the man who vies with the hero for the heroine, one would suspect an unsympathetic character, but Fairbanks could not, even at this young age, be cast as a villain. "Lord Canning—" his character says, in one scene, "although it's against my—own interests, I—I wish you luck . . . I shall keep out of the way—I won't move a step in this matter until I am quite sure the case is hopeless with you." The loser, perhaps—but ever the gallant.

The play had a good, if not spectacular, Broadway run, closing in April after sixty-nine performances. It was never revived and is today only a footnote in theatrical history. It was too close to the end of the season for Fairbanks to find another play. Theatrical seasons began in the autumn, after the summer's heat that made packed theaters insufferable had eased. But a young Douglas Fairbanks was scarcely daunted by such a thing. He decided that Wall Street was a way to riches and found work as an "order man" at the brokerage house of De Coppet & Doremus. ("The name Coppet appealed to me," he later claimed.) A 1916 reporter actually went to the firm to verify the story and came back with a report that "he is still remembered in that office, fondly but fearfully. He did his work well enough; in fact, there are those who insist that he invented scientific management."

When asked about this later, Fairbanks recalled that this was pure bluff. "For five days in the week I would say, 'Quite so' to my assistant, no matter what he suggested," he said. "On Saturday I would dash into the manager's office, wag my head, knit my brow, and exclaim, 'What we need around here is *efficiency.*' And once I urged the purchase of a time-clock."

Dramatic coach Margaret Fealy recalled encountering her former student at this time, shortly after her return from London: "I shall never forget the day I met him on Broadway when I returned. How young and happy and handsome. And how he lifted me off my feet in his greeting . . . bless him!"

Such exuberance was typical of him, as was what followed. "I was seized with a restless spirit," he recalled later. "If life had some prize package for me, I wanted it tied up and delivered at once. . . . I thought of London. Of course! One could not expect adventure to dwell in this prosaic land. One must cross the Atlantic." He made good on the decision by quitting his job and working his way across the Atlantic with two companions—football players by the names of "Little" Owen and "Jack" Beardsley—on a cattle boat.* They had, he claimed, fifty dollars each. "I walked from Liverpool to London, from London to Dover, from Calais to Paris and even from Paris to Brussels," he said. "I worked with street gangs, unloaded cobblestones from barges and formed amazing contacts with all sorts of people. By absorbing or at least examining their point of view I corrected and broadened my own."

Even more, the trip provided fodder for Fairbanks's acting repertoire. It would be almost two decades before *The Three Musketeers* was produced, but friend and author Robert Florey claims that it was on this

---

* Normally, this is the sort of claim that would make the most gullible of biographers suspicious, and the paucity of crew manifests for this period makes the date impossible to confirm. But history has strange ways of providing proof, and for Fairbanks (and us) it came on his honeymoon voyage in 1920. Upon landing in Southampton, England, he was greeted not only by the international press but also by a sweaty but stalwart stoker who recognized him from the cattle boat trip nearly twenty years before. Cameras recorded the happy reunion, and one myth, at least, was confirmed as fact.

trip that Doug observed and learned to adopt the tics and mannerisms of the Frenchmen he encountered, to hilarious results. But as the call of travel beckoned him, so did that of the theater, and he returned to New York late that summer in time to be cast in his second Broadway play, *A Rose o' Plymouth-Town*, which had its New York opening on September 29, 1902, after three weeks on the road.

A work of historical fiction that purported to demonstrate that the Pilgrims were not as staid as rumored, the play was the first starring role for Minnie Dupree, who years later was asked to comment on playing with a young Fairbanks. "I think," she famously said, "that he was about the nicest case of St. Vitus's dance that ever came under my notice." He played the heroine's likable younger brother—the first of many such portrayals. He won praise as "boyish, natural and interesting," but the play itself was not well received. Once it reached the Manhattan Theatre, it lasted only twenty-one performances. The only point of interest in the piece is that the plot involved a sword fight. (Dueling Pilgrims—who knew?) But even then the producers dropped the ball. The man who would become the icon of swashbuckling was not a participant, thus marking the play for posterity as being one large missed opportunity.

Having a play close this early in the season was unfortunate, but Fairbanks found another role quickly. *Mrs. Jack* was a successful comedy starring Alice Fischer as the recent widow of a millionaire who, in dealing with his estate, is surrounded by the usual assortment of undeserving and scheming relatives. To their horror, she welcomes into her society many of the beneficiaries of her late—and eccentric—husband's will. When the play went on tour of the Northeast in late November, Fairbanks was in the cast, playing an uncharacteristic role of a cad "with a good deal of judgment," in the eyes of at least one critic.

But he was not with the show for long. He played in Syracuse, New York, in late November 1902; Jersey City, New Jersey, in January 1903; and Boston, Massachusetts, in early March. By the time the tour reached Washington, DC, on April 13, Fairbanks had departed the company.

The family attributes this rapid exodus to Doug's high spirits. He was by then "feeling quite at home in the theater," reported niece Letitia

Fairbanks, and was "up to his old tricks." His lifelong love of pranks began to creep into actual performances. A villain's hat would be loaded with an eight-pound shot, ruining the man's exit. Doug would add stage business and improvise lines, much to the chagrin of the play's manager. "Finally," his niece wrote, "after an unusually exuberant performance in which he played a whole scene exclusively to a front row of young ladies, the manager 'called' him in the presence of the cast. The verbal battle that followed resulted in his resignation and the manager's immediate acceptance of it."*

This experience left him rattled, and in his characteristically rash manner he decided to quit the theater. But not quite yet. He joined a group of young actors, including William Courtenay, performing in stock company work in Albany, New York. The only evidence of that summer is a program for *Men and Women*, a piece performed in July 1903 as a one-night benefit for the Albany City Homeopathic Hospital and Dispensary. The play had a number of major names attached: it was written by Henry De Mille and David Belasco and codirected by beloved character actor Thomas A. Wise. It was heady company for a young actor just discharged from a touring company.

Nothing else turned up. He had brief employment at the Russell and Erwin Manufacturing Company, makers of hardware in New York City.†

---

* Fairbanks would later soften his memory of this period and claim, incorrectly, that he had played a supporting role in *Mrs. Jack* for "a whole year."

† Nineteen years later, at the height of his fame, he got a letter. Someone had unearthed his 1903 employment card from the company. It revealed little beyond his signature, his salary (he was paid five dollars a week), and his address: 119 West Ninety-Fifth Street. Was it the same Douglas Fairbanks? A studio employee dutifully replied, confirming that yes, it was the same man, adding, "Mr. Fairbanks wishes to thank you for your very kind inquiry, and says he is sure no one in your organization would remember him if it depended upon his ability along hardware lines." Kenneth Davenport, as unofficial studio biographer, would later write: "He had thought to become a captain of industry and had enlisted as private, donning overalls—picturesque ones, you may be sure,—and learning all about the manufacture of bolts, nuts and hinges. But the rewards of the particular captain that came within his range of vision did not seem alluring enough to warrant Doug's continuance in the hardware regiment. Certainly if one is to leap there must be something worth leaping for."

Next came the law. Possibly inspired by his father, he worked as a law clerk for three months in the firm of E. M. Hollander and Sons, also in New York. But discovering that "it would not be possible to become a brilliant attorney by Christmas," he claimed to yield to the lure of travel. He would go to the Orient. He would fall in love with a geisha girl. Or at least, this is the version of events he would tell his family and press agents in later years.

There is no evidence via ship manifest or passport application that he went to London that summer, as he alleged. It would be hard to imagine his fitting a term at a hardware company, three months of law clerking, and a trip to Britain into the spring and summer of 1903. This overseas jaunt was likely part and parcel of the series of cheerful half-truths that made up the Fairbanks myth.

At least he spun a good yarn: his plan, reportedly, was to sell the rights to a patent for an electric switch, as a way of raising money to go to Japan. Once in Great Britain, he claimed to have met an English beauty and suddenly felt no need to raise money to go anywhere. He represented himself to her as a successful Broadway actor—a white lie, at worst—playing the part until his funds began to dwindle. Claiming the need to return to the Great White Way to take a part in a play, he left the young woman behind. The fable ends with his fib turning into truth: he was placed under contract to famed producer/manager William Brady, and cast in his production of *The Pit*.

William Brady was one of those larger-than-life figures that the turn of the prior century seemed to produce. Fairbanks friend Kenneth Davenport said of him, "No orchestra ever played loudly enough to suit him, no mob ever shouted vigorously enough to suit him." He was forty years old, had made and lost several fortunes, had managed two world heavyweight boxing champions (James Jeffries and "Gentleman" Jim Corbett), and had produced dozens of plays, including the favorite of his generation, *Way Down East*. He possessed "more charm than was right for any one man to have" and knew how to use it to a showman's best advantage. He even had—for 1903—a fairly extensive background in motion pictures. He had acted as timekeeper when Thomas Edison filmed the boxing match between James Corbett and Peter Courtenay in his famed Black Maria studio in 1894 and was involved with the filming of subsequent fights during the 1890s. By the turn of the century he was, in association with an ambitious young immigrant by the name of Adolph Zukor, an exhibitor of Hale's Tours, described by film scholar Edward Wagenknecht as travel films shown in small theaters constructed to resemble railway coaches: "The 'conductor' stood on the back platform to receive your ticket, and when you went inside and took your seat you really seemed to be settling down for a journey. Presently the lights were extinguished, the car rumbled and swayed, and on a small screen in the front of the coach, you saw Yellowstone Park or the Yosemite or whatever locality might be on exhibition that day. Since the film had been taken from the platform of a moving train the illusion was complete."

Films took a great leap forward in 1902–1903, when Edwin S. Porter, inspired by France's Georges Méliès, began to string a series of successive shots together to progressively construct a narrative. "Porter distinguished the movies from other theatrical forms and gave them the invention of editing," wrote Lewis Jacobs in 1939. *The Life of an American Fireman* in 1902 was followed late the next year by *The Great Train Robbery* and the blossoming, the year after, of nickelodeons. What was a gimcrack novelty suddenly reached a tipping point. Movies learned to tell a story, not simply document movement, and the fuse for what was to become a popular culture sensation was lit.

Accordingly, Brady's involvement in film would grow over the course of the next ten years, but for the present his main occupation—his prestige occupation—was as a theatrical manager in "the legitimate." And for "the legitimate," *The Pit* seemed to hold promise.

Based on a major novel, *The Pit* dealt with the Chicago Board of Trade and the risks of commodities speculation. Brady's plans for it were ambitious. Sets were elaborate: transportation of scenery for the pre-Broadway run in Philadelphia, Jersey City, and Chicago took four train cars, in an era when most major productions required only one. There were fifty speaking parts and four grand opera singers. Most notable: the two hundred to five hundred extras for the climactic scene in "the pit"—the room where brokers traded and fortunes were made and lost. Brady would plaster the town in advance with posters asking for "500 men of good appearance to take part in the wheat scene." This had the happy effect of generating advance publicity, as well as a built-in audience of wives, mothers, and sweethearts.

The play toured through the fall and winter of 1903. Its Chicago run was at the New Garrick, a block from the Iroquois Theatre, the site of the worst theatrical fire tragedy in history. Brady describes how on that fateful day (December 30, 1903) he left *The Pit* to check out the competition, leaving the doomed Iroquois mere minutes before the fire broke out and hundreds of patrons—mostly parents with small children—were killed. It was during the matinee performance. An arc light sparked, a cotton curtain ignited, and within a shockingly short time a wall of flame and smoke roared into the auditorium, killing patrons in their seats. Hundreds more were killed by being crushed at tight exits with locked or inward-opening doors.

It was a horrendous demonstration of the effects of fire, and the cast and crew of *The Pit* were witness to the devastation. Bodies were piled like cordwood on the street; improvised first aid stations were set up in nearby restaurants and shops. The smell of burned flesh, the scores upon scores of dead children, the general scenes of terror and grief—all potent reminders to every actor and stagehand present that they worked every day in wooden firetraps, that what had happened to Eddie Foy and the *Mr. Bluebeard* company could happen to them and their audiences at any time. Fire was to remain a constant hazard throughout Fairbanks's career, even after he left the theater. Every few years he would find himself fighting yet another one, and with each he must have remembered that cold December day in Chicago 1903. He never spoke of it.

The mayor of Chicago shut down all theaters, and Brady responded by having the Chicago company take over the schedule of a planned second company, moving through towns such as St. Louis and Milwaukee. Despite this major setback, the play did well, arriving on Broadway in

February 1904. By this point the pit scene was so successful that within a week of the play's arrival at New York's Lyric Theatre, it was being burlesqued in a sketch at the Green Room Club, with *The Pit*'s star, Wilton Lackaye, as referee and Brady as leader of the bulls.

And in the midst of all this mayhem was Doug, cast as Landry Court. While not the lead, his was a major character in both the novel and the play. Author Frank Norris's description of the character makes Brady's casting decision clear:

> This was Landry Court, a young fellow just turned twenty-three. . . . He was astonishingly good-looking, small-made, wiry, alert, nervous, debonair, with . . . dark eyes that snapped like a terrier's. He made friends almost at first sight, and was one of those fortunate few who were favoured equally of men and women. The healthiness of his eye and skin persuaded to a belief in the healthiness of his mind; and, in fact, Landry was as clean without as within. He was frank, open-hearted, full of fine sentiments and exaltations and enthusiasm. Until he was eighteen he had cherished an ambition to become the President of the United States.

Brady got it right. Reviews of Fairbanks's performance were positive, noting that Doug played "with refreshing spirit."

The Pit was to provide Fairbanks with a lifelong friend, a fellow player fated to become the first member of his entourage. Kenneth Davenport lent Doug his coat one frigid night and, the story goes, caught a chill himself when he had to go out without it. This led (at least in Fairbanks's guilty mind) shortly thereafter to a diagnosis of tuberculosis, and from that point forward Doug felt responsible for the man. It would be a number of years before he was in a position to employ anyone, but once he was, Davenport became his secretary-companion and, eventually, his ghostwriter.

"After a season of what I thought was a very successful work in this vehicle," Fairbanks was later to claim, "Mr. Brady decided to reduce my salary, but I assured him that this could be avoided by the simple expedient of detaching me from the payroll, which he did." Brady's recollections were less politic: "There were some stormy aspects in the handling of Mr. Fairbanks. On one occasion I tore up his contract in front of him."

One does not know whether to attribute Fairbanks's behavior to extreme confidence or extreme temper. It cannot have been a wise thing for a twenty-one-year-old novice to engage in a battle of wills with one of the top producers on Broadway. Whether due to an excess of self-assurance or self-will, the breach occurred. He had to find other work. *The Pit* stayed at the Lyric until late April, when it moved to the Academy of Music. Just when the rift with Brady occurred is not clear, but Fairbanks's next play, *Two Little Sailor Boys*, opened at the Academy of Music on May 2.

This was a revival of a British comic melodrama, featuring two young ladies (variably described to skeptical critics as being between twelve and fifteen years of age) as the nautical lads. Doug played the character role of "Jack Jolly, able seaman" and was, in the view of the *New York Dramatic Mirror*, "boyish, roistering, likable." The play had a dramatic rescue at sea, effected with the aid of the members of the Fort Hamilton Division of the United States Volunteer Life Saving Corps, who nightly performed the act of pulling the drenched "boys" from a large tank of water. But neither the charms of wet costumes clinging to teenage girls nor the roistering likability of Douglas Fairbanks made the play a decided hit, and it closed after thirty-two performances.

The early summer of 1904 was idle, from a theatrical standpoint. "Discouragement isn't the word that expressed my feelings at all," Fairbanks claimed later. "I didn't know what to do. And in those days whenever I was in doubt, I always went to London, so I took passage on the first cattle boat out."*

He was likely to have been telling the truth in claiming that on this trip he met Lee Shubert, who engaged him for *Fantana*. He returned

---

* Except, of course, the "cattle boat" was a passenger ship, and his mother was along. But it sounds less than heroic to say that you went with your mother to London.

to New York City late in August 1904, where he joined rehearsals for Shubert's musical spectacle, which had started four weeks earlier. Ever since *The Mikado*, Japanese-themed operettas had been all the rage, and *Fantana* was another in this species. "In the first act the entire dramatis personae go suddenly mad on the subject of Japan and decide to emigrate en masse to 'That fair island of Asia,'" wrote Douglas's niece of such productions. "Somebody conveniently has a yacht and it seems the most logical thing in the world for the entire population of Newport to embark upon it." Family myth describes Fairbanks as merely a member of the male chorus in this production—his niece recalled his claim that he was "one of the most emphatic in voicing the cry 'To Japan, to Japan!' but after that line he would get hopelessly off key and flounder around in a maze of other people's melody."

While the description of Doug's singing may have been correct, the designation of his role was understated. He was again the heroine's brother. His name was prominently placed in the cast listings, and he was noted not only for an unusually fine voice but to have "acted with distinction and had more than the usual share of manly good looks." What's more, he sang a solo, "Just My Style," directed at the play's ingénue, and he was featured in the cast portraits on the sheet music that was issued with the musical's success.

Evidently it was something more than the "manly good looks" that caught the eye of Grace George, wife of producer William Brady, when she saw the production after its New York premiere in mid-January 1905. (The play had had a successful pre-Broadway run in Chicago in the fall.) "He's not good-looking," she is reported to have told her husband. "But he has a world of personality—just worlds of it. His name is Douglas Fairbanks."

The story, one suspects, is just a little too pat—the sort of theatrical myth that artistic personalities like to construct. Brady liked what he saw, plucked the youngster out of the chorus, signed him to a personal contract, and gave him a starring role in his next production: *A Case of Frenzied Finance*. In fact, Fairbanks had already played an important role in Brady's *The Pit*, and Brady was very familiar with the actor's virtues and flaws. And he was more than a mere chorus boy in *Fantana*. But the essentials are true. Brady acknowledged that it was his wife's influence that caused him to once again sign Fairbanks, and it was Brady who was to play a major role in the next phase of his theatrical career. Brady cabled Fairbanks to offer him a contract. Fairbanks, recalling the Sturm und Drang of their last encounter, thought it a practical joke. He wired back to ensure that Brady was serious. He was. *Fantana* went on to a long run, but Douglas Fairbanks was not to run with it—at least for a while.

As with *The Pit*, the theme of *A Case of Frenzied Finance* dealt with the financial markets and the "reigning craze for watering stocks and getting rich quick." Indeed, the term *frenzied finance* carried as much weight in 1905 as *irrational exuberance* would a hundred years later. The story was a comedy, and plans for its opening were announced in mid-March. It was a modest production, requiring nothing like *Fantana*'s nine weeks of rehearsal, and opened at the Savoy Theatre on April 3.

Fairbanks was the lead: an ambitious bellboy at the Van Billion Hotel who has, in the words of the *New York Times* reviewer, "made up his mind to be a power in the world, and who reiterates that fact at every opportunity with face upturned to the gallery and clinched fist extended skyward." The gesture—hackneyed even in 1905—was one that the world was to see many times ahead. As Zorro, cajoling the caballeros from atop a table, his right fist would extend upward; as Robin Hood, it would be clutched, pointing upward, always upward, from thousands of brilliantly colored stone lithograph posters. Even twenty-five years later, in the early talkie *Reaching for the Moon*, it is still there, surrounded by ticker tape, its owner older, perhaps, but no less determined.

This reaching, this grabbing for success, this declaration that it would come, it *must* come, was emblematic of Fairbanks through most of his life and for his entire active career. He doodled the word SUCCESS on scratch pads the way others drew random squiggles. He relished the fight: "When there were no natural obstacles in my path, I used to create them, just to get used to going over them," he wrote twenty years later. A brazen ambition but somehow a likable one as well. Even the *Times* critic grudgingly admitted that Doug was "pleasing when he was not spouting platitudes." Others wrote of his "fervor and enthusiasm."

It seemed to be paying off. He was not yet twenty-two, was signed by a major theatrical producer for fifty dollars a week, and had his first leading role on Broadway. He rented a carriage and drove his mother slowly past the theater so they could relish the sight of his name up in lights. And who could blame him?

Still, it was good that he did so on opening night. The play, for all its topicality, was too broad a comedy, badly staged, and with a spotty cast. The farce, wrote one critic, "shows the hurried pitchfork in its construction." Brady moved the production from the Savoy to the Princess Theatre after its first week, shortening the title to *Frenzied Finance* in an attempt to save it. "I think the play is one of the best comedies we have had in years," he declared, "and I am willing to back my judgment." It was a losing bet. It lasted only until late April. Little remains of this play—even the script is missing from the Library of Congress, suggesting that Brady did not consider it worth the bother of registering. But one trifle has washed up on the shores of history: four pages from a young theatergoer's album. The young lady attended the April 10 performance. The cast list from the program is on the first page. Douglas Fairbanks's name is underlined seven times. A cabinet photo of Fairbanks in costume on the second page is followed by a production still. Finally, a page of written criticism: The leading lady, it seems, was "too old." But Doug? The young woman was a fine judge of star power: "Douglas Fairbanks," she wrote succinctly, "simply great."

She was not the only one who felt this way. One astute critic captured the essence of Doug's engaging cheerful narcissism: "Douglas Fairbanks . . . did excellently when he was not obliged to spout of his ambitions, the 'spirit of the age,' and his love for an heiress whose name he had not learned," the *Morning Telegraph* reviewer wrote wryly. "The audience liked Mr. Fairbanks. Mr. Fairbanks liked himself, and everybody was satisfied."

The short life of his first leading role did not appear to discomfit him. By mid-April he was announced as the romantic lead in the upcoming revival of *Trilby* at the New Amsterdam. *Trilby*, the story of Svengali and his beautiful, hypnotized victim, had been a great success ten years earlier, and Brady's plans were for a two-week revival with the original cast. The original romantic hero was not welcome, however, by virtue of having divorced the leading lady two years prior, and young Douglas Fairbanks appeared an opportune substitution.

But it was not to be. Perhaps he was too young for the star's comfort. Whatever the reason, when the play premiered on May 8, 1905, Fairbanks was not in the role of Little Billee. He was silent on the subject, never mentioning the play, or his proposed part in it, in any interviews or autobiographical writings about his theatrical career. Perhaps it was a sore point. Or perhaps it was of little importance to him.

But he must not have been pleased to return to *Fantana*, on May 4, and his cries of "To Japan, to Japan!" History does not record how long he stayed with the production the second time around (the play was a prodigious success, running 298 performances on Broadway). But it cannot have been long, for by early September, he was in Chicago, in a supporting role in another Brady hit, *As Ye Sow*.

As Ye Sow was a New England melodrama, cut from the same cloth as *Way Down East*, replete with shipwrecks, lost husbands, and stolen babies. Brady knew his stuff: the producer leaned heavily in his advertising on the fact that a minister of the Gospel had penned the story; he even held a special matinee to which he invited every cleric in Chicago. ("The general public will not be admitted.") Over a thousand men of the cloth bravely overcame their historical aversion to the evils of the stage and attended.

Doug played Lute Ludlam, once again half of a juvenile pair in a secondary love story—one of the comic New England characters surrounding the long-suffering heroine and her minister-love. The play was a tremendous success in Chicago that fall, and within three days of premiering it was booked into a Boston theater for an indefinite run. It arrived there in late October and was unstoppable. Even the abrupt death of the leading lady (she developed sudden deafness in those pre-antibiotic days and died in surgery in a Boston hospital in late November) did not slow it down, and it stayed for three months.

On Christmas Day, it opened on Broadway at the Garden Theatre. New Yorkers, however, prided themselves on not being susceptible to "robust fun of the usual huckleberry flavor." "If the minister portrayed in the play could have been secretly strangled and drowned in some of the real water which fell in the storm scene the whole situation would immediately have gained in sincerity," was the dry report of one New York critic. Brady's publicity releases claimed that the crowds at the Garden were the largest in five years, but *As Ye Sow* ran for a modest thirty-four performances on Broadway.

Still, a shrewd Brady knew where the money was. He booked the play for an extended road tour of New England. While Fairbanks may have participated in some of the tour, by the summer of 1906 he was back, in a sense, where he started: Denver, and Elitch's Gardens, where eight years before he used to run to be the first to open the gates for Hobart Bosworth.

Elitch's Gardens, a thirty-minute trolley ride from the heart of downtown Denver, was only sixteen years old the summer that Fairbanks played there, but already it was famous for its theater and resident stock company. Tyrone Power, Sarah Bernhardt, and Minnie Madden Fiske had all appeared there—in fact the Divine Sarah came there for the 1906 season after the San Francisco earthquake destroyed the theater at which she had been scheduled to perform that summer, playing *Camille* in matinees and *La Sorcière* at night. History is silent on whether Mr. Fairbanks ever met Miss Bernhardt. Cheerful social-climber that he was, it would be surprising to imagine that he would trod the boards with the greatest actress of her generation and say nothing about it.

But in writing about that summer a decade later, he was diffident in tone: "In my home town I played a number of unimportant parts as a member of the stock company that was a fixture at Elitch's—a company in which every Denver actor is expected to appear at least once in his career." Clearly it was a step backward, and it is unclear why it was taken. He had a contract with Brady. He could have continued to tour with *As Ye Sow*. Perhaps Ella was homesick. Certainly it was an opportunity for reunions; Maude Fealy, his first theatrical compatriot, was playing stock for the summer at Elitch's, and their adult encounters were always replete with reminiscences and laughter.

At any rate, a summer of rotating juvenile roles in plays such as *The Little Princess*, *Old Heidelberg*, *Sherlock Holmes*, and *The Little Minister* appears to have done his career no harm, and by autumn he was back in the East, supporting Grace George (Mrs. William Brady) in her next vehicle, *Clothes*.

Clothes, a social comedy, opened in early September. Fairbanks's part was small—so small, in fact, that when he was briefly needed in late October to fill in for his old role in the still-touring *As Ye Sow*, his friend Kenneth Davenport was able to step in for him with a single rehearsal. Still, he was noticed by the critics: "Douglas Fairbanks gave his customarily truthful picture of a particularly superfluous American youth," wrote one. "Douglas Fairbanks . . . played an unimportant part well," stated another.

Superfluous. Unimportant. These are not the characteristics of a role that could contain his boundless, youthful energy. It had to emerge, and it did. Noting that the set included a long staircase (handy for casting villains down to their fates), William Brady wrote, "During rehearsals, which always wore everybody else to a frazzle, Fairbanks' idea of resting up was to walk up and down that flight of steps on his hands. He was an instantaneous success."

So was the production, running over one hundred performances. Again, Fairbanks did not stay for the run of the play. By early October 1906, Brady announced that Doug was cast in *The Man of the Hour*.

The Man of the Hour was a political drama, and Fairbanks once again played the part of the heroine's brother. Initially, Brady sandwiched the production into the Manhattan Theatre, where *Clothes* was still playing, by running it at matinee performances. The play premiered in New York City on Sunday, October 28, before an invited audience ("the simplest way," commented the *New York Times*, "to avoid any infringement of the Sunday law"), a day after a single performance in Albany. It played briefly in Trenton, New Jersey, before finding its rightful home and formal opening at the Savoy on December 4. Reviews were generally strong; they demonstrate that the Fairbanks persona was starting to be recognized. The *New York Sun*'s critic wrote that Fairbanks "had the audience with him from the time his smile first appeared," and the *Times* critic noted, "Douglas Fairbanks played his now familiar, breezy, attractive youth."

Contemporary photographs suggest his charisma. In the midst of gesticulating actors in costumes of the period, Fairbanks stands out, modern and natural. Brady must have recognized this unusual quality and planned to capitalize on it. By the third week of December, he had contracted with George Sandhurst, *The Man of the Hour*'s author, to write a play specifically for Fairbanks. There would be no more heroines' brother parts for Doug.

It was at this point that the love-hate relationship between actor and producer hit another major bump in the road. By December 30, 1906, Doug announced that he was leaving the stage—for good. He was in love. What's more, he was engaged.

Her name was Anna Beth Sully. She was soft, plump, and fair of skin, in an era when these attributes were closely linked with the definition of beauty. She was born in 1886 in Rhode Island. She had not been born to great fortune, but by the time she was a teenager her father, Daniel Sully, an iron-willed speculator of the robber baron variety, had cornered the market in cotton and become a multimillionaire nearly overnight. The family built a sprawling summerhouse in Rhode Island (named Kenneth Ridge, after an older brother who died young) and occupied a mansion off Fifth Avenue in New York. She had the trappings of wealth. In the words of her son, Douglas Fairbanks Jr., "She epitomized that upper-class world in which he felt very much at ease, and which his mother [Ella] had always thought their due."

The exact circumstances of their meeting are in dispute. Fairbanks Jr. believed that they met after Beth saw him during the Boston run of *The Man of the Hour*. Since the show didn't play Boston until early

1908, this is unlikely. The version that played in the popular press at the time of their marriage was that father and daughter attended a matinee of *The Pit*. If so, it was a case of art imitating life, for two days later, it was said, the cotton market collapsed—and with it much of Daniel's fortunes. In fact, by the time he gave his consent to their marriage, Papa Sully's establishment was running on fumes.

But this was not evident to the young couple, who were determined to wed. Daniel could posture that a family of his status could hardly have an *actor* join their fold, and Fairbanks was either too politic or too uninformed to point out that the Sully fold was very much of the nouveau riche. And perhaps not so riche at that. He became ardent in his pursuit, and Beth's father began to soften. In one contemporary account: "Opposition to the suit aroused the fighting blood in Mr. Fairbanks and Mr. Sully loves a fighter." Sully would reconsider his refusal—*if* Fairbanks would come to work for his current business venture, the Buchan Soap Company. Doug agreed. But Daniel was only half of the equation. Brady had Fairbanks locked into a five-year contract, and this would have to be broken.

Here Doug reverted to a tactic that had worked for him in the past. Much as he sent Ella to plead his case with Frederick Warde, he now sent Beth to do the same with Brady. Her backbone was of the same quality steel as her father's. "At the conclusion of the conference, manager Brady retired, wearing the expression of a martyr and the five years' contract torn to tatters reposed in the wastebasket," went one account. "He had agreed to release Fairbanks at the conclusion of the present season."

So Fairbanks did double duty starting in early 1907—evenings and matinees on the stage, and all other working hours at Buchan Soap's Brooklyn plant. The prospect of a rising young Broadway star working in a soap factory for his ladylove roused some interest in the press, and contemporary photographs show him in crisp white coveralls, his hair getting progressively more mussed as he doggedly worked his way through all the steps in the manufacturing process. He could never do anything halfway; rumors abounded that during his time on the sales force, he would cheerily take a bite out of the soap to demonstrate its purity.

The June wedding was timed to the end of the theatrical season. The sun parlor at Kenneth Ridge, banked with maidenhead fern and daisies, was arranged to represent a miniature chapel. Two hundred seats formed a central aisle. The bride wore white princess satin and carried orange blossoms. The groom—perhaps to tweak his father-in-law—had Broadway star Vincent Serrano as his best man. A simple Episcopal service was followed by a reception in the living room. The couple left for a European honeymoon. It could not have been more proper.

Film historians often claim that Fairbanks returned to the stage upon the collapse of Buchan Soap. But Doug did not wait nearly that long. Perhaps he was persuaded by Brady's plea ("I think you are making a great mistake abandoning a professional career which indicates so bright a future for you for any other occupation or career," he wrote Fairbanks at the time). Or perhaps he had never planned to leave the stage but waited until the marriage was a fait accompli. More charitably, it may be that the family's dwindling assets were becoming evident. Whatever the reason, he returned to *The Man of the Hour*, still chugging along at the Savoy, on September 2, 1907. His agreement with Brady called for him to remain in the play throughout its New York run; in exchange, Brady would produce a new play specifically for him, and "he will be launched as a full-fledged star on or before September 1, 1908."

3

Stage Stardom

T HE SUMMER OF 1908 was significant in the theatrical world, and not because it was the summer when Douglas Fairbanks was launched as a stage star. Rather, it was because one of theater's greatest failures took up a new profession.

David Wark Griffith was seven years older than Douglas Fairbanks, born in 1876 in rural Kentucky. He wished to become a playwright, so he left home at the age of nineteen to become an actor and learn the trade. He failed in both professions. He knocked about the world of Victorian melodramas and starving stock companies until 1907, when he was in such a diminished state that he was forced to seek work in moving pictures. He tried to sell a screenplay to the Edison Studios.

He failed again. But he was hired for a day or two as an actor in an Edwin S. Porter film, *Rescued from an Eagle's Nest,* wherein he rescued a baby and fought a stuffed eagle (whose wires were readily apparent) against the painted theatrical backdrop typical of the earliest films. From this experience he moved into the universe of the unsuccessful actor, supporting himself in "the flickers." One of the studios at which he found work was the American Mutoscope and Biograph Company, known to his peers as "the Biograph." The company was in a creative slump, producing story films of no particular merit. The director, Wallace McCutcheon, had a drinking problem. Not that it mattered much; no one thought that directors were important—they just told the actors what to do. It was the cameraman who counted, and one of the company's two cameramen (Arthur Marvin) was the boss's brother, the self-described "Captain of the Good Ship Take-it-Easy." In fact, so unimportant were directors in the relative scheme of things at Biograph that when the studio head decided they needed a second one, he took a flier on one of the hammier actors in their stable: Griffith.

It turned out to be a brilliant choice. Griffith may not have been able to act to save his life, but he changed the face of motion pictures. Over the course of the next five years he directed over 450 short films, one- and two-reel melodramas and comedies (far more of the former than the latter). Revisionists enjoy quarreling today to determine who else might have come up with any particular innovation first, but few disagree that whether alone or in parallel with others, Griffith developed the essential grammar of film as *film*—the fluidity of shot placement, staging, editing, and performance that remains the blueprint of movies up to the present day. He fought for innovations in camera placement (close-ups were rare in 1908) and creative use of lighting, including backlighting. He fought vehemently for films longer than ten to twenty minutes, realistic sets (as opposed to painted stage flats), and location shooting. Under his influence, films evolved from essentially filmed stage performances to true cinema.

It would take seven and a half more years for the cinematic explosion to occur at a complete societal level with the release of his *Birth of a Nation* in early 1915. Still, the introduction of D. W. Griffith as a film director in the summer of 1908 was akin to lighting the fuse.

Fairbanks, about to be launched as a theatrical star—on Broadway, no less—was of course unaware of this development. It had taken almost a year from the time of Brady's announcement, but rehearsals for *All for a Girl* began August 3, 1908. *All for a Girl* was an improbable romantic vehicle, even by 1908 standards: a wealthy heiress, weary of male gold diggers, impersonates a poor secretary on holiday. The hero, an upright young man, meets the girl, falls in love, and the predictable comedy of mistaken identities ensues. It was a tepid endeavor. Still, Fairbanks's qualities were increasingly recognized. "Another star burst forth in the theatrical firmament on Saturday evening August 22," the *New York Clipper* critic commented. "And although the glare resulting therefrom was not a blinding one, Douglas Fairbanks, the young man in question, may console himself with the comforting reflection that he landed solidly." The *Washington Post* was a little warmer: under the subhead DOUGLAS FAIRBANKS MADE A STAR the critic wrote that Fairbanks "is extremely clever in the personation of everyday, good-humored, sharp-tongued, boyish young fellows." Most perceptive of all, perhaps, was the *New York Times* critic, who wrote, "Mr. Fairbanks is not beautiful. He has, however, the very pleasant personality. Fortunately for his own future and for those who will have occasion to sit in judgment on his future efforts, he has something more."

This was the essence of the matter: Doug may not have been the handsomest matinee idol treading the boards, but he had *something more*.

All for a Girl, however, did not last long. "I played the part of a speedy young chap named Harold Jepson," Fairbanks wrote later. "I regret to state as a chill and bitter fact that Harold's speed took him straight off the boards . . . after a brief run of a month."

Still, Fairbanks used the play thirteen years later as a central point around which to weave a tale related to his then internationally famous smile. He had lunch with a friend on a bright June afternoon, so his story goes. The friend told him a "tremendously funny" story. The story stuck with him, and during the day's matinee of *All for a Girl*, at "the one really serious and dramatic moment in this play," it leaped back into his mind.

He grinned—"a genuine convulsion which spread itself wantonly over my whole face. . . . The more I tried to control myself, the worse I got." The play was in the dwindles, "and so close to the margin of complete failure that only a little shove was necessary to send it over. I knew I had given it this shove." But instead of the expected reproaches, his story continued, he received only accolades from his producer. "He wanted to know why I had been holding back on him and concealing this marvelous smile until it was too late to do the drooping fortunes of the play any good. Advertisements were promptly prepared counseling

the public to Come and See the Famous Fairbanks Smile." He continued in a self-deprecating tone: "I now think that the public response
to this appeal represented correctly the proper valuation of the smile.
It brought in box-office receipts of thirty-seven dollars and fifty cents,
and shortly after this the play failed and was withdrawn. But the harm
was already done."

No evidence of such advertisements exists, of course. The play ran
for one month in August, so there was no "bright June afternoon."
But what are trifling facts to interfere with glorious myths? Note the
charming mixture of self-effacement within the larger portrait of success.
His first true starring role was a short-lived fizzle. It was neither such a
glorious flop to be worthy of the *Hamlet* story ("Mr. Warde's company
was bad but worst of all was Douglas Fairbanks as Laertes . . .") nor a
triumph to be reveled in. It was—there is no kinder word—a mediocrity.

But mediocrity was not Fairbanks's middle name. So in looking back
on the experience, he transformed it. It became the launching point—the
inadvertent launching point—for the Famous Fairbanks Smile. It became
the reason he moved from his plans for grand drama to light comedy. A
boy couldn't help it. Never mind that he had been succeeding in light
comedic parts up to this point. Fate, in the form of a remembered joke
and a flashing smile, had provided a turning point during *All for a Girl*.
And this is how he would choose to remember—or at least present—his
indifferent star debut. But he would have no cause for rationalizations
with his next play. *A Gentleman from Mississippi* was a bona fide smash.

Mississippi was much like *Mr. Smith Goes to Washington*, if Mr. Smith
had been a three-hundred-pound, wise old southern widower. The title
character was played by Thomas Wise; the celebrated character actor had
also coauthored the play with Harrison Rhodes. Fairbanks had the Jean
Arthur role: the worldly wise newspaper reporter who takes the senator
under his wing and guides him through the corrupt system. Like *Man
of the Hour,* the play had political machinations to spare, but unlike
Hour, it addressed them with wit instead of melodrama.

Just as Brady had played on the politics of New York and Tam-
many Hall by previewing *The Man of the Hour* in Albany, he premiered

Mississippi in Washington, DC, at the New National Theater on September 21, 1908. The press loved it, the crowds roared, and Teddy Roosevelt, nearing the end of his second term, reportedly declared the play to be "Bully!" and "A corker!" Better yet, as far as Doug was concerned, he got to meet his idol when the cast was invited to the White House.

Theodore Roosevelt was his hero, the embodiment of just about everything that Fairbanks was or wanted to be. In many ways, they were identical. In the words of historian Richard Zacks, Roosevelt was "energetic, stubborn, opinionated, with a fondness for manliness—boxing, hunting, military history." A contemporary of Roosevelt could have been describing Fairbanks when he said of the president: "He was tremendously excitable, unusually endowed with emotional feeling and nervous energy, and I believe his life was a continual effort to control himself."

Fairbanks was the genuine personification of Roosevelt's edict of living the strenuous life. He set many of his films in the West, in part, historian Alistair Cooke was to write, "because it was the best [background] to demonstrate how he felt about the enervating effects of modern plumbing." Later in life he would attempt big-game hunting in emulation of his hero. And where his history did not match Roosevelt's, he rewrote it. He claimed to have attended Harvard (Teddy was a Harvard man) and actively worked to present an image of himself as coming from a respectable Protestant family—the sort of family, like that of the Dutch Roosevelts, that was old money and represented all that was traditional and wholesome and good in the eyes of America at the turn of the twentieth century.

He was, as was his idol, the antithesis of a *mollycoddle*—one of the late president's favorite terms. Ten years after this meeting Fairbanks would spend the equal of twenty years' salary for an average American simply to retain the term *mollycoddle* as a film title. One of the many strains in his relationship with his father-in-law was over Roosevelt. Fairbanks told a reporter at the time that Sully "loves Roosevelt about as much as a newborn kitten adores the Atlantic Ocean." Still, "I knew 'way down in my heart that I admired him [Roosevelt] more than any man I ever knew."

Still, at the time of the meeting Fairbanks anticipated the usual platitudes. After all, he and his troupe were merely actors, and this was *Roosevelt*. "I expected he'd howdy do me and tell me that he liked the show and enjoyed my acting; and that he thought the drama was a wonderful means of expression . . . and all that old stuff," he recalled. But the president, with his prodigious memory and iron-grip handshake, took him aback. "I never got such a surprise in my life. He knew all about me, every play I had ever been in, all about my family, where they came from, who they were, all about my wife's family. In fact, he reminded me of things about myself that I had forgotten," he said. "I'm for him to the end. He's got them all beat. He's a wonder."

From Washington, the company moved to New York City and the Bijou Theatre. Critics were ecstatic. The success of the play was assured, the *New York Dramatic Mirror* claimed, "before the first act was half over." All agreed that Fairbanks was not playing a supporting role but that he and Thomas Wise—an odd couple, they—were truly costars. The *New York Times* critic wrote that Doug's "fresh, breezy, wholesome way of saying things made just the right foil for the easy-going Senator." There were *twenty* curtain calls on opening night.

It remained a smash throughout the winter. Brady started giving out souvenirs for the one hundredth, two hundredth, three hundredth performances. By May, the play was novelized. When the summer season came, and with it time to shut down the dramatic theater, Brady did something unprecedented: he moved the play to the roof garden of the New Amsterdam Theatre. While Ziegfeld and his Follies girls could stage musicals on a rooftop theater, never before had any straight comedy or drama been presented in such a setting. All costumes and scenery were totally revamped, and the company performed under the stars throughout July and early August.

By the time they hit their four hundredth performance, they were back at the Bijou. In late September 1909 the company moved *in toto* to Boston and the Park Theatre, where they stayed for a record-breaking run, moving to Philadelphia in mid-December.

It was a propitious time to start a family, and Beth gave birth to a nine-pound son, Douglas Fairbanks Jr., on December 9. Her father had advanced the young couple the funds to rent an apartment at the Apthorp, on the Upper West Side; *his* first grandchild was not going to come home to a theatrical hotel! It was not a wise move for a man whose financial fortunes were crumbling, but it seemed the time for a grand gesture, and his extravagant daughter (and, in the words of his son, "equally extravagant actor-husband") were not disposed to decline.

Late February 1910 the play returned to Washington for a week at the Columbia Theatre. By this time at least four touring companies were playing *Mississippi* around the country. By April, when the original cast was playing in Syracuse, there is evidence that theatrical audiences were recognizing Doug's unique charms. Three hundred students attended the opening night performance, and after curtain speeches "the student body compelled Mr. Fairbanks to jump over a chair and walk down a flight of stairs on his hands, a feat which was greeted as the top-notch dramatic event of the evening."

Fairbanks finally left the play that summer, arriving in Great Britain in late May with Beth and their new baby, staying in Bourne End, on the Upper Thames. By all accounts, Doug was a proud new father. He was photographed with the billiard-ball-bald infant* almost as often as was Beth, who shared Ella's mania for portraits of her son. One charming photograph of Junior during his first summer shows the exuberant father lying on his back on a British lawn, feet in the air, his delighted baby held straight into the sky. They enjoyed a rented Tudor cottage, the International Horse Show, and the revived London social season. (They were just in time for the relaxation of official mourning for King Edward VII.) *Mississippi* had increased Fairbanks's newsworthiness: their international comings and goings were being reported for the first time in the *Times*—as were Fairbanks's heroics.

On Derby Day, welching bookmakers robbed visiting Americans— among them, A. G. Vanderbilt—of thousands of dollars in winnings.

---

* Fairbanks Jr.'s self-description.

But the day was not totally lost, for the press reported that "Douglas Fairbanks, the actor, chased a 'bookie' across the field and made him disgorge." There would be many more rescues and spontaneous acts of athletic heroics in following years, but in the age of press-agentry and ballyhoo, it is difficult to separate fact from fiction. Fairbanks was at this point not yet a world-famous figure, and this report smacks of truth. He wanted for neither physical courage nor impulsiveness. What he lacked was a press agent. That would come with Hollywood.

At any rate, there appear to have been no other colorful incidents while abroad, and the family returned to the States to enjoy Connecticut in August while Fairbanks entered rehearsals for his starring role in *The Cub*, which previewed in Boston in mid-September 1910.

The Cub was a farce based on the Hatfield-McCoy story, demonstrating a typical Kentucky feud, in which twenty-one mountaineers lost their lives over a quarrel about a pig. Fairbanks played a cub reporter, "fresh from college . . . sent by his editor to 'cover' the feud . . . because his boyish enthusiasm and supreme confidence in his own abilities strike his editor as fitting the requirements of the assignment—those of being just plain 'fool.'"*

Fairbanks's entrance into the Kentucky hills was comically inauspicious: he arrived, Quixote-like, astride a donkey with a license plate above its tail. Inevitably, he falls in love with a beautiful mountain girl—who prevents, in the dry words of a critic of the time, "the further progress of the ass." Ultimately the feud is settled on the $1.50 pig by the payment of $1.37, the remaining cents being waived in exchange for one of the clans getting the opportunity to thrash our hero reporter for falling in with the wrong side.

Producer Brady remembered this production as the first in which he recognized Fairbanks's athletic ability. (Presumably he'd been absent during curtain calls for *Mississippi*, and for purposes of the narrative he conveniently forgot that his star had walked down steps on his hands

---

* The plot device of eager reporter and cynical editor would be lifted by Fairbanks nearly a decade later for *Say! Young Fellow*.

between acts in *Clothes*.) "In one scene he had to run upstairs in a two-level set and save somebody's life—probably the heroine's," he recalled years later. "Run?" he quoted Fairbanks as asking. "What's the matter with jumping?" Brady was dubious. There was a "twelve-foot gap between stage floor and upper floor."

Fairbanks declared this no challenge at all. "Why, that's simple," he said. He "took a little run, caught the edge of the flooring by the stair-opening and pulled up as easy as an alley-cat taking a fence." Curiously, Brady claimed to have missed the appeal of this thespian approach. "That made a tremendous hit with the audience, but I didn't get the idea," he claimed. "I never did see what an asset Fairbanks' acrobatics were until the movies pointed it out to me."

Perhaps his claim of an inability to recognize Doug's particular charms related to his personal dislike of the actor. The relationship between the two men was often stormy; Brady claimed he did not take Fairbanks back after his turn in the soap business until "my lawyers had made sure of him." But evidence argues that Brady *was* making great hay out of his star's physical skills. (Once Brady was quoted as saying, "Put him in a death scene and he'd find a way to break the furniture.") By the time *The Cub* was touring, advance publicity was playing up this angle heavily. "It requires the physical endurance of a trained athlete to do the stunts demanded in the part," read one article. "In his contact with the feudists Steve [Fairbanks's character] is handled roughly, and in the last act he makes a dive into a bed that is not only an acrobatic wonder, but also that looks like he must break an arm or suffer some injury. It is a dive few actors would care to take eight times a week."

Thus Doug began to distinguish himself from all the other light comic leading men in the field. The combination of remarkable physical skills with the willingness (*Why, that's simple!*) to subject himself to the nightly risks and bruises made him stand out. But even without his athleticism, he was garnering glowing reviews. A New York critic wrote, "The audience was kept almost continually in laughter every time he spoke. His winning smile and dashing manner made him a favorite before the play was half an hour old."

The Cub ran for three months in New York, shuffling between theaters as Brady's requirements dictated.* In early April 1911, Brady announced that Doug would be starring in *A Gentleman of Leisure*, but first his entire stable of stars would be featured in a limited-run revival of *The Lights o' London*.

The Lights o' London had been a tremendous hit when it premiered in 1881. It was an early entry in what was then the latest theatrical craze: melodrama. Thomas Wise (still soldiering on in *The Gentleman from Mississippi*) had portrayed the villain in a touring production in 1884. Brady himself played the policeman in the same production. It was the sort of play of which everyone had fond, nostalgic memories. F. W. Bert, Brady's right-hand man, treasurer, and confidential adviser, had been the first to produce the piece in the States, and it was he who urged Brady to put it on as a revival. After all, it was "the prize melodrama of 30 years . . . time-proof." Brady assembled a formidable cast, including Fairbanks, Thomas Wise, and a young Marguerite Clark, and premiered the revival at the Lyric Theatre on May 1.

Perhaps, somewhere in the annals of theater history, there was a more disastrous opening night. After all, the theater didn't burn down around the patrons' heads. By the end of the evening, however, Brady might have wished it had. The audience came expecting to bask in the glow of warm memories. Instead, they discovered that youthful memories weren't what they used to be: what was great then was suddenly old-fashioned now. Where they should have gasped, they laughed.

---

* In the cast as one of the feuding clan members was a young actor roughly the same age as Fairbanks—Elmer Booth. He would appear with Fairbanks in future plays and vaudeville acts, but he is best remembered for his brief contribution to film. Although he was to die in an automobile accident in 1915, his immortality was assured by his performance as the Snapper Kid in D. W. Griffith's *The Musketeers of Pig Alley* in 1912. In 1910, he was a second-string performer who, in between stage engagements, sought employ in the flickers. He must have felt a case of déjà vu that same year, when Griffith cast him as—little surprise—a member of a feuding clan in *A Feud in the Kentucky Hills*. It differed from *The Cub* in every other way. This being Griffith, the story was not a comedy. And the lead was a young woman, herself on the brink of fame and fortune: Mary Pickford.

Circumstances did nothing to help. The opening curtain went up too early, revealing nonplussed stagehands. The villain was to murder the elderly uncle in the dark so as to lay the blame on the hero. The stage lamp stubbornly refused to darken, and the hapless uncle was murdered in bright light. At one point, the troublesome curtain came down on a cluster of extras dressed as policemen, leaving some inside, some out, and the remainder entangled in the folds. Brady himself was backstage, assisting in the setup of the large set for the London Bridge, when part of it dislodged, striking him on the shoulder. He took his curtain call with an arm in a sling. His actors were taken aback by the cheerful hisses for the villains and laughter for the rest of the cast. They threatened to quit, without the customary two weeks' notice. Brady held them back by promising to update the script.

The week became worse for Brady. He and his aged treasurer were walking down Broadway to deposit the second night's box office receipts when F. W. Bert collapsed. Brady caught him as best he could (his arm was presumably still in a sling), but by the time the old man was dragged into a nearby druggist's, he was dead. If ever there was a jinxed production in this most superstitious of worlds, this was it.

And then something happened. Brady made touches here and there, cutting down some of the more emphatic *Curse her*s. But that isn't what did the trick. The actors decided to have fun with the piece.

Fairbanks, ever the masterful practical joker, led the charge. His character was offstage for the climax of the play, a dramatic rescue in which the hero leaped off the London Bridge and, clinging to a spar with one hand, held a rescuee by the other. In one performance, Doug armed himself with a basket of fish, opened a trap door behind the hero, and "one after another, sent a perfect shower of fish over the two actors. From the front it looked as if flying fish were leaping out of the water." Not only did the audience explode in laughter, but the actors, too, had trouble keeping straight faces to finish the play.

In the finale, Fairbanks was posed nonchalantly leaning against a fence while the hero and heroine embraced. The clinch was a prolonged one, made worse for the hero by the fact that on one particular night,

Doug rigged up a small rubber tube attached to a faucet. Just as the hero clutched the heroine, Fairbanks put the tube down the back of his collar. The actor "was not to be balked, but certainly played a very damp love scene that evening."

That is not to say that Fairbanks didn't get as good as he gave. Doug played Philosopher Jack, a costermonger. In a reverse twist on the eight-pound-shot-in-the-villain's-hat trick that he played during the run of *Mrs. Jack*, some wag filled his basket of potatoes with paving stones. When it came time to lift the basket, he couldn't. The line of the man playing opposite him was "What have you there, my good man?" His reply should have been "Potatoes." "But this evening," Charles Richman, the play's villain, reported, "without a waver, he looked cunningly at the innocent inquirer and answered, simply: 'A little 'eavy 'umor, Sir.'"

Brady's recollection of Fairbanks was not always fond, perhaps because of such hijinks. "No doubt Fairbanks' temperament had a good deal to do with the way he got across to an audience," Brady recalled twenty-five years later. "But its regardlessness did not make him popular with his coworkers on the stage, which was unhandy for everybody, including me as a manager. It did come in very handy once, however." Near the end of the play was a tremendous fight. Charles Richman recalled: "The last act was a riot. Folks got so they dropped in for the finale alone. They would fill the house a little after ten."

"His big scene was in a market where he jumped out from behind a cabbage wagon and started battling a crowd of supers single-handed, the curtain coming down on the shindy at its height," Brady wrote. "It was a fine thing, being just Fairbanks' dish. All the finer because the supers all had it in for him and it was usually anything but a fake fight. Eight times a week they ganged up on him and gave him a good two minutes of brisk battering."

Richman elaborated: "In the fight scene he stirred the whole stage up to a fearful pitch. He really fought and one night, the word was passed, 'This is the evening when Doug gets his.' It was passed too frequently and Fairbanks heard about it so he want to Columbia College and got three football men to mix in among the stage hands, in overalls. The fight that evening rivaled the slaughter in the sunken road at Waterloo and the scrapping on the pass of Thermopylae. One of the Columbia fellows had his nose broken and had to be taken in an ambulance to the hospital. One of our stage hands was knocked unconscious. Fairbanks was knocked down and seized by the feet, was dragged from the stage, yelling. That ended the riot, for the management sent back word that humor was going a little too far."

"Anybody else would have complained to the management, with some justification," Brady wrote. "But not Fairbanks—he loved it, and gave the supers just as good as they sent all the way." Richman summed it up best: "There was no holding Douglas Fairbanks down."

The play ran the intended four weeks on Broadway, and an extra week in Brooklyn. In the end, it grossed Brady an astonishing $60,000.

Rehearsals for his next play began on August 3, 1911. *A Gentleman of Leisure* began life as a novella, *The Gem Collector*, written by a struggling young P. G. Wodehouse in his pre–Jeeves and Bertie days. The original story featured a reformed jewel thief who had since come into an inheritance. The plot progressed to a *Raffles*-like adventure complete with a British castle, a dimwitted lord, and a diamond necklace. In 1910 the story was revised—our hero was no longer a thief—and published in book form as *The Intrusion of Jimmy*. Wodehouse and John Stapleton then converted the story to play form, and Brady snapped it up.

It is easy to understand why. Once the character was decriminalized, the part seemed custom-made for Fairbanks. The hero was "a young man of medium height, whose great breadth and depth of chest made him look shorter than he really was. His jaw was square and protruded slightly; and this, combined with a certain athletic jauntiness of carriage and a pair of piercing brown eyes very much like those of a bull-terrier, gave him an air of aggressiveness which belied his character." Wrote Wodehouse, "Jimmy was one of those men who are charged to the brim with force. Somehow the force had to find an outlet."

Brady knew how to provide this outlet. In the original text, when the hero encounters a housebreaker, he overcomes him with a single tackle. On opening night (August 24 at Brady's Playhouse Theatre), "the audience was treated to one of the most realistic fights on a darkened stage the town has seen in a long time."

But Fairbanks was not to fight on that particular stage for long. Brady started playing musical chairs with his plays, moving *A Gentleman of Leisure* to the Globe Theatre in mid-September, in order to make room for his production of a drama titled *The Rack*. *The Rack* failed miserably, but Brady did not return Fairbanks to his flagship theater: the producer was saving that space for a play featuring Grace George—his wife. To add insult to injury, by late September it was announced that *Gentleman* would again have to find a new home, as yet another piece was coming to the Globe.

Perhaps this is what set off the break. The story Doug told his family went thus: *Gentleman* was not the success that Brady had hoped for, and "after the final curtain," Brady summoned Fairbanks to his office and asked him to cancel his contract early, "through no fault of his." Letitia Fairbanks wrote of her uncle, "It was typical of him that he could always see the other fellow's side. In a spirit of genuine friendship and good feeling, he stuck out his hand."

This does not smack of the truth. Brady's final attitude toward Fairbanks, as expressed in his autobiography, was not that of a man in debt to an actor who graciously ended a contract early. It was that of a producer with a nettlesome star, likely a valuable star, who had left him in the lurch early in the run of what was, up to then, a successful play. Both Brady and Fairbanks remained diplomatically mum on the subject, but by early October a split was announced. Brady, from the Playhouse, stated that he and Mr. Fairbanks were still the best of friends. (The reporter unhelpfully failed to note if this statement was produced through gritted teeth.) Mr. Fairbanks, from his dressing room at the Globe, echoed the sentiment. He simply wished other opportunities. A change in management might do him good. He was considering offers. Cohan & Harris were interested, very interested. But they didn't have a play ready for him on such short notice. Then there was Charles Frohman. He had a piece, *Jack Spurlock, Prodigal*, "prepared with him in view."

So the pattern that Brady and Fairbanks had established for themselves (split, reunion, split) played itself out for the third time since their initial breach during *The Pit*. One suspects that there were even more near misses within those seven years. In January 1909, for example, very early in the run of *A Gentleman from Mississippi*, Fairbanks had announced that "Western capitalists" were planning to build a theater for him. Every detail was announced: the location, the architect, the opening play, the seating capacity. These Western capitalists were, no doubt, his brothers.

He was, even at this early stage of his career, developing a view of show business that gave equal weight to the *business* of the show. It was said that he hung around the counting room, "anxiously watching the till fill up." He was exasperated by the concept that the public owed its attention to the struggling arts. "The public owes no more toward the theater than toward grocery stores, canning factories or livery stables," he said. "The theater with theatergoers is a matter of what Falconbridge calls 'commodity' and nothing else; it has never been anything else and never will be."

Nothing more was heard of the plan—likely it was a negotiating tactic with Brady—but his confidence here is evident. He felt himself, even at that early stage of his career, capable of not only production but also theater ownership—what was, in a sense, the whole ball of wax in the world of live theater and what would become, in time, two parts of the holy trinity of the film business: production, distribution, and exhibition. In less than a decade, he would come to revolutionize this model with the formation of United Artists.

But this was yet to come. By early October, Fairbanks had given his last performance in *A Gentleman of Leisure* and still had no contract signed. Without the charismatic actor, the play lasted only another two weeks. As short as its run was, whatever his role had been in killing the play early seemed to cause no resentment on the part of its author. Wodehouse was later to republish *The Intrusion of Jimmy* under the title of *A Gentleman of Leisure*. He dedicated the book to Fairbanks.

Ultimately, Fairbanks signed with Cohan & Harris, but it was not a smooth transition. George M. Cohan was all of thirty-two years old in 1911, but he already wore the mantle of "the man who owned Broadway." A vaudevillian since childhood, he had been a superstar since *Little Johnny Jones* in 1904. With partner Sam Harris he produced more than fifty plays and musicals in the years leading up to 1920. He was one of the few individuals in that century who could legitimately enter into competition with Fairbanks as a force of nature. On paper, it looked like a brilliant shift of management. As it was, Cohan & Harris would produce only one play with Fairbanks, and his theatrical career was never quite as stable after he left Brady's management.

Initially, things looked promising. Though the producer team did not have anything immediately at hand, Cohan pledged that they would have a piece for him ready to open by Thanksgiving: "The typical young American, winning fame, fortune and female over insurmountable odds," he promised. It sounded perfect. There was just one hitch: Cohan did not produce the script.

Inactivity did not suit Fairbanks well. He manifested a behavior that he was to repeat throughout his life. Whether at loose ends or at wit's end, he got out of Dodge. "I got the wanderlust so bad that I couldn't stand it any longer, and I just 'beat it,'" he recalled. "I took a steamer to Cuba and walked across the island from Havana to Batabano, about one hundred and twenty miles." With him was friend and costar (in both *The Cub* and *A Gentleman of Leisure*) Elmer Booth.

From there he took a ship for the Yucatán Peninsula and walked from Progresso to Mérida. History does not record whether he was footsore or tanned and rested on his December arrival in New York, but he returned to the news that Cohan had still not produced the promised play. "I've got the young man in the drawing room and I can't get him out," Cohan reportedly offered by way of excuse.

Never patient, or perhaps in need of money (he had already returned his family to their former digs, the Algonquin Hotel), Fairbanks next did the unexpected: he signed with Arthur Klein, a vaudeville manager. At first glance, this seems astonishing. Fairbanks had been in "the legitimate" since 1902. Even as a teenager on the touring circuit, he had never set foot on a variety stage. But theater historian David Mayer clarifies the issue:

> It was not uncommon to find . . . major stars playing cut-down versions of their vehicles to vaudeville audiences. Sarah Bernhardt, for example, contrived to make a vaudeville sketch from a medley of roles in which she had formerly toured American legitimate houses. To appear in vaudeville was not a descent from the lofty heights of the legitimate stage to the degradation of the itinerant variety artiste which some film and theatre historians might imagine. Rather, stepping into vaudeville was, in the closing years of the nineteenth century and the early decades of the twentieth, a conventional tactic for prolonging the life of a stage play whose popularity was marginal or visibly waning. It was a favored way of earning a theatrical livelihood when the national economy, and with it, the legitimate stage, experienced fallow periods. Actors of stature—the entire Drew and Barrymore clan . . . moved their dramas onto variety circuits when business slackened, then returned to the theatre when conditions improved or new roles beckoned.

Such appears to have been the case with Fairbanks. February 17, 1912, initiated what was billed as "Star Week at the Fifth Avenue." Both Fairbanks and his *Mississippi* costar Thomas Wise premiered sketches at the theater, in what *Variety* called the "first instance of record where two 'names' have made their metropolitan debut simultaneously."

Fairbanks was in a twenty-five-minute sketch titled *A Regular Businessman*, playing "a young lawyer, with nothing but debts and a pretty stenographer." The opening was a hit, and as Doug was taking his bows at the conclusion, the elder Wise joined him on the stage, patted him on the head, and informed the audience, "He's the greatest kid in the world." No one demurred, and plans were made for an extended run, to be followed by a tour. But it was not to be. The powers-that-be at Cohan & Harris huddled and decided to send Fairbanks west to Chicago, to star in the Chicago production of their Broadway hit *Officer 666*.

Officer 666 was a step up from two-a-day back to the legitimate, but it did not represent a full return to his starring days on Broadway, suggesting again that his departure from Brady was made with more haste than consideration. True, the production was the inaugural show for George M. Cohan's Grand Opera House in Chicago. But it was a second unit for a play already running on Broadway, and Fairbanks was second billed.

He played a role very similar to that in *A Gentleman of Leisure*, a bored millionaire "who finds his money a nuisance and hungers for a thrill." Nearly stealing the play from Fairbanks was John Miltern, playing the suave thief who has assumed the identity of Fairbanks's character. Literally stealing the spotlight one matinee was Doug Jr., sitting in a box with his mother. ("I was about three then and a dumpling of a boy," he recollected later.) He suddenly noticed his father in a moonlit love scene and shrilled, "Oh, Mummy! Look what Daddy's doing with that lady!"* It took some time for both audience and players to recover.

The play had a long, successful run in Chicago, and Fairbanks remained with it until August, when he assumed the part—second billed—in the New York production. Cohan announced at the same time that his star would stay with the production only until his next play, *Hawthorne of the U.S.A.*, was ready for rehearsals.

Despite its Cohan-esque title, *Hawthorne of the U.S.A.* was an adaptation of a British play. In it the hero, now a true-blooded American, travels to a European kingdom, where he falls in love with a beautiful woman—who, of course, turns out to be the princess. He saves the kingdom from a revolution, mostly by way of fisticuffs; restores a grateful king; and ultimately wins the hand of the fair maiden. It was in time to serve as a template for some of the Fairbanks films to come and to be virtually copied for one: *His Majesty the American*. Fairbanks himself referenced it often in the course of interviews—frequently

---

* It is possible that Fairbanks Jr. has melded two separate events together. The play description sounds more like *Hawthorne of the U.S.A.*, which also played in Chicago when Junior was three.

misremembering Brady as the producer of the play but always recalling the climactic fight scene. "I made my first appearance by vaulting a wall, and at the end of the third act I sprang from a balcony to the throat of the villain," he said later. "It went all right, but an actor can't put up as good a fight every performance of a play as he can for the movies, where he can afford to take a chance on being laid up for a while."

Out-of-town tryouts began in late September in Washington, DC. By the time the production reached Philadelphia, trouble was becoming apparent. Preview audiences were not up to expectations, and the show was pulled for revisions by play doctor Winchell Smith. The company returned to Washington, where puzzled critics noted that the revised fourth act was "most-ill-advisedly written in American slang," and was almost a transcript of the last act of another Cohan play, *Get-Rich-Quick Wallingford*.

But Fairbanks himself was garnering praise. The adjectives came flowing: buoyant, breezy, daring, agile, enthusiastic, intensely earnest, peppery, live, wide-awake—the play may have been lacking, but its star was not. Burns Mantle of the *Chicago Daily Tribune* even coined a phrase for the occasion. Doug, he wrote, was "one of the most skittenish and happy of our younger stars."

The opening night on Broadway on November 4, 1912, went well. The house was packed, and "a tumultuous greeting was accorded the young star." Fairbanks had a large and loyal following, and they turned out in droves. They were not disappointed. "No matter who condemns the piece or praises its entertaining qualities," wrote *Variety*'s critic, "one will admit that the power behind the throne is Fairbanks. He has the pep, ginger and dynamic force to back up a personality that hits any audience straight between the eyes."

But a star, skittenish or not, is not enough to keep an indifferent play running for long. The play was pulled from the Astor Theatre the first week of January and began a peripatetic existence for the next three months, moving from the Grand Opera House to the Montauk Theatre in Brooklyn and then, mid-January, to Cohan's Grand Opera House in Chicago.

To be fair to Cohan, he was aggressive in promoting the piece. Newspapers carried tales for the credulous of Fairbanks's injuries during the fight scenes ("to date the young star has been badly wounded twice with a sword; dislocated his wrist once; thrown both shoulders out; is never without a broken finger and has just escaped water on the knee several times"). Cohan's team mailed HAWTHORNE, U.S.A. postcards to theatergoers and printed special foldout paper suitcases with photos advertising the play.

But business was still shaky. A month into the Chicago run, *Variety* reported that the house was still top-heavy—selling cheap seats in the balcony but not the higher-priced ones on the main floor. Fairbanks reportedly started making bets with the house manager on the house take for the week. By the end of February, the actor playing the king left the cast abruptly, due to a quarrel with the star. A week later, *Variety* stated that Fairbanks would close his season in two weeks. "There is said to be a straining of the entente cordiale between star and management."

Strain or no, the company went on, playing short stays in St. Louis; Columbus, Ohio; and finally, in early April, Boston, where the play closed and was released for stock companies. To add insult to injury, George M. Cohan finally got the hero of his long-promised play out of the drawing room but gave himself, not Fairbanks, the role. Cohan's *Broadway Jones* was a hit, running 176 performances on Broadway.

Cohan was vague about a follow-up to *Hawthorne*. In late April there was a brief trial of a play titled *Cooper Hoyt, Inc.* in Atlantic City. It was a tale of a "popular chap who is not successful financially"—until his friends incorporate him. But by the time the reviews hit the paper, Fairbanks and family, including Ella, were already on the *Olympic* sailing for Europe. He announced various plans: He would play London vaudeville in *A Regular Businessman*. He would travel around the world.

In the end, he simply haunted the theaters in Paris and London, trying to catch every show possible. When he returned in mid-July, plans were announced that he was to enter rehearsals for *Cooper Hoyt, Inc.* Nothing came of this. Two weeks later, Cohan announced that his star had been reassigned and was now to be in a piece titled *Something for Nothing*. Nothing was all that resulted.

So, it appeared as if he would have to return to the variety stage. This was not likely to endear him to Cohan & Harris, who at last account were "unalterably opposed" to any of their stars appearing in vaudeville. But Fairbanks had not only a wife and child to consider but increasingly dependent in-laws. Since the failure of the soap company in the spring of 1908, Dan Sully had been reduced to renting out his estate in Watch Hill, Rhode Island, as a high-end boardinghouse. Fairbanks assembled a company and, with a production called *Dollars and Sense*, started the weary rounds of the New England variety circuit: Springfield, Massachusetts; Portsmouth, New Hampshire; Boston. He was undoubtedly a headliner, and a matinee idol as well: in Boston the handsome star drew audiences that skewed heavily female, three women for every man. But it was a relief—a significant relief—when producer Joseph Brooks, in association with Klaw and Erlanger, tapped him for a revival of the famed play *The Henrietta*. Fairbanks was so eager to return to the legitimate that he began rehearsals while still under contract for his vaudeville engagements. The *Henrietta* company rehearsed in the mornings and early afternoons, with Doug "jumping back and forth" to make his vaudeville appearances.

The Henrietta was a storied success from the moment of its premiere in Union Square in 1887. The tale was that of a father and son: the father, a crusty multimillionaire, and his son, Bertie (a.k.a. "the Lamb"), a tepid milquetoast. The father, played by William H. Crane, cuts the ineffectual Bertie off with a mere five hundred thousand and trusts his business affairs to an unscrupulous son-in-law. While the father is off on a yacht wooing a widow, the son-in-law engineers the old man's ruination on the stock market—until bumbling Bertie wanders onto the trading floor and throws his half a million dollars into the fray to save the family fortune.

Bertie had only ever been played by one man, Stuart Robson. After the long Broadway run, he purchased rights to the play and became as closely identified with the part as Maude Adams was with Peter Pan.

When he died in 1903, so, it seemed, did the role. Accordingly, there was much curiosity (and preemptive knife sharpening) on the part of critics to see what Fairbanks would do with the part in the revival, now named *The New Henrietta*. After all, he had built his career and his reputation on, as one wrote, "his own very virile, positive personality." How could anybody, but especially this handsome young live wire, step into the shoes of the late Mr. Robson? It "seemed almost a sacrilege."

In the end, there was no need for cutlery. Both in out-of-town tryouts and at the Broadway premiere at the Knickerbocker Theatre, Fairbanks garnered the best reviews of his theatrical career. He "surprised even his most intimate friends with the excellence of his performance." It was "the best role the popular young actor has created." Seeing a Crane-Fairbanks collaboration along the lines of the Wise-Fairbanks one during the spectacular *Gentleman from Mississippi* run, producer Brooks announced that Fairbanks and the elder veteran would partner on the stage. They would play *The Merry Wives of Windsor*, Richard Sheridan's *The Rivals*, and Oliver Goldsmith's *She Stoops to Conquer*. The partnership, he declared, would run for at least five years.

Except, of course, for the fact that the play, despite rave reviews, was a financial disappointment. The New York engagement was scheduled as a limited run, and the play closed on Broadway on the last day of January 1914. It toured through the winter: Boston, Syracuse, Baltimore, Washington, DC. But by mid-March the theatrical pages were announcing that the play was being withdrawn, and Mr. Crane would be at leisure until next season. Mr. Fairbanks would return to vaudeville. There was no more discussion of a Crane-Fairbanks partnership.

Fairbanks gritted his teeth and completed the contracted touring engagements through April and May, appearing in such venues as St. Louis and Detroit. *The New Henrietta* seems to have been more successful as the company moved to the center of the country, and Klaw and Erlanger decided to renew the tour in the fall. Fairbanks was not to join them. George M. Cohan might have nothing for him, but manager A. H. Woods did, and by mid-May 1914 Fairbanks announced yet another change in management. He would premiere *He Comes Up*

Smiling in the fall season. The hero of the play is a voluntary hobo, cheerfully wandering the romantic roads until a mix-up with a suit of clothes and a swimming hole has him impersonating a reigning "Cotton King." Fiction being fiction, he soon falls in with a traveling party consisting of the competing Cotton King and his beautiful daughter. The party whose suit he is wearing has evil designs on Daddy's fortune, but all ends well with our hero cornering the cotton market and—surprise!—winning the girl.

But before then, it was back to vaudeville. There would be no summering over the Atlantic; Europe was no place to be in 1914. At least he had the consolation of playing at the top: New York City's Palace Theatre. Most vaudevillians spent their entire careers in hopes of playing the Palace, and Fairbanks opened his new sketch there in mid-May. It was titled *All at Sea* and was a curious mixture of *A Regular Businessman* and *The Henrietta*, set in the wireless room of a ship. The constrained setting and single act gave little room for Fairbanks's "peppery maneuvers," and within a month he was back to his *Regular Businessman* standby. June and August found him at theaters in such towns as Atlantic City and Brighton Beach.

Rehearsals for *He Comes Up Smiling* started in late June. Out-of-town runs were prolonged by script doctoring, but it finally premiered on September 16 at Broadway's Liberty Theatre to favorable reviews. The *New York Times* referred to the "whole-souled sunniness of a manner which is neither of town or country. Mr. Fairbanks brings an infectious affability to his new role, but he brings something more. He brings a great deal of spirit and a lively sense of comedy." The only objection was to the final act. The original book had the hero retain his hobo ways. "But in the play the knight of the road has 'made good' by playing the cotton market and he comes up wealthy." It was, in the view of the critics, "not true to the blithe spirit of the people and the story of the play." True, no doubt. But to have the hero end up in a dinner jacket "with no end of money in his pocket and the girl of his heart in his arms" was truer to the mixed bourgeois/bohemian spirit of Fairbanks.

Smiling, like *Henrietta*, was not the success that the insiders felt it
should have been. It did better than most new plays on Broadway that
season, but that was saying little. The European war, combined with an
economic downturn and an autumn heat wave, resulted in an almost
unbroken line of failures that season. Even if houses were full, the sales
came through half-rate ticket agencies.

By early November the play was pulled, and after a week's run
in Brooklyn, Woods decided that the play did not have the legs for
a road tour. Back again—for the fourth time!—Fairbanks returned to
vaudeville. It was the same old rounds with *A Regular Businessman*. The
tour took him from Maryland to Pennsylvania to New York throughout
November and December, and early in the latter month he shared the
bill with Fanny Brice. No one seemed to mind seeing the same material; reviewers noted that Doug added some additional acrobatic antics
and noted that he "can easily go over the same route a second time,
through his very breezy playing." Happily, this was a short interlude
before his final Broadway production was to begin.

Doug's last play began its existence as *The Spotlight Man*, migrated
to *In the Limelight*, and finally premiered on the last night of 1914 as
The Show Shop. It was a backstage comedy, telling the tale of a young
millionaire who is in love with an actress. The stage mother will not
let them marry before her daughter has appeared on Broadway, so the
hero conspires to front the worst possible play and, to better ensure its
failure, is cast in the lead. Just as in *The Producers*, sixty years later, the
flop is so terrible that it is a runaway hit.

The Show Shop was itself a hit, but paradoxically this did not mean
that it was a financial success. The Broadway that the play satirized was
a Broadway that was vanishing. The world of the legitimate was being
changed by two forces.

The first was the aforementioned cut-rate ticket agencies, selling
what were indelicately termed "Those Moe Levy tickets."* By the tenth

---

* After Moe Levy, whose advertisements for cheap suits were part of the New York landscape for decades.

week of the play, such cut-rate "People's League Tickets" and "Special Play-goers' Vouchers" were being offered for nine Broadway theaters from the basement of the Fitzgerald Building. By the end of April, the number of theaters was up to twenty. Fairbanks observed the phenomenon and didn't like it. "We are doing that awful thing—" he groused in private correspondence. "Selling cut rate tickets which cause our house to sell out the last part of [the] week." Ticket prices were as low as twenty-five cents.

At the same time, one theater was enjoying the opposite experience. The Liberty Theatre (where he had starred in *Smiling* a few months prior) was attracting capacity audiences every night and matinee. Originally just the box seats were to be offered at the peak two-dollar rate, but demand was so strong that the greater part of the floor seats could also be offered at the full fare and be sold out every performance. Better yet, the management had little cost beyond the lease of the hall. There were no actors to pay, no sets to maintain, no costumes to rent.

On Broadway, in a legitimate theater, these seats were being filled by a motion picture: D. W. Griffith's epic *The Birth of a Nation*.

Fairbanks was not blind to this—nor to its implications. In *The Show Shop*, a failed producer could proclaim, "I guess I'll tackle the ten cent movies. If I can't be the Erlanger of the drama, I'll be the Woolworth." But Griffith's film, for all its considerable moral flaws, was a compelling argument that motion pictures could be art and could command full prices. Broadway, on the other hand, might produce art, but its potential for financial return did not have the scalability of motion pictures. *The Birth* was breaking records not just in one theater but in hundreds. On Broadway, returns were diminishing.

Fairbanks would claim ever after that it was seeing *The Birth* that convinced him to try motion pictures. He would also paint an elaborate trail of coy reluctance to enter the world of the flickers. But the truth is that Douglas Fairbanks and the movies had been circling each other cautiously since 1912—and they were about to embrace.

4

Triangle (as in Company)

T HE VERSION OF "How I Got into the Movies" that Fairbanks proffered for family—and, through them, to all subsequent historians—was simple. He was walking through Central Park one day in 1914, family in train. A motion picture cameraman *just happened* by and took some footage of Doug obligingly hopping over park benches. He, of course, forgot all about the incident until (continuing the tale of happy coincidences) Harry Aitken, producer for D. W. Griffith and president of Triangle Films, *just happened* to see the footage. He approached our hero. Would he care to star in motion pictures? (The myth conveniently ignores the fact that Triangle was yet to be formed, and thus Aitken was hardly recruiting Broadway stars at this juncture.)

Would he? Well, perhaps. The money was good, true. But, oh—to enter the *flickers*! Every biography quotes his exchange with good friend and Algonquin proprietor Frank Case: "A short time later Fairbanks told me he had an offer of $2,000 a week to go to Hollywood but did not know whether to accept or not," wrote Case. "Two thousand dollars was very much more than he could possibly hope for in the theater; moreover, the employment and salary were to be continuous, fifty-two weeks in the year, not for an indefinite season as in the theater. When I pointed out to him that $104,000 was a handsome amount of money, he said, 'I know, but the movies!'"*

---

* Case had it wrong. Fairbanks's original contract was for ten weeks.

Of course, our hero relents, and the history of motion pictures is changed forever.

An alternate version that Fairbanks offered during the height of his fame had him grasping the potential of the new medium immediately: "The night that I saw *The Birth of a Nation* I knew that I wanted to be in the pictures. I had much the same sort of vibration or thrill that I had when I saw the Grand Cañon for the first time. . . . Both left me wordless. Accordingly, when D. W. Griffith offered me a ten weeks' contract I was quite willing to leave the stage for a while."

The truth manages to be more prosaic and more interesting at the same time—a neat trick. Fairbanks was not an unwilling recruit nor a sudden convert to motion pictures. He had been studying the industry and trying to break into it for a number of years. While his personal narrative always made everything he did seem effortless, in truth he engaged in as much advance preparation and study for entering the film industry as he did with his stunts.

In late December 1912, while still appearing in *Hawthorne of the U.S.A.*, Fairbanks made a late-night "sightseeing" visit to the studios of Carl Laemmle's IMP (Independent Motion Picture) Company. "It has grown to a fad almost, for parties to watch the manufacturing of a movie," reported *Variety*. Accompanying the article describing the visit is a photograph of Fairbanks, dapper and complacent in a white tie, sitting, arms folded, in the front row. He is surrounded by the IMP stock company and their director, Herbert Brenon (later famous for directing such films as *Peter Pan* and *Beau Geste*). Brenon later recalled, "I went along [directing] as usual and he watched and he asked me if I was 'of the theatre.' I told him I was. He asked many questions and was fascinated by what he saw."

His interest continued into the summer of 1913, when he encountered Brenon on the *Olympic*. "We had many chats," Brenon said. "And he was then fully determined to take a 'fling.'"

By the fall of 1913, he had progressed to filming a screen test, directed by J. Searle Dawley, who was at the time directing Mary Pickford in *Caprice*. Using one of the film's sets and a script devised by

Dawley, Fairbanks was filmed at a game of cards with two other men. Doug entered the room, leaped over the back of an empty chair, and started dealing. Dawley's widow, Grace, recalled that Mary Pickford watched the test being filmed. This is possible, but if so, the lady in question had no recall of the event. Adolph Zukor offered Fairbanks a contract on the basis of this test. "I know nothing about business," Fairbanks was said to have replied. "You'd better discuss it with my wife. She manages all my business affairs." This was true. Beth, both bossy and intelligent, was handling her husband's career and finances. From the moment she stormed William Brady's office in 1907, she had been decidedly in charge—a sore point with mother-in-law Ella. Although Zukor's offer was said to be tempting, it was not tempting enough for Mrs. Fairbanks, who decided that her husband should continue on the stage.

Still, Fairbanks remained fascinated. "My many questions must have bored everyone at the studio, but they all humored me," he recalled. "When they photographed what is technically known as a 'test' and I first saw it projected, I pinched myself to see if I were awake. The idea of seeing myself on the screen seemed uncanny. Of course I had seen many Motion Pictures previous to this test; but it was the idea of seeing *myself* walk around, fumble my coat nervously, and try to grin—with a number of people looking on."

His first public film appearance was in early November 1913, during the run of *The New Henrietta*. He and the other lead *Henrietta* cast members appeared in a Kinemacolor film depicting the cast "in their social hours." While the prospect of seeing a thirty-year-old Douglas Fairbanks in color is tantalizing, the film is currently considered lost. Kinemacolor did not have wide distribution, and it is unlikely that many saw the film, even in 1913.

By the fall of 1914, with *He Comes Up Smiling* playing to dwindling audiences, he tried again. Victor Eubanks of Essanay Studios approached Fairbanks. "He agreed to come with Essanay on any sort of a contract I agreed to make," Eubanks wrote. "I wired [company head] Spoor at

Chicago and received the following reply: 'Don't want Fairbanks now. Can you find a good scenario writer?' Imagine my embarrassment when I had to tell Fairbanks the fatal news."

Undaunted, Fairbanks continued putting out feelers. His agent contacted film company Bosworth Inc., to no avail. Jesse Lasky and Sam Goldwyn, of Famous Players, contemplated signing him for a film version of *A Gentleman of Leisure*. Nothing came of this, but by November he appeared in a short produced by the Mutual Film Corporation: chapter 47 of a weekly series titled *Our Mutual Girl*. His appearance in this film, *Our Mutual Girl Sees the Yale-Princeton Game*, amounted to little more than a celebrity cameo.* The heroine is driven to the game by Fairbanks "in his racing runabout." He has a matinee, however, and leaves her to fend for herself for the rest of the short film.

Still, by early 1915 it was clear that he was going to be snapped up by *someone*. Stars from "the legitimate" were being signed by film companies throughout the spring. It was a matter of matching the man to the company; through luck or planning, Fairbanks started at the top. He signed a contract with Harry Aitken.

Wisconsin-born Harry Aitken was thirty-seven years old in the summer of 1915 and had been in the film business for ten years. He was the owner of thirty-five film exchanges (entities that would purchase short films from producers and rent them to theaters) and had, in the words of historian Richard Schickel, "a quick mind and a ready tongue." What he lacked, in Schickel's view, was patience. "He loved new beginnings but was bored by the day-to-day business of managing his creations." He had been, until May, president of the Mutual Film Corporation. His most famous accomplishment to date: wooing D. W. Griffith away from Biograph and helping fund *The Birth of a Nation*. This was done without the consent of Mutual's board of directors, on whose behalf he had pledged $40,000—forcing

---

* Of note is the fact that D. W. Griffith, in his early days after departing Biograph for Harry Aitken and the Mutual Film Corporation, directed some of these films. It is unlikely that he directed this episode, however.

him to take out loans against his Mutual stock and provide the money himself. The fortune this made him turned out to be ephemeral. He was constantly robbing Peter to pay Paul. "[His] financial affairs were sufficiently complicated to baffle a team of certified public accountants," Triangle historian Kalton Lahue recounted. "He owned many pieces of various organizations on paper, but then again, he really didn't—one had been mortgaged to buy another which in turn was used as collateral for a third and so on."

But this was not known at the time. What *was* known was that in departing from Mutual, Aitken had signed the production companies of D. W. Griffith, Mack Sennett, and Thomas H. Ince to form the three points of a production and distribution entity to be called the Triangle Film Corporation. Sennett had his collection of slapstick comedians, Thomas Ince had cowboy star William S. Hart, and Griffith had a homegrown stock company populated with such luminaries as Mae Marsh, Bobby Harron, Lillian and Dorothy Gish, and Owen Moore—husband of Mary Pickford. But for Griffith's Fine Arts unit, Harry Aitken wanted only the best. He wanted Broadway stars. Until this point, only those actors who could not make it in "the legitimate" were reduced to appearing in motion pictures; only for the past few years had cast member names even been listed on the films or in the advertising. Actors had been ashamed to be known as "movies" (the term applied to the performers before ultimately settling on the films themselves). But stars emerged from anonymity, led primarily by Mary Pickford and, within the past year, by a young British comedian by the name of Charles Chaplin. To be a star in moving pictures was no longer a shameful thing but was, in fact, quite lucrative. Mary Pickford was paid $2,000 a week, with a $10,000 bonus for each film completed. Chaplin made $1,250 a week at Essanay and by the end of the year was to sign a contract with Mutual for almost ten times that amount. Such salaries tempted even the haughtiest Broadway talent to take a flier in the flickers, and Aitken in short order had signed DeWolf Hopper, Raymond Hitchcock, Eddie Foy, Billie Burke, Weber and Fields, and Sir Herbert Beerbohm Tree. Thus, while the

Triangle Film Corporation would ultimately fail (in large part because of the desertion by Griffith and Fairbanks in the following year), it stood, in 1915, as a credible threat to such companies as Paramount and Universal. It had the top directors in the industry and was now recruiting the top stars of stage.

The terms Fairbanks (or, more likely, his wife) negotiated were excellent: $2,000 a week for ten weeks and first-class transportation to and from the West Coast for not only him and his family but also his domestic staff. The return trip was to be via San Francisco (so they could visit the Panama-Pacific International Exposition); work-related travel expenses were to be covered; and scripts were to be in keeping with Fairbanks's "talents and professional standing." Most important, direction of his films was to be supervised by D. W. Griffith.

He could not have been launched on better terms. It could be truthfully said that he started at the top and went up from there. Still, he hedged his bets. Journalist Gilbert Seldes encountered him that spring, walking down Broadway. Yes, Doug acknowledged, he was going to Hollywood. But he didn't want it to get around. "I don't want my reputation spoiled," he said. "I want to come back next year." Given how long and carefully he tried to get into the moving picture industry, one cannot but think that this was a case of a man who doth protest too much.

Aitken, more than Griffith, was an astute judge of male star quality. Alistair Cooke famously quotes him as saying, "We picked Douglas Fairbanks as a likely film star not on account of his stunts, as the majority think, but because of the splendid humanness that fairly oozed out of him." It was a pick both shrewd and fortunate, as Aitken was staking the Fine Arts portion of the Triangle Film Corporation squarely on Fairbanks's broad shoulders. Cooke and many subsequent biographers have fostered the argument that Aitken signed so many major Broadway stars that Fairbanks was, in effect, an also-signed. The fable continues with the claim that *The Lamb*, his first feature, was considered second-rate stuff by the studio but went to the theaters because there was no other film yet available from the Fine Arts division. At its premiere, the story continues, it was an unexpected hit.

This is as much a Fairbanks fable as the disastrous Duluth *Hamlet* or the break-in to Frederick Warde's dressing room. Aitken had several Fine Arts features in the can before Fairbanks completed his first film, including *The Martyrs of the Alamo*, a film frequently misattributed to Doug but which had finished production before his arrival in Los Angeles. The reality is that Fairbanks was Triangle's highest-paid performer and Aitken was banking Triangle's fortunes on the strength of *The Lamb* and its young, muscular star.*

By the summer of 1915 Douglas Fairbanks bore little relation to the thin, wiry nineteen-year-old who had stormed New York thirteen years before. He was five feet nine inches (give or take), broad of shoulders, and slim of waist.† His torso resembled a pyramid balancing on its point: the ideal build for a gymnast, or an acrobat—strong with a low center of gravity. His hair was brown, his eyes a light hazel. His gaze was sharp and his smile dazzling. His gait was so unusual— a widespread, almost straddling walk, with arms swinging and palms pointing to the rear, chest concave, and chin extended to meet the world—that young men were imitating it before it was ever recorded on film.‡ He exuded strength, charm, youth, confidence, and—here he was differentiated from the normal run of leading men—a loopy sense of humor.

He arrived in Hollywood the last week of July 1915 replete with enough extra luggage to incur an additional $52.44 in baggage fees. D. W. Griffith was not there to meet him. He too had a hankering to visit the Exposition in San Francisco and, having finished principal

---

* Star director D. W. Griffith, by comparison, was collecting $400 a week at this point, although he had a profit-sharing clause.

† His height is based on what he declared on his passport. Comparisons to Chaplin suggest that he was an inch or more shorter.

‡ One 1914 story by author Edna Ferber has the heroine's likable younger brother tell his mother: "They call it the juvenile jump, and all our best leading men have it. I trailed Douglas Fairbanks for days before I really got it."

filming on *The Mother and the Law*,* elected this week to do so. This would characterize the relationship between "the Master," as his acolytes called him, and the charismatic stage star for the duration of the Triangle contract—and perhaps beyond.

Perhaps it is understandable. Griffith, a failed stage actor, had been instrumental in the explosive growth, both financially and artistically, of the new medium of films and had done so with a stock company of fellow stage refugees. Having created an original and powerful art form, and having created stars—film stars—out of the very people who were rejected by "the legitimate," he was now being told by Harry Aitken that the secret to Triangle's success would be through the costly recruitment of stars from the Broadway stage. "It is an interesting question whether 'legitimate' stars or the so-called 'stock stars' of film organizations will prove the more serviceable in making the highest quality of pictures," Griffith said at this time. It was clear where *he* thought the answer would lie. The stock star "has the advantage of having been trained in all the niceties of the new art. Generally he has years of experience in picture making to his credit. He has nothing to unlearn. . . . It would seem that artists like Mae Marsh, Lillian and Dorothy Gish and Robert Harron are on a par with the best sent us from the theatrical world." In the short term, Griffith was proven right. His band of youngsters had, under his progressive tutelage, developed a naturalistic style of acting that was ideally suited for the intimacies of the screen. The stage giants, of course, arrived on the scene and, unschooled in this new universe, continued for the most part to play to the rafters. To be fair, Griffith's actors did the same in 1908, and he and they learned together. But now it was 1915, and he was at the peak of his powers. His treatment of these theatrical "greats" over the next year would reflect this ambivalence, and Fairbanks was no exception.

Doug seemed to take no notice, or at least no offense. He stayed at the Alexandria Hotel until he could lease a two-story California-Japanese

---

* This film would ultimately grow like Topsy with the addition of three additional stories and become *Intolerance*.

bungalow on North Highland Avenue, and he settled into the new town. Hollywood in 1915 was a new town indeed, or at least a town in the midst of transition. A mere five years before, it had been a sleepy village of retirees and orchards, acres of fruit trees cross-hatched by dirt roads, interrupted by the occasional cottage. D. W. Griffith had come out to Los Angeles for winter shooting beginning in 1910, and the Hollywood hills and the surrounding valleys made for scenic backdrops for such one-reel films as *Ramona*, with Mary Pickford.

Griffith was not alone. Several film companies discovered the virtues of Southern California at that time, not only for the climate and the near-continuous string of sunny days but also for the distance from the Motion Picture Patents Trust and its camera-wrecking crews. The following year, Hollywood saw its first year-round studio, when the owners of the Blondeau Roadhouse, suffering from a recent ordinance that made Hollywood a dry town, leased their Sunset Boulevard building to the Centaur Film Company. The Nestor Studios, as it was named, was soon joined by a host of others: Mack Sennett's Keystone Kops began their antics in nearby Edendale, Thomas Ince's production unit was based in Culver City, and Universal opened a studio in the valley. Griffith, upon leaving Biograph in 1913, set up production at 4500 Sunset Boulevard, where Sunset and Hollywood Boulevards meet.

It was the work of these pioneers in the intervening years that resulted in the boom that was turning Hollywood into *Hollywood*. The influx of the production companies and the creation out of whole cloth of an entirely new industry resulted in the growth of a supporting social infrastructure. The Hollywood Hotel, on Hollywood Boulevard between Highland and Orchard Avenues, frequently housed peripatetic actors until they rented or—if truly successful—built homes. The Alexandria housed no less than D. W. Griffith, who preferred its food to any other in town. Cafe Nat Goodwin dangled over the Pacific Ocean on a wooden pier in Santa Monica, competing with places like the Sunset Inn and Baron Long's at the Vernon Country Club for the likes of Wallace Reid, Roscoe "Fatty" Arbuckle, and Charlie Chaplin to fill their tables. Bungalows, such as that leased by Fairbanks, no longer dotted the landscape but started to fill up blocks. All those property men and carpenters and cameramen had to live somewhere, and they found that Hollywood fit the bill. Growth was rampant.

Take Griffith's Fine Arts studio, where the phenomenal success of *The Birth of a Nation* resulted in an influx of cash. A new open-air stage, 190 by 70 feet, had been constructed on the lot. Cotton cheesecloth was hung overhead to diffuse the sunlight and soften the shadows on actors' faces. Men who served as assistant directors under Griffith were now directing features on their own under his supervision. The stage was crowded with various sets, each with its own director, assistant directors, cast, and cameraman, all filming simultaneously—the competing sounds of production (and construction) serving as no problem in the world of silent movies. Fairbanks loved it. "Hollywood is a world being made," he said later. "Topsy-turvy. Bums, college athletes, prize-fighters, professors; all out there; all tossed together as if by an eruption, by a volcano."

The year and a half that Douglas Fairbanks was to spend at the Fine Arts studio would be pivotal. He entered this world with no more knowledge of motion picture production than the experience described above, but in less than eighteen months he would master his medium. He starred in thirteen films, shooting on both coasts. He established a template for his characters and a successful formula for his stories; he learned the elements of production and identified individuals who could optimally write, direct, and film him to full advantage. He determined what genres were to be avoided. He initiated business relationships that would permit him to obtain financing for his own production company and engage in a profitable distribution arrangement. He also found his best friend in Charlie Chaplin, and met the woman who would become the love of his life, Mary Pickford.

A busy time, indeed, and it started with *The Lamb*, which began production immediately upon his arrival. Billy Bitzer, Griffith's cameraman, claimed in later years that the film's crew resented the intruders from the Broadway stage and therefore plastered Fairbanks with enough white paste makeup to make him look like a corpse. Most historians have since discredited this story, with good reason. Bitzer, like many a film veteran, was never afraid to let the truth get in the way of a good yarn.* Also, there is no difference in Fairbanks's face makeup in any of the early Triangle features. He looks unnaturally pallid in all of them, but so did every other leading man of the time.† The gradual move to more natural coloring, followed by the other extreme, the tanning craze, was a direct result of the choices that Fairbanks was to make over the course of his film career. In time, leading men would look tanned and hearty, but in 1915, at the tail end of the era when only the proletariat were brown, silent film players were lily white, with black kohl lining their eyes.

In fact, Fairbanks's arrival was heralded by the crew with a minor flurry of excitement. "I swear that during my first week here I signed over a hundred photographs," he recalled in early 1916. "Every one in the place from the office boy's assistant to the chief mixer of scenery paint has given me the old, old story of me being their favorite actor and all that tommyrot, and ended it up with the old plea for a picture—signed. . . . I sprained my right hand in the first scene of the 'Lamb' and it'll never get well if I don't steer clear of the pen and ink."

The Lamb was originally conceived as a two-reel film titled *Blood Will Tell*. Playing off Fairbanks's acclaimed performance as Bertie the Lamb in *The New Henrietta*, *The Lamb* recast its lead as a milquetoast named Gerald. The plot bore no relation to the original (nor was it supposed to, no rights having been paid for the stage play). Still, the production company worked to associate the piece with the play, including publicizing photographs of Fairbanks and director W. Christy Cabanne on the Fine Arts lot entertaining its author, Winchell Smith. Anita Loos collected twenty-five dollars for writing the intertitles and thus provided the irreverent tone that was to characterize Fairbanks's films for the

---

* He famously claimed, for example, that *The Musketeers of Pig Alley* was shot in the tenements of New York City, confounding film historians for years until Russell Merritt proved in 2002 that it was staged on the then-bucolic streets of Fort Lee, New Jersey.

† Film historian Kevin Brownlow explains that this white paste makeup was necessary because of the qualities of orthochromatic film. "If you wore none, orthochromatic film, over-reacting to red, made you look 'colored.'"

next five years. Cabanne, one of Griffith's serviceable assistant directors, was assigned to direct.* William Fildew was the cameraman. Filming began in the studio, with a sequence in which Fairbanks's character, having shamed himself before the heroine by an act of cowardice, now determines to learn boxing and karate. The last two weeks of production were spent on location work in the Mojave Desert. Cast and crew stayed at the Porter Hotel in San Fernando. Perhaps here is where Bitzer's recollections have some basis in fact. The cowboys hired for the cavalry parts were prepared to treat the Broadway actor with derision. But they quickly learned that Fairbanks was no tenderfoot. His skills as a horseman had been honed not only by his years in Colorado but also by many a bout of polo with the Rhode Island set—and "he rode and shot with the best of them." The nights were reportedly filled with moonlight coyote hunts and tall tales around the campfire. Fairbanks returned to the studio, by one contemporary account, "brown as an Indian, lively as a grasshopper and excited as a small boy can be." He was delighted to have met authentic cowboys. "Probably there never will again be such a bunch of real, veteran punchers together," he enthused. "It was a taste of the life that every kid dreams about and that people say has passed and wasn't true anyway. It is true and I've seen it."

The Lamb was one of three Triangle films to premiere at the Knicker-bocker Theatre in New York City in late September 1915. The program contained one film from each of the production units of Triangle. With it came Harry Aitken's gamble on the future of motion pictures. Certainly he and Griffith had proven earlier in the year that a grand epic of the scale of The Birth of a Nation could command two-dollar seats at a major theater. But epics like The Birth could not be produced weekly. Could a weekly program of more modest films do the same? "No event of the season has been so fraught with interest from the exhibitor as the test of 'two dollar pictures' on the New York public," opined the edito-

---

* Joseph Henabery, an actor on the Fine Arts lot at this time, and later a director himself, characterized Cabanne years later as "a good fast director; the type that would be in demand by anyone that had to make 'em quick and cheap."

rial staff at the *Motion Picture News*. And not just New York: Aitken had extended his gamble to theaters such as the Studebaker in Chicago and the Chestnut Street Opera House in Philadelphia. The program consisted of Dustin Farnum in *The Iron Strain*, Raymond Hitchcock in *My Valet*, and Douglas Fairbanks in *The Lamb*, each with an orchestral score composed by William Furst. Usherettes had pantalets with triangle-shaped lace visible beneath their skirts, coordinating with the triangular hats tipped across their brows. The audience was padded with a proper quota of names: William Randolph Hearst, James Montgomery Flagg, and Ignace Paderewski were among the throng.

And the verdict? Apparently, it was Fairbanks by a blowout. The other films were proclaimed perfectly satisfactory, but critics fell over themselves in praise of *The Lamb*. It was no *Birth*, acknowledged *Photoplay*; nothing could be. Still, it was "a rollicking, typically American melodrama, presenting Douglas Fairbanks, one of America's best known, best liked and most continually agreeable stage personalities." The *Motion Picture News* wrote: "*The Lamb* . . . is by far the high spot of the program. . . . An excellent actor on the spoken stage, transplanted to the screen [Fairbanks] becomes a delight to the eye."

In retrospect, it is hard to see how this modest effort produced such an enthusiastic response. But here the advantage of hindsight handicaps us. Knowing what Fairbanks was to produce so soon after *The Lamb* makes his first feature a pale shadow of what is to come. But even that shadow was, to the contemporary eye, new and arresting. The audience, expecting to see a Griffith drama, separate and distinct from the Sennett Keystone on the bill, instead got this strange new hybrid of comedy-drama, with a hero who invited our laughter as much as our awe. There is, of course, the pleasure of seeing the stage performance of Fairbanks as Bertie being replicated as he enacts the part of Gerald. The series of hesitations and fumbles and the constant apologetic little cough are understated—even delightful—and quite unlike the usual gesticulations of the stage or even the screen of the time. It is to a typical performance as a miniature is to a mural.

But we don't see the timid Gerald for long. Following an act of cowardice (he hesitates, and his rival beats him to the punch and rescues a drowning woman),* we get the reformed Gerald—a different creature altogether. Taking boxing and jujitsu lessons, he is enchanted to discover that he has earned a black eye. He shows it in triumph to his mother, his butler, and anyone else who will look at it. In pursuing his sweetheart west (another leitmotif that would be replicated in these films—the physical journey from east to west paralleling the spiritual journey from fop to hero), he is lured away from his train by Indians selling trinkets. No respectable hero in 1915 would be caught buying a trinket. But Fairbanks's hero is, evidently, an exception. He purchases a cheap necklace, and when later in the story he is captured by banditos, it is torn from his neck by the chief kidnapper. This will not do. Pettishly, Doug steals it back. Granted, all of these acts may have been scripted, not improvised by the star. Still, a strong argument can be made for Fairbanks's contribution to the scenes. This sort of tomfoolery was only to increase as Doug's control over his pictures grew. And in instances where the shooting scenarios survive, they document that such moments were often unscripted. His son told film historian Kevin Brownlow that "*The Lamb* was his first picture, and in this he was unsure of himself. But even then there was this dominating leadership complex." This resulted in the leading man evincing behavior unlike that of a standard hero—particularly a Griffith hero.[†]

But hero he was in the last reel of the film. His heroics were minor by the standards that he himself was to establish in the next few months. But the reviewer for the *Motion Picture News* waxed rhapsodic: "One incident which is 'sure fire' is a jump by Fairbanks from a thatched

---

* Paradoxically, this is the most outrageously overacted portion of the film. Fairbanks mugs tremendously, throws his arms in the air, and flings himself upon the sand after his fiancée accuses him of cowardice.

† No less an authority than Russell Merritt wrote in 2004 several arguments in favor of *The Lamb* having been actually supervised by Griffith, before concluding: "But that was before I actually saw the film. Now I've looked at it and I'm ready to recant."

roof, onto the shoulders of a Yaqui pursuer, and the disarming of the belligerent."

It was not a particularly high jump. And he disarmed but a single Indian in the course of it. But with that single leap, the audiences and critics sensed that there was something different about this performer. "Transplanted to the screen he becomes a delight to the eye," continued the reviewer. Others agreed. "Columns of praise would not do justice to *The Lamb*," wrote *Variety*. It is no wonder the Triangle people signed up Fairbanks for a period of three years at any salary within reason. They would even have been justified in stretching a point to secure Douglas. He 'registers' on the screen as well as any regular film actor that has ever appeared in pictures and more strongly than most of them."

This issue of "registering" on film is not a minor one. Those traits that would serve a performer across the arc lights of a stage were not, as Aitken was to learn, the same as those that worked on the screen. Mary Pickford is a case in point. As early as her Biograph films for D. W. Griffith in 1909, she demonstrates this quality. She may be part of a crowd; she may be standing alone. It matters little. The eye is drawn to her. In fact, one finds oneself looking at no one else. It is inexplicable: there is something about her that the camera loves.

So it was with Fairbanks. Something about his cheerful face, his engaging personality, his exuberant willingness to look foolish one moment and throw his body off a roof the next, made all the other pasty-faced leading men up to that time seem like anemic fops.

Aitken, if not Griffith, recognized this. He signed Fairbanks to a three-year contract before *The Lamb* even opened, with salary increases of $500 per week every six months for the duration of the term. Fairbanks missed the premiere, not only being in the midst of moving his family to a larger rental on La Brea Avenue but also having begun production on his second feature in the third week of August.

Double Trouble, rarely seen today, stands as a curiosity. Because Fairbanks essentially found his formula by his third film (*His Picture in the Papers*), *Double Trouble* provides a chance to see Fairbanks enacting the part of a character other than what would become his norm—two separate characters, in fact. The story was of the knocked-on-the-head dual-personality variety, an aging trope even then. Still, it affords the fascinating opportunity to see Fairbanks play a villain, albeit a comic villain. Here he channels his recently deceased friend Elmer Booth.* He is all swagger and proto-Cagney, tipping his hat forward and elbowing his compatriots in the ribs. As his opposite, Florian, Doug is in full flutter: wrists extended, pinky-biting, Sunday school–teaching, woman-fearing prissiness.† Neither performance is subtle (Fairbanks would be far more understated—and thus more comic—suggesting unmanliness as Don Diego in *The Mark of Zorro*), but each is intriguing. We will never see them again. Once *Double Trouble* is in the can, we shall see Fairbanks stray from what will become his sure-fire character only once more, in *The Half Breed*.

The film was quickly made. Fairbanks's time on the production amounted to twenty-two days. Cabanne, again directing, took over the small town of Santa Ana, incorporating the fire and police departments, as well as the municipal band and polling booths for the election parade sequences. Anita Loos again collected twenty-five dollars for writing the titles. Better yet, when by mid-October Fairbanks was preparing to go east to film his third feature, the clever twenty-two-year-old Loos was not merely punching up the titles. She had written the entire story.

His Picture in the Papers was a gem of a little film, one that got everything right and would serve as a model for Fairbanks comedies for the next five years. It not only had Anita Loos's witty script, which poked fun at vegetarians and commercial food manufacturers but also had her future husband, John Emerson, as director and—of all people— Erich von Stroheim as both art director and featured performer. The cast and crew arrived at Triangle's studios in Fort Lee, New Jersey, in early October, filming exteriors ranging from Riverside Drive to Atlantic

---

* Booth died in an automobile accident in Los Angeles weeks before Fairbanks's arrival.

† Although women make him sneeze involuntarily, the character is not gay, as demonstrated in a scene where a homosexual bellhop makes a proposition and is rewarded by a kick in the seat of the pants, a surprisingly candid scene for 1915.

City.* A boxing match was filmed at the Sharkey Athletic Club, and Broadway's leading performers cheerfully went "slumming it" as extras in support of their friend. Famed boxer Terry McGovern did a cameo as a referee. Cartoons of Fairbanks in boxing shorts and gloves were featured in the New York papers.

Doug starts the story as a lovable goof, the sort of man who hides his martini mixings in his desk drawer and his olives in the earpiece of his telephone. His father ("a self-made man who adores his maker") is the manufacturer of twenty-seven varieties of vegetarian food products. Fairbanks, as Pete Prindle, is a meat eater. Loos retained the film's original script until her death, a fine documentation of both her sparkling wit and Fairbanks's improvisational skills. In one sequence, as originally scripted, the heroine was to spot Fairbanks from her window, then rush outside to hand him an umbrella. Doug, who never saw a house without giving thought to how to climb it, evidently felt the sequence could be more interesting. He clambered up the side of the building for the cameras in a single, uncut shot, meeting the young woman at her second-story window and retrieving the umbrella there. It was not simply stunts that he improvised. After intentionally crashing his recently acquired junker of a car ("Take me home for $83.99!"), Fairbanks not only stages himself in the scene per the screenplay's instructions but also places the sign prominently on his chest—another bit not included in the script. Thanks to his contributions, the film was full of stunts, creating a hero who was undeniably a screwball and yet capable of performing remarkable feats of prowess at the same time. Audiences and critics were dazzled. "His personality is so all-pervading," wrote one, "that he is like the sun when it rises in a sky of morning stars, the light by which some of them glow, the light which causes them all to fade. His is apparently in a class all by himself, at once an athlete of resource and daring, and a subtle interpreter of the amusing side of

* Triangle used both the Willat-Triangle studio in Fort Lee and another facility in Riverdale. It is unclear which studio Fairbanks used at any particular time, but historian Richard Koszarski is confident that portions of *His Picture in the Papers* were shot at Fort Lee.

human nature." Critics at the Knickerbocker premiere noted that the crowd applauded with his first appearance on the screen.

Of equal note is what was in the script that Fairbanks, his power growing, left out. Anita Loos was a brilliant, funny, accomplished woman who would go on to do great things, but she was also a creature of her time, complete with its ugly biases. The script has such unsavory references as "a coon pushing a wheelchair" and even goes so far as to have an intertitle state "I am Peter Prindle. I was raised on Prindle's Products and I have just licked five coons." Fairbanks, for this film and many films going forward, eliminated all such references. This is not to say that there were no occasional "Yassuh" Stepin Fetchit characters in his movies (his last film for Triangle, *The Americano*, has a particularly painful example), but all references to "niggers" and "coons" that were in his scripts were removed and the characters replaced by whites or simply played by African Americans with no particular comment on their race.* It is to Fairbanks's credit that he used his influence in this manner. He made no particular point of his liberalism; in fact, he was of the era before actors and politics mixed. But he was of a uniformly democratic bent, as affectionate and welcoming to a table of cow herders one night as he was slavishly devoted to a household of royalty the next. "He had a varied assortment of friends, ranging from cowboys to kings, and found interesting qualities in them all," wrote Charlie Chaplin fifty years later. He respected accomplishment and would back a black extra on *The Thief of Bagdad* to become a prize fighter with no more thought to his race than that of the Native American to whom he lent money or the white family of child actors at Triangle whom he helped support during the Depression years.

His Picture in the Papers was completed before autumn turned to winter, and when Doug and Beth found themselves with a free weekend in November 1915, they decided to accept an invitation for a weekend house party in Tarrytown, New York, at the estate of friend and fellow

---

* *Down to Earth* and an early treatment for the sound version of *Reaching for the Moon* are the most painful examples of utterly casual racism in early film scripts.

theater star Elsie Janis. Janis was a sparkplug of a woman, the sort of friend who would tie her skirt in a knot and match Fairbanks in hand-walking in the lobby of the Algonquin.

En route, the Fairbankses were passed by a staid black limousine. Inside, in strained silence, sat Owen Moore and his wife, Mary Pickford, headed to the same party. Pickford recalls seeing the "low-slung foreign car with a half top" and the couple within, "a leopard rug over their laps." Her first memory was of disapproval. The car was showy. The lap robe was flamboyant. When Mary and Owen's chauffeur lost his way, their car stopped at a crossroads and Owen got out to look at the signs. The roadster pulled up and "a very agile young man jumped down and joined Owen," Pickford wrote. "I saw them beam in recognition and shake hands." Owen brought Fairbanks over and made the introductions. That crossroad, she was to say later, "was also a crossroad of my life."

Once at the estate Mary found herself settled in a corner with a magazine, her eyes gazing periodically at "a laughing huddle in the center of the large reception room . . . I found myself disapproving heartily of the exuberant Mr. Fairbanks."

Janis recalled events a little differently. "Miss Pickford thinks Mr. Fairbanks will do wonderful things in films," she wrote later, using the present tense. "Mr. Moore echoes, 'Wonderful.' Mrs. Fairbanks thinks everything Mr. Fairbanks does is wonderful." The hostess, on the other hand, nursing what she termed a "pash" for Doug "that dates back to *Fantana*," was scheming how to get alone with him. Finally, she suggested a walk, expecting only Fairbanks would be willing to go out in the dismal weather. She was wrong. Doug and Owen were both game to go. Unwilling to leave their spouses in the clutches of the estimable Miss Janis, Beth and Mary followed suit. Doug elected a route to discourage any woman in fashionable shoes, and Mary, in a black velvet hobble skirt and kid leather Russian boots, qualified. Doug cast a glance at both Elsie's and Mary's footwear. "Humpf!" he said. "Women are just about as companionable as a pipe without any tobacco in it!" ("Of course," Mary recalled, "this rather piqued us, so without even glancing down at our shoes, which were destined to be ruined, we assured him in one breath we were quite equal to any athletic feat he would propose.") The puckish Doug not only proposed but "he disposed of us with equal alacrity, for he dared us until we had walked through muddy pastures, passed the brambles and had climbed over barb-wire fences." Beth dropped out when the group reached a crossing of the Pocantico River that required crossing stepping-stones and a log. It was too cold; she for one would return to the house. Mary persisted. As she placed her first foot on the log, Elsie taunted her: "You'll ruin those beautiful new shoes of yours!"

"What's a pair of shoes to losing a husband?" Mary retorted, and took a few cautious steps. But midstream, she froze. Her panic was rising when she saw Douglas Fairbanks on the log, smiling at her. "Do you mind?" he asked succinctly. No, it seemed. The lady didn't mind a bit.

And in that moment, Douglas Fairbanks quite literally swept Mary Pickford off her feet.

5

Mary and Charlie

I T IS IMPOSSIBLE TO state how extraordinary Mary Pickford was—both as a person and as a phenomenon. She was, in the words of one scholar, "the focal point of an entire industry." It was more than that. For a decade and more in the nascent commerce of cinema, she was the center point of the world's affection.

She was born Gladys Marie Smith in Toronto in 1892 to an alcoholic father and a fiercely loving mother. Her father deserted the family when Gladys was three and died a few years later of a blow to the head. There were three children now: Gladys, Lottie, and the youngest, Jack, and all ended up in touring theater companies to keep the wolf from the door. Little Gladys was the most talented of the brood, and, as they endured frequent separations and the grim hardships of the road, she became, in a sense, the father of the family as well.

At fifteen, her talent and tenacity got her an audition with David Belasco, the great Broadway impresario. He renamed her Mary Pickford and gave her a supporting role in *The Warrens of Virginia*. While newlywed Douglas Fairbanks was playing in *The Man of the Hour* and *All for a Girl*, teenage Mary Pickford was playing Betty Warren both on Broadway and on tour. She made twenty-five dollars a week and lived on five, using the rest to support her mother and siblings. But by the time the company returned to New York City and Doug was in his long, triumphant run of *A Gentleman from Mississippi*, seventeen-year-old Mary Pickford was unemployed and contemplating how to feed the family. Desperation drove her to motion pictures.

She was wise enough, or lucky enough, to start at the top: the American Mutoscope and Biograph Company, where the then thirty-two-year-old David Wark Griffith was busy turning a novelty into what would become an art form.

She haughtily told Mr. Griffith that she was a Belasco actress. He haughtily told her that she was too little and too fat—but that he would give her a try at five dollars a day, only for those days when she was needed. She insisted she must have a guarantee of twenty-five a week. Pickford biographer Eileen Whitfield eloquently captured the essence of the creature Griffith was attempting to stare down at that moment: a formidable young Mary, "whose face seemed to move from round good humor to unsettling beauty. Her hazel eyes held a melancholy sweetness. Her bones were fine, her build small. Her back fairly dripped with springing curls. She stood up proudly on size-five shoes; the longest finger on her hand was two and a half inches. Yet she spoke with the aim of a torpedo."

He put her in costume and gave her a trial. By the time the day was over, she insisted on ten dollars a day. (If she had to do something as dreadful as act in motion pictures, they had better make it worth her while!) They settled for a guarantee of forty a week. Griffith knew he had someone extraordinary here.

And she was extraordinary in the Biograph films. She registered on film as had no one else up to that time. She played prostitutes and scrubwomen, ingénues and wives—a range of roles she was never to enjoy again. Under Griffith's tutelage she gradually learned to shade her performances, to remove the stage mannerisms of the time and adjust to the intimacy of the camera, which, as Griffith matured the form, moved ever closer to the actor. She was not truly the first performer to have a close-up; they are seen in American and European films as early as 1903. But hers was the one many film historians remember.

While working at Biograph, she met and fell in love with a tall Irish actor—twenty-two-year-old Owen Moore. Mama Charlotte did not approve—he brooded, and he drank. She could tolerate the drinking—the Pickfords were a rather wet lot—but she could not abide the brooding. No one liked a mean drunk, and Owen would turn out to be just that. As 1910 moved into 1911, Mary did two things. She eloped with Owen and departed Biograph for greener financial pastures at Carl Laemmle's IMP Company. She was important enough to successfully insist that her new husband's employment (as both actor and director) be part of the deal. By the time she moved—briefly—to the Majestic Motion Picture Company, her pay was up to $225 a week. But the production standards were so inferior at these two companies that in January 1912 she took her first, and only, reduction in salary. She returned to Griffith and the Biograph Company for $175 a week. She took the pay cut gladly. Money was important, sure. But, to her discerning mind, so was quality.

It was in the summer of 1912 that a group of Biograph players, along with their director, took a busman's holiday to see a Broadway play (Mary mistakenly remembered it as *A Gentleman of Leisure*) and the twenty-year-old laid eyes for the first time on Douglas Fairbanks. According to her recollection a mere four years later, Griffith remarked, "Now there's a young fellow who will someday make a great impression in pictures." She agreed: "He was so full of life and expressive pantomime, with health, spirits and a fine athletic figure."

The world that summer was starting to change. Moving pictures were no longer just for the poor, urban immigrant. Middle-class families were now going to them, increasing the size of the audiences nationally. And everyone, everywhere, was in love with that Biograph Girl: the Girl with the Curls. David Belasco was a shrewd producer who recognized the power of films to create a star, and in November 1912, he lured her back to "the legitimate." Now Mary Pickford had the lead role in his Broadway play *A Good Little Devil*. Her last film for Griffith, *The New York Hat*, was also the first screenplay by an unknown nineteen-year-old writer, Anita Loos.

While the play had a respectable run, from January to May 1913, its star did not go on the usual post-Broadway tour. She had been wooed back to films, this time by producer Adolph Zukor. Now her salary was $500 a week, and she would be making feature films—no more shorts.

She was not yet playing children, although this is how, one hundred years later, most think of her, if they think of her at all. Many hold a vision of some sort of rosebud-lipped, Victorian Valentine of a girl—all mincing goodness. In fact, the appeal of Mary Pickford was that she was very far from this stereotype. She played scrappy, intelligent young women facing adversity with humor and an authentic quality that can best be described as spunk. She could break your heart or make you laugh, but no one ever confused her with the run-of-the-mill heroine that characterized her era. She was unique.

Further, now her name was on the films themselves, and in the advertising. Now everyone knew who the Girl with the Curls was. The emergence of feature films, the creation of a new type of periodical (the movie fan magazines), and the golden halo of Mary Pickford and her ability to resonate with an audience created a perfect storm. Seemingly overnight, she acquired a level of fame that is hard to fathom. It is often written that more people saw Mary Pickford in one night than had seen Sarah Bernhardt or Eleonora Duse in their entire careers. It matters little if this is apocryphal; the truth is that the tremendous fame that was thrust upon her in her very early 1920s was without precedent until Charlie Chaplin came upon the scene the following year and Douglas Fairbanks the year after that. There was no template for this level of acclaim and very little for the sudden acquisition of the associated wealth. More astonishing than the fact that it happened is the fact that she handled it so well.

Certainly it would be a challenge to any marriage. But here her spouse was a fellow actor; a male in an era when the man was supposed to support the woman; an insecure, bitter, evidently unlikable, handsome drunk. One could hardly blame anyone, much less someone as young and vulnerable as Mary Pickford, for being taken with the prospect of the dashing, charismatic Mr. Fairbanks lifting her into his arms and carrying her to safety.

She was to claim in later years that she didn't think of the episode in a romantic light ("and I'm quite certain Douglas didn't either. It was a gesture he would have made to any woman in such a predicament"). But there was no fooling Elsie Janis. They may have started the walk as Mr. Fairbanks and Miss Pickford, she noted. But by the time they returned, they were Mary and Douglas.

Mary continued her attempts at denial. "I don't recall giving him much thought after that meeting," she wrote. "I buried myself in my work, and in fact tried to do as little thinking as possible about myself." She was kidding only herself. Shortly thereafter, Frank Case, the Algonquin's manager, invited her to a dance he was giving. Her invitation (Case was one of Fairbanks's best friends) was no accident. Neither was her acceptance. This was the sort of event that she normally would skip. Still, she noted, she "did the unusual thing of accepting."

Doug, of course, was there and, between dances, shone the full wattage of his charm upon her. She (and Chaplin), he told her, were the two greatest artists of pantomime. "You do less apparent acting than anyone else I know," he said, "and because of that you express more." She remembered that conversation to the end of her life. She "hugged the echo of his words for days, repeating them over and over again to myself." Like so many others, she described Fairbanks in terms of light: "I had been living in half shadows, and now a brilliant light was suddenly cast upon me, the sunlight of Douglas' approval and admiration." Smarting under her alcoholic husband's constant belittling, she could not help but be drawn to this glorious, handsome source of esteem. It was characteristic Fairbanks. Actress Lila Lee said it best: "He was just about the best morale booster I ever ran into."

Still, there was something else happening here. Mary was the top woman in her industry—the top person, for that matter. "People of attainment fascinated him," she wrote. "He sought them out, not because he was a snob, but because of his lively interest in how they had made their names; how they accepted their successes; how it had influenced them." Actress Bessie Love had a similar recollection of Doug at this time, recalling, "He told me to observe cultured people, how they talked, walked, conducted themselves—not to copy them, just to learn how the other half lived." Best friend Charlie Chaplin admired Fairbanks's candor on the subject: "I found him disarmingly honest because he admitted that he enjoyed being a snob and that successful people had allure for him." That alone might have made Mary Pickford a source of interest. Yet there was more. She was ambitious and hardworking. They were in the same field. They both had strong ties to their mothers. She was vulnerable. She was beautiful.

It was the maternal tie that Fairbanks used as a pretext for their next meeting. Charlotte should meet Ella! It was only natural! (Every sentence he spoke seemed to end in an exclamation point.) He invited Mary and her mother to tea the next day. It was a shrewd move. There were many ways to Mary Pickford's heart, but the quickest, the surest, the best was through her mother. She gladly accepted. He, of course, had done nothing to clear this with his own mother, but reportedly he showed up the next morning at the Seymour Hotel with the gift of a new sealskin coat in hand and the query "How would you like to have Mary Pickford and her mother here to tea?"

There was little an astonished Ella could do if she didn't like the idea. But she did. "I knew you would," Doug is reported to have replied. "They'll be here in half an hour." A caterer from Sherry's arrived with service large enough to feed a platoon. Florists came with bowls of flowers. The tea went swimmingly; the mothers got on famously. By the time the guests departed, Doug turned to Ella and said, "I suppose you know how I feel about Mary."

She knew. She gave the usual maternal advice. No one could help how they felt. But everyone was accountable for how they acted. He needed to be careful. "Sometimes we pay dearly for the unhappiness we cause others," she reportedly said, having reason, perhaps, to know.

He had had, it was said, multiple dalliances in the past. "He didn't smoke or drink much, so he thought he had the right to some kind of vice, so he chose women," Anita Loos claimed. "He went after every girl who crossed the Triangle lot." His son wrote that the numbers of his "extracurricular fancies" were "surprisingly large." Neither individual was an unbiased source at the time they made their statements, and in the case of Fairbanks Jr. this was a case of the very black pot casting aspersions on the kettle's complexion. Still, one suspects the truth of their claims. The double standard was ubiquitous; actors were raffish, and Fairbanks was wealthy, handsome, and charismatic. Casual affairs were very likely the order of the day.

But this was different and he knew it. This was the type of thunderbolt that could ruin marriages, careers, lives.

And yet, he pursued it. He was heedless, in fact. He next invited Mary to the Netherland Hotel to "meet the family." This, given the subtext of their attraction, seems a bold, almost callous move, but it made sense. How better to pretend that there was nothing untoward going on—as indeed was the case at this point—than to have Mary meet Beth and "the boy"? This she did, with some apprehension. To the end of his days, Douglas Fairbanks Jr. recalled the circumstances. He was on the floor, playing with toy trains. Upon the introduction, the six-year-old stood and bowed, meanwhile wondering how it was that someone essentially his own size (Mary was five feet tall) could be considered a grown-up and go around by herself. She joined him on the floor with the trains and, in his words, "Mary had made another conquest."

But the romance, the full-fledged romance, did not begin right away. They were to circle each other throughout 1916, yearning, wishing, longing, but not acting. For now, he and she were to focus on work.

His next film, *The Habit of Happiness*, brought him a collaborator who was to direct more of his films than any other: Allan Dwan.

Toronto-born, Notre Dame–educated Allan Dwan was two years younger than Douglas Fairbanks. An athlete in college, he trained as an engineer, and it was this training—by way of his work with the Cooper Hewitt Light Company—that first led him to the motion picture industry. He graduated from scriptwriter to director, a task for which he was well suited. He was, in the words of the great film scholar Kevin Brownlow, "a man with a strong dramatic sense whose clear and logical brain and rich sense of humor ensured for his pictures the highest standards of entertainment and craftsmanship." He and Fairbanks felt a kinship. When asked how he influenced the molding of the Fairbanks persona, he replied, "I was a little bit like that myself when I was young—a restless, athletic type." And as a college-educated engineer, he was, in some respects, what Fairbanks only pretended to be. He was an important figure in Fairbanks's history but also a source of obfuscation. The problem is this: the older Dwan got, the more colorful his stories. By the time he was in his eighties and nineties, his tales were getting pretty tall. Film historians and biographers lapped them up. What could be a better way to demonstrate D. W. Griffith's thinly veiled aversion to his upstart Broadway star than the following? Dwan (he himself claims) and Fairbanks are sitting on the Triangle lot. A lion wanders by, scaring both men into paralysis. Griffith follows, approaches the (tame) lion with the phrase, "Come, little pussy cat!" and thus one-ups the company's top male star and his rising young director.

One wants to believe such tales. They embody everything about Griffith's antipathy toward Fairbanks, or any strong male. And while there were no lions in *Intolerance*, a trained lion was used at that time at the Fine Arts studio for a DeWolf Hopper comedy. Griffith was even photographed with it. So it might have happened.

Still, such a story sounds too good to be true. One struggles to separate fact from creatively embellished fiction. *The Habit of Happiness* is a case in point. Filmed in Fort Lee, New Jersey, the movie was an attempt to capitalize on Fairbanks's growing reputation as "Old Doc Cheerful." It was a slight story of a millionaire's son whose egalitarian instincts drive him to a New York flophouse to teach its inhabitants how to laugh. It was Dwan's assertion (then echoed by others, including Adolphe Menjou, who was an extra in the film) that the Bowery bums who were bused in for the scene would not laugh at Doug's jokes on camera. Upon Dwan's urging, Fairbanks advanced the smuttiness of his stories until they were quite blue. Finally the men demonstrated the proper mirth. A reasonable enough tale and likely true. The problem comes with the denouement. According to Dwan, the lip readers in the audience objected to the scenes. "We had to call the picture back and make different shots of Doug," he claimed. "And that's how I learned to be very careful about what actors said even in silent pictures."

As appealing a tale as this makes, there is no documentation in the financial records of the Triangle Film Corporation to support it. There were no reshoots, no change in negative length, no evidence that this was anything but a fable.*

Perhaps Dwan was simply trying to milk an interesting story line out of what was essentially a very minor film. *The Habit of Happiness* was studio-bound and—except for a brawl in the last reel and a sequence where Fairbanks slings the solidly built actor George Fawcett over his shoulders and runs him up a flight of stairs—short on physical action. Loos's titles helped (she collected another twenty-five dollars for her efforts), but there was really no disguising the thinness of the plot. The critics concurred. *Photoplay*'s critic wrote, "My criticism is leveled . . . against the growing habit of making Mr. Fairbanks—who happens to be one of the very finest young actors on our platforms—depend wholly on his strong chin, chortling ivories, belligerent movements and snappy eyes."

The Habit of Happiness was the first of many films that director and star would make together, and the association was to prove fruitful. Dwan was a skilled and sensitive director, although he was never truly considered an auteur. But for Fairbanks, this was one of his strengths. He was cooperative, creative, and collaborative. Kevin Brownlow noted in 1962, "Douglas Fairbanks, Senior employed a number of directors, almost all of whom made their best pictures under his control. But once away from Fairbanks they were never really able to repeat this success."

---

* It is possible that Dwan confused incidents or chose to embellish them. There is a brief sequence in the film where Fairbanks is breaking up a fight between feuding millwork- ers. He defuses the situation with a joke. We never see the joke being told, but we get the following title card: "'That reminds me. Did you ever hear the story about . . . ?' Note—We'd like to let you in on this story, but it takes Mr. Fairbanks himself to put it over right." It is conceivable that there was some colorful language in *this* sequence, which was handled in postproduction by this intertitle. But this title was in the premiere print, so there was no "calling back" of the prints to insert it.

These are strong words; even stronger are those of his son: "My father had great respect for directors of other pictures, but none for those of his own. These were largely friends who would carry out exactly what he wanted."

This does, perhaps, a disservice to men like Victor Fleming* and Allan Dwan—particularly, perhaps, to Dwan. What Dwan brought to Fairbanks was the idea that his stunts should not demonstrate the extreme of what the star was capable of accomplishing but that they should look unforced. "When Doug did any of his stunts, he was essentially graceful. That's one thing he struggled for and I insisted on: there was never to be any evidence of an effort on his part," said Dwan. "He floated through the air, and everything we did was based on measurement of his reach. Heights of tables, heights of stair rises; we had stairs specially built so he would gracefully go up and down them. . . . He could take three of them without effort and anybody else would be stretching." Dwan, an engineer, would help Fairbanks design the setup for the stunts so that his leaps would become graceful arcs across space, almost balletic in their control. "Stuntmen have tried to imitate him and it always looks like a stunt when they do it. With him, it always looked very natural." In time, this tendency would grow, reaching its apogee in *The Thief of Bagdad*, where the star's movements were dancelike throughout the film, not merely in the stunts.

But this was to come. Fairbanks was still learning. "At Triangle, he was studying the business, finding his errors, watching what was being done, choosing what he thought was good, eliminating what wasn't and planning for the future," said Dwan. "Dreaming up things he ought to do." The dreams caught hold. He would soon make much better films than *The Habit of Happiness*.

---

* Fleming, of course, was famed as the principal director of *Gone with the Wind* and *The Wizard of Oz*. He was Fairbanks's primary cameraman at Triangle and was to continue with him through his time with the Artcraft Pictures Corporation and into the United Artists years, when he was given his first directing opportunity with *When the Clouds Roll By*.

To be fair, the film had its modest virtues: Doug's character (Sunny Wiggins) is introduced in a tight iris shot, sleeping soundly in bed. The iris widens, and we see that there is a vagrant snoring peacefully on either side of him. He awakens, and instead of being startled, he looks delighted. Subsequent shots demonstrate that both bedroom and bath are full of homeless men. He forces them to bathe, herding them into the bathroom like a Japanese subway pusher, before bringing them downstairs and feeding them breakfast at a table set for his sister's society friends. (Loos's title tells us that the Wiggins family "have risen to the plane where they are snubbed by all the best people in town.") Alistair Cooke proffered a theory: Fairbanks's screen character was such a close fusion of his actual personality "that it was no longer possible to say where 'Doug' began and Fairbanks ended." *The Habit of Happiness* may serve as an example of this. Margery Wilson, a fellow performer at Triangle in these years, later recalled, "He was once in a Chicago hotel that faced a park where old men sit about on the benches waiting, waiting, no one knows for what. Fairbanks watched them until he could no longer stand the thought of their hunger and cold. He sent his brother over to collect them to eat as his guests." Was Fairbanks emulating his movie character or was the character written to reflect the man?

It can be argued that once he had control of his scripts—and he began to have control by his third film—he inserted for his character those feats he had never accomplished, or those he hoped to. It was unlikely a coincidence that the hero of *The Americano* was a "breezy American mining engineer" (to quote the publicity) who attended the Massachusetts School of Mines, as Fairbanks falsely claimed to have done at its Colorado counterpart. Similarly, he had traveled little farther than the civilized parts of London and Paris, but his heroes donned pith helmets and strode confidently through the jungle, native guides forming a train behind.

This is not to say that he was merely playacting his life—he would turn some of those visions into reality in later years, although admittedly these were more of the pith helmet than the academic variety. Like Sinclair Lewis's Dodsworth, as a young man he envisioned himself "riding a mountain trail, two thousand sheer feet above a steaming valley; sun helmet and whip cord breeches; tropical rain on a tin-roofed shack; a shot in the darkness as he sat over a square-face of gin with a ragged tramp of Noble Ancestry." And once he had the wealth, and the luxury of time, he would get there. But not yet. His destination now was back to Los Angeles.

A visiting reporter captured the essence of Fairbanks at this juncture. He was in his suite of rooms in his hotel unwrapping parcels: a rake, a hoe, a lawn mower, a bushel of seeds, a trowel, garden gloves, a hat, and even overalls. "I'm going to have a bungolaoh [*sic*] and be a bungaloafer," he was quoted as saying. The reporter could not resist the obvious question: why buy everything in New York and end up paying the freight charges to California? "Somebody in the next room gave an approving sniff of scorn," he wrote. "It was quite evident that this subject had already been thoroughly discussed in the Fairbanks family." His first wife was not, evidently, as indulgent of his boyish whims as his second would turn out to be.

Whatever Beth's feelings, it is clear that he had become popular with the gang in Hollywood. He returned to Los Angeles in late January, met at the station by an enthusiastic group of his peers anxious for news and gossip of Broadway. ("What the actor didn't know, he promptly made up," said one source. "And thanks to its being a very hilarious party, no one was any the wiser.") Both Dwan and Emerson were among the group. It was Dwan who was slated to direct his next film, *The Good Bad Man*. Seventeen-year-old Bessie Love was selected as the leading lady, reportedly at the behest of Beth.

Beth's influence as her husband's manager extended beyond mere casting decisions. Her father, his fortunes continuing to decline, decided to get involved in his son-in-law's career—at least to the extent of cashing in. Beth got Daniel on the Majestic payroll.* Buried deep in the ledgers of the US Majestic Motion Picture Company is a page titled "H.E. Ait-

---

* Majestic was one of the many holding companies that preceded the Triangle Film Corporation. For purposes of this discussion, it is synonymous with Triangle's Fine Arts.

ken Special a/c (D. Sully)." The "salary" Sully collected monthly varied, typically being $1,200 and rising some months as high as $2,500. (For context, consider that the average annual family income in this decade was $750.) But it was not to last. This particular chicken was to come home to roost within the year.

The Good Bad Man was to be one of Doug's strongest Triangle entries. It was a gently comic western, in which Fairbanks's protagonist commits sundry nonviolent robberies and distributes the take to father-less children. "He makes a specialty," one character tells another, "of helpin' kids that's born in shame." The theme of illegitimacy haunts our hero, whose belief (mistaken, as the unfolding story reveals) that he is among those unfortunates causes him to declare, "There's no decent place for me in the world 'cause I never had no father." In the end, of course, he learns that his mother and father had been married and that his father was murdered, and before his character rides off into the sunset with sweet Bessie Love, this crime is avenged.

It is easy to read too much into the theme of this story, except for one fact. While Fairbanks never had the patience to actually sit and type a scenario, he crafted the plot of the film.* It became common for him to work with his team to create a story line. He would sketch out themes that he wanted the narrative to contain, and a scenarist would write the script. During the course of the filming, Fairbanks would then develop the action sequences as both the setting and the story permitted. *The Good Bad Man* is the first documented case of this method being employed by the star and his director. He had a significant say in the making of this film, and it shows.

There is, of course, the risk of proposing the auteur theory pre-maturely. Sometimes a film has no great meaning in an artist's canon; people are given stories to film by their superiors, after all, and often have no say in the matter. To use the Freudian metaphor, sometimes

---

* Someone must have done the typing for him, as the Triangle records at the USC Warner Archives document a canceled check to Fairbanks for $300 dated March 17, 1916, for the scenario (File 2721A).

a cigar is just a cigar. Still, in this case there is a suspicious amount of smoke.

The theme of the absent father, the fear of illegitimacy, the hero's internal redemption in learning that all was fine and proper and the way it should have been—all play conveniently as a form of wish fulfillment. We will never know if Fairbanks knew that his mother's marriage was invalid, that his father was a bigamist, that he was, in the technical sense, as illegitimate as the film's hero believes himself to be. But we do know that his father was absent for almost all of his childhood and that he spent his adult life working to cover up this inconvenient fact. He hid his mixed (by nineteenth-century standards) parentage and the fact that his father was Jewish by attempting to blend with the WASP standard of the upper crust. His dinner jackets (one would never call them tuxedos) were bespoke, not off the rack; his stationery was custom engraved, not plain foolscap; his name was Fairbanks, not Ulman.

But this is speculation and has nothing to do with the fact that audiences who saw the film had a grand time. Both Dwan as director and Fleming as cameraman were at the top of their games, and the movie, filmed in Mojave, California, is as engaging as it is beautiful to watch. The critic from *Variety* stated, "In his writing for the screen Mr. Fairbanks discloses a fine sense of what the public wants in pictures and he gives it to them." The *New York Times* critic was more specific: "*The Good Bad Man* might have been designed by Penrod Schofield* with flashes by a sentimental chambermaid, but it is full to the brim with Fairbanks. His expressive face, radiant toothsome smile, immense activity, and apparent disposition to romp all over the map make him a treasure to the cinema. No deserter from the spoken drama is more engaging in the new work than Douglas Fairbanks. May his shadow never grow less."

The film was the opening picture for the Rialto Theatre in New York City—a trivial fact, but for a bit of symbolism. The Rialto was built on the site of the late Oscar Hammerstein I's Victoria Theatre in

---

* The mischievous eleven-year-old hero of a series of books by Booth Tarkington.

Times Square. It was, the *New York Times* noted, "a motion picture house, pure and simple." Unlike the Knickerbocker, a legitimate theater converted for film exhibition, or the Strand, a movie theater built with the ability to be converted to stage performances (should the film craze run its course), the Rialto had a screen placed plumb against the back wall of the building. "Built," the *Times* concluded, "in the conviction that the American passion for movies is here to stay." Fairbanks, like the Rialto, also had made an irrevocable commitment to motion pictures. And he, too, was here to stay.

This was not the case with most of the luminaries who had been recruited from the Broadway stage by Aitken. Near the end of filming *The Good Bad Man*, Fairbanks hosted the farewell banquet for the esteemed Sir Herbert Beerbohm Tree. The great thespian's inability to tone down the theatricality of his performance for the intimacy of the camera became the stuff of legend among the crew at the Fine Arts studio. He had come at a steep price tag, but it was clear to all that genius in one medium did not necessarily translate to genius in another. Beerbohm Tree—and most of his peers—had been a costly mistake for Aitken, all the more reason to keep Fairbanks, and Beth, happy.

The "employment" of Daniel Sully served the purpose for Mrs. Fairbanks, but not for her husband. Walter Green, the president of the Artcraft Pictures Corporation, later stated that Sully had been meddling in his son-in-law's business affairs, to the latter's disgruntlement. Harry Aitken likely shared his feeling. But as Fairbanks's films were keeping the studio alive, he paid the piper.

What Doug required was family—his family. He was waging a campaign to convince Ella to move to California, as her health had been failing. In this he never succeeded, but he was edging toward victory on another front. His oldest brother John was a guest at Sir Herbert's banquet, the result, to quote niece Letitia, of "persistent phone calls and telegrams—plus the fact that no one in the family could ever deny Douglas anything he wanted for very long." It was a jolt for John to contemplate leaving the Morey Mercantile Company of Denver and take a flier in what must have seemed a very fly-by-night prospect of working with his young brother in motion pictures. He had worked for the Morey family since he was nine. But he was just what Douglas needed: a sober, dispassionate business mind who had his brother's best interests at heart. For even at this early stage of the game, Douglas Fairbanks had an idea. But he wasn't going to act on it until his conservative brother had kicked the tires.

In the meanwhile, there was work.

Reggie Mixes In (produced under the working title *The Bouncer*) was his next project, and again it costarred Bessie Love. Although she was young and inexperienced (one critic wrote, "She should learn that panting in a close-up doesn't resemble deep emotion"), Fairbanks contemplated using her as his permanent female costar. The diminutive Love stood only five feet in heels. "So next to me Mr. Fairbanks looked six foot tall," she recalled. Indeed, the image of the petite Bessie, her arms looped around his neck, her trusting face looking up to his, was so appealing that it was exploited in posters and publicity for their films together.

But she was to costar with him in only one more film. Perhaps this was because of the woman who played the bad girl in *Reggie*. Alma Rubens was to die at thirty-three years of age from complications of addiction to cocaine and narcotics. At this point, however, she was nineteen years old, clear-eyed and healthy, with dark hair and sultry eyes. She made the perfect screen villainess, exotic beauty, or tempestuous Spaniard. She recalled location work on *Reggie*: "a trip to Balboa, during which the ever-agile Doug, apparently smitten by my charms, tried in every way to impress me."* Fairbanks may have been besotted with Mary Pickford, but (at this stage, evidently) this did not prevent him from attempting to captivate other young actresses. While Rubens implied that he did not succeed, there was more to come.

Reggie Mixes In ("who but Mr. Fairbanks could mix in with the name of Reggie and get away with it?" queried the *New York Times*) was certainly one of the minor Triangle films. Directed by the less-than-

---

* The Balboa sequence was cut from the final release, but Triangle retained two reels of beach scenes as stock footage.

stellar Cabanne and largely filmed in the studio, it was the slight tale of a rich playboy who fell in love with a poor young woman who was reduced to working as a "café hostess" to support her mother. While there was little in the way of interesting stunts, the major attraction was a knock-down, drag-out fight between Fairbanks and the film's villain. Here Aitken was working to exploit the reputation Fairbanks had established on the stage in such productions as *The Lights o' London, A Gentleman of Leisure,* and *Hawthorne of the U.S.A.* The fight is short but brutal—even by modern standards of Hollywood violence—and well choreographed. Audiences who had been dazzled by Wallace Reid's fight as the blacksmith in *The Birth of a Nation* were suddenly recognizing the difference between theatrically staged blows and—what at least appeared to be—the real thing. In fact, it seemed to be the real thing, squared. Take the fall-across-the-table gambit, a standard in any movie barroom fight. Here there were two tables. In a single spring, Fairbanks leaped over the first, which was between him and his opponent, tackled the man, and drove him backward in a joint somersault over the second. No less a source than the *New York Times* wrote of this scene: "It is quite probable that if there were many more like Mr. Fairbanks in the movies the Boxing Commission would be made film censors and the sporting department sent to write about them. Never was such a fight seen on the screen. The audience fairly gasped."

The writer also observed the first use of a stunt that Fairbanks was to deploy in the future: "Once when he sees a gangster coming down a passageway to get him he dodges back around the corner, darts up the wall of a building like a fly, and hangs suspended above the door till his prey comes beneath him, when he pounces upon him with the swiftness of a tiger." Cabanne may have been a pedestrian director, but he let Fairbanks choreograph the action, which was all, in this instance, the film required.

Released on the same bill as *Reggie* was Fairbanks's next film, *The Mystery of the Leaping Fish.* This two-reel farce was one of the strangest films of Fairbanks's career—or of any career, for that matter. Normally the Triangle release schedule consisted of one film each from Ince,

Griffith, and Sennett. Substituting for the Sennett slot, *The Mystery of the Leaping Fish* was dubbed a "Triangle-Komedy." The sudden and unexpected provision of short comedies from the Fine Arts division, as opposed to the Keystone arm of Triangle, came about as a result of exhibitor complaints that the biweekly Triangle program lacked variety. Griffith historian Russell Merritt wrote:

> Patrons complained of undiluted Keystone shorts, when other theaters added the spice of newsreels, cartoons, hand-colored travelogues, and sing-alongs. . . . As theaters began to break away from Triangle, Aitken desperately strove to revamp and modify his plan. He shortened the overall weekly program, ordered one-reel shorts from both Ince and Griffith to help offset the steady Keystone diet, and contracted with the A. W. McClure company for a seven part series called The Seven Deadly Sins—one sin per week.

The film became a cult classic in the 1960s and '70s, much as did *Reefer Madness* and other drug-related films. Fairbanks plays a Sherlock Holmes type dubbed "Coke Ennyday." Sporting an overcoat with monstrous black and white checks (curiously, an exaggerated version of a checked coat he wore in *Reggie*) and a huge mustache, he injects himself frequently with drugs drawn from a syringe-loaded cartridge belt. A large can labeled COCAINE is prominent on his desk. Fairbanks's character is in fact so hopped-up that he spends the last half reel conducting his fights and rescues in a continuous state of dance—a strange, skittering, wild flinging of the legs associated with a rigidly held upper body that makes him look like Michael Flatley on steroids.

His was hardly the first film to spoof illegal drugs, nor would it be the last—Chaplin famously did so in *Easy Street* a year later, sitting accidentally on a loaded needle and, after a series of comic twitches and jerks, acquiring superhuman powers. Other elements of *Leaping Fish* would also be co-opted—most famously the apparent wall safe that is really the office exit, used by Buster Keaton to great comic effect in

*Sherlock Junior.** In what was clearly meant as a tongue-in-cheek spoof on *Reggie*, seen in the same bill, the film climaxes with Fairbanks and the villain entering a darkened room to have a fight to the finish over lovely Bessie Love. Sixty years later Love would recall that "Mr. Fairbanks was a perfectionist: 'I can't seem to get the right voice for this character!' he would say in his quick, breathy way—in spite of the fact that it was a silent film."

Because it was bundled with *Reggie* on the distribution and exhibition schedule, it is difficult to assess what would have been the success or failure of this odd little film had it been on its own. But one thing was clear: Fairbanks would spend the rest of his days disavowing the end product. This was not simply an assertion of good taste (although that alone could be argued as just cause). In time he was to claim in a legal forum that he had never made any two-reel films.

This claim related to an episode in the 1920s, when a distributor by the name of Hyman Winik reissued Fairbanks's Triangle films as two-reel comedies. Chopping each five-reel feature down by 60 percent, he rewrote the titles and took extreme liberties with the plots of many.[†] Fairbanks sued, and since he had no ownership of the Triangle releases, he based his legal argument on the premise that he had made only feature films. To be associated with two-reel films, he maintained, was detrimental to his reputation. The mere existence of *The Mystery of the Leaping Fish* wiped out his argument, so he conveniently chose to forget the film's existence.[‡]

One can hardly blame him, although some critics were kind. The *Motion Picture News* deemed the film "refreshing nonsense, farcical to

---

* He also would borrow Fairbanks's leap from the door frame in a sequence ultimately cut from *The General.*

† In the abridgment of *The Half Breed*, for example, Fairbanks ends up with the white Jewel Carmen and not the Spanish Alma Rubens. Also all mention of racism—the main point of the original film—was expunged.

‡ It was to little avail; Fairbanks appealed up to the Supreme Court of New York, losing every time on the grounds that he was an employee, not a producer, of Triangle and thus had no say in the ultimate fate of the properties.

the last degree." *Variety* was more direct, stating, "John Emerson staged the travesty." While we may presume the term was used in the sense of "farce," it may be argued that it works both ways. In the words of Bessie Love, the film "didn't quite come off."

Emerson's putative direction is another source of interest. Bessie Love's albums note that Christy Cabanne was the initial director on the film and that Emerson replaced him after the film was completed, necessitating that the film be reshot from scratch. Triangle financial records offer little in the way of clues. Fairbanks features were costing between $25,000 and $30,000 as a rule, or $5,000 to $6,000 per reel, on average. *Fish* had negative costs of roughly $12,600—or $6,300 a reel. While this is slightly over the norm, it does not suggest that the entire film was reshot, even with the possibility that sets were reused. The greatest expense on any Fairbanks Triangle film was that of the star's time, and this would have doubled had the film been entirely reshot. Further, Cabanne was hardly banished to the Fine Arts doghouse—he went on to direct Fairbanks's next film, *Flirting with Fate*.

Flirting with Fate was a screwball comedy before the genre had been officially invented. Fairbanks played August Holliday, a starving artist. He falls in love with Gladys, the standard-issue heroine, wooing her with such claims as "The play of light on your hair and nose remind me of the works of Rosa Bonheur at her best."* In short order, his world collapses: the heroine rebuffs him over a misunderstanding, his prized painting is stolen, and the rent is overdue. In despair, he does the only logical thing: he hires a paid assassin to kill him when he's not looking. Soon, however, fate rectifies every catastrophe, and he now has to dodge the killer—who, of course, has since been reformed by the Salvation Army.

It was on such gossamer plot threads that Fairbanks began to string the pearls of his stunts. *Flirting* contained several of what were to become fixtures in his films: extended chase sequences. In this one, Fairbanks

---

* "Suddenly," the intertitle tells us, "Gladys remembers that Rosy never painted anything but horses."

performed a forward somersault into a moving car before leaping from that vehicle into another. He climbed several buildings, in one instance ending up on the top by impromptu catapult, and in another by pulling himself up by a drainpipe. While this particular chase was conducted by a lone, somewhat stout policeman, the motif was to evolve. Over the course of the years, the pursuers would grow into various hordes: soldiers, lynch mobs, cannibals. The pursuers mattered little; the joy was in watching Fairbanks elude them. Richard Schickel put it best: "To see Doug at bay and fighting off his enemies the while casing the joint for possibilities—that staircase there, that balcony yonder, that chandelier above, how can I put them together to befuddle these fools?—this was the moment of high deliciousness in all his work." *Flirting with Fate* was, like most of the Triangle films, a modest endeavor—"melodramas decorated by acrobatics," in the words of Alistair Cooke. But Fairbanks looked like he was having a hell of a good time throughout, and audiences found this quality infectious. The film was, as were all its predecessors, a solid hit.

To the surprise and dismay of all in the organization, however, his next film, *The Half Breed*, was a rare failure. On the surface, it is easy to see the cause for astonishment. Much time and effort had been invested in the movie, and it showed. The source material was Bret Harte's story "In the Carquinez Woods." In February 1916, Houghton Mifflin publishers were paid $1,000 for the story rights.* Allan Dwan was assigned to direct, and the entire production was filmed on location in Calaveras County, including in the nearby redwood forest, where the company staged a forest fire. The film's cost was $22,906, almost double that of *Flirting with Fate*.

The results justified the expense. Even today, the film is an absorbing story of racial discrimination in the American West. (Fairbanks played the title character, whose mother was a Native American.) The intertitles were intelligent and incisive, the two female leads played characters

---

* In contrast, $500 was paid for *Flirting with Fate*, both story and finished script, a mere two months before completion of that production.

who were complex and nuanced—an unusual event in any era—and the settings and photography were, in the words of cameraman Victor Fleming's biographer, "pictorially ravishing."

And yet the returns were a disappointment. "We, who had a hand in its making, regarded it as a 'knockout,'" wrote Fairbanks two years later. "But the public . . . couldn't see it."

The problem was this: as interesting, deserving, and well made a film as *The Half Breed* was, there was no *Doug* in it. Bret Harte's hero is stoic, literal, and stolid—the opposite of the star's natural traits. Fairbanks elected to communicate these (and, evidently, all other Indian qualities) by the frequent folding of his arms. His famous grin was rarely seen. Stunts were few. The *Motion Picture News* noted, "There is also less than the usual footage given the star." The film's weakness (or strength, depending on your point of view) was that its engaging, complex story rose above the charms of its leading man. And it was these charms that the audience had paid to see. As an indictment of racism, as a retelling of a Bret Harte tale, and as a narrative of two complex women, the film succeeds. The fact that it failed at the box office was because it was none of the things that it should have been to serve the Fairbanks persona. Audiences recognized this; word of mouth spread, and they stayed away. Alma Rubens said it best, two years after the film's initial release: "Douglas Fairbanks in a heavy dramatic role! Can you imagine that today?"

Shortly before her death, Rubens revealed more about her experience making the film. She attributed her casting to the fact that Doug "apparently had liked me ever since our trip to Balboa. This," she added primly, "despite the fact that I had not encouraged him in the least." The company was quartered in shacks in a mountain resort, she recalled. She was in bed at 2 AM, quavering under the covers at the sound of coyotes, when there was a tap at her window. "I heard a husky whisper from the outside: 'Alma, Alma . . . Open the window and let me in.'" Quite logically, she demanded to know what he wanted at that hour. "We've got to talk over the story" was the improbable reply.

She opened the sash. He flew in feet first, and, in her words, "wasted little time talking about *The Half Breed*, offering me, instead, the opportunity to accompany him back to New York where he was to play the lead in *Manhattan Madness*. He painted a glowing picture of my future, in this event. 'Six months in New York,' he explained, 'and you'll be made. Your name will be in the electric lights along Broadway. You'll have jewels, gowns, a Rolls-Royce—everything. I'll make you the leading woman in every picture I play in. You'll be getting a thousand a week.'" Of course, the lady in question may have been exaggerating. But one can almost hear the percussive quality of Fairbanks's voice as he painted this verbal portrait of fame and wealth. These were things he valued.

Her response (be it verbal or physical) Rubens discreetly left for her audience to imagine. But a proposal of a permanent costarring role made to Alma Rubens in her bedchamber at two o'clock in the morning was a different kettle of fish from the far more proper (yet similar) offer he made to Bessie Love. Love (or her mother) either declined or, being under contract to Triangle, was in no position to accept. She recalled: "I didn't know of any difference between the standing of one actor and another in the whole theatrical business. (Once my mother asked Douglas Fairbanks if he'd been cast yet for another picture, and poor Doug almost had a stroke.)" One suspects his motive in the latter case related to Love's size and frailty helping him look large and heroic on screen. His motive in the case of Miss Rubens may have been less seemly. We shall never know.

What we do know is that the reviews of *The Half Breed* were glowing. *Photoplay* declared that it was "Up, above the ordinary level of mere narrative. Up, above ordinary pictorial beauty. Up, in sheer daring of caption and situation. Up, in the way it gets you." And there was still some Doug that crept through all the stoicism of the character. The *New York Times* commented that his tree-trunk-dwelling character "looks rather more like Peter Pan than not."

Fairbanks's tracking of the varying box office receipts for his Triangle films was as careful here as in his theatrical days. Noting that the far more modest *Reggie Mixes In* ("It didn't look good at all and we dreaded the coming of the verdict") was a tremendous success when *The Half Breed* failed, he wrote, "We were beginning to get an idea as to what the public wanted to see me in." To the extent that the miscalculation was his (and this is unknown), he would not make it again. For the next decade and more, his films stuck to a formula. The flavor of the formula varied—now a modern Loos screwball comedy, now a western, now a Ruritanian romance—but the rule was the same, going forward: the story served the star, not the star the story.

His next film—*Manhattan Madness*—shot largely in New York,* again directed by Dwan, was a prime example of how to get the formula right. But before Doug's departure east, there was another event of note.

This was his participation in a one-night, cast-of-thousands out-door production of *Julius Caesar*. Staged in Beechwood Canyon on May 19, the play was a benefit fundraiser for the Actors Fund of America. Tyrone Power, DeWolf Hopper, Theodore Roberts, Tully Marshall, William Farnum, and other theatrical heavyweights appeared. Originally Fairbanks was slated to play Octavius, but his packed work schedule evidently intervened, so he appeared in the smaller role of young Cato. Forty thousand spectators attended as the five thousand actors and enthusiastic extras staged battle scenes over the open acres. Fairbanks did not know it at the time, but it would be his last major live performance.† It is fitting, perhaps, that it was conducted on a stage of epic scale. No mere proscenium arch could hold him anymore.

His arrival in New York City on June 15 to begin East Coast production was typically Fairbanksian. With no particular explanation, he wired the studio manager at Fort Lee: ARRIVE AT 9:40A.M. MEET ME WITH SEVEN TAXICABS. FAIRBANKS. While Doug's predilection for excess baggage was well known,‡ even he couldn't bring *this* much. Still, the staffer knew better than to question the instructions. The seven cabs

---

* Shots for the western sequences were filmed in California in late May.

† He would appear in a few local fundraisers during World War I, reenacting his old vaudeville sketches.

‡ A tendency that director Dwan would later playfully document in *Mr. Fixit*.

were waiting. Fairbanks arrived with twenty people: assistants, actors, cameraman Victor Fleming—to whom he had taken a fancy—and director Allan Dwan. Within a day the entourage was at Fort Lee working on the film. The decision to relocate and house so many members of a production crew to shoot in the East would at first seem like an expensive impulse, especially in light of Doug's recent declarations to the press that he would remain in the West indefinitely for filming, both for reasons of weather and for the varied exteriors. But the script of *Manhattan Madness* cried for shots of the big city; indeed, an entire sequence was written contrasting the allures of the East and the West. Audiences were treated to the sight not only of their hero breaking a bucking bronco and driving a stagecoach across the desert but also of him atop a Fifth Avenue bus and galloping through Van Cortlandt Park. Of course, it is entirely possible that there was another reason why Fairbanks was willing to cross the country to shoot his next two films. Mary Pickford was in New York.

She was living in Larchmont, a village north of New Rochelle, while she filmed at Famous Players' East Coast studio. Nearby was Broadway songwriter/performer Clifton Crawford, a friend of Fairbanks. Thus it was that Doug and Beth elected to summer in a cottage nearby. It is likely that this happy coincidence was abetted by the fact that John Emerson was then directing Pickford in *Less Than the Dust* and perhaps mentioned to Mr. Fairbanks where his star was summering. The lady in question certainly seemed surprised and pleased to discover that the Fairbanks family would be close at hand.

She first caught a glimpse of him when she accompanied Elsie Janis and a group of friends to see *Reggie Mixes In* at the Rialto. "A pleasant surprise took us quite off our feet as we turned away from the theater. It was Douglas Fairbanks himself, just returned from California," records her daily column.* "What attracted our attention to him were the remarks passed by a group of people who were pushing their way

---

* The column was ghostwritten by her friend and scenarist Frances Marion but was based on Pickford's recollections of her day.

past us. A voice said 'Ssssh! Look at that man over there in the corner! Surely it isn't Douglas Fairbanks!'

"'Douglas Fairbanks! I should say not!' replied one of the ladies. 'That fellow's as black as an Indian—why, for land's sake! I do believe he is an Indian!'" A vigorous debate among the crowd was not resolved "until he smiled—and no one has had or could ever have just such a smile as Douglas Fairbanks."

She and Elsie teased the smiling Mr. Fairbanks about the case of mistaken identity. He was unapologetic about his unfashionable coat of tan. "He had just come from God's own country, where he had lived in the out of doors like a real western cowboy," she wrote. He was never happier in his life, he told her. He had bought a small yacht that carried nine. He loved being in the movies: "The only thing about them is that I hate to call them work—I enjoy every minute."

And he (and she) seemed to enjoy every minute of the summer. There were boating trips on Long Island Sound. On one stormy day the sailboat capsized; the ladies were dunked, and the picnic basket lunch was lost. (Mary recalled hearing Doug cheerfully cry, "Let's hope the mermaids enjoy it," before she ended up in the drink.) There were dinner parties at Elsie Janis's Tarrytown estate, games of charades with the likes of Billie Burke and Florenz Ziegfeld—Mary put on pants and portrayed Charlie Chaplin. It was all perfectly proper, always with starstruck Beth and others making up the company. There were long conversations. Doug confessed ("with a twinkle in his eyes") that he had urged Mary and Elsie to take that long muddy walk the prior November because he knew Mary had qualms about her dainty new footwear.

It was a courtship, of a sort. He was hardly pitching woo, it is true, but he was exposing her to a healthy dose of Doug. And she found, perhaps against her will, that this was irresistible. He began to pop up in her daily column more and more. "The man of him has never lost sight of the boy of him," she wrote in one. She recounted a tale Beth had told her. Having finished *The Good Bad Man*, Fairbanks had invited the participating cowhands to a farewell dinner at the town's hotel. The cowboys were stiff and awkward in the unfamiliar social setting. Doug saw this, and immediately started dining as if he were on a roundup. He ate from his knife. He dropped his bread into his soup. He picked his teeth and cheerfully planted his elbows on the table. This did the trick; the cowboys relaxed, and the meal was enjoyed by one and all. Mary was enchanted. "There are so many stories to tell about Douglas Fairbanks one scarcely knows where to begin: of his generosity, his kind heart and his love for humanity, which is reflected in that genial smile of his," she wrote. With Beth's unintentional help, she was starting to fall in love with him.

The cowhand's banquet served, in a way, to document the theme of *Manhattan Madness*. The dynamic between the East and the West, between the civilized and the wild, was to govern Fairbanks's career for its first five years, and, some would claim, defined his appeal. Those of a more sociologic bent make the argument that as the nation was changing its essential character from rural to urban, there was a fear that there would be an associated diminution of its vigor and hardiness. The West had been settled, the cowboys of a mere generation before were a dying breed, and the modern man was increasingly to be found wearing a coat and tie instead of chaps and bandana. There was, it is said, a certain level of national angst over this in the first years of the past century. Modernity, it was feared, was making America soft.

Douglas Fairbanks was a one-man antidote to this ailment. With effortless grace he carried—as did his adored Theodore Roosevelt—the opposing characteristics of the city and the wilderness. He was as competent a cowboy as one could wish. Yet at the same time he was the white-tied citizen of Broadway, the man who would come to live in New York and London, who would mix easily with presidents and kings. He was no everyman but rather an über-man, one who reassured Americans that to be an eastern elite did not equate with being effete and that there were, at the same time, still plenty of cowboys out there who could pack a punch. Very few stars were able to cross this divide, falling more usually into either the eastern (think Cary Grant) or the western (think John Wayne) mold. Fairbanks spanned it routinely, usually with an engaging wink or an impish grin. George Creel wrote in *Everybody's Magazine* of his popularity, "It is a good sign, a healthful sign, a token that the blood of America still runs warm and red, and that chalk has not yet softened our bones."

In *Manhattan Madness*, Fairbanks's character (a western rancher appropriately named Steve O'Dare) is stoutly of the opinion that the merits of the East are nothing to those of the West. He returns to his college club in New York and drives his friends to distraction extolling the virtues of the western lands. One perspicacious pal bets him $5,000 that within a week New York will offer thrills to equal those of Nevada. The bet is taken, and adventures ensue at a mysterious mansion. The estate used for the shoot served as a cautionary tale to any young celebrity. It had belonged to theater star Clara Morris for thirty-seven years, until blindness and poverty forced her to sell. Now its mansard roof and windowsills served as a virtual jungle gym for Doug to play upon.

And play he did. The level of the stunts in *Manhattan Madness* was ramped up to a degree not yet seen. He climbed up the home's three stories; he climbed down, in and out of windows, running along the rooftop, firing guns, leaping to nearby trees, down to the ground, and back up the building again—all while wearing an absurd little bow tie at formal odds with his open, free clambering. He performed various standing leaps: onto the back of a horse, over a chair, over a group of men. He ran across the top of a moving train, rode a bucking horse, and in general demonstrated, in the words of one reviewer, "that as an all-around athlete Douglas Fairbanks puts Jim Thorpe way back stage."

One wonders if his athleticism may have become tiresome to his fellow actors. Art director Ben Carré was asked by Dwan to create the interior of a Fifth Avenue club for the sequence where Fairbanks reunites with his friends. "The set was ready; plenty of actors were standing in it having been placed there by an assistant director," Carré recalled. "I saw Douglas Fairbanks all dressed up in evening clothes but with a five gallon hat on his head, not yet on the set. He came over to speak to Allan Dwan who, in answer to his question, said 'Go to it.' Fairbanks went on the side of the set to make his entrance. Dwan called 'Camera' and Fairbanks made a quick entrance, saw a man walking and dived to tackle him. The man went down with a surprised face."

The unsuspecting extra may not have seen the charm of Mr. Fairbanks, but the audience did. The film was a marked success. The only dark spot in its production was a corneal burn that its star suffered when a prop gun was fired too close to his left eye. ("If Mr. Fairbanks had not swung quickly around when he saw the man turning the rifle upon him, he might have gotten the full blast in his face and had his eyes put out," Pickford reported somewhat breathlessly in her column.) But corneal burns heal quickly,* and contrary to modern rumors, he was able to perform all the stunts in the film. In fact, he used the reported injury to his advantage. When he bounded onto the stage on *Manhattan Madness's* opening night at the Rialto and, in the words of the *New York Times* reporter, "with hands in trouser pockets stood smiling at a large audience," he stated modestly that "he thought the picture was pretty good, that he nearly lost his eyesight during the taking, but that the picture on which he was now working would be better, because he had already been hurt more times than in the former." Every injury emphasized to the audiences that what was being done was real, not trickery, and what's more, it was being done by Doug himself.

The volume of injuries he suffered over the years was imposing. There would be broken bones of his hands and fingers, dislocated bones, torn ligaments, stab wounds, sword slashes, and contusions. His brows and lashes were burned off in the forest fire sequences of *The Half Breed.* An ankle injury incurred during filming of *The Americano* sent him to the hospital. Each time, he took the position that the injuries were not only to be borne, but the mere fact of them made the picture authentic and the volume of them spoke to the volume of risks taken. Each injury, he argued, made a better movie.†

---

* His son recalls that he wore a black eye patch and "rather fancied the dashing look it gave him."

† Jackie Chan, one of the few authentic film athletes whose skills are comparable to those of Fairbanks, takes the same position, showing outtakes at the end of his films documenting the injuries he sustained during the course of shooting. Fairbanks, on the other hand, never lifted the curtain to actually let the audience see him getting hurt. The illusion of effortlessness was maintained on the screen, while the press reported the injuries.

It is hard to argue that his next film, *American Aristocracy*, was better than *Manhattan Madness*, but no one save the occasional critic seemed to care. The exteriors were filmed at Kenneth Ridge, Beth's family home in Watch Hill—likely a further opportunity to line her father's pockets. Moreover, Junior made his first film appearance, playing a bit part as a newsboy. A series of publicity photographs taken at this time shows the little family sitting on the steps at Watch Hill, Beth proud and plump in a white cotton frock, Junior awkward and doughy in a white sailor suit ("no real newsboy ever looked like that,"* he was to comment, seventy years later), and Doug, pipe clenched between his teeth, stern-faced, trying to look the role of the paterfamilias. One wonders what each was thinking.

His son certainly had not yet developed the ambivalence toward his father that would characterize the majority of his life. He was still in awe of the man—when he actually saw him. He wrote, "Dad was absent so often I hardly noticed, although everything, including me, brightened and bustled when he returned." Junior had the vague sense that he, roly-poly and perpetually dressed in sissy clothes by his mother, was an embarrassment to his athletic father—or worse, of no interest. Richard Schickel quotes Beth's recollections on the subject: "Senior was perfectly tender and nice, he just did not have the instinct of being a father. . . . He used to come into the house, day-in day-out, and he wouldn't know the child was there. Unless I asked if he was going up to say goodnight to Douglas or unless somebody wanted to see the child, Senior displayed no interest in him—he didn't care; he was just bored."

This certainly seems at odds with his general approach to children. Triangle had a collection of children about for use in films as the "Triangle Kiddies" or for whenever a stray child was needed for a regular feature. "Fairbanks and his lasso divide their spare time about evenly between a bunch of old-time cowpunchers with a taste for boxing and wrestling and the children," wrote one witness at the time. "They adore him." He set up a class in rope tricks, taught them string puzzles, and

---

* The director of *American Aristocracy* must have agreed. Contrary to Junior's memories, he wore overalls for his actual scene in the film.

engaged in boxing matches. "Francis Carpenter and Fairbanks had a boxing bout," continued the account. "Francis is four, going on five. It was a lively bout. Francis closed in and landed a body blow. His antagonist sank limply to the stage, and Francis stood over him and counted him out. When Fairbanks was up, Francis came back and held out his hand. 'Mr. Fairbanks,' he said, 'I'm willing to call it square, if you are.'" Eunice Woodruff died at ten years of age in 1921, but during Doug's reign at Fine Arts, was also one of the children on the lot. Her mother wrote that Fairbanks "loved Eunice, then only six years old. He would have the extra boys run a race from the studio to Vermont Ave and Eunice would be on his shoulder and hold the money for the winner."

This behavior was not restricted to children around the studio. Assistant cameraman Glen MacWilliams once pulled into Fairbanks's driveway for a meeting, carefully leaving his children in the car so as not to disturb his boss. Learning that they were out there, Fairbanks would have none of it. He brought the children into the house and proceeded to romp, chase, and conduct imaginary sword fights up, over, and around the furniture, giving them a memory that they would cherish to their graves.

So these recollections are difficult to square with those of Beth. Junior was clear that he enjoyed mightily the "jolly and vigorous but infrequent" presence of his father. "His home appearances were rarely anything but pleasant. He would come, to my secret delight, and go, to my secret regret, and rarely seemed to be more than vaguely aware of my presence. . . . He was never unkind or unjustly stern with me. . . . But alas, I was too shy, too plump and awkward, and he was such an evanescent sprite." He was not only shy around his father, he was a little afraid, as timid children will be. True, his mother was more prone to explosions of rage and thus more frightening to him. But Doug, too, would occasionally have an outburst. The difference, his son noted, "was that it was always a summer-like thunderstorm followed quickly by grumpiness and then his personal rainbow."

And his father might not have been as neglectful as he thought. Jesse Lasky Jr. recalled being seven years old and working feverishly with a friend to assemble a "coaster" for a race down La Brea scheduled for the next day. His father approached him with a request that the boys include a new boy, Doug Jr., in their activities. Junior was the son of a dear friend and neighbor, he said.

The boys protested. The race was the next day! Doug Jr. wouldn't have a coaster! Lasky, according to his son, pondered the problem. He would pass this information on to Junior's father. The next morning, the boys were assembled for the race.

> Then our ears caught a suspicious sound. A small sputtering like a motorcycle, a chugging up the hill. We strained in horror to watch the approach of a coaster. But no ordinary affair like ours, stuck together from boards, sheet metal, and old wheels. This was a small automobile with its own gasoline engine, snorting up the steep incline under its own power. Behind the wheel, Doug, a scant year younger than I, but by right of ownership of such a vehicle, far elevated in social status. It was the unlikely start of a beautiful friendship.

The father, evidently, was working behind the scenes in the interest of his child.

Junior remembered worshipfully watching his father shave his heavy beard in the morning, using a straight razor and singing:

> I'm so—goll-darned tough,
> I'm so—goll-darned rough,
> That I—shoot—
> My goll-darned
> Whiskers off!

And he recalled that during the filming of *American Aristocracy*, Senior was "sport enough" to permit Victor Fleming to shoot a short film starring Junior and his playmates.

American Aristocracy was, according to his son, also partially the product of his father's creative hand, being, in his words, "a fluff-weight fable concocted by Anita Loos and Dad." While Loos got the sole authorship credit,* an argument can be made that both contributed to the plot: the film was essentially two movies—the first an incisive caricature of America's bean-can nobility, the second a spy adventure. The two, in the minds of the critics, did not mesh. They universally loved Loos's contribution. "Satire is an advanced form of literature," commented *Photoplay*. "Her satire on Newport Society ('American Aristocracy') is perhaps the greatest stride movie literature has made." Indeed, Loos's titles remain as sharp and funny today as they did one hundred years ago.

But the second half of the film came in for much critical ennui. "It drivels out into a mere vehicle," griped the *Moving Picture World*. "Would it not be possible to give Mr. Fairbanks more opportunity as an actor and less as an acrobat?" *Photoplay* agreed. "Mr. Fairbanks is being completely eaten up by his jumping ability. He leaps into his chairs, over his motors, onto his horses, out of his difficulties, like a godson of St. Vitus. Acrobatics and agility are good, but in this picture they are driven into the ground, to the exclusion of much better stuff of which he is entirely capable."

The *New York Times* took to listing the feats of derring-do: "He vaults a dozen walls and fences, swings like a Darwinian ancestor from the top branches of trees, plunges headlong down embankments, drives an automobile at wild speed, flies in a hydroaeroplane, and performs other feats of athletic skill and prowess." The critic also noted evidence of Fairbanks's puckish humor in the course of this film: after scaling innumerable walls, "he makes ready to leap at a window ten feet above the ground, and then suddenly opens a basement window and climbs in easily instead."[†]

---

* Files at the Margaret Herrick Library and USC Warner Archives indicate that she was paid $500 for her story and script.

† The incident never fails to get a laugh, even today, much as does the scene in the first *Indiana Jones* film where Harrison Ford, braced to engage in a sword fight with a villain, pauses—exasperated—then simply pulls out his pistol and shoots.

The critics might have felt that *American Aristocracy* was a "nondescript vehicle" for Fairbanks, but audiences overruled them. The box office at the Rialto, where the film premiered in New York City, recorded the highest weekly take the theater had ever seen. Hundreds milled outside in the cold November rain, waiting to get in. Nobody seemed to think that Doug was jumping too much. They enjoyed watching him use the world as his personal playground, and the film was a solid success.

He returned to California in late October, wiring Harry Aitken on the day of his arrival "that he craved two boons—first, that John Emerson act as his director; second, that Anita Loos . . . write the titles for his plays."

He got one out of two. Loos wrote the script, but his next film, *The Matrimaniac*, was directed by Paul Powell, who was famed for nothing in particular.* Still, as always Fairbanks had fun during the film's hasty construction and production. When some exteriors were shot near the Lillian Way studio, where Charlie Chaplin was producing his Mutual comedies, Chaplin interrupted his own shoot to rush out, sit on the curb, and watch his friend. "Now make me laugh, Doug," he was reported to have said. "I'll be your audience."

They had met earlier that year. Constance Collier, who was Lady Macbeth in Sir Herbert's Triangle production, had been talking up Fairbanks to Chaplin. "From Constance I had heard much about Douglas Fairbanks' charm and ability, not only as a personality but as a brilliant after-dinner speaker. In those days I disliked brilliant young men—especially after-dinner speakers," he recalled drily. Still, she persisted and arranged an introductory dinner at Fairbanks's house in Hollywood. Chaplin came prepared to fake a headache and leave early. Fairbanks, uncharacteristically nervous, retreated to the billiard room the moment the doorbell rang. "That night," Charlie wrote fifty years later, "was the beginning of a lifelong friendship." In the other, each found the perfect complement. Fairbanks's warmth and extraversion drew the diffident Chaplin out of

---

* He would go on to direct Mary Pickford in *Pollyanna*, but this was one of her least favorite films. He was largely known as a competent studio hand but little more.

his shell. "He had extraordinary magnetism and charm and a genuine boyish enthusiasm which he conveyed to the public," Charlie said. He summed up the relationship with an almost poignant cynicism: "Doug Fairbanks was my only real friend and I was a showpiece for him at parties." Chaplin meant far more to him than that, of course. For many years they were inseparable, whether there was a party or not. And Fairbanks was a trusted sounding board. He would laugh with unfeigned delight as his friend worked out new routines—no matter how many times repeated and no matter how many subtle variations. "Sweet Douglas," Chaplin said. "He was my greatest audience."Chaplin was happy to return the favor.

This is not to say that every aspect of *The Matrimaniac* was unabashedly joyful. Anita Loos reports that Doug was confounded by one simple scene. The opening sequence required him to stick a hat pin into the tires of a car. This, she wrote, brought out "an incredible cowardice in Doug; he tried over and over to do the stunt and finally said, 'I can't do this scene, Nita; I'm scared.'" If this was the case, it doesn't show on film, where he stabbed the tires with apparent aplomb. And at this juncture, at least, she found no other cause for complaint. "Douglas Fairbanks," she said, "could conquer any living space. . . . He never sat when he could stand, never walked when he could run; and, to Doug, chasms were built to jump over."

It was fortunate that he enjoyed running, for *The Matrimaniac* is essentially one extended chase scene. The heroine's father and his suitor of choice chase Doug and the delightful Constance Talmadge as they elope on a train; Doug and a minister (whom he has plucked out of his bathtub) chase the train with the bride on board; injunction servers and the young woman's father chase the groom over hill, dale, fences, and buildings, all attempting to prevent the ceremony. "It would have made a whopper of a two-reel Keystone," the *Variety* reviewer commented drily.

Thrills aside (and Fairbanks stepped up the stunts to an astonishing degree in *The Matrimaniac*, in one instance walking across telephone wires, slipping and almost tumbling to the ground in the process, then slowly, carefully regaining his position on the wiggling lines and continuing his progress), the film had comic appeal. Fairbanks's behavior throughout the crazed proceedings remained impeccable: he assiduously left IOUs for every item stolen or borrowed, and took tender care of his abducted minister throughout the chase. No matter the obstruction, he remained doggedly cheerful.

One contemporary reviewer tried to characterize this phenomenon. "Fairbanks represents physical agility and temperamental optimism, and it is really the latter quality that wins. His leaping and climbing feats would soon pall if he did not perpetually demonstrate that life is good and growing better, in spite of all pessimistic claims to the contrary. Therein lies the true charm of Fairbanks." Alistair Cooke should be credited for preserving a quote from an obscure French critic who said it best: "Douglas Fairbanks is a tonic. He laughs and you feel relieved."

Fairbanks's last film for Triangle (although the company did not know it at the time) was *The Americano*. Anita Loos (and, reportedly, John Emerson) adopted the plot of *Blaze Derringer*, a 1910 novel by Eugene P. Lyle, an author who specialized in western adventures. Here the original story was the tale of a wealthy young man who had run through the money allotted to him by his father and thus was tempted by a $100,000 reward to free the deposed emperor of a fictitious South American country.* In the original the hero is accompanied by a pair of notorious jail breakers. In the Loos rewrite, all distasteful elements of the plot are removed: Fairbanks's unnamed character—he is known to the audience only as "the Americano"—is motivated not by money but by love for the captive's daughter. It is no longer an emperor they are freeing but a republican *presidente*. This being Doug, he cannot be accompanied by professional jail breakers; he performs his heroics with the aid of an elderly minister of the deposed government and a splay-footed, rabbit's-foot-clutching employee of the mining company, played in blackface by Tom Wilson. And, instead of being a college dropout, our hero is a graduate of a mining school. Other than the main setup of the plot—the need for a jailbreak, and the prisoner's daughter—no plot elements of the original text remain in the film. This scarcely seems to

* In the film the location is moved to Central America.

matter; as source material, it is pretty weak stuff. Fairbanks was learning that in his sort of movie, the more intricate the plot, the more screen time wasted on exposition, and the less to let him play. Adapting Bret Harte had taught him this lesson.

The exteriors were shot at the San Diego Exposition, which served as a picturesque stand-in for the fictional Latin American country of the story. The film was a cheery little spy story, with a moderate amount of stunts. Fairbanks, for the first time in a film, incapacitates a villain by engaging him in a scissor lock between his legs.* As in *American Aristocracy*, he spends a fair amount of time scaling tall walls. Still—and this may be hindsight only, of course—there remains a sense that he is phoning it in, not fully engaged with the making of this cloak and dagger feature.

If this is indeed the case, it is understandable. It was December 1916, and he was contemplating his exit from the Triangle Film Corporation. He had been with the company less than eighteen months.

D. W. Griffith had departed earlier in the year, having bought Aitken and Triangle out of their ownership stake in his epic *Intolerance*.† Aitken's house of cards was starting to totter. Fairbanks would later tell of a dinner meeting Aitken arranged for him and John Emerson with a certain Mr. Parker, of the American Radiator Company. Parker, Aitken hoped, would put money in the company. The radiator man, however, was more interested in the creative side of the business. He produced two paperback books, "saying that these were the money-making things," Fairbanks later stated in an affidavit. But Doug had no interest in advice from a radiator manufacturer. Normally polite to a fault, he cracked. This was absurd, he told the man. He might just as well expect Fairbanks to suggest ideas about radiators as for Parker to suggest ideas about screen

---

* A trick he first demonstrated on stage in *Hawthorne of the U.S.A.*

† *Intolerance* was released as a "road show" picture—traveling from major city to major city, orchestra and publicity in tow, much like a major theatrical production. The timing, for Griffith, was unfortunate. A paean to pacifism, it came out just as America's isolationist leanings toward the Great War were turning. It took an achingly long time to break even. Griffith ended up signing a distribution deal with Adolph Zukor at Paramount.

productions. The books, Fairbanks said, "were unadulterated bunk." There is no record of whether Mr. Parker stuck around for dessert.

Then Aitken had hired an efficiency expert to trim waste around the studio. "All the actors and actresses who had been selected by Fairbanks were let out and inferior ones procured," reported the *Exhibitor's Trade Review*. Wilbur Higby, "who usually played the parts of bartender, gunman and rough neck was chosen to play the part of a modern millionaire." Actors wore their own clothes for modern roles at that time, and Higby's dress pants were patched. This became evident during a scene in *The Matrimaniac* where the actor, playing Constance Talmadge's outraged father, was required to descend a ladder. The patch showed, and the take was ruined. Worse—at least in Doug's mind—the car with the tires that required puncturing was eight years old. Own an eight-year-old car? "No modern millionaire would do that!" he groused.

The state of Triangle's finances created a pressure on him to crank out films faster than he wished. He did not yet have the sort of ambitions that moved Griffith to build massive sets and make lengthy epics. But he did have a desire to take the time to make his films better. The Triangles, with rare exception, demonstrate the haste of their construction: interior sets had often looked flimsy and thrown together. But now the pinch was really on. Fairbanks had filmed both *The Matrimaniac* and *The Americano* in the six-week period between November 1 and December 16, 1916. Three weeks per feature was not the pace he wished to keep, nor did it result in films that he felt were of substantial quality. He could, conceivably, negotiate new terms with Aitken to obtain more control of his productions. But given Triangle's financial straits, this scarcely made sense.

The answer, it seemed to him, was to have a production unit of his own and to seek a better distributor. He had been considering it for some time—thus the recruitment of brother John to the fold. In early October, after the completion of *American Aristocracy*, a *Chicago Tribune* reporter found him in a contemplative mood, businesswise. "There's a lot of opportunity ahead, and I think 'state rights' is the big thing in releasing," Fairbanks said. "Your pictures have got to circulate, and that is the coming way to make them. You do a good picture and sell it on its merits and you keep making money on it. Then you don't need to make another picture until you can do a good one." In fact, the state's rights model—in which a film is leased to an organization or individual covering a territory instead of to individual theaters on a piecemeal basis—would not turn out to be the model of the future. Vertical integration, in which a powerful studio system would control production, distribution, and exhibition, would dominate the industry until the Supreme Court determined the model to be a violation of antitrust laws after Fairbanks's death.

But his essential thinking was correct. Take more time, invest more money, make better pictures, and let the market determine their merit on a case-by-case basis. He also thought he knew the formula for better pictures. "I'd be happy if I had a studio and Anita Loos, who writes the funny captions, and John Emerson to direct me," he said. "That's all I ask for." Loos and Emerson, being romantically involved, came as a unit. But it was Loos he really wanted. "Time and again I have sat through plays by Miss Loos and have heard the audience applaud her subtitles as heartily as the liveliest scenes," he said later that autumn. "There have been cases I can mention where her comments outshone the scenes themselves. This has convinced me of the great value of the kind of work she does."

It was not, in point of fact, all he asked for. He was beginning to feel his oats. It has already been demonstrated that upon arrival in Los Angeles he wired these requests (demands?) to Aitken. But the fact of his cross-country trip was in itself outside of Aitken's original plans. He was supposed to stay out east that autumn. But, a *Moving Picture World* reporter wrote, "He left New York in a hurry when they told him to get ready for a picture. He said he did not want to work in the East, and that they could find him in California if they wanted to use him in any of the scenes."

Aitken tried to meet his demands. By early December it was announced that Loos would be writing the intertitles for all his future productions. But as Christmas approached, Aitken found himself repeatedly denying that Fairbanks was going to leave Fine Arts to form his own company. He (rightly) pointed out that Fairbanks had signed a three-year contract with Triangle in September 1915. He conveniently left out the mention that this contract, as with his ten-week contract, stipulated that D. W. Griffith supervise his films. Griffith was gone.

Fairbanks, in turn, started getting his ducks in a row. He engaged Dennis "Cap" O'Brien, who—little coincidence here—served as Mary Pickford's attorney. He brought on Bennie Zeidman as his "special representative" for publicity. And, on January 2, 1917, he notified the Triangle Film Corporation that he was severing business relations with it.

His summer with Mary Pickford had consisted of more than picnics and charades. There were·serious business discussions as well. The story of how Mary discovered, in the summer of 1915, that she was being cheated on the profit-sharing component of her contract by the practice of "block booking" is now the stuff of legend—at least among those who study the history of films and finance. Her contract, negotiated in January 1915, called for her not only to double her salary to $2,000 a week but also to share in 50 percent of the profits of her films.

All well and good. But how was that 50 percent being calculated? Adolph Zukor, head of Famous Players, was much beloved by Mary Pickford as a father figure. But this did not stop him from being a sly fox when it came to all things financial. He had set up a system with his distributor, Paramount (in time the production company would assume the name), to offer films in packaged groups. Lesser films were accepted by exhibitors in order to ensure getting the Pickford features, which were goldmines. By spreading the revenue that the distributor (and, downstream, the producer) netted across a block of films, Zukor was artificially underreporting the profits on the Pickford films.

In the summer of 1915, when Douglas Fairbanks was heading to Hollywood for the first time, Mary Pickford was living and filming in New York City. Daily, her driver took her past the Strand Theatre, where crowds were lining around the block to see her latest feature, *Rags*. When the bill finally changed and another Famous Players film was at the Strand, the sidewalks were, she noticed, empty. She then did something that most actresses would not: she went in the theater and counted the house. At this point, she sweetly asked her dear Mr. Zukor to check the books. What was the rental for each film? The cat was out of the bag. Zukor had been charging theaters essentially the same for her hits as for the others' duds, thus directing profits away from her films.

When her contract was up for renegotiation in the spring of 1916, dear Mr. Zukor was in for a trial. The contract, which took four weeks to negotiate, influences film industry deals to this day. Pickford was given her own production unit (albeit with Zukor as its president) and a guarantee of $10,000 a week against 50 percent of the profits—whichever was greater. Of equal importance, a separate distribution company was established as a division of Paramount. Artcraft, which ultimately would serve as distributor for both Douglas Fairbanks and D. W. Griffith, booked each Pickford film on an individual basis—no block booking. Zukor, to finance this venture, merged his Famous Players production company with that of Jesse Lasky, the other main producer to distribute through Paramount. The combination—Famous Players–Lasky, ultimately known as Paramount Pictures—became the largest motion picture company in the world.

Fairbanks's Triangle salary had progressed through scheduled biannual raises to $3,250 a week. This was, of course, an enormous sum, and he asked for no pity. (*Photoplay* magazine stated puckishly, "No self-respecting actor can afford to labor for a paltry 3,000 iron men a week when potatoes are soaring around $4 a bushel and onions are almost ungettable.") But consider his peers. He, Mary Pickford, and Charlie Chaplin were the three most popular stars in film. In February, Chaplin signed his record-breaking contract with Mutual for $10,000 a week, with a $150,000 signing bonus—but no profit sharing. Mary, four months later, matched Chaplin's weekly salary and topped him by obtaining the unprecedented profit-sharing clause. Within the context of his value in the industry, Fairbanks was grossly underpaid. The free market recognized this as well. It started in late December, when Famous Players–Lasky put out a feeler to Fairbanks for $7,500 a week to leave Triangle.

He let it be known—by way of a front-page headline in *Variety*—that he was open to offers. Triangle, he said, had been in breach of contract. "One story," wrote *Variety*, "is that Griffith has given no further attention to any Fairbanks release and never looked at one of the Fairbanks films before release excepting the first, when Griffith remained one day at the studio."[*] He would entertain offers of $15,000 a week, he said. That, or he would produce his own films at a cost to the distributor of $200,000 a film, with a promise of eight films a year.

The offers came. Novelist Rex Beach, who produced films based on his stories, offered $10,000 a week. Universal topped this with an offer of free distribution. Fairbanks declined. He needed, he told *Variety*, $15,000 weekly to "ensure against any judgment Triangle might obtain against him, if suit were to be brought . . . for breach of contract." Louis B. Mayer, whose production company bore his name, approached Cap O'Brien with an offer of $15,000 a week.[†] Sam Goldwyn offered a comparable flat weekly rate, but learning that Fairbanks wanted to produce the films himself, offered a minimum guarantee of $225,000 per picture, against a division of 72.5 percent of the gross receipts to Fairbanks and 27.5 percent to the Goldwyn Pictures Corporation.

A generous offer, indeed. But by the first week of February came the public announcement that Artcraft would distribute Douglas Fairbanks films. The original contract was with Fairbanks personally: a minimum guarantee of $200,000 per picture, against 72.5 percent of

---

[*] Curiously, when it came time for the legal filings, Fairbanks took the opposite tack. It was hard to prove that he wasn't being supervised, and easier to point out that Griffith had left the company, so his once-critical supervision was now absent.

[†] In a 1923 affidavit related to a tax case, Mayer asserted that the "deponent is familiar with the earnings of the pictures of the leading stars during that period—among whom he considers Douglas Fairbanks—and he is of the opinion that $25,000 per week would not only have been a fair and reasonable compensation for Douglas Fairbanks to have been paid during the years of 1917 and 1918, but that as a producer, he would have enjoyed a substantial profit under such a contract."

the gross. (The split on international revenues was to be 60/40.) Why did he take the Paramount deal instead of the (presumably) richer one from Goldwyn? One can only speculate. He might have felt that the Famous Players–Lasky combine had a stronger distribution network. More likely, he was following in the footsteps of his fascination with Mary.

It can certainly be stated that Beth Fairbanks, who formerly prided herself on managing all of her husband's negotiations and contracts, was not involved in this process—a considerable source of family strife. John Emerson later detailed this in a deposition asserting that:

> Mr. Daniel Sully, the father of Mrs. Beth S. Fairbanks, had been busy in the affairs of Douglas Fairbanks, and that Douglas Fairbanks was very much opposed to the same. That Mr. Sully was employed by the Majestic Motion Picture Company, and that upon . . . Fairbanks serving notice of cancellation of his contract with the Majestic Motion Picture Company, the President of that company handed such notice to Mr. Sully, and later Mr. Sully sought Douglas Fairbanks and endeavored to have him recall such notice.

None of this, of course, sat well with Harry Aitken. He filed an injunction in New York against Fairbanks appearing in any Artcraft releases. Fairbanks, already at work on his first independent production, was served with papers at Lake Placid, New York, on Valentine's Day. Further (and perhaps more to the point), by stopping Daniel Sully's "salary," Aitken opened a can of family worms. Sully claimed that his son-in-law had a personal contract with him. He, Sully, would negotiate a $10,000 a week contract for Doug. Fairbanks would keep $7,500 of it, and he would "enjoy a profit of $2500 a week thereby." The contract, of course, had never been made with Douglas Fairbanks. If it existed—and this is questionable—it had been negotiated between father and daughter.

Cap O'Brien, who, with Douglas's brother John, was handling the actual negotiations, stated: "Sully then sought to influence his daughter . . . to have her husband recall his written resignation. . . . Sully constantly interfered with all negotiations that were subsequently pending for the employment of Douglas Fairbanks, through influencing his daughter."

Sully was betting on the wrong horse. When it came to business, Mary Pickford, Cap O'Brien, and John Fairbanks were the voices Douglas Fairbanks was heeding now. Enraged, Sully got a lawyer, who attempted to serve papers on O'Brien.

This would never do. Although he already had established contracts with Anita Loos, John Emerson, and Victor Fleming (for scripts, direction, and cinematography, respectively), Fairbanks was now required to build a legal firewall between himself and his angry father-in-law by forming the Douglas Fairbanks Pictures Corporation.

The entity served simply as a pass-through vehicle, having no independent source of income other than what came into and went out of it from Paramount and, later, United Artists. The contracts the corporation made were identical to the deals he had struck as an individual. Emerson and Loos were to be compensated both by way of weekly salaries ($1,000 per week for Emerson, $250 per week for Loos) and profit sharing (15 percent of net, capped at $10,500 per film, for Emerson; 7.5 percent of net but with no cap for Loos). Brother John also got 10 percent of the profits and even cameraman Fleming was awarded a 1 percent share, meaning that Fairbanks in effect retained two-thirds of the company's profits and shared one-third with his creative and business team. It was an extraordinarily generous arrangement—and not typical of the industry. Chaplin was notorious for his penurious salaries, and while Mary was not as bad, she was extremely careful about every nickel.

This served to protect Doug from his father-in-law. He settled, in the end, with Aitken. Triangle's books have a single page titled "Douglas Fairbanks Indemnity a/c" showing a payment of $12,673.81 on April 30 and $15,000 on July 23. How this odd sum was calculated is a mystery. The funds paid to Daniel Sully had totaled $9,800. But however derived, the amount satisfied Aitken, who dropped his suit and injunction against Fairbanks.*

For West Coast production, Douglas leased space from Jesse Lasky at his Hollywood lot for $12,000 for the first fourteen weeks and then at a slightly reduced rate of $833.33 a week thereafter. Lasky would charge time and materials for set construction. The deal would work out strongly to Fairbanks's advantage. He had no upfront, fixed costs in staffing or managing a lot, or in obtaining and maintaining props and sets. By late November, Famous Players–Lasky general manager Cecil B. DeMille grumbled in a letter to Lasky that they had already lost over $8,000 on the deal due to increased costs of material and overhead.

Even if he had lost money on the arrangement, one suspects that Doug would have stuck with it. For at the same lot, within one city block, were the production offices of Mary Pickford. The last two weeks of December 1916 did not merely bring about his rupture with Triangle and his union with Artcraft. They were to contain other momentous events. He would lose one woman who had been seminal in his life, and he would gain another.

---

* Not so with Artcraft Pictures, however. Aitken pursued this case until losing at the appeal level, when Judge Learned Hand wrote, "Nobody has ever thought, so far as we can find, that in the absence of some monopolistic purpose every one has not the right to offer better terms to another's employee, so long as the latter is free to leave."

6

Triangle (as in Love)

JUST BEFORE HIS TRIP to New York in December 1916, Douglas Fairbanks stopped by Charlie Chaplin's studio to bid him farewell. They clutched each other for the cameras, Chaplin in full tramp costume, his left arm around Doug's shoulder, his right clamping Doug's left forearm, his head drooped on Doug's chest. Fairbanks, in turn, had his normally irrepressible smile turned upside down into a mock expression of grief. *Photoplay* would soon publish the picture under the title "A Couple of Wall Nuts."

But in very short order, Fairbanks was to find his faux grief turn into the genuine article. On his train trip east, on the day before Christmas Eve, he received a telegram telling him that Ella was dead of pneumonia. Ella, whose favorite he had always been; Ella, who sold her jewelry to fund her move to New York from Denver when he wanted to be on Broadway; Ella, from whom he had recently been gently, though decidedly, estranged.

The issue had really been between wife and mother. Both were strong-willed women, and each prized what they felt to be their influence on Doug. This competition—over some long-forgotten issue—had grown to a head over the course of 1916. The outcome suggests a maternal source for Fairbanks's lifelong struggle with the bête noire of his existence: jealousy. "Ella's natural instinct to hold on to her son caused her frequent pangs of jealousy when other things and other people came between them," observed Letitia Fairbanks. "Inevitably, Beth revolted." Ella, who had a strong a sense of the dramatic, gave her son an ultimatum: choose between them.

Douglas Fairbanks was many things: impetuous, impatient, impulsive. But he was no man's fool. He sided with his wife. In the words of his niece, "He wasn't a mother's boy and her apron strings bound no one but herself." It wasn't a complete estrangement; there were frequent wires and presents, and he telephoned often. But what he said at the time of the breach—"I can get along without you, Mother. But I can't get along without Beth"—must now have added to the complexity of his feelings. For, of course, the separation from Triangle was proving just the opposite, at least as far as his wife of nine years was concerned. He had chosen wife over mother, and now mother was irretrievably gone. And did he even want his wife?

Publicist Bennie Zeidman was with him on the trip and reported to his family that Fairbanks remained locked in his drawing room until the train arrived in New York City. The funeral services were held at St. Patrick's Cathedral on the day after Christmas. Once they were over, and with nothing left to do, he found himself trapped with his thoughts—never a comfortable situation for a man who preferred action. Robert later related that Douglas "paced up and down his room at the Algonquin like a caged animal" before suggesting, unexpectedly, that they go to the theater.

Robert was shocked: how would it look? His younger brother replied, "Tutu would understand." And so they went, slipping in after the lights were darkened and leaving before they came up. To the end of his life, Douglas would never remember having gone to a play that night. But he would never forget what came shortly thereafter.

Mary Pickford heard, through mutual friends, that he was grieving. She sent a note of condolence to his hotel. Here, depending on the source, the story varies in detail, but not in essence. He asked if they could meet. Either she picked him up with her car and driver or he drove to fetch her. It was evening—perhaps later. The vehicle ended up in Central Park. He spoke of his mother and, under the influence of her sympathy, finally broke down into hoarse, racking sobs. From here authors often extrapolate. His hands clutched her curls, one will write, forgetting that she never wore her hair down except when making a film. She discreetly stared out the window while he cried, another will claim, having no direct knowledge of just what exactly happened in those minutes. Did the moment climax in a kiss, or a declaration of love? We shall never know and perhaps should not speculate. Even for the most public of public figures, some things are private. Certainly Pickford was not explicit in her account of the event forty years later.

But all versions—those from Mary and those from Doug, by way of his family—agree on this one thing: After the sobs diminished, they both chanced to look at the automobile's clock. It had stopped—stopped at the moment of his breakdown, by all accounts, and at the very hour and minute of Ella's death, by some others.

That moment for them came to be summarized by the expression "by the clock." It was used by one to the other in speech, in letters, in telegrams for the rest of their lives. The phrase was one of the last to ever pass his lips before his death. It came to mean all that they meant to each other and, to his mind, was a sort of passage of the care of his soul from his mother to Mary. After this, it was clear that there was no going back. Whether spoken or unspoken, their love for each other had now been declared.

A year later, he would send her a note on his personal stationery. They were in the midst of their secret love affair at this point, with all its associated ups and downs, guilt and raptures. He had taken scissors to a family portrait, cutting out Beth and Junior and leaving only himself and Ella, and enclosed the trimmed piece in the letter. "Don't be blue," he wrote. "I love you as I never loved you Dear. I will do anything you want . . . so do be happy Dear, especially on this day. Remember mother left you to me. I worship you."

Exactly when their love extended to a physical affair is also a source of speculation, and pursuit of an exact date is likely unnecessary, and even unseemly. Suffice it to say that the love affair began around this time and that time failed to perform its usual task of causing an emotional attachment to diminish in intensity. It only grew.

Letters and notes—and even telegrams—came to her often. He was improvident and reckless, leaving what would have been a very damning paper trail had any of these missives been discovered. She was his "little nearly-an-armful." Her voice on the phone was like heaven. "A mere thought of you stimulates as nothing else can," he wrote. "You have grown sweeter—lovelier—bigger. . . . I can't tell you how thrilled I am at all times—your intelligence, your beauty—your kindness, your sense of justice—oh I am simply wild about you. I feel positively sure that no man could love a woman more than I love you my beautiful—"

He poured his heart out on the pages. It was passion, pure and simple. In the current era, when romantic communication seems to the jaded eye to consist largely of scantily clad selfies and more-explicit-than-we-want-to-see sexting, his words evoke a different form of nakedness, having no qualifying irony or detachment. "I want you to know how wonderful I think you are—how beautiful, how sweet—how fine—how womanly and how dearly I love you," he wrote, "—a love that can never die Darling and will last in the life beyond."

He tried to overcome her hesitations. She was married, after all, and a new industry and a new era had combined to create of her an accidental icon of virtue and purity. She took this reputation and its implied social responsibility seriously. It was not that she had been living the life of a plaster saint before he arrived on the scene. She had consoled herself during her intermittent separations from her abusive husband in the arms of fellow actor and director James Kirkwood. Mama Charlotte had hired a former vaudevillian named Edward Hemmer as a "fixer" for these situations: in 1915 he reportedly pulled Mary out of Kirkwood's apartment in the wee small hours, at Charlotte's behest.

And it appears that Kirkwood was not her only source of consolation. Of the personal correspondence that she held until her death, most was from Doug. But a single letter from a different man was retained. It was written from New York City in March 1917, when her affair with Fairbanks was in full throttle, and after both she and he had left

New York to film in California. It was unsigned. The handwriting was not that of Kirkwood, nor Fairbanks, nor that of her favorite director Marshall "Mickey" Neilan, who wrote on his deathbed that he had been so in love with Mary during these years that he finally had to quit directing her.* Still, she kept it, suggesting that she had more than just a bad marriage to untangle in the face of her new and all-encompassing relationship.

> Darling
>   Just a few lines in a hurry. Please forgive me for not writing you before this but you know I am afraid you will not receive my mail and I cannot write you as I feel and think for fear some one else may read my letters. This is Sunday afternoon. It is snowing and miserable almost as blue as myself. Nothing to do but think of you and feel that I am the most lonely creature in the world. It seems like you have been away as many years instead of weeks I miss you sweetheart more than I ever have before. I am like one shipwrecked always thinking and wondering when you are going to rescue me from this awful solitude. Have been trying to settle up my afairs [sic] so I could take a little trip out to see you if only for a few days, yes even for a few hours just to see you and hear you say you are happy to know I love you and are pleased to think I had made that long journey just because I had been miserable for the sight of you. Love if I do not see you very soon I will die of too much Mary. The proposition I have in view for making two reel comedies looks very bright. Everybody is very keen about it. Bowman thinks I would be a big hit, am trying to interest Kauffman as he would be a big help with his standing. He is trying to get out of his present position. But darling I can't think clearly or do much until I have seen and held you in my arms once more. I would sacrifice everything love to be with you a short while. That is mostly all I think of these days.

---

* He wrote: "Mary I was so stuck on you I couldn't see straight and I knew I simply had only one way to keep things straight and that was go east so east I went."

Are you happy and do you like the studio? Don't allow them to do anything with [*sic*] you do not want. Everybody says *The Poor Little Rich Girl* is wonderful, the best you've done. I feel so badly because I can't go see it tonight. Have had a long previous engagement to go to the Lambs Gamble [*sic*].* However there is that much happiness to look forward to all day tomorrow. Oh, I supposed I will go more than once. Will wire when I see it.

I hope you will get this letter but am not sure. Am at the Biltmore. Was too unhappy to return to Algonquin.

You beautiful darling you are all and every thing to me. Have been thinking things over since you left. What is the use of worring [*sic*] and struggling for all this power and ambitions. Life is quite wonderful if we would only try to find the secret instead of conquering it. Am feeling fine and taking very good care of myself. Kiss me sweetheart until we meet again. I love you.

Your lonely man

Handwriting and circumstances aside (he was not a man wanting to make two-reel comedies), it is clear that these are not the words of Douglas Fairbanks. *He* would not worry about struggling for power and ambitions—ambition was his cheerful stock in trade. And he never hesitated to write what he thought and felt for fear it would be discovered. The identity of this poor, soon-to-be spurned lover may forever remain a mystery, which, given the outcome of his grand passion, may be considered a mercy. Clearly Mary dealt with him, and he suffered his broken heart quietly, never to emerge as a source of heartburn to Mama Charlotte, or income to Edward Hemmer.

The same cannot be said for Doug. He kept Mr. Hemmer busy. Eighteen months into the affair, Charlotte paid him to go to Denver to convince (read: pay off) local newsmen not to write of Doug and Mary's "friendship." In another instance he reportedly chased Doug from Mary's dressing room with a gun. Fairbanks escaped by sprinting over the studio fence. But most of the time the lovers successfully met

---

* He is referring to the Lambs Club event called the Lambs Gambol.

in private, either by wearing improbable costumes (dusters and driving goggles, floppy hats, and, on his part, the occasional prop beard) to drive up into the Hollywood Hills or by meeting at brother Robert's or publicist Zeidman's house. Between illicit rendezvous, dodging henchmen and donning disguises, it is remarkable that either of them found time to make motion pictures—but they did.

Fairbanks started his first independent production before he had even officially formed his production company. *In Again, Out Again* was scripted by Loos and directed by Emerson and was a redoubtable virgin effort. Not only was it the sharpest and funniest film Fairbanks had been in to date, but also it documented how firmly the star had his fingers on the American pulse. Filmed in January and February 1917, the story poked fun at pacifists; its late-April release—mere weeks after America's entry into the First World War—was a publicist's dream, and the mirror image of what D. W. Griffith had experienced with his epic *Intolerance*. Artcraft played up the relevance of the film's plot with full-page ads in which Uncle Sam congratulated Fairbanks on "his great patriotic picture . . . the most timely feature in months, teeming with action, patriotism, thrills and laughs."

The major plot of the film—to the extent that such a light froth can be burdened with plot—involved Fairbanks's character (named Teddy, in a clear nod to his favorite president) being jailed for public intoxication and falling in love with the jailer's daughter. Through a series of events, he is released early and spends much of the film comically trying to get back *into* jail. Stunts were notched up to a new level of creativity; almost every reviewer wrote about the sequence where Fairbanks, trapped on a roof by a lynch mob, grabs a rope, lassoes a telegraph pole thirty feet away, swings onto a wagon, and from there deposits himself in a coal chute. ("The single stunt," wrote the *Moving Picture World* reviewer, "is worth all the hours he has spent in rope rehearsal.")

The plot also involved terrorist bombings of domestic munitions factories, and here we find the involvement of art director and location scout Erich von Stroheim.* Von Stroheim was to later claim that the combination of his German name and the fact that he was scouting for munitions factories created suspicion, and that "I was discharged on account of Doug's apprehension about having a man with a German name in his employ when even German-fried-potatoes had to be rebaptized 'Liberty' potatoes."

It is possible that von Stroheim's recollections, over the years, were muddled. He was not discharged from the company—far from it. He returned west after completion of production, working on both *Wild and Woolly* and even appearing in *Reaching for the Moon*. His association was with John Emerson, however, not Fairbanks, and his tenure did not outlast that of Emerson. The episode he recalls more likely occurred later that same year when he was working as an assistant director and performer in *Sylvia of the Secret Service* with director George Fitzmaurice. Cameraman Arthur Miller distinctly recalled that it was in the production of *this* film, involving Germans dynamiting an ammunitions dump, that von Stroheim got into trouble. He "went to New York to research the names of the different explosives to be painted on cases stored at such a place. . . . Between his appearance and the sort of questions he was asking it was no time at all before he was in the clink," Miller said.

The film demonstrates the remarkable progress Fairbanks had made once in charge of his own productions. Contrast the drunk scene from *Double Trouble* with that in *In Again, Out Again*. The quality of Fairbanks's performance is essentially the same—he made a very comic drunk. But the staging of the sequence, the sets, the quality of direction, as well as the very nature of the script (in the later film, Doug and character actor Frank Lalor, playing the helpful pharmacist who provides the hooch, alternate throwing raw eggs at every advertising poster of women in the place) are worlds apart, although little more than a year separated the staging and filming of the sequences.

---

* Rutherford, New Jersey, ultimately provided the scenes for the location shoots. A short newsreel was made of the mayor and the local theater owner meeting Fairbanks and Emerson. The film was shown in local theaters and is, at this writing, presumed lost.

Another difference was to be found in the level of marketing support provided by Zukor's Artcraft Pictures Corporation. Take the press book. Triangle had released a two-page "press sheet" with articles and photographs. The campaign book for *In Again, Out Again*, in contrast, devoted seven pages to eighteen separate press stories, each handily perforated for ease of reproduction. In addition there were sixteen "cuts"—line drawings that could accompany an ad or article—as well as reproductions of all the posters. The poster selection was dizzying. Each film had two one-sheets, two three-sheets, a six-sheet, a twenty-four-sheet (essentially a billboard), as well as a window card and half-sheet. Doug's face was plastered everywhere, including on the poster boards of some Triangle theaters, which must have given Harry Aitken a case of agita. Triangle theaters were supposed to be showing only Triangle releases, but theater managers didn't care. It was Fairbanks they wanted, regardless of who the distributor was.

Making his debut in *In Again, Out Again* was a comically homely, acromegalic, cauliflower-eared mountain of a man by the name of "Bull" Montana. Born Luigi Montagna in Italy, he had labored splitting wood for seven cents a day in his homeland before coming to America. He soon was earning fifty dollars a night as a wrestler. Fairbanks needed an "outstanding pug-ugly" to play a fellow prisoner, and he found that Bull fit the bill brilliantly. He provided not only ready workouts for Fairbanks but also comic relief in several Fairbanks films. He made an admirable foil. Adolphe Menjou recalled:

> He was a huge fellow, built like a Sherman tank, with enough muscles for three men. By prearrangement, Montana used to stooge for Doug whenever visitors came on the lot. He would come up to Doug and start an argument in broken English. The argument would grow in fury until finally Montana would make a rush at Doug, whereupon, with a twist of the wrist, Doug would toss him over his shoulder and the big wrestler would land sprawling on the ground. Then he would plead, "Please don'ta hurt me, Meester

Fairbank." Probably Montana could have broken Doug in half, but he loved to play straight man for the boss.

What's more, the amiable Bull formed part of the nucleus of what was to become the original Hollywood entourage. "Spike" Robinson, an ex-prizefighter who became an all-purpose sparring partner, also returned to Hollywood with Doug after *In Again, Out Again* was completed. Added to these two was Kenneth Davenport, his actor friend from his days in *The Pit*, who was brought on as studio biographer, personal secretary, and, among other things, ghostwriter of a series of short inspirational books directed at young adults. *Laugh and Live* was the first of these, followed in short order by such masterworks as *Whistle and Hoe—Sing as We Go* and *Youth Points the Way*. While the language is of the sort found in second-rate youth literature of the time, the ideas are pure Fairbanks. It is evident that Davenport (having survived the case of tuberculosis that had made Fairbanks feel so guilty) was sitting down with his friend and taking notes of his thoughts before hitting the typewriter. The percussive quality of Fairbanks's speech survives in these little homiletic tomes, as does the simplistic, albeit enthusiastic, advice (Keep on Moving! Marry Early! Laugh! Live!). This steady stream of cheerful doggerel not only was profitable (he netted almost $2,000 in royalties in 1919) but also was an early example of cross marketing. *Laugh and Live* was distributed free to exhibitors showing *In Again, Out Again* as a premium for off-hour shows. In return, the theater owner was asked to advertise the book.

Also in the gang was trainer Chuck Lewis, a former All-American from Cornell, and Tom Geraghty, a writer. In later years, columnist Karl Kitchen was added to the mix. From virtually the start, there was also Charles Stevens, a Native American who appeared in every Fairbanks production filmed on the West Coast, from *The Lamb* to *The Taming of the Shrew*. While Stevens did not travel with Fairbanks, he was part of a general crew of cowhands and Indians who hung around the studio, and his presence in a film in time came to be viewed by Doug as a sort of lucky charm.

Finally, there was Bennie Zeidman, a pint-size dynamo from Philadelphia whom Fairbanks had brought on as publicist the prior December, when he was not yet twenty-two years old.

Algonquin owner and friend Frank Case described the functions some of these friends served:

> Douglas, like royalty, seldom or never carried money in his pockets, so one of his staff was a sort of almoner, who complied with all requests within reason. Another of his entourage was a fellow adept at breaking up conversations that threatened to become lengthy or serious. Others were volunteers, who happened to be around and liking to be seen with him, just came along, so that when he started out on foot, he was like a locomotive, as Al Parker said, trailing a string of empties.

This attached posse could be an irritant to Case. "I don't think Douglas was conscious of their presence, certainly not aware that it was anything unusual," he wrote, "but to a man of different temperament they were a decided bar to conversation of any degree of intimacy." Once, when Fairbanks came to visit his friend in New York after an absence of a year, Case was irked to notice that "he brought a squad of five with him." With cheerful narcissism, Fairbanks assumed that no one minded this. When a few days later Doug called and invited him over for a talk, Case showed up at the Ritz with his engineer, porter, bellboy, and a waiter. When he invited them to draw up chairs, Doug took the point. On all future visits, Case recalled, "the regiment was always bivouacked downstairs in the lobby."

Men of accomplishment or autonomy chafed under Fairbanks's assumption that they would be happy to be one of the "string of empties." Edward Knoblock, author of *Kismet*, fell into this category. "I disliked the idea of drawing a salary just for playing the companion to a celebrity," he wrote. "I felt as if I were being kept—which was a new experience to me and somewhat absurd at the age of forty-eight. But he saw things differently. Once the lords of the movie-world engage anyone, they feel they possess them body and soul and cannot understand, no matter how generous they may be, that this sort of attitude ends by proving humiliating to anyone who has been used to disposing of his own time, once his daily work is done."

But as there are always those happy to fill such positions, Fairbanks had no shortage of followers. Director Ted Reed's daughter recounted, "Fairbanks was, as my father described him, a sort of vagabond king. He expected his courtiers to follow wherever his sense of adventure took him. This they did gladly because he was so alive, so exciting to be with, and so generous." Not all were sycophants or court jesters; some, like publicist Bennie Zeidman and writer Tom Geraghty, were men who performed significant functions in the all-encompassing enterprise that was Doug. But all were men who operated best as satellite planets, surrounding their ever-bright, ever-shining personal sun.

In Again, Out Again was a marked success and a strong start for his production company. All attendance records were again shattered for the Rialto,* and *Variety* reported that at the 81st Street Theatre audiences left right after the movie, even though there were two vaudeville acts and a Keystone film to follow. After making the film, Fairbanks remained in New York only long enough to obtain the Manhattan-based shots needed for his next film, *Wild and Woolly.*† He returned to L.A. by way of a reserved train car with a party of seventeen, including Emerson, Loos, Fleming, brother—and now business manager—John, assistant cameraman Glen MacWilliams, the tireless Bennie Zeidman, and a young woman who would become his new leading lady for the rest of the year, Eileen Percy. According to Loos, the presence of Percy constituted the moment "when Fate edged up and nudged me with its elbow." Describing the blonde Percy as "a Broadway cutie who was being imported to Hollywood for a screen test," she went on to bemoan:

> That girl was a lot bigger than I was, but she was being waited on by every male in our troupe. If she happened to drop the magazine

---

* The Rialto alone grossed $17,880 the first week, against a rental cost of $3,000.

† Originally titled *A Regular Guy.*

she was reading, several of them would jump to retrieve it, whereas I was allowed to tug heavy suitcases from their racks while those same men failed to note my efforts.

That girl and I were both in the pristine years of early youth; we shared about the same degree of comeliness, and mine was less contrived, for she was a quite unnatural blonde. Concerning our mental acumen, there was nothing to discuss; I was the smarter. But there was some mystifying difference between us. Why did she so outdistance me in feminine allure? Could her power, like that of Samson, have something to do with her hair?

Loos pulled out her yellow notepad and started to scribble furiously. From this seed was to ultimately sprout one of the defining novels of the Roaring Twenties: *Gentlemen Prefer Blondes*.

But she did not, evidently, produce the plot for *Wild and Woolly*. The story was attributed to Horace B. Carpenter, which is curious, as Carpenter was a bit player at Famous Players whose credits include such memorable roles as "Mexican Henchman" and "Talkative Old Timer." The script is Loos through and through, and since she was contracted to provide the stories as well, one suspects that either this was a Fairbanksian practical joke or the actor actually said something to suggest the plot.* Regardless of where the story originated, it formed one of Fairbanks's best early films, and—for a long time being one of the few pre-swashbucklers available for public view—also shaped much of the critical discussion of the themes of his films. In *Wild and Woolly*, Fairbanks's character, a Manhattan son of wealth who has taken to heart every cowboy dime novel written, finally gets the chance to travel to Arizona. Decked out like an extra in a Hoot Gibson nightmare, he heads west, where the local townspeople, anxious to get his approval on an extension of his father's railroad line into nearby mines, camouflage

---

* Another clue is suggested by a *Motion Picture News* review: "One is easily able to understand why Mr. Fairbanks picked *Wild and Woolly* to star in, even though submitted anonymously. It is, however, extremely difficult to draw any line between the work of Horace B. Carpenter, author of the story, and that of Anita Loos, who did the scenario."

themselves and their town to look like the West of the 1880s. In the course of the phony events, a corrupt Indian agent creates real dangers for the good townsfolk, and Doug ends up saving the day. He does so by way of some dazzling new stunts, including more lariat work, which he had been avidly practicing even while in Manhattan. (One reporter described finding him, in full dinner dress, idly lassoing the doorknob at the Algonquin while waiting to go out.) Ed Burns, who had served for seven years as foreman at "Buffalo Bill" Cody's Wyoming ranch, was hired to cull the authentic cowhands from the pool of aspiring extras.

Burns also contributed to the current and future productions by selling to Fairbanks a stunt horse named, appropriately, Smiles. In *Wild and Woolly*, the animal received a good indoctrination into what it meant to be owned by Fairbanks. Doug made several leaps onto the horse, including a standing vault from the rear that has been copied in scores of westerns since. He also dove off the animal with aplomb, once to tackle hapless Charlie Stevens and once to board a moving train. He even shot his gun while hanging from the side of the horse at full gallop, Indian-style.* Smiles was never featured as a cowboy costar, à la Trigger or Tony (there was only one star in a Fairbanks film, after all), but remained stabled and much-cosseted at the studio and employed by him in multiple films, skillfully and cooperatively participating in sudden leaps and falls, the firing of blanks near his ears, and the slinging of villains and maidens across his willing back. He even would stand still for the *Photoplay* photographer while Doug performed a headstand in the saddle. Smiles, it can be argued, was the original white horse that young boys for decades associated with the good guy.†

Wild and Woolly also saw the addition to the company of Joseph Henabery, a Griffith stalwart who was best known at that time for portraying Lincoln in *The Birth of a Nation*. He was functioning initially as an assistant to John Emerson and proved invaluable on several fronts.

---

* He had previously done this stunt in *The Good Bad Man*.
† Zorro, of course, rode a black horse, so the villains rode white ones, but that was the exception, not the rule.

For *Wild and Woolly*, he recalled of the script, "I could see that it was being written without much consideration for cost. Emerson, like many directors from the legitimate stage, was not very concerned about the technical side of picture making. . . . I began to think about using an existing small town that we could transform into an Old West town, then restore it to its modern state. . . . To cover the modern oil pavement, I would have to bring in truckloads of earth."

He selected the little-known town of Burbank, in the San Fernando Valley. The mayor, fortunately, turned out to be a Fairbanks fan, and that, combined with a judicious $500 contribution to the local library from Doug, bought them the right to turn downtown Burbank into the Old West for a week.* Henabery also directed several sequences in the film. This stemmed from the need, per Henabery, "to produce pictures more quickly to fulfill the contract. . . . Emerson confined himself to shooting with Fairbanks, while another director helped plan production and shot episodes in which Doug did not appear. Later, such jobs were called second-unit directors."

He recalled that Fairbanks especially liked making westerns. "Doug loosened up more with the fellows who worked in Westerns than he did with the ordinary breed of actor," he wrote. "We had used many Western riders in . . . *Wild and Woolly*, and he had become acquainted with some of them when he worked at the Fine Arts Studio. Most of these people had been born and raised in Western cattle country, and they were tops in their lines. Some had specialties such as bronco riding, some were trick riders, and others were expert ropers. Many had ridden with Wild West shows and rodeos. They could tell tales by the hour." The feeling was clearly mutual. One of these cowboys was arrested for shooting a man who had the gall to claim that Fairbanks did not do his own stunts. "The judge was amused by his loyalty," went the news report of the time, "and, being a Fairbanks fan, dismissed the case from court."

---

* The town leaders decided to welcome filmmakers from that point forward, leading, perhaps, to the "beautiful downtown Burbank" (as Johnny Carson used to so aptly phrase it) of today.

Fairbanks clearly spent a fair amount of time with the broncobusters, who trained him for the sequence in which the hero daydreams himself into a painting and rides a bucking bronco. "You might hang on if you could grip the pommel of the saddle like grim death and think of nothing else, or if you were permitted to keep both feet in the stirrups. But that wouldn't be ethical," he recalled. "You have one foot in the stirrup and with your free foot you keep on scratching your mount's ribs with the spur. At the same time you fan his ears with your sombrero with one hand, and with the other gripping the rein, you try to hold his head up. I was pretty well discouraged by my semi-aeronautical bronco busting attempts, until a cowpuncher came along and took me in hand."

Perhaps the most impressive stunt was when Fairbanks, trapped in a room, leaps, grabs a ceiling beam, and repeatedly chinning himself, kicks a hole through the ceiling to the room above. The continuity, as written by Loos, demonstrates a rare attempt by her to insert a stunt into the script instead of creating the situation and letting Fairbanks and his director develop a solution. But instead of using his feet, she has the hero use his *head* to butt through the flooring.*

It was around this time that he started to collect western art, including paintings and bronzes by Frederic Remington and paintings by Charles Russell. His fascination with the West was to remain with him his entire life, although he would stop making westerns before the decade was out. There were some who would mourn this fact. Russell himself sent Fairbanks a hand-painted letter shortly after *The Three Musketeers* was released in 1921, depicting himself in cowboy gear and waving his hat to Doug, who is dressed in musketeer garb. "I know that D'Artagnan's name will fit you as well as his clothes. But Doug don't forget our old west," he wrote. "The old time cowman right now is as much history as Richard The Lion Harted [*sic*] or any of those gents that packed a long blade and had their cloths [*sic*] made by a blacksmith. . . . The west had

---

* She did not attempt to script any stunts after this endeavor, instead sticking to story and titles.

some fighters, long haired Wild Bill Hickok with a cap and ball colts could have made a correll [sic] full of King Arthurs men climb a tree."

Russell's entreaties were in vain: Fairbanks's last western was in 1919. And while he was to make other westerns after *Wild and Woolly*, none ever quite matched it. This was the western that set the typical western on its ear, and it would remain the archetype of the comic anti-western that was to be found later in such films as *Destry Rides Again* and *Blazing Saddles*.

He was in his prime that spring. On his thirty-fourth birthday, Beth arranged a surprise party for him. "The wily Douglas through some mysterious channel kept in touch with the plans of the conspirators," wrote one reporter. "Hence when he walked into the 'trap' he reversed the surprise by distributing handsome gifts to every person present." He was given a pair of heavy silver spurs upon which his smiling face had been engraved. Bull Montana declared it a very "suspicious occasion."

He was enjoying stardom immensely. No complaints came from *him* about irksome intrusions on his privacy or the burden of answering fan mail. In fact, he answered a prodigious amount of it personally and, until he hired a secretary, did so without the aid of a typewriter. A letter from the summer of 1916 serves as a charming example. One young female fan was evidently worried that a request for a signed photograph might result in a stamped photo—a common and time-saving practice at the time.* A small cabinet photograph with a slightly smudged signature accompanied the following, which had no introductory greeting:

> Did you ever see a self respecting autograph stamp which <u>blotted</u> instead of dotted its "i-s"? My secretary chains me to a chair and I proceed to indulge in a general attack of autography—And does my secretary open up my mail? She's much too busy taking my pipes and rucksacks to be mended and tracing things I've left behind to think about the mail. Now are your questions answered?
> Douglas Fairbanks

---

* As was having an assistant do all the signing, a practice that Fairbanks disdained.

His passion for automobiles was given free rein in the open streets of Hollywood. A local teen wrote his father in 1916: "We . . . saw Douglas Fairbanks in his little Mercer Raceabout. He was racing a green Abbot Detroit. He pooped all over it. He looked like a darn nice guy. He didn't have any hat on and he was in his shirt sleeves and had his shirt open at the neck.* He looked like an Indian he was so brown but he sure could whirl that little Mercer wheel."

He was tireless. As a fundraiser for the American Red Cross, he autographed ten thousand photographs to be given to donors. Not content to merely sign, he took the time to write on each, "Yip! Come across for the Red Cross!"† He was one of the few stars, along with Mary Pickford, Lillian and Dorothy Gish, and William S. Hart, who did not request money to cover expenses when a fan requested a photograph.

Fairbanks began to be photographed with Mary. These were always publicity shots—they were, after all, working on the same lot and both distributing through Artcraft. And usually in the picture was his best pal, Charlie Chaplin. *Photoplay* referred to them as "the golden triplets." But it did not take long for everyone in town—Mrs. Fairbanks excepted—to be in on the secret of the romance. The *Moving Picture World* published a photograph of Doug, Mary, and Charlie in early June 1917. Charlie, in tramp costume, is smiling at the camera. Doug is doing the same. He is leaning in toward Mary, who is looking up at him as if he were the only man on earth. The accompanying note stated, perhaps a tad archly: "Taking it by and large, it sure is a most interesting picture, one possessing almost limitless possibilities in the way of speculation—taking that last word in any old sense you like."

This must have raised concern. Up until this point, Owen had been kept out of the picture. Mary was starting to portray children now, and Zukor enforced a very youthful persona: she was never to be seen with

---

* Doug popularized informal dress in an era when men wore celluloid collars and even hoboes wore jackets.

† These turn up on eBay periodically, documenting that each is uniquely written, not stamped.

a drink in her hand; a pencil or a piece of chalk could be mistaken for a cigarette; her nails must be kept short. But now Owen was allowed back and moved into the house she shared with her mother. It is unlikely that he was allowed to share her bed. Pickford biographer Scott Eyman writes of an episode when Owen rented a suite at the Biltmore Hotel: "Charlotte surveyed the suite, nodded and said, 'Very fine, Owen. You take that room in there and Mary and I will sleep in here.'" Mary was either giving the marriage one last try or diverting suspicion away from her relationship with Fairbanks. One suspects the latter. *Photoplay* featured a photo spread: "Our Mary and Her Owen." They were photographed in front of their car, playing golf, and lounging on the porch swing. It was clearly staged—their clothes are unchanged in each circumstance—and the body language is telling. Mary leans away from Owen or is turned away. Neither is smiling. But they were together, and the public was permitted to see that "Our Mary" had a husband.

Certainly Owen knew what had been going on. Pickford quotes him as telling her, "I'm going to kill that climbing monkey." And conversely, Fairbanks's jealousy was infamous.

Mary was up in Pleasanton, California, filming *Rebecca of Sunnybrook Farm* when Doug began his next film, *Down to Earth*. In mid-June, he went to Yosemite to catch some mountain-climbing shots for the film but also ostensibly to have a peak named in his honor.* He evidently managed to sneak in an overnight with her before arriving at the park. The next day brought a letter in his usual telegraphic style, speaking not only to the heights his passion was reaching but also the jealousy that was eating at him.

My Darling—Just two million thoughts are running madly through my brain—I can't begin—it is so jumbled—but it all means I love you and you alone. Darling girl I felt so near to you last night—I have never known such happiness—I mean just that—<u>I</u> <u>have</u> <u>never</u> <u>known</u> <u>such</u> <u>happiness</u>. I do hope that soon I will be normal and

---

* This appears to have been a publicity stunt and not an official act of the government.

that I will cause you no more disturbing moments—these petty jealousies etc. I am so sorry Dear—and don't think me silly Dear the way I behaved this morning—I was rather ashamed—when I had left you—please forgive me—

I am so utterly miserable and lonesome for you tonight—I can't think—I want to tell you many things but I can't seem to collect myself—perhaps you would like me with a bit more poise—I can't help it—really honey I am indulging entirely in self pity tonight and rather enjoy it—I have just read over this letter and it is not a practical [*sic*] the way I want it—can't you understand, don't you feel dear <u>what</u> I want to tell you—you seem so many miles away my heart aches—I feel so desolate. You must never leave me again it is not right—the rest of the world means nothing to me—here I am in the midst of one of God's most beautiful gardens and it means nothing to me without Mary my Mary—you just you I want—some may say that memories are sufficient in our lifetimes but it is not true—I must be with you my own and when you die I wish to go to [*sic*]—you have so completely taken possession of me—I cannot live without you—I feel sure Darling I can make you happy—do write me often—if you feel it—do think of me—know that I love you only—believe me my soul belongs to you Mary and you must love me in return before heaven—

Please take care of yourself & go to bed early—and be very careful of your food—don't worry—be nice to your dear mother—work hard—and think of me once in a while because every beat of my heart is for you my dear and forever and ever

Good night

Douglas

Down to Earth featured a story of Fairbanks's own creation and Anita Loos's execution. It was a five-reel Fairbanksian sermon for Teddy Roosevelt's "Strenuous Life," the famed 1899 lecture in which Roosevelt proclaimed, "Those who do not embrace the strenuous life . . . do not live meaningful lives."

The heroine of the tale rejects the hero at the beginning of the film in favor of a jaded urbanite. While he deals with his heartbreak by cutting through jungles and climbing mountain peaks, she, laced with caffeine and cigarettes, suffers a nervous breakdown. Fairbanks's character comes to visit her at a sanitarium. There he discovers a place full of self-absorbed, comic neurotics whose ailments are clearly all in their heads. He buys the place, lock, stock, and barrel, and takes its entire population out on his yacht (Fairbanks used his own boat). He then stages a shipwreck on a "desert island." Here the patients must learn to chop wood, find food, and live Teddy Roosevelt's "strenuous life." Of course, in short order they are cured.

The film's release was delayed by the death of a cast member, *Variety* reported—the unfortunate having fallen off Doug's yacht and drowned off the coast of Catalina. It was a cast member, true, but the player in question was a small spotted dog. While he may have dog-paddled to shore, an extensive search failed to turn him up. Equally bad, he was a rather distinctive-looking mutt, and since no matches could be found to substitute for him, the sequences in which he appeared needed to be reshot.*

The film was probably the best example of Fairbanksian wish fulfillment. In it he is a college football hero, a polo player, the owner of a Wyoming ranch, a mountain climber, and a jungle explorer. Even more to the point, it is the embodiment of the Fairbanks philosophy, that there are no ills that cannot be cured by a healthy dose of exercise and the great outdoors. The film had very little in the way of stunts, which the critics were quick to note. "But the producers have looked to his off-cited personality to hold the interest, which is like using the Rock of Gibraltar for the foundation of a house," wrote the critic from the *New York Dramatic Mirror*. Others were equally effusive. "Book it, Mr. Exhibitor," *Variety* wrote, "and if it fails to draw, it will just about be time to hail a few carpenters and make a garage of your place." Only

---

* It may be that they were reshot with no dog instead of a substitute. There is a dog in the film. He is seen as Fairbanks rescues him and brings him on the yacht and later gets him to land on the "desert island." From there he simply disappears from the story.

a few voices in the wilderness suggested that the film was not up to his most recent standard. "If we are to look closely at the story and judge it from the standpoint of a dramatic critic, we will, no doubt, say that something is lacking," wrote the *Motion Picture News*. "It isn't a masterpiece in this respect. But it must be remembered that Douglas Fairbanks' strong points do not include Shakespearian repertoire. They are comedy, thrills, smiles and personality."

It was with *Down to Earth* that early cracks began to appear in his relationship with Anita Loos and John Emerson. Of his first three independent productions, Loos provided the story for only the first. This is not to say that she didn't provide script proposals; Loos's papers reveal, among other treasures, a script in which Fairbanks is a peppermint-eating product of divinity school who is sent out by a reformed dissolute to take the latter's fortune and right all the wrongs he (the dissolute) has committed. One longs to see what the team would have made of this tale, but to Loos's probable frustration, it was never to be. A staff writer must yield, one supposes, if the producer wants to provide the story, and there was likely a marketing argument that could be made for the fact that Fairbanks not only starred in a film but also created the plot. But to have the screen credits and all advertising for *Wild and Woolly* attribute *that* film's story to an unknown bit player must have been galling.* Fairbanks also made alterations to her scripts beyond merely improvising and developing the stunts. As heretofore mentioned, *Down to Earth* was an especially egregious example of Loos's casual racism, and scenes such as one where the villain, in search of faux cannibals, asks a black waiter, "Where can I find some niggers?" were possibly never filmed,[†] and the cannibals were replaced by a single white actor.

---

* Curiously, Henabery never demonstrated the least bit of resentment when Fairbanks was credited in all print advertising as having written the script for *The Man from Painted Post*. Apart from publicity value, it is not clear why Fairbanks took the credit here. The handwritten notes on file at the Margaret Herrick Library document that the work was entirely done by Henabery.

† As was the corresponding scene where Fairbanks's character actually was to say (in the proposed title), "You niggers come down here," to learn that the villain had hired

This, evidently, was beginning to chafe. In May of that year, Loos gave a lecture at Columbia University. One journalist reported that she claimed "the leader [series of introductory titles] was of utmost value in photoplay work and suggested in effect that the action could be used to advantage merely to lead up to a succession of clever titles." In a later issue, an editorialist grumbled about "Miss Anita Loos, who appears to believe that the Fairbanks comedies are rather clever illustrations for her decidedly clever leaders."

It wasn't simply Loos—it was Emerson as well. "Emerson and Doug were a little bit at loggerheads," recalled Joseph Henabery. "Since I was not concerned, I kept my nose out of the business." But unaware though he may have been, he soon became involved in the drama. Doug wanted to make another western. Emerson and Loos were trying, at his behest, to create a scenario based on "Silver Slippers," a Jackson Gregory story published in the November 1916 *Adventure* magazine. They "were getting nowhere, but Doug was really enthused about the West and he urged them not to give up." After a trip to see the Cheyenne Rodeo in Wyoming, he returned to discover that they had made no progress. Since he had just made arrangements for most of the rodeo's contestants to appear with him in this now-unscripted western and had contracted to use a Wyoming ranch* for the locations, "this caused some friction," Henabery recalled. "Even earlier, things had not been as smooth between Emerson and Doug as they could have been. In some way, Mrs. Fairbanks was involved."

She was, indeed. Beth had begun to suspect her husband was having an affair. Long, late "story conferences"—a ready excuse, apparently—

---

them. One must be careful, however, in drawing the conclusion that the sequence had not been shot. The original script has the sequence. The press book plot summary does not. But the six-sheet poster for the film shows Fairbanks being held at gunpoint by the film's villain, who is backed up by a group of "cannibals." The sequence might have been in the film at some point. Existing prints have a relatively abrupt jump from the villain's plotting to hire the faux cannibals to his encounter with Fairbanks on the beach, at which point Doug thrashes him. (To make it fair, Fairbanks elects to do so with one hand tied behind his back.)

* The Riverside Ranch, which was on 160,000 acres of land thirty miles from Laramie.

turned her suspicions to Anita Loos. "Anytime that Douglas and Mary wanted to see each other I had to stay home and pretend I was working in case Mrs. Fairbanks would do any—er—detective work," Loos recalled decades later. "And this went on for quite a while and we used to giggle over the situation." The puckish Loos recalled, "I would notice when we happened to meet, I would get a very frosty reception; and I finally went to Douglas and said 'No, look, this has gone far enough.'" Fairbanks appealed to her loyalty. "'Listen,'" Loos recalled him saying, "'you're the only one I've got that I can depend on. You're my main alibi; you've got to stand by,' and so I did."

But Beth was a born manager (or meddler, depending on one's perspective) and decided to pull some strings behind the scenes. "I was surprised to be asked to her home for a talk," recalled Henabery. "She was a very refined, nice woman. She began by telling me how much they liked my work, and then she got down to the point. Doug wanted to make the Western picture Emerson and Loos were struggling with, but John Emerson was not happy about it. Mrs. Fairbanks said that Doug had made up his mind to do the story in Wyoming, and she questioned me about taking over."

Henabery had already accompanied Fairbanks on his trip to Yosemite for *Down to Earth* and had obtained the shots of Doug climbing the "Alps"—his first time directing any footage with the star. He discovered that shepherding Douglas Fairbanks was memorable, but it could be terrifying as well. "The publicity man for the company wanted some still photographs to show Doug's athletic ability," he recalled. "I was arranging a camera setup below, and when I climbed back to our base, I saw Doug doing a handstand on the edge of the famous Firefall Rock. Firefall Rock is about 3,500 feet above the valley below. I was afraid to yell or shout, so they got that picture, but no more."

But now he was being asked to write the script for, and direct, an entire Fairbanks feature. And he was asked to do it on the fly, as the lease on the ranch was active. Two Pullmans and three freight cars brought cast and crew—including Smiles and twenty additional horses—to Laramie, but the company still had no scenario.

"All the movie people were to sleep on straw in the loft of a massive barn made of logs. . . . The mosquitoes were terrible," Henabery recalled. "I had no story except the Western tale in magazine form—a story not designed to fit Doug's style. What was more, I had no time to develop a new one." He started to write, shooting "sequences that offered few problems" by day, and working on the scenario at night. Fairbanks occupied himself for two full days during this time, signing the ten thousand pictures for the Red Cross. Henabery's story notes survive, scribbled over several pages of blank daily report sheets, a testament to the frantic haste with which the film was put together.

It is a measure of Fairbanks's impetuosity that he would lease an entire ranch and hire every trick roper, broncobuster, and champion rider of the West without confirming that he had a satisfactory script. It certainly was a demonstration of his anger over Loos and Emerson's failure to have one ready for him that he would assign both direction and script to a largely untested assistant director. Still, he had a habit of taking people and advancing them beyond their original roles: under his management, Victor Fleming went from cameraman to assistant director to full director. Future luminaries such as Howard Hawks and William Wellman also got their starts on Fairbanks sets.

The Man from Painted Post was the first appearance in a Fairbanks film of theatrical star Frank Campeau. Campeau, best known for playing the evil Trampus in the stage production of *The Virginian*, was to spend the next several years ably serving the same function of villainy for Fairbanks. He was soon to discover that film acting had its challenges. Unaccustomed to riding a horse, he chafed his legs raw and was reduced to making a nightly thirty-mile run into Laramie to lubricate his woes. Henabery found himself acting as an impromptu fire marshal, getting the lantern out of Campeau's drunken grip every night to prevent him setting the barn ablaze.

Joseph Henabery was never to be a star director, but he was a competent one who got the job done. Time was of the essence after principal photography on *Painted Post* was completed. Henabery and the company's editor, William Shea, booked two compartments on an eastbound train and used the five-day trip to edit the film. The arrangement had been that Loos and Emerson would meet them at the Paragon Film Laboratory to review the edited print and to write the titles. They were a no-show and, in a sort of sit-down strike, made certain that they could not be found. "I had to write them myself," Henabery recalled. "Writing titles is not simple at any time. Further, when you're under pressure on account of a release date, it's very hard to do an acceptable job." As a screenwriter, he was no Anita Loos—no one was. The titles are traditional, stilted and formal, in the manner of Henabery's original mentor, D. W. Griffith. Fleming biographer Michael Sragow summed it up when he wrote, "It's the sort of square Western that the hero of *Wild and Woolly* would devour; it's as if Fairbanks made his revisionist Western comedy, then decided to do the straight version. But it's a well-paced shoot-'em-up, and a feel of fresh air courses through it."

Critics at the time recognized this as well. An unsourced clipping in Fairbanks's personal scrapbooks states of *The Man from Painted Post*, "What we get is a ranch and 'rustler' picture, no better than dozens of others of its general kind and not nearly so good as some. Without Fairbanks it would attract no particular attention. With him, the thought is inevitable that he is having difficulty in living up to past achievements. It seems that Fairbanks wrote and helped direct this photoplay himself, as he did his previous one, *Down to Earth*. Both prove that he should leave authorship and direction to others and pay attention closely to his own knitting. He can't do it all."

When it comes to critical reviews of his films, Fairbanks's personal scrapbooks are enlightening. His tendency was to include reviews only when they were negative. Much like the financial returns at the box office, this was something that he tracked closely—and from which he continued to learn. With *The Man from Painted Post*, the messages were decidedly mixed. "It was made in a hurry, without the aid of a worked out scenario—just made up as we went along," Fairbanks wrote the following year. "Yet according to the financial boys, it's probably the best money maker of all those I've done for Artcraft. And the verdict of the 'fan mail' has been generally favorable."

Returns of early films are impossible to determine by modern methods. Today we get automated reports on box office returns, essentially telling us a film's gross. How the money is divided after that is of little interest to anyone outside the industry. But for a film one hundred years ago, the data of individual box office returns is unavailable. We may know the producer's cut, and what his return is from the distributor. We even may know, without having to divide the producer's return (by 0.725 in the instance of Fairbanks's deal), what the distributor collected. But the distributor may have had a patchwork of deals, leasing the film on a geographic basis (state's rights) or renting a film by the week for a flat rate to a theater (as described above for *In Again, Out Again*, where a single week at the Rialto returned over $17,000 to the theater owner against a rental fee of $3,000). And if there were negotiated "splits" of the box office take, which was rare at this point, there was nothing to prevent the exhibitor from underreporting his box office returns.

Thus, for the Fairbanks Artcraft films, we have only the records of the Douglas Fairbanks Pictures Corporation to guide us. The "financial boys" were correct; *The Man from Painted Post* was the most profitable Artcraft release until 1918's *Mr. Fixit*.

With box office returns pointing in one direction and critical response in another (much as with *The Half Breed*, except there the reviews were strong and the box office tepid), what was Fairbanks disposed to do? Shoot for higher financial return or try to make a better film?

He elected to improve the quality of his films. He evidently felt that he had locked down his formula and did not need the box office to guide him in this instance. He was grateful to Henabery and gave him further opportunities to direct, but he knew the director he wanted to supplement—or possibly replace—Emerson. Even before *The Man from Painted Post* was released, he had signed Allan Dwan, who had directed four of his best Triangle films. The terms were generous: work with Fairbanks on scenarios and direct a total of five films for $100,000.

But Loos and Emerson were still on the payroll. Fairbanks was likely furious over their no-show on the titling of *Painted Post*—a contractual violation. Loos never referred to any of this in her various autobiographies, instead claiming that "worldwide acclaim had made Doug touchy; his male chauvinism had been bruised when the *Ladies' Home Journal* published my picture with the caption 'The little girl who made Doug Fairbanks famous.'"

This does not jibe with the evidence. In fact, Fairbanks had been actively promoting Loos as the wit behind his muscle. The major fan magazines and the publicists for the top producers in the industry had a naturally symbiotic relationship. Fairbanks, for example, wrote a monthly column for *Photoplay* beginning in 1917. It was *Photoplay* that helpfully published the pictures of the blissful Mr. and Mrs. Owen Moore that same year, and it was also *Photoplay* that featured a full page with Loos, Emerson, and Fleming in March 1917, essentially trumpeting the message that *here* was the talent that produced the Fairbanks magic. It is difficult to imagine that Fairbanks would object to the *Ladies' Home Journal* providing the same message a few months later. This is not even taking into account the many times that he readily acknowledged Loos and Emerson's contributions in print interviews during this time. As late as the January 1918 issue of *Photoplay* (which was created in November 1917), he featured a photograph of Loos in his full-page personal column. But if the couple were suddenly failing to contribute—not producing a continuity for *The Man from Painted Post* and intentionally refusing to title the film—then *that* was a different kettle of fish.

Loos did have another story up her sleeve, and this became Fairbanks's next film. *Reaching for the Moon* was the last film that the team would make for the star. The title and idea for a Venetian canal–like location was the original work of Henabery. "Then it was decided to let Emerson and Loos take over the next picture," he recalled philosophically. "They wanted to write their own story, but they liked my title *Reaching for the Moon*, and they wanted to use the Venetian settings and the gondolas. I knew that it would have been much more expensive for the company to have Emerson and Loos drawing pay for doing nothing rather than me, so I devoted my time trying to get ideas for another Fairbanks story. Hardly anyone outside the movie business can realize how much constant thought and effort is expended in finding or developing scenes for a star like Doug."

Anita Loos early in 1918 used *Reaching for the Moon* to illustrate how the process worked for their particular team:

> The first conference concerning *Reaching for the Moon* was held in the Fairbanks dressing-room in Hollywood, and began something like this:
>
> Mr. Fairbanks—"You know, folks, I have always wanted to play the type of young chap who has tremendous ambitions; who wants to go out and conquer the world overnight."
>
> Mr. Emerson—"We ought to be able to find a theme that will fit that character, but let's have one that we can satirize."
>
> Miss Loos—"I know! Poke fun at New Thought. That's not been done yet!"
>
> Mr. Emerson—"That's all right, but we must be careful how we handle it, for after all there is something real in this New Thought idea."
>
> Miss Loos—"Well, suppose we give this young man a false idea of New Thought and then poke fun at *him!*"
>
> Mr. Fairbanks—"I can see this young chap as a typical American, full of energy and with boundless ambition. I like to see a chap like that put right into the midst of a whirlpool of excitement! Go to it! I've got a couple of broncs that have to be broken by lunchtime."
>
> Exit Mr. Fairbanks.

Filming proper began with a quick run to New York City to pick up a few location shots. To bring wife, child, and twelve company members on a ten-day round-trip journey to spend only three days shooting exteriors might seem extreme, but Fairbanks said, "One thing you can't reproduce with scenery is New York City." His press agent was along for a day's shooting and gave a flavor of the cheerful chaos as the team shot an exterior scene:

Just as the Czar of Russia, the Minister from Argentina, a Prussian spy, a French monsieur and a Swedish masseur alighted from a big closed car in front of a mysterious-looking house* and prepared to steal up to the door, a yellow racing car dashed up the street and spoiled the whole picture. Then from the yellow car alighted a man who rushed up to Mr. Fairbanks and, seizing him by the hand, cried: "Doug, when did you come East?"

"Only yesterday," replied Doug.

"Why didn't you let me know?"

"Well, you see, I came in a hurry."

"You haven't changed a bit, Doug. Say, you look good to me."

"So do you," countered Doug with his most hospitable smile.

"Say, let me get in your picture, will you?"

"Well, we're not doing much today, but come around to-morrow, and we'll fix something up."

"All right, and you look me up tonight, won't you?"

"Sure I will. Where are you now?"

"Same place. Haven't moved. So long; I'll see you to-night," and the yellow racer was off.

Douglas turned to John Emerson for enlightenment. "Say, who the devil was that?"

The press agent also noted that Emerson, like Henabery, had to keep an active eye on his star. "The front of this mysterious house was decorated with little stone ledges and during the afternoon Douglas cast longing glances at this edifice, but said nothing. Finally . . . he said, 'I'm going to climb that house.' To which the director unfeelingly replied: 'You're going to do nothing of the sort. You're going down to Rector's and take those tea scenes.'"

The filming also included shots at the Plaza Hotel in what was then the Champagne Porch. One observer noted, "One 'close-up' which he did yesterday was merely to walk out of the Plaza Hotel and smile. By

---

* These were actually the ministers of "Vulgaria," the fictitious country of the story. Erich von Stroheim, if you look closely, is among them.

the time he had repeated this two or three times a crowd had assembled, and some shouted, 'Let's see you do some of your stunts!' So 'Doug' obligingly leaped up eight steps, striving to please, with the camera wasting perfectly good film on the exhibition, which was not required by the scenario."

As to the scenario: Loos and Emerson took Henabery's title and location and worked up a story about an ambitious button factory employee who learns that he is really a king. As Loos intended, the story had good fun with the concept (which evidently recycles as a vogue every fifty to one hundred years) that if you concentrate upon a goal, it will materialize. Once our hero reaches his kingdom of Vulgaria—which has a minister named Badinoff (suggesting that some jokes don't take a hundred years to recycle)—he is subjected to multiple assassination attempts. This gives Fairbanks free rein to clamber and jump over the buildings and canals of Venice, California, site of the location filming. Most critics thought the film delicious satire, although *Variety* grumbled that it was "a series of fist fights. Mr. Fairbanks must be running out of scenarios."

One who had no objection to the fisticuffs was assistant cameraman Glen MacWilliams. He was dutifully cranking his camera that autumn as Fairbanks staged a fight with Bull Montana, "Strangler" Lewis, Spike Robinson, "Kid" Fleming, and the other usual suspects. A young woman watching the action fainted. MacWilliams abandoned his camera, unbeknownst to the combatants, to attend to the lady in question—who was reportedly very pretty. The actors were not pleased to have the shot missed, but evidently Miss Marie Campbell of Minneapolis was quite appreciative. The young couple became engaged the following February, with plans for Fairbanks to serve as best man and his band of Vulgarian assassins as ushers.

But Doug's marriage with the team of Loos and Emerson was coming to an end. On December 1, each signed a termination agreement, giving them their contracted percentages on all Artcraft films up to and including *Reaching for the Moon*—even *The Man from Painted Post*.

"When John asked for a cancellation of our contracts, Doug was relieved to be rid of us," Loos wrote years later.

Herein lies a challenge. With Loos, especially in later years, one has to keep one's saltshaker close at hand. Fairbanks would die at fifty-six, and history fails to record that he had anything to say about the matter. This does not appear to stem from restraint; it simply appears not to have been a grudge that he nursed. He had higher mountains to climb. Anita Loos would also progress to massive fame with the publication of *Gentlemen Prefer Blondes*. But, for the purposes of film history, the last person one might wish to offend is the one with the scathing wit, for wit is a more effective weapon than venom alone. In this department, Loos was well armed.

And she lived a very long time. During those years, she took her history with Douglas Fairbanks and reworked it, shaping the details of the story, altering events, combining scenes, and in general constructing what would have been a very fine film script. It was a script in which John Emerson ("a pimp") was blasted and Fairbanks emerged largely as the creature of her creation. ("We *made* Douglas Fairbanks," she once told Kevin Brownlow.)

Griffith was going to fire Fairbanks in the early days, she would claim. Or, worse, turn him over to Keystone. Enter John Emerson, who stumbled across a veritable goldmine of clever scripts that Loos, then working at Fine Arts, had submitted. Griffith knew they could never be made into films; he just liked to read the funny titles. Loos and Emerson then took Fairbanks in hand and filmed *His Picture in the Papers*. (Her contributions to *The Lamb* and *Double Trouble* were conveniently forgotten.) The story got even better from here. *His Picture in the Papers* was thought to be a stinker, until it was accidently shipped to the Roxy Theatre in New York City* and the hall "fairly rocked with laughter." A star was born. She implied that she wrote all of Fairbanks's early films

---

* The Roxy, of course, didn't even exist until twelve years later. But Sam Rothafel (the original "Roxy" in question) did book Fairbanks films in his New York theaters in the teens. Loos was characteristically loose with her facts.

from that point forward, and that Emerson directed them all. Allan Dwan is written out of her history of these years. But, then, she tells us, things changed. Doug didn't want to share the credit. So they left. He was getting snooty, anyway. Took himself too seriously. Started eating off gold plates.

Certainly her explanations when Fairbanks was alive were quite different. "One always dislikes giving up associations that are pleasant," she told an interviewer in March 1918. "But Mr. Fairbanks decided to get away from satirical comedies and try a new type of play. We do our best work in satirical comedies. That's our specialty, so naturally we ventured forth to pastures new." Emerson gave a different reason: "Of course we liked Mr. Fairbanks and regretted leaving him, but the real reason, speaking for myself, was that I wanted to get away from California. I never felt well there. I was never myself. 'Perpetual sunshine' sounds very poetical, but it isn't—it's too hot to be poetical."

Almost everyone in the film industry, Fairbanks included, shaped his or her narrative. Whether it was Fairbanks's false modesty and his habit of disguising his own origins, Dwan's colorful exaggerations, or Loos's thinly veiled resentments, small lies would be told over and over until it is likely that all participants came to honestly believe them. While historians have uncovered many of Loos's misrepresentations, the fact is that a witty female pioneer of the industry who was still giving interviews into her nineties was a challenging force to overcome.

And she *was* critical to Fairbanks's early career; no one should take that away from her. But Fairbanks was looking for more. He had ideas that did not jibe with those of his first creative team—more action, fewer laughs from the titles but more from the situations. In less than three years he would take his career in such a different direction that it is hard to imagine Loos wanting to write his sort of films. He would stumble down a few blind alleys on his way to his swashbuckling future, and there are many who would argue that the early films of 1917–1919 are as good—or even better—than the later works. But that is a matter of taste. And the taste that counted was *his*—the funding producer and star. The rift began when he wanted a western and his creative team did not. He was the master of working with a team, a talented collaborator, but at the end of the day, his was the only vote that counted. So they parted ways. Loos had the satisfaction of channeling her wit into a great comic novel, and Fairbanks had to console himself with being, for a heady decade, the King of Hollywood—the original swashbuckling icon of the century. Neither lost, if seen in those terms. Their lines were not parallel and crossed for only two and a half years. But while they did, they created real magic. It is unfortunate, then, that the accomplished Anita chose, in small ways, to act as a sore loser.

She and Emerson were still on staff when Allan Dwan arrived in the fall of 1917 to shoot Fairbanks's next film, *A Modern Musketeer*. Here Dwan's history of tall tales returns to challenge the historian. According to him, Owen Moore's threats impelled Fairbanks "to get away from Los Angeles and that embarrassing situation." Dwan was on a westbound train when he received a telegram from Fairbanks: IMPERATIVE MEET ME IN SALINA KANSAS AND WE WILL RETURN TO NEW YORK. Dwan disembarked, met Fairbanks on the next eastbound train, and retraced his route. "Between Salina and New York," he recalled, "we cooked up the idea of *A Modern Musketeer*." Dwan described the main character: "A young fellow who's very restless in his little Kansas hometown. He dreams of riding out like D'Artagnan on a horse . . . he gets into a series of adventures we invented as we went along."

Well and good, except that Fairbanks showed no evidence of hiding from Moore. He hosted a banquet for Dwan upon the latter's arrival in Los Angeles. (Loos and Emerson were pointedly absent but had wired their felicitations.) And the film was scarcely made up on the fly. A full scenario exists in the Joseph Henabery papers at the Herrick Library documenting a well-laid-out story, based on the short story "D'Artagnan of Kansas" and scripted, evidently, well in advance.* But Dwan was correct when he asserted that the story of the film bears no relation to the

---

* A contract was made with Eugene P. Lyle for $250 for his story, which appeared in the September 1912 issue of *Everybody's Magazine*. The contract was dated October 19, 1917. The fact that the issue was five years old seems to contradict Booton Herndon's claim that Fairbanks and Dwan found the story in a pile of magazines that John Fairbanks had brought on the train, suggesting instead a conscious search for appropriate material in older publications. Things were more organized than Dwan suggests.

story that inspired it. Fairbanks and Dwan appear to have taken all their inspiration from the title, and the film shares only the hero's given name (Ned), his Kansas origins, and the fact that his mother drew prenatal inspiration from *The Three Musketeers*. The story is, like so many Fairbanks films of this period, two different tales, the first being a delicious comedy of a chivalrous young man who goes to great ends to play the gallant and protect women, and the second an action story staged at the Grand Canyon and the Canyon de Chelly, involving Fairbanksian heroics.

The film, long lost, has been largely recovered and restored in the past decade. It is a fortunate find—*A Modern Musketeer* is a formidable entry in the Fairbanks body of work. As the (perhaps hyper-caffeinated) *Photoplay* critic wrote, "Fairbanks makes the Dumas swashbuckler seem a popinjay, a milksop, a wearer of wrist watches in times of peace, a devotee of the sleeve handkerchief, a nursery playmate, an eater of prune whip, a drinker of pink lemonade, a person susceptible to hay fever, a wearer of corn plasters, an habitué of five o'clock teas, a reader of Pollyanna." It is well known as being the first film in which Fairbanks appears in swashbuckling garb: he walks straight up to the camera in the opening sequence in full D'Artagnan regalia, strokes his mustache, fingers his curls, and gives us a wink, as if to say, "Don't worry, folks. It's *me* underneath all this horsehair."* The sword fight that follows is an over-the-top, joyous romp of a battle involving not only rapiers but also a lot of throwing of furniture and climbing of walls.

Fairbanks was so pleased with the result that after an initial screening of the film he gave Dwan a Twin Six Packard. Being his usual prankster self, he did not simply present the car but instead suggested that he was considering its purchase and asked Dwan to give it a test drive. Dwan complied but was pulled over by a police officer—a Fairbanks plant. When the "cop" demanded license and registration, Dwan had to confess that the vehicle

---

* Lip readers will note that Fairbanks literally says, "Yes, it's me." This was not the first time that Dwan had Fairbanks walk straight up to the camera, break the fourth wall, and wink at the audience. He did the same in *Manhattan Madness*, in which Doug reveals himself to be the "bad man" of the story within the story.

wasn't his. The faux policeman then checked his records and informed the director that the car was indeed registered to Allan Dwan. Doug then emerged from hiding, and Dwan got the point. The same point presumably was not lost on Anita Loos and John Emerson. They were still working with Fairbanks at this point, but there were no new cars for *them*. One wonders if they regretted their behavior during *The Man from Painted Post*.

A review of the *Musketeer* script reveals sequences that appear to have been filmed but that are lost from the restored print. There was a set piece of a ten-year-old Ned (Fairbanks's character) beating a bully for dipping a little girl's hair in an inkwell. Further,there was a sequence of Ned as bank teller, holding up the line while he wipes silver dollars: "There is a lady on every dollar—she represents the spirit of Liberty. I tremble to think what filthy hands she may have encountered," he says. (An impressed customer wipes his hands before taking a coin.) Ned then leaves the line to carry bundles home for a girl (existing stills reveal that this was ZaSu Pitts, whose unexplained appearance later in the Kansas sequence now makes sense). After he is rebuffed for trying to carry kindling for an elderly lady, Ned returns to his bank, where he moves women and children to the front of the line.*

The script also documents those elements that were constructed post-scenario. The sequence where Ned, learning that he is going to finally get out of Kansas, climbs to the top of a church steeple was not defined in the script, which called simply for "a stunt" to demonstrate his joy. And Fairbanks clearly did some improvising on location at the El Tovar Hotel at the Grand Canyon. Where the script calls for him to enter the building to speak with the heroine's mother, Fairbanks instead jumps off his horse and scrambles up the side of the structure to meet her on a second-floor porch.

For the trip to El Tovar, Fairbanks was accompanied by his wife and son. Beth had elected to remain in New York and do some shopping after

---

* The children included his son and brother John's two daughters. Here, still photographs reveal Junior to be in the sailor suit that he recalls from *American Aristocracy*, suggesting that the sequence was filmed. Their pay was donated to the Red Cross.

the Manhattan trip for exteriors for *Reaching for the Moon*. A bad cold had progressed to pneumonia, and for a while it seemed to be touch and go. Upon hearing the news, Fairbanks had rushed back from California to be at her bedside. Guilt, perhaps, or a newfound solicitude caused him to bring his family along on location for *Musketeer*. This, combined with the fact that Owen was in residence with his wife in Hollywood, made communicating with Mary difficult. Still, he managed to get one note out in early November. It was written on El Tovar stationery, and he used the expedient of getting someone else to address the envelope to Mrs. Owen Moore so that his handwriting would not be recognized—an uncharacteristic act of discretion. "Leaving here for the Painted Desert tomorrow," he wrote. "Be back in Hollywood one week from today—I wonder if you have changed—if I could only hear one word . . . I would be so happy. Will not be possible to communicate after we leave here—please please please Dear—I am just as you want me to be—forever and always."

The heroine in this film was played by Marjorie Daw, who had recently been featured with Mary Pickford in *Rebecca of Sunnybrook Farm*. Daw, who was turning sixteen, was to replace Eileen Percy as Fairbanks's leading lady for the majority of his pre-swashbuckler films. Several years later she would serve as Pickford's bridal attendant upon her marriage to Fairbanks—one of the few present at the ceremony. Fairbanks Jr. cast a curious aspersion on her in passing when describing the wedding in his autobiography, referring to her as "Dad's once or twice leading lady, rumored to have been, at an earlier time, 'a great and good friend.'"

This is the kind of report that shakes one's faith in Junior as a source. He gets the location of the wedding wrong—placing it at Pickfair—as well as most of the guest list. And Daw costarred with Fairbanks in nine films—more than any other actress—hardly making her a "once or twice leading lady." And while it is true that she was Mary's witness at the 1920 wedding, her earlier presence as Fairbanks's leading lady suggests less an illicit affair (as Junior implies)* than the possibility that

---

* He is the *only* source, incidentally, to imply such a thing.

Daw was enlisted as a sort of "beard" for the love affair between Doug and Mary. Her employment as Fairbanks's costar made this plausible and convenient. In a 1921 interview, Mary identified Marjorie Daw as "really the only intimate [woman] friend I have." She and Doug hosted Daw's 1923 wedding to director Eddie Sutherland at their home. And it is unlikely—highly unlikely—that Fairbanks would have had a fling with her before his affair with Mary began. Apart from the fact that this would have made her a highly implausible choice as maid of honor, Daw was fourteen in 1916 and still playing children's roles. (She makes a very convincing twelve-year-old in *Rebecca of Sunnybrook Farm* for this very reason; she was not far removed from twelve herself.) Fairbanks and Chaplin shared many interests in common, but an attraction for underage girls was not among them.*

Daw, one suspects, was grateful for the work. However, she learned very quickly that working for Fairbanks had its risks. Production on the film was delayed when, astride a horse in the Canyon de Chelly, she suffered a collision with another rider, seriously injuring her knee and requiring weeks to recover. Worse, Daw's mother died within twenty-four hours of her stretcher-bound daughter's arrival in L.A.

It was likely these calamities that resulted in the casting of a different leading lady, Katherine MacDonald, for his next feature, *Headin' South*. Here we do have a candidate for a prior romance. MacDonald had been a prominent model in New York City in the 1910s and could very well have had a relationship with Fairbanks at that time. Also, she was to appear in two Fairbanks films but was his romantic interest in only one, qualifying her as a "once or twice leading lady." But this is speculation and, in the absence of hard facts, will remain so.

There is an absence of a different sort in the discussion of *Headin' South*—the film itself. It is, as of this writing, lost. A small fragment survives in a Paramount documentary from the early 1930s, *The House*

---

* To say nothing of the fact that Daw spent three years of her adolescence in a body cast for scoliosis, making her an improbable candidate, even if someone had been interested in an underage seduction.

That Shadows Built, but it only serves to tantalize. The story was a variant on *The Good Bad Man,* in which Fairbanks portrays a bandit who joins a gang headed by Frank Campeau. By the end, it is revealed that our hero is actually a Canadian Mountie in disguise. The film was directed by Arthur Rosson, another Triangle refugee, who had been originally brought on as Dwan's assistant director. Henabery was now the director who would alternate projects with Dwan, but he was tied up writing and planning what would become *Say! Young Fellow.* This left Dwan stretched, so he worked on the script and acted in a supervisory capacity to Rosson, who was promoted for this film to principal director. In the last week of January 1918, he shepherded eight passenger and twelve freight cars to bring over two hundred men and horses to Fort Lowell, near Tucson, Arizona. Included with the cowboys were future western stars Art Acord (a champion bulldogger) and Hoot Gibson (a champion broncobuster). Ginger, one of Fairbanks's Alaskan malamutes, came along as the company mascot—a move that might have made some cast members leery, considering the dog had bitten Eileen Percy on the arm during the filming of *Down to Earth.**

No leading ladies were harmed during the making of this film, but a Sioux Indian chief by the name of Eagle Eye was, when he fell from his horse and broke his leg during filming. Because the man was deemed permanently disabled from this injury, Fairbanks readily pensioned him for the rest of his life. The gesture loses a little of its dramatic punch with the knowledge that Eagle Eye was, at the time of the injury, in his ninety-ninth year.

Henabery recalled that Fairbanks requested his help postproduction. "He said 'Go down and look at that and tell me . . . see what to do with it.' I went down—and he had piles of good action, piles of good

---

* Dogs were always a significant element in his life. In addition to Ginger, he had Rex, a prizewinning malamute. By 1920 he had a full kennel with at least five of the same breed. He bought a pricey Airedale for Mary (*Zorro*) and through the 1920s had a Saint Bernard named Robin, after Robin Hood. There was no end of studio mutts that he adopted, one of whom, dubbed Rooney after the Pickford film *Little Annie Rooney,* costarred with him in *Mr. Robinson Crusoe.* His final dog was a Great Dane named Marco Polo.

material out of Rosson, who was a very good man, but I mean they had unfortunately, a jumbled up story. . . . So I said this is going to be a big trouble because we've got to cut out one faction in here because to start with nobody knows who's chasing who. I can't tell. We have to simplify the story—get out some of the junk, you know, to point up some of the gags a little bit. . . . I didn't shoot anything new for it at all. Just re-edited and simplified it."

Even so, as in *The Man from Painted Post*, the critics were beginning to demonstrate some discrimination. "The Fairbanks smile is carrying a load under which it almost collapses," wrote the usually sycophantic *Photoplay*. "With anyone else in the leading role, this would be a reversion to the wild west picture of five years ago." The *Motion Picture News* wrote, "Whereas *A Modern Musketeer* was the perfectly balanced combination of comedy and melodrama, *Headin' South* has too much of one and too little of the other, regrettably to the detriment of each element."

Once again, audiences didn't care. Grosses on the film were excellent, although because of cost overruns, the profits for Fairbanks were the weakest to date. Transporting and housing two hundred extras did not come cheap ("Mr. Fairbanks is prodigal in this respect," commented *Variety*), and it was time for a retrenchment.

He and Dwan did so quickly with what was to be his least expensive Artcraft production, *Mr. Fixit*. *Mr. Fixit* was a studio-based, modern-dress film with a plot that had Fairbanks's character stepping in and impersonating an Oxford chum with his American family—a bunch of elderly stuffed shirts. Because, until the last reel, there are no large action sequences, it is a film of small charms, but these are worth watching for.

Fairbanks is typically seen in terms of the large gesture, be it the broad ones of the late theatrical style or the grand ones of his swashbuckling greatness. In this, modern audiences often miss the small movements he makes. This is easy to do—particularly for the post-1930 eye, accustomed to voice, sound, and music to provide a cue as to when to pay particular attention. Fairbanks's films are full of small, quick gestures that are full of delight. In *Flirting with Fate*, he runs to the police department, frantic to notify the authorities that he has hired an assassin to kill him. Blink and you will miss him drink from the inkwell on the sergeant's desk. He meets Bessie Love in *The Good Bad Man* and, in a flash so quick one might not notice it, punches a hole in her hair ribbon with his pilfered conductor's punch. He attempts to kiss the heroine's hand as it rests on a table in *Wild and Woolly*, only to have her pull it away at the last second, leaving him to smooch the tabletop. *Mr. Fixit* was rife with such moments. And if Fairbanks was largely restricted to the set that comprised the family manse, audiences still could find pleasure in counting the number of ways he elected to descend the central staircase (skipping with five children on his back, on his belly like a snake, walking on his hands, jumping clear over the balustrade, and in a full log roll down its length).

Mr. Fixit was made on the fly, and all shots involving Fairbanks were interiors or taken on the back lot in order that the company could work days and into the nights. He was in a hurry and needed to finish the film in a very short time. The country was at war—and Uncle Sam wanted Doug.

7

Citizen Doug

THE YEAR 1918 WAS like no other for Fairbanks. It would represent the peak of his endeavors, not as a movie star but as a public citizen. Ever since Frederick Warde had established the template for civic duty for him two decades before, he had been involved in organized good deeds. The causes demonstrated no discernable pattern; the Federation of Jewish Charities in Brooklyn was as likely to be supported as the Irish Parliament Party Fund. Building funds, funds for out-of-work actors, fundraising drives for widows of dead actors—if it had the word *fund* in its name, he was there. At the Actors Fund Fair in 1910—an event opened by no less a personage than President Taft—he donned overalls and clerked at the "Country Grocery Store" booth alongside Jack Barrymore.* When he wasn't performing, he was buying tickets or, once flush, whole boxes to charity events.

If he was not at a fundraiser, he was joining an organization. He was a lifelong joiner—a cosmopolitan Babbitt before the character had sprung from Sinclair Lewis's pen. He was an avid member of the Lambs Club—participating in all of their Gambols, which in no way prevented him from also attending Friars Club events. And if there wasn't an organization to join, he founded one. In February 1914 he was a founding

---

* They also conducted the barn dance, but no photographs are known to exist, thus depriving history of the surreal prospect of the Great Profile in denim overalls, square dancing with Douglas Fairbanks.

member of the Sixty Club, a society of theatrical stars formed largely for the purpose of holding dances every Saturday night at the Hotel Astor. He covered vaudeville as well, cofounding the Fortnight Club the same week.

His energy was boundless, and when the War to End All Wars finally came to the United States in April 1917,* he devoted a tremendous portion of it to the cause. As with many of his charitable acts, it was somewhat of a scattershot affair at first. Still, as 1917 turned to 1918, Fairbanks found his energies directed increasingly to two areas: the Red Cross and the sale of Liberty Bonds. His efforts on both accounts were prodigious.

It began in the summer of 1917. Fairbanks was one of the celebrities at a fundraising concert for the Red Cross. A woman in the audience held out a check for one hundred dollars, saying that she would donate it if Doug jumped from the roof of the bandstand. He promptly shimmied up the supporting pole and made the twenty-foot jump. ("Five dollars a foot," reported one contemporary. "Doug says he is glad the lady didn't offer a thousand dollars.") He was one of the four men (also including industry pioneer Edwin S. Porter) composing the imposingly titled Committee of the National Association of the Motion Picture Industry Cooperating with the Red Cross. They prepared and distributed one thousand trailers to theaters nationally to recruit members to the organization. He spent a day in San Diego, twenty-five Red Cross nurses and fifty Boy Scouts trailing him in ten automobiles, traveling between department stores, movie houses, and major street corners, selling Red Cross memberships. He personally bought memberships for the newsboys in town.

But this was, in his mind, penny-ante stuff. In January 1918, he sponsored a rodeo for the Red Cross. It was an elaborate event, for which Fairbanks covered all expenses. A stagecoach loaded with cowboys paraded through downtown Los Angeles giving out handbills. Boxes were sold at a premium of $500. (Mary Pickford bought out a special

---

* Europe, of course, had been embroiled since 1914.

section for 165 children from the Los Angeles orphanage.) Fairbanks's motto was "$10,000 or bust!" Given that most tickets sold for fifty cents to two dollars, it was an ambitious expectation. They exceeded it, making $18,000. Twenty thousand spectators listened to military bands, watched William S. Hart hold up a stagecoach, bought favors and treats from movie stars, and saw Doug ride a bucking bronco and shoot glass balls. A tribe of Sioux Indians did war dances, Anheuser-Busch brought its Clydesdales, and trick rider Helen Gibson slid down the side of her racing pony and picked up a peanut from the ground with her teeth.

It was such a success that Doug then paid to move the entire enterprise—two hundred cowboys, the Indians, and "a lot of Mexicans"—to San Francisco. Astride Smiles, he led a parade down Market Street. He met the mayor while "balancing on his hands on the hood of an automobile and kissing the stars on the American flag painted on it." The mobs at Ewing Field could not all be accommodated; therefore, a second rodeo was agreed to the following day. Even with no advertising, it was a sellout. An additional $38,000 went to the coffers of the Red Cross.

Fairbanks contemplated touring nationally with the rodeo, but a much greater cause intervened. The federal government needed money to conduct the war and raised it by issuing a series of bonds. Four groups of Liberty Bonds were sold during the conflict; a fifth, postwar bond issuance was deemed the "Victory Liberty Loan" in 1919. The first two Liberty Loans, in April and October 1917, received relatively tepid receptions. Many bonds were sold at a discount. Fairbanks participated in efforts to promote the second Liberty Loan, traveling across the country and speaking at a few meetings in New York City in October. He raised a million dollars, $100,000 of which was his personal subscription. He, along with Mary, William S. Hart, and female impersonator Julian Eltinge appeared in a half-reel film promoting bond sales, variably titled *War Relief* and *The All Star Production of Patriotic Episodes for the Second Liberty Loan.* It was one of only five bond films produced for the drive.

By the time of the third loan issuance, scheduled to begin on the first anniversary of the US entry into the war, Treasury Secretary William McAdoo decided that a more aggressive marketing campaign was in order. He enlisted Fairbanks, Pickford, and Chaplin, as the three most popular movie stars in the nation, to participate in a national tour to promote bond sales. They readily agreed.

The three, accompanied by Charlotte Pickford chaperoning her daughter Mary, departed from Los Angeles on April 1, 1918, taking a train designated the "Three Star Special" to Chicago. Bennie Zeidman preceded the group by a couple of days, arranging rallies and events at the major stops. But at every stop, no matter how short, one of the stars would address the assembled crowds from the back of the train. Chaplin, exhausted from staying up nights to finish editing *A Dog's Life*, slept straight through the first two days. It was during intervals between speeches that he and Doug invented a game they titled "Three Minute Man." One would pick a topic, and with no preparation or warning the other would be required to give a three-minute discourse on the theme. The subject would be chosen for either obscurity or banality—"window shades" being an example. They played it evenings at Pickfair for years.

The trio arrived in Chicago on the fourth and were greeted with a large rally. "His million-dollar grin was piloted through the cheering throngs of Chicago's admirers in a Haynes 'Fourdore' roadster," noted one observer. The four doors were unnecessary. As they reached the Liberty Bond Station on LaSalle Street, Fairbanks leaped through the car's open windows and onto the roof, exhorting the crowds through a megaphone, leading a rousing chorus of "Over There" and promising to sign the receipts of any and all who bought bonds in the next hour.

They left for Washington that night, resuming their speeches from the observation platform of the train at every five-minute whistle-stop on their path. Night or day, it did not matter; they were there for the crowds at Fort Wayne, Altoona, Harrisburg, York, and every stop in between. Their arrival in Washington, DC, on the sixth was a major event. Pulled in horse-drawn carriages, they (along with star Marie Dressler) paraded down Pennsylvania Avenue—Mary in one carriage, Doug and Charlie in another. They sold bonds on the Capitol plaza, on the ellipse at the White House (where they briefly met President Wilson), and at a large football field, where Chaplin recalled that in his enthusiasm he fell off the speakers' platform, dragged Dressler with him, and landed on top of the then little-known assistant secretary of the navy—Franklin Roosevelt. It was Roosevelt who bought the first bond that Fairbanks sold in Washington; their smiling exchange was captured in the rotogravure section of the *Washington Post*.

Then it was Manhattan. Upon arrival each was served in a lawsuit: Pickford by a woman who wanted $103,000 commission for securing Mary's contract with Artcraft (the sort of nuisance suit she and her handlers repeatedly dealt with); Chaplin in a suit from Essanay over his contract move to Mutual; and Fairbanks (along with Anita Loos and John Emerson) in a suit from Scribner's publishing house. The assertion was that Fairbanks's last film for Triangle, *The Americano*, was based not on *Blaze Derringer* but on a Richard Harding Davis novel, *The White Mice*. The claim is understandable. The film bears a far greater resemblance to the story line of the Davis novel than it does to the reputed source material.* Still, naming Fairbanks was a hollow gesture—he was an employee of Triangle, a de facto producer, not de jure.

Of more lasting resonance in his life's story was a decision he made as he arrived in New York City. Instead of going to the Algonquin, where Beth and Junior were waiting, he went to the Sherry Netherland. Beth's suspicions of his infidelity had never quieted, and sometime in late 1917 she confronted her husband directly. A telegram dated October 9, 1917, speaks to this time in their lives: WIRED YOU AFFAIR WAS OFF BECAUSE YOU THOUGHT IT WAS ON YOU HAVE MISJUDGED ME TERRIBLY [*sic*] THERE NEVER WAS ANYTHING WRONG WILL FINISH PICTURE AND LEAVE FRIDAY FOR EAST CAN YOU MEET ME IN CHICAGO WANT TO SEE YOU ALONE AM WORRIED ABOUT YOUR CONDITION WIRE ME HOW YOU ARE LOVE DOUGLAS.

This was disingenuous, especially considering that in the same period he was wiring Mary: RATHER BLUE SPLENDID MOON TONIGHT BUT NO

---

* In the Davis novel, the hero is a mechanical engineer; the captive is rescued by way of a tunnel and even communicates the existence of the tunnel via the same code used in the film.

ONE TO SHARE IT WITH and, a week later, AM SO HOMESICK FOR THE
MOON FOR YOU FOR OUR DREAMS EVERYTHING. He was playing both
ends against the middle, and it could not last much longer.

Beth and Junior had moved to the Algonquin in New York in the
fall of 1917, ostensibly so that the boy could go to school there. There
was no official separation. Beth's family, according to her son, assumed
that the household would reunite when Fairbanks was finished filming
in California. No one, not even Beth, expected him to be a no-show
at the Algonquin.

His first day in New York City was spent uptown. One spectator
recalled years later:

> Mary Pickford sold one of her famous gold curls, then the symbol
> of all the sweetness and light that he-men wanted in their women,
> to the highest purchaser of bonds. She stood on the landing of the
> little stairway leading up from the back of Lord and Taylor's and
> the store was so packed that doors had to be locked to keep the
> rest of the crowd outside. Afterwards she joined Fairbanks, who
> did his bit by turning back somersaults, walking on his hands
> and going through a lightning series of fantastic gymnastics, and
> Chaplin, who made a speech on a platform in front of the Library
> on Fifth Avenue. Crowds filled the avenue and 40th street, entirely
> blocking traffic, and the trio got more applause than the soldiers
> who paraded the preceding day.

The second day they were in the financial district, where they stood
in front of the Treasury Building. Wall Street was packed with faces as
far as the eye—and cameras—could see. "I think the three of us all got
stage fright down at the New York sub-treasury that day," Fairbanks
recalled a month later.* "Chaplin and I were there together, and I held
him up with one arm. Now, Charlie's not hard to hold, because he's
light, and because he is a handy little acrobat and knows how to bal-

---

* Chaplin and Fairbanks were together on the day in question. Pickford made a solo
  appearance at the Treasury Building two days later.

ance himself to perfection. But after our speech-making he said: 'How do you do it, Doug? Do you realize you held me up there for almost three minutes?' It was just sheer nervousness that enabled me to do it."

The *New York Times* published a photo of the moment: Doug, grinning broadly, holding a teetering and somewhat anxious Chaplin high over his shoulder. The photo is usually cropped, but if one sees the full still, one can recognize Junior, muffled in an overcoat and hat, smiling at the antics from the rear of the platform—a perfect, privileged bird's-eye view for a little boy. His father had turned up at the Algonquin after all, and not merely to pick up Junior for the rally. It was for the purpose of confessing. He and Mary were in love, he told Beth. More, he continued, it was the one big love of their lives—*nothing* else mattered in comparison.

History does not record Beth's immediate response. But it does tell us her delayed reaction. As her husband left for his solo, midwestern portion of the national tour (Mary was to tour the Northeast, and Chaplin the South), she stewed. On Thursday, April 11, she acted. She met with a reporter, and she named names. She spoke of the "one big love," adding, "Now I am big enough to stand aside until they have time to find out if it really is that big a love. For twelve years I have thought only of my husband's happiness, and now I have decided that there is only one thing for me to do—to let him take it as it came to him, while I wend my separate way with my boy. There will be no divorce."

She continued, "I cannot defend any woman with whom my husband's name has been linked. . . . I have made up my mind that I will no longer act as a shield for her. For the last eight months whenever gossip raised its ugly head I was the one who kept denying and defending and explaining. Now I am through. . . . The gossip has a foundation in fact."

The news caught Fairbanks unawares. He was in Flint, Michigan, having just given a speech at a rally, when reporters asked him for comment. It was, he insisted, the work of "German propagandists," continuing, "Why, I have been reported shot three times since I started campaigning for the Liberty loan." Most newspapers were not so brave as to publish Mary's name directly in the article, but all sought a quote from her. She obliged, saying, "I have not the remotest idea that my name has been brought into any difference between any man and his wife."

This did not sit well with Beth. "I am sorry the woman who has caused all this unhappiness in our home is not willing to acknowledge to the world as she has acknowledged to her friends and her family, her love for Mr. Fairbanks."

Owen Moore now chose to chime in. "I deeply sympathize with Mrs. Fairbanks, who by years of devotion and service to her husband in matters connected with his profession, has done much to bring about his success, at the same time as a loyal wife and mother catering to his domestic happiness. It seems doubly unfortunate that in the present state of her health, Mrs. Fairbanks should be compelled to bear public humiliation in a situation where she cannot face the world with her husband at her side. As for myself," he added darkly, "I can only say my attitude at this time has been prompted by motives that I do not wish to discuss at present."

Beth was asked about the "German propaganda" claim on Doug's part. She replied drily: "It was like him to add this. . . . It is much to have a husband with a thoroughgoing sense of humor."

The denial was met with derision elsewhere. The *Moving Picture World*, normally an unabashed booster, published a still photograph of Fairbanks running to catch a train. Observing pettishly that the train was not in motion at the time of the photograph, the caption writer added, "Then, too, comes the lingering suspicion that Mr. Fairbanks, in thus hurriedly diving into the steps of a standing passenger-coach, is trying to escape the pro-German propaganda said to be so relentlessly pursuing him." *Variety* observed that while Beth's statement yielded admiration for her simple dignity, her husband's denial "had the opposite effect." Another columnist for the paper noted that Fairbanks's image was hissed when a "coming attraction" slide featuring him was seen at a theater in Los Angeles.

Meanwhile, back in the heartland, Doug wasn't doing much laughing. He was, however, doing a lot of shouting. Accompanied by brother John, Bennie Zeidman, and his valet, Naoki, he was on a grueling whirlwind tour of the Midwest. Naoki recalled, "Of the country, I see nothing. Mr. Fairbanks, he change his clothes ten times a day, and all I have seen is the inside of taxicabs and hotels. I have I think much pride when I say I have carried twenty-one bags from coast to coast in the interest of the Liberty Loan; I have pressed 326 suits; I have shined 140 pairs of shoes, found the collar button 96 times, and have been taken for Sessue Hayakawa eighteen times."

On the day Beth announced the separation, Fairbanks was in Detroit, Flint, and Saginaw, Michigan, and Buffalo, New York. He did not reach Buffalo until 8:40 PM, yet still "he rushed about the city like mad for a couple of hours, urging audiences to buy bonds until it hurts." Journalists were already noticing that near-constant speech making—it was an era before microphones—was making his voice husky. By the end of the day he could only whisper, but still he offered to climb to the roof of one of the theaters if someone would buy a $50,000 bond. By the next day he was in Ohio, where he was markedly hoarse but continued to deny any separation. Saturday he was in Indiana and was totally voiceless. "The only thing left for him to do in putting over his bond message was to convey his thoughts in actions rather than words. And this he did by occasionally punctuating a few sentences with a leap over a chair or some other Wild West maneuver," wrote one observer. By noon of the same day, he was on his way to Louisville, Kentucky, where he spoke (or tried to) at fifteen-minute intervals at each movie house in the downtown region. But he went beyond this: "Mr. Fairbanks also talked at Macauley's Theater, and some that were not down on the published schedule, which included the Alamo, Strand, Majestic, Walnut, National and Mary Anderson," wrote a reporter, adding—perhaps unnecessarily—"In fact Mr. Fairbanks was a glutton for work and covered as much territory as it was possible to do."

But the strain began to be evident. "He showed the result of his long trip and continuous campaigning for the Liberty Loan," wrote the Louisville reporter. "However, the vim which characterizes his picture productions was also shown in his patriotic talks." Vim alone couldn't carry him, however. A Cleveland reporter noted, "When here he was on the verge of a breakdown. He was obliged to cancel many engagements and kept only those absolutely necessary." By April 15, in Evansville, Indiana, he threw in the towel. The folks in towns such as Racine, La Crosse, and Milwaukee, Wisconsin, were to be disappointed. All visits were canceled, and Doug went to the French Lick Springs resort in Indiana to rest his voice and catch his breath. He returned to Los Angeles in early May "a nervous wreck."

From there he retreated to Montana, spending five days on a ranch surrounded by his favorite people—cowboys—and far from the eyes of the curious press. It may have been more than the loss of his voice. The emotional strain of having the marital break go public at last was taking its toll. He wanted to be liked, no, *loved* by everybody. A nasty divorce and scandal threatened a film career that was less than two years old. Further, Fairbanks never handled confrontations head-on. He was far more inclined to retreat. Things were getting dirty indeed: Owen Moore was now threatening to sue for a quarter of a million dollars. Paradoxically, this backfired on Moore. Columnists began to refer to him as "Mr. Pickford Moore." Arthur Brisbane went further, writing, that Moore "hadn't proved anything, and that in all probability his sensitive heart is mistaken." If Moore was going to collect, he was going to have to do so sub rosa.

Mary had toughed out the entire loan drive, hiding her fears like a consummate professional. Upon returning to Los Angeles, she found herself having to deny reports that she intended to quit making movies. "If anyone thinks I am about to retire from motion pictures they should take a peek over the fence at the studios tomorrow morning. I'll be there bright and early and ready to start on my next picture," she said firmly. There was no doubting her pluck. A reporter then asked her for a statement on the Fairbanks separation. "Of that I have absolutely nothing to say. The less said about it by me, the better," she replied.

Fairbanks returned to work, laying low. In May, for example, every industry leader, including D. W. Griffith, Mary Pickford, Lois Weber, Charlie Chaplin, Cecil B. DeMille, William S. Hart, Mack Sennett, Jesse Lasky, Maurice Tourneur, Billy Bitzer, and William Desmond Taylor attended a mass meeting at Clune's Theatre to form the Motion Picture Relief Organization. This was just the sort of thing that was up

Fairbanks's alley. Although he was elected vice president of the group, it was in absentia. He telegrammed his regrets and pledged his support.

When he did emerge, in June, it was strictly for war work, such as a fundraising carnival at the Lasky studio. He competed in a "drinking bout" at William S. Hart's western bar, staggering away, reportedly, after his fifth ice cream soda. Undaunted, he boxed world champion Kid McCoy but fell into the swimming pool adjacent to the platform after two rounds. He supported the United States Balloon School in Arcadia, California, not only with money but also by funding a luncheon for all of its students. He promoted the "Smileage" campaign, which subsidized entertainment—including motion pictures—for soldiers in training camps and in the field.

Motion pictures were a critical source of sanctioned recreation for the troops. One soldier wrote home to his mother:

> Our amusements here are limited. American movies are paramount (not a pun.) I was watching Doug Fairbanks in some of his latest stunts the other night, when the show was interrupted by the boom of guns and the clang of bells. . . . Of course the show was off, and right in the midst of the interesting part of it, too. I was disappointed. I can see an air raid on any star-lit night, but a movie, and a Fairbanks one at that, is an epoch here.

Fairbanks devoted most of the spring and summer of 1918 to production of just what the doughboys wanted: more films. Joseph Henabery provided the script for the first.

Say! Young Fellow is another lost film. Contemporary reviews suggest that the loss is acute. Fairbanks played a cub reporter who was guided at critical moments by a miniature version of himself who would appear on his shoulder and give advice (always prefaced by the film's title). Assistant cameraman Glen MacWilliams recalled, "There was a lot of 'trick stuff' to do. Doug's character had an alter ego, a 'hunch' personified by a tiny figure of Doug. This tiny miniature man would advise him in times of problems or indecision. In these scenes the little guy would tumble out of Doug's ear, advise him, and then dive back into his ear, tumbling and somersaulting all the while. We worked out a system of double-exposure using black velvet and a matte."

Henabery created the character not only for comic purposes but also because he felt that Fairbanks films should all have a moral theme. "Hunch" was prone to such pearls as "Stick to what you're doing and what you're doing will stick to you" and "Never miss an opportunity if you would win success." Success and the hero's desire for it were visualized "in a kind of allegorical way," in the words of one contemporary critic. "It shows a chasm the sides being formed by steep mountain walls with the word 'success' in the distance and Mr. Fairbanks after it." The film also had its climactic action sequence in a factory, with Fairbanks battling the villains while whirling around on pulley belts and perched over flywheels. One yearns to see it.

Henabery recalled that during the shoot, "Doug was as happy as I've ever seen him." The worst, it seemed, had happened, and his world had not come to an end. He was fortunate in his era. A mere fifty years later, the cozy relationship between the print and the film media would never withstand such an interesting scandal. The top male star separates from his wife, who names the top female star? The press would have a field day. But after the first week's flurry of press—nary a mention. It is possible that Doug and Mary's critical importance to the war's fundraising activities resulted in subtle pressure on the part of the government to avoid the topic. That, or Charlotte Pickford's abilities with a well-placed bribe were underrated. Whatever the reason, the storm passed, and Fairbanks was, evidently, as popular as ever. No more was he a nervous wreck: on the last day of filming, which took place on a set adjacent to the Lasky pool (the same pool he had taken a dunk in while boxing Kid McCoy), Fairbanks cried, "I double dare you!" and ran, fully clothed, into the drink. Henabery and the rest of the crew followed suit—all except Bennie Zeidman. This was soon corrected by Doug and the gang, who threw him, protesting, into the water. They were then required to fish him out, as the poor publicist did not know how to swim.

The schedule was so close to the bone that Henabery was still editing the print on the night of its premiere at Sid Grauman's Million Dollar

Theatre. He brought the film in with the last three reels unscreened, fresh from the cutter's. Fortunately all went well; the picture opened to rave reviews. Henabery, who lived to eighty-eight, cherished the clippings until the end of his days.

Dwan directed Doug's next film, *Bound in Morocco*. This picture is also, as of this writing, lost. It was a vehicle designed for Fairbanks's comedic skills: at one point, to rescue the American heroine who has been kidnapped for a sultan's harem, Doug disguised himself as a veiled attendant. The film contained the usual quotient of Fairbanksian stunts, but it was the ending that caused comment in most critics. Fairbanks had rescued the girl and her mother, and they rode off in a cloud of sand. A title then appeared: ONE HUNDRED YEARS LATER. It was followed by a shot of tombstones in the corner of a graveyard.

Buster Keaton was to do the same thing ten years later in *College*, and in his hands the message was sardonic and bittersweet—a nod to the futility of all our comic thrashings in life. Critics did not read the same moral from Fairbanks. Framed by his sunny heroics, the graves suggested rather that boy and girl stayed together to the end of their days. Doug—or his cheery popular image, at least—did not brook anything approaching irony.

His nose to the grindstone, he had produced two feature films in short order that spring and summer. But he experienced a setback on Independence Day. A stray firecracker thrown onto the roof of the editing room at the Famous Players–Lasky studio caused a fire. Fairbanks's dressing room burned, along with the Scenario Department. The blaze destroyed a print of *Bound in Morocco*—and, worse, the European negative of *Headin' South*. The negative for *Swat the Kaiser* was also lost.

Swat the Kaiser was a Liberty Loan film made for the third bond drive. While the second Liberty Loan had only five associated fundraising films, the third drive, that spring, had thirty-five. Much as he had chosen to use the powers of Hollywood for in-person fundraising in the spring of 1918, McAdoo elected to ramp up the bond film program as well. He asked all seventeen thousand theaters in the nation to run the half-reel trailers at every screening. By the fourth drive in the autumn, every theater had a new four-minute film every three days. Fairbanks's contribution to the spring drive was an allegory in which burly Bull Montana represented Prussianism; Tully Marshall, Death; Helen MacKern, Justice; Frank Campeau, the Devil; German Gustav von Seyffertitz, Uncle Sam; and Doug, Democracy. It was set "in the boxing ring of humanity" and asserted that every Liberty Bond purchased represented a blow to the Kaiser. Joseph Henabery directed the film, which was released to theaters during the April bond drive.

In the fall of that year, for the fourth bond drive, Fairbanks produced *Sic 'em Sam*. This was also an allegory but one more elaborate in nature, with a set labeled THE HOME OF NATIONAL LIBERTY. Prussianism (again, Bull Montana) attacked Liberty while Propaganda distracted Democracy (Doug). Prussianism then set fire to the house, and it wasn't until Doug telephoned the world to enlist the Allies as firemen, and thrashed Bull for good measure, that Liberty was rescued.

The Victory Drive in 1919 also yielded a film: *Knocking Knockers*. It picked up where *Sic 'em Sam* left off. Prussianism, having seen Liberty rescued, hid in the Hall of Justice. Doug as Democracy jumped through a skylight, attacked him, and, seizing a fire hose from one of the Allied powers, washed Prussianism down the sewer. He then did battle with those peacetime foes Dissension, Seditious Propaganda, and Brute Ignorance, defeating them in typically Fairbanksian ways.

It is inevitable, perhaps, that Douglas Fairbanks would represent democracy in these little parables.* He had come, to many, to embody America with a capital A. Even before the war, *Photoplay* wrote of his

---

* It is likely that there were others. The surgeon general asked him in February 1918 to make a film to communicate to the recruits that "clean living and physical fitness are, after loyalty and obedience, the prime requisites of the soldier." Fairbanks pledged to do so, and he and Allan Dwan worked on the project. There was a bond film for the fifth Canadian Victory Loan Drive, which occurred at the same time as the fourth Liberty Loan in the United States (possibly some variant of *Sic 'em Sam*), and a film made at the request of Herbert Hoover, who was then functioning as the US food administrator. He was also asked to make a "pep" film for the cantonments in the summer of 1918 and "morale pictures" in the early postwar months of 1919.

on-screen persona, "The good-bad loveable chap Douglas Fairbanks always plays *does* represent America and the biff-bang Americanism for which we are justly and unjustly renowned." George Creel, head of Woodrow Wilson's Committee on Public Information during the war, was quoted in 1918 as saying of Fairbanks: "He is what every American might be, ought to be, and frequently is not. More than any other that comes to mind, he is possessed of the indomitable optimism that gives purpose, 'punch' and color to any life, no matter what the odds." Edward Wagenknecht, perhaps, said it best: "He was the Yankee Doodle Boy whom George M. Cohan had put on the stage when the eagle screamed more lightheartedly than he does today, but he performed on a larger stage than was ever available to Cohan."

Chaplin was British; Mary, "America's Sweetheart," was Canadian. So the mantle of Americanism during the nationalistic fervor that engulfed the country during the Great War lay principally on Doug. He wore it easily, as if born to it. Whether it was his actor's narcissism that permitted this or a sense of patriotic duty is a matter strictly of opinion.

By July, he had increased his public presence, acting as the grand marshal at a Los Angeles event dubbed "the Big Parade." But the requirement to make films for Artcraft as well as the sundry public service split-reel creations for the government kept him largely in the studio. He brought on his brother Robert in mid-July as an "efficiency expert." Robert would spend the next twenty years managing Doug's finances and studio operations. He was deemed a "technical director" until John was disabled by a stroke in the mid-1920s, at which point Robert assumed the position of general manager. Both brothers were reliable anchors to their younger sibling's flights of enthusiasm, providing a level of prudent, disinterested advice that most film stars of the era lacked. Charlotte served the same function for Mary, whose luck in relatives was otherwise scant. Brother Jack and sister Lottie (now also bearing the name "Pickford" both personally and professionally) were infamous good-time Charlies and a financial drain.

The other major source of support in Mary's life was her dear friend and frequent screenwriter Frances Marion. Marion was smart, beautiful, talented, successful—and one of the few people in Hollywood who did not like Douglas Fairbanks. Her distaste was enhanced as the years progressed and the Pickford-Fairbanks union caused anguish to her beloved Mary. Near the end of her life, she was to say of Fairbanks, "He was more spit than fire. He was artificial—phony—social climbing. A cheater. He loathed the fact he was a Jew. Minute the door was closed he went limp. He was such a toady to people with money—title crazy."

A scathing indictment, managing, with a writer's skill, to find every weak point in Fairbanks's psyche, real or perceived, and sum them up in a mere forty-one words. And there is no denying that there was truth in some of her observations. The issue of Jewish roots is the simplest to confirm. While officially he would not be considered Jewish, as the lineage was not from his mother's side of the family, by the racially insensitive standards of the era, any Jewish blood made you a Jew. And to be a Jew was only a step up from being a person of color. Even immigrants—Christian immigrants, that is—were higher on the social scale. His son wrote:

> My father, though not in the least religious in a formal sense, sometimes found it useful to recall, even boast about, his Roman Catholic baptism and upbringing. He was embarrassed by whatever amount of Jewish blood he had. Both my mother and stepmother Mary told me (on separate occasions years apart) that there were days of spiritual agony before he could bring himself to "confess" to his mixed-up ethnic origins. Both Mother and Mary tried, but failed, to persuade him either to be proud of his roots or, alternatively, not to be so ridiculously self-conscious about them.

But Frances Marion's distaste for Douglas Fairbanks was not yet at its peak in July 1918, when he hired her to write the screenplay for his next project: *He Comes Up Smiling*. This was the first and only film he made that was based on one of his stage productions. He paid $10,000 for the rights—an impressive sum for the time.* Two of the five reels of the film exist as of this writing and document the scenarist's considerable skills in "opening up" the stage production. In the play, Fairbanks exists from act 1, scene 1 as a voluntary hobo—a man who has given up the world of the desk and pen for the joys of the road. But Marion devotes one reel of the film's five to show us how he got there.

The opening shot is of Fairbanks in a human-size birdcage. Sparrow-like, he hops from perch to pen and back before pulling the bars apart and emerging from his prison. But it was all a vision; the next shot demonstrates that our hero is still trapped in the cage of a bank teller. But the birdcage is not entirely a figment of his imagination: his elderly boss has a beloved canary in the bank, and Doug is put in charge of it.† He puts the bird through a series of "Swedish exercises," sings for it (using the chain link gates in the bank as an impromptu harp), plucks it free of fleas, gives it a shower, and air towels it dry. All is going well until he is distracted by a customer and the bird escapes.

A mere three minutes into the film Fairbanks is in full flight: scaling buildings, jumping from roof to roof, popping into and out of windows, and launching himself from the top of a ladder. When he finally catches his prey, he is out in the country. There he meets an elderly hobo who convinces him that both bird and bank clerk need their freedom. From here the story proper begins. Fairbanks's house at the time, set on a fifteen-acre lot in Beverly Hills, served as the film's Country Club setting. The estate featured tennis courts, an outdoor pool, stables for horses and kennels for dogs, a "war garden," and a view of the Pacific Ocean. It predated Pickfair, which was to be a simpler house. Allan Dwan's property in the Sierra Madres was also used in the film when the plot required a hunting lodge. This portion of the film remains lost.

Also missing from the existing reels is footage of a remarkable set. Akin to a large dollhouse, it showed four rooms and two hallways

---

* In contrast, the rights for *Arizona*, a far more famous play, cost $5,000.

† The little canary was one belonging to Marion, who trained birds as a hobby. She employed another one of her aviary friends in 1926's *The Scarlet Letter*.

simultaneously, through which Fairbanks chased various characters. Buster Keaton was to employ a similar device two years later, when he filmed *The High Sign*, but because *He Comes Up Smiling* has been lost for decades, most are unaware that Fairbanks beat him to the punch.*

The critics of the time were enraptured. The *Motion Picture News* labeled it "a knockout—and then some." *Wid's Daily* declared it "the fastest and funniest thing Doug had ever done." He had hit the last three films out of the park. Perhaps it was the law of averages, or simply a confluence of circumstances, but things did not go well with his next, *Arizona*.

Partly this was related to the source material. *Arizona* first made its appearance the same year that Doug set foot on stage with Frederick Warde, arriving on Broadway as Warde entered his twentieth, and Fairbanks his second, theatrical season. It was a drama set on a military base at the time of the Spanish-American War. In it the hero takes the blame for a jewel robbery in order to protect the reputation of his beloved commander's wife, who has been having an affair with the villain. He is drummed out of the military until circumstances of the plot (and a few heroics) restore his good name. The play had legs and was a standard in the American repertoire. Frank Campeau, the all-purpose Fairbanks villain, was as well known for playing the heavy in *Arizona* on the stage as he was for the role of Trampus in *The Virginian*. The play was revered as serious drama. Doug, having learned his lesson from *The Half Breed*, worked with Allan Dwan to add comic elements to the script. The play's author, Augustus Thomas, asked Fairbanks in November of that year how they were "getting on with his drama." Fairbanks's cheery response: "Fine! You won't recognize it when we've finished."

---

* This is not to disparage Keaton's genius. All the great comics of the silent era played variations on sundry leitmotifs, and to see a device pop up here versus there was not considered plagiarism. It was more akin to hearing different jazz musicians performing a riff on a theme. The melodies may be the same, but the result is unique to each. Maurice Tourneur was said to have used the same device in a film two years prior to *He Comes Up Smiling*, although it is unknown if Fairbanks's creative team was aware of this.

This must have been discomfiting to Thomas. Something—likely we shall never know what—was also bothering director Dwan. In the middle of the production he quit—or was fired. Columnist Karl Kitchen hinted at the atmosphere on location when he visited the Fairbanks set during the filming of *Arizona*:

> When he was not "kidding" his unhappy director or teasing his pet bear, he was playing tricks on the former Mexican Generals who were now working for him. The great joy in Fairbanks' life is to play jokes. He will shove a six-shooter into the pit of your stomach and fire another gun behind his back, with the result that you need a flatiron to keep your hair down for the remainder of the day.

Just what was making Dwan unhappy is not clear. But his unhappiness must have been acute to cause such a break. Dwan biographer Frederic Lombardi suggests that the decline of Dwan's marriage combined with the workaholic hours caused Dwan to quit. Certainly these were contributing factors, but Lombardi also points to evidence of a personal rift. *Photoplay* reported: "The parting of star and director was such that not even a Wilson speech at a Versailles conference could ever bring them back—except as combatants."

One suspects that the offender in this dispute was Fairbanks. Dwan was of an easygoing nature, patient with his rambunctious, effervescent, practical joker boss. But patience, even that of Dwan, is not infinite, and Fairbanks was not of a temperament to back down in the face of a quarrel. Possibly there was a dispute in front of cast and crew, much as the time in 1903 when the *Mrs. Jack* stage manager called out Fairbanks for his pranks in the presence of the whole company. If, as an unknown neophyte with everything to lose, he was willing to quit rather than endure such an indignity, it is probable that once at the top of the heap, he would be even more unwilling to back down under similar circumstances.

Dwan and Fairbanks would heal the breach within a few years—each needed the other more than he needed his pride. But as of

September 1918, Dwan signed an early termination letter with the Douglas Fairbanks Pictures Corporation.

The date of September is of note, for this was the month of the third and final draft registration for the war. All men aged eighteen to forty-five were eligible, and for the first time, Fairbanks fell into that category. He had already seen his production company go one by one in the earlier drafts: director Joseph Henabery to Fort McDowell, cameraman Harry Thorpe to the Aerial School of Photography, editor Billy Shea to Camp Kearny; even burly Bull Montana ended up training men at a submarine base.

Fairbanks had been active in getting his men placed, if possible, where they could do the most good. Joseph Henabery serves as a good example. Fairbanks worked to get Henabery his heart's desire of joining the photographic division; on July 2 he sent a telegram to Al Kaufman in DC:

> JOE HENABERY WHO HAS JUST SIGNED A CONTRACT WITH YOUR COMPANY, THE GOVERNMENT, IS VERY ANXIOUS TO GET INTO YOUR DEPARTMENT. BELIEVE ME, I COULD NOT RECOMMEND ANYBODY THAT I KNOW, IN ANY CAPACITY, MORE THAN I CAN RECOMMEND HENABERY. I WOULD ESTEEM IT A GREAT PERSONAL FAVOR IF YOU WILL DO YOUR UTMOST TO HELP HIM.

He also wrote Henabery a general letter of recommendation that was typically Fairbanksian in tone:

> Believe me, it is a tough job, this saying anything about anybody else, because when you do, you lay yourself open. I mean by this, that should I be wrong, I get the brunt of it. If the party you say is all right, is not all right, then you are not all right. But here is a man that I truly, at the moment, think I can go the limit on.
>
> I read "The Message From Garcia" by Hubbard and if I had known Mr. Joseph Henabery, I would say that it was an incident in his life, and I mean an incident. This may sound superlative, but anything Mr. Joseph Henabery says he can do, you may rest assured he can, and I mean this.

According to Douglas Fairbanks Jr. (who had, perhaps, little direct knowledge at the time), his father had been raring to go into active service since the war's inception. Frances Marion shares the recollection that Fairbanks was avid to stop playacting and go to war. Announcements began to appear in the papers: Doug was joining the Navy! No: Doug was joining the Marines!

No: Doug was going to Washington. "Dad's efforts to enlist in one of the nation's armed services were discouraged on the presidential level," wrote his son. He was of more service to the nation selling Liberty Bonds. Thus, Fairbanks halted *Arizona* production mid-shoot to leave for Washington, DC, and participate in the fourth Liberty Loan drive.

He could not have picked a worse time. The greatest medical holocaust in world history—the "Spanish" influenza—was about to reach its second, and most deadly, peak that autumn. Thirty percent of the world's population was infected, and 10 to 20 percent of those affected died—suddenly, rapidly, and horribly. Fever would develop, followed by bleeding from the nose, mouth, ears, and bowels. Secondary pneumonia would often ensue—a deadly outcome in those pre-antibiotic days. Those most vulnerable to the virus were young adults between twenty and forty—those who were traveling for the war, in the trenches, or aggregated in large, contagious groups at military camps. The death toll was greater than that of the war itself, killing more people in a year than the Black Death did in a century.

Places of public assembly were closed. Ten thousand movie theaters—80 percent of the total—were shuttered for a period of one week to two months, resulting in an estimated revenue loss of $40 million. All film production was shut down on the East Coast; in California, 60 percent of production was stopped for four weeks, and along with it salaries. Harold Lockwood, who had been Mary's leading man in *Tess of the Storm Country* and *Hearts Adrift*, died, as did scores of the less famous. *Variety* started devoting pages to "Epidemic Casualties," chronicling the deaths of chorus girls, studio technicians, drummers, bookkeepers, theater managers—all young, most with families dead or dying at the same time. Metro star Viola Dana was so ill from her case of influenza that she did not learn of her husband's death until after his funeral.

Among those threatened was Bennie Zeidman, Doug's publicity agent. They left Los Angeles together on October 8, heading to Chicago. The trip was made with scant notice: Treasury Secretary McAdoo wired Fairbanks the day before requesting that he join the fourth Liberty Loan drive—the same date that the Board of Health closed down all theaters in Chicago, where the pandemic was then at its peak. By the time they reached the Windy City, Zeidman was manifesting symptoms of the deadly disease. Fairbanks hustled his staggering friend to Michael Reese Hospital and submitted himself to a blood transfusion—a heroic but likely futile gesture. Blood transfusions, even from the hale and hearty Mr. Fairbanks, did little to stem the course of the illness. (That said, Bennie, after surviving a touch-and-go fortnight in the hospital, demonstrated himself to be the consummate professional by stoutly issuing a press release upon his discharge that credited his survival to his boss's "lifesaving" gesture.)

Bereft of his right-hand man, Doug proceeded east on his own. He repeated his fundraising speech-from-the-rear-platform at every stop, with no Mary or Charlie to share the honors. Upon arriving in Washington, he wrote Mary from the Willard Hotel: "I am positively sure that no man could love a woman more than I love you my beautiful—happiness—real happiness Dear is ours—just care for it—watch it and it will grow even more—the idea of counting the seconds or just existing till I see you is positively a truth—I really could be happy if only to look at your beautiful face—to watch your slender body as you moved if even I could not touch you or talk with you—I love you so."

He was getting closer to his goal of obtaining her. Beth had agreed to a settlement. It was generous: a $500,000 lump sum payment (in a year when the average family income was $1,500), with full custody of Junior. It represented a large portion of his savings. His gross income in 1917 was $470,000. War work kept his production down in 1918, and his income took a corresponding dip to $391,790.* The divorce was obtained quietly, in November. Beth was to gratify his reputation by remarrying a childhood sweetheart the following March, mere days after the decree became final. Mary's name was kept out of it.

And it was this that was foremost to him. As to the money and the risk to his career, he didn't care one whit. Any cost, in his mind, any risk, was worth it. Anita Loos—never an entirely reliable source—quoted him as saying, "Why shouldn't I divorce? Caesar did it. Napoleon did it."

Grandiose words, if true. And—almost—understandable, given what was happening in his life at that time. In a fundraising publicity stunt, he departed Washington for New York on October 16 on the US Mail plane, tagged as mail, Third Class. He went immediately to Wall Street, hoping to match a million-dollar subscription he had obtained from Barnard Baruch. He got it within five minutes. He visited every large brokerage house, and within short order had the total up to $3 million. From there he went to the Public Library on Fifth Avenue and raised several hundred thousand more from the assembled throng. "Mr. McAdoo then instructed the crowd in a 'yell' for Doug, which was given with a will," wrote a reporter. "'Douglas Fairbanks, Douglas Fairbanks, Douglas Fairbanks, Fighter! Fighter! Fighter!' yelled the crowd, in perfect unison, as Doug stood on his hands by way of appreciation."

The next day was even more intoxicating. A reporter wrote:

Fifth Avenue, the great highway of New York, known everywhere of all men who know any highway, uncovered something new under the sun on the afternoon of October 17. Even as this is being written the throngs are filling the famous thoroughfare at Forty-fourth street. The sounds of cheering and handclapping come down the avenue and turn into Forty-third street. . . . Doug Fairbanks is out there selling Liberty Bonds.

---

* An additional $1,872 came from sales of his books, enough to support an average family of four in 1918, but of little consequence in his overall finances.

This actor-man came up Fifth avenue as a himself parade—
and the town stopped work to see and hear. Fears of contracting
influenza through mixing in a crowd apparently deterred none
from jamming in around him. Escorting Doug were the full police
band and six mounted policemen, the latter in pairs. . . . This was
probably the first "one man parade" New York ever witnessed, for
Doug was the whole parade.

One wonders what the effect of this sort of adulation would be on
a normal psyche, much less that of one of God's own happy narcissists?

He took this heady show on the road, traveling back to Washington
and from there to Charlotte, Spartanburg, Greenville, Atlanta, New
Orleans, San Antonio, and finally Los Angeles. There he retuned to
Arizona—the film, not the state.

Albert Parker had appeared as the villain in *American Aristocracy* and
In Again, Out Again. He also had directed a number of films, including two with Gloria Swanson. It was as a director that he rejoined the
company in late August, directing *Sic 'em Sam*. He now took over and
completed the western. *Arizona* was ultimately to be a film without
a credited director—neither posters nor press books nor news articles
ever acknowledged one—leading some historians to mistakenly ascribe
direction of the film to Fairbanks himself.

If the film's reviews are to judge, no one would want to claim the
credit. "That Mr. Fairbanks is alone in the high-speed comedy field—a
class by himself, in fact—no one will question. But when it comes to
appearing in heavy drama, that is different. Then he is in shallow waters.
In the latter case, either the star's ability to entertain will suffer, or else
the dignity of the drama. In *Arizona*, both suffer," wrote the *Motion
Picture News*. Critics did not appreciate Fairbanks's interjection of his
own personality into that of a well-known character. "His performance
of Lieutenant Denton is not a characterization," grumbled the *Moving
Picture World*. "The athletic star has, as usual, put his own personality
into the picture, and acts Douglas Fairbanks with his customary life-like
perfection. A new breed of United States army officer is the result."

Most discouraging of all was a clipping that he kept in his personal scrapbook:

The truth about "Arizona" is so bad that we have to stop and say our prayers before we utter it. For though we went twice to see what a Fairbanks' performance of Lieutenant Denton would be like we never did see. It wasn't there. In its place was just a sort of smear across the film, as if an automobile had shot past and vanished. . . . Time was when he achieved with little conspicuous movement a great variety of expression; now he achieves movement all the time with no expression at all. Finally, to the mania for doing something every moment he has added the mania for doing it so fast that nobody can see what he does do.

Yet in the occasional seconds—all funereal—when his head is still enough for us to see his face, that face is crossed by none but the most obvious changes and few enough of those. The comic and serious elements of his Denton form not a blend but a sandwich. The seriousness he plays as solemnly as he would Othello; he does the lighter scenes as if he were a mechanical toy. And not only do the mechanical toy and Othello never blend into one, but no communication ever takes place between them; they live in absolutely separate air-tight boxes.

What to make of this? He did not know. There was no immediate change in the essential nature of his movies. But it was around the time of *Arizona* that he began to rethink his films. It would be understandable if after *Arizona* he had simply drawn the conclusion to stay away from the classics, to revert to form. After all, the three films prior to *Arizona* had been critical darlings. And critics aside, *Arizona* performed as well as the others at the box office.

But there was something in his nature that could not accept this. "Success, particularly if easily won, is a very dangerous quality which only a strong constitution can survive," he wrote years later. "I would rather be what the world calls a failure and be making vigorous motions to get along than the kind of success who has come to a stand-still." It was the negative clippings of *Arizona* that he kept, and, one suspects, it was the negative clippings of *Arizona* that he mulled over. If there was one thing that Douglas Fairbanks never did, it was stand still.

Neither did the country. The war was now over. It was not of long duration, but it had changed the American people. The calendar may have claimed that 1918 was turning into 1919, but as far as the national psyche was concerned, the Roaring Twenties were about to begin.

To many, of course, Fairbanks embodied America—its rash, bullyboy, jingoistic patriotism, its cheerful youth and strength and essential goodness. But the simple mirror analogy—Doug reflects America—does not work. Nor does the reverse: America reflects Doug. Rather, America in the decade ahead was to become a house of mirrors, with multiple characters—gangsters, bootleggers, chorines, ballplayers, movie stars, preachers, police—all bouncing about in the funhouse that was the Jazz Age.

He was to measure the pulse of the country as often as he was to set it, but in the end he was to transform his image in that decade to the one by which he is best known today: not a mere swashbuckler but *the* swashbuckler—the mold from which all others were cast.

But not quite yet. His first film after *Arizona* was *The Knickerbocker Buckaroo*, the last of the lost films. Albert Parker again directed. At first glance, this film appears to be cut of the classic cloth: an enthusiastic easterner (once again named Teddy) heads west on a program of planned generosity. ("Teddy decided to go out and do something for other folk, hoping to develop an interest in life thataway," declared the press book.) He swaps clothes with a hunted bandit and ends up in hoosegow, where he meets the beautiful heroine, who has been jailed on a trumped-up charge by a corrupt sheriff. He rescues the fair maiden and restores to her and her brother the fortune the sheriff was trying to steal. The film had new stunts, including one where Fairbanks pulled himself out of the window of a speeding train, ran along the top, jumped onto the swing-arm of the water feeder, and landed on the back of his horse.

Making his first film appearance was future superstar director William Wellman. Fairbanks had noticed him back in his theater days, when one of Doug's productions was having its Boston run. The teenage

Wellman, who, like Fairbanks, had been expelled from high school, was playing professional ice hockey. The handsome athlete caught Doug's attention, and they formed an acquaintance. When the war began and young Wellman joined the Lafayette Flying Corps, Fairbanks followed his exploits in the newspapers. He wired Wellman that when he returned, a job in Hollywood was waiting, at $250 a week. ("Hell, I would have committed murder for that kind of money," Wellman claimed later.) And while the second lead in a Fairbanks picture is a redoubtable start, Wellman discovered that he hated acting. He was, however, taken with directing. That he succeeded is clear: within ten years his production of *Wings* would win the first Oscar for best picture.

Also making a cameo in the film, as one of the clubmen at the East Coast setting, was Ted Reed, scenario editor and future Fairbanks director. Fairbanks met him on the third Liberty Loan drive, when Reed was a reporter for the *Detroit Free Press*. They struck up an immediate friendship, and Reed joined the actor on the remainder of the tour. From there Fairbanks offered him a job in Hollywood. He readily agreed, moving his wife and three children away from the land of cold winters and wartime coal rationing. He wrote titles and edited scripts, progressing to assistant director and, ultimately, director of Fairbanks's last silent modern-dress comedy, *The Nut*.

The Knickerbocker Buckaroo was different from all the other Artcraft releases, however. It was the only one to lose money. Paradoxically, it had the highest gross of any of Fairbanks's productions to date. The answer, of course, lay in the cost of production. Fairbanks spent a lot of money on this film. He built an "idealized Mexican village" on the side of a hill, rather than use the studio back lot. This alone cost $40,000. Five weeks were devoted to the script—normally the entire allotment of time for script and production. The press book, the official source of studio publicity, quotes John Fairbanks as saying *Knickerbocker* cost over $200,000—more than twice the normal cost for a Fairbanks Artcraft film. In fact, it cost almost $300,000, while the normal Artcraft productions hovered around the $150,000 mark. Although the returns were greater, the net result was that Fairbanks took a $50,000 loss on the production, his first as a producer.

The film with the greatest profit of the thirteen he filmed from January 1917 to April 1919 was *Mr. Fixit.* This is not because it had an impressive gross; rather, it was because it was filmed so quickly and cheaply in advance of his Liberty Loan tour. It would have been entirely understandable if he had reviewed the financials of his first baker's dozen of productions and elected to reduce costs, retain his formula, and increase profits. But he did not. He was to do the opposite: invest more in productions and ultimately change his formula. Moreover, he would change or, rather, enlarge his job description. By the time he finished filming *The Knickerbocker Buckaroo* in April 1919, he was well down another path. He was now going to not only produce but also distribute. He, his best friend Charlie Chaplin, his best girl Mary Pickford, and the industry's founding director, D. W. Griffith, joined to form United Artists.

8

United

THE ALEXANDRIA HOTEL WAS not yet thirteen years old in January 1919, but with its luxurious Palm Court ballroom, it was considered *the* destination for anyone visiting downtown Los Angeles. On the sixth of that month fourteen men of note entered its lobby.

They were all white and middle aged. Most were stout. Harry Schwalbe of Philadelphia was secretary-treasurer of the group. A toupee perched, hatlike, on his very, very broad forehead with the jaunty assurance of two gerbils kissing, countering the suggested gravitas of his pince-nez. Aaron J. Jones of Chicago bypassed a hairpiece in favor of a comb-over, which did little to distract from the uncomfortable fact that he was pop-eyed. Their president, Robert Lieber, was a graying gentleman from Indianapolis of serious mien and long upper lip. The Los Angeles representative, T. L. Tally, had the weathered face and walrus mustache of an aged cowboy. They constituted the board of directors of the First National Exhibitors Circuit, the second-most-powerful entity in the film business.

They were in town for a general convention but had arrived early. They spent the following three days huddled in Parlor A on the mezzanine floor, a guard at the door. The meeting, it was said, had been called suddenly, leaving the town, in the words of one wag, "full of rumors, conjectures and hand-woven and fancy embroidered guesswork." The organization, an association of independent, first-run

207

theater owners, had been founded a mere year and a half before. As with so many activities in the early days of motion picture history, the very existence of this company was the result of the actions of Mary Pickford. Her spring 1916 contract with Famous Players required Adolph Zukor to merge his firm with Jesse Lasky's production company to form Famous Players–Lasky. This combination then became the largest provider of films to the distributor known as Paramount—which it then acquired.

Because of this, Paramount stood as the eight-hundred-pound gorilla in the industry. Cecil B. DeMille and Jesse Lasky ran production, Hiram Abrams handled distribution, and Zukor ruled above all. In mid-1917 he was able to boast having Mary Pickford, Douglas Fairbanks, and star director D. W. Griffith under contract. Having Griffith meant having his stock company, which included Lillian and Dorothy Gish. In addition Paramount distributed the comedies of Roscoe "Fatty" Arbuckle, featuring an up-and-coming Buster Keaton, and had fan favorites such as handsome Wallace Reid under contract.

This near monopoly of top talent (only Chaplin was excluded, still releasing through Mutual in 1916 and 1917) meant that Zukor could jack up rates to exhibitors. Partially this was not his fault; stars such as Mary and Doug were essentially setting their own price, and their price was what the market could bear. Further, the cost of their productions was going up; while a Triangle Fairbanks feature cost less than $30,000 to produce in early 1916, an Artcraft Fairbanks film from 1917 and 1918 averaged over five times that amount. There was an essential tension of conflicting incentives: Producers such as Pickford and Fairbanks wanted to make longer and better films. Distributors such as Zukor and Paramount wanted a larger volume of films, inexpensively made. But needing the stars to fill the seats, Zukor signed the Pickfords and Fairbankses and simply passed on the extra costs to exhibitors, while managing his financial risk by block booking the rest of his studio product.

The more astute exhibitors saw where this was going. If Zukor had no reasonable competition on the distribution side, they were going to be in trouble.*

The answer seemed clear: the major exhibitors of first-run theaters throughout the country should combine and form their own distribution firm. This entity, in turn, would negotiate with the major stars. They still might pay top dollar, but they would enjoy the profits of distribution, instead of merely bearing the costs. It was perhaps inevitable that a competing entity would be formed, as the First National Exhibitors Circuit was, in the spring of 1917.

They started with a bang, snagging Charlie Chaplin in the summer of 1918. Chaplin was contracted to provide First National with eight two-reel comedies for a total of $1 million. Additional reels within a film (Chaplin had ambitions for three-reel and longer comedies) were to be compensated at the paltry rate of $15,000 a reel.

In November 1918, First National scored a second major coup, wooing Mary Pickford with a three-film contract. She was to receive $675,000 base pay, with 50 percent profit sharing and full authority on her films, from script to final cut. The separation from "Papa" Zukor was a monumental event in both of their lives. He had served as a father figure and mentor to her, while her films had been the cornerstone of his company. In her autobiography, Mary quotes a Zukor adviser: "Let her go to First National; I guarantee you it will deflate her swelled head, destroy First National, and bring her back to you on her knees."

But she was getting advice, too. Doug wrote her from Washington, pleased about the deal. "I am really very happy about Zukor because with the forming of your new company to produce you will have enough

---

* Companies such as Universal did not, in their minds, constitute reasonable competition: Carl Laemmle operated on a factory model, with no-name stars and modest production values. He did not yet have Erich von Stroheim and Lon Chaney to justify "super-productions." Metro, Fox, and Goldwyn were not yet major concerns. Triangle, without Griffith, Fairbanks, and Hart, was in its death throes.

worries," he wrote. "Again it argues my little sweetheart's value of which I am most proud."

Fairbanks's own contract with Artcraft and Zukor was coming up for renewal in February 1919. The trade magazines of the time indicated that Fairbanks was in as much demand as he had been in late 1916: "A dozen different representatives of film concerns are hanging around the Fairbanks studio endeavoring to secure his name to a contract," wrote *Variety* on January 15. But Chaplin recalled a darker picture. He had gone to the First National board that week to make a plea for additional per-reel compensation for longer comedies. He met a room full of cold shoulders. "Exhibitors were rugged merchants in those days," he wrote, "and to them films were merchandise costing so much a yard. . . . I might as well have been a lone factory worker asking General Motors for a raise." This confounded him. "I could not understand their attitude, as I was considered the biggest drawing card in the country."

Chaplin's brother Sydney put the finger on the rumors associated with the First National convention. Just what *were* the board members doing in L.A., anyway? Speculation was rampant. They were meeting to sign D. W. Griffith! (Griffith issued a denial.) They were planning to sign Douglas Fairbanks! (Fairbanks did not address this rumor directly.)

The most interesting—and, to the stars, troublesome—rumor of all was that First National was in town to vote on a merger, possibly with Paramount. This, as far as the producer-stars were concerned, would be disastrous. If First National and Paramount were to merge, all the major and midsize exhibitors would be tied up as neatly as a Christmas package with a silk ribbon—but there would be only empty stockings for the artists.

Anxious to determine if the rumors had a basis in fact, Chaplin and Fairbanks agreed to engage the Pinkerton Detective Agency to get to the bottom of the matter. Chaplin's account of hiring "a very clever girl, smart and attractive-looking" who engaged the interests of a major production executive, "a glib braggart in an esurient state of libido,"* sounds too theatrically perfect to be true. But Chaplin biographer David Robinson, with full access to the actor's papers, was able to document that this is indeed what happened, even sharing the typed reports of "Operator 8."†

The report, according to Chaplin was sobering. "[Zukor] and his associates were forming a forty-million-dollar merger of all the producing companies and were sewing up every exhibitor in the United States with a five-year contract. He told her they intended putting the industry on a proper business basis, instead of having it run by a bunch of crazy actors getting astronomical salaries."

This would never do. Something would have to be done—but what?

One answer lay with Hiram Abrams, Adolph Zukor's head of distribution, and Benjamin "B. P." Schulberg, Zukor's publicist and personal assistant. Will Irwin's 1928 account is the closest we have to the events in question:

> From the first, the aggressive Abrams and the dominant Zukor worked badly in harness; by 1918 came friction so severe that it began to burn out the bearings. Zukor took the extreme course: he discharged Abrams. Now Schulberg, as he says himself, is a one-man dog. In old days he had been fiercely loyal to Zukor; serving under Abrams, he transferred his allegiance. He sat half that night in Zukor's house, quarrelling with the Boss.
>
> "If he goes, I go," he said.
>
> "Very well, Ben," replied Zukor, at the end of his persuasiveness, "but you'll come back some day."
>
> . . . Burning for eminence and revenge, Schulberg and Abrams sat for days analyzing the motion-picture business in its larger

---

* Chaplin, who had been raised in London workhouses and grinding poverty, had the self-educated man's pride in a hard-won vocabulary.

† Evidently there were multiple agents employed to shadow and eavesdrop on the likes of Samuel Goldwyn, Adolph Zukor, and the First National board. According to Robinson, the accounts of both Operator 8 and Operator 5 "read like operetta."

aspects, looking for an opening. "And we found one as wide as the Grand Cañon," said Schulberg.

The idea? United Artists (UA)—a company that would be owned by the stars and which would serve as the distribution arm for their production companies. The pair sat up through the night, typing up a manifesto entitled "Eighty-Nine Reasons for United Artists." They then bundled up their respective families, loaded them on a westbound train, and headed to Los Angeles—the same week as the First National convention was meeting. They had five superstars in mind; the "Big Five," as they termed them, were D. W. Griffith, Charlie Chaplin, Douglas Fairbanks, Mary Pickford, and William S. Hart, the western star who followed Fairbanks's path from Triangle to Paramount.

Young Budd Schulberg was not yet five years old when his father walked the family into the lobby of the Alexandria Hotel, but he remembered the moment. "How vast and grand it seemed," he recalled. "From that crowded, overly ornate lobby sprang the new spirit of the new industry being born before our eyes."

Schulberg and Abrams set their sights on Chaplin first, "because he was the best combination of artist and money man," according to the younger Schulberg, whose father clearly had not dealt extensively with Charlotte Pickford. Chaplin was more than happy to meet with two former Paramount executives. The idea intrigued him, and he brought it to Pickford and Fairbanks. (Schulberg approached Griffith separately, hinting at the dynamic that would serve Griffith ill for the next decade. The aloof "Master" was always somewhat of a lone child in this particular sandbox.)

It was around the time of this meeting—whether just before or just after is unclear—that the group of entertainers staged a little guerrilla theater. "We decided that the night before their convention we would appear together in the main dining room of the Alexandria Hotel for dinner, and then make an announcement to the press," wrote Chaplin.

On that night Mary Pickford, D.W. Griffith, W.S. Hart, Douglas Fairbanks and myself sat at a table in the main dining room. The effect was electric. J.D. Williams unsuspectingly came in for dinner first, saw us, then hurried out again. One after another the producers came to the entrance, took a look, then hurried out, while we sat talking big business and marking the tablecloth with astronomical figures. Whenever one of the producers appeared in the dining room, Douglas would suddenly talk a lot of nonsense. "The cabbages on the peanuts and the groceries on the pork carry a great deal of weight these days," he would say. Griffith and Bill Hart thought he had gone mad.

Private detectives, secret (and not-so-secret) meetings—Fairbanks was having the time of his life. These were the sorts of shenanigans that appealed to the perpetual boy in him. Reporter A. H. Giebler wrote of visiting Fairbanks at his studio when the negotiations were at their peak: "Doug was sizzling around like a bottle of old-fashioned soda pop." But Fairbanks could be serious, as well. When a meeting was scheduled at Mary Pickford's residence (she had come down with influenza), he demonstrated the essential duality of his nature. "While our lawyers haggled out legal technicalities, he would cut capers like a schoolboy," recalled Chaplin, "but when reading the articles of incorporation he never missed a comma."

Certainly there were forces attempting to woo them back to Paramount, or to First National. "One night I was up against Zukor," Fairbanks recalled. "When he had me going and I felt like crying, I would go out into the hall and read over my copy of the Eighty-nine Reasons until I got a grip on myself." Hart was ultimately to decide against the risk and remain with Paramount.

The "Eighty-nine Reasons" may have helped Fairbanks hold firm against the blandishments of Adolph Zukor, but in the end they were not to serve Hiram Abrams significantly or B. P. Shulberg at all. Fairbanks and his fellow artists felt that Abrams and Schulberg's request of 20 percent ownership for the idea was excessive. Abrams was granted

2 percent, as the resident expert in distribution, and offered the position of general manager. Schulberg was offered a salaried position as assistant general manager—but no ownership. Stunned, he accepted, but by April he had resigned.*

For president of the new entity, Fairbanks wanted his friend from the bond drives, William Gibbs McAdoo. McAdoo was not only head of the Department of the Treasury and director general of railroads but also President Wilson's son-in-law. He, with his wife and daughter, was wintering in Santa Barbara at the time. Doug kept the bread of his friendships with the rich and powerful carefully buttered.[†] He had met McAdoo at the train station with a brass band and, hearing that the former secretary was fond of mountaineering, sent him two climbing ponies.

The national prestige, the links to the very office of the presidency—these seemed to Fairbanks's mind more appropriate attributes for the leadership of the company handling the four top luminaries in the industry. After all, Fairbanks reasoned, B. P. Schulberg had been merely a publicist and personal assistant, whereas McAdoo had run the railroads during the Great War. To say nothing of the Treasury Department, saving the national economy when European nations were liquidating their American assets and converting them to gold. "The railroads and the treasury were at best only a two-star combination," opined *Photoplay*, "but now he has four." McAdoo, in the end, did not accept the presidency of the organization but proposed Oscar Price, his former assistant, assuming for himself the position of general counsel.

---

* Whether Schulberg truly was part of the creation of the concept of the company will never be definitively known. Schulberg sued Abrams for his share of the commissions in 1920, but the case was settled out of court for what Schulberg's son declared to be a very modest sum in 1922. Cap O'Brien, who represented not only Pickford and Fairbanks but also Abrams in this matter, noted in private correspondence: "Schulberg has the tendency of writing, talking, and claiming too much." He was ultimately to return to Adolph Zukor and to help discover and promote such luminaries as Clara Bow and Gary Cooper.

† For example, he was to send Woodrow Wilson a film projector after the latter suffered a stroke. It was used in the East Room, thus creating the first White House movie theater.

Still, the association of McAdoo's name removed any raffish associations with the endeavor. "McAdoo's reported connection with the industry is entirely consistent with my conception of the dignity and importance of the business," wired one exhibitor to *Wid's Daily* in early February. "Fifteen thousand motion pictures theaters could elect a Presidential Ticket composed of McAdoo and Fairbanks."

The United Artists train picked up speed. *Variety* provided the first hints on January 24, writing of the rumors: "The air is filled with bombs and when the stars' barrage is lifted, there may be an explosion that will rock the film world." The following day, the Big Five announced their plan to form United Artists: "We believe this step necessary to protect ourselves, as well as the exhibitors who play our pictures, from injurious combinations between the various producing concerns now operating and to protect the exhibitor from having poor pictures forced upon him."

This was a bombshell indeed. It produced two schools of thought, the first embodied best by the famous phrase "The inmates have taken over the asylum." A sizable number refused to believe that any group of artists could pull off such an endeavor. "There is certain to be tremendous jealousy in any 'all star' combination and no one believes the film stars will stick together," wrote a *Variety* reporter. Samuel Goldwyn, for one, was openly disgusted. "The star is the cause of more trouble in this business than all other troubles combined," he said. Others speculated that the founders' existing contracts would make a new company impossible to get off the ground. Pickford owed First National three films and Chaplin owed the company five, while Griffith owed Zukor two. Further, each one's current contract expired at a different time.

The second school of thought ran along the lines of *How can I get on this gravy train?* There were reports (only some of which were denied) that Henry Ford, J. P. Morgan, and the du Pont family were all interested in providing capital investment. William Randolph Hearst telegrammed each of the owners, trying to land distribution rights through his International Film Service Company. Indeed, Chaplin asserted that the dinner and public announcement in late January had simply been a ploy, that there had been no real intention of forming a distribution firm.

They had simply hoped to scare the major combines from merging. But the positive reaction caused them to, in essence, call their own bluff.*

It is unlikely that Fairbanks saw it as a ploy. When the agreements were signed, he defined the event to the press as "legalizing their emotions."

The memorandum of agreement was signed on January 15, 1919, and the full articles on February 5. The signing was restaged on February 6 at the Chaplin studio, on a set dressed to look like an office. The four were then filmed by photographers outside Griffith's studio, yielding a series of images that are now irrevocably linked to the organization: Chaplin in tramp costume; Griffith in a snappy fedora and tweeds; Mary with her curls pinned up, a fur collar and pearls speaking to quiet wealth; Doug in a light-colored double-breasted suit.† While Griffith stood back and maintained his dignity, Doug lifted Charlie in the air repeatedly for the cameras. Occasionally Mary stood at his side as he lifted Chaplin. They looked like a quartet at the peak of success. But they were not. Improbably—and happily—each had greater heights to scale, although Griffith would be the first to take the painful tumble into the depths. In fact, even at this point, his position was the most tenuous.

For one thing, the United Artists were funding themselves. Each of the four was to subscribe to one thousand shares of stock at one hundred dollars per share to cover start-up costs—20 percent of this sum due every month for the first five months.‡ Second, there would no longer be a Harry Aitken (unreliable though he may have been) or an Adolph Zukor to finance their films. Each would have to fund their productions

---

* This is hard to confirm. Griffith's attempts at an autobiography never got past 1915, and Fairbanks never lived to contemplate writing his. Pickford makes no mention of such reasoning, but her account of the formation of United Artists is very abbreviated.

† The makeup man at the Chaplin studio was used to slapping whiteface on clowns, not foundation on leading men. Fairbanks looks as pale as any specter in these photographs, with a clear makeup line on his neck.

‡ Initially, each founder had a 20 percent share, with McAdoo owning the final fifth. He sold out his share within a year, however.

with monies earned on the returns of prior films—a process that often took one to three years.

A mere week after signing the agreement in principle to cofound UA, Griffith signed a three-picture deal with First National. "Movie producers are liars," he told columnist Karl Kitchen at this time, and, given his prior denials, his partners could hardly beg to differ. This could not have been anything less than exasperating to them. They were reaching into their own coffers for the seed money to fund their stock and their future productions. Griffith could not. Lacking the resources, he increased his outside commitment from two films to five, significantly delaying his ability to contribute films to the fledgling firm.

And motion pictures were what they needed—a minimum, they figured, of twelve a year (three from each). Why twelve, when organizations such as Universal and Paramount were releasing a new movie to exhibitors weekly?

They reasoned that the films produced by these top artists had broken the model of how long a motion picture would stay in a theater. In the earliest days, to keep a film in a theater more than half a week would be akin, today, to running the same episode of the same television show nightly for a month. *The Birth of a Nation* was the most famous exception, but it was not issued as part of a major studio release schedule but instead was exhibited—depending on the region of the country—on either a "road show" or a state's rights basis. The typical prewar release schedule was seen with Triangle: In 1915 a Fairbanks film with a Keystone short was booked in a Triangle theater for three days—whether it packed the house to the rafters or the hall was empty. The Thomas Ince/Kay Bee films would fill the other three days. (Blue laws kept most theaters shuttered on Sundays.) This was the case even with theaters in the largest cities, such as New York. But this would change. By the time Fairbanks's third Artcraft film, *Down to Earth*, was released, his popularity was such that *Variety* reported that the 81st Street Theatre in Manhattan was going to abandon its "split-week" practice and run the film for an entire week. As his reputation grew, and with it audience affections, the Artcraft films continued to push the envelope of staying power, progressing to two weeks and—by the time *A Modern Musketeer* hit the screens—to three. The same was happening with the Pickford Artcrafts. This spoke, of course, to their tremendous popularity. The norm for other films in 1919 was still one week.

This was something that Doug and Mary dearly wanted. They were, after all, participating in profit sharing on these films. The longer they could stay in a theater, the better. The flip side of this coin was apparent to both: the better they could make the films—the higher production values, the better script, the better (in the case of Fairbanks) stunts—the longer the booking and the higher the profit.

The major studios were built on the opposite model. The bill was to change weekly. They wanted to fill the houses for that week, but they didn't want the film to linger more than a week and drive the audiences who had already seen it to a theater they didn't own. Vertical integration—the combination of production, distribution, and exhibition—created an incentive to make midpriced films.

Accordingly, the UA founders took a public and vociferous stance against block booking, but not for the same reasons as two years prior. At that point they hadn't wanted their returns to be diluted by the prices exhibitors were forced to pay for lesser films in order to get theirs. Now the reasoning was that they didn't want the exhibitor to be precommitted to a schedule of films, the most recent of which would bump their latest endeavor out of theaters prematurely.

They found themselves walking a tightrope. They needed to have product, but, except for Fairbanks, no one would be able to produce a film immediately. Even a Douglas Fairbanks could not expect to make a film in January and February 1919 and have it still be in theaters nine months later, when his partners might conceivably contribute to the endeavor. (Not even the most avidly optimistic film executive could have predicted in 1919 that a mere four years later Fairbanks's *Robin Hood* would stay at some theaters for six months and more.) Further, even if Doug had a film ready immediately, the organization had no infrastructure. There was no distribution network, no exhibitors signed up, no contracts with lithographers for posters—not even an office with a phone number. And unless he was going to release a film through Zukor, he didn't even have a studio to work in.

Thus it was that although his contract with Artcraft/Paramount ended in February 1919, Fairbanks went on to film and release *The Knickerbocker Buckaroo* through Artcraft later that year. It was distributed as a "special"—not a programmed release. At seven reels, it was two reels longer than his norm. Zukor was able to claim bragging rights to Fairbanks for another three-quarters of a year, and Fairbanks bought time. Technically, Zukor might have claimed that Fairbanks failed to deliver the eight films a year that his contract had required (*Knickerbocker* was the fifth feature to be released during the second year of his contract), but he could hardly do so without being unpatriotic, with so much of Fairbanks's time occupied in war-related work during 1918. In addition, the volume of government-requested short films that he produced extended beyond the Liberty and Victory Loan drives. In January—that same, busy January that saw the birth of United Artists—Fairbanks was tied up making morale films for Uncle Sam.

"[The War Department] laid down four principles for my guidance and told me to get busy," Fairbanks said. "These principles are 'purity of purpose,' 'cheerfulness,' 'steadfastness' and 'willingness to sacrifice.' That's what they gave me to work on, and it's *all* they gave me to work on." He and his team were understandably stumped at first. "I didn't see how on earth I was going to make a picture out of that," he said.

Finally, the idea came for an allegorical film ("It isn't named yet, but it will be finished within a week") about the tree of Democracy:

We open with Democracy, a young tree, sheltered and tended by Washington, and we show what our forefathers did that Liberty might live. They're sure to like that, and it's a good thing for all of us to remember just now. And then we go on to the time when the tree, a sturdy sapling now, is in danger from winds from the South and the North, which threaten to rend it. Lincoln hedged it about and saved it. Then we work in the idea of steadfastness, the principle that had its finest demonstration in the "Message to

Garcia."* The tree of Democracy is established and deep rooted by this time, ready to afford shelter to weaker, needy brethren.

And at last we show the tree grown to its full height and full of fruit. It's a castor bean tree, this time, and Uncle Sam is forcing the beans, plenty of them, down the throat of the Kaiser, for his own good.

This curious little film—reportedly a full feature—may or may not have included Fairbanks. It is probable that he made an appearance (likely the fellow shoving the castor beans down the Kaiser's throat), but at this point it is unknown. The film—whatever it was named—is, as with the other Fairbanks films issued on behalf of the government, lost. Still, it is evident that Fairbanks used his final months at the Famous Players–Lasky studios to full effect.

By March, he had found a new home for his production facilities, leasing the Clune studio at the corner of Melrose and Bronson in Los Angeles, with occupancy to begin in the first week of April. The fifteen-acre property required significant improvements—an indoor stage, an administration building, a carpenter shop—all of which prudent John Fairbanks negotiated for Clune to provide.

And as he prepared his first release for United Artists, Douglas Fairbanks again was working with Uncle Sam as his copilot. *His Majesty the American* was scripted and directed by Joseph Henabery, who, along with cameraman Victor Fleming, had recently returned from the war. "Doug promised to include in his next release some favorable propaganda in behalf of President Wilson's League of Nations idea, which

---

* Modern readers are unlikely to be familiar with the "Message to Garcia," an allusion Fairbanks used not only in this film but also in recommending Joseph Henabery to the military higher-ups. It was a reference to an incident in the Spanish-American War, in which a heroic captain brought a message from President McKinley to a rebel leader. The story was published in booklet form and was generally known and wildly popular, with over forty million copies in circulation. The phrase, which is reportedly still in use in some military circles, came to mean the taking of initiative above and beyond the norm, a characteristic that Fairbanks associated, of course, with his young country.

was hailed as world lifesaver," Henabery recalled. "Doug wanted me to write a story that would incorporate some of the President's ideas in the upcoming picture."

Combining an administration's political agenda in an adventure-comedy was a challenge. "The writing job was no easy one," groused Henabery. "The Government wanted some emphasis given to each of Wilson's proposed Fourteen Points. The danger was that propaganda could easily overburden the story, unless great care was taken to weave it in subtly."

Here we are on curious ground. The marriage of Hollywood and Washington is something that is generally acknowledged during wartime. But the ready agreement to promote a particular administration's peacetime agenda sets an interesting and possibly dangerous precedent. But Fairbanks, whether intoxicated by his proximity to the halls of power or simply from a form of carryover patriotism, seemed to have no qualms on the topic. The Government (capital G) wanted him? He was there! And so poor Henabery lumbered on with the story, a Ruritanian romance very similar in tone and incident to *Hawthorne of the U.S.A.**

Once the script was finished and approved by the Feds—an eight-week process in total—production began with a will. Instead of maintaining the normal pace of shooting, in which players and director wait between camera setups and lighting changes, or even the accelerated program of having a second unit director, Fairbanks's team had three separate production crews working simultaneously. Each had its own pair of cameramen, set of electricians, and director. While Henabery was responsible for the overall direction, Arthur Rosson was directing the second unit, and young cameraman Victor Fleming got his directorial start on the third. Fairbanks would change costumes and rotate from set to set. In the words of a *Wid's* reporter: "As soon as he finishes with one bunch he jumps to another gang that is all set up and waiting for

---

* Curiously, George Barr McCutcheon, a novelist who specialized in "mythical kingdom" books, threatened a plagiarism suit. The author of *Hawthorne*, on the other hand, was never heard from.

him." With this pace, filming was completed by August, giving Henabery a full month for editing.

"Hard work and money went into making it," Henabery said of the film. Then political reality set in. "Wilson's Fourteen Points went down the drain, and I, in a way, went with the Fourteen Points. I could conceive of no way to salvage the picture without doing damage by the removal of material relating to the propaganda, but the job had to be done. Luckily, some excess material, for which there was no room in the first cut, was available."

The film was Fairbanks's longest release to date, at eight reels. It also reflects a slight retrenchment from *Knickerbocker* in terms of cost. Tax and accounting files document that *His Majesty* cost $254,017.07 total (including production, negative cost, and promotion), while *Knickerbocker* ran $292,442.26. It opened with a title card that read, over the names of the four founders: "It is our hope and desire to attain a standard of entertainment that will merit your approval and continued support." The title was revealed to be life-size, as Fairbanks burst through it with a somersault. Then, fists pumping, winking and smiling, he said, by way of intertitle: "Listen, Folks—they made me start the ball rolling. So here's the first picture. Gee whiz!—I hope you'll like it."

The opening titles introduce Bill Brooks, a "Fire-eating, Speed-loving, Space-annihilating, Excitement-hunting Thrill Hound." His adventure seeking is readily demonstrated in the first reel when he climbs three stories up the side of a blazing tenement building, swings on a rope to a window across a courtyard, and rescues a mother and three children. (He even obligingly returns to the burning room to recover a kitten.) He then heads to another part of town and breaks up a white slavery ring. Again the gambit of the six-room dollhouse cutout set was employed, with trap doors, windows, and stairs forming part of the action.

A reforming DA cleans up New York, which is unfortunate for our thrill-seeking hero, who is forced to pursue adventure in Mexico. Finally, a full half hour into the film, Fairbanks arrives in the mythical kingdom of Alaine. Here he rescues the king, falls in love with his beautiful ward, and discovers that he himself is heir to the throne. Ever the smiling American, he converts the country to a democracy.

The resulting film is a mishmash. It is intertitle-heavy—uncharacteristic for Fairbanks—with expensive sets but a badly wandering plot. There are some gratifying chases and stunts in the last twenty minutes, but the production was overlong and cried out for the tight directorial hand of an Allan Dwan. Contemporary critics recognized this; the *Motion Picture News* called it "another routine Douglas Fairbanks celluline cyclone. . . . The star dashes from mantel to balcony and from housetop to window-ledge with his customary dramatic power. In other words, *His Majesty the American* is just another Fairbanks comedy of the usual sort."

Henabery was equally scathing. "My feeling about that thing was always that it was a bunch of hash."

It scarcely mattered. Even a month before its release, the film was heavily booked, some towns having competing theater chains showing the film blocks apart, simultaneously. In New York City, the entire Fox circuit and entire Loew's circuit booked the film, and unprecedented three-week advance bookings were arranged in multiple cities. The Capitol Theatre in New York paid a record price in film rental—$7,000 a week, with a 50 percent interest on the gross over $35,000. Certainly, Fairbanks had reason to be pleased from a financial standpoint. The return to the Douglas Fairbanks Pictures Corporation was $579,894.53, yielding a net of $325,877.46, more than three times the return of his most profitable earlier film and six times the average return of the prior thirteen. Clearly, being a distributor had its benefits.

Still, he knew he could do better from an artistic standpoint. His next film, *When the Clouds Roll By*, would have no government input and was a dazzling return to form. It was the story of a comically superstitious young man who was slowly being driven mad by his evil-scientist neighbor. The most memorable and striking sequence of the film occurred in the first reel: the nightmare scene. Film historians have been lavish in handing credit to fledgling director Victor Fleming for this witty, surreal sequence, but they are mistaken. This section was shot by Joseph Henabery for *His Majesty the American*. The press book for *Majesty* referenced the "wild and delirious nightmare," including the slow-motion chase and the moment when Fairbanks entered a ballroom full of matrons clad only in his underwear. A correction slip had to be published and included with each *Majesty* press kit, urging exhibitors to eliminate any reference to the nightmare. Henabery's recollections were specific:

> The revolving room—that was my idea. I made this barrel-like thing, had the hawsers around it to revolve it so that when he was running on the ceiling he was really running on the floor. The camera was upside down.* It wasn't used because we had too much film. Another thing we had in that . . . where Bull Montana is socked in the nose and fell down and comes up again. . . . I had a counterweight on him so he was pivoted on the floor. You'd push him down—course he was aided by a wire—but the weight below would bring him right back up. In other words, Fairbanks couldn't knock him down.

A sharp eye will note the reproduction of the pajamas and the right side of the bedroom set from the first film to the second. The omission of the nightmare from *His Majesty* deprived Henabery of some rightful credit, but the sequence fits in splendidly with the story of *When the Clouds Roll By*.

The opening credits set the loopy tone—Fleming filmed the scenarist, himself, the cameramen, even Fairbanks with his favorite Alaskan malamute, Rex, to accompany the names on the titles. The intertitles followed suit. That which introduces Fairbanks's character reads:

> It is midnight along New York's water front. It is also midnight in the Wall Street district. However, this has nothing to do with our

---

* The revolving room innovation, where the set was an open cube that rotated much like a hamster wheel, created the illusion that Fairbanks was walking the walls and cutting capers on the ceiling. The effect has been famously reproduced twice since (without attribution)—in *Royal Wedding* with Fred Astaire and in certain shots in the modern thriller *Inception*.

story, except it is likewise midnight uptown where we first meet Daniel Boone Brown—an average young man.

Our tale proper opens with the eating of an onion—

The titles' backgrounds were painted by popular illustrator Henry Clive and were written by Thomas Geraghty. The issue of authorship came into brief contention shortly after the film's release. Louis Weadock was a newspaperman and short story writer who reportedly joined the scenario staff before *Clouds* was produced. He leaked a story to *Variety* that both he and Thomas Geraghty were "rather incensed over the fact that the employer-star failed to give them credit for having evolved what seems to be the greatest hit that Fairbanks has had in a year." This was met with a quick denial by United Artists.

> The story was the original idea of Douglas Fairbanks and the sce-nario was written by Tom Geraghty. Numerous articles have been published giving Louis Weadock mention as part author and as assistant in the screen preparation.
>
> Weadock, it is declared, was engaged by the Fairbanks orga-nization as an apprentice at a small salary, and was present at the studio during the making of the story. His ideas, however, did not come up to the standard required by Fairbanks and before the completion of the production he was removed from all affiliation with the company. He was not placed under a long term contract, as has been announced, and is not affiliated in any capacity with the Douglas Fairbanks organization.

This, for all intents and purposes, appeared to settle the hash of the disgruntled writer, who was not heard from again.*

Fairbanks pulled out all stops in the last reel of the film. Four enor-mous electric pumps drew more than a million gallons of water from the Sacramento River into an elevated reservoir in the Cascade Range. Once

---

* Possibly because his palm was appropriately greased. Fairbanks biographer Jeffrey Vance notes that Fairbanks paid Weadock $500 to settle a claim of libel.

released, the flood washed out the town, a convincing combination of miniatures and life-size buildings. For the postflood sequence, a flooded plain near Seal Beach was filled with trees, houses, and even a floating church (handy for the provision of the minister at the film's happy ending).

The film was a strong success. "If he had begun his United Artists' career with it he would have given that new connection a boost which *His Majesty the American* failed to impart," wrote the *Photoplay* critic. The returns were $531,418.18 on an investment of $256,681.65—a little less than *Majesty* but the second highest of any of his productions to date.

Tom Geraghty found himself sharing screenwriting credit on Fairbanks's next film, *The Mollycoddle*, despite the fact that the story was entirely his and an uncredited Doug's creation. The team was almost two months into production on the film when an author, Harold MacGrath, contacted the studio. He had published a story of that same title in a May 1913 issue of the *Saturday Evening Post*. Fairbanks, whose mania for everything Teddy had not diminished, did not want to lose the Rooseveltian turn of phrase for the title of his film, so he paid MacGrath $5,000 for full rights to his story. He wanted no more lawsuits along the lines of the one engendered by *The Americano*.

He worked to make it up to Geraghty, of whom he was genuinely fond. He took out a quarter-page ad in the trade papers, declaring:

DOUGLAS FAIRBANKS
Biggest production and best picture of his career
"THE MOLLYCODDLE"
SCENARIO BY
TOM. J. GERAGHTY
Suggested by Harold MacGrath's story

This feature is even better than
"WHEN THE CLOUDS ROLL BY"
By Douglas Fairbanks
Scenario by
TOM. J. GERAGHTY

This was the first (and likely only) time that a scenarist's name would be featured in a larger typeface than Fairbanks's own. He also brought Geraghty out to New York for the opening of *The Mollycoddle*, and he had Bennie Zeidman plant squibs in all the trades informing the world of Geraghty's trip, as author of the story.

The film was the tale of an American-born, English-raised fop who amuses a group of American tourists in Monte Carlo. They kidnap him as a joke, and he ultimately finds himself in Arizona, breaking up a diamond-smuggling ring being run by Wallace Beery. The film has charm and excitement to compete with *When the Clouds Roll By*, and the additional novelty of a short animated sequence, which explained graphically the villain's diamond-smuggling plot. Victor Fleming again took the helm, building a replica Monte Carlo and taking the entire cast and crew on location to a Hopi reservation to film Doug dancing with the natives. An avalanche provided the natural catastrophe that the plot required.

Production on *The Mollycoddle* began in late February 1920 with yachting scenes taken in San Francisco Bay. Filming was delayed by an injury that Fairbanks incurred on the Arizona location during the first week of March. A horse upon which he was vaulting startled and ran, leaving him to crash into the ground on both outstretched hands. He ended up back in Los Angeles, nursing two sprained wrists and a broken index finger on his right hand. Thus it was that the most noteworthy stunt of the film—a leap from the edge of a cliff onto the villain, who is perched high on a tree—was performed by stuntman Richard Talmadge.

Talmadge (born Silvio Metzetti) acknowledged to biographer Booton Herndon that he performed the leap in Fairbanks's place to keep the film on schedule. Fairbanks kept him on staff for his following three films: *The Mark of Zorro*, *The Nut*, and *The Three Musketeers*. That Talmadge trained Fairbanks in new techniques, everyone agrees. He would often perform a stunt repeatedly for his boss to study and perfect before Fairbanks would then execute it for the camera. But just how often he stood in for the star is up for debate.

Allan Dwan was adamant that in his films, at least, Fairbanks did all the stunts—with a caveat. "There just wasn't anyone in the world who could do things with such grace. . . . But that doesn't mean we were silly enough to risk tying up the completion of a picture, with all its expenses, by injuring the star. So there were plenty of times when it was just good sense to use a double or a stunt man. You don't think he was actually riding the horse in the jousting scenes in *Robin Hood*, do you?"

Costar Mary Astor recalled the use of a double in one shot in *Don Q, Son of Zorro*:

> He did almost all of his own stunts himself, except when the risk might mean an injury that would delay the picture.
>
> Once during the filming of *Don Q, Son of Zorro*, while he was watching his double do a jump from a wall onto a running horse, he said, "It's not good, he's too soon, he ought to swing out more." He stopped the camera and told his double, "Let me show you, Jim. Go on back to where the camera is. I'll show you, you've got to *lean* away from the wall, like this." And with everybody watching and no camera running, he did the whole stunt, and the crew and everybody laughed, and the double said, "Why don't I just go home?"

For most shots, it is reasonably simple to determine that it is indeed Fairbanks performing the stunt. He had a slight kyphosis, or curvature, of the spine at the base of his neck, which caused his head to tip forward at an abrupt angle. From the side and back, this yielded a slightly hunched appearance that makes his profile distinct, at least to the clinical eye. The vast majority of the time it is Fairbanks you see; and when it is not, it isn't because he was incapable of performing the stunt. It is because the director did not wish to risk the film's staying on schedule.

The Mollycoddle may have been the film that caused producer Fairbanks to rethink how hard to push star Fairbanks. He was hurt twice during the course of filming. In late April, the avalanche special effect was triggered prematurely, resulting in further injuries that held him up for another two weeks. The production dragged on "an unconscionably long time until the entire company were . . . sick to death of it," said featured ingénue Betty Bouton.

The injured hand and wrists caused aggravation not only to Fairbanks but also to his attorney, Cap O'Brien, who found himself doing battle with the IRS over the eighty-dollar deduction Fairbanks took on his tax return for the doctor's bill. "If a horse which Mr. Fairbanks was riding while engaged in his work should stumble and injure itself, there can be no question that the cost of such veterinarian attention as was necessary to restore the horse to workable condition might properly be deducted by Mr. Fairbanks as a business expense," he wrote in exasperation to the IRS, but to no avail.

Fairbanks had further aggravation in January: his estate suffered $20,000 worth of damage when a flaw in his chimney flue resulted in an early morning living room fire. The Beverly Hills volunteer fire squad arrived to find Fairbanks standing on a cabinet phonograph player, chopping at the ceiling with an axe, while Tom Geraghty and playwright Winchell Smith were busy with fire extinguishers. Several Remington paintings, as well as a piano, were damaged or destroyed. But Doug retained his sunny reputation: he sat the firemen down to an impromptu dinner in another part of the house after they had put out the flames. Perhaps he was cheerful because he knew he would soon be moving to his newest home—a former hunting lodge in Beverly Hills that he was in the process of revamping and expanding.* And he knew that he wouldn't be there alone for long. While he was on Summit Drive, urging the workmen on, bringing in studio arc lights so they could work into the night, Mary was in Nevada.

---

* Fairbanks bought the property on April 22, 1919, for $35,000. At the time of the purchase it was a six-room hunting lodge.

9

Love and Marriage

MARY HAD TRAVELED TO New York City in December 1919 to meet with Owen and her lawyers and negotiate for the divorce. Even this meeting, so necessary and hoped for, threw Fairbanks into fits of jealousy, as he wrote:

My own darling beautiful

Please dear when you close your eyes tonight know that you are my only love—my first and forever and ever—I will think constantly of you—and I am sure you will <u>feel</u> that I am yours alone. Oh Darling what wonderful happiness you have brought into my life. There has been a corresponding misery with it but that is necessary and I am sure when we work it out it will be a perfect union—my little <u>wife</u>—that seems so good to say—my own—just think to possess you—my angel. Why I am cold all over writing it—and if it were really so I think I should die—

Be a dear good girl while you are away—be careful about your sleep and food—<u>don't worry</u>—love me—come back soon—Good night—God bless and keep you for me—I love you so—

I am so <u>miserably</u> jealous.

Good night—I worship you—Douglas

Owen had finally set his price—$100,000—and an indignant Charlotte Pickford dug into the vaults and produced it. She then accompanied her daughter to Nevada in mid-February 1920, where on March 2, Mary swore before a judge in Minden County, Nevada, that Owen had been cruel to her, and that yes, she planned to live in Nevada for at least six months. "Mother has been suffering from rheumatism," she said, by way of explanation. The judge did not recognize Gladys M. Moore as anything but a "frail little matron who had just dried her eyes of the tears that flowed so copiously during her recital of her husband's desertion." He was reluctant to grant her a decree without alimony, which she steadfastly refused. "Do you think you will be able to earn your own living?" he asked incredulously, not realizing he was speaking to the highest paid woman in the world. She assured him she would. Immediately upon receiving her decree, she returned to Los Angeles.

The press swarmed about her. She was Catholic: wasn't she worried that she would be excommunicated upon remarriage? "Then I shall never be excommunicated," she replied. Did she not intend to marry that dashing Mr. Fairbanks? "That rumor is absurd," she declared. "My divorce does not signify that. I just wanted to be free—free as I have wanted to be for years."

Mr. Fairbanks, upon returning home with his broken finger, was asked about marrying Miss Pickford. He smiled. It was beautiful weather but bad for outdoor work, he replied. The question was repeated. The response: his hand hurt like blazes and he believed it was time for the doctor to put on a new dressing. A few more cycles of this and the reporter gave up.

But Mary was not to be free for long. Doug had been wheedling, begging, and threatening since the day of his divorce, and he wasn't going to be stopped now, even though she insisted that she should wait a year. He would have none of it. On Friday, March 26, he hosted a dinner party. Among the guests were Mary; R. S. "Cupid" Sparks, the local marriage license clerk; and the Reverend Mr. J. Whitcomb Brougher, a Baptist minister. Fairbanks posed a question to Mr. Sparks, who was understandably suspicious of being asked to dine with movie stars: could he issue a license but keep it secret for a few weeks?

"I had a hunch I might be asked for something in the license line when I was invited to the dinner, so I took along the necessary documents," he recalled later. "When they brought the subject up I said, 'I knew I'd get you two sometime.' And Fairbanks laughed. After I had made out the papers I said, 'Well, that's my masterpiece in marriage licenses. You can shoot me now. I never can stage anything better than this.'"

With the paperwork done, Doug, of course, wanted to be wed on the spot. But Mary vetoed this plan. It was a Friday; she wanted to be married on a Sunday. And she was dressed in black. Her first marriage had been conducted at a Jersey City clerk's office, in street garb. She wanted to be married in a white dress. Doug had waited this long—an eternity for his impulsive nature. He would wait two more days.

The culmination of his romantic yearnings finally came on Sunday, March 28. He was seen that day, clad in old golf clothing, watching the automobile races at the Los Angeles Speedway. He looked, one reporter wrote in hindsight, "far from the way a man usually looks who is to be married in a few hours to one of the most widely known women in the world." But at ten thirty that night, the wedding party met at 1331 West Fourth Street in Los Angeles, the home of the Reverend Brougher—who, for his pains, received $1,000 and the threat of having his name withdrawn from nomination at the election of officers at the Baptist Convention in Buffalo three months later.* Doug wore evening clothes. Mary wore a white tulle dress edged in apple green trim, with a single string of pearls. Both were reportedly nervous. Marjorie Daw, faithful friend and former costar to each, served as Mary's witness; Robert stood up for his brother. It was a double-ring ceremony. The reverend was asked to read from Ella's Bible and selected Ephesians 5:22–32. Charlotte was there, of course. Accounts vary as to the remainder of the guest list—some say Mary's brother, Jack, was present; some say Edward

* He survived censure by a vote of 699 to 422 and remained on the executive committee.

Knoblock, others Bennie Zeidman.* Dr. Henry Miles Cook, assistant pastor, also was on-site, presumably as pinch hitter. Mrs. Brougher happened to have her mother and son at hand.

Upon returning to the house at 1143 Summit Drive, soon to be irrevocably tagged "Pickfair," Douglas announced that the property was his wedding gift to his bride. The next day, Mary returned to work on the set of her current production, *Suds*, with cloth tape over her wedding ring. She fooled no one. The Sunday after the wedding, they held a reception at Pickfair to announce the happy news to friends. By April 1, word was out to the press: Douglas Fairbanks and Mary Pickford were married. The couple jointly held their breath and waited to see if their careers would grind to a halt.

Certainly the attorney general of the State of Nevada had something to say about the matter, filing suit that the Pickford-Moore divorce should be invalidated. After all, he huffed to any reporter within earshot, Mary Pickford, under oath, swore she intended to become a resident of Nevada, but within hours of getting her divorce, she returned to California and, within days, married a California resident. Furthermore, Owen Moore had conveniently been within a mile of the county seat, available to have papers served upon him. Something was rotten in Denmark—or at least in Minden County. Mary stoutly (albeit unconvincingly) denied all. There had been no collusion with Owen Moore to permit her to divorce! It was a coincidence that he was in Nevada! Certainly there had been no financial settlement between them!

Nevada had been the go-to site for fast, convenient divorces for years—director Allan Dwan and his wife had divorced by the same route, in the same county, in front of the same judge, shortly before. Everyone knew that the Nevada courts winked at the Californians' claims that

---

* Mary recalled that John Fairbanks stood in as best man, though most accounts (and the marriage certificate) claim it was Robert. Knoblock was not yet working for Fairbanks, and Bennie had recently resigned his position as publicist. Knoblock writes nothing in his memoirs about attending the wedding, making his presence less likely than that of Zeidman, who was along for portions of the honeymoon. Most contemporary accounts claim that Jack and sister Lottie learned of the marriage when the news broke in the press.

they had been, or were going to become, residents of the state for the required six months. Towns like Reno would, within a decade, make their bank on the divorce industry. This incident cemented the opinion of most of Hollywood. The attorney general, the town consensus ran, was simply grandstanding because he had a newsworthy celebrity upon whom to forge his reputation.

The governor of Nevada found his office deluged with telegrams supporting Pickford and demanding that he stop the investigation. Even Owen Moore chimed in: without his aid, the Nevada officials could prove nothing, he said. And *he* (figuratively patting his newly enriched pocket) "was not inclined to make trouble for his former wife."* To put an exclamation point on the sentence, Mary then had a reported "nervous collapse," leading to briefings and bulletins to the press in which sundry physicians and "nerve specialists" declared that she was resting comfortably, thank you very much. This, however, made her unavailable for interviews on the part of Nevada officials about the divorce investigation. "Her state of health forbids the slightest worry or annoyance," Doug said darkly to reporters.

Undaunted by lack of access, the attorney general filed a complaint almost sixty pages long, including Fairbanks in the conspiracy charges. Mary, no fool, hired Gavin McNab, the famed trial lawyer best known by history for his defense a few years later of Roscoe "Fatty" Arbuckle on manslaughter charges.

There were a few holdouts. Joseph Henabery recalled the moment when Fairbanks told him of his impending marriage. "I can't honestly say I was completely surprised, but the announcement shook me up, and I must have shown it. . . . I liked the existing Mrs. Fairbanks very much, and the whole situation made me unhappy," he recalled. Decid-

---

* He did, however, manage to create further inconvenient headlines for her by failing to pay his attorney's fees. Possibly he expected her to pick up the tab, which was an outrageous $15,000 (curiously, exactly 15 percent of the settlement, suggesting that Moore engaged them on commission). The attorney filed suit against Moore in July, putting Mary back in the headlines.

ing to retain his allegiance to Beth, who had a hand in getting him his first directing job, he quit the Fairbanks organization. He explained his reasons to Robert and John but not Douglas. "I don't think what Doug would say to me would make any difference, anyhow," he said over forty years later, "because this is the way I feel about it. . . . And he was quite disturbed about it when I quit because I had failed to live up to my agreement with him. And I felt that his brothers should have taken steps to thoroughly acquaint him with the fact that I had been in a—sort of over a barrel. I didn't want to make his troubles greater."

There were also brief and early rumblings on the part of the clergy. The Methodist Episcopal Church in Los Angeles issued what it termed a "White List" of motion picture actors—those sufficiently well behaved to merit the nickels and dimes of their congregation. Included in the list of the suitably virtuous were Wallace Reid (later to die of drug-abuse-related causes) and Roscoe "Fatty" Arbuckle, who was less than seventeen months from a scandal that would threaten the entire industry. Conspicuously absent were Fairbanks, Pickford, and the recently divorced Chaplin. *Variety* wrote a long and indignant editorial, decrying those who "are claiming certain sections of the Protestant church as their cloak and shield in their advance on a more or less defenseless woman who has brought happiness and charm into the lives, not of thousands, but literally of millions."

The public seemed to agree. Thousands of telegrams of congratulation poured in. *Photoplay* pointed out that Beth had helped proceedings immensely by remarrying a mere eight days after her divorce decree had been granted. "They're married now—let 'em alone!" the columnist wrote. "And we hope the matter will rest there and that Mary Pickford and Douglas Fairbanks may be permitted to have a real-life honeymoon that will last a long, long time."

Indeed, the couple planned their honeymoon to begin May 19, when they were finished with their current productions. Charlotte took ill, however, and Mary refused to leave her. Knowing better than to cross his new and redoubtable mother-in-law, Doug assented to the delay. Thus it was not until early June that they started their cross-country trek, stopping first at the remote reservation where Fairbanks had filmed the Hopi sequence for *The Mollycoddle*. As they arrived at the rail station in Holbrook, Arizona, one scribe set the scene:

> Except for a small coterie of thirty or forty friends, camera men, business managers and newspaper reporters from Los Angeles . . . the two honeymooners were practically unattended, as they got off the train. . . . Doug himself wore cream-colored riding breeches and high tanned riding boots, and a sort of blazer coat which combined the splendor of a Navajo rug and a California sunset. Mary wore a gray corduroy skirt, a white sweater and a small straw hat with a champagne-colored veil . . . Mrs. Pickford . . . might have been on her way to the Ritz.

The next day the caravan, complete with a print of the film and a projector, drove one hundred miles across the desert to the reservation schoolhouse. The nighttime screening went across well with the Hopi, until a recently deceased member of the tribe appeared on the screen. "A positive bellow of savage and strident sound rose from the audience . . . some of the more excited Hopis leaped to their feet and threw out their arms in wide, menacing gestures, which seemed distinctly to include the white members of the audience," wrote one nervous reporter.

The happy couple emerged from this incident unscathed, however, and continued their progress east. In Chicago, where they were obliged to change trains, they pulled a gentle prank on the hundreds of people who were hoping to catch a glimpse of them:

> They have only been married a few weeks and there they came pushing a baby cab. What was more to the point, there was a baby inside the cab.
>
> But before the tense situation reached the bursting point, a mild little woman stepped out from behind the famous "king and queen" of the "movies" and smilingly took the cab in hand.

Then the joke became apparent. Douglas and Mary simply had assisted baby's mother in alighting from the train by taking temporary charge of her infant.

"Somebody asked me if the baby was mine," said Mary, "and it gave me a regular heartache when I had to say no." But the wistful moment passed quickly. Doug had, by this time, donned a taxi-driver's cap and was calling, "Keb, sir? Taxi-any-part-of-the-city?" to the delighted crowd.

They advanced then to New York City, and the Ritz. There they held a press conference, complete with lemonade and ice cream for the reporters. He posed with Mary on the roof of the hotel, doing a handstand while she watched indulgently. They assured reporters that their marriage was the *real* thing. They had found absolute happiness. "It's great, simply *great* to be the happiest man in the world," said Mr. Fairbanks.

"He's been like that since I married him," added Mrs. Fairbanks. "He plays with all the kiddies on the train, slides down banisters in the hotels and is so youthfully happy that I feel like a kiddie myself." They smiled blissfully at each other, and the world smiled with them. They popped down to Washington for a day, to pay a call on the White House, and to have their passports issued. They were going abroad.

On June 12, they boarded the SS *Lapland* bound for Southampton, England. Upon their arrival a tugboat brought a load of photographers: "Men with cameras seemed to appear in the ship from nowhere," recalled Fairbanks. "They sprang out of the deck and down the masts." Planes flew low over the deck—one dropped a parachute with a message of welcome; another dropped roses. Not a single flower hit the deck; Fairbanks leaped and caught each one, to the delight of all present. Throngs surrounded them as they disembarked—a sign of what was to come. The boat train arrived at Waterloo Station, and the mob, correctly guessing that the car with the drawn shades contained the couple, swarmed the carriage. One observer, a trifle sardonically, captured the essence of the experience:

> Door opens. Mary appears, registering fright. Women seize her. Mary disappears in swaying mass. Doug jumps out. Places arm around her. Police drive back crowd. Mary again separated from husband by surging mob. Doug does football rush to reach her. Crowd third time rushes between them. Doug leapfrogs over backs of six cockneys. Once more rescues Mary. Repeats rescues twenty times before reaching taxi stand.

Humor aside, they encountered real danger from the loving mobs at a theatrical garden party on the Chelsea Hospital grounds. They were in an open car, and Mary made the mistake of extending her hand when someone in the crowd asked her to shake. "Immediately I felt it lock in an iron grasp," she recalled. "Then someone else grabbed my other hand, and two or three people reached for the rest of me. I was quietly but surely sliding over the back of the moving car, when Douglas turned his head and quickly lunged out for my ankles."

He won the tug-of-war and retrieved his terrified wife, but was then obliged to perch Mary on his shoulder as they emerged from the car. All the British papers published the photo the following day: Doug looking as worried and determined as in any of his movies, with Mary disheveled and frankly terrified. He staggered through the mob, balancing her and barely dodging a low-hanging branch that threatened to unseat her, finally reaching a tent populated by two elderly matrons and many pots of jam stacked for display. The mob soon made short work of this. "In no time at all we were all walking around in a sticky goo that seemed inches deep," Mary said. MARY HAD A LITTLE JAM, read one British headline.

Fairbanks tried to be politic about the incident. "At first, when I saw the 'entire British nation' advancing, I wondered what was up," he told a London paper a few weeks later. "It soon developed that the advance was friendly. All they wanted was to kiss Mary. I had to tell 'em that's my job."

The garden party experience drove her back to the Ritz to rest her jangled nerves, but Fairbanks remained supercharged. He headed to Soho Square for a private screening of newsreel footage taken onboard the *Lapland*. But getting there turned out to be a challenge, according to the *Daily Mail*:

> As the motor-car turned out into Piccadilly a young, bright-faced girl jumped on to the side of the car and said, "Take me with you, Douglas." He looked perturbed, but the motor-car was gaining way, and the girl got inside. She was panting with excitement and as she sat down beside him, she put her arm through his and explained that she was dying to act with him if he made any films in this country.
>
> Douglas was extremely diplomatic, but the girl was not to be so easily put off. "If you are so persistent all through your life," said Douglas with a smile, "Gee, you'll do great things." The girl dogged his footsteps into the private theatre. There trace was lost of her, but Douglas said he was certain that could not be the last of her.

The mobs were tremendous; from their hotel window they could see thousands. Words were inadequate to describe the phenomenon— this first demonstration of the worldwide fame that came with motion pictures. The British tried to find analogies. Why, these were greater crowds than ever seen for the Prince of Wales! It had never happened on this scale before, no, not with royalty, not even with Jenny Lind. No one had anticipated this; no one, perhaps could have. Movies were silent and intertitles were in the local language; everybody in the world felt that they knew, firsthand, DougandMary.

And DougandMary they were to be—or, more properly, Maryand-Doug, as her fame was of longer duration and quite arguably greater. The next fourteen years of their lives would find them inextricably linked in print and in the perception and the hearts of the public. They were the golden couple, or, to resort to the oft-quoted line from Alistair Cooke: "They were a living proof of America's chronic belief in happy endings."

The crowds drove them to the Isle of Wight, where a certain Lord Northcliffe offered succor.* Mary awoke the first morning, looked out the window, and discovered "the ten foot brick wall surrounding the cottage was black with people," all of whom had been sitting quietly since dawn. At the sight of Mary in her nightgown they applauded heartily, which woke Doug with a start. Fond though he was of the applause of thousands, it was disconcerting to hear it from his honeymoon bed.

They connected with scenarist Frances Marion and her new husband and went to Amsterdam. Marion recalled: "A welcoming committee met us with plans a yard long for 'Mr. and Mrs. Pickford.' Doug laughed, but his laughter was hollow. Mary's heart stood still; ghosts of her first unhappy marriage rose before her. Could another marriage survive if her career outshone her husband's?"

At the end of the day, that never turned out to be a problem. Fairbanks was the top male star internationally for most of the 1920s. It is rather like the second-wealthiest person in the world marrying the wealthiest. By the time one is in that stratosphere, differences are minor.† Or, cheerful and feverish collector of the rich, famous, and royal that he was—and this particular malady would not abate until his death—her marginally greater fame may have made her all the more desirable a prize. One can only speculate. This is not to say that jealousy was not an issue for him. It was a profound issue, and a significant character flaw. But it played out in other ways. In fact it would rear its ugly head at their next destination.

---

* In her autobiography, Pickford recalled the visit to the Isle of Wight as preceding the disastrous garden party. Contemporary accounts reverse the order.

† There were only two accounts to ever suggest that Fairbanks was jealous of Pickford's greater fame: the Frances Marion anecdote described here and an Anita Loos account that Fairbanks once asked her at a premiere if the cheering was louder for Mary than it was for him. Loos, as already discussed, had an axe to grind with her former boss. Also, she was not attending premieres with Fairbanks when he was publicly escorting Pickford.

After renting a yacht and sailing among fishing villages in Holland, the couple drove to Germany, on the theory that, their films not having been seen there throughout the Great War, they would be unrecognized. They were correct. Mary recalled:

> After a day of shopping and sight-seeing, during which we did not catch a single flash of recognition on anyone's face, Douglas asked me: "Frankly, Mary, how do you feel about it? Do you like being left alone?"
>
> And I said, "I definitely do not, Douglas. Let's go some place where we are known. I've had enough obscurity for a lifetime."
>
> I'm afraid we were already becoming spoiled.

They advanced to American-occupied Coblenz, where they were gratified by being recognized by one and all. They were quartered in a German home and invited to join the troops at a Fourth of July dance. Here is where the trouble began. Fairbanks, on their wedding night, had extracted a pledge from his bride: "I don't expect any 'twosing' with anyone but me at dinner tables, in theaters, or on dance floors. Have I your word?"

She gave it. Unfortunately, she also gave her hand that night to the commanding general for the first dance. Fairbanks seethed, his ungovernable jealousy refusing to permit speech. At the evening's end, he walked her to the door of their borrowed lodgings, then turned on his heel and stalked off into the night. She was alone for only an hour, and he was apologetic upon his return, but it was a very long hour for a woman who had been so prominent in anti-German propaganda. She was terrified. She never made that mistake—if mistake it was—again. Princes and dukes might ask her to dance, but for the next decade she would dance with no one but Douglas. She adopted the party line with the press, saying, "Douglas doesn't like it [dancing], and I think it is rather silly myself. . . . A lot of foolish flirtations start. I suppose Douglas is a bit jealous; most brunettes are. As for me," she added, "I am a blonde."

Germany was followed by a rail trip to Switzerland. Here Fairbanks learned that their train did not offer private sleeping quarters:

> Our tickets for Basle had been purchased with the assurance that we would be provided with sleeping accommodations on the train. And we were, only the accommodations were what is known as "couchettes." Three persons occupy each compartment and of course they sleep with their clothes on.
>
> If we had had the entire compartment it wouldn't have been so bad, but we found a long-bearded Frenchman on one of the "couchettes" when we boarded the train, and forgetting that he might be able to understand English, Mary and I exchanged some heartfelt views on railroad management in France. When we concluded the Frenchman explained in excellent English that he understood our predicament and with true Gallic politeness offered to give up his place and stand in the corridor of the car. Naturally we would not hear of that and after we had apologized for our tactless remarks, we took our respective places on the "couchettes" for the night. But Mary didn't sleep a wink and I dreamed of wagon loads of long whiskers.

Upon arrival in Lucerne, they had no more than checked into their lodgings before he was off. He returned, according to Mary, "in a brand-new car, driven by a paragon of a chauffeur immaculately clothed in a perfect-fitting uniform. In one brief hour and a half, Douglas had purchased the car, secured all the accessories, engaged the chauffeur, had him measured for the uniform he wore . . . 'Such a thing never happened before in Switzerland,' gasped our landlord. 'It is a record. Ach Gott! You move just like your pictures.'"

They drove to Italy, where he was delighted to learn that he was known as "Lampo"—the Italian word for lightning. In fact, their guide made such a fuss over Fairbanks that he went out of his way to point out that Mary was not just equally but, in fact, *more* famous. "*Si, si,* but of course," replied the guide. "The name of Maria Pinkerton is known all over Italy." Delighted, Doug called her "Maria Pinkerton" for the rest of the honeymoon. In Venice they took a motorboat for an impromptu late-night visit to an American cruiser lying in the Adriatic, astonishing the starstruck sentry at the gangplank, who reportedly exclaimed, "'Ully gee! Douglas and Mary!" Their whirlwind tour continued in Florence and Rome, followed by the French Riviera, then Paris—reportedly a small shock to the essentially conservative Fairbanks. "Some of the things women wear abroad give you the feeling of being lost on a forest of September morns," he said. "Paris is no place for a married man to take his wife on a honeymoon. I was shocked the first day."* A visit to a French open market resulted in another fan crush. Mary was obliged to be rescued by some helpful butchers, who scooped her up in their beefy arms and threw her into a nearby meat cage.

They sailed for home on the *Olympic*. Their arrival on July 29 demonstrated that New Yorkers weren't going to let London get the best of *them*. Competing bands struck up songs as a welcoming committee of luminaries found themselves overwhelmed by the thousands of ordinary citizens who surged through the police line and surrounded the couple. Mounted reinforcements were required to get them into a waiting car. A procession headed by six motorcycle police progressed to the Ritz. Mary's personal maid at the time recalled the heady day:

> Those marvelous memories—when in 1920 the whole population of New York City went wild, on their return from their Honeymoon!
>
> Thousands and thousands of people, greeting them on the Dock, police unable to hold back the maddening crowd, cordoned off, and leaving a tiny lane to forge through the throng! I was hanging onto Mr. Fairbanks, who in turn piloted Mrs. Fairbanks a step ahead of him!

---

* This might, of course, be a case of a man who was being coy. He certainly did not have that complaint upon his first visit to the City of Lights.

My dress was toren [*sic*] and one of my earrings pulled off—a human, mad crowd, mad for joy to greet the greatest lovers the world has ever known!

Driving up 5th Ave, to the Ritz, traffic was stopped—sirens shrilled—16 motorcycle cops escort*—3 huge sightseeing busses crowded with bands playing—confetti strewn from all the 5th Ave windows—for it was a New York Holy Day,[†] for Mr. and Mrs. Fairbanks.

Yes! How proud I was, sitting in the cariage [*sic*] with Mrs. Fairbanks, Mr. Fairbanks sitting atop the hood, 6-8 newspaper men hanging with their teeth on the running board.

Photographs capture the moment: the car is pulled up to the Ritz to release its precious cargo. Mary, in a white Jeanne Lanvin dress and hat, her kid gloves halfway up her forearms, is standing in the rear of the open, flag-draped roadster. She is waving—not the restrained "queen's wave," where the back of the hand faces the crowd, but palm up and out, as if she would grasp them all if she could. Douglas is on the running board by her side, his left arm in perfect parallel to hers, holding aloft his straw boater. The July sunshine is beaming on them as they bask in it, and in the warmth of the adoration around them. They are—remarkably—both exultant and relaxed. They have gambled everything, their reputations, their fame, even their careers, to be together. They have gambled, doubled down, and won.

Their marriage would assume, in a way, biblical proportions, at least in the sense of Pharaoh's dreams of kine and corn. There would be seven rich years, seven years in which everything went from good to better, seven years of success and acclaim and gratification of every wish. Then would come the seven lean years—the emotional and career famine, seven years of follies and slow failure.

---

* Contemporary newspaper accounts give the motorcycle count at six. In the excitement of the moment, it probably felt like six hundred to Madam Bodamere.

† The good lady probably meant "holiday," but it can be argued that with the worship of celebrity coming to full bloom, she may have had it right, at that.

Fairbanks did not have the wisdom of a Joseph, did not know how to store the corn from the years of plenty to carry them through the years of fasting. This is not literal—there was never to be any shortage of money for either husband or wife. But they would spend their emotional capital, and when the hard times came, they found that their prior fame and success ill equipped them for the storms ahead.

But in July 1920 there was only sunshine.

10

"Having Made Sure I Was Wrong, I Went Ahead"

THE COUPLE LINGERED IN New York City long enough to enjoy a Friars Club dinner in their honor, and to see themselves portrayed in a Ziegfeld Follies number, before boarding a westbound train for home.

It was on this return trip that Doug finally read a story that his team had recommended. Mary, ever inclined to do homework, even when it wasn't hers, had read the serialization during the voyage to England, liked it, and urged him to consider it for his next film. He trusted her judgment; without even looking at it, he wired instructions to buy the property. They were still in Europe when the trades reported that *The Curse of Capistrano* would be his next production.

The train trip from New York to Los Angeles was a long five days, and this enforced captivity aided Mary in her attempts to get her book-adverse husband to sit still long enough to read.* Even then, she had to

---

* Margaret Case (daughter of Frank) wrote, "Douglas Fairbanks was a man who never read *anything*. Even his method of deciding on scripts was to glance over them rapidly and then hand them to someone more fond of reading than he. . . . Douglas would do *anything* to get out of reading the printed word. It was not lack of intelligence or intellectual curiosity that prevented him—simply the fact that he couldn't bear to sit still long enough. Father once said to me, in a bewildered kind of way, 'I don't know how I can be so fond of a man who has never read a book.'"

promise to play two games of Hearts with him before he would tackle the task. Finally, he settled in to see what, exactly, his money had bought. *The Curse of Capistrano* was a story written for a pulp magazine—one of those monthly journals that furnished the young and the working class simple tales of escapism and adventure. Many of his earlier successes had come from such sources.

The resulting film would, as movies do, undergo many name changes before production was finished. It was known as *The Curse of Capistrano*, then *The Black Fox*. Finally Fairbanks decided on the ultimate title of the film that would, for him, become a career changer: *The Mark of Zorro*.

Much has been written about the transition that Fairbanks made from "coat and tie" films to swashbucklers in the 1920s. Scholars, running the gamut from Alistair Cooke in 1940 to Jeffrey Vance in 2008, all agree that the postwar psyche called for a new form of escapism. And although costume films after *The Birth of a Nation* had largely been financial failures, they also point to a small but meaningful renaissance in the genre with the successful release of the German films *Madame DuBarry* and *Anna Boleyn*.

But here the logic gets circular: the former was not released in the United States until December 1920 and the latter was not seen on American shores until April 1921. It is certainly possible Fairbanks had screened the films, or knew about them by reputation, before making the leap into his first full costume picture. But he did not have the reassurance of the American box office—his major source of revenue at this point in time—to bolster him. In fact, it might be argued that the success of Fairbanks's first costume film contributed to the American willingness to give the Ernst Lubitsch films a try, and the tail, in this instance, ended up chasing the dog.

But this discussion is academic and, when trying to retrace the decision-making process of Douglas Fairbanks, likely futile. With Doug, intellect took second place to intuition. He demonstrated a pattern of following his gut, and happily for his reputation and bottom line his gut was to be a reliable measure of the vox populi for the decade ahead.

The scholars tell us *why* his decision was right for his time. But they do not tell us *how* he got there.

Vance and Herndon both provide one tantalizing clue: a letter from Cap O'Brien outlining exhibitor complaints. There was not, they said, enough romantic love interest in Doug's films. Women populated matinee audiences, and women wanted romance. This was a valid observation; Fairbanks had a horror of love scenes. Anita Loos spoke of his sex appeal and his aversion to addressing it: "He had 'that thing' when he was in pictures, yet he never played love scenes. I used to travel with him, with the company, and his fans virtually tore him to pieces if he dared appear on the street. Yet he'd come to me and say: 'Look Anita, don't write any mush in there for me.'" When he did play love scenes, he would often do so for comic effect.

It is true that *The Mark of Zorro* contains more love scenes than do his earlier films.* But this is no explanation for the change in genre, unless one is to make the leap from romance (as in wooing) to that of *the* romance (as in tales of distant lands and times). O'Brien's suggestion may have triggered this line of thinking, but we have little evidence one way or the other.

Certainly, Fairbanks had known for some time that a change was in order. When *The Lamb* was released, it took only a simple leap from a low slanting roof and a few fisticuffs to enchant audiences and critics. He had developed and enhanced the level of stunts in successive outings, and the production value of his films had increased tenfold—now floods and avalanches rained down upon the protagonists. But what had dazzled before was insufficient now. He had been aware of this at least since the reviews came in for *Arizona*.

Some missed the satiric touch of Anita Loos. "Since parting company from Miss Loos, his comedies have lost their magic touch,"

---

* Enid Bennett, who was later to play Maid Marian in *Robin Hood*, was married to *Zorro* director Fred Niblo. In 1967 she told historian Kevin Brownlow, "Doug was timid about doing a love scene. The first time he had a love scene was in *The Mark of Zorro*. Fred insisted, and got it out of him."

groused *Photoplay* in 1918. "His plays now consist in jumping off roofs and climbing porches." A year later, the same source continued its dire warnings: "Douglas Fairbanks has not 'slipped' in personal appeal, but he has slipped tremendously as a reliable purveyor of dramatic amusement simply because of his vehicles and his manner of playing. . . . Most of his other pieces in the year 1919 have not been satisfactory entertainment, and unless Mr. Fairbanks follows a different line he will lose steadily."

This feeling was not universal, of course. The editorial writer at *Motion Picture Magazine* opined:

Now some of the critics are beginning to hop on Douglas Fairbanks because of his "sameness." In other words, they want him to cover up the personality which has endeared him to millions. Don't do it, Doug. Stick to your smile and your personality, old boy! We have plenty of actors on the screen and not enough personalities. . . . Your stories could be better, old top, but yourself, never!

It was clear that he was aware of the issue. He wrote of it later— satirically, and a tad ruefully:

I admitted freely that when it came to the matter of smiling I could give anyone else a couple of teeth and win, going away. I smiled . . . through twenty-one screen productions [but] when I wanted to attempt a different sort of part, which would give my face a rest and give me an opportunity to be serious again, friends, producers and associates laughed at me. I might not be much of an actor, they as much as hinted, but as a smiler I was a knockout. The public, I was told, wanted to see me go on smiling, and I must do it however gloomy it made me feel. I do not know that I can seriously blame the public for their unconscious cruelty, for it was something I had started myself. So the ghastly thing went on. I kept on smiling. Measured by film length, I have smiled over twenty miles. And I feel as if I had smiled twenty thousand.

The same, it seemed, applied to acrobatics:

I found that I had once more started something I couldn't stop.
If the public wanted acrobatics, I decided that I would give them
what they wanted. I would show them what I really could do if
I tried. I quite forgot, myself, why I had started all these tricks.
They began to possess me, almost as completely as the smile. . . .
I romped, jumped and skylarked through one play after another.

All of this smiling, and all of this jumping, was in his mind a
substitute for what he really wanted to be doing. He didn't want to be
just a personality; he wanted to be an *actor*. And the role he wanted to
play, more than any other, was D'Artagnan of *The Three Musketeers*.
He spoke of it constantly while on his honeymoon in Europe. The film
must be made in France, he said. He would make two other films back
home and then return to Europe to film it.

But a period piece—a famous one, at that—would be both expensive
(if done right) and risky. Accordingly, he took a careful, intermediate
step. "I was a little timid and did not wish to risk *The Three Musketeers*, so I put out as a feeler another costume play, *The Mark of Zorro*,"
he wrote two years later. *Zorro*'s location was Southern California. It
would be no more costly to create sets for it than it had been for *The
Knickerbocker Buckaroo*.*

Zorro would not be a total departure from his earlier films; it had
romantic elements but also comedic ones. Fairbanks's Don Diego, the
Zorro alter ego, is a prime example. He is not so much effeminate
or fey as he is gently sleepy. Nothing will rouse him. Even the broad
corduroy of his suit suggests nothing so much as striped jammies with
footies. His silly, gentle magic tricks with his handkerchief ("Have you
seen this one?") interest no one but himself.†

---

* Less, in fact. *Buckaroo* cost $292,442.26, while *Zorro* cost $266,209.28.
† It is not the first time he used this device. In *Mr. Fixit* he is sitting next to the woman
 his family has arranged him to marry. She, being in love with someone else, is in a woe-
 ful state. Trying to roust her into a smile, he pulls out his handkerchief for a trick and

But for Zorro, the caped avenger of the oppressed native Indian, the jokes are always on the other fellow. He will carve his trademark *Z* (an invention of his own devising) on his opponents' cheeks—both facial and posterior, so to speak. He is a figure of romance and adventure, a newer, higher level of hero.

Production began that summer at the Clune studio, with location work in the San Fernando Valley. Fairbanks had included fencing in his general training regimen since *A Modern Musketeer* but went to the additional effort of hiring Belgian world fencing champion M. Harry Uttenhover. Uttenhover had trained him for *A Modern Musketeer* and would now train not only Fairbanks but also Robert McKim and Noah Beery Sr., his film opponents. New to his company was director Fred Niblo. He was no Allan Dwan yet he was competent at staging the action and keeping Fairbanks in the frame. Marguerite De La Motte had her first turn as his leading lady, and she fit the bill splendidly.* The clever script, Fairbanks's dual performances, and the engaging action sequences did the rest.

Zorro was to outlive his creators in the American psyche. The idea of the double-identity hero was not original to *The Mark of Zorro*, having first been seen at the turn of the century with *The Scarlet Pimpernel*. But a young Robert Kahn (later Bob Kane) had never seen the Pimpernel play or read the book. Still, like all little boys, he did go to the movies, and like all little boys he worshipped Douglas Fairbanks. It was *The Mark of Zorro*, with its subterranean hideout and dual identities, that served as his inspiration for the creation of Batman.† Superman, too,

---

says, "Have you seen this one?" He loved practicing magic tricks, and tales of him doing so at Hollywood parties go back to 1916, the same year he demonstrated his affinity for them in *The Good Bad Man*.

* Orphaned at sixteen, she had been dancing at Grauman's downtown Los Angeles theater (the Chinese and Egyptian theaters were yet to be built) when she was seen by Fairbanks. This led to her first film role, in *Arizona*. (Marjorie Daw had the female lead in this lost film.) De La Motte was to serve as Fairbanks's feminine lead more than any other actress during his swashbuckling years. The suicide of her first husband by drowning has been said by some to be the inspiration for *A Star Is Born*.

† He also credited the 1930 film *The Bat Whisperers*.

sprung from the influence of Fairbanks, although here it was an amalgam of his swashbuckling heroes, not just Zorro. In 1933 Joe Shuster adopted Fairbanks's "hero stance"—legs apart, elbows out, knuckles on hips, cape flying—in his early versions of Superman.*

Zorro got everything right. The blend of humor and heroics remains the benchmark that other action films try to reach. The climactic chase was the epitome of the Fairbanksian series of escapes from the befuddled collective constabulary, and it is extracted in film compilations even today.†

Fairbanks introduced the new persona to filmgoers with care. Every variant of movie poster had not only an image of Zorro in costume but also a large oval portrait of the star in modern clothes. United Artists wanted no confusion as to who that masked hero was. They needn't have bothered.

Audiences adored the film. Fairbanks could not have asked for a more emphatic vote on his change of tack. In its first week, *Zorro* broke all attendance records at New York's Capitol Theatre, with over ninety-four thousand tickets sold in that theater alone. The film returned $725,035.02 to his production company, for a net of $458,825.74.

The profits were none too soon for the struggling UA. Far from achieving the original goal of three films per year from each founder, the organization was starving for product to release. The year 1919 saw only three films: two from Fairbanks and *Broken Blossoms* from Griffith.‡

Things were just as tight in 1920. Mary had fulfilled her First National commitment and released *Pollyanna* for UA in January, but

---

* Clark Kent, however, was based on Harold Lloyd.

† Most recently, large portions of it were used in 2011's *The Artist*, with actor Jean Dujardin cut in for close-ups, substituting for Fairbanks.

‡ This last was a bit of a fluke. It originally was produced for Adolph Zukor and Artcraft, but Zukor thought that the film's tragic ending made it noncommercial. He didn't want to release it, yet he had the product-hungry UA over a barrel. Still smarting from the loss of his top stars, he charged them $250,000 for the distribution rights. The joke ended up being on him, since *Broken Blossoms* was a smash hit, ultimately netting $700,000 for the organization.

the organization was forced to go outside its ranks and pay Mack Sennett a $200,000 advance guarantee for distribution rights to *Down on the Farm*. The only other non-Pickford/Fairbanks releases of 1920 were *The Love Flower*, a minor Griffith effort, and the "Griffith-supervised" drama *Romance*, which was a flop. Thus 1920 saw only seven UA films, with the triumph of *Zorro* coming very late in the year, on December 5.

Having so few releases made it hard to get exhibitors to commit to bookings. UA historian Tino Balio writes:

> UA's product could not be sold a season in advance of production, as was the output of the larger corporations using the block-booking method of distribution. Because pictures were sold to exhibitors separately on an individual contract, not only was a greater effort required of the sales staff, but also it took longer to exhaust the market for each picture. A UA producer could be well into his third picture before he could hope to recoup his investment on the first. In short, the owners did not have unlimited capital with which to furnish the company its requirements.

One approach to the problem was to ask the exhibitors for pay for the full rental fee at the time of booking. This was an undue burden to most theater owners, who were accustomed to paying 25 percent down on booking and the remaining 75 percent a week before the first screening date. The reluctance of most exhibitors to sign up for this plan, Balio states, meant that "in its early days, UA's pictures played in many second-rate theaters. In some areas of the country, the company was shut out completely"—making the resounding returns of the Pickford and Fairbanks features even more remarkable.*

---

* Michigan exhibitors organized, refusing to pay the high rentals on *Robin Hood*. They came to regret it. Hiram Abrams simply negotiated with the Masons and the film was shown in Masonic lodges in the state. The theater owners missed out on one of the highest-grossing films of the decade.

UA was to provide each of its artists with $200,000 of seed money per production. A mere three years earlier this was considered a lavish sum, but now both Fairbanks and Pickford had grander ideas.* Accordingly, Abrams changed negotiating tactics with the exhibitors. Instead of asking for the full rental fees up front, he structured deals in which the exhibitors paid a base rental rate with a split of returns above a predetermined figure.†

One thing was clear early in the life of United Artists: McAdoo and Price were expensive superfluities. By the summer of 1920, both men had resigned from the organization, and Hiram Abrams was moved into the presidency. He was to remain in that position until he died of a heart attack in November 1926.

Fairbanks did not have the luxury of waiting for the response to *Zorro* before starting his next production. Conservatively, he reverted to his former model, and *The Nut* would become his last silent "coat and tie" comedy. Its ectopic placement between *Zorro* and *The Three Musketeers* contributes to the neglect it suffers today, which is a pity, for it represents an unusual genre in the silent era: a screwball comedy. The film starts out with a sequence of its inventor-hero being tossed out of bed, tipped into his bath, and guided by a series of Rube Goldbergesque machines through his toiletries and into his clothes.‡ Modern audiences get half the joke, for the bit stands well on its own. But contemporary audiences got the full point: Fairbanks was spoofing the elaborate bathing sequence that Cecil B. DeMille constructed for Gloria Swanson in *Male and Female*.

---

* Griffith, too, wanted bigger budgets. He attempted to skin the cat by going public, forming D. W. Griffith Inc. in the summer of 1920, a tactic that would ultimately fail him.

† Because this figure would vary by film, theater, and city, it remains a challenge to determine the total box office grosses of the films. We can discuss the revenues only in terms of the return to the Douglas Fairbanks Pictures Corporation as a taxable entity.

‡ F. Scott Fitzgerald, evidently a fan, lifted this sequence almost whole and put it in his short story *A Diamond as Big as the Ritz*.

From there the film progresses into surrealism worthy of Buster Keaton. Fairbanks is trapped outside in his underwear,* so he trims the number "23" off a large theater poster, tacks it to his back, and jogs past the police as if he were running a marathon. When this fails, he cuts out a life-size suit from a billboard advertisement and attempts to wear it home. At one point in the absurdist events, Fairbanks, for the purpose of a plot too convoluted to explain, hijacks figures from a wax museum. After thoroughly ruining his sweetheart's fundraising event, he finds himself in the hoosegow, where he frantically begs everyone—jailor, janitor, and fellow inmate—to "Please call up Miss Wynn, Gramercy 35. Tell her I'm heartbroken about this—I adore her—I think she's wonderful—and—just say 'honeybunch' at the end."

Production was held up for several weeks when Fairbanks once again hurt himself. Shooting a leap through a courthouse window near the end of the film, he caught his foot on the sill and crashed six feet onto the pavement. This time it was his left hand that sustained multiple fractures. That, plus a badly wrenched back and neck, delayed the film's release from February 22 to March 1.

History has been unfair to *The Nut* in another manner. Fairbanks's earliest serious biographer, Richard Schickel, dismissed the film as "one of his few commercial failures," which has influenced thinking since that time. The film was not a failure. It was as successful as many of his UA modern-dress comedies—beating *When the Clouds Roll By*—and more successful than any of his Paramount or Triangle films. It returned $506,313.74, for a net profit of $300,231.60. If this was failure, it was the sort of failure any other filmmaker would have given his or her eyeteeth to endure.

Jeffrey Vance is more on the mark when he refers to the "relative failure" of *The Nut*—relative only to the smash success of *Zorro* that preceded it. And until the returns came in for *Zorro*, Fairbanks was

---

* Publicity for the film trumpeted that audiences should come to see Fairbanks running down Broadway in his BVDs. The makers of BVDs lodged a protest—the underwear Fairbanks was wearing was a different brand.

still undecided on how next to proceed. While recovering from his injuries, he and his publicist put out feelers as to his next film choice. It would be *The Virginian*, he said. He purchased the rights from Famous Players–Lasky for $55,000 in December 1920. No, he claimed next, it would be a story called *The Melancholiac*, written by the team that wrote *The Nut*. This never came to be.

Hindsight having twenty-twenty vision, his choice to make *The Three Musketeers* feels inevitable. But in January 1921, this was still a bold decision to make. The industry was in a terrible slump, one that would continue through the entire year. Of the major studios, only Fox and Universal were active that month. "There is a shortage of money," wrote *Variety*. "And none of the banks in this section is willing to finance any picture proposition. The interest rate on money is at seven percent at present in the banking houses, but there is not a penny available for anything in films." Stars were being released from their contracts. Even super-luminary Lillian Gish was abruptly let go by D. W. Griffith, her former lover and lifelong mentor. "You know as much about the high cost of making pictures as I do," he said to her peremptorily. "With all the expenses I have, I can't afford to pay you what you're worth."

As spring arrived, things worsened. Extras Starving as Slump Goes On, headlined *Variety* in April, adding, "Right now the studio is as much a place of the dead as Hollywood Cemetery." By July, an industry-wide strike nearly crippled production. "The Ince plant issues a statement Saturday it would close for the next four weeks," wrote *Variety*'s reporter. "Yesterday there was not a company working at Goldwyn or at Roaches' [studios] which completely killed the Culver City end."

But *Variety* noted one small bright light in a very dark universe: there was no strike at either the Pickford or Fairbanks operations. They were beloved—and evidently generous—employers. Indeed, Mary was in the midst of production of *Little Lord Fauntleroy*, and Doug was filming *The Three Musketeers*. Fairbanks recalled finalizing his decision to go ahead:

I had always wanted to do *The Three Musketeers*, but I was a little reluctant to undertake a costume film. The impression of the business was that a costume story just would not do.

Every now and then someone of the overhead—I mean someone from the business office—would come in to tell me that an exhibitor, or group of exhibitors, wished to talk to me. Among other things I always asked them how they would feel about booking a period or costume play in their theaters. They were immediately apprehensive. They were sure their patrons, when they saw the billing up in front of the theaters, would walk to the next movie palace. I sent some men out to ask questions and they made a unanimous report against the undertaking. No costume picture need apply.

Having made sure I was wrong, I went ahead. I felt that if there was enough good melodrama the interest could be held in spite of dress. Also the people must be kept human. Costumes change, but customs do not to any great extent.

The production was to be his grandest to date. Not only the Clune studio but also the Brunton studio, essentially across the street, were rented to accommodate all the sets the film required. (The Clune studio was at the site of the present Raleigh Studios. In 1926 Paramount would relocate to the site of the Brunton studio, where it remains to this day.) Edward Knoblock (the playwright responsible for *Kismet*) was hired in March to write the adaptation of the Alexandre Dumas novel, spending many a day and night at Pickfair. "Nothing could have exceeded the happiness of Mary and Doug," he recalled of that time. "They were both full of ambitions and plans for better things to be done. They lived a quiet life, devoting themselves almost entirely to their work and a little intimate circle of friends." Britain's Lord Mountbatten, in his later years, said of it, "Pickfair was about—certainly, the most, best taste house, I should think, in Hollywood, and run very much on English country house lines. . . . In fact, they really kept court there. It was like Buckingham Palace in London; it was the house that everyone wanted to go to. . . . To be asked, they would have to be more or less passed certain standards of behavior generally. Things were very proper and correct."

Indeed, they were happily settled in Pickfair. And they were not alone. The 1920 census reveals a host of live-in servants even before Mary arrived with her retinue: two maids, a butler, a majordomo, and an Irish stableman to care for the horses. This did not include the day help who lived off-site—gardeners, cooks, handymen. Japanese valet Tanaka had been replaced by Rocher, a faithful manservant who would attend Doug for the next decade and more. Tanaka had vanished one day, and all attempts to locate him failed. His disappearance was perhaps understandable: keeping up with Doug's exploits required both infinite patience and nerves of steel. (A year prior he had found himself surrounded by a swarm of rattlesnakes while setting up camp for Fairbanks in the mountains and had to be rescued by his boss.) When they finally located the misplaced manservant, he was in Japan, working for the Teikoku Motion Picture Corporation, having parlayed his experience in Hollywood into becoming a full-fledged movie magnate.

Mary may have been as wealthy as her husband, but Victorian sensibility reigned when it came to who paid the bills. Doug covered all operating expenses related to Pickfair. "He's old-fashioned enough to want to do this without aid from his wife," Pickford said. The estate was comfortably furnished in American walnut and overstuffed floral chintz sofas. Fairbanks's private suite included bedroom, bath, large walk-in closet (his wardrobe was prodigious), hall, and sleeping porch. Mary's suite was in lavender, with dull green furnishings. It included a bathroom and sleeping porch. Two additional guest rooms were on the second floor; one dubbed "the rose room" was reserved for Charlie Chaplin, who slept over several nights a week. The table was set every night for fifteen, as the staff never knew just how many cowpokes or visiting dignitaries their impulsive boss was going to bring home to dinner. A bronze casting of Adolph Weinman's *Rising Sun* was on the lawn—a birthday gift from Mary to Doug.* It was under this statue that Knoblock, Fairbanks, and scenarist Lotta Woods were photographed, basking in the spring sunshine and pecking away at a typewriter. (It might be more proper to say that Knoblock and Woods were writing. The photographic evidence suggests that saddle-shoe-clad Fairbanks spent a lot of time atop tables, brandishing a sword in various cheerfully heroic postures.)

Knoblock worked on the continuity of *Musketeers* for five weeks, turning in what he felt to be a version extremely faithful to the original book. "Although D'Artagnan figured throughout as the hero, I had also developed the story of Milady," he wrote. "The famous scene of branding her on the arm I had naturally retained. But this Douglas discarded."

At the time, Knoblock was livid. He felt that he had been employed as an artist; he had no sympathy for the notion that the motion picture industry was an amalgam of commerce and art. He also had no understanding at that time of film censorship. But Fairbanks did. The heroine Constance was now the niece of the innkeeper, not his wife. And there would be no sexual congress with, much less branding of, the villainess Milady. With tincture of time, Knoblock cooled down. "He may have been right," he wrote ruefully. "He certainly carved from the novel a part and a story which suited his own particular personality." The author spent the rest of the production helping the costumers and the art director, which, curiously, he found more gratifying than writing for the film.

Knoblock contributed to the casting as well, suggesting the then little-known Adolphe Menjou to play Louis XIII. "Working in a Fairbanks picture was quite an experience," Menjou recalled. "In some ways

---

* It is not clear if this was the actual bronze that topped the fountain at the Panama-Pacific International Exposition of 1915 in San Francisco, as was claimed in the press at the time. Weinman cast multiple bronzes of the image, many of which are in museums today. Similarly, the china that Fairbanks gave Pickford was popularly believed to be that which Napoleon gave to Josephine. The auction of Pickfair furnishings early in the current century proved that it was the identical pattern but not the actual china of the emperor and empress.

it was like going to a Hollywood masquerade party instead of to work. The set was always crowded with visiting celebrities and Doug's friends. Between shots Doug was likely to feel the need of a physical workout, so he would hold an impromptu gymkhana with some of his athletic buddies."

Menjou's first day of filming was one of the later scenes in the film—the scene where the cardinal is poised to expose the queen's affair to the king. Multiple takes were ruined as actors felt themselves being suddenly stung by some unseen insect. Finally, Menjou discovered a small lead pellet at his feet—and laughter from the overhead rafters revealed Jack Pickford. He had been shooting birdshot at them from between his teeth.

Jack Pickford, Mary's ne'er-do-well younger brother, was no stranger to trouble. During his service in the war, he had barely avoided a court marshal and dishonorable discharge when he was part of a scheme to get rich young men who wanted to avoid battle to pay for slots in the naval reserves. Strings were pulled from on high; Jack turned state's evidence against his coconspirator, and the government was spared the embarrassment of having headlines besmirching the name of Pickford during the period when Mary was one of its top fundraisers.

Six months before America's entry into the war, Jack had eloped with Olive Thomas, a beautiful showgirl who at twenty-two was already a divorcée and one of Florenz Ziegfeld's many conquests. She moved into motion pictures, making films for Paramount, Triangle, and Lewis J. Selznick Productions Inc. The marriage of the beautiful Olive and the ferret-faced Jack would seem an odd combination at first, but he apparently had charms beyond those evident when he was fully clothed. They spent the next four years happily practicing the usual vices while trying to invent new ones. Thus it was that they found themselves, drunk and tired, returning to their Paris hotel room in the early hours of September 6, 1920. The exact sequence and nature of the events that followed will never be fully known. Either by accident or intent, Olive ingested mercury bichloride, a toxic chemical used in that pre-antibiotic era for topical treatment of the sores associated with syphilis. Despite immediate hospitalization, she died a few days later of renal failure.

Coming on the heels of Mary's contested divorce, this was a scandal that neither the family nor the industry needed. The newspapers had a brief heyday—*Was it suicide? Just what was that mercury doing in the medicine cabinet?*—until the French authorities labeled the case an accidental ingestion and the press had no choice but to accept the improbable claim that the chemical had been a cleaning solution left in the bathroom by the hotel maid.

Now Jack was back in Hollywood, delaying production on his brother-in-law's most expensive film to date,* and acting very unlike a man in mourning. Ostensibly, he was codirecting Mary in *Little Lord Fauntleroy*, but he was off on drinking binges as often as he was in the director's chair.

Menjou argued that the horseplay did the production no harm. "Doug invariably got the very best performance out of his actors," he wrote. "I think that was because they were relaxed and having a good time. And the spirit of fun that prevailed at the studio always seemed to show up in Doug's pictures. There was a tongue-in-cheek, devil-may-care sort of quality in all his films that nobody else has ever been able to duplicate."

Doug knew that in wedding Mary, he was marrying her hard-drinking, hard-living family as well. Mary's younger sister, Lottie, was to wed four times. Her first marriage produced a daughter in 1915, but her wild ways ill suited her for motherhood. Grandmother Charlotte legally adopted the child in 1920 (while Mary and Doug were in Europe on their honeymoon tour), changing her name from Mary Pickford Rupp to Gwynne Rupp. Mary and her mother shared the childrearing duties while Lottie partied through the 1920s.

Mary recalled that during this time, "Sometimes we worked so late at the studios that we would come home in our make-ups and our

---

* Fairbanks's investment in the film was significant: $748,768.76. His publicist, of course, claimed it was a million.

household became quite accustomed to seeing Fauntleroy come bounding up the stairs, followed by D'Artagnan in all his plumed glory. And when we had company I used to wrap D'Artagnan's velvet cape around me in deference to my guests and it made quite a respectable train."

For the role of D'Artagnan, Fairbanks grew a mustache that he was to keep for the rest of his days. Until then, all film heroes had been clean cut; only villains had facial hair. But, as with his tan skin, Fairbanks's appearance was broadly influential. Soon heroes like John Gilbert and Antonio Moreno were sporting mustaches. Eventually even desperado John Dillinger (who reportedly idolized Fairbanks) grew one.

The film's narrative developed at a leisurely pace, establishing the story of the queen, her jealous king, her ardent lover Buckingham, and the scheming cardinal. Fairbanks's D'Artagnan does not even appear until the second reel. He makes a suitably comic first impression: britches too high, boots too low, scraggly feathered hat atop, and bony buttercup-colored horse beneath. His performance is funny and fierce, and very French. French film historian and Fairbanks friend Robert Florey attributed this to Fairbanks's 1901 visit to Paris:

> Thus Douglas had learned to know France and to like the French. An observer both fine and subtle, he quickly adopted some tics and manners of the French for his future repertoire. At the present time it is not unusual to see him imitate a street vendor, or a Parisian omnibus conductor. In these imitations he surpasses the boundaries of the height of comedy. He dangles a cigarette butt on his lower lip, looks at the end of his feet, rolls up his moustaches with a back of hand, then buries his hands at the far end of his pockets and begins relating a story in which he inserts the French argot that he knows.

There is an enhanced theatricality to his performances in the costume films: he will tap the side of his nose and sniff the air in an "I smell a rat!" gesture when he detects betrayal; his stance is broader, and his arms are flung in wide arcs of acting. The artificiality of his performances would increase over the course of the 1920s—the grander the film, the broader is our hero's performance. Knowing the naturalism of which he was capable, it is clear that this was done with intent. It is an impish theatricality, not of the formal, Frederick Warde variety. A case in point: in escaping from the cardinal's guards in the film, he not only slides down a bannister like a ten-year-old but actually gives a little *skip* as he beats them to the forecourt of the palace. By the time he portrayed Robin Hood, he and all his merry men hop about like rabbits drunk on ragtime.

Still, not all acting was easy. Fairbanks was to claim that he was unable to generate proper tears for the scene early in the film in which he is not permitted to join the musketeers ("We had to resort to the good old glycerine squirter"). The final print demonstrates no tears at all: D'Artagnan barely has time to give a hard swallow before noticing his archenemy ("The man from Meung!") outside the barrack window. Menjou recalled that Fairbanks "went completely unorthodox" during the fencing sequences, despite Uttenhover's training. "He was all over the set, jumping over chairs and on top of tables, slashing away with his rapier as though it were a broadsword. The fencing instructor . . . tore his hair. Never had he seen such an exhibition."

This makes the fight sequences sound more boyish and impromptu than they actually were. Outtakes from Fairbanks's swashbuckling films document that every movement of the blade and leap upon or over furniture was carefully choreographed to prevent the actors from being sliced to ribbons. It is worth noting that the individual shots within the fencing sequences were sustained in length. Most Hollywood films keep sword-fighting sequences to a maximum of three moves per shot: thrust, parry, counterparry. More than this and untrained actors can get hurt. But the Fairbanks sword fights not only involve glorious and creative fight choreography but the sustained clash of blades that can come only from continual and painstaking rehearsal. Menjou, it seems, was weaving a good tale.

Filming took place in the spring and early summer of 1921. They were dogged throughout the spring by printed reports that Mary was pregnant and due to deliver in the fall. Fairbanks, after repeated denials, finally labeled the rumors as "untrue and unkind." This confounded reporters: "Untrue, perhaps, but why unkind?" one asked. They had no way of knowing, but Mary was now sterile. While married to Owen Moore in her teens, she had become pregnant. Rumors of an abortion have tantalized biographers for years and were ultimately confirmed by Owen's nephew Thomas, who was a welcome guest at Pickfair in the 1960s, when time and scotch had loosened Mary's tongue. "Her mother made her get an abortion," he recounted. "She [Charlotte] didn't want any part of Owen Moore, not even as a grandchild."

Abortions in the pre-antibiotic era could often lead to infertility. Now that she was finally in the position to have a baby with the man she loved, Mary was unable to conceive. It was heartbreaking for her. She wanted children: "Not less than four babies—two boys and two girls—is the ideal family," she said. She did not want to be childless. "An old age without children about is horrible," she told a reporter that year. "The loneliness of it all."

Doug tried to comfort her. Over and over, he left her notes: she was his "darling little baby girl" and "my own darling baby." *He* needed no baby as long as he had her. And, in marrying him, she did get her own Peck's Bad Boy to scold and indulge. That, and the shared care and raising of Lottie's Gwynne, would have to do for now.

But June also brought good news—Mary had won the first round in the Nevada divorce wars. The appeal court justice ruled that the state could not properly attack the divorce, as it had missed the opportunity to do so at the time of the awarding of the original decree. Friends gathered at Pickfair to congratulate the couple. Fairbanks issued a statement that his bride "was very much gratified," while the Nevada attorney general, in turn, vowed to appeal to the state supreme court. He did, and the following June, Mary triumphed a final time.

The first bullet neatly dodged, they traveled to New York City in late August to premiere their respective films. Fairbanks optimistically leased the Lyric Theatre (site of his long-ago musical performance in *Fantana*, as well as *The Pit*) for an unprecedented eight weeks. Still, there were challenges. One came with the reissue of a 1916 Thomas Ince Triangle film *D'Artagnan*, retitled *The Three Musketeers*. This was opportunistic poaching, pure and simple. Worse, the Alexander Corporation, which had acquired the rights to the film in the wake of the demise of Triangle, took the unprecedented stance that since *it* had copyrighted all 515 scenes of the 1916 film, Fairbanks's version was in violation of copyright if it contained *any* similar action. More audacious yet, Alexander filed suit in federal court to restrain exhibition of the Fairbanks film.

This argument, a pugnacious example of the best defense being a good offense, did not fly. The story was public domain, and while the images and performances were copyright protected (film piracy was a lively practice even in the first years of the industry), the portrayal of the narrative was not. Cap O'Brien brought the case to the Federal Trade Commission. The issue hinged on the failure of the distributors of the 1916 film to advertise it as a reissue, which the FTC had required since 1918. (Reissues needed to be clearly labeled as such in all billings, which was not the case with the Ince film.) The commission ruled in Fairbanks's favor.

This turned out to be a minor distraction in what was a triumphant premiere. Chaplin, present for the event, recalled:

> The crowds were gathered for several blocks on every side of the theater. I felt proud that I was in the movies. Though on this night with Douglas and Mary I feel that I am trailing in their glory. It is their night.
>
> There are cheers. For Mary. For "Doug." For me . . . We get out of the car and the crowds swarm. . . . "Doug" takes Mary under his wing and plows through just as though he were doing a scene and the crowd were extras.

Chaplin had viewed a screening of *Musketeers* the day before at the orchestra rehearsal. He felt that the film needed some severe edits: "Charlie found at least five places in the picture which he thought

ought to be out; the fight in front of the Luxembourg ran too long; there was too much of the scene where D'Artagnan asks Buckingham for the jewels; and there were many other glaring faults," Mary recalled. "Charlie would say to me, 'Mary, that scene must come out, it will ruin the picture. Whatever you do, don't let Douglas run it that way. Take your scissors and go right up into the projection room and see that it is taken out.'"

Chaplin acknowledged this. "I suggested a few changes and several cuts which I thought would improve it," he admitted. "I always do. They listened politely and then let the picture ride the way it was. They always do."

He recanted fully upon seeing the film with the audience on opening night. "When the pandemonium of the audience was at its height at the end of the first duel, Charlie put his fingers in his mouth, boy-fashion, and whistled so shrilly that it hurt my ears," Mary wrote. "And when the show was over, he was generous enough to admit that he had been entirely mistaken about the cuts,—that in his judgment the film was perfect."

"Fortunately, the changes I suggested were not made and the picture is a tremendous success," Chaplin admitted.

Tremendous, indeed. The film returned $1,358,259.03 to the Douglas Fairbanks Pictures Corporation, a profit of $609,490.27. Its success was critical as well as financial. One reviewer wrote, "*The Three Musketeers* with Douglas Fairbanks is not only a great picture—it is stupendous. It is no child's play to lift a story of this magnitude out of its atmosphere of four centuries ago and transfer it with its multitudinous scenes and its daring action to the screen. Yet that is what the Fairbanks forces have done; and they have done it without an anachronism and with a completeness and fidelity to the book that is amazing." Another wrote: "Search high and low and you will find no actor better suited to the role of D'Artagnan. He is the hand; the role: the glove."

Critics also noted that Fairbanks had made anticipatory changes for the censors. "Liberties have been taken with the original Dumas story, it is true," wrote *Motion Picture Magazine*, "but in these days of censorship there was no choice in the matter. Mr. Fairbanks and his assistants undoubtedly felt that it was wiser to eliminate certain colorful episodes themselves—eliminate them carefully and cautiously—than to have them boldly lifted from the high points in the story by censorial shears." Fairbanks acknowledged later that this was the case. "There was one whole phase of the book, one of the most interesting and significant phases, that was hardly touched on in the screen adaptation. It had to do with the relationship that existed between men and women in that day. . . . If I had tried to reproduce conditions as they existed the film would have landed in the scrap heap."*

By 1921 the issue of film censorship was acute. The first municipal censorship board was established in Chicago in 1907. On Christmas Eve 1908, New York mayor George B. McClellan (son of the Civil War general) closed all motion picture theaters in the city. In the words of historian Kevin Brownlow, "His excuse was safety; his true concern, public morals." Emergency injunctions reopened the theaters, but then the city council banned all children under sixteen from attending motion pictures unless accompanied by an adult.

This sufficed to put a proper fright into producers, distributors, and theater owners, and they initiated a move to police themselves. In early 1909 the New York Board of Censorship of Programs of Motion Picture Shows was formed. According to Brownlow, this board "acted as an enlightened censor in the hope that the more vicious variety might be neutralized by its existence. . . . Exhibitors could show a film rejected by the board, but they risked arousing the wrath of the local authority (thereby losing their license) or the exchange (losing their supply of films). On the whole, they toed the line, because the board was liberal—far too liberal for many people."

Attempts to overcome censorship by way of the courts failed in 1915, when the US Supreme Court rendered a decision that First Amendment rights did not apply to motion pictures.† Motion pictures were

---

* He was likely referring to D'Artagnan having sex with Milady under a false identity.
† *Mutual Film Corporation v. Industrial Commission of Ohio.* This ruling was not reversed until 1952.

"a business pure and simple . . . originated and conducted for profit, like other spectacles, not to be regarded . . . as part of the press of the country or as organs of public opinion."

The country was full of reformers at the turn of the century. They had successfully pushed through prohibition, and now they were setting their sights on motion pictures. When the New York Board of Censorship demonstrated itself to be too enlightened for their taste, the clubwomen and reformers adopted another tactic, demanding state censorship. Four states passed censorship laws in 1916. Pennsylvania was especially rigorous. Mothers-to-be could not even be shown knitting booties. "The movies are patronized by thousands of children who believe that babies are brought by the stork," claimed the board, "and it would be criminal to undeceive them."

This was a nightmare for film producers. Their prints would travel the circuit, subject to the shears of every regional censor, each of whom had a different bête noire. One would cut scenes of drinking; another any that implied sex. Police could not be shown in a comic light in some areas; crime could not pay in others. Fairbanks was not immune. One Chicago exhibitor wrote of *Headin' South*: "A sure money-getter. Douglas performs some great stunts in this, but the local censor board cut it somewhat, I'm sorry to say."

If the ever-wholesome Fairbanks was suffering cuts, nothing was sacrosanct. "In the early June pea that the censor fondly refers to as his brain, the principal idea seems to be that film producers are a bunch of vicious, depraved chumps, who spend large sums of money in an endeavor to put themselves out of business by making productions that no decent person will patronize," groused *Variety* in late 1917. "Imagine pinheads like these daring to try to edit the work of master craftsmen like David Griffith, William Brady, the DeMilles, Thomas Ince or Lois Weber, or to pass judgment on the humor of a Sennett, a Fairbanks or a Chaplin?" Even Dorothy Parker entered the fray, penning a poem in 1922 that went (in part):

There are the Movie Censors,
The motion picture is still in its infancy,—
They are the boys who keep it there.
If the film shows a party of clubmen tossing off ginger ale,
Or a young bride dreaming over tiny garments,
Or Douglas Fairbanks kissing Mary Pickford's hand,
They cut out the scene
And burn it in the public square.

Fairbanks, as the touchstone of all that was wholesome and respectable in films, had a dog in this fight. He took a strong public stance against censorship, going so far as to participate in a film titled *The Non-sense of Censorship* produced between *The Nut* and *The Three Musketeers*. He was the only actor to do so: all other participants in the film were authors and playwrights, including Rupert Hughes, Edward Knoblock, Samuel Merwin, Thompson Buchanan, Rita Welman, and Montague Glass.

The film was a series of vignettes. Most featured the famed authors voicing their disgust for censorship. "The moving picture is about 15 years old," wrote Rupert Hughes for the camera, after setting down a booklet entitled *The Rules of the Censor*. "Sin is somewhat older than that, yet the censors would have us believe that it was not Satan, but Thomas A. Edison who invented the fall of man."

Samuel Merwin's contribution read, "This censorship, if applied to literature, would destroy Shakespeare, Dickens, the Bible itself. It is stupid, ignorant, vulgar. It puts an intolerable limitation on workers in the new art of the screen. Carried only a little further, it will abolish free speech in America."

Fairbanks's piece came at the end of the film and was more visual than verbal, according to *Variety*:

Douglas Fairbanks walks in on a cue from "Abe's: Bank Robbers," and entering from the opposite side strolls on a tough looking individual who bumps into Fairbanks with teeth-rattling force, but the athletic "Doug" makes no effort to retaliate. The tough then proceeds to shove "Doug" all over the lot, and finally Fairbanks musters a sickly grin, swallows hard, and says:

"Say, I'd like to mop up the floor with this bird, but the censors won't let me fight."

The producer/censor impasse might have remained static for years were it not for a series of events that, in the words of Brownlow, "burst like depth charges in the very heart of the film world." The first was Mary's divorce from Owen Moore and rapid remarriage to Doug. Because of the public's enchantment with the union, opposition never progressed much beyond stern Sunday sermons. The second was also, indirectly, in the house of Fairbanks. But the death of Olive Thomas faded from the headlines after the coroner ruled it an accident.

The third scandal was a torpedo that almost sank the ship of the industry. It occurred on Labor Day weekend of 1921. As Doug and Mary were in New York City, basking in the glory of their dual premieres for *The Three Musketeers* and *Little Lord Fauntleroy*, Roscoe "Fatty" Arbuckle was in San Francisco, checking into the St. Francis Hotel for a long holiday weekend. Arbuckle was the former Keystone/Triangle comic who was now the leading comedy star at Paramount. On Monday, September 5, he and his friend, director Lowell Sherman, held a daylong party in their three-room suite. Among the guests consuming large volumes of bootleg liquor was a minor actress, Virginia Rappe. Accompanying her was a woman named Maude Delmont, among whose many accomplishments were bigamy and blackmail.

All the elements for disaster were in place, and sure enough, fate cooperated. As the party was at its peak, Arbuckle went to his bedroom to wash and change for an appointment. Per his court testimony, he discovered an intoxicated Rappe on the floor in his bathroom, vomiting. He wiped her off and put her on top of one of the twin beds in his room. Shortly thereafter she began clutching her abdomen, tearing her clothes, and screaming. The entire party spilled into the bedroom and administered the sort of home remedies one might expect from a room full of drunks. She was dangled by her ankles, had an administration of ice to her private parts, and was dunked in a cold bathtub. She failed to improve (although hanging by her ankles did serve to stifle her screams somewhat). Ultimately a separate room was engaged for Rappe and Delmont, and the party continued.

Virginia Rappe received physician visits and nursing care in her hotel room—including a glass tube catheterization of her bladder—until Thursday, when she was transferred to a maternity hospital. She died the following day. An unauthorized autopsy was performed, revealing a ruptured bladder. Her reproductive organs were removed and destroyed, making it impossible in retrospect to rule out a missed tubal pregnancy or venereal disease.

Delmont went to the papers, claiming Virginia was raped and brutalized by Arbuckle. San Francisco's district attorney, his eye on the mayor's race, issued an arrest warrant.

The result was absolute chaos. This was the first international scandal, one that was far more interesting to the average American than was the Teapot Dome imbroglio in Washington. Politicians, after all, were far away. But people went to the theaters and paid a visit to Roscoe Arbuckle every six weeks. And this involved whiskey, women, jazz music, and, best of all, sex. It was irresistible. The newspapers—particularly the Hearst papers—ran with it.

Scandal was not then so ubiquitous that the public would respond with a world-weary cynicism. Box office receipts plummeted. Women's clubs and the clergy revolted. Paramount saw its stock drop from ninety dollars to forty dollars a share. Within a week of the event, Arbuckle's films were banned in six hundred theaters in New York, as well as statewide in Missouri, Kansas, and Pennsylvania.

Republicans in Congress fronted a proposal to set up federal regulation and censorship of films. It was a move prompted more by loss of taxes on liquor sales than anything else, but it was conveniently timed to ride the wave of public indignation over the Arbuckle scandal.

Even *Variety*, an industry booster if ever there was one, fell on the side of outraged virtue:

> For several years now the name of Hollywood has been a stench in the minds of the decent people of the screen . . . those who must band together now, immediately, without delay and clean up thoroughly, wash out back alley and avenue, studio, lot, apartment, home and house.
>
> If they do not, some Hercules from the outside will cleanse these Augean stables and cleanse them good. The lion of popular indignation is aroused, the innocent will fall with the guilty, the patiently schemed fabric of a great industry will rock and crack in the mighty hands of its patrons, for these patrons have been fed by a hundred sob-sister written fan publications with ideas of the sanctity of home-life in pictures, the chastity of the heroine, the chivalry of heroes, and finding themselves mistaken, their emotions will blow ruinously the other way like a fire caught up and flung back by an unexpected wind on those who started it.

Arbuckle's first trial (there would ultimately be three before he was exonerated) came quickly, in November. The jury repeatedly voted eleven to one for acquittal, the lone holdout being a woman whose lawyer husband was associated with the DA's office.* Hollywood had expected—*needed*—a quick acquittal.[†] When it did not happen, the effect was overwhelming. There were forces in the film industry who believed, truly believed, that it was possible the entire industry could vanish or be banned. If this seems improbable a century later, recall that nationwide theatrical exhibition had existed as such for less than twenty years. The product was ephemeral, and the business might be as well.

---

* The final count was ten to two for acquittal.

† This was a rightful expectation. Any evidence against Arbuckle was later proven to be manufactured by the DA's office after discovering (too late) that Delmont was not a credible witness. Arbuckle's innocence is widely agreed to today.

Four days after the first Arbuckle trial ended with a hung jury, the studio heads took a page from Fairbanks's book and looked to raid Washington for a solution—or a figurehead, depending on your point of view. Will Hays was then postmaster general, and despite having a face that only a mother could consider being fond of in an era when, for the first time, being photogenic mattered (see Warren G. Harding), he was a master politician.* He was hired to be the head of the newly formed Motion Picture Producers and Distributors of America (MPPDA— more readily known as "the Hays office"). As such, he created a model of self-censorship within the industry. This bought everyone time and survival, but, in the words of Brownlow, "by restricting subject matter so that many of the vital topics of the day could not be touched upon, by rejecting scripts which were 'too provocative' and by anesthetizing anything political, Hays ensured that American film stories would suffer from arrested development. Had he been in office a decade earlier, there might have been no *Birth of a Nation*, no *Intolerance*."

Fairbanks's films were pure escapism, so this did not affect him as it might those filmmakers who were dealing in social issues or pushing other envelopes. Still, he was invested in the debate. His view on how to address the problem was more forward thinking, and in 1924 he proposed the model that would ultimately be adopted forty-four years later:

> I have always believed that censorship should be worked out upon a system of signals or guides to the public. Now, when a film is passed, you know nothing about it, except that the censors in your state, if there is censorship, have found it harmless, or according to their ideas, have made it harmless. This does not protect the mother who, because of its name, takes her children to see a film version of Ibsen's *A Doll's House*. A system of flags or other general warnings that would show into what general class a film belonged would be far more helpful.

---

* Brownlow describes him looking like a "startled mouse." Arbuckle biographer Greg Merritt noted that he had "teeth like mixed nuts."

Chaplin, who had worked with Arbuckle in 1914 at Keystone, was on his way to Europe when the scandal broke. Doug and Mary had accompanied him to the pier to see him off, and it was there that the old familiar wanderlust struck Doug again. Chaplin was taking the *Olympic*, the ship upon which the couple had sailed for their honeymoon the year before. "From some mysterious and unknown place in the offing," Fairbanks recalled, "a still small voice whispered in my mental ear: 'How would <u>you</u> like a trip to Europe?'"

Mary would have none of it. She "in effect, dragged me by my physical ear into the waiting taxicab and said: 'Nonsense, we have too much work to do.'" But the siren call was beckoning, and he began to wheedle. "Persistency," he wrote cheerfully, "is the mother of ocean travel." It would be easy, he urged. They would get into their car and motor south. Their plans would call for no plans. No fuss, no muss.

Of course, she capitulated. And of course, they were incapable of traveling without fuss or muss. By the time they departed on the *Olympic* in late September 1921, ensconced in the same suite they had shared on their honeymoon, it was the usual Fairbanksian parade. "If Mary and I had been traveling alone there would not have been so much to do," he mused. "But we started out like a party on a Cook's tour."

On their arrival at Cherbourg, they were met by a boat from an American battleship and invited to visit the sailors. They happily obliged. The sailors gave Doug some of his favorite brand of cigarettes, resulting in a tussle at customs. The French wanted duty paid on the twenty cents' worth of cigarettes, and Doug, per his norm, had no money at hand. Still, he refused to throw his new gift away. "But it's always that way with Douglas—he never thinks of money. It just doesn't seem to enter his life. As a consequence, he never has any when he goes out," Mary wrote later. "We probably would be gesticulating with the French customs officials yet if I hadn't found some change I didn't know I had in the bottom of my bag."

Such delays would cause a normal person to miss the train to Paris. But they were not normal people; the crew held the train for them. Still, the delay had its costs. By the time they arrived at the Hôtel de Crillon the dining room had closed, and they went to bed hungry.

The next three days were devoted entirely to interviews. Finally they broke for a day's visit (accompanied by Robert and Charlotte) to Fontainebleau, followed by a trip to the Follies Bergère. Mary was not impressed with the chorus girls. "As I saw them cavorting around the stage with their stockingless legs and cold blue knees, I rather pitied them," she recalled. "They looked as if they would so much prefer being home, plump and forty, to trying to appear sweet sixteen."*

In a fit of nationalistic, albeit cinematically misguided, pride the French refused to let *The Three Musketeers* be exhibited in their country, instead issuing their own version of the story. But the same did not apply to *Zorro*, which Doug learned was being shown at *sixteen* theaters at once in Montmartre. He managed to attend a screening in a small theater in the Apache district.

Chaplin was in town and came to visit. He remained a source of exasperation for Mary. "Poor Charlie—I don't believe he'd had the fun of a good argument since leaving Hollywood," she wrote. "'You're not having a good time,' he insisted, 'the only place you could possibly have a good time is at the studio working.' Well, I did my very best to convince him but it was no use. Again black was white with Charlie."

She must have been glad to be quit of him, as they left Paris bound for Basle on the Swiss frontier, with a stop at Dijon. "In Switzerland," Fairbanks recalled later, "everything looks as if it were put away at night and spread out in the morning." In Lucerne, they encountered the same landlord from the year prior, when Doug had bought a new car. They visited Mt. Pilatus, the Lion of Lucerne, and, best of all, went to a circus.

"Douglas was a school-boy again," Mary said. "One of the acrobats did some stunts that immediately won his admiration, and at the close of the performance he went to the dressing-tent and prevailed upon the performer to teach them to him. Probably he would be traveling with

---

* History has failed to note whether, in later years, she had the insight to see the irony in her words.

that circus now if I hadn't dragged him back to the hotel by main force."
The pattern of mischievous schoolboy and loving, scolding mother was
to repeat itself many times.

On they progressed. They visited a hotel at Interlaken for a quiet
and—it was hoped—anonymous lunch, only to discover that their waiter
was from the Algonquin Hotel. He "immediately decided not only to
reveal our identity but to turn the hotel upside down in our honor as
well," Mary recalled. "We appreciated his kindness, of course, but just
the same we wished he had stayed in New York." They motored through
St. Gotthard Pass and stayed several days in Lugano. They sent the car
ahead to meet them in Florence and took a train to Venice.

In Venice, they encountered the same old problem: Doug didn't
carry money and counted on someone else to handle details. "We stayed
at the Grand," he recalled later. "But to vary things we went to luncheon
one day at the Danelli. All went well until it was time to pay the check.
. . . Robert, who was the family banker, was 'out on location,' so to
speak. And I hadn't the slightest idea where. The only thing I could
think of was to order more coffee. Undoubtedly the waiter wondered
how I could drink it all, and if he had kept a close watch he might
have noted the simple and deft twist of the wrist with which I pitched
it into the canal below our balcony. . . . Finally I left Mary to stand
off the waiter while I went in search of Robert. In due time—which
was about an hour and a half—I located him in an obscure restaurant
experimenting with a new brand of spaghetti. He rendered financial aid,
and I departed to rescue Mary. But when I asked with a grand flourish
for the check the waiter said, 'That's perfectly all right, Mr. Fairbanks,
you don't have to pay the check. You see, the Grand and the Danelli are
under the same management so the check will be charged on your bill.'"

From there: Rome. They toured as many highlights as could be fit
into four days and left, as he said, with "a shamed feeling of sneaking
away." Even more fascinating was Naples, where they were permitted
access to freshly excavated portions of Pompeii not yet open to the
public.

Next, they took a steamship from Naples Harbor to Palermo, Sicily. From there they sailed to Tunis. Why Tunis? Mary had the answer: "Camels!—he was crazy to see camels." But Tunis brought him more than that. It planted early seeds in his mind for what would become *The Thief of Bagdad*. They stayed in an older, less modern hotel. "The architecture of the building itself was a feast for the eyes, with its mosaics, its Moorish windows and its fantastic Oriental designs," Mary wrote. "We were constantly being treated to sights that were strange combinations of street carnivals and scenes from the Arabian Nights."

Scenes indeed. At the bazaars in Tunis, their guide offered to take Mary into a harem. If this wasn't discomfiting enough, he stared fixedly at her pearls. Nervous, she slipped them off and handed them to Doug, who tucked them away in his pocket.

The ruins of Carthage were "an anticlimax" after Pompeii. More gratifying was the motor trip to Constantine, Algeria, where at last Doug encountered his desired camels. He was enchanted with them—and with all things Arabian. From Constantine to El Kantara to Biskra; *everything* served to enthrall. "We visited all the places of romantic interest," he wrote afterward. "But I think I enjoyed the wonderful nights under the starry heavens more than anything else. Because of the peculiar quality of the atmosphere more stars are visible here than anywhere else in the world, and a night in the desert is an unforgettable experience."

The opening shot of *The Thief* would reflect this, with the wise man telling a tale to a child in the desert at night and the stars combining to spell out the moral of the tale: Happiness Must Be Earned. It is likely that Doug opened and closed his film with scenes of the starry skies in the desert at night because of the effect these nights camping in the desert had had on him. But even the desert near Biskra "was too close to civilization to give me the thrill I longed for." He vowed that the next time he came, he would "go far up the Blue Nile and camp out on this wilderness of sand for many days."

As usual, his wife was a far more hesitant traveler. "Mary had her first and last camel ride," he recalled. "Certainly the camel enjoyed it far more than she did."

They retraced their route to Constantine and from there went to Algiers. The passage to Marseilles on the *Timgard* was the roughest the ship had ever experienced, and instead of a single day's voyage, they spent two days of misery aboard. The waves swept away most of the lifeboats, and they were driven almost to the coast of Spain. "I ate very little on that trip," Doug recalled philosophically. "In fact I might say, 'On the contrary.' As for Mary, I know she will never trust the Mediterranean again."

Paris was far more civilized. Mary got to visit her couturier, Jeanne Lanvin. More amusing for Doug was the process of buying perfume. "The perfumes are brought out to you in tiny samples and placed on the show tables like precious jewels. The vendeuse draws out the stopper, waves it in front of you, and with a long drawn out 'a—a—a—ah!' steps back to note the effect," Mary wrote. "They fascinated Douglas and every time he went out he bought me a bottle of perfume." It was not just for his bride that he obtained fragrances. His dressing room at home was a veritable bottle shop of aftershaves and pomades.

After ten days, they went to London to arrange for the premiere of *Musketeers* and *Fauntleroy*. Doug and Robert flew across the English Channel, while Mary and Charlotte, more prudent, took a boat. The starstruck pilot let Doug take the controls for part of the flight. Ever boyish, he tipped and dipped the plane with abandon, until finally Robert passed a note to the cockpit: "If you don't care anything about yourself, please remember that I want to get back to Hollywood." Fairbanks later confessed that watching Robert's face during this experience was his favorite part of the trip.

Fairbanks rented Covent Garden for the two premieres, stirring up, to quote Mary, "considerable commotion . . . all because this fine old place had in the past been sacred to opera and royal entertainments." More interesting than this fuss, to Doug, was his visit to old Temple Church, where several crusaders were buried. He had not yet settled on *Robin Hood* for his next film. In fact, when he left for this trip, he had decided against it. But the sight of these graves moved him. Perhaps, he thought, if the Crusades could be worked into the story . . .

Mother, Ella, and father, H. Charles Ulman. Each was married multiple times—and not always legally. *Howard Gotlieb Archival Research Center, Boston University*

Thicker than thieves. Brothers Robert, left, and Douglas, right, were partners both in mischief and in business. *Howard Gotlieb Archival Research Center, Boston University*

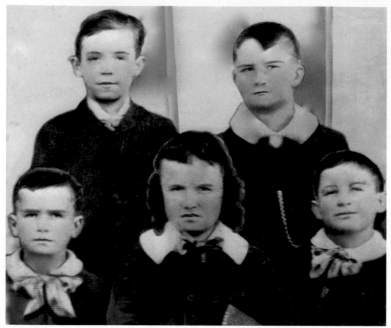

His first nemesis. Patrick McGovern, front row center, is surrounded by Douglas, front left, and Robert, front right. Douglas was jealous of Patrick's finery, so he tugged at his curls, earning himself a bloody nose and a reputation for being unafraid to take on larger opponents.

His first mentor. Thespian Frederick Warde reunites with Fairbanks during the filming of *The Three Musketeers*. The old actor retained a great affection for his student, whose fame was ultimately to surpass his a thousandfold.

The soap factory, 1907. In order to obtain permission to marry heiress Beth Sully, Fairbanks had to agree to quit the theater and work in his father-in-law's soap factory. As with any and all things in life, he performed with a relish.

Stage star. With Ruth Shepley in *A Gentleman of Leisure*, 1911.

His first studio. Sets at Triangle were cheaply constructed. Hand-painted plywood stood in for marble. The glimpse of the outdoors visible to the left of the set demonstrate that shooting was open-air. From *Flirting with Fate*, 1916.

Clowning behind the scenes of *The Half Breed*.

The unsmiling Doug was not what audiences wanted to see, and *The Half Breed* was a rare failure. He would not repeat the mistake of breaking character again.

On location for *The Half Breed*. Alma Rubens, far left; Fairbanks, front center; Allan Dwan, in goggles.

The original bromance. Doug and best friend for life Charlie Chaplin outside the offices of the Douglas Fairbanks Pictures Corporation in Hollywood.

With Doug Jr. at Watch Hill, Rhode Island, on the front porch of Daniel Sully's estate, 1916.

Fairbanks and Elsie Janis, competing with a saw for the prize in toothiness. It was at Elsie Janis's Tarrytown estate that Douglas Fairbanks met Mary Pickford in 1915.

Mary Pickford in 1919. The most famous and beloved woman on the planet.

Fame and fortune. There were Douglas Fairbanks cigars, Douglas Fairbanks paper dolls, Douglas Fairbanks notebooks . . . He, Mary Pickford, and Charlie Chaplin were ubiquitous in the prewar years.

Fairbanks signed ten thousand photos for the Red Cross while waiting to film *The Man from Painted Post*.

With cowboys at a Wyoming ranch. Fairbanks was always at ease with cowpokes and trick riders, and he was as likely to have them to dinner as royalty.

A tale of two directors.

ABOVE: John Emerson, seated, on the set of *Down to Earth*, was replaced by Allan Dwan after Emerson and Anita Loos staged a strike over *The Man from Painted Post*.

BELOW: Doug, Allan Dwan, Tully Marshall, and brother Robert Fairbanks amid the post-"tornado" destruction in *A Modern Musketeer*.

Creating the illusion that they are out to sea in *Down to Earth*.

On the set of an unidentified film. Fairbanks's personal charm was experienced by all who worked with him.

His first foray into a period costume, and his first appearance as D'Artagnan, in *A Modern Musketeer*.

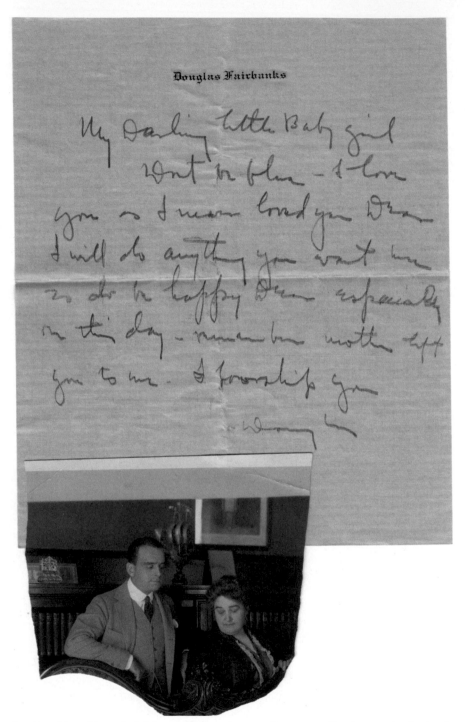

Cutting his wife and child out of the picture. One year after his mother's death, Doug sent Mary this letter. He trimmed Beth and Junior out of the accompanying photo, leaving only Ella.

Clowning around.

ABOVE: Doug polishes the shoes of assistant cameraman Glen MacWilliams, while Charlie gives a brush to Paramount star Thomas Meighan.

BELOW: Cauliflower-eared Bull Montana has *Mollycoddle* Doug in a tight spot.

Brother John was a lifelong adviser and aide to his younger brother, Doug.

Caught in oversize jammies by a ladies' club in *When the Clouds Roll By*. There was a loopy humor to Fairbanks's heroics that made them unique.

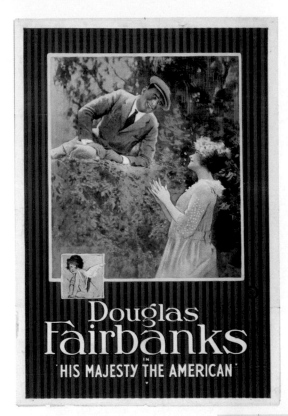

Douglas
Fairbanks
IN
"HIS MAJESTY THE AMERICAN"

His Majesty the American was the first release for United Artists, cofounded by Fairbanks, Mary Pickford, Charlie Chaplin, and D. W. Griffith.

DOUGLAS
FAIRBANKS
IN
"THE MOLLYCODDLE
SCENARIO BY TOM GERAGHTY
STORY BY HAROLD MacGRATH

The Mollycoddle. Fairbanks was so taken with Theodore Roosevelt that he paid $5,000 to retain the term *mollycoddle* in his film because it was a favorite term of Teddy's.

Return from a triumphant honeymoon. Doug and Mary arrive in New York on July 28, 1920.

The mobs did not always make it easy. Terror at an English garden party is reflected on Mary's face as the throngs overwhelm them.

Pickford and Fairbanks are barely visible among an adoring mob in Spain, 1924.

With the 1920s came the switch to swashbuckling roles and an exponential increase in his fame and success. LEFT: As D'Artagnan in *The Three Musketeers.* BELOW LEFT: As *The Thief of Bagdad.* BELOW RIGHT: As *Robin Hood. From the collection of the International Movie Poster Archive.*

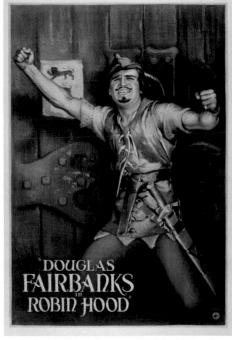

Floats like a butterfly . . . Fairbanks did the vast majority of his stunts himself.

Doug versus the censors. This shot from *Robin Hood*—his greatest success—was one of many that were trimmed by censorship boards across America.

Caught unawares. Doug and Mary's love was deep and sincere, until his ungovernable jealousy undid them both.

Visitors were always welcome at the Pickford-Fairbanks Studios.

ABOVE: Doug and Mary give a tour to visiting dignitaries.

BELOW LEFT: the general public was allowed to watch filming and, if very lucky, would get their pictures taken with the star

BELOW RIGHT: Washington Senators pitcher Walter Johnson and slugger Babe Ruth join Fairbanks in a game.

Life's a beach. Doug, Mary, and little dog Zorro enjoy the sunshine in Santa Monica.

Douglas Jr., far right, outgrew his chubby phase and became a competitive force on the silver screen.

Joseph Schenck, center, was the force that kept UA successful. Sam Goldwyn was the fly in the corporate ointment. From left to right are M. C. Levee, Fairbanks, Samuel Goldwyn, Schenck, Norma Talmadge, Buster Keaton, and Edwin Carewe.

The Gaucho was the beginning of the end of everything.

ABOVE: Unsubstantiated rumors of an affair with costar Lupe Vélez damaged his marriage.

RIGHT: Snide implications that our hero was less than perfect were beginning to be published.

THE PASSING OF AGILITY

BELOW: Contemplating a stunt, as only Fairbanks could.

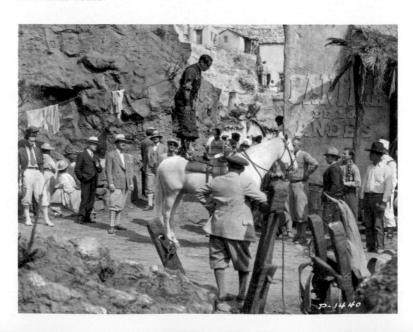

Fallen idol. After he left Mary, nothing seemed to go right.

Doug and Sylvia. He is reduced from hero to lapdog, carrying her jewelry case.

Doug and the Nazi Joseph Goebbels, far left, were in adjacent cabanas in Venice, August 1939. Goebbels, one of history's most notorious anti-Semites, was likely unaware that he was tipping off the half-Jewish Fairbanks to the Nazi plans to invade Poland. Fairbanks was able to get his wife's family out of England just in time.

Meeting Sylvia, her sister, and her sister's children after getting them safely to America. With his Great Dane, Marco Polo, who was with him at his death.

They spent the final days of the trip in Paris. Mary caught a cold en route, and by the time she was in their hotel, she was suffering from a fierce case of tonsillitis. Still, she soldiered on. They visited Versailles and the Little Palais at Trianon, as well as Malmaison. Lottie's four-year-old daughter, Gwynne (still called "baby Mary" at this point), was rightfully indifferent to these spectacles but loved the Punch and Judy shows in the parks along the Champs-Élysées.

Finally, they sailed from Havre on the *City of Paris*. "Whoever selects a ship because of the excellence of the cuisine makes a grave mistake. It is much better to examine how soft the couches are," Doug wrote of the return journey. "The French deck scrubbers are so expert that they can almost miss a person with a bucket of water every time they throw it."

They arrived in New York City with a case of indigestion. Two weeks at the Ritz were spent, in his words, in "conferences, conferences, conferences. Lawyers, interviewers, authors, interviewers, actors, inter-viewers, photographers, interviewers, members of our own organization, interviewers, prize-fighters, and more interviewers—always interviewers." The city began to chafe, as did all big cities for him. "They cramp me, give me a sensation of being handcuffed," he wrote.

They decided enough was enough. They would go home for Christmas, and Doug would finalize the decision on his next film at the New Year. Nineteen twenty-two would bring him much: his biggest commercial success, *Robin Hood*, and with it the wherewithal to create his greatest artistic achievement—*The Thief of Bagdad*.

The sun was shining brighter.

11

Prince of Thieves

FAIRBANKS AT FIRST RESISTED the idea of making what would become the biggest financial success of his career. In the fall of 1921 he was still considering *The Virginian*, in addition to *Monsieur Beaucaire*, or a sequel to *Zorro*.* Credit must be given to Allan Dwan, with an able assist from Fairbanks brothers Robert and John, for changing his mind.

Sometime in the prior year or so, Fairbanks and Dwan had mended fences. Whatever disagreements *Arizona* brought were forgotten.† In fact, there had been reports at the time of preproduction on *The Three Musketeers* that Dwan was slated to direct the Dumas story, causing the director to release a statement saying that while such an arrangement would be a very pleasant one to him, he was tied up with another organization. But by December 1921 he was free and signed a contract to direct Fairbanks's next film.

Prior to formalizing the contract, Dwan had been directing at the Brunton studio across the street from Clune's. As previously noted, *The Three Musketeers* was filmed at both studios, while Mary's production company was also filming at the Brunton stages. It was this proximity that aided Dwan in interesting Fairbanks in *Robin Hood*. The idea, when

---

* Fairbanks sold his rights to *The Virginian* in 1923 for $70,875. He sold his rights to *Monsieur Beaucaire*—purchased for $30,000—the following year for a modest profit.

† As with the case of Loos and Emerson, Fairbanks never spoke of the quarrel.

first suggested, met firm resistance. "The spectacle of a lot of flat-footed outlaws in Lincoln Green, a few paunchy friars and a homeless minstrel or two singing a roundelay in the shades of Sherwood Forest did not strike me as anything to make a picture about," Fairbanks wrote. Dwan, to his credit, saw the problem in Fairbanksian terms: "He couldn't see any agility in the character," he observed. But happily, Allan also knew his man.

Dwan persuaded John and Robert to buy archery sets, and he and Jack Dempsey, accompanied by an expert archer, would stroll over to Clune's at the noon hour to practice. Studiously ignoring Doug, they started shooting. "Well that was a contest, so Doug got interested," Dwan recounted. "He wandered over and tried a bow." Untrained, he released the arrow, and "the thong of the bow struck his wrists as they always do if you don't know how to avoid it—and made it hurt. And he thought: this isn't so pansy-like after all."

As with any athletic activity, Doug wanted to learn. The expert worked with him and soon, Dwan recounted, "Doug got better than anybody else and"—more importantly—"whether he did or not, we saw that he did." As Fairbanks improved, Dwan launched his pitch. An enemy could steal an apple and you could shoot it out of his hand. Or hit him in the pants! Or pin him to a tree! Think of the tricks you could do!

Doug's eyes, according to Dwan, "sparkled a bit." Yes, he admitted. That would be great. Dwan pressed his case. "That's Robin Hood. . . . That's the guy we want you interested in."

"I don't know," Fairbanks replied. "I don't want to have anything to do with it."

Finally, the idea of the Crusades provided the hook. The December visit to the Temple Church had had an effect. Mary reported that Doug "was tremendously interested in the graves of the crusaders." Fairbanks himself reported:

I came by chance upon some old manuscripts of the period of Richard the Lion-Hearted and the Crusades. The robust, heroic figure of Richard . . . stirred me at once. The period contained every dramatic element: a strong religious impulse, a kingdom undermined by treachery at home while the flower of its knighthood sought adventure in foreign lands, fair maidens won by valor in war or tournament and left behind by their knights . . . all the romance, the chivalry, the color of the adventurous Middle Ages.

That did the trick—almost. He still did not want to play Robin Hood; now he wanted to play Richard the Lion-Hearted. Somehow Dwan talked him out of this but convinced him that they could combine the Richard story with the Robin Hood tale. Fairbanks wrote later that "if, instead of sentencing him to an indefinite term in Sherwood Forest, I could involve him in the stirring history of the period, I would have a real story." Proof of this sudden burst of enthusiastic creativity, in the form of a one-page scenario, has been reproduced in several prior Fairbanks studies, with good cause. His fountain pen fairly blots with his excitement.

"We had nothing real to go by," Fairbanks wrote, "except in the one case a loved character and the knowledge of the period he lived in and certain deeds and exploits which incidentally I had done again and again in modern guise." Today audiences are accustomed to the idea of Robin Hood associated with evil Prince John and the return of rightful power to Richard the Lion-Hearted. Dwan claimed that none of this existed at the time. "There were just tales of the man who robbed the rich to feed the poor. We invented all the knighthood, invented the fact that he was off on the Crusades and had to come back to save the throne for King Richard from his brother John." This may or may not have been true (Dwan seems to have conveniently forgotten Sir Walter Scott's *Ivanhoe*), but with his characteristic loose grip on the facts, Dwan went on to state: "Lady Marian was invented."* Biographers frequently

---

* Maid Marian preceded Dwan and Lotta Woods's creation by centuries and was even present in a 1912 film version of the story. Furthermore, an operatic version of *Robin Hood* played on Broadway in 1912 just down the street from where Fairbanks was playing in Cohan's *Officer 666*, and it also featured Maid Marian. Possibly Dwan was referring to Maid Marian's elevation to Lady Marian and her placement in Richard's court.

quote a Fairbanks observation that many people complained that the film's story wandered too far from that of the book: "If these critics know what book they are talking about, they have a distinct advantage over me." Doug, as previously noted, was never one for reading. The book all were referring to was Howard Pyle's 1883 *The Merry Adventures of Robin Hood*, a staple for every little boy in the late Victorian and Edwardian eras.

Fairbanks saw other challenges to overcome. Paris-born Robert Florey was to become a journeyman director in the studio system of the 1930s and '40s, best known for directing the Marx brothers in *The Cocoanuts*. In the 1920s he was a film journalist and Fairbanks publicist, writing for French-language magazines about the movie industry. He was close to Fairbanks, and his contemporary reports often serve as a more reliable account of events than do the later, embellished memories of others. He recalled Fairbanks raising the specter of further obstacles: "The sets worried him in particular. Where would one find a feudal castle in California? *Robin Hood* meant moving the whole unit to Europe."

As late as Christmas Fairbanks still favored *The Virginian*. A week later, on New Year's Day, things were different. Smoking nonstop, lighting one cigarette from the remains of the last, he addressed his assembled team at Pickfair.

"I'm going to make *Robin Hood*. We'll make all the sets in Hollywood. I've made up my mind!"

The energetic delivery of this phrase by Douglas will always stay with me. His fist pounded on a small table and everyone was quite silent while he explained at length . . . "We must buy a new studio where we will all work together; I have in mind the old Jesse Hampton Studio on the Santa Monica Boulevard—round the studio are fields and nothing but fields. There we will build enormous sets: Nottingham as it was in the 12th century, Richard the Lion Heart's castle, a Palestine town, Sherwood Forest, the bandit's cave. Inside the studio we will build all the interiors and in the big field to the south we will set up the Crusaders' camp in France. We'll have several thousand costumes designed from contemporary documents, we'll order shields, lances and sabers by the thousand, we'll restage a tournament, we'll . . ."

"How many thousands of dollars will we spend?" interrupted John Fairbanks.

"That doesn't matter," Doug went on. "*Robin Hood* should be made lavishly or not made at all."*

Preparations for the film began at the old Clune studio. Twenty-two hired experts assembled a 250-volume reference library. Fairbanks reportedly lingered hours at a time with the books—an uncharacteristic behavior. Florey reported that Doug even let his regular training slide: "I can recall the broken-hearted expressions of Bull Montana or Jack Dempsey or even 'Kid' McCoy waiting in vain for their friend at the running track." Wilfred Buckland, art director of many of Fairbanks's Artcraft productions, made models of all the proposed sets. Florey recalled that "Douglas decorated his personal apartment with them, and the man who was generally so restless would stay peacefully seated for hours at a time looking at [them]." Fairbanks doodled little drawings of crusaders and their horses, the latter, in Florey's words, "looking like horned beasts. Fortunately the cross he drew on his knights' chests got the idea across."

When they purchased the Hampton Studio at the corner of Santa Monica and La Brea for $150,000, they acquired not only studio space but also a large back lot. The modest plant underwent extensive improvements to meet the requirements of the two superstar producers. Assistant director Bruce "Lucky" Humberstone, who worked at the studio in the later part of the decade, recalled, "Mary had a complete bungalow that not only had an enormous living room, [but] a dining room, two bedrooms, a library, a kitchen and service porch. And she kept servants on the lot all during production. We always went to her bungalow for

---

* Any inconsistencies between this rendering of Florey's story and those in other accounts relate strictly to differences in translation. The source is the same.

lunch, and it was like dining at home. . . . You had a butler that would
serve you luncheon that was cooked by her cook or chef in her own
kitchen, and we'd sit down like ladies and gentlemen." Doug, instead
of a bungalow, occupied a third of the first floor of the administration
buildings facing Santa Monica Boulevard. He had an office, dressing
room, barber shop, makeup room, playroom, bar, and a saltwater plunging pool. A gymnasium was in a separate building perpendicular to the
administration complex, backing up to Formosa.

There was a reason behind his willingness to headquarter in the
long, barracks-like administration building. Fairbanks, it seems, liked to
emulate the earliest Olympians and run in the nude.* This, of course,
was impossible in a busy town—but he found a solution. Workmen
built a concrete-lined trench running parallel to Santa Monica Boulevard—over six feet deep, almost two city blocks long, and wide enough
for Fairbanks to turn around in, enabling him to run multiple laps. It
was isolated from view both from the street by a solid wall and from
office windows by a trellis. An interior staircase within the building
provided him access to his private running track.†

The only other nudity at the studio occurred in the steam room,
located at the east end of the administration building. Here Fairbanks would sit in mint-green-tiled splendor, joined by friends and
whatever stray (male) royalty was in town, demonstrating that to the
democratic Douglas at least, cowboy and king were all the same under
their skivvies.

The studio yard provided a ready source of exercise as well. It
was littered with rings, bars, wooden horses, and sundry other fitness

---

* He appears to have been comfortable with public nudity—as long as there were no women
  within hailing distance. Multiple photos have surfaced of him sunbathing in his birthday
  suit in secluded and shielded sections of yachts or in native waters in remote lands.
† Evidence of the interior staircase—torn out sometime in the years after his death—can be
  seen beneath the first floor of the building fronting Santa Monica Boulevard. Fairbanks
  could descend the private staircase to the trench entrance, shed his garb, conduct his
  run, and return to his offices with staff none the wiser. A portion of the trench survives
  to the present day, befuddling those few who stumble across it.

paraphernalia. "I never cross the yard without improvising and overcoming some obstacle," he said.

His company moved into the newly christened Pickford-Fairbanks Studios on February 11. Nine days later, he and Mary departed for New York City. "We went with him to the little station at Pasadena and as the train was moving off his last words were still instructions about *Robin Hood*," recalled Florey.

The following day, John Fairbanks brought in more than five hundred workmen, masons, and carpenters to start building the sets, which would ultimately take up a full acre of the twenty-acre back lot. By February 23, wooden scaffolding outlined the castle and village. While the castle foundation consisted of blocks of rock, the walls were not stone. Two hundred workmen constructed panels of four-inch-thick molds for the "stone" of the walls. Into these molds were poured 252 tons of liquid plaster mixed with wood shavings and cement. Another 125 tons were required for the village of Nottingham.

The statistics continued to pile up and were staggering. One million feet of lumber. Thirty tons of nails. Twenty thousand yards of "heavy velvets and rich cloths." Each of the eight castle towers had a capacity of 276,000 gallons of water. The stock of three tanneries was needed to make the shoes. In the end, it is enough to say that everything about the production was big—and the castle was biggest of all.* Its main facade was 620 feet long, with a steel-framed drawbridge and a thirty-foot moat. The plaster stones were painted to give them age; moss and ivy were then planted in the crevices. Work continued into the nights, aided by large searchlights and impeded by the mosquitoes they attracted. The inner banquet hall (an outdoor set) was larger than the waiting area of New York's Penn Station.

Doug saw none of this. He was in New York, providing moral support to Mary as she testified in court on a case that had been dog-

---

* A painted glass matte made it appear taller yet for distance shots. The castle was not a single set piece but a series of interlocking pieces that could be arranged as needed. It was the largest physical set built in the silent era, outstripping that built for the Babylonian sequence in *Intolerance*.

ging her for four years.* ("This suit's been going on since Grant was a cadet," Fairbanks said, waggishly.) The civil suit, for which she had been served papers that long-ago day when she, Doug, and Charlie arrived in New York for the war bond drive, was finally coming before a jury. Cora Wilkenning, an agent, claimed that Mary pledged her a 10 percent commission—over $100,000—if she could get competing offers from studios during her 1916 negotiations with Adolph Zukor. Both Mary and Mama Charlotte testified indignantly that this was not the case. Since it was a she said/she said situation, the jury took less than a day to side with America's sweetheart, and the Fairbankses were free to return home. They arrived in Hollywood on March 9. "The train was on time, and Douglas on the platform in one leap," Florey recalled. "His first words were 'Well, then?'"

He paused long enough to clown for photographers, putting the hook of a walking cane over his bent arm, flexing his biceps to make the cane jump, then catching it midair. But it was clear that he was impatient to get to the studio.

What happened next has become part of silent film folklore—possibly true, probably not. We come to the Fairbanks-almost-shelved-the-film myth. Allan Dwan immortalized the story by repeating it to Kevin Brownlow, whose seminal *The Parade's Gone By* dedicated an entire chapter to Fairbanks's *Robin Hood*. The tale, now oft told, goes like this: Fairbanks saw the huge sets and, overwhelmed, told Dwan that he was canceling the project. "I can't compete with that," Dwan reported him as saying. "My work is intimate. People know me as an intimate actor. I can't work in a great vast thing like that." By the time Dwan was retelling his story to Brownlow a few years later for the *Hollywood* series, Fairbanks never even got into the studio. "He got as far as the

---

* Sitting still in a courtroom was challenging for Fairbanks. While present and accounted for during the critical testimony, he reportedly spent much of the proceedings out in the hallway, sitting on a radiator, smoking cigarettes, and watching the New York skyline. He had been reluctant to make the New York trip just as *Robin Hood* was taking shape, and only his love for Mary could separate him from the project.

gate of the studio and he told the chauffeur to hold up and he took a look in through the gate at these big sets and he backed the car off and he said 'Take me home.' And he told his brothers who followed him, 'You can forget it,' he said. 'I wouldn't go near those damn things. . . . They'd swamp me.'" Dwan, by his account, took a day or two, asked him to come back to the set, and won him over with a tapestry-covered playground slide and a trampoline. He showed his star how, trapped on a balustrade forty feet in the air,* he could escape Prince John's encroaching troops by sliding down a long drape. ("He did it a thousand times—like a kid," Dwan claimed. "He jumped off that balcony 'til he practically wore out the burlap.") He could appear at a remote window by vaulting a moat (thus the trampoline) and climbing up vines placed on the castle wall. "These were the things that finally made him buy *Robin Hood*," Dwan concluded. "But it wasn't easy to get him to do it."

Dwan little suspected that his own version of the tale to students at Columbia University in the fall of 1922 would survive him. And he forgot, or never knew, that Robert Florey had also provided a contemporary account. The reality, it seems, was less dramatic than Dwan would have us believe.†

It is true that the trip to the studio from the station was planned so that the sets would hit Fairbanks's eye all at once. Every account agrees: they took Highland Avenue to Hollywood Boulevard, then La Brea to Santa Monica, thence to the corner of Santa Monica and Formosa. Dwan told the Columbia students, "I purposely engineered it so he would not see it until, when we drove around a corner, the set would loom up. He looked at it for nearly a minute. I said, 'What do you think of it?' He said, 'Heavens, you have taken me seriously.'" And that, it seems, was all there was to the story when Dwan recounted it in 1922.

---

* I choose this number as an average. The height of the balcony seemed to increase ten feet with every retelling. In fairness to Dwan, it *was* very high.

† It is of significance that Dwan biographer Frederic Lombardi agrees that Dwan's later version of events was a fabrication.

But Florey was also in the car. His recollection was that upon seeing the castle, Doug's eyes widened and he exclaimed, "Gosh!" followed by "Ah! Isn't it wonderful?" The rest of his account in no way suggests a man daunted by the size of his sets:

> Without even wasting his time changing his traveling suit, Douglas rushed onto the set to get a closer look at the huge construction. Everyone followed him. . . . For more than an hour Douglas walked about among the sets; he was interested in everything and looked in detail at the work on each one; he questioned the workmen who, greatly flattered, replied in great detail. At last, around 3:30, Douglas made his first appearance at his offices, but he was much too excited to take note of the mass of personal mail waiting for him, and he kindly, but firmly dismissed the army of secretaries who were waiting for his orders and ready for him to sign a pile of letters.
>
> The great star sat in an armchair near the bay window which looked out on the castle façade, and started to talk to his devoted collaborators. During the New York trip, Douglas had given a lot of thought to his scenario and was already thinking about making certain slight alterations. He explained all the new stunts he'd thought up during the last five days' train trip.
>
> He had even already rehearsed a scene with Paul Dickey who was to play the part of the villain Guy of Gisbourne, and showed his audience the way in which he intended to kill Guy of Gisbourne in the last part of the film. "I shall break his back, like that, against one of the castle pillars," he explained. "Look—his body goes round the pillar; with one arm I hold his throat; with the other his heels and I slowly break his back."

There is little likelihood that, having seen the sets, Fairbanks contemplated shelving the project. For one thing, over $248,000 had been spent on materials, labor, and architects. Furthermore, the industry recession was, if anything, worse. No bank would fund a film project, not even from the estimable Fairbanks. It was his own money in those plaster walls. He knew there was no going back and did not need a playground slide to convince him. From that date until shooting began, Fairbanks devoted himself to practicing his stunts and sword fights, doing screen tests with actors, and making costume tests.

He was careful, however, not to announce that the project was the tale of Robin Hood. The story would be too easy for a competing studio to produce cheaply, stealing his thunder. Photos and press releases went out showing Doug practicing on his bow and arrow, announcing that the next Fairbanks release would be a film entitled *The Spirit of Chivalry*. Mindful of the troubles they'd had with the alternative version of *The Three Musketeers*, Cap O'Brien suggested that the film, upon release, be titled *Douglas Fairbanks in Robin Hood*.*

The casting of Little John perhaps revealed a small chink in our hero's armor. Assistant director Richard Rosson hoped to have Maurice Bennett "Lefty" Flynn—a friend and Yale athlete—cast in the part. He gave Flynn explicit instructions: "If he is going through his daily workout and invites you to join him, play along but don't do your best. Always let Doug win. Show him that you are a good athlete but not too good."

Flynn was nervous at meeting the great Fairbanks and required a few shots of bootleg gin to steady his nerves. He forgot his instructions and hit a tremendous home run during a pickup game of softball. Adolphe Menjou recounted:

> Doug slapped him on the back and told him he was great. So Lefty decided that Rosson had been completely wrong.
>
> Then they started high jumping. Doug jumped 5 feet 6 inches, but Lefty cleared 5 feet 7 inches. Doug grinned and slapped him on the back. Lefty thought he was making a big hit. When they tried broad-jumping, Lefty beat Doug by 2 feet. He beat him at

---

* His advice was taken. Note that in the case of *Musketeers*, the competition was a retitled five-year-old film. But the risk of simultaneous releases of films with identical titles and plots was not a new one. Dual versions of *Carmen* and *Romeo and Juliet* had duked it out just a few years before.

pole-vaulting, at shot-putting, at everything, and Doug kept giving him his famous grin and telling him what a wonderful athlete he was. But next day Doug cast Alan Hale in the part of Little John.

The story, of course, may be oversimplified. Hale may have been a better actor. But Menjou's commentary remains: "Doug was always a little jealous of his own special accomplishments."*

Then there was the matter of Doug's wig. Florey reports that Fairbanks tried twenty or more before finding one that worked. An initial glance at the unstructured mop of hair would suggest the opposite, but our eyes have been trained—fooled, rather—by years of foppish helmet-haired pageboys that subsequent movie swashbucklers have worn. Fairbanks, for both *The Three Musketeers* and *Robin Hood*, wanted hair authentic to the period, hair that was blunt cut with the edge of a knife, not styled by scissors, curling iron, and spray. Yet it could not look like a wig; it had to move as real hair would. Apparently dissatisfied with the wig he had worn in *The Three Musketeers*, he assigned costumer Mitchell Leisen to solve the problem. Leisen recalled, "One of the tough things was to get Douglas' wig, the long hair, to fall naturally. It was always so stiff; no matter what you did with your head, the hair stayed there." The solution finally came from the patriarch of the famous Westmore family, who crafted a wig of the finest toupee hair. "Real hair," Leisen said. "And he worked and worked and worked with it, but the result was: if Doug shook his head, the hair just flew all over the place."†

Leisen was also in charge of the costumes, which numbered in the thousands. Chain mail armor was too heavy for modern Californians,

---

* Not all agreed with Menjou. Ralph Faulkner, who visited Doug on set the following year, wrote: "He is delighted when they beat his records. It spurs him to greater efforts. . . . I'd hate to be the man who would try to get in right with Doug by throwing one of these contests."
† George Westmore had worked with Fairbanks before. In the 1910s he had devised for him what was then a novel haircut—layered so that it would not flop over his eyes during his stunts. Westmore's sons became heads of the makeup departments of major studios in the 1930s and '40s.

so he devised a method of knitting hemp, ironing it flat, and adding silver leaf.*

The castle and other exteriors were not yet completed when filming began on the morning of April 3, 1922. The first scenes were shot in the tent of Richard the Lion-Hearted. Musicians played mood music as Doug, playing the Earl of Huntington (later Robin Hood), asked his king to permit him to leave the Crusades and return to England. Six takes and Dwan was satisfied.

Filming went very smoothly. "The war made *Robin Hood* easy," said Dwan. "There wasn't a single man on the lot either in the capacity of an extra or on the technical staff, who had not had military training. They knew the importance of obedience. They knew how to take orders and, in turn, how to give orders; every mother's son of them." Those portions of the rushes—when the slate board is being held up to the camera, or the actors are resuming their positions—show a happy and laughing crew. "Doug would hold up the work at any time, at heaven only knows what expense per minute, to do some absurd or ridiculous thing if it promised a laugh," Frank Case recalled. "Often there was a method in it, for if the actors were tired and . . . things not going well, Doug would suddenly be missing and as suddenly reappear in a costume that had nothing to do with the picture or the period, accompanied by some strange derelict he had picked up at the gate, or by a live bear on a chain, or a monkey. Then all work would cease for half an hour or so." The bear (a tame animal, reportedly) featured in a practical joke Fairbanks pulled on one particularly high-strung staffer.† A friendly arm-over-the-shoulder gesture from Doug provided the requisite honey on the jumpy gentleman's posterior, and the bear soon followed, hoisted through the window of his office. The ensuing chase was good fun for

---

* Dwan had misremembered the chain mail costumes as painted burlap in his interview with Brownlow for *The Parade's Gone By*. Leisen, in a later interview, set the record straight.

† Case identifies him only as "Benny," making the victim possibly the long-suffering but amiable Bennie Zeidman. If Bennie could be thrown in a pool and almost drown, a bear going after his nether regions might have seemed like just another day at the office.

all—except the unfortunate victim. And even he "took it in good part," according to Case. "He knew that life on that lot was give and take. If you could put one over on Douglas, that was fine, too. If you could."

Mitchell Leisen concurred. "He played all the time," he said. "When some athlete came by, he would stop everything and race or play tennis." He invented his own racquet game—a more athletic version of badminton—that he named "Doug."

He opened the studio to the public on June 11, as a fundraiser for an entity identified only as the Assistance League. He enjoyed this so much that soon visitors weren't restricted to charity events. They were so common that signs were placed about the complex (Welcome/Follow Robin Hood's Arrow →) to guide them to the back lot. There Fairbanks had bleachers built so they could watch the filming without being underfoot.*

This is not to say that things were simple; Doug simply made them look easy. Outtakes are revealing. In one series of shots, Fairbanks loops his bow around a hapless Charlie Stevens, lifts him up bodily, and in one swift, graceful move, hangs him on a protruding rod over a doorway. In the completed film, it occurs in a merry blink of an eye. The rushes, however, show him lifting Stevens, shot after shot, high above his head, and hanging him on that rod. He had no trouble hitting his mark for most takes. (Getting the bow over the rod with Steven's dead weight at the bottom could have been no easy task in itself.) The challenge was to do it in a manner both quick and fluid. There could be no hesitation, no jockeying to get the top of the bow threaded over the rod. He tries repeatedly, but it is never just right. One is exhausted just watching him.† So too with outtakes of Fairbanks fighting Prince John's men in the castle. Here he was not fencing but hacking with a

---

* Hosts of family albums in the 1920s were graced with photos of children and maiden aunts smiling shyly as they pose in front of the sets. The luckiest were able to snap Fairbanks, Dwan, and the production team huddled for an impromptu conference on King Richard's throne or strolling the village of Nottingham. These turn up periodically in online auctions, providing an intimate glimpse of the experience, almost one hundred years later.

† In the end, Dwan elected to break this up into three separate shots.

broadsword, again and again, take after take. Knitted hemp or no, he must have broken quite a sweat.

He and the rest of the crew also broke a sweat two weeks into the production, when fire—that ever-present threat in a studio filled with flammable materials—broke out in the costume department. Doug headed an impromptu bucket brigade, and the blaze was extinguished with only slight damage to the over $82,000 worth of costumes.

Another challenge related to a scene where Prince John's falcon kills a carrier pigeon. A trained falcon was purchased for $250 and imported from England. It arrived with a list of instructions: keep it in the dark, feed it only raw meat, and ("especially important") bathe the bird twice a week. It is unknown who inherited these tasks, but the falcon performed beautifully. It was the pigeons that wouldn't cooperate with cameraman Arthur Edeson. It took a hundred takes to keep both pigeon and predator in the frame as the falcon took down its prey. It is undocumented how many pigeons gave their lives in the service of art.

Animals (or, rather, one very little animal) forced a reshoot of another sequence. In one scene, Wallace Beery, playing Richard the Lion-Hearted, was eating meat and throwing the bones to his dogs. Prominent among them was a little Airedale that Doug had given to Mary the year before. Originally named War Bond, the pooch—a rare breed at the time and purchased for $4,000—was rechristened Zorro. He became part and parcel of the little family, coming along on European trips and even being featured on the couple's custom bookplates. But one place he didn't belong was on the *Robin Hood* set. Airedales, it seemed, had not existed as a breed in the twelfth century. When this was pointed out during the screening of daily rushes, Fairbanks, dreading anachronisms, ordered the scene be reshot.

Another scene that was shot multiple times was a sequence in which Fairbanks climbed the chain of the castle's drawbridge. Brother Robert, per his daughter, "had neither interest nor ability in athletics himself, [thus] he worried constantly over the risks Douglas took." Because of the sizable investment in the film, he convinced a reluctant Fairbanks to yield and permit a stuntman to perform the scene. "When the scene was rehearsed and the double climbed the chain, the expression on Doug's face was not pleasant," Letitia Fairbanks recalled. "Obviously the double was lacking in the usual Fairbanks grace so the scene was called for the day and Robert was instructed to find another double."

Later that afternoon, Chuck Lewis and Kenneth Davenport held their breath and watched Fairbanks climb up and down the chain. "After that he felt better," Letitia recalled, "for he had always maintained he would never ask anyone to perform a stunt that he couldn't or wouldn't do himself." The following morning when the scene was to be filmed with a new stuntman, Doug refused to watch. He would be working out new routines in his private gym, he said sourly, and disappeared. The new double did a few trial runs and was judged to be satisfactory. While the camera setups were arranged, the man returned to makeup for touch-ups. Letitia wrote, "Robert thought the double was excellent when he dashed back on the set. Moreover, he thought he even looked like Doug as he quickly climbed up the chain while the cameras turned. And when the double reached the top and flung out one hand in a characteristic gesture accompanied by a broad grin, Robert dropped limply to the nearest chair. He knew then that Douglas had put one over on him and doubled for the double."*

Principal filming was completed in early August, and a rough cut screened for cast and crew on the tenth. The newly completed studio projection room was silent throughout. At the end, "a veritable tempest of applause broke out," wrote Florey, "and they raised three cheers in honor of Douglas." Everyone gathered to shake his hand, but Fairbanks was modest. "He replied to his collaborators that he deserved no more than they."

In late September, he and Mary began a cross-country trek to premiere the film. They went by way of Vancouver and the Canadian Pacific Railway, stopping at Lake Louise in Alberta and in Banff, Winnipeg, and Montreal.

---

* In case one should doubt the story and still suspect the stunt to be doubled, *Ladies' Home Journal* had a special photographer on the set that day to take a photograph for the September 1922 issue. The man halfway up the drawbridge chain is unmistakably Fairbanks.

The Chicago premiere was on October 22. The publicity campaign was representative of how the film was promoted in road shows across the nation. Placards were posted along highways two weeks before the film's arrival, announcing, ROBIN HOOD IS COMING! LOOK OUT FOR HIS ARROW! Following this, thousands of paper arrows fluttered from every doorknob, car, and available window in Chicago's downtown, announcing the theater and the date; 150 billboards (twenty-four sheets), 250 eight-sheets, 200 three-sheets, and 200 trolley car cards alerted the public to the upcoming film. In case they had failed to take note, one hundred more billboards were added the day the film opened at Cohan's Grand Opera House.

Tie-ins were made with various businesses. One-sheets were provided to all the Columbia Phonograph stores, along with stickers pitching not only the movie but also the various *Robin Hood*–related records for sale. A photograph of Doug, jauntily perched on a tractor and brandishing a lance, was given to each Ford dealership in the region. Special match holders advertising the film were provided to all the local automobile clubs and affixed by suction cup to every Ford sold during the film's run. Twenty thousand blotters touting *Robin Hood* were distributed to every office building, hotel room, and government agency the week before the premiere. Department stores were lent costumes from the film to create window displays. Best of all, perhaps, was a hat-related promotion. The Wormser Hat stores placed cards in their windows: WEAR THE MARK OF CHIVALRY! THE *ROBIN HOOD* FEATHER. ONE WITH EVERY WORMSER HAT. The trend caught on, and soon other stores were selling *their* versions of the *Robin Hood* hat, eventually leading to an entire generation of baby boomers wondering why their grandfathers wore little pheasant feathers in their fedoras.

The visit to New York City for the premiere at the Lyric Theatre was eventful. Fairbanks and Pickford were staying at the Ritz. A *Christian Science Monitor* reporter described the scene: "The telephone in his suite rings constantly, and his secretary patiently answers requests for everything from a signed photograph of either star to requests for 'a chance to act in the movies.' The suite itself gives away the personality of its occupant, and reflects something of his volatile and numerous interests. In one corner are stacked high several long bows used in *Robin Hood*; arrows tipped with feathers lie carelessly on the dressing table, a sword just brought from England by Edward Knoblock, the playwright, for use in *Monsieur Beaucaire*, Mr. Fairbanks' next picture, occupys [*sic*] an otherwise comfortable armchair. A model of an airplane flippantly tops an open wardrobe trunk."

It was on the roof of the hotel that Doug posed with a bow and arrow for photographers. There, to quote Dwan, "some deviltry within him made him let go of the arrow and away it flew." The story, from here, diverges. Certainly, there is no disagreement that the steel-tipped arrow soared a respectable course over the Manhattan skyline, from Fifty-Ninth Street all the way to Forty-Sixth and Fifth. And all agree that it flew through an open window, striking an unsuspecting furrier by the name of Abraham Seligman. Most accounts from this point put their faith in the family's version of events. Like the "Doug got himself expelled by putting green bows on the hallway statues on Saint Patrick's Day" story, it makes its protagonist seem to be one who causes mischief, not true harm. The story goes like this: The arrow hit Seligman straight in the bottom. The poor immigrant, convinced that Indians had launched an attack on Manhattan, ran yelping about the worktables and onto the street, where he was finally taken to Bellevue and the arrow extracted. It was a mystery! Who was firing arrows in the air? Two and two were put together; Fairbanks manfully confessed and paid the dazzled and (now evidently lucky) man a handsome $5,000.

A gentle and comic little tale, for tale it was. True, the arrow did travel that prodigious distance, and it did hit Mr. Seligman. Unfortunately, it hit him in the chest. Frank Case was present when Fairbanks learned the awful news from reporters:

> Conversation and laughter ceased suddenly. We were all terribly distressed, especially Douglas, who paced the room in torment. Meanwhile the press, still waiting, had to be seen and no newspaper man, even with the best heart and intentions, could be asked

to smother, or even tone down, a story of Robin Hood shooting a furrier with a longbow half a block from Fifth Avenue. That couldn't be expected. . . .

It was three in the morning before Cap [O'Brien] managed to get the furrier or one of his family on the telephone and arrange a meeting for the next day. Happily it turned out that the man was not seriously hurt physically, so satisfactory arrangements were made to soothe his outraged feelings, and quite properly outraged it seemed to me—for you can't expect a man to be pleased at having an arrow stuck in his ribs while he is sewing up a mink.

As a matter of history, later on when the man learned who it was that had pinked him, and when he had lunch with Douglas and two choice seats for the opening, he seemed quite pleased about the whole thing.

Well, everybody was much relieved when Cap signaled all clear the following afternoon. But the hours between midnight and the receipt of Cap's message (we stayed up all night) were hours of distress filled with misery.

Fairbanks was lucky—and a beneficiary of the laws of physics. The distance the arrow traveled ensured that it struck its victim with little force. Still, it was a careless act; he had well earned his long night's agony. He could have killed the man. Apart from the moral burden this would impose for the rest of his life, it would likely have led to a manslaughter charge, and no amount of smiles, charms, or stunts would have helped him escape *that* brush with the constabulary.

The industry was still staggering under the weight of recent scandals. True, Roscoe Arbuckle had finally been acquitted on his third trial in March of that year. But Will Hays banned him from America's screens nonetheless. And weeks before the acquittal, Paramount director William Desmond Taylor was murdered in a case that was to destroy the careers of comedienne Mabel Normand and Paramount's Mary Miles Minter. The vilification of "movie people" that this engendered was significant. "It isn't safe to admit that you know anyone in Hollywood except Jackie

Coogan," Fairbanks quipped. When he and Mary were questioned on the Taylor murder, he was quick to distance them from the misdeeds in town: "We don't know anything a-tall about this affair," he said. "You see, we live in Beverly Hills, and that's seven miles from Hollywood."

They both positioned themselves as representatives of the better-behaved class of filmdom worker. "The whole motion picture industry should not be condemned because a few persons do not conduct themselves as they should," tsk-tsked Mary, as her husband added, "Real motion picture stars know no more of dope rings and drug parties than they do of the eight-hour law, and unless the public sticks to facts rather than fancies, there soon will be no motion picture industry in this country."

His solution to the crisis was simple, as one reporter discovered when trying to pin him down on the subject:

> "What," we asked, "should the industry do to meet the yellow newspaper attacks on Hollywood?"
> "Make good pictures," said Mr. Fairbanks.
> "What about censorship and blue laws in general?"
> "Make good pictures," said Mr. Fairbanks.
> "What do you think about the business situation?"
> "Make good pictures," said Mr. Fairbanks.

The censorship train was still rumbling down its tracks, despite all his efforts to derail it. Since *The Three Musketeers* was released, New York had instituted a state censorship board, and *Robin Hood* was not spared. The censor's cuts mostly related to scenes of Prince John's minions torturing the sundry townsfolk, but Doug's beloved scene of Robin Hood breaking Guy of Gisbourne across a stone pillar was also trimmed. "Eliminate actual choking by Robin Hood of Gisborn [*sic*] where eyes bulge," wrote the New York State Motion Picture Commission. Its reasoning? Such scenes were "inhuman." Fairbanks was not pleased. "These atrocities of King John are a part of history, and they should have been a part of the picture," he grumbled to the *New York Times*.

"And because I could not [show them,] there was a certain force gone out of it that nothing else could replace."

But censors or no, *Robin Hood* was a smash. A second showing was staged at midnight after the New York premiere to accommodate not only the stage actors who could not attend an eight thirty screening but also the mobs waiting on the street. The film, including negative and promotional expenses, cost $961,129.12. The return to the Douglas Fairbanks Pictures Corporation was $2,219,478.70. No film he would ever make would gross more, and his net was staggering. It is important to emphasize again that the net return to the producer is a fraction of the rentals a film accrues. Everyone was making profits along the way: the exhibitors, the distributor, even the publishers of the little tie-in *Robin Hood* books that were sold in the theaters.*

The reviews were glowing. Some surly few suggested that the first half—the medieval castle/Crusades story—was a tad too slow and stately. But they seemed to be in the minority. "Douglas Fairbanks in *Robin Hood* out-spectacles all that we have seen before on the screen," wrote the *Wid's Daily* critic. "No part that we can think of would fit an actor better than this title role falls about the athletic shoulders of Fairbanks."

Doug and Mary returned to Hollywood by way of Chicago. Waiting for them upon arrival on November 28 was a new weekend house, built on a beachside lot in Santa Monica at 705 Ocean Front Drive. It was a four-bedroom dwelling; Wallace Neff designed a private garage and servants' quarters on the 90-by-150-foot lot. The wide-plank wooden floors had hobnails that evoked the era of Robin Hood, as did the Tudor windows. The house was, in time, to consume as much of his life as did Pickfair. In the end, he would die there. But that sunny Christmas season, the end must have seemed very, very far off.

Superstitious though he may have been, he took no meaning from the discovery of a suicide victim under the Santa Monica pier two days after their arrival at the beach house. When they thought the man might be resuscitated, they assured the press that they would give the desperate

---

* Fairbanks's return on the *Robin Hood* booklets was $2,160.09 in 1923.

stranger work at their studios. When it was declared hopeless, they left money for flowers.

Their Christmas cards for 1922 were custom designed and engraved. They depicted crusaders, flags flying, marching past a castle gate into a bold future. Fairbanks had just completed what would be his greatest financial achievement and, with the spoils of this effort, was on the verge of launching his greatest critical triumph: the film, more than any other, for which he would be remembered to this day.

12

The Fairy Tale

B Y MANY MEASURES, 1923 was the best year of Douglas Fairbanks's
life. *Robin Hood* was road-showing its way through the major
metropolises, spinning off money and accolades for its creator at a prodigious rate. The intelligentsia had weighed in: the smiling, jumping
cavalier had created Art with a capital *A*.

His marriage was still in an endless honeymoon phase. Mary couldn't
even sit for a portrait without interruptions every ten or fifteen minutes
from her besotted swain. He wanted to buy her everything—jewels, furs,
cars. ("But Douglas," the portrait artist recalled hearing her say over the
phone, "I have enough pearls now. . . . Yes, I know, dear, but where
would I wear a chinchilla coat?")* "That he is very deeply in love with
Mary no one who sees them together can doubt for an instant," Samuel
Goldwyn wrote at this time. "Not by any means a self-effacing person,
he is nevertheless always trying to turn the spotlight upon her and her
achievements. Of the latter he is inordinately proud."

Further, his bromance with Charlie Chaplin continued, abated only
by the comedian's current mad affair with Polish film star/diva Pola
Negri—a source of much amusement to most in the press, and likely to
Fairbanks as well. Chaplin purchased a lot adjoining the one on which

---

* He settled for ermine, which she politely tried on but sent back to the furrier. No Peggy
  Hopkins Joyce, she.

Pickfair stood in late September 1922, telling his aide de camp Tom Harrington, "I've just bought a hill. Get me a house."

And having hit the sweet spot, the magic trifecta of critical, financial, and personal success, Fairbanks was then emboldened to take his greatest leap ever, both financially and artistically. He would, he decided, top himself. He would make a film greater than *Robin Hood*.

In a way, he had little choice. One astute columnist wrote, "In the case of Douglas and Mary, it is a plain case of weeping for more worlds to conquer. They can't very well back down from big pictures to little pictures, and they don't know where to go on from pictures like *Robin Hood*." But it wasn't the critics' voices he heeded. It was his inner voice, that part of his nature that urged him ever onward to better work, to greater things. It was that same hypomanic, cheerleading-through-a-megaphone voice that wouldn't let him reduce the costs on his early Artcraft productions simply to increase their profit, the same rousing call that was shouting inspirational phrases to him as surely as "Hunch" had done years before in *Say! Young Fellow*. For all his flaws—and there would turn out to be too many before his days were done—it was this sturdy enthusiasm that made him neither a run-of-the-mill star nor an ordinary producer. It was a part of his greatness.

It was a greatness that would run its course in a mere fifteen years, true, but it can be argued that he exercised it within the confines of an art form that existed for barely more than twenty. Every force that encouraged him to continue to reach beyond his grasp was at its peak in the early winter months of 1923, and Douglas Fairbanks did not require much prompting to stretch his arms wide and try to grip all that the world could offer. No soul seeking fame, wealth, or even the more laudable aim of creating true art ever really gets as close to the goal as desired. But Fairbanks's reach in 1923 would be farther than he would ever again achieve.

Part of this related to his self-proclaimed, cheerful narcissism. "I'll tell you about me," he confessed to a reporter, tongue only partly in cheek:

If I had my way about it, I could make myself very happy all the time. My big ambition is to pack up and take Mary to the Riviera. There I would like to step out for a stroll around about 8 o'clock in the morning and hear everybody say: "There he comes now; that's Fairbanks, the great motion picture star!" Then I'd go right in, change my suit and come out again. They'd say: "Why, there's Fairbanks, the famous cinema actor; here he comes now!" And I'd like to change my suit once an hour all day long and hear them say: "Here he comes now!" until I got sleepy. Then I would like to go to sleep and get up in the morning and have it all over again.

In considering an actor, perhaps, this should not astonish. Many a leading man had more than a healthy dose of self-absorption. But none were willing to invest as much, risk as much, as was Fairbanks. This may have constituted courage, or it may have come from the fact that he had suffered little in the way of failure along the way. He had been climbing that metaphoric mountain with nary a misstep for two decades; why should he not climb higher? It is easier, perhaps, to not fear cliffs if you have never fallen off one.

Still, there were early warning signs that there might be stumbling blocks on the trail ahead. Wallace Reid, Paramount's handsome leading man who had risen to stardom at the same time as he, became hooked on morphine provided by a studio doctor for an injury. In late January 1923, he succumbed to endocarditis. "The motion picture has sustained an irreparable loss," Fairbanks told reporters, acting, as always, as the industry's de facto spokesman. Less than a week later John Fairbanks suffered a devastating stroke. John had always been the strong, sensible brother, the first Douglas had called upon when it was clear that he was going to make a life and business in the film industry. While Robert had been his peer in age and his youthful coconspirator in mischief, John had been the male adult figure in the household. As such, he had been made general manager of the Douglas Fairbanks Pictures Corporation, to Robert's production manager. The stroke robbed John of much of his speech and motor function, and he was to die within four years, at the age of fifty-three. Robert's daughter related an anecdote in which Doug took his stricken brother out for an airing in the car. As they passed a cemetery, John pointed with his left arm (the stroke had totally paralyzed the right side of his body) and said, "Jack there." Normally ebullient, Doug was nevertheless prone to periods of gloom—his "black dog." This incident depressed and demoralized him.

Whenever sorrow threatened, he did not find his succor in contemplation but in motion. "When I keep moving I'm in harmony with the force that drives the world," he said. "When I stop, the brunt of that power hits me. If I stopped long it would destroy me." And so he hastened on, planning his next epic.

When in New York, he was still convinced it would be *Monsieur Beaucaire*. By the time he had reached Chicago, he had declared that it would be a pirate film. He seemed certain this time; Mary even gave him an antique replica of a pirate galley for Christmas. He started growing his hair long and set his team to work on creating a script. The draft that resulted was a cumbersome story, bearing a closer relation to 1927's *The Gaucho* than to *The Black Pirate*, which was to be filmed in 1925. It also included elements of an Arabian tale: the protagonist was a descendant of Moorish kings, whose personal philosophy of vengeance was based on his reading of the Koran. But this heavy-handed jumble of slave revolutions, burning plantations, coups d'état, and piracy was quickly abandoned.

There followed a brief and heady period when he contemplated a toga tale. "There hasn't been a good picture showing ancient Rome since *Cabiria*!" he declared to Robert Florey. "Last night I thought up a *great* story that happens during Caesar's time. Can't you see the chariot races? The battles? That great old Roman architecture?"

Pictures of pirate galleons came down from the walls of director Raoul Walsh's office. Up went images of the Roman Forum and Pompeii. The team buckled down to this epoch, until the day when Fairbanks popped his head into a staff meeting and declared, "Let's do an *Arabian Nights* story instead!"

Scenarist Lotta Woods described the researcher's job on a Fairbanks production as being that of "a graduate engineer who charged fifteen cents for starting a stalled motor and $499.85 for knowing how." Robert's daughter claimed: "Doug never heard any complaints; his staff simply swept everything into the wastebasket and started afresh. It wasn't the first time the boss had changed horses in midstream and it wouldn't be the last." Kenneth Davenport had warned Florey that this would happen during the Roman craze. "You'll see," he said. "This devil will change his mind three times—if not more—before we start shooting." Even the press reflected this confusion; some early news accounts described *The Thief of Bagdad* as a pirate story inspired by *Captain Kidd* and *Captain Blood*.

But the *Arabian Nights* idea stuck. ("I had to find a picture to fit my hair," Fairbanks said with mock seriousness.) The project he envisioned was to be grand in scope. A ten-acre tract of land behind the studio was acquired to expand the back lot. The walls of Bagdad,* incomparably designed by the twenty-six-year-old William Cameron Menzies, were erected on the stone foundations of the *Robin Hood* castle. All the settings in the film remain a marvel today. Undoubtedly, the production's art direction was heavily influenced by the German expressionist films of the time. Shades of Paul Leni's *Waxworks* can be seen throughout. But Menzies had a gorgeous visual sense of his own, and it can be argued that the work of the Germans served merely as a starting point for his genius. Fairbanks recalled:

A special problem that faced us for *The Thief of Bagdad* was my desire that a dream city should not look too well anchored on its foundations. It is easy enough to make a thing fantastic and unreal, but I wanted it to seem light in addition. By using a somewhat weird design, by painting trees and branches black even when we had real ones, by the use of light backgrounds instead of the cus-

---

* The spelling of Baghdad has, for the sake of consistency, been changed to match that used at the time of the film—Bagdad.

tomary dark ones which are thought to bring out the figures more clearly, by confining our colors to gray, gold, silver, black and white for everything except the actual costumes, we obtained an unusual effect; but sets built on the ground will *look* as if they were.

To get away from this solidity, we painted our buildings darker at the top than at bottom. This seemed to make them less solid and heavy at the bottom. We also built upon a highly polished black floor that had reflections. The vertical line of a house meets the horizontal line of the ground and ends there. Our polished floor reflects the building lines and lifts our city. And this black floor caused considerable extra work. There was endless brushing and polishing week after week.

Indeed, those floors were a constant source of worry. One visitor to the set recalled: "The whole scene immediately lifts us from the commonplace to the ethereal heights of the futurist influence in art. But we are brought back to earth by the most plebeian of notices which reads: 'Are your feet clean?' Whereupon, before we go on the set an attendant hands us a pair of loose-fitting sandals which we slip on over our shoes."

John's stroke had resulted in Doug's temporary assumption of the position of general manager,* a daunting task in itself. Still, he was tireless. "It isn't easy to work with Doug," director Raoul Walsh wrote wryly. "First, you have to find him. He's doing a thousand things at the same time. He's banging at a typewriter; he's on his gymnastic rings like some school kid; he's with the Art Director. . . . When he goes from office to office, he jumps over everything in his way. . . . If he does stop for a second, it is to bill and coo with 'our Mary.'" Walsh went on to describe the experience of finally pinning his boss down for a meeting. In the middle of an intense discussion of how to best punish the story's villain, Fairbanks suddenly jumped up and started playing with the light switches. Another visitor to the studio during production remarked, "While he was dressing, Doug was constantly in motion. He

---

* Robert ultimately assumed the job long term.

paused, dressed as Adam, to see if he could jump a high-backed chair. He could."

Edward Knoblock (with Lotta Woods) again played a major role in creating the scenario, which in the end wasn't produced as a shooting continuity so much as it was a working grid—a spreadsheet conveyed by way of a large cork bulletin board. In the "Set Plot" grid, the sets were listed across the top in columns, with the actors' names in a left-sided row. If an actor was to appear in a scene on that set, the corresponding cell had an *X* in it. Running in parallel with this was a tightly worded "Shooting Schedule," which defined, scene by scene, only the minimum necessary to explain the action. In the words of historian Rudy Behlmer, "Of course, breakdown boards and sheets, along with shooting schedules (both still in use), were not a Fairbanks innovation, but his application of the system was unique." Fairbanks, as in *Robin Hood*, provided the general settings and theme ("Happiness must be earned"), but it was left to the likes of Knoblock and faithful Lotta Woods to iron out such niceties as the plot.

Casting in *The Thief of Bagdad* would turn out to have more pitfalls than that of any other Fairbanks film. Evelyn Brent, who had acted in Selznick and Metro productions, was signed as Fairbanks's leading lady. Early publicity emerging from the studio declared that Mary had helped make the selection and that Evelyn was "a perfect type of screen beauty." She was originally hired in contemplation of the pirate film, but as winter advanced into spring and still no production was underway, Brent began to get restless. She was living at the time in a house across the street from the Chaplin studios, with her fiancé, Bernie Fineman. "I just didn't like the part of the princess in *Thief of Bagdad*," she recalled years later. "I remember going to Bernie and saying, 'I cannot do that part.' After I had been in the studio and talked and done still pictures with Fairbanks holding me up in one hand and all of that silly stuff. I just didn't like the setup." She asked to be released from her contract.

This would have caused no particular fuss, except for a squib in *Screenland*, one of the lesser fan periodicals.

There seems to be a difference of opinion over why Evelyn Brent took her make-up box and left the Fairbanks lot. *Evelyn* said that she had signed with Doug to work in pictures, and that so far she had been the world's champion rester.

Doug said that his *Thief of Bagdad* had to be an airy, ethereal sort of picture, and that Evelyn was a bit too voluptuous to match the picture.

But Dame Gossip says that Mary put her pretty little foot down and told Doug to get another leading lady. For be it known that Doug has an appreciative eye for feminine pulchritude, and Mary knows the weakness of sex.

The same thing is said to have happened when Doug was casting for *Robin Hood*. Marguerite de la Motte had been eminently satisfactory to the public, and to Doug, and Fairbanks expected to retain her for *Robin Hood*. But Marguerite had been announcing fondly in print that all she was and all she hoped to be she owed to Douglas Fairbanks, or words to that effect. So Mary changed his mind and picked out Enid Bennett, a lady who was safely in love with her own husband.

So there's three stories. You pay your money and you takes your choice.

This, Brent recalled, caused the predictable response from the Fourth Estate. "One morning I went out horseback riding about 6:00 in Griffith Park and I came back and the house was surrounded by reporters. I was living there, they said, because it was near Chaplin's studios and Fairbanks could go to the studio ostensibly to see me. It was absolutely untrue. There was no basis to it at all. As a matter of fact, I didn't even like him! But have you ever tried to deny a story to a bunch of reporters who are looking for a headline?"

The response of Pickford and Fairbanks was swift. They notified Cap O'Brien to file suit against the magazine and made certain that every journalist in the country was apprised of the fact. Not only did such gossip harm their brand (although the term in this context was not in use at the time), but it also appears to have been authentically untrue. In later years—and not so much later, at that—there would be rumors of infidelities, rumors that were ultimately authenticated. The response at the first sign of *these* rumors was a retreat into a wall of no-comments and denials. But no lawsuits. Here the indignation was real, as well as the desire to go to open court and face the wagging tongues. (On a lesser note, the supposed charge that Fairbanks let Brent go because she was too zaftig for the role made him appear ungallant—a point of pride.)*

"And what started it I don't know," Brent said years later. "That thing followed me for ages, and people would not believe me. I had three personal contacts with them—one at the Algonquin, one when I came out here and they asked me to come to some story conference or something, and Mary was not there but he was . . . among the executives and Mary's mother and the whole bit! Then I was told to come and make the still pictures. Those were the only contacts I had with him." Brent in later years remained friendly with Mary and saw her often when Pickford was visiting the Motion Picture Home (officially the Motion Picture Country House and Hospital, cofounded by Mary herself) to see director Mickey Neilan. Mary, she reported, was warm, "but we never discussed it." Brent remained puzzled to the end of her days about the episode. "You don't know what starts these things," she said ruefully. Willowy Julanne Johnston, who had originally tested for the slave role played by Anna May Wong, replaced her in the part.

Anna May Wong went on to greater fame than any other of the film's supporting cast. The daughter of a Chinatown laundryman, Wong was only eighteen during production, but her appearance as the duplicitous slave girl made a huge impression, and she became the first female Asian American star—Japanese actor Sessue Hayakawa having preceded her on the male side by almost ten years. Fairbanks had seen her in the first two-strip Technicolor feature, made as a demonstration project by the Technicolor Corporation. There had been some discussion of film-

---

* And Mary seemed to have no problem with Marguerite de la Motte, who reprised her role as Constance in *The Iron Mask*, although Fairbanks recast two of the three musketeers.

ing *The Thief of Bagdad* in color, and Doug, always keeping up with technical developments, was fascinated by the process but rejected it for his film. Yet the young actress impressed him, and he insisted a part be found for her. According to Wong biographer Graham Russell Gao Hodges, "He had to get past Wong Sam Sing first." After promising her father that he would personally keep an eye on the young beauty, Doug received permission for her to appear in the film.

Another casting attempt was to prove even more disastrous, although not generally known to the public then, nor to film scholars today. Fairbanks was looking for unconventional casting and was intrigued by the prospect of having Japanese German poet and critic Sadakichi Hartmann in the film. He arranged a test for him in the relatively minor role of the Indian prince, one of the suitors for the heroine's hand in marriage.* He tested well. Fairbanks declared, "You have the eyes of a saint; the rest of your face is that of a villain," and offered him the far larger role of the Mongolian prince. Hartmann, an asthmatic with tuberculosis, thought the work would not be too taxing, and he accepted.

Thus the troubles began. Shooting started in mid-July. Production required Hartmann to arrive at *nine* and stay until *five* o'clock—eight hours! ("I did not fancy it. . . . To obey the whims of some director is an imposition.") He was not asked to participate in the conferences with writers, director, and star. No one listened to his unsolicited advice. ("When there isn't any needle's eye, thread is not of much use.") His costume was too heavy ("What is this, I demanded to know, something to advertise linoleum?"); his hat was too small; his shoes were too high. He didn't want to shave his head.

Furthermore, all the costumes were in bright colors. What was the point of that? Also, the costumes of the extras were too "pretentious

---

* Stills of Hartmann in the Indian costume remain and are often misidentified as representing him playing the court magician, the role that the final cast list claims for him—a misrepresentation that acknowledges his presence in the film without having to answer sticky questions about his departure.

and conspicuous"; they shouldn't compete with those of the leading players! (Read: *his* costume.)

He, an *artist*, had already planned out the action of his first scene to be shot—a sequence late in the film in which the villain enters a fishing village, buys a magic healing apple, and has a fisherman poisoned to test its efficacy. He would be on the prow of the ship, pointing at the town. The townspeople would all gather in silent awe as he approached. But the director! The director wanted a shot from the point of view of the villain in the back of the boat, in which he gestures for the sail to be lowered, revealing the town.* That ridiculous town which "would have made a great chop suey restaurant in some world's fair."

The director, art director, scenarist, costume designer, and even humble extras begged to differ. Fairbanks remained above the fray—in fact, Hartmann couldn't get his way, he claimed, *unless* he complained to Doug. "Sadakichi Hartmann was not very cooperative," Julanne Johnston said, in an understatement. "Fairbanks humored him." Hartmann did not know that his boss couldn't bear to be perceived as unlikable and relied on his team to do any tasks involving unpleasant confrontations.

Robert Fairbanks was more than happy to help and did so in a style worthy of Machiavelli—or of the prankish Fairbanks brothers of Denver. He "seemed to have a strange predilection for the delicate art of poisoning as an occasional luncheon topic," Hartmann recounted. Food was often sent as gifts to the studios, tempting Mary, but she was not permitted to eat any, Robert said lazily. After all, the foodstuffs could be poisoned by mad fans. Then there were the postage stamps. Fans could send a request for a picture, along with the required postage. But the stamps could be poisoned so that when the star licked them to mail the picture, well . . .

With the word *poison* ringing in Hartmann's ears, the next act was staged. Some "play-all" actor,[†] "an old standby of Fairbanks's

---

* Raoul Walsh, of course, got his way. This is exactly how the sequence plays on film, and it is very effective. The town was reworked from the Nottingham set in *Robin Hood*.
† Likely Charlie Stevens.

productions, a veritable crack-a-jack in losing his identity in minor parts," came up to Hartmann and offered him a bottle of rum. He was forced, for politeness sake, to take a swig or two before quickly deciding that it was no good. Bootleg booze in the 1920s often was methanol, which could lead to blindness and death. ("Angels and ministers of grace, defend us!") Next, another bottle of hooch was brought to his home by a studio employee, courtesy of the film's wigmaker, who happened to run a side business as a bootlegger. To Hartmann's suspicious mind this too was bad whiskey. It likely was spiked but with little more than vinegar.

The deed was done. Hartmann departed in a huff. The scheme, if scheme it was and not merely an unfortunate series of coincidences, has all the earmarks of the practical jokester Douglas rather than the far more phlegmatic Robert. Still, it is likely that any and all were delighted to participate in getting rid of the troublesome artiste a mere three weeks into the production. Sôjin Kamiyama (billed simply as "Sôjin") stepped into the role, playing in all but the fishing village sequence. Frame blowups document that Sôjin is missing a front tooth whereas Hartmann is not, and the hated hat ("such as some Chinese Pavlova may wear") is propped high on Hartmann's dome but sags down over Sôjin's ears. The fishing village sequence was abridged to minimize Hartmann's appearance; for ninety years few noticed that the lead villain in Douglas Fairbanks's most famous film was played by two different men.*

Happily, the remainder of the casting was uneventful. Snitz Edwards, the silent film era's most ubiquitous character actor, rejoined Fairbanks as his companion in crime. (Edwards had first appeared with Fairbanks in *The Mark of Zorro* as the timorous barkeep.) His daughter recalled the scene where first Doug, then Snitz, climbed a clinging vine over forty feet up the wall of Bagdad's castle:

---

* Sôjin and other Japanese members of the cast suffered some frantic hours in late September when a major earthquake struck Tokyo. It took days to hear by cablegram if family and friends were safe.

My father adored Douglas Fairbanks—thought him the most genial, good-natured, unaffected, down to earth man. Snitz was very athletic, too. They told them "stunt men will do this."

"Ridiculous—we'll do it!" and they climbed up the creepers up the wall. . . . It was like a game.

Unable to find a stout male actor to satisfy him, Fairbanks cast a rotund Frenchwoman, Mathilde Comont, in the role of the Persian prince.* He had seen Comont that winter as she played Mary's mother in *Rosita*, directed by Ernst Lubitsch.

The story of the sly, witty Lubitsch, fresh from Germany, and his trials working with Mary Pickford have been meticulously detailed elsewhere. Both Fairbanks and Pickford were enthralled with his German film work (and Chaplin, as previously mentioned, was equally enamored with his former star, Pola Negri). But the early months were an uncomfortable fit for the director and his female producer. He was accustomed to telling actresses what to do, not reporting to them. Language and temperament were barriers between two otherwise very vital, creative, and engaging people. Before settling on *Rosita*, Lubitsch and Pickford were divided on what film to make together. Mary wanted him to direct *Dorothy Vernon of Haddon Hall*. Lubitsch wanted to make *Faust*. Mary claimed that her mother nixed the plan because the tragic female lead commits infanticide. This is highly probable. But Lubitsch claimed another reason. In his mind there was only one man to play Mephistopheles: "Mephisto must have humor and charm," he told a columnist. "Douglas Fairbanks would be the greatest Mephisto who ever played the part. He has humor and lightness and vivacity; yet he has dramatic power. He would go through Faust like a stroke of lightning—flashing dangerous, vivid and intense, yet brilliant. . . . Ach lieber Gott, he would be such a wonderful Mephisto." Both she and Lubitsch went so far as

---

* Three extraordinarily corpulent gentleman who appear to have tested for the role were instead used as eunuchs guarding the princess's bedroom, to wonderful comic effect.

to urge him to take the part, Mary claimed, but "he always countered with 'Can you imagine anyone taking me seriously as the devil?'"

He was right. America's Sweetheart was not going to strangle a baby, and her dashing husband was not going to depict Satan. By the time *Thief* was in production, Mary had completed *Rosita* and was filming *Dorothy Vernon of Haddon Hall* with a different director. The plump Frenchwoman was the only remnant of the Lubitsch experiment to carry over into *The Thief of Bagdad.*

One cast member was a mere extra—and a teenager at that—but his presence on the set had resonance for Fairbanks. A stunt that had required months of preparation and practice was a scene in which Fairbanks (with the aid of hidden trampolines) leaps into and out of a series of huge jars. It required perfect timing and placement, yet on the day of filming, one of the takes was spoiled when a young extra failed to pull his camel out of the shot in time and—worse yet—the camel managed to soil the precious black floor.

An assistant director was giving the boy holy hell when Fairbanks bounded over. With a start, he recognized the youngster underneath all the body paint. It was Jesse Lasky Jr., slumming as an extra to pick up some pocket money.

Nothing could have made him happier. According to Lasky, "He threw back his head and spilled laughter upward." Here, in the form of a gangly youth, was poetic justice. Young Lasky's father had recently created a firestorm in the Fairbanks household by hiring Douglas Fairbanks Jr. to star in a film for Paramount.

The problem was this: Beth and her son were living in Paris, where the American dollar stretched very far, not so that Junior could study art and learn French, as she claimed, but because they were nearly broke. The large sum that Doug had settled upon her was gone, wasted in bad investments by her second husband, James Evans. Jewels were pawned and then sold, and, according to Junior, they had started skipping meals. When the offer for $1,000 a week for six weeks' work came, they felt that they had little choice. Also, Junior noted, "I think Mother saw at once a way that she could again supervise a career and involve herself in business."

Fairbanks had learned of the plans by way of a letter from Lasky and was livid. Lasky and Zukor both had been stung by Pickford and Fairbanks's departure from Paramount, and Lasky acknowledged that hiring Junior constituted "sort of a minor revenge on the senior Fairbanks." He would, Junior recalled, "be bound to be embarrassed to have his overgrown thirteen-year-old son around as an All-American boy with similar athletic ability."

A few years later, as his son shot up in height and even wore a glued-on mustache for the final scene of 1926's *Stella Dallas*,* Fairbanks *was* concerned about the prospect of appearing old in comparison. But in 1923, this was not the issue. Junior at that point was still outgrowing his plump, awkward stage, and the only threat he constituted was of embarrassing them both. Fairbanks was vehement. His son was being used for his name and—worse—was abandoning his education. Beth used the dubious strategy of sending Junior alone to the Hôtel de Crillon to thrash it out with Senior during Doug and Mary's Paris stay in the autumn of 1921. There father and son had a vituperative argument. Senior, in authentic belief that his ex-wife and son were very comfortably provided for, wanted him to go to Harvard (as he himself claimed—falsely—to have done) and then on to Cambridge. ("I often thought back on that idea," Junior recalled, "and had reason to wish it had worked out. I think I would have liked it.") His son, armed with strict instructions not to reveal their financial straits, instead stubbornly clung to the line that he could do as he chose. The quarrel escalated, and for the first time in his life, Junior was actively rude to his feared and revered father. He would later confess that he had behaved so "because I was more afraid of Mother's reaction if I lost the day than I was of my father's." Once the deal had been signed, Doug sent Beth a telegram demanding that the boy continue his schooling, adding tersely: DOUGLAS FAIRBANKS' SON WILL HAVE SUFFICIENT MONEY TO LIVE ON WITHOUT WORKING IN THE MOVIES.

---

* Try though he might, the sixteen-year-old could not grow one for the part.

There ensued a considerable strain in father-son relations, scarcely intimate to begin with. But the majority of Fairbanks's anger was with the executives whom he felt were endangering the future of a thirteen-year-old boy for the purposes of payback. The use of children, in his mind, was not fair play. But here, right in front of him, was young Lasky, already in Arabian garb, having brought himself to the studio. It was too good to resist.

Company photographers were summoned, and multiple shots of the star and the costumed teenager were taken—and released to the press. Lasky Sr. now enjoyed a taste of his own medicine. The early headlines—Douglas Fairbanks Jnr. Works for Lasky; Lasky Jnr. for Fairbanks—required some effort on the part of Paramount to squelch. But Doug had made his point. A soft truce was called.*

His son's first film, *Stephen Steps Out*, was a failure. "The picture was terrible," Junior recalled seven years later. Upon its screening, his father, evidently deciding that a public stance against the film would appear churlish, wired his congratulations. Paramount did not hesitate to take out full-page ads in the trade magazines trumpeting the fact.

Comfortable in the belief that this was the end of Junior's film career, his position softened, and during the production of *Thief* his son was a frequent visitor to the set. But the following summer, when Doug and Mary were again in Paris, Junior once more approached his father. "I asked him to withdraw any opposition he had to my becoming a screen player," he recalled.

> He said he would give me a regular monthly allowance that would enable Mother and me to live properly if I would study art. I declined the offer.
>
> He told me to go to the devil and I told him to go to hell. He disowned me as a son and I disowned him as a father!
>
> Two days later I received a message from him, asking that I come to see him, and I went back to his hotel where, in the presence of several newspapermen, like the gentleman he is, he apologized

---

* Curiously, he and Lasky Sr. remained friends.

to me. He announced, publicly, that he would no longer oppose my efforts to become an actor, admitted that I was right in my ambition and that he had been wrong.

Whether Douglas was truly at peace with this or merely bowing to the inevitable is unclear. Mary's gentle hand may have played a part. But what is evident is that in 1923, his son was no longer out of sight and out of mind but present. Further, what he felt was the boy's exploitation, by both Beth and Paramount, was very much top of mind.

Another notable extra in *Thief* was an extremely tall African American named Sam.* He was a striking presence, with a body as chiseled as Fairbanks's and a turban that added another foot and a half to his height. The two men became friends, and Doug sponsored the extra as a professional boxer. Accounts of set visits at the time often describe Sam, side by side with his boss, playing Fairbanks's version of follow the leader—a contest that involved a great deal of climbing, swinging, and jumping over gymnastic equipment scattered around the lot.

Sam was the victim of an unfortunate incident involving his body makeup. Cameraman Arthur Edeson, looking for a certain effect, experimented extensively on Sam with multiple compounds. When no ordinary makeup served his needs, he resorted to varnish. This was a grievous mistake. Sam patiently tolerated its application, but very shortly thereafter studio workers were startled by the sight of a screaming giant, skin gleaming like polished obsidian, running across the lot. He ended up in Fairbanks's plunge. Soap and water were ineffective in removing the lacquer, and in the end, the unfortunate man had to undergo a benzene rubdown and a vigorous scrubbing with a horsehair brush. His high-pitched cries could be heard across the compound.

And yet, his personal grit and affection for Fairbanks were such that he was back the next day. Graphite was applied, and varnish was never again suggested as a way to create a photogenic sheen on a black man.

---

* Multiple references are made to this gentleman during this period, but none give him the dignity of identifying his last name.

As with *Robin Hood*, the studio was open to visitors during filming. The process had evolved: managers of all the major local hotels were provided a limited number of passes. Guides then met the scheduled groups and gave them forty-two-minute tours (someone timed them). This was followed by the opportunity, if they were fortunate, to see Pickford or Fairbanks actually filming. In the end, over twenty-three thousand spectators got inside the studio gates.

This was not to Raoul Walsh's liking. "I did not encourage outsiders when I was making a picture—Fairbanks' love of an audience sometimes irked me," he wrote. Still, the spectators "appeared to put more snap into Doug's performance."

Also aiding performances were the set musicians. Ever since stage star Billie Burke had used a violinist on set to help her overcome her camera fright, small musical ensembles had come into general use during filming. Each had its own particular repertoire; Mary requested "Roses of Picardy" when she needed to draw tears. Doug had employed his particular ensemble of bass, piano, and violin (named, of course, "the Fairbanks Trio")* since 1921. The group, which would come to Pickfair often to play for screenings and social functions, was headed by a Miss Douglas, who reported that Fairbanks preferred peppy tunes, favoring especially the Spanish folk song "Cielito Lindo." Whether he was in fifteenth-century France, Sherwood Forest, or the streets of Bagdad, cheerfully anachronistic strains of "*Ay, ay, ay, ay / Canta y no llores*" would follow him.† Unless, that is, Raoul Walsh had his way. Upon reading the script for *Thief*, Miss Douglas had purchased seventy-five dollars worth of what she deemed "Oriental music"—only to find that Walsh would request "Mother Machree" or "My Wild Irish Rose" to evoke the mood he wanted. Because Mary's brother Jack was also filming

---

* Other sources claim it was a quartet: Euretta Wolf Douglas, violin; Elizabeth Mason, violin; Berniece Neale, cello; and Ruth Chambers, piano.

† Those of a certain generation will recall the song best as a Fritos jingle in the early 1970s: "*Ay ay ay ay /* I am the Frito Bandito . . ." The character, and the song, were withdrawn later in the decade on grounds of cultural insensitivity. On the flip side, the song was used to great emotional effect in 1943's *The Human Comedy*.

on the back lot, an elaborate set of signals were developed so that one company's mood music would not conflict with the other's.

Whatever the music, there is no doubt that Fairbanks's performance was akin to dance. The naturalism of the Douglas Fairbanks of the pre-war films was entirely gone, replaced by broad, flowing movements and figurative gestures that even the earliest silent films never demonstrated. This is particularly evident in the opening scenes of the film. If he was hungry, the flat of his hand rotated in broad circles over his belly. If astonished, both arms went straight up, feet kicked outward. He was trying to make a film as universal, as primarily symbolic, as dance.

It was, without doubt, his boldest move—bolder yet than the staggering investment in sets and costumes. The naked torso, the flowing harem pants, the lyric, fluid gestures—only an actor with a reputation as masculine as Fairbanks's could have pulled this off and not been the butt of crude jokes. But pull it off he did; the critics were largely in agreement about that. One wrote of "the new grace which has crept into the movements of Douglas Fairbanks, a sort of dancer's grace of rhythm and line, a mimicry of movement such as the old harlequins used to boast." There have been, of course, dissenters—particularly in the intervening years, when the last vestiges of stage dramatics died with talking films. "Fairbanks' stage training never counted much until the period of the costume films, when he relied too often on an acting style that a younger 'Doug' had once lightly tossed out of the movies," Alistair Cooke groused in 1940, adding that the film "suffocated the old beloved sprite in a mess of décor," and "the more theatrical convention of acting which he had restored to his costume character froze the gaiety of 'Doug' into stage cameos."

Filming was completed in early January 1924, with the complicated trick shots of the various fantasy effects filmed last. Then it was time for the annual trek east for the New York premiere. Doug and Mary arrived on February 15, accompanied by the appropriate royal retinue: Mary's mother, maid, and secretary; little Gwynne (now six years old) and her governess; Kenneth Davenport; and Rocher, Doug's faithful valet.

They stayed this time at the Ambassador Hotel,* where the couple was photographed seated companionably together on a sofa, fully absorbed in a daunting pile of correspondence, separated only by little Zorro.

The film opened in New York, at the Liberty Theatre on March 18. By now the ritual was becoming familiar. Throngs blocked Forty-Second Street, bringing out police for crowd control. Showman Morris Gest handled the road show presentation of the film, complete with the appropriately extravagant quota of harem girls, oriental carpets, and incense. The film was chosen the best picture of the year by a *Film Daily* poll of critics—like the Photoplay Medal the year before, a singular honor in the pre–Academy Award days.

And yet. There was a hint in the reviews, a sense that while Fairbanks had again outdone himself and created not simply Art with a capital *A* but ART with all caps, things were somehow just a little less fun. Worse, historians as early as 1931 were claiming that *Thief* was in some measure a disappointment.

One has to be careful not to label *Thief* as a box office failure. Quite the contrary. The return to the Douglas Fairbanks Pictures Corporation was $1,803,640.77—two and a half times that of *Zorro* and a third more than *The Three Musketeers*. As far as the audience, United Artists, and most exhibitors were concerned, the film was one of the smash successes of the decade.† It was to Fairbanks the *producer* that the film was barely a break-even project. The total cost of *The Thief of Bagdad* was $1,701,630.23, meaning that the net to his production company was $102,010.54. This was less than his share of the profit on the modest *Mr. Fixit*. While his average Artcraft release had a profit of $62,000, he had averaged more than six of those films a *year*. Now with *Thief*, and a larger fixed cost in the form of studio overhead, he

---

* Perhaps the association of the bow and arrow incident and the roof of the Ritz was too painful.

† Hiram Abrams negotiated brutally high rental fees with a requirement for upfront advances on both *Thief* and *Robin Hood*, causing many exhibitors to barely break even. Still, they booked the films, not wanting the competition down the street to get their hands on them.

had created a masterpiece, but one with a very thin profit margin. In order to do as well as he had done with *Robin Hood*, the film would have had to have twice *Robin Hood*'s return. Only one or possibly two films in the decade even matched *Robin Hood*, and they had distribution networks far superior to that of United Artists. To double that film's returns was impossible. He had pushed the envelope as far as he could without taking a loss. Now he knew his limits.

There were no immediate concerns. He had been averaging $734,000 in profits per year since 1920. *Robin Hood* had provided a significant padding with its $1.2 million margin. He was not going to starve. In fact, his personal income in 1923 and 1924 was as high as it was in the 1917–1919 era—likely higher, in fact. In those early years of personal income tax, his accountants and attorneys were—as the rest of the nation—trying to figure out what was acceptable in the way of deductions. By the mid-1920s, they were more aggressive in skinning that particular cat. Therefore, while his taxable income looked the same between these two periods, his actual, pre-deduction income was higher.

But the *Thief* returns would not be fully known for another year. Now it was time to celebrate what appeared to be yet another triumph. In keeping with their 1920s pattern of make a movie/go to Europe, Pickford and Fairbanks departed for London on April 13. As they embarked on the *Olympic*, Doug merrily told reporters there was no doubt as to whose star shone brightest in the family. "When I get on the other side," he declared, "they all say, 'Oh, there goes Mr. Pickford!'" Their arrival in London must have felt familiar: the mobs, the royalty, the acclaim. They were hosted by Lord Mountbatten and enjoyed balls and receptions thrown in their honor by the likes of the Duke and Duchess of Sutherland and Sir James Barrie.

A hot industry topic that summer was the casting decision on Paramount's *Peter Pan*. Author James M. Barrie was widely rumored to want Mary to play the role—a choice popular with the public at large. She had already played a little boy to perfection in *Little Lord Fauntleroy*, and had she been willing to make a film for a production company other than her own—something that she had not done since 1916—she would have been a shoo-in for the part. Jesse Lasky was at that moment en route to London, bearing with him the *Peter Pan* screen tests. He was careful enough to hedge when pressed by reporters, given that Mary had held several conferences with Adolph Zukor in the weeks before she sailed. "From the first we decided that *Peter Pan* need not be selected from within our own organization—but the choice rests entirely with Sir James." Could this signal a merger of United Artists and Famous Players–Lasky? Could *Peter Pan* and Mary Pickford be the fulcrum upon which yet another industry shift occurred? Zukor was anxious to bring Doug and Mary back into the fold. Speculation was rampant, but no answers were yet to emerge.

Next came Paris, where the now familiar drama of Doug saving Mary from the surging throngs was enacted, as was his private quarrel with his son over the latter's proposed acting career. Perhaps he was particularly cranky because of having to stay in bed for a few days with a case of *la grippe*. As Mary nursed him back to health, they contemplated a visit to Copenhagen. Their press agent worked with a local newspaper to contact the Danish royal chamberlain to see if they could meet with the king. "Who are Fairbanks and Pickford?" demanded the functionary, thus ruffling American feathers. "Quite sufficient cause for war if we didn't have a presidential election coming on," groused the *Daily Register Gazette*, demonstrating that the good people of Rockford, Illinois, at least, knew the real royalty from that fancy-pants European kind.

But before Denmark, they stopped in Berlin, followed by their first visit to Spain. The outpouring there was tremendous; five thousand were on hand when they arrived in Barcelona.* A mounted troop had to be called for crowd control. Their personal photo album shows them on the balcony of their hotel, smiling down at the multitude, and provides a striking point-of-view shot of the people below, thousands of them,

---

* The king and queen of Spain, upon arriving in that city a few days before Doug and Mary, received a much lesser reception. It was reported—although impossible to prove—that this contrast was too painful to the royal egos, and the stars were asked to move on to a different city, which they promptly did.

necks craned in symmetry, staring back. Other pictures document the couple, dapper and gorgeous (Fairbanks could pull off a pair of spats as few could), touring, attending bullfights, hobnobbing with royalty. This last incident occurred at the American embassy in Madrid, where the king of Spain most famously satisfied his curiosity as to whatever had become of "Fatty" Arbuckle,* and all present insisted that Doug and Mary make their next pictures there.

It was unlikely that Fairbanks would do this—his well-oiled machine at Santa Monica and Formosa was not to be discarded lightly, and the contretemps that Metro was suffering that summer in the Italian shoot of *Ben-Hur* was widely known. But he was not averse to Spain as a setting. The idea of bullfights intrigued him. His next film, indeed, would draw from his experience during these weeks in San Sebastián, Madrid, Seville, Toledo, Granada, and Barcelona.

They went next to Copenhagen, where the mobs that greeted them disrupted the tramway service, proving that the people of Denmark knew more about motion picture stars than did their royal chamberlain. Then it was back to Paris, to enjoy the 1924 Olympic Games. There Doug was awarded a medal by the French government—the Palme d'Or, an award making him an officer of public instruction. (Charlie Chaplin had been given the same award three years earlier.) No amount of ribbons could help him shortly thereafter when he, Mary, and the American ambassador to Spain were stranded in an upscale restaurant, flummoxed by Doug's habitual inability to remember to carry money. After waiting an hour in the hopes that someone they knew would happen by, they made a plea to the waiter—could they not send a check? They were Doug! And Mary!

The waiter was underwhelmed, replying, "Tell that to Sweeny"—the French equivalent, apparently, of "Tell it to the marines." Finally, an exhaustive search turned up a stray twenty-dollar bill in the ambassador's possession. The waiter gave them a usurious exchange rate, and they escaped with their hides—and another tale for their press agents to feed to their adoring public.

---

* An anecdote that, for Fairbanks, never got old.

Their return to America on the *Leviathan* was made eventful by their fellow passengers, movie diva Gloria Swanson and violinist extraordinaire Jascha Heifetz. Pranksters both, they disguised themselves as a steward and stewardess and entered Doug and Mary's stateroom while they slept. Speaking in garbled faux French, they noisily began to clean the room until the sleeping couple (Swanson rather cattily noted that Mary was wearing a chin strap) awoke and got the joke.

As they gathered for an impromptu breakfast, Mary told Gloria that she really (in Swanson's words) "had it in for Paramount because they hadn't given her *Peter Pan*," but that Zukor would only give it to her if she signed for two additional pictures.

This wasn't the only complaint they had upon their return to New York City on July 20. The *Peter Pan* rumors vis-à-vis Mary were still filling the trades, not because Zukor or Pickford had said anything to confirm this (the part, in fact, would ultimately go to a luminous teenage Betty Bronson) but because D. W. Griffith had just signed a three-picture deal with Paramount.

If ever there was an exasperating partner, it was Griffith. His sins against his partners had been ongoing. When he released *Way Down East* in the fall of 1920, he did not immediately hand the film's distribution, with its 20 percent fee, to UA. Instead he elected to road-show the picture—renting legitimate theaters, providing a full orchestra score, going from city to city with publicity and premieres, and garnering 100 percent of the profits for himself and his production company. *Way Down East* was a blockbuster—the only one he would have during these years,* and one the fledgling company needed badly. Fairbanks at that time wired Griffith an angry and direct message:

THIS RECENT ACTION OF YOURS WITH WAY DOWN EAST IS MOST UNFAIR. IT SEEMS TO ME THAT IF YOU HAD APPLIED A SENSE OF

---

* The film ultimately returned $1 million to Griffith. *Broken Blossoms* is excluded from this discussion as while it was distributed by UA, it was originally produced under the 1917 contract he had with Paramount.

JUSTICE TO A MATTER WHERE HONOR HAD SOMETHING TO DO WITH
IT YOUR ASSOCIATES WOULD HAVE GOTTEN A BETTER DEAL. I SEND
YOU THIS TO LET YOU KNOW HOW I FEEL AND THAT IT MIGHT HAVE
SOME EFFECT ON YOUR FUTURE.

Griffith did not budge.

Well and good. What was good for the goose, Fairbanks reasoned.
. . . He and Mary would road-show *their* productions, and did so, from
The Three Musketeers onward. And when Chaplin was finally free of his
First National contract, he could do the same. What Griffith lost and
his partners gained, by the different level of profitability of their films
during the first half of the 1920s and the lost revenue to UA—revenue
that they would have shared equally—certainly was one of the factors
contributing to D. W. Griffith's ultimate financial collapse. That collapse
meant little to him in material terms—he had always lived modestly.
But it had tremendous repercussions in terms of costing him his creative
freedom, something he prized dearly. By shortchanging his partners, he
learned the consequences of having them shortchange *him*.

By 1924, Griffith's financial situation had worsened. The high overhead involved in his studio in Mamaroneck, New York, was on the verge
of bankrupting his production company. He was largely the agent of his
own destruction, but he did not have the insight to see this. Instead, he
engaged in the very human practice of choosing to find fault elsewhere.

He shared the partners' dissatisfaction with Hiram Abrams's sales
techniques, but for different reasons than theirs. He felt that Chaplin,
Fairbanks, and Pickford formed a California triumvirate and were getting preferential treatment from the UA sales department. Mary, at least,
whose *Little Lord Fauntleroy* was kept out of most large cities for two
years because of Abrams's standoff with exhibitors, begged to differ. She
argued that Griffith, with his East Coast studio, had superior access to
UA's home office, and if anything *he* got preferential treatment.

Each side had instances that they could point to. Griffith argued that
The Love Flower yielded better exhibitor returns than Mary's *Suds*, an
argument skewed by his selection of one of Mary's few underperforming

films. Fairbanks countered that Griffith's *Broken Blossoms* had been sold on more favorable terms than Fairbanks's *His Majesty the American*. In truth, it all had to do with the quality of the product. Films such as Griffith's *The Love Flower* and *Dream Street* sold for less because of free market forces, forces that the bickering partners could, and did, use to quote examples in both directions.

Regardless of who had the moral high ground in this argument, trouble was brewing. Within a week of Doug and Mary's February arrival in New York to promote the premiere of *Thief*, news of Griffith's dissatisfaction had been featured in a *Variety* article. An annual UA stockholders' meeting was held two weeks before their departure for Europe, and on March 28, 1924, a reassuring, jointly signed press release resulted. All four partners, to quote the release, "unanimously decided to not only carry out their existing contracts, but to renew and extend their contracts for a period of three years, except Charles Chaplin who has 8 pictures still to deliver."

Griffith, evidently, did not consider his vote at the stockholders' meeting or his signature on this document to be binding. While Doug and Mary were touring Europe, and Charlie was in Los Angeles filming *The Gold Rush*, he was conducting secret negotiations with Adolph Zukor. He signed a $250,000 deal to produce three features.

This was too much. Fairbanks certainly made his feelings clear in a sharply worded telegram. Deeming Doug's wire "antagonistic," Griffith wired back, in part:

HAVE FELT FOR SOME TIME THAT I WAS IN A HOPELESS MINOR-
ITY. . . . IT HAS BEEN SPOKEN THROUGH UNITED ARTISTS BOOKING
OFFICES THAT GRIFFITH PICTURES WERE NOT EVEN PRICED AS HIGH
AS SOME OTHERS. . . . KNOWING WHAT I CAN DO WITH MY OWN
PICTURES, WOULD LIKE VERY MUCH TO WITHDRAW ENTIRELY FROM
UNITED ARTISTS.

His reasoning reflected that, as a businessman, D. W. Griffith was a very fine director of motion pictures. (It can be argued that even in this arena his skills were beginning to ossify.) It was naive to expect films such as *One Exciting Night* or *The White Rose*, with their smaller budgets and lesser leading players, to command the sort of prices from exhibitors as super-productions such as *Robin Hood* or *The Thief of Bagdad*. And Griffith's recent attempt at an epic, *America*, was a flop. Even Adolph Zukor would not have charged theaters as much for a Griffith programmer as for expensive studio productions such as *The Ten Commandments*.

Abrams, Fairbanks, Pickford, a Chaplin representative, and Griffith's lawyer, Albert Banzhaf, met at Doug and Mary's suite at the Ritz to attempt to thrash out the issue. (Griffith had conveniently escaped to postwar Berlin to film *Isn't Life Wonderful*.) Stern words were exchanged over the topic of Griffith's 20 percent stock ownership. In the end, a public statement was released, over the vehement protests of Banzhaf, stating that United Artists considered Griffith's signature on the March 28 pledge to be a binding contract.

They had just cause to adopt this stance. The company was not consistently profitable. UA's problem continued to be a lack of films to distribute. Chaplin took so long to fulfill his First National contract that he had, to date, made only *A Woman of Paris* for UA release—a drama in which he did not appear except in an unrecognizable cameo. The film was a critical darling but a financial failure.* They needed Griffith's steady stream of product. His films may have made no money for him, but they did for UA. And now Griffith was going to fly the coop. Something would have to be done or Doug and Mary would find themselves back in the arms of a Paramount or First National.

Help came in the form of Joseph Schenck. Schenck was approaching forty-six years of age in the autumn of 1924 and was that rarest kind of

---

* Chaplin still would not have fulfilled the original 1919 nine-film requirement by the time of Fairbanks's death in 1939. The partners had agreed to decrease the requirement for the number of films from Chaplin, as he had moved from two-reelers to features during this decade. But the fact remained that once releasing through UA, he moved to a "genius schedule," making films at a glacial pace.

Hollywood mogul: a beloved, honest, and trusted figure. A Russian Jew who immigrated to New York City at the age of fifteen, Schenck, with his younger brother Nicholas, began by running concessions at the Fort George Amusement Park. With entrepreneurial skill and tenacity, and financial help from theater owner Marcus Loew, the brothers bought the Palisades Amusement Park in New Jersey. From there their paths diverged. Nick stayed on the exhibition side, going on to head Loew's Inc. and the merged entity now known as Metro-Goldwyn-Mayer. Joseph became an independent producer, luring Roscoe Arbuckle away from Keystone in 1917. He also produced dramatic features starring his wife, Norma Talmadge, and light comedies starring her sister, Constance. A young Buster Keaton was such a success supporting Arbuckle that Schenck gave him his own production unit upon Arbuckle's departure to Paramount in late 1919.

Since 1920, UA had been trying to woo Schenck into the fold. The partners had always had a warm and fruitful relationship with him, and as an independent producer he shared many of their aspirations and challenges. Early in 1923, a brief skirmish occurred in the larger war of the two models: the studio system/factory model of film production versus the cottage industry/independent producer model. The battle lines were drawn over the effectiveness of Will Hays in his role as head of Motion Picture Producers and Distributors of America. The independents did not think him worth the money. Fairbanks led the charge in January 1923 with a statement: "Mr. Hays has nothing whatever to do with the art or morals of the motion picture industry. He is simply the hired intermediary or 'fixer.' He has done wonderful work in straightening out the censorship tangle, but that, and only that, is his function. . . . The public ought to be informed that 'moral uplift' was not his role." Zukor and the large studio heads fell into line supporting Hays. Schenck joined the ranks of Fairbanks. The dust settled quickly on this scrap, but allegiances were defined.

Further, as a director of the Bank of Italy, a major source of financing to filmmakers in the 1920s, Schenck helped Pickford and Fairbanks that same year. A side venture, Associated Authors, established to provide content to UA, had stumbled and was under threat of loan foreclosure by the bank until Schenck stepped in. Thus it was perhaps inevitable, and certainly fortunate, that he would come to join United Artists. The negotiations and announcement came in November 1924. Schenck was made chairman of the board and admitted as a full partner with a thousand shares. In return, he would deliver six Norma Talmadge films a year for UA to distribute, with the option to provide six more with other stars, on the condition that UA would provide half the financing. It was an extremely happy turn of events and likely saved the company.

But try as he might, Schenck could not save Griffith. Even before he took the helm, he tried, offering to secure loans to take the heat off the embattled director. But Griffith was getting business advice from his brother, Albert Grey. Of Grey, Griffith biographer Richard Schickel wrote: "Perhaps the younger man had an unconscious desire to wreck his brother's career. Or maybe the captaincy of a derelict ship struck him as better than no captaincy at all. Or perhaps he was simply an idiot." Many argue that Schickel's third theory applies. The offer was rebuffed. Griffith's *Isn't Life Wonderful* and the Paramount-funded *Sally of the Sawdust* were distributed by UA. Then Griffith left the organization, his stock in escrow, the path of his downward spiral now irreversible.

He would not be the only founder to take this ride. Of the four, Chaplin was the most fortunate. Like Mary, he would retain his riches, but unlike her, he died surrounded by a loving family and with a reputation that was, after the furor of the 1950s, once again brightly burnished. Mary lived long—terribly long—as an alcoholic and a recluse. Douglas, loved by both, would take an intermediate path down the mountain of success, one not as humiliating as Griffith's impoverished end as a washed-up has-been or as long and painfully sustained as the slow, dreadful demise of his beloved Mary. But down he was going to go.

He would not have believed this in the late autumn of 1924. Things at United Artists were turning around, and he had plans for his next film. *Don Q, Son of Zorro* was going to whip—literally, whip—things into shape.

13

Buckling Down

NINETEEN TWENTY-FIVE WAS THE year that Douglas Fairbanks got
back to work. Company coffers needed refilling, and United Artists required a turnaround. No small order. Still, it was a merry grindstone to which he returned, producing two major swashbucklers in a
twelve-month period. One was a pioneering effort that saved the nascent
Technicolor Corporation, the other a tremendous financial and critical
success that is all but forgotten today.

Don Q, Son of Zorro, the forgotten blockbuster, was announced as
a project in January 1925. It would combine his recent fascination with
Spain with the surefire box office draw of his *Zorro* character. He had
been toying with the idea of a sequel to *Zorro* as early as 1921, but each
time the opportunity arose, he would instead elect a more novel idea.
At that time sequels were largely unheard of—certainly for big-budget
productions with major stars.* But the safety of a sequel—a concept
Hollywood would ultimately come to embrace ad nauseam—seemed
just the ticket. *Thief* was finally working its way to the smaller cities
and towns as the year dawned, and it was becoming clear that the film's
rural returns were not going to match those of *Robin Hood*. "*The Thief
of Bagdad* is one of the biggest things in the movies, but it is surprising
to learn of the great number of people, especially in the small cities,

---

* An exception might be the Tarzan films with Elmo Lincoln.

who would have none of it," wrote one Philadelphia columnist. "We of the big cities fail to take the likes and dislikes of the small cities and towns into consideration."

Neither he nor Mary was going to repeat *that* oversight. Mary, having stretched herself with two adult-role costume dramas, *Rosita* and *Dorothy Vernon of Haddon Hall*, elected to return to young girl roles that year, filming *Little Annie Rooney* and *Sparrows* in succession. Doug's return to Zorro reflected the same conservatism. They were artists, true, but also businesspeople, each an intelligent and thoughtful producer willing to invest and risk but, unlike Griffith, not to the point of ruin.

Fairbanks's character in *Don Q* was, of course, not Zorro but his son. The film gave him an opportunity to play both parts on the screen, repeating Mary's brilliant split screen work from *Little Lord Fauntleroy* and anticipating Valentino's final film, 1926's *The Son of the Sheik*.* The story was not Johnston McCulley's but was derived from the pulp novel *Don Q's Love Story*, written by one Hesketh Prichard, a British explorer and wartime sniper with a weakness for boys' adventure fiction. The character of Zorro was simply shoehorned by Fairbanks into the plot as the hero's American father. Fairbanks had a requirement that his films' themes be simple enough to be summarized in a single sentence. For *Don Q* it was: "Truth crushed will rise again—if you have the *yeast* to make it rise." Donald Crisp, a stalwart favorite in the industry as both an actor (*Broken Blossoms*) and a director (*The Navigator*), was chosen not only to play the film's villain but also to direct. Nineteen-year-old Mary Astor, who had costarred with John Barrymore in 1924's *Beau Brummel*, was tapped for the female lead. She was, to put it delicately, a young woman of sensual interests, then embroiled in a torrid affair with Barrymore. She found the happily married Fairbanks unsatisfactory on this front: "I looked forward to meeting this man who was something of a legend around Hollywood, but I found the man himself to be less

---

* Valentino signed a three-picture deal with United Artists early into the filming of *Don Q* but lived long enough to make only two. Later accounts claim the contracted number was five films.

exciting than the legends. For one thing, I was put out by his attitude toward me. He was nice to me, in the way a sophisticated man about town would be nice to a small and reasonably well-behaved child. I felt that I merited more attention than that!"

Still, she liked him. It was hard not to. "It was all fun for him," she recalled near the end of her life. "He wasn't an actor at all. To me, he was an effect; he was a wonderful effect." She recalled particularly his intense training on the Australian bullwhip with expert Snowy Baker—six weeks of unceasing practice. "While I was making up in my dressing room . . . I could hear the repeated swishshshsh—SMACK of the whip," she recalled. "He could soon do all the tricks with the bull whip, and he was boyishly proud of his accomplishment." Proud, indeed. He would delight to show his hand calluses to anyone who would take the time to admire them.

> Snowy was hired to wield the whip for the close-ups of shots like the one where a cigarette is detached from a surprised face, but Doug would always say, "Let me try, Snowy. Then if I can't, you do the next take."
>
> Feeling an impulse to show off one day, and wanting to please my "star," I refused a "double" for a scene in which Doug was supposed to teasingly crack the whip and let it slither around the girl's shoulders when she was not aware of his presence—a strictly Fairbanksian method of saying "BOO!" . . . Of course Mother objected, and there were conferences, and I insisted that I was not afraid; and Doug beamed and reminded us that it would be much more effective if we could get the whole sequence in one shot. Finally it was left up to me, and I said I wanted to do it. So I did. Two takes went uneventfully; the leather slid harmlessly around my shoulders, I was properly startled, and Doug leaped to untangle me. But Doug wanted "just one more"; it had to be perfect. And Doug miscalculated. After all, the whip was twenty feet long, and I don't see how he ever *did* calculate. But this third time I heard the crack, and knew it was too close to my head, and then I felt a sharp burning pain as the whip lashed around my neck. Doug was

incoherent in his remorse; doctors were fetched; there was a chaos of noise and confusion. Donald Crisp, the director who was also acting in the picture, suffered the same accident at Snowy Baker's hands a few days later, and the edict went out, "From now on we stick to dummies."

Besides learning the whip, Fairbanks became the student of what was, for him, a new discipline: dance. Dance is something that few associate with silent film, but in truth the fusion of music and movement was very much a part of the medium. Dancing scenes were surprisingly common. Valentino's tango in *The Four Horsemen of the Apocalypse* four years earlier had created a sensation. But Fairbanks was not—at least at this time—looking to generate any sexual energy with his dance. While he did a few tango steps,* most of the dancing scene was broken up by expository shots of action in the café or demonstrated the irrepressible Doug clicking his heels boyishly, hopping up on the table and dancing a solo jig, leaving his Latina partner to her own devices. It is of interest that this sequence was the very first to be shot for the film, suggesting the possibility that he just wanted to get it over with.

Filming began on January 26 and was completed by late April— a brisker shooting schedule than any of his earlier swashbucklers. Even Donald Crisp's broken foot midproduction (he was stepped on by a horse while filming the castle sequence) did not cause delay. They soldiered on, taking only close-ups and midshots and working back to the long shots later. Work on exteriors in the San Fernando Valley was delayed by a day when a nearby wildfire required all in the production to aid in extinguishing the flames. Still, it seemed that filming had scarcely begun before Doug was celebrating the production's end, photographed sunnily wielding an oversize knife at a large cake sculpted to look like the head of a bull.

His sense of urgency, his desire to turn around a quick hit, was understandable. The last thing he wanted was the perception that he was slipping. After all, pretenders to the throne were encroaching. Col-

---

* It was reported that he took tango lessons for four weeks.

umnist Herbert Howe, who returned to Hollywood in 1925 after a long absence, noted some weather changes:

> For years the pioneers held the claims. Mary Pickford, Mabel Normand, Douglas Fairbanks, Chaplin. . . . This old order is rapidly fading, and the past year has seen the greatest shakedown. Mary Pickford now acknowledges that the crown has passed to Gloria Swanson. It's the popular decree written in the indisputable letters of the box-office. Of the men, Harold Lloyd is the acknowledged champion. . . . Fairbanks has kept going only by the Herculean effort of endeavoring to make each picture better than the preceding. He has passed beyond close-ups, and he realizes that his place in the sun can be maintained only as a producer.

Harsh words for a man who, in the winter of 1925, was forty-one years old and about to produce a film less lavish than his last. Small wonder, then, that interviews began to appear that claimed just the opposite. DON Q TO SURPASS THIEF OF BAGDAD, barked one headline, the article quoting Fairbanks: "From the standpoint of costly production, this picture is very apt to more than rival *The Thief of Bagdad*." It was far from true. *Don Q*'s cost was $834,589*—less than half that of *Thief*.

Still, at the end of the day, such fibs were unnecessary. Everyone, audiences and critics alike, welcomed enthusiastically what they felt was a return to form. "Without doubt one of the best that Doug has had in some time from an all around entertainment and picture house standpoint," wrote *Variety*. *Photoplay* added: "It is guaranteed to drive little boys into frenzies of stunts until they break an arm or a new fad comes along."† The verdict was clear: while many saw much to admire

---

* This figure is "all in," representing production costs as well as negative and print costs, publicity, and contingent commissions.

† A young Marion Morrison, later John Wayne, was among the juvenile set who worshipped Fairbanks. He tried to emulate him by jumping out a second-story window, clinging to a grapevine. "I ruined a beautiful grape arbor," Wayne biographer Scott Eyman quotes him as saying.

in *Thief*, what they really wanted from Fairbanks was to *enjoy* him. The grand settings, the thousands of extras, the glorious costumes were all well and good. But *Don Q*, everyone seemed to feel, was just more fun. "If *Don Q, Son of Zorro* is not as good a picture and better than *The Thief of Bagdad*," insisted one small-town critic, "Bull Montana is the queen of Siam." The film returned $1,616,872 to Fairbanks's production company's coffers, independent of its return to UA. Only *Robin Hood* had a greater profit.

And, indeed, the film *is* a lot of fun, draped though it is under a fairly heavy load of sets and costumes. But our boy was peeking out from underneath the finery, wooing the fair lass, whipping his whip, and in general raising sunny hell.* The film's pace and pep went a far way toward squelching the "he's getting too old for close-ups" argument. One reviewer, who had written, "As the years pass and age begins its inroads, Douglas Fairbanks becomes a little too strenuous at times for this admiring onlooker," now rhapsodized, "Doug has never leaped so high, moved so quickly or kept in such constant motion so long before. The man isn't human, that's what he isn't. He's perpetual youth, a three-ringed circus, the personification of all juvenile heroes, all rolled into one. . . ."

The film's New York premiere broke precedent on two fronts. First, it took place in the summer. Historically, summer was the worst time to open a film; audiences did not want to sit in sweltering theaters in an era when few had air conditioning. But *Don Q* packed the house in the eight weeks it was at the Globe Theatre, which had no cooling plant. The run was intentionally short, with the general release date set for August 30. This was for the benefit of United Artists. The departure of Griffith and the arrival of Schenck changed the dynamic within the

---

* Today most prefer *The Mark of Zorro* to its successor. A plain backdrop, it can be argued, best set off the form of the hero and his stunts. And *Don Q* suffers from an association that would have been impossible to predict at the time. Fairbanks's wig, waved and combed straight back, suggests the style later adopted by Richard Nixon. This, combined with the fact that the only available copies are badly damaged 16mm prints, has deprived the film of much of its luster.

partnership. Members began acting for the good of the organization, not simply themselves, and the early handoff of what was to become his second-most-profitable film to date was a good faith gesture to the new leadership. But even this abridged Broadway run was agreed to only after what *Variety* deemed "a stiff fight." After all, no Fairbanks film was going to go *straight* into general release.*

Further, Fairbanks did not attend the New York premiere. This was a significant break in pattern. It is easy to be lured into seeking meaning where it may not exist: his cycle of swashbuckler/Broadway premiere/ trip to Europe was broken for the first time, one might assert, in the interests of getting more product out. And, one is tempted to argue, this also represented a power shift from East Coast to West. The Broadway premiere was becoming less the imprimatur denoting the legitimacy and importance of a film. Hollywood would serve just fine.

Fairbanks had a different explanation. Mary was editing *Little Annie Rooney*, he claimed, and he was not going to leave her, declaring, "If I had five pictures opening there on the same night, I would not go without Mary." But none of these explanations reflect the truth. In fact, there was a kidnapping plot afoot, and Mary was the intended victim.

It was early May. Mary remembered being alone at Pickfair when Douglas called. Where was she? "Rowing down Hollywood Boulevard in a golden gondola," she replied wryly.

No, he insisted impatiently, his sense of the dramatic never failing him. This was *important*. "Call the butler and the gardener and tell them not to leave the house. Go immediately to your own room and lock the door. Do you hear?"

She obeyed, with no little curiosity. When she unlocked her door fifteen minutes later, it was not only to her husband but the chief of detectives, George Home. The police, through a combination of a helpful informant and some timely keyhole peeping,† had discovered

---

* And none did, until *The Iron Mask*.

† The detectives actually used a stethoscope to listen through the walls of a hotel room.

a scheme. Kidnappers, dressed as conventioneering Shriners, were to waylay Mary's car as she departed the studio. Counting on the transfer of their victim to look like general merrymaking, they would abduct her and hide her in a cabin in the mountains. They wanted a $200,000 ransom from Doug. They had considered nabbing little Jackie Coogan or the grandchildren of a local oil magnate or even Buster Keaton, but they settled on Pickford as the easiest to snatch. Yet an arrest could not be made, the detective asserted, until the kidnappers made their move.

Thus began a tense two weeks. Mary had a bodyguard on the set, but in traveling to and from Pickfair, she needed to present the appearance that she was ripe for the picking. She drove in her two-seater Rolls-Royce ("the last word in daintiness") and waited. Her film double, Crete Sykle, would don Mary's hat and coat and drive periodically about town during the course of the workday in an attempt to lure the kidnappers to strike.

One evening in late May, the couple began the drive home in the little Rolls, Fairbanks at the wheel. Mary noticed a convertible a few blocks back, storm windows up, suspicious faces peeking through the curtains. The car followed them as they moved north from Santa Monica Boulevard and proceeded west on Sunset. The Rolls, being of British make, had the driving wheel on the right side of the car. As they accelerated, the convertible did the same, pulling up to the right. Between Doug and Mary's seats rested a sawed-off shotgun and a Colt .45. She recalled her husband's voice as feverish. "If the shooting starts, Mary, drop to the floor of the car!" Pickford, being of a plucky bent herself, secretly resolved to do no such thing. She would grab that .45 if trouble came and get in a lick or two of her own.

> We were now doing all of eighty miles an hour. I kept telling Douglas not to get ahead of the other car, but he was frightfully excited, and evidently didn't hear me. Douglas swerved sharply to the other side of Sunset Boulevard ahead of the convertible, and in so doing cut directly into the path of a shining brand-new Ford,

set, like all other Fords of that period, high from the road. I saw it rock perilously from side to side, and for a moment I was sure it would capsize.

He pulled into the driveway of the Beverly Hills Hotel, followed by the convertible, and leaped out of the still-rolling car. Mary recalled him as "bathed in perspiration and white as death." Cocking the shotgun, he stood between their pursuers and Mary, shouting, "Throw up your hands!" The occupants did so. They were, however, the police. The kidnappers were in the Ford that had almost overturned.

Enough was enough. "I will not subject my wife to any more of this danger," he declared. Hollywood was a fiefdom, and the police were wise enough to know who ruled. The next day, when the kidnappers turned up outside the studio and planted themselves to watch and wait, the detective walked up to their car, peremptorily knocked the driver unconscious with the butt of his gun, and enquired politely of the others, "Will you take it the hard way or will you come quietly?" They went quietly. It was a different era.

Justice came quickly. Fairbanks testified before a grand jury the following week, and conspiracy indictments quickly followed. The trial began on July 22, and he attended faithfully.* The first day he sat quietly with the prosecuting attorneys, assisting, when necessary, those ladies who required drinks at the nearby water cooler. The run on thirsty damsels drove him in following days to working in the judge's chambers. When finally his turn came on July 29, he was on the stand for twenty-five minutes, testifying to having seen the defendants loitering near the studio grounds on several occasions.

When the men were convicted and condemned to ten years to life at San Quentin, neither Fairbanks nor Pickford had any sympathy to give. "I think in sentencing them the law was lenient in the extreme," Mary wrote a quarter century later. "The public has no idea of the things

---

* Mary was still filming *Little Annie Rooney* and was in court only when needed for testimony and for the verdict.

that we and others were subjected to before those men were arrested," Fairbanks told reporters the day of the conviction. "I am anxious to have an example made of this case."

It wasn't simply the fear he had felt for her safety. When reports of the plot first came out, some cynics claimed that the story was nothing more than a publicity stunt. It took denials from the police department, the stars, and even the Shriners* to overcome this skepticism. By the time the perpetrators were sentenced, reporters were obliged to acknowledge that the couple's vindication was on more than one front.

This episode was not their first brush with the criminal element, nor would it be their last. Eighteen months earlier, in the final months of production of *Thief of Bagdad*, Fairbanks received several threatening letters from a man who had been turned away from work at the studio. Harry Dunlap was the disgruntled job seeker, an ex-convict now wanted for stopping automobiles by the ruse of a police badge, raping the female occupants, and then robbing and sometimes killing the men.

Doug took to toting a sawed-off shotgun (very likely the same one he carried in the Rolls) and offered a reward for the "Badge Bandit." By January 1924, he and Mary were accompanied everywhere by armed guards. The criminal was traced to Beverly Glen but eluded the local posse.† Ultimately he was captured in Detroit and returned to Los Angeles, where he received a 214-year sentence. Two murders and thirty-seven rapes suggested that Fairbanks's attachment to his shotgun was not unreasonable. "Mary and I have decided that we are the target for all the nuts who come to Los Angeles," he said, and stepped up the security at the studio and Pickfair.

But even home was not safe, as they were to learn four months after the kidnapping scheme. On the morning of September 25, Tony Vanera, the Pickfair night watchman, came across two men attempting to pick the lock on the front door. Vanera, a former immigration

---

* Fairbanks held nothing against the organization and even staged a rodeo for their conventioneers within two weeks of the arrests.

† Led by film cowboy Tom Mix.

agent who went by the nickname "Black Tony," was armed. A shot—either very skilled or very lucky—took the flashlight from his hand and bullets began to fly. It was later estimated that twenty-five rounds were exchanged. Doug, gripping his .45 revolver, emerged on the scene through a window—demonstrating that what he lacked in prudence, he made up for in dumb physical courage. He and the watchmen chased the two men, who eluded them by virtue of a getaway car and driver. Vanera was confident that he wounded at least one of them; a blood trail was found on the lawn. Doug's contribution to the kerfuffle was to almost shoot Mary's little Airedale Zorro, who was hiding in the bushes.*

Nothing was lost in the episode, except more of the dimming innocence of the early days of Hollywood. Fame now began to require isolation. Stars retreated to their homes and double-locked the doors.

Not that home was such a bad place to be, as Fairbanks discovered one morning that year when he popped out for his morning swim. There, on the bottom of his pool, was a strange round container. He dove in to investigate and discovered an aquarium cum miniature pirate city. It was then that he recalled the date: May 23. Upon emerging, he noticed new lawn furniture, pirate's heads custom-carved into the arms. His birthday surprises from Mary were not over. When he arrived at the studio, he was met by an eight-foot-tall pirate crafted of wooden planks, accompanied by a set of throwing knives.

She had misjudged when, in Christmas 1922, she gave him a model galleon, but this time she was on target. He was finally going to make the pirate film. What's more, he was going to cross another frontier. He was going to make it in color.

Fairbanks's encounters and uses of color photography did not, of course, begin with *The Black Pirate*. After all, his first film appearance was in a Kinemacolor actuality in 1913. Kinemacolor was the first truly photographic color process. All earlier color had been rendered on film by way of stencils, tinting, and toning, all labor intensive—particularly

---

* Many at the studio would not have minded had he plugged the little dog. Zorro, it seems, was a biter.

the stencil process, which required work on portions of each frame of film. The Kinemacolor process used alternating frames of green and red, which were then projected through a rotating color filter onto a custom "color fixed" screen. But Kinemacolor was not the ultimate color solution. The images flickered to the point that the audience could endure only short viewing sessions. Eyestrain became associated with color film and would haunt its reputation for the next fifteen years and more.

Fairbanks's films up to this point were not truly black and white. Almost no films were. Feature films were "tinted," which is to say the developed film was washed in chemical baths to give overall colors to different scenes. Nighttime scenes were typically tinted blue, outdoor daytime scenes were soft yellow, and fire sequences were often red.

A later, more sophisticated technique that came in use around this time was one developed by an engraver, who would, in the words of Technicolor historian Fred Basten, "etch, print or hand block a 'register print' of the portion of the film selected for color treatment." A color plate would be created, much as color plates were created for use in the stone lithographic printing of posters. Because of the expense and the labor involved, this process only worked for short, relatively static portions of films. It was used in Griffith's *The Birth of a Nation* and *Intolerance* and in DeMille's *Joan the Woman*. Fairbanks reportedly employed it for a sequence in *The Three Musketeers*.*

Then came Technicolor. Herbert Thomas Kalmus was only thirty-three years old when he founded the fledgling Technicolor Corporation in 1915, but he already had degrees in physics and chemistry from MIT and a doctorate from the University of Zurich. He was methodical, organized, unusually deft at business for a scientist, and doggedly persistent. Working with a small team, initially out of an old rail car that served as a laboratory, he had—after some fits and starts—devised a two-color process that did not require special projection equipment. The colors captured were reds and greens, each recorded by a camera that would split the optic beam, permitting separate exposures of each

---

* The search for an extant tinted print of the film is ongoing.

color to register onto separate filmstrips. In 1922, the company invested in its first full-length demonstration film.* Filmed in Hollywood, *Toll of the Sea* was made with the cooperation of Joseph Schenck, who lent Kalmus the production facilities, cameraman, director, and actors.† The lead actress was the then-unknown Anna May Wong.

Toll of the Sea succeeded, and the two-color process began showing up in short sequences in such major films as *Ben-Hur*, *The Phantom of the Opera*, and *The Merry Widow*. Jesse Lasky had given it a full-length try in 1924 with the western *Wanderer of the Wasteland*, now lost. The film made no particular impression, either critically or financially. Technicolor was stalled. It was, in the words of Basten, "a puzzling situation. Hollywood was churning out hundreds of films, but few producers were willing to take a chance with color." What Technicolor needed, Kalmus felt, was a major personality with sufficient gravitas and reputation to endorse the process. "The fact remained," Basten wrote, "Technicolor needed a star."

Enter Doug.

Fairbanks was all Kalmus could have hoped for: innovative, fearless, and deep pocketed. After rejecting color for *Thief*, and not even considering it for *Don Q*, Douglas Fairbanks had at long last decided to make his pirate picture. And, to his mind, it had to be in color.

Preproduction work on *The Black Pirate* began in May. Much of the effort was directed toward Technicolor tests. The challenge was, reportedly, "to take the color out of color." He did not wish to replicate the effect of *Toll of the Sea*, which had been filmed to demonstrate the extreme potential of the color process. The film was ripe with plummy reds and jelly bean greens. In Fairbanks's mind, the color needed to supplement but never distract. If more attention were paid to the effect

---

* It is of note that there were competing color processes at the time. *The Glorious Adventure*, filmed in Prizma Color in Great Britain the same year, was the first feature film to use a subtractive color process, and it featured blues and reds.

† A 1917 film, *The Gulf Between*, had been filmed by the Technicolor team using an earlier process. A small portion of Griffith's *Way Down East* was also produced in the two-color process, but the color sequences are believed lost.

than the narrative, it would be no more than an expensive novelty. Fairbanks was to later claim that his first response to the idea of color was to think, would you rouge the lips of the Venus de Milo? But then he had a second thought: What was it about color—apart from the early challenges associated with the flickering—that made him leap to that conclusion? And could that phenomenon, once identified, be reversed? "We were afraid that the public might at first be more intrigued by the colors than by the story itself," he said. "So we decided to practice restraint."

They elected to model the film's coloring on the paintings of the old masters—Rembrandt, in particular. Either out of aesthetics or necessity (Technicolor could not capture blues or yellows), they elected to use a color palate of greens and browns. The task was not simple. Six months of tests were conducted. Dual sets of costumes had to be made, as it was discovered that they photographed differently under artificial lights versus outdoor sets. Even outdoor shooting required supplemental lights to capture colors at the levels desired. Fairbanks had always been bedeviled by a heavy growth of beard—requiring shaves twice a day and occasionally three times during prolonged shoots—and now whenever a five o'clock shadow threatened, his lower face would photograph green. Extra red powder was added to his beard area to neutralize this effect.

This principle did not just apply to Fairbanks's beard. Any item would be dyed or otherwise colored so that it came out the proper color on the two-strip Technicolor film, as opposed to the color that it demonstrated to the naked eye. Their efforts paid off: the film had a muted, lovely palate that did not compete with the story. The occasional flash of bright red (as in a bloody sword in the film's opening sequence) served the narrative function rather than competing with it.

Casting the film had none of the challenges associated with *The Thief of Bagdad*. Interested in the possibilities of color as early as 1923, Doug had screened both available color features as soon as he could. *Toll of the Sea* is the film that brought lovely Anna May Wong to his attention; *Wanderer of the Wasteland* introduced him to Billie Dove.

Dove was a Ziegfeld Follies beauty who had appeared earlier in the year with his son in Paramount's *The Air Mail*. Her coloring, he felt, was perfect. She recalled being offered the role by Fairbanks over the phone, without even a screen test.*

The George Eastman House has in its archives a lovely and fortuitous piece of film: color footage of Mary Pickford, wearing Billie Dove's costume and wig. Pickford replaced Dove in one of the final shots of the film, when the hero kisses the heroine. What was an inside joke to the production company—Doug plants a very enthusiastic kiss on the princess, a rare sight in a Fairbanks film—provides succeeding generations the pleasure of seeing Mary Pickford in color in 1925.†

The most engaging part of the casting process, for Fairbanks, at least, was finding the background players to play the crew of the pirate ship. Here was an opportunity to dip into the deep pool of his friendships with boxers, athletes, and grizzled cowhands. Jack Dempsey's former sparring partner, Jimmy Dime, was among those hired, as well as a boxer named Bob Roper, proud possessor of a broken nose, cauliflower ear, and permanently split lip. "Stubby" Kruger, a member of the 1920 Olympic swim team, joined Fairbanks's constant trainer and companion, Chuck Lewis, as a pirate. Broncobuster George Holt was hired because

---

* Multiple camera tests were taken of Dove after she was cast, as part of the Technicolor testing. And there is evidence that many screen tests were taken of other hopefuls, so the good lady's recollection might not be complete. Rudy Behlmer, in his definitive write-up of the production, states that Fairbanks reviewed Dove's color tests as well as *Wanderer of the Wasteland* before casting her. The idea of an actress being cast for simply looking good in Technicolor is not as odd as it sounds. Certain performers—think Katharine Hepburn, Greta Garbo, Marlene Dietrich—photograph better in black and white than in color. The angularity of their faces, the ravishing planes and shadows, disappear or are minimized with color photography. Conversely, other faces were found, as three-strip Technicolor came into broader use in the 1940s and '50s, in which the opposite rule applied. Rhonda Fleming and Maureen O'Hara fell into this category, the latter carrying the nickname "the Technicolor Queen." Even at this stage, Dove was being touted as "the Color Girl of the Movies."

† At the only public screening of the footage, at the San Francisco Silent Film Festival, the audience made an audible gasp when she appeared.

his bowed legs suggested scurvy. Fairbanks himself cornered a traffic cop at Santa Monica and Fairfax whom he felt possessed a suitably piratical air, recruiting him to join the motley crew.

Donald Crisp played a sympathetic one-armed pirate in the production but did not direct. This task was assigned to Albert Parker,* the villain from *American Aristocracy* and director of *The Knickerbocker Buckaroo* and *Arizona*. Parker, who had known Fairbanks since his *Gentleman from Mississippi* days, was the definition of a company man—and a staunch admirer. "You don't know—nobody can know, without working with him—how he is loved and admired by the people he gathers around him," he told a columnist the following year. "You don't know the power he has developed by which he can get the best that a group of experts have to give, and yet be able to weld their efforts into a splendid unity which has his own, personal stamp on it. . . . He gets the best work out of people by telling them the *result* he wants, and then letting them work it out, in their own way."

Donald Crisp would later assert that *he* had been the original director of *The Black Pirate* but had been replaced by Parker when he and Fairbanks had a falling out. One scholar argues that Fairbanks's annoyance with Crisp for casting Doug Jr. in *Man Bait* might have been the source of the change at the helm. There are two problems here. First, Crisp was never at the helm. Albert Parker was identified early in the press as the film's director and was documented to be in preproduction meetings as early as July 1925. Second, *Man Bait* could not have been the cause of any staffing change. Junior was cast by Crisp in *Man Bait* late in 1926, more than a year after preproduction began on *The Black Pirate*.†

Crisp himself claims that the falling out was over who would do the most famous stunt in the film (and, some argue, in Fairbanks's career).

---

* Director Hugo Ballin claimed that he was offered the post ahead of Parker but was not able to free himself from his Paramount commitments.

† This is not to say that Junior's casting by Crisp wasn't a source of strife. Letitia Fairbanks reports in her biography of her uncle that he angrily told Crisp, "There's only *one* Fairbanks." It is possible, if not probable, that Crisp was her source for this tale.

This is the knife-in-the-sail slide, in which our hero travels from the main topsail yardarm to the main yardarm by means of plunging a dagger into the topsail and slicing his way down. He then repeats the exercise with the mainsail, disabling the ship. Historian Booton Herndon muddies the historical waters in reviewing this stunt, quoting Donald Crisp's suggestion that it was Chuck Lewis, not Fairbanks, wielding the blade and sliding down the sail.

This merits discussion. Crisp appears to have developed a Frances Marion–level distaste for Fairbanks late in his life: "He was always striving to be something he was not," he groused to Herndon. "He would have killed himself showing off." Crisp had distinct recollections of working with Chuck Lewis on the stunt, running a wire through a plaster cast on his knife arm and chest and pulling him down through the canvas with a wire. Child actor Robert Parrish claimed that Fairbanks showed him the device during filming of *The Iron Mask*—a baseball bat in lieu of the knife, operated by a pulley behind the sail. Kevin Brownlow in subsequent years deciphered the mechanism of the stunt: the sail was angled at forty-five degrees, with the camera tipped in parallel, to give the illusion that the sail and mast were fully upright. The fabric had been pretorn and loosely stitched together. A counterweight rose as gravity pulled Fairbanks down, thus controlling his rate of descent.

It is likely that all accounts are correct. Trial and error was a significant part of designing the stunt, and many mechanisms—plaster, wire, pulleys, baseball bats—were likely tried. Similarly, much as Richard Talmadge would help Fairbanks design stunts in the early 1920s, Chuck Lewis helped Fairbanks now. "We had a place on the lot where we tried out all these things," he told Herndon fifty years later. "I did it, Charlie Stevens did it, Doug did it, everybody did it." Outtake footage shows repeated takes of Fairbanks performing the stunt. And the form sliding down those sails in the final print of the film is also Fairbanks. The cervical kyphosis that causes his neck to jut forward at an anterior angle is distinctly recognizable to the clinical eye.

Crisp may have resented Fairbanks in later years; certainly in 1925 he had just cause to feel jinxed in working with him. Barely recovered from *Don Q*'s whip burn and foot fracture, he proceeded to dislocate a finger filming *The Black Pirate*. He was hardly alone in his misfortune. Production manager Ted Reed broke his leg when he fell down a ship's hold, and Anders Randolf, who shaved his head for the role of the evil pirate captain, suffered both sunstroke and a blistering scalp burn after his first day's filming. Fairbanks himself separated a rib from his sternum in early October while lifting Billie Dove to the roof of the ship's cabin. He also experienced an accidental slice to his arm shooting a fight sequence with Randolf and received another gash perilously close to his left eye while filming with fencing master Fred Cavens (who stood in for his opponents in over-the-shoulder shots). Outtakes reveal Doug scowling in annoyance at the first injury;* for the second, however, he had an audience. Sailors from the HMS *Capetown* and HMS *Patrician* were studio guests, and upon the scene being halted, he turned to the visitors and cheerfully exclaimed, "Pirates always were a bloody lot." The public Doug never scowled.

While preproduction lasted six months, filming took only nine weeks, five of which were devoted to exteriors. Fairbanks purchased and had restored an 1877 clipper ship, the *Llewellyn J. Morse*, to house the cast and crew by night and double for one of the film's ships by day.† The *Morse* wasn't the only ship in the shoot—a reproduction Spanish galleon was built, as well as a one-hundred-foot-long galley (this latter being Doug's "particular brain child").‡ Mary came along for three weeks of the location shooting—the location in this instance

---

* Complete with expletive.

† The ship snapped her hawsers during an early winter storm, damaging much of the equipment and necessitating multiple tugboats to save it as it drifted out to sea. Steel cables replaced the rope hawsers, and, off camera at least, twentieth-century ship safety replaced that of the nineteenth. A miniature of the *Morse*, about the size of an automobile, was constructed for a sequence in which its powder magazines were set on fire and it exploded and burned. In addition, a stranded lumber schooner, the *Muriel*, was redressed to resemble a seventeenth-century galleon and was blown up for the cameras.

‡ He named the galley the *Yo-Ho* and christened it with a bottle of bay rum. Parker recruited men who had participated in the Pacific Fleet boat races in order to find men able to handle its oars.

being twenty-five miles off the coast of Catalina Island. They declined the offer of the use of a yacht (likely Joseph Schenck's), instead taking up quarters in a cabin constructed especially for them on the *Morse*. Two tugboats served as supply ships from the shore, and speedboats carried actors and directorial commands from ship to ship. Evenings and lunch breaks were spent enjoying boxing and wrestling matches conducted between members of the pirate crew. They returned in time for the company to spend Christmas Eve with their families.

Doug and Mary had each produced two features that year and survived a kidnapping scare. As far as Fairbanks was concerned, they had earned a holiday. Mary hoped to start yet another film but saw the writing on the wall. "Right here at Christmas time I am going to begin a new picture and Douglas will have nothing to do; and I will have this big boy of mine on my hands, with nothing to do—wanting me to play with him all the time," she said. She would rather have remained in California; she hated travel. "I love my home, and I really want to stay in it," she admitted. "But of course I want more than anything else to please my husband."

And so Doug's wishes prevailed. They leased their studio to Joseph Schenck for the upcoming year and scheduled $2.5 million in improvements to be made during their absence. Norma and Constance Talmadge moved into Mary's bungalow, and Schenck himself took over Doug's quarters.* The couple would spend a year abroad, they announced. Perhaps two. They would travel through Europe, Russia, Siberia, and possibly the Far East, perhaps even making a film together. They would depart, they declared, on February 2, accompanied by Robert and his family, Charlotte, little Gwynne, and their usual retinue of retainers.

But then came the first cloud on the horizon.

---

* Schenck formed a business entity in combination with Pickford and Fairbanks to lease out space, sets, props, and equipment from their jointly owned studio in order that the plant and facilities could continue to generate revenue during their down times. Soon Goldwyn would be leasing space from them. Many of his classic films were shot at this location.

Charlotte was ill. A tumor in her breast had been discovered. Mary, in the mode of the firstborn child who assumed responsibility for all, blamed herself. Her mother had been looking for black fabric for a mourning dress for Mary's character in *Little Annie Rooney*. The trunk lid fell on her, striking her breast. In fact, this was a serendipitous accident that caused her mother to discover the mass, but in the 1920s, there was a prevalent folk belief that trauma could cause a tumor. Charlotte kept the news largely to herself throughout 1925, resisting the advice of physicians to have the lesion removed. Finally, shortly after Christmas, she consented to an operation. Doug and Mary delayed their trip.

Fairbanks occupied himself playing host to the adult children of Lord Asquith—Elizabeth, now Princess Bibesco, and Anthony, soon to become a film director of considerable visual power. The princess briefly made headlines when she fell from a horse while riding on the Pickfair grounds. No one seemed surprised. Doug and Mary were always entertaining minor royalty, it seemed. It was remarkable that more of them hadn't fallen off horses or into the swimming pool by sheer force of bumping into each other.

Pickfair had, by this time, assumed a character and status of its own. An invitation there was more prized in some circles than a summons to the White House. Mr. and Mrs. Fairbanks were excluded from Southern California's social register, true, but it scarcely mattered. They made blue books irrelevant. Theirs was the hardest invitation in town to get. Fairbanks remained a cheerfully unrepentant snob about hobnobbing with the rich and famous. They needn't even be dukes or princes—in keeping with the new century, he recognized the ability of fame and fortune to drape upon those lucky few the mantle of de facto royalty. He and his wife, after all, constituted one of the best examples of this phenomenon in the new century—this postwar century, where democratic values and the power of a meritocracy began to outweigh those of the aristocracy. He would be seen playing tennis with a Vanderbilt or dining at the Park Avenue apartment of Condé Nast as often as he was pictured with a Lord Mountbatten or the Prince of Wales. "He drew successful people to him wherever he went," Mary recalled. "In fact he almost seemed to be collecting them." But much as he relished his time with Babe Ruth, Jack Dempsey, and other members of the meritocracy, he harbored a special soft spot for royalty.

Between her procrastination and surgeon's squabbles, Charlotte's surgery did not take place until late February 1926. Fairbanks stayed by her side during the procedure (sterility practices being, evidently, looser in those days), while Mary paced outside the operating theater. When, in the first week of March, the patient was declared to be out of danger, he could wait no longer. He and Mary departed for New York, arriving just in time to attend the premiere of *The Black Pirate*.

The film was another triumph. Columnist Karl Kitchen declared, "*The Black Pirate* is everything one has come to expect from a new Fairbanks picture. In addition it is the most beautiful photoplay that has yet been made. This briefly sums up the consensus of opinion regarding this new picture, which came to the Selwyn theater last Monday night."

"Up to now, the Technicolor process has never been particularly successful, due to its insistence on the more violent reds, oranges, yellows and greens," wrote *Life* critic Robert Sherwood. "*The Black Pirate* marks a definite advance in the development of this new movie medium. Its tints are deliberately subdued, so that the most brilliant color in the entire film is the glowing bronze on Doug's well tanned skin." Another critic summed up the color experiment with a succinct headline: DOUG GETS AWAY WITH IT.

The normally reserved critic from the *London Times* perhaps said it best: "He can have nothing of boyhood surviving in him who has no pleasure in *The Black Pirate*." For color or no, a film still lived or died by its story, settings, and performances. And here the film also excelled. *The Black Pirate* enjoyed a tight story that contained every archetype of pirate tales without an overly complex plot. Only seventy-eight intertitles were required to tell the story.* But this was part of the film's strength. It was a fable, pure and simple, a Howard Pyle–inspired tale of buried

---

* Film critic Robert Sherwood recalled overhearing one patron at *The Black Pirate*'s premiere remark, "I never saw a movie that taxed the intelligence of a ten-year-old boy."

treasure chests and heroes forced to walk the plank. It was, perhaps, Doug's last truly joyous production.

Before leaving the country, Fairbanks and Pickford attended an event at Madison Square Garden. Mary (along with forty-eight other professionals) was elected an honorary member of the American Women's Association. Speaking to the assembly, she acknowledged that she was indeed a businesswoman and a professional. Still, she managed to straddle the nineteenth and twentieth centuries by suggesting that her husband also be inducted, as she "never went anywhere without him."

At this, Doug was thrust before the crowd of twelve thousand women and induced to say a few words. He tugged nervously on his mustache at the prospect but managed to rally. "I am married to an organization, you know," he acknowledged modestly. "But when I married I insisted on retaining my maiden name." This served to charm one and all. He was elected the group's sole male member.

They departed for Italy in early April on the *Conte Biancamano*. Charlotte, unwell from her cross-country train trip, had to be carried aboard. Mary, worried her thirty-four years would show, was reluctant to pose for the newsreel photographers. "Sunlight in films makes one look so old," she lamented. She had no such complaints upon their arrival in Genoa, where both posed for the cameras wearing the colors of Italy's flag in their buttonholes. The usual crush of the crowds blocked their automobile, and police were required to get them from the port. They attended the premiere of *Little Annie Rooney* in Rome and decided that Italy had improved under the leadership of Benito Mussolini. "We met Mussolini at every corner," Mary said. "Not personally—I mean we encountered evidences of the extraordinary changes he had wrought in Italy. . . . Everywhere we went we were made to realize the tremendous force for good this comparatively young man of 43 years of age had become." Fascism was not yet a bad word to the politically naive. Many—Doug and Mary among them—were impressed simply because the trains ran on time. "I would like to see the Prime Minister Mussolini," Fairbanks said, when asked, apparently unaware that his title had already been changed to "Dictator": "I would like to express the changes I've found in Italy's national progress. The people are full of American 'pep'!" They were photographed, gracious guests always, giving the fascist salute.

Here was the flip side of fame's virtues, if, indeed, fame has virtues. Talent and charisma did not necessarily come with wisdom or mature political judgment, yet the opinions of celebrities on matters of governance were sought by an avid press. Mary would harden in her conservatism, praising fascism and Mussolini even into the late 1930s. Fairbanks gave it far less thought. He was simply drawn, as the proverbial moth, to fame. The inherent contradictions in admiring Benito Mussolini as he did Teddy Roosevelt never occurred to him. He was intelligent but neither literate nor prone to careful thought on issues outside his immediate sphere. He recognized the many responsibilities that came with fame (no one was a more sober corporate citizen than he), but speaking out on political issues of which he knew little was a serious omission in judgment—one repeated by celebrities ever since.

They met Mussolini—Il Duce gave them a thirty-minute audience— and Mary was suitably cowed, hiding her autograph book behind her back and later declaring him the most interesting person she met on their trip. Doug was more generic in his praise: "He's a great man and we had a most delightful visit with him." One wit, at least, saw the event for what it was worth: "When Douglas Fairbanks met Premier Mussolini, it was not exactly two Greeks getting together, but just the same they both know their publicity onions."

They better served the interests of their nation in Germany, where they attended the Berlin premiere of *Little Annie Rooney*. The orchestra played "The Star-Spangled Banner" for the first time since the war's end, and the German audience stood and applauded. "Tonight I am not Douglas Fairbanks," he told the cheering crowd. "I am Herr Pickford."

Things were stickier in Spain. There was general objection, it seemed, to the fact that the villain in *Don Q* was a Spaniard. Of course, all the characters in the film (the hero excepted) were Spaniards, but this did not seem to matter. Neither did the fact that no one in Spain had seen the film yet. The artists, the government declared, "surely had no intention of slandering the Spanish people by means of exaggerations and buffoonery, but merely displayed bad taste in a desire to bring out the picturesqueness of Spain."

Still, they somehow survived this diplomatic crisis (Mary helpfully pointed out that the film was very popular in Italy, due to the fact that the main character wore a black shirt, just as did the *fascisti*) and moved on to Paris. An automobile tour through Great Britain followed; then it was back to Berlin, and to Warsaw, as the entry point to a long-anticipated visit to Russia.

To visit Russia in the 1920s constituted a major event. American films were wildly popular there, albeit heavily edited. Any reference to or depiction of wealth was either entirely cut or retitled to fit the "worker versus parasite" theme the government espoused. Gloria Swanson, she of the designer gowns and DeMille glitz, was scarcely known in the country. Doug, however, was—in the words of a foreign correspondent—"nothing short of a national hero." *The Thief of Bagdad* was a phenomenon. Motorcyclists raced across Moscow, shuttling the reels back and forth so a single print could run simultaneously in multiple theaters. Critic Alexander Wolcott wrote, "At last accounts, the movies taken under the auspices of the Soviet Government were unfolded nightly to empty benches but it was hard to buy seats, even in the eighteenth month, for *The Thief of Bagdad*." Both Doug and Mary had the Soviet government stamp of approval. "He typifies not only physical prowess but a type of joyous abandon which they like their people to see," wrote one scribe. Mary, of course, typically played poor, plucky youngsters, often in rags—in perfect keeping with the Soviet proletariat.

Still, there was some degree of trepidation. Mary recalled that two mysterious men came to Warsaw to warn them that the trip was too dangerous to undertake. Fairbanks, with his characteristic mix of the pragmatic and the dramatic, made arrangements with Floyd Gibbons, the *Chicago Tribune*'s war correspondent, to stage a rescue mission by air if the couple had failed to return by a certain date and time.

His worries turned out to be unfounded. They were treated, literally, as royalty. Upon reaching the Russian border, they were removed from the Polish train and transferred to a car on the wider-gauge Russian tracks. It was the private coach of the late czar and czarina. The mob that awaited them when they reached Moscow the following morning was estimated to have been over a hundred thousand people. As Mary was strong-armed through the crowd by a pair of bureaucrats, Doug single-handedly tried to push his way through the throng behind them. The officials passed through the wooden gate of a government building just in time for the doors to slam shut on Doug. Frantic, he scaled the gate (likely to the delight of the crowd) and made a blind leap over the top, landing directly into a car full of flowers and strawberries. It made for a good story after the fact, but at the time it was a harrowing experience.

In Russia, they got to meet young Sergei Eisenstein, whose *Battleship Potemkin* they had just seen in Berlin. Fairbanks had been dazzled by his work and actively promoted the film upon his return to the States. "The finest pictures I have seen in my life were made in Russia," he declared. "They are far in advance of the rest of the world." He arranged for the picture to be screened for critics and the press and relentlessly promoted the young director. "I used to think I knew something about movement in the films," he said. "I used to think I knew a lot about conveying emotion through movement. But when I saw Eisenstein's work, I realized I hadn't begun to learn." He announced that Eisenstein had been signed to direct a film for United Artists.

It was not his first foray into adopting artists. In 1925 Charlie Chaplin was taken with the fledgling effort of a young Josef von Sternberg; he convinced Fairbanks to buy a quarter interest in *The Salvation Hunters* and distribute it through United Artists. Fairbanks, a purveyor of the joyous and light, had an honest appreciation for those whose work he thought reflected a deeper form of art. In the case of the lugubrious *Salvation Hunters*, he saw what the industry as a whole would not recognize for another half decade—the visual genius of von Sternberg. In the case of Eisenstein, of course, it was the brilliant editing of the Odessa steps sequence: the mis en scène and the visual montage—terms that would very soon become common currency in cinema studies, a field that he would help pioneer a few years later with the founding of the first bachelor's program in film studies at the University of Southern California. Both von Sternberg and Eisenstein would become the staple of film curriculums.

There is irony here. The life and career of Douglas Fairbanks is a topic that is never taught in film schools. There is no hesitation to cover the somber and the dramatic, and no one begrudges the hours that are devoted in some quarters to Biograph's 1909 short *A Corner in Wheat*. The past fifty years have even seen academic respectability conferred on the world of slapstick; there is no lack of literature on the existential meaning of Buster Keaton or the anticapitalistic impulses of Chaplin's Tramp. But academics ignore Fairbanks. One can make an argument of elitism. Using the universe of literary criticism as a parallel, it would be as if critics were devoted to deconstructing *Ulysses* while ignoring Twain or Dickens. There is something too popular about Fairbanks, too appealing to the multitudes.

Certainly the Russian populace knew which films *they* preferred. *Potemkin* made no impression on the Soviet masses, but Doug and Mary did. In fact, newsreel footage of their visit, combined with a shot of Mary kissing a young comedian, was woven into a Russian film released under the title *A Kiss from Mary Pickford*. The second half of the story dealt with the consequences of the kiss—the hero is pursued everywhere by people wanting to see the lipstick on his cheek. But the first half told the tale of the hero as a humble movie usher whose sweetheart, like every other woman in Russia, was mad for Douglas Fairbanks. Portions of *The Mark of Zorro* were included in the film, as was a sequence where the hapless hero attempts to replicate Fairbanks's insouciant pose on the film's poster. The Russian newsreel footage of Doug and Mary documents Fairbanks, tanned as black as he ever would be, wearing a native headdress, drinking coffee, running, jumping, and posing up in a tree, looking, as always, as if he is having the time of his life.

Mary was enjoying things far less. The strain of travel was wearing her down. Her husband would eat eyeball of yak with gusto; she could hardly choke down an aged saltine. He offered little consolation. "If you are taken ill in a foreign country, the best way to get well is to eat the same sort of food the natives of that particular land do," he lectured. "You'll keep your liver right—and consequently your disposition." Her liver must not have been right; nervous exhaustion drove her to stay in their room at the Metropole while he toured the Kremlin. He finally had to find a translator to ask the mobs outside their window to please be quiet, as "Marushka" needed rest. The crowd applauded silently, by bringing their hands together without touching, and tiptoed away.

His head was still swimming with the glories of Russian cinema when they arrived back in the States in late August. His impulsiveness extended to his tongue: "In Russia, the moving picture is controlled by the government, which is a good thing. The plan could be followed in the United States, and would mean that we would have good pictures to educate our children," he said—odd words from a man who had been a vigorous opponent of censorship boards. These comments, foolish and impetuous, were received with all the merit they deserved. "Does Mr. Fairbanks hold the opinion that the United States government is equipped in any sense of the word to design or advance or regulate or in any manner supervise any art product, or that it ever will be so equipped?" wrote one editorialist. "Doesn't he know that the government is no more qualified to control the movies than it is to control the theater? . . . Mr. Fairbanks was either seeking publicity, which he does not need; or he was heralding his retirement, which is not to be believed; or he was just talking, which is the only plausible explanation. A man making several hundred thousand dollars a year can't believe in Sovietism or Bolshevism."

Fortunately for Fairbanks, his comments were lost in the general hullabaloo over the death of Rudolph Valentino at age thirty-one, which occurred while they were en route home. They said all the proper things at the time—Fairbanks even served as an honorary pallbearer. But Mary later recalled Valentino as yet another source of her husband's ungovernable jealousy. "One day Rudolph Valentino made an unexpected appearance on the Pickfair lawn, which, in the warm months, was our outdoor living room," she wrote. "I never saw Douglas act so fast, and with such painful rudeness, as he did in showing Valentino that he wasn't welcome."

Valentino's untimely demise did affect their travel plans. They canceled their trip to the Far East and settled in to provide more product for United Artists.

Multiple efforts had been made to add more producers to the core group at UA. Negotiations with Cecil B. DeMille stalled early in 1925, but in March of that year they finally lured William S. Hart into the fold. This, unfortunately, was late in the arc of the fabled cowboy's career. The flashy Tom Mix films had replaced the authentic westerns of Hart, and *Tumbleweeds*, his swan song, did indifferent business.* Schenck signed John Barrymore, and he even conferred with Erich von Stroheim, whose terms were so onerous that Schenck broke off negotiations. Of more consequence was the affiliation with Samuel Goldwyn, the independent producer of fine taste and irascible temperament.

It was Goldwyn, working behind the scenes, who scuttled Joseph Schenck's next plan: a merger of the distribution arm of MGM with UA. This would increase the distribution volume to UA by a robust fifty films a year and would wipe out the company's current debt. Even better, the merged entity would be able to charge distribution fees of 35 percent. From a business standpoint, it was brilliant. "It is almost certain to go through," Fairbanks stated. "They have said what they wanted and we have said what we wanted. I believe the agreement can be reached, and within a few days."

He did not count on Samuel Goldwyn getting Charlie Chaplin's ear. UA historian Tino Balio argues that Goldwyn feared losing preferential treatment if films to distribute were plentiful, and he worked his influence on Chaplin, who, in turn, went public with vehement objections. To sign such a deal, Chaplin claimed, would be to form a trust—the very thing that UA was founded to prevent.†

---

* Hart sued UA for inadequate promotion, a suit that was not resolved in his favor until after Fairbanks's death.

† It is possible, too, that Chaplin's judgment was clouded by his antipathy for Louis B. Mayer, with whom he once engaged in fisticuffs in the lobby of the Alexandria Hotel.

The deal could have gone ahead without his vote. But at the inception of the company, the four partners had agreed that all major decisions would be unanimous. This incident caused the first—and probably only—strain in the friendship between Fairbanks and Chaplin. Doug, according to Balio, was livid and called Charlie a "kicker." Charlie returned fire by calling him nothing but a "jumper."

But they seemed to have gotten over it quickly. Nothing could really break the friendship between these two. Chaplin never required an invitation to Pickfair, where he stayed so long and so often that he had his own assigned bedroom. "He was always welcome to come and play with us, and we were just as happy to have him as he was to be with us," Mary recalled. "The two of them would romp all over Pickfair like ten-year-olds. I couldn't count the number of times I stayed behind to entertain one or another of Charlie's wives, while they would go wandering up and down the surrounding hills."

And Fairbanks would never, ever be anything less than a lifelong cheerleader and booster for his best friend. Chaplin cameraman Roland Totheroh recalled for Chaplin biographer David Robinson:

> Charlie was always so proud when he was building a set. We had the lousiest looking sets I ever saw, a side wall and a back wall. He'd build something with a little balcony or something and he'd get ahold of Doug Fairbanks or somebody and say, "I want you to see this set I'm building." . . . Fairbanks had the most spectacular sets of anybody. And Doug used to say, "Oh, gee, that's swell Charlie." He always wanted to encourage Charlie in whatever he did.

Mary, on the other hand, was less inclined to forgive and forget. She recalled arguing with Chaplin: "But Charlie, you know Schenck is a good businessman." "I'm as good a businessman as anybody else!" was the retort. Her conclusion: "Of course poor Charlie was no businessman at all."

Very soon—a matter of less than a few weeks, actually—none of this would seem important. Fairbanks was about to enter a dark period in his life. The single cloud on the horizon had been joined now by others, and they were about to merge.

14

Death . . .

F AIRBANKS STARTED 1927 IN a frenzy of activity. Possibly this was
simply his way, but even by Fairbanksian standards, he was feverishly occupied. He may have required distraction; the Saturday before
Thanksgiving 1926, John suffered a second stroke and died the next
day. As he escorted his brother's body back to Colorado for burial,
Doug might have suspected that the worm was about to turn. Perhaps
not. His was not a reflective nature.

He spent the early months absorbed in his latest project, one that
would ultimately be known as Rancho Zorro. He had had the full-
blown vision for it as early as 1925. He would buy land, thousands
and thousands of acres, and stock it with herds of cattle and expanses
of fruit trees. There, like the grandees of old, he would build a majestic
estate: adobe-walled, "behind which life will drowse along as it used to
be, to the drone of browsing cattle, the round-up song of the vaquero,
the thrum of guitar and banjo in the near casas of the Mexican and
Indian retainers."

Beverly Hills, he claimed, was getting crowded. In 1920 Pickfair
had been the only property in the area. Now it was surrounded by
houses of other movie stars, and curious fans trying to scale the walls.
Recently, they had shooed a hot dog vendor away from their front gates.
But Fairbanks was not planning simply to construct a remote getaway.
Ever the producer, he planned a miniature *world*. "I like the colorful

361

life," he claimed. "When I plan anything I want it to be romantic."
The house would be lit by candlelight ("Candle light is so beautiful.
Electricity is modern and harsh.") The only nod to modernity would
be in the plumbing—the faithful Mexican and Indian retainers, living
in small adobe huts scattered around the Casa Grande, might don the
studio-designed native costumes but would presumably balk at emptying
chamber pots. No automobiles would be permitted. Guests would arrive
via a specially constructed airfield, and the cars that ferried them to the
property would be abandoned outside the gates. They would travel the
rest of the way on horseback or in oxcarts. "The whole place will have
a Spanish tang," he declared cheerfully.

He, Robert, and Ted Reed searched for over a year and, in late
1926, settled on property that was, in their minds, perfect. The nine-
thousand-acre Rancho Santa Fe had been deeded more than a century
before by the king of Spain to Don Juan María Osuna. The property
was beautiful—gently undulating acres of what was to become San Diego
County, picturesquely placed between ocean and mountains, sliced into
delectable green valleys by the San Dieguito River. It was protected by
the surrounding lands so as to be cool in the summer and warm in the
winter. The soil was rich. Upon the death of Osuna's childless son, the
deed passed to the Santa Fe Railroad and thence to the Santa Fe Land
Improvement Company. Doug, seeing property that had well-developed
roads, water, sewage, and even a pending telephone exchange, pounced.
He bought 847 acres in late 1926, quickly followed by 160 acres of
adjoining land, then, for $125,000, another 2,700. Before he was done,
he owned Black Mountain, visible from Escondido.

Property improvements began immediately. Wells were drilled, and
the largest private dam in the country was built, creating an eleven-acre
lake. A pump house was constructed at the base of the dam to provide
irrigation for the 125 acres cleared for cultivation. Fifteen thousand
Valencia orange seedlings were installed in the new nursery, and eight
thousand mature trees were planted. The overhead sprinkling system
was said to be the largest installation of its kind in California. Apart

from the land costs, improvements on the property were reported to be $250,000.*

Plans for the house were worked on variably by George Washington Smith, Carl Jules Weyl (later famed as the art director of such Warner Bros. classics as *Casablanca* and *The Big Sleep*), and Wallace Neff. It was not going to be cheap. "It has been planned to have the house, which will serve as our home, cost something better than $150,000," he told a reporter. "But if the ideas of Mrs. Fairbanks and myself are carried out that sum, I fear, only would be a starting figure."

He was more right than he knew. The place was a money sieve. Dollars poured into it—irrigation systems, farming implements, rodent control, trucks—but scarcely any came out. His magical dream of a great self-sufficient ranch with a glorious hacienda staffed by cheerful peons was just that—a dream. The golden house was never built;† and the ranch ran in the red every year but one.

Still, the dream seemed viable in the early months of 1927. Money was plentiful, and Fairbanks never hesitated to spend it in the name of quality. When varying builders quarreled over who should be compensated for subcontracted work on the sprinkler system, he simply wrote a check for $11,810.14 and gave it to the court to disperse as its judgment determined. The check was written from his house account. "He didn't have to draw on his regular account—he just took this from the sum he sets aside monthly to pay the grocer and the meat man," the deputy county clerk declared, holding the check up for the admiration of the suitably awed crowd.

The first half of the year was consumed not only with Rancho Zorro but also with a wealth of other activities, each in itself sufficient to serve

---

* Rumors were more extreme than the facts. In 1927 his cost for improvements was slightly over $89,000. Still, he reached that higher sum eventually. Improvement costs in 1928 were $44,000 (excluding depreciation); 1929 cost $72,000 against the property-produced income of $14,000; 1930 cost $85,000 against the property-produced income of $17,700.
† At least in his lifetime. A front facade for a ranch house was sketched for Fairbanks by Neff in 1928. Architect Peter Choate followed Neff's sketch and constructed a version of the house decades after Fairbanks's death.

as an obituary header for any normal man. In May, he participated in the cofounding of the Academy of Motion Picture Arts and Sciences. The organization was not his brainchild; Louis B. Mayer conceived the idea at a January 1927 get-together with director Fred Niblo, actor Conrad Nagel, and producer Fred Beetson. But he was in the room a few days later when thirty-six industry leaders met at the Ambassador to hear of the idea. As with just about every other institution created by the entertainment industry to foster civic good, Doug was elected president. Although the Academy is known today primarily for its annual awards ceremony, its purpose was (and is) multifold, with stated goals of not only the bestowal of awards for excellence but also the union of the different branches of the industry: actors, producers, writers, directors, and technicians. Fairbanks headed up the inaugural banquet for the organization on May 11, 1927, taking in enough $100 subscriptions (with $5 per month in membership fees pledged thereafter) to put more than $25,000 in the organization's coffers. Will Hays led the speeches, warning the members that "dishonorable or unethical conduct, or the commission of any act involving moral turpitude, shall be sufficient cause for expulsion from the academy."*

The organization served a useful function during the summer of its inaugural year, when producers threatened an industry-wide 10 percent pay cut. The proposal was a continuation of the struggle that dated back to 1919 and the formation of United Artists: producers loathed paying astronomical star salaries. Jesse Lasky led the charge, declaring that the industry had "been making pictures at ridiculous prices for high-priced and unreasonable stars and directors whose names were a mirage rather than a reality. No longer will we be dazzled by the very names we have created. We can tell them to deliver our way or get out."

On the opposite side of the battlefield were the actors, directors, and writers. They began joining the Actors' Equity Association and fostered a few demands of their own, including eight-hour days and closed-shop contracts.

---

* By some miracle, the room did not immediately empty.

Fairbanks, under the auspices of the Academy, assembled a series of meetings throughout July between the producers and the other specialties to brainstorm cost-saving measures. "The Academy . . . has been organized primarily to unify the various branches of the motion picture industry, so that if at any time any particular branch should be confronted with difficulties we shall be able to confer among ourselves," he said. "As is the case now, producers feel that the cost of production has reached its highest peak and, being an actor and writer as well as a producer, I am in a position to know this, but our first and most important obligation is to try to improve the quality of pictures at all times. This we owe to the public."

It was difficult to argue with this. He could, and did, see things from the point of view of each party, having assumed each role in turn—and often simultaneously. Compromises were reached, and announced at a July 27 Academy meeting at the Biltmore Hotel. Producers agreed not to cut salaries. Actors, in turn, had to promise to indulge in no more fits of thespian temperament. They would respond to studio calls promptly, they pledged, even if shooting was scheduled for the middle of the night or early in the morning. And none would disparage their producers by referring to them publicly as "button-hole makers."*

The Academy continued to work behind the scenes to improve conditions for its rank and file. Under Fairbanks's oversight, work was begun to develop a standard contract for freelancing workers in the industry. Actors wished to be paid from the point at which they reported to the set in makeup, not when cameras began rolling. Further, they wished also to be paid without deductions for those days when they were not called for filming and to be compensated for a six-day workweek.

And it was under the mantle of the presidency of the Academy that Fairbanks worked to found the first academic film curriculum at the University of Southern California. He even gave the inaugural lecture,

---

* Sam Goldwyn started out as a glove salesman, William Fox worked in the fur and garment industry, and Adolph Zukor was a furrier's apprentice. The "button-hole makers" crack hit home.

on "Photoplay Appreciation." One can almost hear his voice in the press releases: "Courses in acting for the screen are not what the Academy has in mind. . . . Men and women [need training in] chemistry, optics, art and architecture, with particular bearing on the chemistry of motion pictures, the optics of motion picture camera work, the artistic and structural elements of motion picture set design, and elements of motion picture writing. In other words, schools of motion picture engineering and art comparable to the schools of mining, civil engineering, architecture and the like." Only Fairbanks, one feels, would draw a comparison of a film school to a school of mining. Reflecting his pragmatism, night courses were set up at USC in order that already-employed industry workers could improve their skills and knowledge.

And, in keeping with his vision of the Academy as a professional organization, the first banquet held by the organization to confer honors was not the May 1929 affair at which the then-novel statuettes were distributed but an April 1928 event at the Roosevelt Hotel in honor of the Society of Motion Picture Engineers. Fairbanks stood before the assemblage and cheekily stated a universal truth rarely acknowledged:

> Those of us who get our names in electric lights are inclined to forget the debt we owe you. It is by such means as you have provided that the film was discovered and enabled many of us to leave the one night stands, the barber chairs, and the fur business, and amass a fortune sufficient to allow us to take our yearly trips to Europe. And so we bow our heads and pay homage.

But his activities with the fledgling Academy and USC were, in essence, white noise in the cheerful din that was his life. It was time to start another film.

He used the site of Rancho Zorro to huddle with his creative team over his next project. As always, he struggled to find a story and setting that were original and that would play to his strengths. At first, he overreached. This would happen often; he would climb a metaphoric cliff impossibly high, before cooler heads talked him down. While at the end of the day he would temper his reach to not exceed his grasp, it still both instructs and amuses to review some of the wilder preliminary stretches.

First, he announced, he would make a film about the progress of civilization since the birth of Christianity. It would be called *The Brotherhood of Man*. He appears to have retreated from this idea by January, as Lotta Woods's diary for 1927 documents that he was by then contemplating a science fiction story. "First mention to me of Martian idea—following Mr. F's talk to Ray Griffith," she wrote on February 4. Two days later Griffith gave a formal pitch for a story titled *Trip to Mars* at Pickfair.* It must have been underwhelming: "Disappointed to find there was no story as yet," Woods wrote philosophically, and that appeared to be the end of the idea.

Consideration was given to a modern-day version of *A Houseboat on the Styx*, a thirty-year-old novel written by humorist John Kendrick Bangs and involving the encounters of famous people in the afterlife. Robert Florey proposed the idea to Joseph Schenck: what if he were to cast all of the UA luminaries—Barrymore, Fairbanks, Pickford, the Talmadge sisters, Gloria Swanson, and Charlie Chaplin—as versions of themselves? This would have been the first true all-star feature. Lotta Woods's diary reflects that the story was being worked on by Emmett Flynn at the same time that Griffith was promoting his Martian tale, but there is little evidence that Fairbanks or Pickford took the idea seriously. Half a decade and more would pass before MGM would score big with the all-star concept when the studio produced *Grand Hotel*.

Doug gave serious deliberation to another story about the Crusades. *Robin Hood* had whetted his appetite for the theme, and he sent his team back to the thirteenth century to explore the history of the Children's Crusade. The story was based on varying legends, each centered on a shepherd boy inspired by a holy vision and leading a band of followers south to peacefully convert Muslims. Doug was to be "a devil-may-care Mohammedan who becomes converted to Christianity." The pending release of DeMille's *King of Kings* was the reported reason

---

* Presumably "Ray Griffith" was silent film comedian Raymond Griffith.

for his abandoning this idea; it is likely that the tragic outcome of the tale—the children were reportedly drowned or sold into slavery—might have had more to do with it. One can scarcely imagine a Fairbanks film where he does not save the day, and a host of little dead Christians was not likely to send 1920s audiences home feeling happy.

Perhaps inspired by his vision of Rancho Zorro, he then announced that he would film a version of *Captain Cavalier*, a romance of early California by Jackson Gregory, who had written the story on which Fairbanks had based *The Man from Painted Post* ten years prior.

But historic California had already been covered in *The Mark of Zorro*, and he prized originality. He continued to circle around a larger, religious theme. One influence was *The Miracle*, which Max Reinhardt had directed on Broadway in 1924. In the first week of 1927, Reinhardt came to California at Fairbanks's invitation to see the West Coast production of the play. The story, as its title suggests, was faith themed, the tale of a nun who ran away from her convent. In her absence, a statue of the Virgin Mary came to life nightly to perform her duties. While Fairbanks had no interest in producing a film version of the play, the idea of a religious miracle was added to his thematic pot. In the end, he combined the various elements—the Virgin, a miracle, a religious conversion of a cheery reprobate, and a vaguely exotic, nonspecifically historic remote setting—into the stew that would become *The Gaucho*. The plot, as were so many of his stories, was a collective effort of his go-to team: Tom Geraghty, Lotta Woods, and Ted Reed. Together, under the pseudonym Elton Thomas, they built a coherent story line around their boss's wild flight of ideas.*

One important element to the narrative was the result of an observation of Pickford's: his films never seemed to have strong female characters. This was irrefutable: the passive, lovely damsels of his efforts to date were largely interchangeable, and they were scarcely memorable. Mary convinced him that his heroines should have "stronger character

---

* The pseudonym was formed from Fairbanks's middle names and served for all of the collective scripts generated by his team through the 1920s.

and bolder relief." And heroines it was to be, as, for the first time, Fairbanks would have two female leads in a film, a virginal saint figure—the adult version of the shepherd child who has a Fatima-like vision at the film's beginning—and the good-bad girl to provide the romantic and comic interest.

The former part was readily cast. Fairbanks invited director Edwin Carewe to an impromptu lunch, but Carewe declined: he had to see a screen test first. Doug sat in on the screening and decided Eve Southern was ideal for the part of the sainted shepherd girl. The timing was fortunate for her: she had been in Hollywood for over ten years but had a history of her performances ending up on the cutting room floor. The tale provided suitable grist for the studio publicist's mill: taking Fairbanks's quip and running with it (Fairbanks's weakness for bad puns was exceeded only by his love of practical jokes), articles appeared claiming Southern was "lunched" to fame.

The role of the spirited mountain girl was originally intended for Dolores del Rio but he was to learn that what Edwin Carewe giveth, he taketh away, as the director cast the actress in *Ramona*. Enter Lupe Vélez.

Vélez, later known as "the Mexican spitfire," was a few months shy of nineteen when she won the role. Her career to date consisted of Mexican vaudeville and a few Hal Roach comedies. She was charming, vivacious, peppery, and the first feminine lead in a Fairbanks film to give him a true run for his money.*

The cameo role of the Virgin Mary could be played, of course, by no one but Mary Pickford. The rest of the cast were Fairbanks regulars, and cameras were ready to roll by June 1.

He had commenced his usual fastidious preparation, undergoing tutelage in the ways of the Argentine gaucho. As he had learned the Australian bullwhip for *Don Q*, he now worked to master the bola—

---

* Rumor claimed that Fairbanks felt the actress too tame for the part during initial tests, until a stagehand plucked her Chihuahua from her arms. Then, the story (possibly the product of a publicity agent) went, she threw a tantrum for the ages, and Fairbanks changed his mind.

a woven leather rope upon the end of which were suspended three weighted balls. The proper throw could wrap the rope around the hind legs of a steer. It could also disable a human opponent, as one poor studio technician could attest. His job was to run across the lot wearing quilted padding and a fencing mask, while Fairbanks would attempt to lasso his feet. And on the subject of steer: six hundred longhorns were shipped in from Mexico for use in the film. Hundreds more miniature, dollsize cattle filled in the background of the stampeding herd.

Color was contemplated for *The Gaucho*, but the experiment with *The Black Pirate* had been costly. Further, projectionists were reporting trouble: the two strips cemented together resulted in "cupping" as the film ran through the projector, moving the image in and out of focus. Exhibitor complaints poured in. While color tests survive of the religious sequences with Mary as the Virgin, in the end Fairbanks elected to bypass Technicolor.

As in *Don Q*, dance was featured. Fairbanks sat for hours, his fingers planted firmly in his ears, watching demonstrations of different Latin folk dances. He wanted to see how the dance registered on the eye in the absence of hearing the rhythmic click of heels on the floor. "It is not always easy to distinguish between those steps that look well, and those which merely sound well," he stated. Fairbanks took his dancing lessons for the tango sequence with Vélez from Henry Brasha. He claimed that he intended the dance to "symbolize the wild life of the South American frontiers during the last century."

In fact, it was to connote that which he had avoided his entire career: sexuality. It was overtly sensual, symptomatic of one of the many ways *The Gaucho* was atypical. Fairbanks's hero was vulnerable, with an underlying wounded quality to his outward cheer. His failings were not the charming ones of his Earl of Huntington; this bandit king was not a'feered of women but clearly enjoyed them rapaciously. He drank. He stole. He scoffed at God. Here, for the first time in a Fairbanks film, was a hero in need of reform.

Also for the first time, here was a star experiencing criticism—the sort of cruel kicks usually reserved for a man already down. Two visiting writers from Great Britain were granted access to the studio during production. They had the thin decency to not identify their host when they wrote:

> Already the famous agile star showed visible signs of Time's fatal advance. In normal dress he was fuller in the face than we had anticipated, and when made up for acting a close examination revealed a subtle reddish tint covering the area between the chin and the throat. This red was less photographic than the rest of the make-up and thus camouflaged the slight bulge which was already beginning to coarsen his profile. He was clearly not the man he had been; the amazing feats of strength and skill which had so delighted the audiences of the world were performed less easily. Once we watched him try to mount his horse with a comrade on his back. Another man would have used a dummy. Not he. Nevertheless the trick did not come off; he strained a muscle, and at last three workmen had to urge him upward, the camera, with nice adjustment, cutting off the long lever inserted under his lower foot.

The accompanying sketch (provided by one of the authors) was less kind, revealing the struggling hero in gaucho costume to be unmistakably Fairbanks.*

These were not the only slings and arrows he was to endure. He was slashed on the leg by a dropped saber in the first week of the production. The injury caused no delays, but that was not the case when Vélez took ill, with an ailment variably described as peritonitis or malarial fever. Her hospitalization held up production for two weeks. The hospital admission was not, as one might reasonably suspect in that era, for termination of a pregnancy. Vélez was a Catholic, albeit

---

* The authors may have been referencing the scene at the end when Fairbanks mounts his horse with Lupe Vélez in his arms. If this was the case, the filmmakers neatly resolved the problem by having him step up on a tree root and from there directly onto the horse's back.

one with generous sexual morals, who later committed suicide due to the shame she felt over an unwanted pregnancy. Evidently abortion was not on her list of options.

Normally the question of a costar's health would be of minor note. But with Lupe Vélez one approaches a biographical quandary. The seven good years of Douglas Fairbanks's marriage were about to end. Conventional wisdom as to *why* centers on the two young costars engaged by Mary and Doug in the late spring of 1927. For *My Best Girl*, which was filmed on a schedule partially overlapping that of *The Gaucho*, Mary had borrowed from Paramount a promising young actor, Charles Rogers. The son of a Kansas judge, "Buddy," as he was known, was genial, gentle, and not yet twenty-three years old—thirteen years Mary's junior. He had jet-black hair (the first thing she noticed about him), Bambi eyes, and was intensely, flatteringly infatuated with her. There were those in the studio who noticed that Mary and Buddy were spending a lot of time rehearsing a kissing scene, staged in a wooden shipping crate. Fairbanks was among them.

Meanwhile, eighteen-year-old Lupe was a dynamic force to be reckoned with. It was clear that if Fairbanks's role had an element of sexual chemistry, that chemistry was with Lupe. Outtakes of the banquet sequence document Fairbanks, after a fluffed take, laughing, grabbing Vélez, tipping her backward, and planting a comic romantic kiss directly on her lips. This from the man who would typically go out of his way to avoid kissing *any* heroine on camera if he didn't have to.

Studio tongues began to wag.

"Lucky" Humberstone, assistant director on both *The Gaucho* and *My Best Girl*, recounted the version of events generally accepted by most biographers:

> If Mary did have or was inclined to like Buddy at the time, she had every right to and a reason for it because she knew, I knew, everybody knew that Doug, her husband, Doug Fairbanks, had been having an affair on the picture he had just finished which was *The Gaucho* and his leading lady was Lupe Vélez. Everybody

knew that Doug and Lupe [were], let's just sum it up by saying fooling around, which if I knew it, Mary knew it. So maybe that's why Mary decided to fool around with Buddy Rogers.

The challenge is to determine if this was, indeed, the case. Up until this point in Fairbanks's marriage, there is no evidence that he had strayed. He and Mary were gloriously happy, glued together like two sweet, warm pieces of toffee. Candid photographs demonstrate the body language of genuine and familiar love—his arm draped protectively over her shoulder, hers around his waist, each leaning into the other.

But in 1927, something changed. The intimacy, the authentic smiles, the unconscious warmth—gone. It might be the power of suggestion; it might be hindsight. But an argument can be made that after 1927, his smiles for the camera never again seem genuine. He was weary, sad, diminished. A trust had been broken, and despite the intervening years and multiple attempts at repair, it was never whole again. So, one asks: who cheated first—and why?

The true answer might be sadder than the popularly accepted one. In fact, it might have been both—and neither.

Consider the evidence: Lupe Vélez was never shy about trumpeting her sexual conquests. She had many lovers, and the world knew about them. Yet she never laid claim to Fairbanks. Years later, Mary may have realized this; she let then-husband Buddy Rogers costar with Vélez in a series of comedies. Vélez was also invited to dine at Pickfair when Doug and Mary were still married. But if studio gossip conflated a flirtation between Fairbanks and Vélez, it is entirely possible that, at the time, Mary had an authentic belief that there was mischief afoot.

Thus, one can argue, she engaged in tender, prolonged rehearsals of a love scene with her young worshipful costar—rehearsals that Fairbanks saw, as she perhaps intended. What was a better way to prevent a husband from straying, in the mind of one schooled in happy-ending film plots, than a warning shot across the bow?

There was, of course, a fatal flaw to this strategy. Fairbanks was pathologically jealous. "I have never known a man to read so much as he did into a simple look of masculine approval," she recalled. Each knew the other to be capable of marital infidelity—after all, had that not been the origin of their romance? Given this, he very likely interpreted her actions as signifying more than they actually did. Then, to his furious mind, all bets were off. From that point forward, if the cat was away, the mouse was definitely going to stray. All sources are adamant that he had manifested none of this behavior before that point; all are equally specific that by the early 1930s he had become a discreet rake. The ball, he told one friend, was out of bounds. He would play another.

It will probably never be known with whom or exactly when Doug first paid Mary back for that which she had not yet done.* But misbehaved he must have, and around this time. Mary retained all her letters from Doug, but there was only one upon which she marked a date: August 11, 1927. The note was scribbled on his studio stationery and used their common nicknames for each other:

> My own darling little baby with a slim-cute figure that looks the vogue in a bathing suit as well as a street dress—my little Frin that has many burdens but also many joys—people love her—Duber worships her—she has great talent—great beauty—she can build a nest as no bluebird can—she speaks French—is going to speak German—she is going to do anything she <u>wants</u> to do—but with it all she has a little Duber.†

He had written to her of his love often in the past, especially in the earliest years of their passion, when they were often separated. But during the first seven years of the marriage, his notes to her had been loving but more domestic in nature: location shooting was going to

---

* Most feel that Mary did not physically stray during the production of *My Best Girl*. "If there was an affair going on between Buddy and Mary, I don't think anybody in the studio, or I should say, on the picture, was really conscious of it," Humberstone said. "I think it possibly developed there, but it didn't mature [until] after the picture was over with."

† Many sources mention their nicknames for each other as "Duber" and "Hipper." Review of their correspondence suggests that he called her "Frin" more than "Hipper."

run long; he had overslept and would come meet her at the studio;
did she want to screen a particular film that evening? A listing of her
virtues without context was an anomaly. There was something about
this missive that sounded strained, even craven. Had he been caught,
conclusively *caught*, being unfaithful?

One can get lost in conjecture and still never land on the truth.
But the overriding certainty remains: at this point in the marriage,
each lost faith in the other. They had some form of confrontation
over this—in 1934 Mary was to write that Fairbanks claimed "that
he had made no demands on me for seven years—which is a plain
damned lie."

To lose one's love is to remove one of the soul's critical underpin-
nings. The possibility of professional decline threatens another. His
spirits were likely tamped down as he attended the November premiere
of *The Gaucho* at Sid Grauman's Chinese Theatre, where he and Mary
had so recently planted their footprints and signatures in the cement.
Lotta Woods recalled that as late as August 31, Fairbanks was displeased
with the film. "He was not thrilled," she wrote. "Had not seen the eleven
reels before." But his mood improved within twenty-four hours, when
he starting trimming. By Friday of Labor Day weekend, she tentatively
wrote that the film had a "favorable prognosis."

Still, he was right to fret. The reviews were mixed. The *New York
Graphic* wrote, "A queer combination of pictorial heights, reached in several sequences, smooth direction, amazing spectacles, thrilling moments
and occasional banalities make this latest Fairbanks film an uneven
accomplishment." The *Herald Tribune* sighed, "It is a tale partly barbaric, partly religious, for only half the time does the agile and smiling
star act himself."

More cruel yet: "Maybe Douglas Fairbanks' ardent fans will find
him interesting in it as he used to be, but he looked to me like the
oldest alumnus trying to get back in the spirit of things at a reunion."

Time, or audience maturation, has since been kinder to *The Gaucho*.
One can argue at length as to what was Fairbanks's finest film, but few
would dispute that *The Gaucho* was his most mature work. Revisionist

thinking now places it at or near the top of his swashbuckling films. The very qualities that audiences did not want from Douglas Fairbanks—a wounded, jaded cynicism; moral ambivalence; character failings—are now the prerequisites of the modern antihero.*

If nothing else, *The Gaucho* stands as a counter to the claim that Fairbanks could not act. There is a wounded subtlety in his character, a depth beyond his normal performance. Film historian Scott Eyman recently commented that he saw Fairbanks as the "paradigmatic American man of the twentieth century, perpetually outward bound, avoiding any reflection but his own in the mirror." Something about *The Gaucho* suggests that, at least this once, he reflected more deeply. And looking in the mirror, he did not like what he saw.

The Gaucho was a financial success, but this is largely forgotten today, for as the premiere approached, events conspired. Sound pictures were coming, and Fairbanks's kingdom was about to vanish. There was no precedent for such a loss. Only once in history has there been an art form that was created, developed to perfection, and then, while at its peak, completely abandoned—all within the span of a lifetime. Yet with the onset of talkies, this is exactly what occurred. The glorious silent world where Fairbanks ruled would disappear within two short years.

The typical shorthand in film history for the onset of sound in motion pictures is to reference the October 1927 premiere of *The Jazz Singer* as the single bullet to the heart of silent films. It is more accurate to say that it was the knockout punch in a progressive series of blows—the culmination of more than two decades of attempts to marry image with sound. There had been a parade of Kinetophones, Cam-

---

* It is harder to get modern viewers, with their postmodern, postironic eye, to see the earlier films through the lenses of their original audiences. The same is true of the best of the early silent Pickfords: before you can be postironic, you need to be ironic; before you can be ironic, you have to see things as purely and with as whole a heart as a child seeing a film such as *The Wizard of Oz* for the first time. That is a mental state that is hard to return to, but it was closer to how the earliest audiences greeted the pure heroics and twinkling charm of Fairbanks's characters.

eraphones, Chronophones, and Synchroscopes, most emerging from the inventors' laboratories and sinking without a trace. But someone was inevitably going to crack the nut, and that someone was Warner Bros., with the Vitaphone process.

It was not that he did not know it was coming. Doug and Mary were in the audience in August 1926, when Warner Bros. staged a collection of Vitaphone shorts—featuring speech and music—in conjunction with the premiere of John Barrymore's *Don Juan*, which boasted a synchronized Vitaphone score.* A little over a year later, Warner released *The Jazz Singer*. Audiences couldn't get enough of it. It was a game-changing success. Why did it succeed when all prior efforts failed? The answer is partially technical—the earliest efforts were rife with flaws—but only partially.

The Jazz Singer was actually a silent film with a musical score, punctuated by some sound sequences of the dynamic stage star Al Jolson singing (and, in one instance, chatting extemporaneously). As a silent film, it was less than mediocre. But even if it had been a masterpiece of the silent art, the crazy quilt of sound and silence did the latter in. There was a veritable *jolt*, a cognitive dissonance that occurred, not when the film moved to the human voice but whenever it would jerk back to silence. The brain processes the spoken word differently than it processes the combination of image and music. One enters a near-hypnotic state if closely attending to a silent film. Once lurched out of the state, it is nearly impossible to return. In the words of historian Scott Eyman, "Talkies were not an evolution, but a mutation, a different art form entirely."

It is not that Fairbanks was opposed to progress. He had explored 3-D technology in the mid-1920s. He embraced color. It was during promotion of *The Black Pirate* that he proclaimed, "In the course of a decade or so I really believe that all pictures will be made in appropriate

---

* This was followed by two more hybrid releases of Vitaphone shorts plus silent feature with score: *The Better 'Ole* with Sydney Chaplin (Charlie's brother) and *When a Man Loves*, again with John Barrymore.

colors and probably synchronized with a machine for reproducing the exact voices of actors and actresses."*

Yet he can be excused if he did not follow the continued advancement of sound in the industry as 1927 waned and 1928 dawned. In mid-November he and Mary moved in with her mother at her beach house and began the long, slow process of watching Charlotte die from metastatic breast cancer. Mary would not leave her side, recalling, "There I remained for eighteen weeks, every day of it, from early morning till late at night, in her company."

When the terminal moment came in late March 1928, Mary went briefly mad. "I was like a wild animal in the jungle," she said. "I am deeply remorseful and ashamed of what I said in that frenzy of anguish. . . . I have a few fitful snapshots of sanity that come back through that maddening cloud of grief: being amazed, for example, at Douglas' lips being as white as they were."

Her grief hung so heavy that she announced that she would make no more films. He issued a denial ("The report is idle street talk"), stopped preproduction on his next film, and, almost literally scooping her up, hustled her off to Europe. In such a hurry was he that he left town forgetting that he needed to appear in court on a traffic charge—his propensity for speeding tickets was renowned—and a bench warrant was issued by the municipal court for his arrest.†

They visited Geneva, Cannes, Paris, and London, where they arrived to no fanfare at all and were able to travel to visit friends in Surrey as anonymously as any other tourist. A young Walter Winchell was among a pack of journalists at their Paris hotel. Mary, Winchell reported, "was brooding over her mother's death. It was up to Fairbanks to amuse the newspaper men, to answer their questions, to pose for their pictures and

* He was forward thinking enough to see that sound on film would come, but he wasn't entirely convinced that the sound would necessarily be speech: "Dialog may and may not be the ultimate result of experiments with sound in pictures," he said in mid-1927. "The proper synchronization of beautiful music may mark the end of all our present-day experiments with talking pictures."

† The court let him off with a ten-dollar fine.

to do the stunts concomitant with getting one's picture in the papers." Winchell decided that the burdens of being a movie star would have been too much for him to tolerate. "To do this Doug had to beam all afternoon. Although it was raining, although he had not had lunch, although his trunks were not unpacked, although his wife was in another room nursing a headache, the film star had to beam—had to flash two even rows of white teeth. . . . Yes to you, sir. And yes to you, sir. And smile smile smile."

Mary's profound grief led her to a nearly irrevocable act upon their return to New York City. Less than a week after their June 16 arrival, she entered a beauty salon on Fifty-Seventh Street and instructed the horrified hairdresser to cut off her trademark curls. It was a move both of wisdom and folly. She was thirty-five years old. She could not continue to play children on film, no matter how convincingly. She stood at risk of becoming a freak show, the sort of character to later come from the overbaked minds of writers of such works as *Whatever Happened to Baby Jane?* And yet to bob her hair, to make the nod to modernity when her core audience wanted her as the last stalwart of old-fashioned virtue in an indecent age, was akin to surrendering to the enemy.

It might have been wiser to simply put her long, luxurious hair up, as she had always done in her private life. The bob did not suit her, and, pushing forty, she was an unlikely candidate as a jazz baby. But she was sorrowing; her mother was dead and her husband possibly unfaithful. She had started to drink. It was not a recipe for wise judgment.

She had told Doug what she was going to do before leaving for the salon. He had been, she claimed, incredulous, not truly believing that she would do the deed. "When I removed my hat and showed Douglas my shorn head," she recalled, "he turned pale, took one step back, and fell into a chair, moaning, 'Oh, no, no, no!' And great tears came into his eyes."

What is more telling is what she said next. "I had suspected, and *probably secretly wished* [*italics mine*], that Douglas would react the way he did," she wrote, suggesting that in some domestic battles, a barber's shears may be mightier than the sword. But it is not clear who won this skirmish. It might be argued that she was Samson and had just surrendered her power.

To return to Hollywood in the early summer of 1928 was to return to an industry in a marked state of flux. Was sound a fad? Would pictures be part talking? All talking? How quickly would theaters rewire their systems to accommodate sound pictures? And, if so, which system would be in use? Fortunes hung in the balance, as well as the fate of actors and actresses who had been visions on the screen—silent visions, with no jarring Bronx accents or nasal twangs. By 1929 the dust would settle. The marketplace spoke in no uncertain terms: people would rather see a bad "talker" than the finest silent film available. And there was no mistake about it—early sound films are truly awful. It took seven years before films found eloquence with sound. Early talkies represented a terrible step backward, replete with dull thuds that took the humor out of slapstick; hissing, popping track; static cameras; and, worst of all, static actors, who delivered their lines with pear-shaped tones and rolling Rs.

Mary, in the same spirit with which she cut her curls, went straight at the issue, making her first sound film an all-talking drama, *Coquette*. The film, in the words of Scott Eyman, "was and is witheringly bad, with performances that derive from the Belasco era of American theater." It was also a staggering hit. Everyone wanted to hear Mary Pickford talk.

But her husband was not ready for change. He doubled down on silence, investing time and treasure with his favorite character, D'Artagnan, and what he hoped would be his last, greatest film: *The Iron Mask*.

The film was an amalgam of several Dumas stories, including *Twenty Years After* and *The Vicomte of Bragelonne: Ten Years Later*, the third volume of which is most commonly known in America as *The Man in the Iron Mask*. The adaptations were loose—very loose—but formed a tight, cohesive narrative followed in all subsequent versions of the tale. While in France, he wheedled famed illustrator Maurice Leloir to come to America to supervise the film's art direction and costume design. Leloir recalls that he and Fairbanks got off to a rocky start. Doug made the assumption that the elderly Leloir had been friends with Dumas père, the author of *The Three Musketeers*, when in fact he was friends with his son, Alexandre Dumas fils. (He would have had to be very ancient, indeed, to have befriended Dumas père. Fairbanks was never strong on literary history, or any form of dates, for that matter.) But once Leloir corrected Fairbanks ("Why not D'Artagnan [as my friend]?" he asked, a little grumpily), he fell under the sway of Doug's charm. "That devil of a man, with his frank and cheerful eyes, his smile so fetching, his aura so wholesome and energetic!" he bemoaned, before succumbing entirely. He was seventy-four years old and had never left Paris. Still, he found himself on the *Isle de France* at its next sailing.

Leloir wasn't the only marquee name Fairbanks brought to the film. He engaged his best director and most frequent collaborator, Allan Dwan. Not only was Dwan the visually strongest of all of Fairbanks's prior directors, but also he knew just how to work with the happy-go-lucky producer/star. Assistant director Lucky Humberstone remembered, "It wasn't unusual for Doug to call in the morning and simply say, 'Don't count on me today, Lucky. I'm going to take off with the boys. And, possibly tomorrow too. You can figure out something to keep the company busy, can't you?' 'Oh sure, Doug, don't worry about a thing, I hope you break 70 today.' What else can you say to the boss?" To Humberstone's recollection, Dwan "just took it as though he sort of expected it, having directed Doug before in *Robin Hood*," and improvised sets and filmed scenes that did not require the star's presence.

Humberstone acknowledged, when pressed, that this happened only two or three times over the course of an eighty-day shoot, but once a visit from British royalty caused another delay and demonstrated Fairbanks's affection for lower forms of physical humor:

> One day he came to me . . . and he said, "Well, I'll tell you, next weekend I have a couple of very prominent guests that are going to be at Pickfair . . . the Prince of Wales and his brother,* and

---

* Contemporary newspaper accounts suggest that the guests did not in fact include the Prince of Wales, only his younger brother, the future King George.

naturally, I want to bring them on the set . . . and amuse them in some way. . . . Have the courtyard ready, have at least fifty horses in there, but you know, get my regular boys in, all those goosey boys [extras who would leap and shriek in a gratifying manner upon being "goosed"] that we put on salary, all those goosey cowboys and you have them here. And so, that day when the Prince of Wales comes out and his brother, and I have them up in the balcony, at a given time, all I let you know when, just have all those cowboys bend over their saddles standing on both feet, bending over with their head in the saddle, and you know what I'll do, the usual routine, I'll just take my stick and run down the aisle real fast and goose every one of them off, and you know what'll happen, they'll all take off and yell and scream and the horses will fly in every direction and possibly it'll be a little amusing for the Prince and his young brother. So that's the schedule for next Monday and Tuesday we'll have to figure out something else for them."

. . . We got out the files and figured out all the guys, and marked down the ones that are goosey and the ones that aren't goosey. . . . Whether the Prince was just acting or what, I don't know, but he and his brother apparently enjoyed it tremendously, got a big boot out of it, [and] laughed like hell.

Humberstone's is not the only account of filming. Papers reported the usual scrapes: a runaway carriage broke some expensive equipment; Lady de Winter dislocated Constance's pretty jaw while filming their fight scene. Best of all, Maurice Leloir's five-month visit to the West Coast produced a charming little volume entirely self-illustrated by the bemused yet alert and observant Frenchman. It provides a wry, insightful look at the backstage experience—Constance and the cardinal both trying to find relief in their heavy woolen skirts by walking the back lot with them raised above their knees; the Mother Superior, cloaked in cross and habit, sitting on the transport bus and smoking a cigarette; a monk with his arm around a makeup girl; actors costumed for the sixteenth century gathered around a radio to listen to a football game or lined up on stools at the lunch counter at a nearby drug store.

The presence of radio on the set was symptomatic of its rise as a national phenomenon. Joseph Schenck had worked to take advantage of this on behalf of UA by staging a nationwide radio broadcast in late March that featured the company's stars. They gathered in front of a six-foot microphone in Fairbanks's quarters. D. W. Griffith (back in the fold after his three-picture deal with Paramount produced three flops) spoke on love and marriage; Barrymore performed *Hamlet*'s soliloquy; Chaplin did dialects; Dolores del Rio sang; Norma Talmadge lectured on fashion; and Doug, who served as master of ceremonies, gave his usual brisk homily on athletics.* Exhibitors nationwide protested—the people who stayed home to listen to a radio broadcast would cost each theater an average of fifty dollars! Radio was poised to become so popular that it might threaten motion picture attendance! Was Schenck giving over to the enemy?

He was yielding to reality. Will Rogers and Al Jolson (*Jolson!*) had scored a big hit in January with an hour-long radio broadcast, and Schenck was loath to fall behind. But while the broadcast was judged a success ("the transmission of the program was almost flawless"), Schenck learned his lesson. His customers were not the public but the theater owners. He could not afford to offend them again and pledged no further forays into radio.

But perhaps the achievement of the radio broadcast softened Fairbanks's view on sound for *The Iron Mask*. It had already been decided that the film would have a musical score, but while in Europe, Fairbanks announced that it would also have human speech. The talking would not be between characters, however—it would be *from* the players direct to the audience, almost, he proclaimed, a Greek chorus effect.

There were two short sound sequences, the first filmed on a theatrical proscenium and featuring the four musketeers. Fairbanks steps forward from the group, tosses aside his hat, swishes his sword, and begins a speech written by Edward Knoblock:

---

* The broadcast was too soon after Charlotte's death; Pickford did not participate.

> Out of the shadows of the past
> As from a faded tapestry
> Of Time's procession slow and vast
> I step, to bid you bear with me
> The while your fancy I engage
> To look upon another age . . .

This continues for several more stanzas. After the intermission, Fairbanks again appears in a sound sequence, alone this time. Twenty years have passed in the tale, he tells us. But the musketeers will have one more adventure together: all for one, and one for all! Preview prints also had Fairbanks speaking over the final scene, as a voice-over. This was possibly removed before general distribution of the film, as most reviews do not reference it.* Preview audiences heard the voice-over:

> And thus it was in France of old
> In fiery days when hearts beat high
> When blood was young and hate was bold
> And sword crossed sword to do or die.
> For love and honor gloried then
> When life was life and men were men.

Soundman Edward Bernds was present during the filming of the prologue and recalled that multiple attempts were required to shoot the long speech. "Finally, we got a complete take, and, as was the barbaric custom in those days, we played it back," he recounted. "When we made that playback for Doug, we had a 'runaway' on the wax playback machine, just fast enough to give Doug a girlish falsetto. I was standing near him when that mincing gibberish came from the loudspeaker. He turned, not pale, but green."†

---

* The audio has been returned to the end reel by the Museum of Modern Art (MoMA) in its most recent restoration of the film.

† Director Allan Dwan confirms this story, but as was his wont, he embellished. "And gosh, we stopped it quick," he said, referring to the playback machine, "and got a good

In fact, his voice was serviceable, roughly the pitch and timbre of a Ronald Colman (though without Colman's accent). Fairbanks's delivery was another matter. It was highly theatrical—not entirely anomalous for a period piece, though one wonders if the period in question was the 1890s. One can almost imagine that one is hearing the stentorian tones and rolling Rs of Frederick Warde.

Assistant art director Laurence Irving has provided an account of this time, a description that has been used as a coda for the end of the silent era by historians as diverse as Kevin Brownlow in *Hollywood* and Scott Eyman in *The Speed of Sound.**

> While we were about halfway through *The Iron Mask* I noticed that instead of the splendid, bronzed Californians who were surrounding us . . . some strange, pale harassed people began to be seen about the studio and in comparison looked like people from outer space. Of course these were the advance guard of the Western Electric Company. . . . One day Douglas came into my room and said "Let's go down and look at one of these sound stages."
>
> . . . The doors of the studio were wide open, rather like an airplane hangar, and it was dark inside—pitch dark in contrast to the rather joyful and light atmosphere that we were accustomed to working. The place was hung with blankets; no lights; the floor covered with serpentine cables and then these things on stands— these menacing microphones . . .
>
> And then Douglas looked at this after a while and he turned and he laid his hand on my arm, and he said, "Laurence, the romance of motion picture making ends here."
>
> And it did, for him.

---

deep voiced fella; hired him to do it." There is no evidence to confirm that this was the case. The voice, when compared with later talkies, is clearly that of Fairbanks.

* While there were tests of sound recordings at the studio before *The Iron Mask*, Fairbanks's company was the first to produce a talking sequence on the lot.

When the end of the silent era and the beginnings of that of sound are documented, there are three go-to scenes. The first, of course, is Jolson at the piano: "You ain't heard nothin' yet!" The second is Garbo—the last silent star (except Chaplin) to be heard—"Gif me a viskey." The third is Fairbanks—not his first scene in sound, but his last in silence. There is an elegiac quality to the final sequence: Fairbanks's D'Artagnan, now an aged hero, is stabbed in the back, the only way any lily-livered villain could defeat him. He staggers to the rear of the palace, dies alone, and joins the ghosts of the three musketeers to greater adventures beyond.

The trilogy of clips plays as a cohesive narrative. The new order was coming, and with it much richness. But the old order was being lost, and with it its treasures. The universal language was about to disappear, and this was the language in which Fairbanks had a remarkable fluency.

He had suggested that *The Iron Mask* would be his penultimate film. Yes, he would probably make a single picture together with Mary, but that would be it. Columnists scoffed at this suggestion, and they were, of course, right. He did not quit. Yet, for the sake of his status as an icon, it would have been a brilliant strategic move.

It is a sad fact of Hollywood that in terms of establishing reputation, timing is everything—including the timing of one's exit. There might not be a Valentino cult if he had died a narcissistic old has-been, thick of accent and hair grease, a relic of the 1920s. It was written in the 1970s that if Chaplin had died after making *City Lights*, Hollywood would be riddled with gold statues of him, rather than left bristling (as it was for a decade or two) with resentment.

A similar thought springs to mind about Douglas Fairbanks and *The Iron Mask*. Perhaps it is hindsight that makes one argue that this film was his last hurrah. There is no evidence that he skimped on his subsequent effort (although after *The Taming of the Shrew* the value of his investments as a producer declined precipitously). Rather, it seems that this was the last film about which he *cared*. He never again made an emotional investment in his films.

In all its particulars, to say nothing of its glorious sum, *The Iron Mask* was his last great work. The production values were immaculate and, when seen on a large screen today, still staggering. It was his final return to D'Artagnan—the only character he would play three times—and the on-screen death of his character represents an epochal moment. If he had died after making this film, his death would have coincided with—and likely symbolized—that of the medium in which he excelled; he would have been seen by the world as dying happily married to the love of his life, a wealthy and beloved man.

In terms of establishing his shining spot in history, it would have been perfect timing. And perfect timing had always been his stock-in-trade.

But it didn't happen that way. He was a human being, not the icon he represented. He kept living. And, for the first time in his life, his impeccable timing failed him.

15

. . . and Taxes

To add to all of life's other woes, in the autumn of 1928 Doug and Mary found themselves in a tussle with the IRS. The dispute was multilayered and of long standing, and it involved them both, not only as a married couple but also as independent producers.

Fairbanks had been at odds with the Treasury Department almost since the inception of income tax. Taxation on personal income was a novelty to his generation when Congress passed legislation in 1913, and his early submissions of deductions were almost quaint in their sparse simplicity. He and the federal government seemed to be figuring the thing out as they went along, and the early quarrels were correspondingly simple. No, he could not subtract the entire cost of his automobile; he could deduct only those costs that were associated with his work. No, donations to a balloon aviation school during war were not deductible, but those to the Red Cross were. Handwritten schedules of his deductions are as revelatory to character as they are to the early days of taxes. His official charitable giving was scattershot and impulsive: the Salvation Army, a nearby orphanage, the American Legion, the National Tuberculosis Association; whatever need happened to be directly under his nose would receive money. But he provided a wealth of unofficial charity as well, constantly lending money to, and writing off bad loans from, an odd assortment of cowhands, ex-boxers, and friends. He gave funds to one Mrs. Austin to "aid in getting artificial limb"; those injured during filming might find themselves one hundred dollars richer; "Slim" Cole needed thirty dollars, as did one Pat Rooney, who required the same sum to get out of jail. Records document that he bailed out a lot of cowhands—literally.

The deductions also offer a fascinating glimpse into some creative schemes that never saw the light of day. The sum of $6.36 was invested in "experimental work on bouncing doll"; experiments in stereo photography were more expensive—$2,618.57 was written off as a loss against these endeavors.

But as the tax system became more complex, so did his quarrels. One related to the fact that his wife was as wealthy as he. For income over $1 million, the tax rate was 55.06 percent—a strong incentive to keep incomes separate, if ever there was one. In April 1922, clearly on the advice of accountants and legal counsel, Doug and Mary drew up agreements specifying that their finances were to be separate during their marriage. Each would file separately, permitting them to take advantage of the portions of their incomes that were accordingly taxed at a lower rate. "It is the desire and intention of the parties hereto that each shall acquire, own, possess, dispose of and enjoy their respective property and in all respects as if no marriage had ever been entered into between them," stated the agreement. Each relinquished any claim on the other's property (except inasmuch as such property might later be bequeathed to the other after death).

Uncle Sam begged to differ. California State law claimed that the husband had control of all community property in a marriage. If Doug could control Mary's money, the IRS reasoned, then he had to pay taxes on it.

It was not as if he were a tax scofflaw. His financial advisers ensured that he took only conservative deductions and paid his fair share. In fact, he likely paid far more than his fair share. In 1924, for example, he paid over $225,000 in state and federal taxes; in comparison, John D. Rockefeller paid $124,266.47 and J. Pierpont Morgan coughed up a measly $98,643.67.

Even of greater resonance for them, and for the industry at large, was a far more complex dispute that related to how independent producers could assign expenses. Large studios, engaging in the practice of block booking, were in a position to assign future revenue to a film on an accrual basis. They knew that they would sell a certain program of films and could write off the costs over time against the future revenues. Pickford and Fairbanks made the following argument: an independent producer would not be in this position, but instead would sell one film at a time, needing to take the profits from the currently playing production and invest them in the next film. From a financial standpoint, these producers needed to be reporting their income and expenses on a cash, not an accrual, basis. They had no way of knowing what would come in for a film in year two or three. Further, they needed to report their income and losses on their productions as a unit. Two films that each cost $200,000 might have different outcomes; one might return only $50,000, while the other might return $350,000. If the returns were summed, the producer would have been at a dead break-even point and would owe no taxes; money in ($400,000) equaled money out ($400,000). But if reported on an accrual basis, the producer would be taxed for the $150,000 profit on the second film, although he or she had not netted a penny. It was the government's stubborn inability to yield on this point that had bankrupted many an independent producer, including Charles Ray, a very successful star in the late 1910s, the failure of whose film, *The Courtship of Miles Standish*, broke him personally.

Finally, Fairbanks had one separate issue with the Feds, related to his production company (the Douglas Fairbanks Pictures Corporation), formed in 1917 as a firewall against a possible lawsuit from then father-in-law Daniel Sully. The organization was simply a pass-through entity, receiving payments and then passing them on to its individual members (Loos, Emerson, Fleming, Doug and John Fairbanks) as per the original profit-sharing plan. Those individuals then paid taxes on the money they received.

The government wanted the production company to pay the taxes. This was all well and good, Fairbanks (and his attorneys) argued; but then all the members were due refunds for all the taxes *they* had paid over the years. In Doug's instance, $551,013 was due to be refunded in payments and interest just for 1918 and 1919 alone.

The government, then as now, was maddeningly inconsistent, both in the interpretation of its own rules and in the administration of them. Fairbanks would win this last quarrel until a few years later, when the government would again reverse itself and ask for all the money back—with interest, of course. He would be engaged until his death (and beyond) in many of these disputes. The only consolation that he and Mary had as they sat through weary tax hearings in late October 1928 was that they were treated better than the average taxpayer. At least that nice Mr. Coolidge invited them to the White House for lunch after the fact.

It was thin consolation. They entered 1929 in an uneasy state, their marriage in broken shards around them and uncertain how—or even whether—to fix it. Work was Mary's cure-all. Travel was Doug's. They started with travel. As with everything else in the last year of their golden decade, it turned out to be a very rocky ride.

He decided that they should see the country from the air. In March he chartered a private, fourteen-seat trimotored Ford monoplane for $175 per hour and assembled a collection of family and friends that included Lillian Gish, Robert and his wife, some spare royalty, and thirteen-year-old Gwynne. They would fly to Phoenix, then El Paso, he declared. Cruise around the Mexican border and watch the promised dustups between Mexican revolutionaries and the federales. Then, perhaps, they would pop over to Florida.

Their plans changed upon landing at their first stop, Agua Caliente, Arizona. Mary, Gwynne, Lillian, and all the other ladies of the trip emerged from the plane green and airsick. Perhaps, he acknowledged, it *was* a tad too bumpy for a pleasure trip. They gave up after Phoenix, settling instead for a mule ride to the bottom of the Grand Canyon.

Upon returning to Hollywood, he was at sixes and sevens. By some measures, he had little to worry about. *The Iron Mask* had opened at the Rivoli Theatre in New York City in early March and had smashed all box office records at that venue, running eight shows a day and crowding the sidewalks early and late. Of note was that these records were broken even though the tickets were at a reduced price—for the first time in his career, Fairbanks did not open a film at the two-dollar mark. "Doug has always managed to feed it to the waiting public at two bucks a smack before he let them get a peek for six bits or less," wrote one New York columnist (who evidently had Runyonesque aspirations). "Just to show Doug that Broadway appreciates this they are kicking in with enough of the six bits to smack the Rivoli house record in a Dobbs topper. Of course, Doug and his boys may have had their own idea in giving *The Iron Mask* direct to the picture house public without the benefit of a legit run in advance. If so they were wise, 'cause there ain't no two bucks worth on tap in this one. But in the picture houses it should wow 'em and probably will."

A Fairbanks swashbuckler without a road show release was unprecedented. But in a market engulfed by talkies, this was a wise strategy, and it eventually paid off. *The Iron Mask* had a negative cost of $1,495,603.02, with additional UA charges of $89,230.02. It did not turn a profit until after August 1930 but was eventually a moneymaker.

Years later, Allan Dwan was philosophic about the film:

It was a better picture [than *Robin Hood*], but from the audience acceptance standpoint, it didn't have the kick that that one had. It just couldn't live up to it. It was a different tempo anyway, here was Robin Hood, kind of a dancing around guy, all the time, doing the most amazing things; whereas the other was kind of a more stolid story. . . . This [*Robin Hood*] had that myth; it had that magic that a picture needs. And you never know when you've got that.

The verdict on Fairbanks's voice was mixed. Many thought it was fine: "He spoke distinctly and with excellent dramatic effect," claimed one critic. Another wrote, "We have not heard many Shakespearian actors do better with heroic declamation."

But the contrarians were strong in their reproof. One wrote that his voice "registered like warm dish water dripping on a tin garage."

Another headline must have caused no little despair: Doug Must Make Actions Speak for His Voice's a Flop.

Further, *The Iron Mask* was competing not only with talking pictures but also with films populated by fresh-faced youngsters—among them, his son.

Junior had remained in Los Angeles after the failure of his first movie, working his way doggedly up the food chain of the studio system, taking a progressively improving series of supporting roles in lesser films. He was no longer pudgy and awkward but long and lean and strikingly handsome. He started getting roles—serious roles—in important projects. In the fall of 1927, the seventeen-year-old starred in a local stage production of *Young Woodley*. Fairbanks, Pickford, and Chaplin were among the supportive and enthusiastic first-nighters. To commemorate the event, Doug gave his son a signed first edition of Henry Irving's *The Art of Acting*. He quoted Shakespeare in the inscription: "Let your own discretion be your tutor—(Hamlet)."

The gift was cherished by the teenager, but in the short term another memento was of more interest: a note from a young actress who was also at the premiere. Joan Crawford was impressed with his performance and wanted to meet. He obliged her, and a romance ensued.

In the spring of 1929, they announced their engagement. She was twenty-three to his nineteen, although she subtracted three years from her age (and he added one to his) when they applied for their marriage license. Their June elopement was no secret to his mother, who attended the impromptu Manhattan ceremony. But to Doug and Mary, the news came as a surprise. A celluloid hero might conceivably have a teenage son; but to have a son who was married—and very publicly married at that—created the unflattering suggestion that he was getting long in the tooth. Not longer was it *DougandMary* the fan magazines were cooing over; *DougandJoan* relegated them to the awkward status of in-laws.

It may have been discretion; it may have been an unexpected serenity. Somehow Fairbanks never demonstrated any public angst on the topic. His son recalled receiving a lengthy telegram when news of the marriage leaked: "It was absolutely charming and full of hearty blessings.

It was in fact so very warm that Billie [Crawford] cried with relief on the spot." Privately, things may have been quite different. "He could not have enjoyed Billie's frequent talk about having children," his son wrote. Nor, for that matter, could have Mary. There was little that united Doug and Mary at this stage, but both agreed that neither was ready to be viewed as a grandparent.

Another area of spousal agreement—they would finally make a film together. There had been talk of this as early as 1923, when reports circulated that Ernst Lubitsch would direct them in *Romeo and Juliet*. But Norma Talmadge was already planning a version, and the gooey-eyed Romeo did not seem a good fit for the ever-cheerful Fairbanks. When in 1924 Mary was asked about a joint project, she replied, "It would be very unwise for me to act with him, as Douglas paints with a broad brush and I with a small one. Also, we have an entirely different tempo or medium of expression. It is as if he were going at sixty miles an hour and I at thirty. We stand for different things on the screen. His pictures are for men and mine are for women."

Still, the question popped up annually, peppered by scattered pronoucements: They were considering a play by Karl Vollmöller, coauthor of *The Miracle*, with Max Reinhardt directing. No, they would make *El Cid*, with Mary's brother Jack at the helm. They even contemplated *Seventh Heaven*, before deciding it was too dark.

Finally, in the spring of 1929, they settled on *The Taming of the Shrew*. Many arguments favored the choice. The play had strong parts for each. Fairbanks's love of Shakespeare survived beyond his childhood, when, in the words of one scribe, he "could do King Lear or Lady Macbeth without change of costume." As early as 1914 he had voiced a desire for his own repertoire company that would perform the works of Shakespeare. But he maintained that he was at a disadvantage. "Mary has made good in the all-talkies and I don't know the first thing about them," he claimed. Nonetheless, the thought of performing the Bard was daunting to Mary. Douglas had extensive Shakespearean experience, she pointed out. She had had none.

It was uncharacteristic. Each was jockeying, trying to explain why the *other* had an advantage. As they met the press on the topic, there was a definite competitive edge to their statements. They were already in a quarrelling frame of mind. "It will be the greatest thing I've ever done," she declared.

"What do you mean 'I'?" came her husband's retort. "It will be the greatest thing 'we' have done."

The topic then advanced to whether this would be their last film. Would they retire? "Doug pretends he would like to retire," Pickford said.

He interrupted. "Yeah, I'd like to be a bum. I'd like to loaf around and not have anything to do."

Mary was quite contrary. "If you have heard that as often as I have, you'd have a good laugh. Douglas always wants to go some place for a vacation and be a bum—he thinks. Every time we get away from Hollywood he yells and yells and yells until we get back. You can say for me that I'm not nearly ready to retire and you can say for Douglas that he isn't either." In another interview she groused, "Right now my biggest worry is that just when we are about ready to start our picture Douglas will decide he wants to go to Europe and drag me over there with him."

Initial production on the film was delayed a few weeks. Schenck was once again working on a merger plan, this time with Warner Bros. The deal was again a favorable one. Warner would buy a 50 percent stake in United Artists for $20 million. The UA stockholders were guaranteed $1.4 million annually, divided on a pro rata basis according to the volume of stock held. There would be cost efficiencies in merging the distribution exchanges, and the problem of the low volume of UA releases would be obviated by combining the Warner product in the distribution mix. Once again, this would have been of immense benefit to the shareholders of UA, and once again Chaplin nixed the deal. He could have been outvoted, but friendship and loyalty kept Mary and Doug from voting against him. This was a particularly generous gesture on the part of Fairbanks: Chaplin had been very explicit with *Variety* about the differences in their respective grosses. *Black Pirate* and *Gaucho* had grossed $4 million each domestically, he claimed, whereas his film *The Circus* grossed $6 million. Who, then, Chaplin demanded, was the better businessman? Of course, he failed to point out that he had produced only two profitable features for UA in the ten years since the company's formation.* Fairbanks had provided twelve. Doug and Mary made a quiet run to New York City in an attempt to save the merger, but in the end it was hopeless. "There is no chance of the deal going through," he told the press upon his return to Los Angeles.

If it was generous on Doug's part to yield to his best friend, it must have been vexing beyond words for Mary. Her affection for Charlie Chaplin was far, far less than her husband's. She must have dearly wanted the acquisition to go through; it would represent millions for the pair, in an era when a million dollars really meant something. But if Doug was not going to vote against Charlie, she could not be seen as voting against Doug. She was trapped. It is very likely that words were exchanged in the weeks before *Shrew* filming began in June, words that strained the uneasy equilibrium they had maintained throughout 1928. From this point, things only got worse.

Lucky Humberstone was still functioning as an assistant director at the studio when they entered production on the film.

> Now [Doug and Mary are] not talking to one another!
>
> We had a director by the name of Sam Taylor who had directed Mary in a couple of pictures. . . . He was one of the nicest men I had ever met. For some strange reason Douglas Fairbanks took a tremendous disliking to Sam Taylor. . . . You could say that Sam was a very dull man because he didn't have a sense of humor, even though he was a comedy director. He was just a perfect, quiet gentleman and Doug Fairbanks was a happy-go-lucky—he loved life, and, well—they just didn't go.
>
> So now I've got a director that doesn't get along with one of the stars, but is talking to Mary. It puts me in a position where

---

* *A Woman of Paris* lost money. *The Gold Rush* and *The Circus* were the two successful films.

anything Sam Taylor, the director, wants done he has to tell me, and I have to go tell Doug what to do with the scene; Doug won't talk to him. So Doug will say to me, "What's Mary gonna do?"

I wouldn't know and I'd have to find out, so then I'd go over to Mary and all I could say was, "Mary, you know what this scene is all about. You know what you're supposed to do, right? You've talked to Taylor."

And she says, "Yes, but what is Doug going to do?"

"Well," I said, "that's the same question he asked me."

So then I'd go back to Doug and then I'd talk to Sam. Doug would generally say, "Well, that's alright with me. I'll do my scene and she can do her scene and we'll get it all right." Fortunately, they came out. But it was a very trying situation. . . . Let's say there was friction, a lot of it throughout the picture. It was probably the toughest job I ever had to do in my life. . . . Through the whole bloody picture, everybody on that set was tense all the time because of the friction, and you could feel it.

Doug's lack of fondness for Taylor may have been related to filming the scene in which Mary was required to heave a three-legged stool directly at Fairbanks's head. There were no Foley sound effects artists in those days; sound was recorded directly from the set onto the film. Her aim was true, the stool hit its mark, and the microphones recorded the woody thunk. But upon playback, Taylor decided that the sound was not right. It didn't sound like a stool hitting a cranium should. Several more takes were attempted, with Doug's skull serving as a sounding board each time. Finally, he could take no more. "Believe it or not," Fairbanks declared, "the noise we heard in the playback is the sound of stool hitting head whether it sounds like it or not *and that is the way it is going to stay.*"

Mary recalled vividly that her husband would show up on the set late—sometimes hours late—and did not know his lines. The former issue is in dispute. As to the latter, Doug fully admitted as much the following year when a friend praised him on his "line readings" in the film.

"That is exactly what I do—read them," he replied. "I couldn't remember them, so I have them written on a blackboard. When I had a line to speak, a stagehand held the blackboard up out of camera range. In one scene a dog kept getting between me and the board. The dog was in the picture, so couldn't be chased away, but we had to shoot that scene a dozen times."

This was beyond exasperating to Mary. Before filming began, she had been very politic. "I am going to be Douglas' leading lady in this picture [as opposed to the star] because I think the man should be at the head of things," she said demurely. But she was as experienced a producer as he, and far, far more careful with her money. Humberstone recalled:

> Mary, in real life . . . was a hell of a business woman. She knew every move that was made on that set from a financial standpoint. . . . On many occasions she would question me. "Well, Lucky, what did this cost? How many electricians have you got up today? Do you have to have that many electricians? And if I happened to say "Well, we've got twelve," she'd say, "Well, couldn't we have done it with ten?"

Not everyone saw the shoot through the Pickford/Humberstone lens. Soundman Edward Bernds recalled, "There were undoubtedly cross-currents of ambition, resentment and jealousy on the *Taming of the Shrew* set, but I was engrossed with the demands of my job and . . . was not aware of them. . . . Doug and Mary worked hard to make *Taming of the Shrew* a good film. There was no self-indulgent coming to the set late, unprepared, and leaving early. They tried hard, but the film had flaws."

One of the challenges of *Shrew* was, of course, that both were financing the film but each had widely disparate management styles. Fairbanks wanted a happy set and paid no attention to the dollars. Pickford also wanted a happy set but watched every nickel. Original plans had been for the film to be in color, but that was nixed, on the grounds of either cost or aesthetics. A color costume test survives, demonstrating Pickford pointedly ignoring her husband and Fairbanks looking as though he would rather be anywhere but where he was.

At the end of the day, Fairbanks had less cause to look miserable than did his wife. The role of Petruchio played to his boisterous strengths. Worse from Mary's perspective (she was, after all, an actress and as sensitive to reviews as the next person) was the fact that the press did not hesitate to point this out. "Fairbanks is truly capital," claimed the *Motion Picture News*. "He loses not one bit of the personality that his public likes. He is full of devilment and tricks. He rides, leaps and when the occasion offers he shouts and roars. His entire performance has that vigor for which he has long been noted." More galling, "he outdistances Mary, perhaps largely because the part gives him that opportunity." And another: "Doug walks away with the whole show. As the swashbuckling Petruchio he is a heroic figure, romantic and picturesque, and dominates every scene, even those with Mary." It could not have been good for their marriage. "I have always thought that he and Mary would never have parted if it were not for *Taming of the Shrew*," mused Herbert Brenon. "I watched them on the set and that was the beginning of the parting of the ways."

All agreed that their version of the story was Shakespeare-lite. One surly wit suggested that the question of authorship—Bacon versus Shakespeare—could simply be resolved by digging up both men and seeing which had turned over in his grave. This was unfair; the condensation was expert, based on a script used by the Stratford-on-Avon Company in its Los Angeles performances earlier in the year, albeit shortened further by elimination of most of the Bianca subplot. For years the story has circulated that an original title card for *Shrew* stated that the play was "By William Shakespeare / With additional dialogue by Sam Taylor." This seemed so pat an indictment of Hollywood's anti-intellectualism that it has been generally accepted as apocryphal.

It was not. Original preview prints indeed carried the infamous title card, but its inclusion was, supposedly, intended to be tongue in cheek. "The studio later became convinced that audiences out about the country might not accept this jesting division of authorship in the joking way it was intended," reported the *San Francisco Chronicle*. Mercifully, the offending credit was removed before the film's general release.*

Audiences were indifferent to the final product. That the film's release coincided with the stock market crash and the onset of the Great Depression did not help. Those who were curious about the stars' voices had already satisfied themselves with *Coquette* and *The Iron Mask*.

Circumstances almost deprived everyone of the opportunity to see the film at all. A fire and explosion at the Consolidated Film Industries laboratory wiped out the original negatives of many films. Initial reports included Howard Hughes's *Hell's Angels* and the Pickford/Fairbanks *Taming of the Shrew* among them. Fairbanks placed an anxious (and expensive) call from the London offices of UA to learn that, fortunately, the negative had been moved to an off-site vault shortly before the disaster.

They were in London that October en route to Lausanne, Switzerland, with plans to put Gwynne in a boarding school. Mary expected a short visit to Italy and England and then to return home. Doug had different thoughts. "We must go to India," Mary recalled him insisting. "It will be a great adventure." His enthusiasm, as usual, was contagious—or, perhaps, overwhelming. Whatever the motive, she agreed to go. Knowing her growing hatred of travel, she deserved ample credit for this.

Never was the saying "Give him an inch, he'll take a mile" so applicable. If they were going to visit India, they might as well go to China and Japan, he reasoned. Once in Japan, "we'll have only to cross the Pacific and we're home." Mary was reluctant. *Shrew* was having its first showings—she needed to get back to Hollywood, to get back to work. But, "Douglas could talk of nothing but tigers and elephants, the climate of the Tropics and the possibilities of adventure in China," she said. Perhaps, she suggested, they could postpone their trip for a year? Linger a little longer in northern Italy? But Doug had his heart set on Egypt and the Orient.

---

* Original preview prints also listed the stars as "Mr. and Mrs. Douglas Fairbanks."

She succumbed to yet a further extension of the itinerary. They would visit Greece, Egypt, Singapore, China, Japan, and points in between. Doug cabled for Chuck Lewis and Albert Parker to join them in Paris. Jack Pickford was already there and game to be included. In London (hosted by the Mountbattens) Doug purchased "enough Jodhpurs to equip the household of an Indian Rajah." Mary noted with some chagrin that the volume of their luggage had doubled and that "we seemed to be preparing for a year's sojourn in an uninhabited country instead of a four months' trip around the world."

The journey proper began on October 26—three days before the stock market crash of Black Tuesday. A special train car—the largest and finest available—was attached to the Orient Express. As the added weight of this car exceeded the pulling capacity of two engines, a third train engine had to be dispatched to help them over the mountains. The resulting six-hour delay in arriving in Athens did nothing to dim the enthusiasm of the crowd at the station; more than two thousand stayed past midnight to cheer the couple's appearance.

For Doug, the anticipation in travel would often exceed the actual event. "I conjure up such mental pictures of the places I plan to visit that instead of finding enjoyment I often experience a slight twinge of regret," he wrote later. But the Parthenon was an exception. He stood, holding Mary's hand, "drinking in the beauty of the scene in a silence of mutual understanding." Finally, he claimed, Mary, overcome by emotion, sank to a sitting position against one of the pink marble columns. An American woman approached. "I understand, dearie," she said. "My feet hurt, too."

They saw the sights of Athens until they had had their fill and then took a small mail steamer to Alexandria. The trip was interrupted when, one hour out of port, they discovered a stowaway hidden in one of the cabins—a young Greek woman who had come aboard to interview Mary.

Cairo, they discovered, was full of flies. Flies and Egyptians. The mob swarmed the streets up onto the running boards of their car, blowing out three of the four tires. "Not content with autographs," Mary recalled later, "some of the men asked Douglas to write his name on the back of their hands and ears in order to have it tattooed on for all time."

Giza and the Sphinx followed. Doug, treating the world as his playground, "scrambled part way up" the rugged side of the Pyramid of Cheops. Even more exciting was a personal tour of the Egyptian Museum conducted by Howard Carter, who had discovered of the Tomb of Tutankhamen. Fame had its privileges. Carter offered—if they would only stay an extra few days in Cairo—to join them on a tour of the tomb itself. But Doug, ever impatient, wanted to start a camping trip. They toured Luxor without Carter, and then headed out, complete with a caravan of camels and tents. Fairbanks's wish for a longer sojourn in the desert, active since their 1921 trip to Tunis, was at last to come true.

Douglas, Mary wrote, "was so delighted with the trip he wanted to engage another caravan to visit the Fayoum." Here she put her foot down. She must have felt that she was the constant naysayer on the journey: At one point Albert Parker found a Nubian bartender who was so good at making New Orleans fizzes that he wanted the man added to the entourage. "With two secretaries, two valets and a maid, we had enough difficulties, without the addition of a Nubian whose only claim to distinction was his ability to shake up a gin fizz," sniffed the ever-practical Mary. The bartender was left behind.

They took the *Cathay* from Port Said ("one of the few places we visited on our trip . . . which we left without regret," Doug commented) through the Suez Canal to Ceylon. At this point his characteristic impatience started to emerge. One day at sea was much like another, he groused. The singing of the dockworkers at Port Sudan was charming, until it kept him up all night. The planned trip to India could not be fitted in with the available sailing dates and had to be replaced by a motor trip through the Federated Malay States. He had been looking forward to riding elephants and hunting tiger—and was thwarted. Yes, Kandy had beautiful scenery, but "one is perhaps more fortunate if he leaves before the novelty of these exotic surroundings has worn off." Feeding the black crows that were considered the scavengers of Colombo quickly lost its charm. The native vendor "soon ceases to be amusing."

The native dinner at Kuala Lumpur was "a tactical error we all regretted later in the evening." The crowds along the stations on the night train to Singapore made sleep impossible. The famous Raffles Hotel was noisy.

They finally found quiet, and respite, on the ship to Hong Kong. Mary thought the colony fascinating but did not enjoy the elaborate meals of sharks' fins and hundred-year-old eggs ("I would have preferred a dish of chop suey"). Doug, ever exasperating in his good cheer, ate with his usual relish, using chopsticks like a native.

Shanghai, according to Fairbanks, was "seething with excitement" the day they arrived—not because two movie stars were in town but because the nearby antigovernment forces had caused the city to be placed under martial law. But Doug and Mary were not to worry, their hosts assured them. "Aside from the danger of being kidnapped, a European was as safe in Shanghai as in Chicago." This did not serve to comfort. Also unsettling was a movement to impose a boycott on Fairbanks films because of the scene in *The Thief of Bagdad* where the villain was strung up by his pigtail. The issue was larger than *The Thief*, of course. Many Chinese were rightly offended by their depiction in most American films.

Doug was all indignant innocence. True, some American screenwriters were misrepresenting the Chinese, he agreed. But not he! After all, the villain in *The Thief* was a Mongolian! This seemed to satisfy his hosts, who probably felt that their point had been made, and the threatened boycott was called off.

That crisis averted, Fairbanks then engaged in a custom-tailoring shopping spree. He bought silk shirts, dressing gowns, and pajama sets by the dozen. "One can have a dozen shirts made to order within twenty-four hours," he reported happily. "Chinese labor is cheap and expert."

But again his timing was off. By the time those words were published, as part of a ten-part syndicated series on their world tour, the stock market had crashed and the Great Depression had begun. Doug did not sense that the unemployed would not be eager to hear about a movie star's silk shirts and world travels. Ever the glad narcissist, he would continue to share his adventures with the public until two years later, when the failure of *Around the World in Eighty Minutes* would demonstrate the Depression-era indifference to these goings-on.

The rest of the Chinese portion of the journey was taken up with touring a local film studio and visiting all the available Great Men in town. At the end of six days, Mary told Doug, "This Shanghai hospitality is rapidly undermining my health." The trip to Kobe, Japan, did little to improve it, as the North China seas were high and the voyage was rough. Equally challenging was their arrival. Mary noted: "The pier was black with people. More than 10,000 thronged the nearby streets." After finally making it to their car, they found themselves trapped in the backseat of the limousine for more than an hour, unable to progress, surrounded by a mob who beat their hands against the car windows "until every moment I thought the glass would break."

Worse was to follow. "Our experience at Kyoto was the most terrifying of our experience," Mary wrote. The crowd milling at the station could not be controlled by police, and only Doug's quick action kept Mary, who had fallen, from being trampled. They staged a hasty retreat and found themselves scrambling through a window into a small storeroom, where they hid until the stationmaster found them. A couple of enterprising photographers, hoping to capture a shot of their general dishevelment, followed them through the window, but they were quickly dispatched by the burly Chuck Lewis.

Japan must have seemed a repeat of China, with its exhausting rounds of studio tours, special performances, and honorary lunches and dinners. Doug received six samurai swords along the way, and saw his first (but not his last) geisha girl. "They are purely decorative entertainers—exquisitely feminine, and like many of our professional beauties, the highest product of uselessness," he commented later, with uncharacteristic dryness. He climbed the base of the Buddha at the Kosuga shrine, and fed the deer at Nana. The crush at the Tokyo station caused another delay, and he resorted to the now-habitual act of carrying Mary on his shoulders to get her through the station safely. Their social schedule in Tokyo was, if anything, even more hectic. Modern Tokyo, Doug felt, was not Japan—"at least not the Japan one travels thousands of miles to visit." They were spent. "Neither Mary nor I could have remained another week in any part of the empire without suffering a complete physical collapse," he wrote. Both were glad to board the ship to Hawaii.

They celebrated two Christmases, by virtue of crossing the international date line. Mary thought it a strange holiday, for the crowds had obliged them to board the ship early, canceling a planned shopping day. There were no presents. The second Christmas Day was even less typical, as the ship held a sukiyaki party and they found themselves eating Christmas dinner sitting on mats on the deck, wielding chopsticks.

Honolulu dazzled them both. Of all the places they visited on their trip, Mary wrote, Honolulu was "the most beautiful and alluring." Doug agreed. "To think we traveled 22,000 miles to find this!" he exclaimed. "Why didn't we ever come here before?" They took surfing lessons from five-time Olympic medalist Duke Kahanamoku. Here Mary's competitive edge stood out. "At least I was able to stand up long enough to get the thrill of the sport," she wrote. "And when I saw how many times Douglas lost his footing, I did not feel that I had acquitted myself so poorly."

Perhaps her pique is understandable. It was now almost the New Year, and she had wanted to be back in Hollywood and working on her next production months before. Instead, she had agreed to a lengthy (and expensive) trip around the world. It was a valiant attempt to rescue a floundering marriage, but it wasn't enough. Each was asked, *when will you take another world tour?*

Doug's reply: "Next year."

Mary's reply: "Never."

Both were correct. They boarded the *Asama Maru* for the mainland, never to travel extensively together again.

16

Mischief and Music

THE COUPLE RETURNED TO Pickfair with the essential questions unresolved. Mary was determined to get back to work. "Four months is long enough to stay away from this fast-moving business of pictures," she told a reporter shortly after their return. And Doug's opinion on the matter? It was difficult to determine. He was out playing golf.

By 1930 his passion for the game had turned into a mania. He had always been a skilled golfer,* but now he was an obsessed one, referring to himself as "the original, Simon-pure, dyed in the wool golf nut." He played almost daily, up to thirty-six holes a day. "Golf is great fun," he said. "What attracts me is that it is so different from the other sports I have followed. Sports which call for quick, instinctive reaction to shifting situations, as in polo, are easy for me. Golf, on the other had, is a deliberate game. A certain rhythm, and a certain harmony of mental and physical action are required to excel in it. . . . Golf is really an art." Mary had tried gamely to keep up, buying clubs and practicing, but found it impossible. "His pace is too much for me," she said. "He goes 90 miles an hour, whereas when I am at full speed I only do 45."

But Mary volunteered a response to the reporter's query. "Doug has decided that he wants, sometime in the future, to spend half

---

* His earliest recorded win was the Theatrical Managers Tournament in April 1915, and by 1916, *Variety* deemed him one of entertainment's "link bugs."

his time each year in London and half on his ranch down near San Diego." She did not say *our ranch*. Equally suggestive: they might sell Pickfair ("which is a huge house") and, on an adjoining lot, build a smaller place: English provincial, white brick, black roof. She had clearly given it some thought. Could it have been envisioned for herself alone?

They were not yet ready to make a decision. After all, there was much to occupy them in the opening months of 1930. Jack Pickford, suffering from tertiary syphilis, was hospitalized again. Calvin Coolidge came to town to see how talkies were made, and Doug and Mary hosted a luncheon for him. Mabel Normand died of tuberculosis and heartbreak, and Fairbanks joined D. W. Griffith, Mack Sennett, and Sam Goldwyn as an honorary pallbearer. And by late February Lady Mountbatten had arrived for a visit. Then came their tenth wedding anniversary. A special celebration was held for them at the studio, and Mary had two sixteen-cylinder cars sent out on approval, so that Doug could take his pick.

He had commissioned the customization of an antique music box. PICKFAIR was embedded in ivory on the cover, along with portraits of each. Doug's was a shot from *The Black Pirate*. Mary's was a photo taken around 1916, featuring her full head of curls. Inside was a silver plaque on which was engraved:

> Dearest Mary
> That is my favorite image of you.
> When you hear this music, please
> Think of how very much you mean to
> This old pirate
> Happy 10th Anniversary
> Doug
> March 28, 1930

Both wrestled with what films to make next. Doug was changeable. At first he planned to remake *The Mark of Zorro* in sound. Equally appealing, for a time, was a film he titled *Days of '49*. He would play Murrieta, "a bandit and a glamorous historical figure."

But it was not to be. He abandoned his plans, releasing his production and office staff—even those old stalwarts whom he had carried on the payroll for years. This hosted a storm of rumors that he intended to retire. He just couldn't figure out a good template for talking films, he argued. "Mary and I looked at a silent picture yesterday," he told Louella Parsons, "and there was no comparison between the way it was produced and some of the talkies we have been seeing. The silent film was so much better that it left me wondering if we hadn't all better find a solution before we went blindly ahead." Worse, he wasn't sure that sound played to his strength. "I find in talkies I can't be active on my feet and talk at the same time."

He couldn't decide on a film, and they couldn't decide on the marriage. His characteristic impulse to travel, to distract, to *escape* kicked into gear, and this time Mary dug in her heels. She would not go. Thus came a trial of the unthinkable: a time apart.

Their unwillingness to be away from each other had been the stuff of legend. Both had come to abolish location shoots to avoid overnight separation, building elaborate worlds within the confines of their studio.* They had slept apart only once in the ten years, when business forced Mary to return from a visit to Agua Caliente a day sooner than Douglas. The first time they dined apart was six years into their marriage, when Fairbanks joined a Masonic lodge. A mere two years earlier, Mary had been quoted as saying, "One thing I don't believe in is marital vacations. If a marriage needs separation to help it along it isn't much of a marriage." Now she would have to swallow her words or at least hope that they had been forgotten.

It was decided that he would sail on the *Mauretania* to see the Walker Cup tournament in England. Mary, who had decided on a script, would work on *Forever Yours*—which included a location shoot in the desert.

---

* Other producers took note of the results—and the cost savings—and followed suit, leading to the studio-bound appearance of films during the 1930s and '40s.

On the eve of his departure, they held a press tea at Mary's studio bungalow. Ever media savvy, they knew that their first separation would cause a firestorm of speculation. One columnist wrote that the event was "just for the purpose of telling them that there wasn't going to be any divorce." Doug suggested that golf was an excuse to get to London and New York to see new plays. He didn't like the current stories he was working on. He would be gone only a few weeks—back before Mary finished her film. "I can't let her get more than one picture ahead of me," he claimed. "I am already accused of doing all the playing for the family while Mary does all the work."

He left the night of April 25 from Pasadena. She wired him at every conceivable train stop: Seligman, Ash Fork, Williams, Winslow Gallup, Albuquerque, La Junta, Dodge City, Newton, Emporia, Chicago. She was an addict, suffering withdrawal after a ten-year binge.

He was the same. "I just live from one telegram to another," he wrote her from Kansas. "They buoy me up—I get very depressed take a nap and Rocher wakes me up with a wire from my baby. We are getting in Kansas City in a few minutes—usually I would come in the stateroom and say 'come on Baby we only have a minute if you want to get out and walk' and now I have no baby with me. Oh Frin-Din-Din!"

He had trouble sleeping without her: "I only seem to sleep in fits—wake up so often and look for my girl—do this all day as well—seem to feel rested but am sleeping as a dog does," he wrote. He began to recognize the role she played in their lives: "Oh Baby—poor little Duber—he did not know what to do—I did not realize how very much you were a part of my everyday life till now—the many decisions you made for me the words of encouragement—your thousand smiles of sweet understanding." Perhaps, he thought, the insight would be good for their marriage: "You have spoiled the Duber and this is going to be good for him and her."

And he missed other benefits of the marriage: "Oh—how I miss the Pull ins! So glad the last night was all pull ins—"

At first, he communicated obsessively. He wired or wrote daily, handing one letter to the tugboat pilot as the *Mauretania* was pulled out of port. "I am going to be happy because I know you would want it and be happier yourself," he wrote. Then, referring to himself in the third party: "But he ain't going to do this again—I am glad I did. It has given me a truer value of things—and I want you to know that I love you with all my heart."

On the ship, he claimed he read, napped, took bridge lessons, and even tried to follow her on her spiritual path. "You will be happy Dear to know that I am taking up Christian Science—I am declaring the truth every second," he wrote. But, he said, he wasn't enjoying the voyage. Although alcohol—the good stuff, not bootleg hooch—was available to all, Doug remained abstemious. "This would have been a good time for me to take up drinking," he wrote. "But I am enjoying my misery."

Still, the ocean voyage was not a total ordeal. He rose early every morning and received impromptu golf lessons from Bobby Jones, superstar captain of the Walker Cup American Team.* And his mood continued to brighten after arriving at the Hyde Park Hotel in London on May 5. "I am so busy here with golf—shopping—[UA executive Murray] Silverstone—telephone—etc—that I don't get a chance to think—London is <u>wonderful</u>," he wrote, quickly adding, "—but I want my baby. I come home to her and talk to her in my room & get all choked up."

He called her nightly. But even this had challenges. "Our conversations probably would have been better," he acknowledged, "if every operator in the United States and England had not listened in." He wrote Mary after one call: "Tonight on the phone you seemed so near. It was most comforting but most aggravating. . . . I get flashes of joy and the next moment flashes of gloom."

In time, the joy started to outstrip the gloom. He went with the American golfers to the Royal Albert Hall to watch a boxing match and was the guest of honor at a dinner party studded with lords and ladies, counts and duchesses. His claims to be in search of a story were hollow; there is no evidence that he saw a single play, either in New York

---

* Jones attributed his general state of fitness over the winter to learning the game of "Doug" from Fairbanks the summer before.

or London. Mary picked up the change in tone in his telegrams and teasingly wired him, DON'T HAVE TOO GOOD A TIME WITHOUT THE FRIN.

She had cause, but she didn't know it yet. There was, perhaps, one too many ladies of title at the dinner party. Or it could be that he met Lady Sylvia Ashley at another time and place; the details of their meeting have never been clear. But within a month of his return, rumors began to circulate. A woman—a titled Englishwoman—had caught Doug's fancy.

Sylvia Ashley, born Edith Louisa Sylvia Hawkes, was twenty-six years old in 1930. Her father had been a stable hand before opening a pub. Her mother worked as a barmaid. She was tall, lean, and beautiful, and possessed a sort of haughty languor that suggested a wealth she did not have. She had worked in her father's bar, then as a model, then in the chorus at the Winter Garden Theatre's *Midnight Follies*. There she was clad in "a garment so sketchy that it was hardly a garment at all." A featured role in *The Whole Town's Talking* followed at the Strand. She caught the eye of one young Lord Ashley, who evidently was a living example of the somewhat dim species of titled Englishman that routinely emerged from the pen of P. G. Wodehouse. His father was the Earl of Shaftesbury; his mother was Lady of the Bedchamber to Queen Mary. He married Sylvia in 1927, despite a madcap chase to the church on the part of his parents to prevent the disaster. His sister, Lady Dorothy Ashley-Cooper, moaned to the press: "Such an alliance is unthinkable."

It did not take long for the young lord to figure this out. Within a year he advertised in the papers that he would no longer be responsible for debts contracted by his wife. Nevertheless, *someone* was paying her bills in the subsequent years, when she (and her décolletage) had little visible means of support. She was on the social circuit and, evidently, on the prowl. Doug, with his love of titles, and his marriage shaky, was attractive—and possibly willing—prey.

Curiously, it can be claimed that Mary had indirect warning. At the beginning of the year, she had a horoscope cast for her husband. She kept it until her death. It said of him:

You have an intensely emotional nature, [such] that you will have much attraction for the opposite sex, but may be somewhat unfortunate in the type of women who fascinates you. Because of your sex lure, you will have many temptations and peculiar experiences with women who are not worthy of you and who would not prove loyal to you. You are more in love with love or a certain type than with the individual. While the physical attracts you strongly, the only woman who can hold you for any length of time would be one who plays the part of a chum or companion, and with whom you are congenial on many planes. . . . You have, however, an almost hypnotic influence upon married women or those older than yourself. Unless you are very discreet and exercise a great deal of self-control, you will find yourself in compromising situations with the opposite sex.

Neither discretion nor self-control was Fairbanks's strong suit. While there is no direct evidence that this is where or when the affair began, his letters and wires home dropped off. By the time he returned on the *Europa*, he had decided that the experience was not as soul crushing as he had feared. He had discovered, he revealed to reporters upon his return, just what he wanted to be: a bum. "But it's no use trying," he confessed. "Mary won't let me."

Mary, meanwhile, was having her own struggles. Her film was stalled, and she was at a crisis point in deciding whether to try to fix it or abandon the project. Doug was—one hopes—unintentionally ironic in describing her woes to the press. The story, he said, was of a woman's life between seventeen and seventy. "Mary got about as far as the thirties and got stuck." Sam Taylor—he of *The Taming of the Shrew* fame—was brought in to try to rescue the film. He advised shelving the project. Doug, on the other hand, liked the film and advised her to finish it.

Mary sided with Sam. Two weeks from the completion of *Forever Yours*, now retitled *Secrets*, she stopped production and released the staff, including director Marshall Neilan. The decision cost the ever-frugal Mary almost half a million dollars.

Much more could have been lost early in the morning of August 4, when Fairbanks faced down a trio of burglars in their Santa Monica beach house. He and Mary had returned late from a visit with Maurice Chevalier. She was in bed; he was descending the stairs to check the lock on the door. There he encountered a young man with a mask and a gun. Behind him were two compatriots.

He switched on a light, and the young thief caught a glimpse of his face. "Gee, you're Fairbanks, ain't you?" he exclaimed, then, embarrassed: "I'm sorry to do this, but I need the money." Then, unable to resist (and clearly a fan), he asked, "Where's Mary?"

Mary was upstairs, Doug explained. Appealing to their gallantry, he asked them not to frighten her by looting the house and making noise. He had no money in his pockets but said, "You wait down here, boys, and I'll go up and see what Mary has." The young thief followed him as he went upstairs and unearthed one hundred dollars. They took it, continuing to apologize as they got into a car and drove away. His quick thinking saved them from losing thousands of dollars in jewelry. But his image had been built on action, not thinking.

The response to this disconnect was revealing. Fans wrote in to movie magazines expressing dismay: why hadn't Doug swung from the balustrades and knocked the villains out? "The least Doug Fairbanks could have done was not report the robbery so he could have remained, in our thoughts, the dark, handsome, strong, fearless man as we movie fans pictured him in our minds," complained one. Will Rogers quipped: "So Doug burgled Mary for one hundred bucks. Came downstairs and turned over $90, keeping 10 percent for commission and overhead. Burglars made arrangements with him to come back as soon as Mary had anything else."

Normally a publicist would have managed this for them, but the week before, their publicist had resigned—upon request.* They had been displeased with a recent spate of articles suggesting trouble in paradise.

---

* This was not Bennie Zeidman, who had moved higher up the food chain by this time.

This had happened in July, when the press got wind of Doug's possible mischief in London. Doug and Mary were going to separate, the reports went. She would file for divorce by the end of the month. Both issued denials, but it was Cap O'Brien who established plausible deniability. "I have heard talk about this woman," he told the press, "and I know personally that there is no truth to it. The woman referred to is Lady Mountbatten." Lady Mountbatten, he went on to add, was a dear friend of both Doug and Mary. She had stayed at Pickfair often. She was in England the same time as Doug, certainly. Why shouldn't he have visited her, and why should she not have returned his kind hospitality?

It was an inspired strategy. The good lady was, as Caesar's wife, above reproach. Reporters seemed to swallow the explanation whole, and no one thought to look for any ladies of the nobility who were ex-chorines. But if it was chorus girls that Fairbanks wanted, his next film, *Reaching for the Moon*, would provide plenty.

It is significant to note that Fairbanks did not produce *Reaching for the Moon*. It was a Joseph Schenck film, and Fairbanks's involvement, technically, was only as a performer, making this the first time he had starred in a film that he did not produce since 1916 and *The Americano*. Fairbanks was reluctant to invest in another talking film until Chaplin's *City Lights* was released, suggesting he was seriously contemplating following his friend's example: continuing to make silent films.

It is tempting to wonder what might have happened had he done so. In one sense, it would be the first backward step he had ever taken. He had assumed the role of pioneer so often and so well—moving from stage to film; embracing production, then distribution; implementing new discoveries such as Technicolor; investing more; building higher; always at the forefront of the new and the better. How could he, *he* who had always represented the new, the fresh, cling to the old?

Yet one can readily read the flip side of this particular coin. There are certain performers, his wife and Buster Keaton among them, who are brilliant in silence but ordinary—or worse—in sound. To watch Mary Pickford's face in a film such as *Sparrows*, where she awakens to discover that the infant in her arms has died, is to feel a primal communion with a performer that transcends words. The moment is incandescent. To hear her speak in *Coquette* is, to put it kindly, the opposite experience. The small, pear-shaped tones of her mouselike voice distract from the visual performance, and we are irritated, dismayed. The very thing that makes watching her a supreme experience is destroyed by the addition of words.

But Fairbanks and his genres, both comedic and heroic, were not truly in this category. His acting—such as it was—was not what elevated the experience of watching him; it was his *body* and the visual wit that he employed in moving it across multiple planes. In a few years, technicians and directors would master the art of sound, placing music under action scenes, for example, or managing the rhythms of screwball comedy, resulting in satisfactory swashbucklers such as *Captain Blood* or the staccato wit of modern comedies like *The Thin Man*. But this was 1930, and Fairbanks was correct: sound films were not yet what silent films had been. He was wise not to invest his money in *Reaching for the Moon*. What he failed to consider in yielding control was whether he also yielded his full say over the end product. *Reaching for the Moon* was possibly a good early musical, but we shall never know. It was stripped, transformed, and very likely ruined before its premiere.

The film originated after the 1929 Wall Street crash, when Irving Berlin got an idea for a story about a wealthy stockbroker and a famous aviatrix who meet and fall in love. On their honeymoon the stock market crash occurs, and they learn of it only when it is too late to do anything to recover. Their love is tested, and happiness wins. Berlin proposed the plot, including several new songs, to his boyhood friend, Joseph Schenck. Schenck, in turn, thought it was ideal for Fairbanks. He had already tried Shakespeare; why not take another tackle at sound with a musical?

Berlin put his heart and soul into the project. He dusted off one number from the files of his singing waiter days: "Love in a Cottage." Then over the course of nine months he wrote twenty new songs, including "If You Believe," "The Little Things in Life," "Just a Little While," "The Brokers' Ensemble," "What a Lucky Break for Me," "It's Yours,"

"A Toast to Prohibition," "Do You Believe Your Eyes or Do You Believe Your Baby?," "Bootlegger's Song," "Wedding and Crash," "When the Folks High Up Do the Mean Low Down," and the eponymous "Reaching for the Moon." He penned multiple iterations of the script, with the original version titled *Love in a Cottage*.* In it the couple honeymooned in a southern cottage and there was heavy employment of "colored servants," Negro spirituals, and enough use of the term *nigger* to cause despair to even the most unenlightened.

Douglas Fairbanks had many weaknesses, but bigotry was not one of them. He had eliminated that particular term and the associated demeaning of black people in the story line from the original script for *Down to Earth* more than a decade prior, and whether through his sway or that of others, the final version of *Reaching for the Moon* had no cottage—and no "coloreds" at all. Instead, the setting of the second half of the film was moved to a modern ocean liner.

As to that sway, at this stage in his career he elected to exert his influence by way of his pocketbook. He struck a deal with Schenck: if he liked the script, he would back the film with his own money and not only assume the risk but also enjoy the producer's profits. If he didn't, Schenck would fund the film. Fairbanks would meet the requirement for product that UA required and enjoy his share of the distributor's profits—to say nothing of his salary for performing ($300,000 for *Moon*). But he would not put his own money into a story he did not like. Mary was of similar mind at this point—or simply more conservative with her funds. Stinging from *Forever Yours*, she agreed to make *Kiki* for Schenck but not to fund it.

But the fact that Fairbanks did not back the film financially did not mean that he approached it without enthusiasm. His choice to do the project was, like so many in those years, a snap decision. He read the script hurriedly, being sold on the idea, reportedly, by the choice of Edmund Goulding as director. Goulding had *The*

---

* The typed scripts still exist at the Institute of the American Musical in Los Angeles, heavily marked with notes in Berlin's handwriting.

Trespasser and *The Devil's Holiday* to his credit, and Fairbanks was a willing student.

"He actually takes direction for the first time in years," wrote one visitor to the set, noting that while Fairbanks had always employed noted directors for his films, he had, until then, invariably directed himself. Here "he listens as though he learned. He shows up an hour before the other members of the cast arrive each day, and consults his director."

Goulding wasn't the only one he consulted. Charlie Chaplin came to the set one late October day to watch the rehearsal of a scene where Doug drank a cocktail spiked by costar Edward Everett Horton. The farce needed a certain tempo, Chaplin declared. It wasn't right.

Goulding invited him to take charge, and he did. The set became crowded with actors, executives, property men, and grips as Charlie first acted out the scene and then directed Doug through the action. Fairbanks seemed to relish the experience. Gone was what one reporter described as his "lethargic indifference to anything pertaining to talkies. . . . In the time I was there," the reporter went on to add, "he smoked only two cigarettes (in Fairbanks a sure sign of mental clarity and peace of mind)."

Goulding also convinced Fairbanks to sing one of the songs. The original cut of the film included four songs, including "A Toast to Prohibition" and "Reaching for the Moon." Fairbanks likely sang the title song, but today the film is best remembered for a promising youngster who sang a single chorus of "When the Folks High Up Do the Mean Low Down."

In the fall of 1930, twenty-seven-year-old Bing Crosby was not yet a star, much less the superstar he would become.* He was singing at the Cocoanut Grove with the Rhythm Boys and Gus Arnheim's orchestra

---

* The New York censor's continuity script—the only resource available to determine the original cut of the premiere print—demonstrates this. "When the Folks High Up Do the Mean Low Down" has four choruses. Each is linked by the censor to the actor or character who sings it, except the second. The censor, not recognizing Crosby, writes simply, "Second chorus sung by a man." It was likely the last time Bing Crosby would go unrecognized in his lifetime.

when someone—he recalled it as Fairbanks; his biographer states it was Goulding—asked him to sing in the film. He described shooting late at night, after his Grove set was finished, with no prerecording (as was typical of early musicals). "I was well paid," he wrote, "which is probably the reason the song eluded the cutter's shears."

It is the only number in the film that did. Schenck's decision could have been based on preview screenings, or it could simply have been a symptom of an industry-wide phenomenon. Film historian Robert S. Bader writes in the documentary *The Dawn of Sound*: "By 1930, the novelty of sound had begun to wear thin. The public tired of static, stage-bound productions, and the market for musicals reached the saturation point. Studios pulled the plug on several major musicals that had already started filming. . . . Song and dance [were] no longer enough to guarantee box office success."

The result, to put it kindly, was a wreck. A musical film stripped of its songs left only the flimsy supporting structure. One has only to imagine an Astaire/Rogers film without the music to recognize that this was akin to throwing away the diamond while keeping the setting. Schenck hoped that what remained could qualify as one of the pre-1920 modern-dress comedies at which Fairbanks had excelled. But the not-yet-sophisticated use of sound recording, combined with the absence of Loosian wit in the script and Fairbanks's advancing age (though in prime physical condition, he still, at forty-seven, could not pass for the young man his character was supposed to represent) resulted in a film that lacked the sparkle of his earlier works. Not even the stunning art deco sets of William Cameron Menzies or the charms of Bebe Daniels and Edward Everett Horton could rescue the effort. It is not even possible to make a clear determination of the virtues it might have had: the musical sequences are all lost, depriving us of an opportunity to decide if Fairbanks's singing voice was as bad as he claimed when recalling *Fantana*, twenty-six years before. Current copies of the film run about sixty minutes, as opposed to the ninety-nine-minute premiere length, depriving modern audiences of much of the narrative and comedy.

Berlin was furious. "If you wanted to see Irving Berlin go ballistic—even at the age of 100—all you had to do was say four words: *Reaching for the Moon*," states Miles Krueger, of the Institute of the American Musical. Berlin never worked with UA again.

Fairbanks missed the premiere, staying on the West Coast in preparation for his next adventure. He would leave Mary again—this time with a small film crew—and make a documentary about his trip around the world.

17

Around the World in Eighty Minutes

T HE IDEA OF MAKING a film about travel—particularly as a twist on *Around the World in Eighty Days*—had been with Fairbanks long before he even entered film. In 1913, when *Hawthorne of the U.S.A.* was on its Chicago run, he announced plans to spend his summer vacation having his travel adventures filmed. "He has such little ideas of catching a boat by swimming to it, taking a 100-yard dash and a flying leap to make a train on time, and other little exciting incidents that the camera operator will be pleased to grab off to show that Doug Fairbanks spanned the globe in 40 days," wrote one reporter. "Mr. Fairbanks," he added, perhaps unnecessarily, "has been reading up on Jules Verne."

Nothing came of this at the time—Fairbanks was always seething with ideas, and not all of them could come to fruition at once without violating the laws of physics. But his passion for travel kept the idea foremost in his mind. In the early years at Triangle he had a similar scheme that involved Bessie Love: "Mr. Fairbanks had the idea of making films abroad, still with me as his lead (his wife and family would go along too)," she wrote. "He loved to go places and wanted to make a complete story in every country he visited." In late 1918, after finishing *Arizona*, he announced plans to pack up his entire production unit and film in France. "It is quite possible," wrote one trade journal, "that he will take his company on a complete tour of Europe for a special scenario which is now being written by Director Albert Parker."

Twelve years later he decided the time had come. In early January 1931 Mary saw him off on the *Belgenland*. She gifted him with a special sleeping bag outfitted with that newfangled contraption, the zipper. With him were trainer Chuck Lewis, director Victor Fleming, cameraman Henry Sharp, and his valet. He and Fleming posed in pith helmets, clutching game rifles, and announced to the press their plans to visit the emperor of Japan, the king of Siam, and "several Indian princes."

They departed on the fourth, and Mary left for New York City five days later, after arranging for two dozen singers in flowered kimonos to serenade her husband's party upon arrival at the Royal Hawaiian Hotel. She was in New York, she claimed, on "a rampage": shopping, visiting theaters, and skating in Central Park.

His first letter to her was a plea to keep working with him on the marriage: "My Goddess—. . . my beautiful girl—my baby—I love I worship you—the greatest thing by far in my life please Dear one love me and remember your promises. I am so proud of our love our future it will be perfect—it is all up to us to guard."

The team got some footage on the journey out—THREE HUNDRED FEET EXCELLENT STUFF, he wired Mary—mostly under-cranked shots of Doug running and climbing decks, leaping, swinging on poles, and ultimately climbing and jumping into a smokestack. But this exercise was undercut by what he termed MANY BLUE SPELLS. He was, he claimed LONESOME, HOMESICK, BLUE, MISERABLE. He sat in his cabin all day, he wrote, thinking of her and working jigsaw puzzles. Surviving footage suggests that he spent a lot more time on secluded sections of the deck, nude sunbathing.

The entourage arrived in Honolulu, where in between Doug's rounds of golf they filmed him surfing. ("I took so much exercise in Honolulu that I had darndest cramps in my muscles all night," he wrote her.) From there they departed for Japan. Four days out of Hawaii, he and Mary set a new record for the longest radio-wire circuit in ship-to-shore

conversation when he called her at her New York hotel. DARLING DAR-
LING THRILLED BEYOND EXPRESSION, she wired him afterward. YOUR
VOICE MARVELOUS I LOVE YOU DARLING. He replied, MUCH HAPPIER
DEAR FELT YOU NEAR ME TODAY.

He arrived in Japan on the twentieth, where he told Mary [I] FIND
MYSELF MR. PICKFORD HERE. They filmed his arrival at Yokohama, standing between Sessue Hayakawa and Sôjin Kamiyama, who replaced Sadakichi Hartmann when the latter departed *The Thief of Bagdad* in an
artistic huff. Hayakawa was also present at a dinner in Tokyo, where
Fairbanks was presented with a suit of ancient Japanese armor.

He still claimed to be homesick in his cables to Mary during the
filming of the Japanese sequences for the film. These were intended
to be comic scenes demonstrating Japanese life, but they do not wear
well. Fleming was filmed peeking into the doorway of a Japanese home.
Fairbanks, inexplicably wearing a ridiculous wool cap, joined him.*
The following shots purport to be from their point of view: a young
Japanese woman was shown getting into socks, then her kimono. "No
underclothes are worn—[*pause*]—so I'm told," Fairbanks said in the
voiceover. Music and dancing lessons were depicted, and then, the narrative claimed, it was bath time . . .

In an especially cringeworthy sequence, Vic and Doug were filmed
as Peeping Toms as the young woman is about to bathe. Being caught,
they scampered guiltily away, until the girl waylaid Doug. As he sup-
plicated an apology, she asked for an autograph. Doug no longer seems
to exemplify America to us so much as he does the Ugly American. In
an interesting conclusion to the sequence, Fairbanks expostulates to
Fleming that the young woman is *wonderful*, and Fleming replies, "I'll
tell Mary on you, young fellow!"

Around the same time, he attended a geisha festival dance on the
island of Miyajima, a sacred island on Japan's inland sea. The festival
was stopped cold when one of the samisen musicians, recognizing the

---

* The narration later has Fairbanks saying: "I told Vic we needed more comedy in this
picture. He replied 'Just keep wearing that hat.'"

star, stopped playing and cried out in excitement. All sixteen dancers and four musicians abandoned their posts to cluster around him.

By early February they were in Peking. Mei Lanfang, China's premier actor, placed his home at Fairbanks's disposal on his arrival, in gratitude for the hospitality he and Mary had shown him when he visited the States. Doug, looking stern in a winter coat and bowler hat, was filmed at the Forbidden City as well as the Summer Palace.

He continued the daily cables to Mary. He missed her. He loved her. It was tragic that she wasn't there. Shanghai without her was just Pomona.* He wanted her suggestions for the film. She cabled back in the same vein. Beverly Hills, she wired, was Newark without Duber. Ever the filmmaker, she also sent her ideas: BE SURE PHOTOGRAPH BARGAINING OLD CHINA PIGEON ENGLISH INTERPRETING TO AUDIENCE IN ENGLISH AND AMERICAN SLANG CONTRASTING MODERN CHINESE YOUTH ALL LOVE.

Next was Manila. His arrival virtually paralyzed business along the waterfront as over eight thousand admirers crammed the pier and thousands more filled the streets outside the dock. As he reached the bottom of the gangplank, he was seized by the crowd and carried a quarter mile to his car, where he was planted on the roof for all to see. He was in the Philippines only long enough to visit the home of General Emilio Aguinaldo, the country's first president. The film contains a shot of Fairbanks pulling the clearly uncomfortable general up to the camera.

Bangkok followed. More documentary footage was taken of temples, canals, sacred white elephants, hacky sack players, and a laboratory that produced snake antivenom. Fairbanks and Fleming were filmed, hot and uncomfortable in their morning suits, attending a tea party at the royal palace. They looked far more at ease later on the golf course, sinking putts with the king. The filmmakers were to supplement shots of Thai dancers in the film with footage of a dancing Mickey Mouse

---

* Perhaps so, but Pomona was not so full of drug dens. By his later accounts, Fairbanks met a regional warlord who ran the local opium trade in Shanghai. He attended an opium party and reported that "it was an interesting experience and I did not suffer any ill effects."

(his eyes briefly converted to cartoon Asian slits)—likely a nod to the fact that Walt Disney was soon to be using United Artists as his distributor.*

Fairbanks loved it. Thailand, he wired Mary, was MARVELOUS COUNTRY MOST FASCINATING YET. He took a four-day flier to Penang, Malaysia, where he watched a ceremonial dance in Kedah. "They beat drums until they are in a frenzy," he wrote her. "And then with skewers stuck all through their faces—walk in this sort of a spiritual dope—slowly through a long path of burning coals." To his chagrin, the light was too weak to capture it on film. Still, he was BLUE HOMESICK WANT MY FRIN. She called him on his inconsistency and wired: BABY PLEASE DON'T BE HOMESICK ELSE NO MORE TRIPS.

Burma was next. "Beautiful—Round of golf and big banquet presided over by Lord Mayor," he wrote Mary in his telegraphic style. "—Speeches—crowds like Russia—entertainment four tea parties—big mass meeting at night—dinner and Siamese dancers and musicians—interesting—sign nine million autographs."

But he devoted little time to Mandalay, either in person or on film. India was next on the itinerary, and with it the prospect of big game. He was there by mid-March, but with his arrival came trouble. First, Victor Fleming was sick—very sick. "Vic has developed a very serious fever—temperature 103—we have to take him off ship tomorrow in an ambulance to a nursing home he may stay a week there—I am very worried—he has been sick off and on the whole trip," he wrote. "I want Baby Fairbanks here."

The mobs in Calcutta made things worse, and the unthinkable happened. "What an ordeal! Worse crowd yet—tore me to pieces—ran over a little boy about 12 years I took to the hospital they fear he can't live—am terribly upset—awful feeling—want my Hipper."

He was devastated. "Boy is still dying . . . poor family am doing everything I can they say not much hope—crowds here are terrible

---

* Disney signed with UA in 1931, and the relationship was profitable for both. UA's share of profits from Disney releases in the 1932–1933 season was $1 million.

1 million invitations—terrible feeling about the boy" he wrote. The child was "a splendid little fellow—a great fan of mine."

Fortunately, both the child and Fleming improved, and with them, Doug's view of India. "Boy took turn for the better he may live," he wrote. "—I am so happy . . . went to hospital tonight—boy looked at me smiled and said this is worth it." Doug golfed, gave speeches, and prepared for big game hunting, buying guns and reviewing the hunting grounds. He saw a veritable zoo: "Rhinoceros—Bear Boar—Pythons—Deer and 300 yards away a huge tiger came out of the jungle went to the river to bathe . . . a great day." The tiger hunt itself caused him to wax almost poetic: "On my elephant deep in the jungle—shouts of the Mahonto—cries of animals—weird sound of . . . birds trumpeting of elephant when they see game—Dubar . . . waiting gun ready—trembly, wild boar—porcupine deer civet cats huge lizards 6 and 7 feet long all mushing on in front of pack."

It was no minor affair to capture on film. "We have about 40 Elephants 6 or 8 that carry the cameras and Vic—Chuck and myself . . . the rest are used for what they call the 'beat'—line up abreast—pass through jungle and drive all animals ahead." He bagged his first leopard three days later. "He had killed a young buffalo and was sitting on his kill," he wrote Mary. "We beat him out—I hit him the first shot wounded him and had to follow him back in the jungle to finish him. I am send[ing] it to Baby Fairbanks—he is 7 feet 8 inches long. This is great sport. I love my Baby." The next day brought his second kill.

Modern audiences hiss at the scenes in the film depicting the big game hunting, and it is easy to see why. But one should look at this episode in the context of its time. It was just twenty years after Theodore Roosevelt's African game hunt—a highly celebrated event in which Doug's hero bagged literally hundreds of animals. And in 1931 the leopard was not yet endangered but in fact was a menace to the local population. Those who hunted it were considered heroic and daring. One of the leopards killed was found to have the toe ring and bracelet of a missing girl inside him.

Even with these caveats (apologies?) in mind, it is clear that very little of *Around the World in Eighty Minutes* stands the test of time. A studio sequence filmed later to pad the hunting scenes did little to help: a tiger attacks a native and drags him (very clearly a dummy) off into the woods. Fairbanks, in his tent, awakens and gives chase. Finding his gun is out of bullets, he hurls it down and wrestles *mano a feline* with the cat. Here the film cuts to Doug wrestling with a tiger-skin rug in his tent. When Vic Fleming wakens him, he cries: "Oh! I dreamt I was Trader Horn!"

The euphoria of killing leopards (and tigers and panthers) did not entirely keep his mind from home. Bad dreams caused him to fret about his finances, and he wired Mary to check into them. ("Always comes to the Baby—don't know what I would do without her.") He asked Robert to fill Pickfair with flowers for their wedding anniversary—their first apart.

He returned to Calcutta and the happy news that the injured boy was out of all danger. He was "as black as an Indian—much blacker" and ready to explore more of the country. Benares, Agra, and Delhi followed. The Taj Mahal was "the most gorgeous thing of any kind I have ever seen—great beyond powers of description." He marveled at the wild peacock, monkeys, storks, and deer visible from the window of this train.

But it was time to head homeward, and they sailed in early April for Venice. Mary plaintively wired, WHEN ARE YOU SAILING FOR HOME DARLING. His reply could not have served to reassure: HOW DO YOU FEEL ABOUT COMING OVER WOULD LIKE PLAY IN GOLF TOURNAMENTS EUROPE THIS SPRING LOVE YOU.

He had not seen her in almost four months but wanted to linger in England to play golf.

No wife could blame Mary for what happened next. During an interview with a *Photoplay* reporter, she began to muse. No one could say what the future would hold, she speculated. Ten years in the future? She and Doug might be separated. Who knew? The papers went to town on the quote, causing Mary to wire mid-April: UNPLEASANT ARTICLE

PHOTOPLAY MISQUOTING ME ABOUT SEPARATION LONDON NEW YORK
PAPERS MUCH EXCITED PAY NO ATTENTION JUST KNOW I LOVE YOU.

Doug's reaction was swift: ADVISE STRENUOUS ACTION AGAINST
LIBELOUS ARTICLE. Mary, knowing that she could hardly sue for what
she actually had said, was soothing in her reply: FORGET PHOTOPLAY
I HAVE ALL LOVE. Adept at managing publicity, she quickly issued a
statement saying that she was referring in general to any marriage, not
in particular to hers.

Doug remained in Rome, golfing, enjoying the sun, and pestering
her to come over. She couldn't come right away, since she had business
with Cap O'Brien. Doug persisted in wiring her the names of ships and
sailing dates. She replied that she was coming as quickly as she could
but that she needed to conduct her business.

By the time he reached London he wired: TERRIBLY DISAPPOINTED
DATE YOU ARE SAILING STOP PLEASE HURRY STOP IN TWO GOLF TOURNA-
MENTS HERE STOP BREMEN LATEST OR WILL COME AND GET YOU ALL LOVE.

She would have been wise to hurry. He had started looking at real
estate, with a mind to buy. She must have intervened, for he wired:
GOT MY ORDERS FROM YOU STOP NOT BUYING HOUSE STOP. She tried
to soften things: NOT ORDERS ABOUT HOUSE DARLING BUT WISDOM. In
mid-May Mary, taking care to have the media present ("Divorce! Well,
not so you could notice it!") telephoned him from New York with her
travel arrangements. After his long absence, she wanted to ensure that
he would be at the dock when she arrived. She smiled gamely in the
photographs, but she looked thin, wan.

On the *Bremen*, she received a wire: HEARTBROKEN ABOUT POSSIBIL-
ITY BEING UNABLE MEET YOU MAKING ALL ARRANGEMENTS FOR YOU TO
COME TO ME ALL LOVE.

The ship docked at Southampton; he was not there. Instead, a new
Rolls-Royce was waiting for her on the pier. She laughed bravely for the
reporters and called the golf course. He could not take her call. He was
in the middle of a match, playing in grim earnest. The largest gallery
of the event dogged his steps—somersaulting boys, mothers cradling
babies, and schoolgirls clutching autograph books. All hoped to see

his famous smile. They were disappointed until the end, when, in the words of a sportswriter, he "marked himself a generous sportsman" by conceding his opponent's final putt, although it was a good distance from the hole. He seemed, the observers thought, to have other things on his mind. He took the first train back to London.

Reunited, husband and wife posed for a joint picture: Doug in his golf togs, relaxing in an armchair, Mary perched on the arm. The wire services released it with the caption A Divorce!—Does This Look Like It? They were on their second honeymoon, they announced. They would visit all the same places they had in 1920. It would be an extensive tour abroad.

It lasted a week. Doug golfed every day. On midnight of the eighth day they booked tickets on the *Empress of Britain* a few hours before the vessel sailed. Five days later they were back in North America, along with twenty-one steamer trunks and nine other pieces of luggage, their honeymoon, evidently, over.

He returned to Pickfair, to a world that had changed even more since his last stint at home. Hollywood, it seemed to him, was losing its old glamour. Sid Grauman's Egyptian Theatre, which opened for business with his *Robin Hood* in 1922, was now showing second-run films on an increasingly seedy Hollywood Boulevard. Even Grauman's Chinese Theatre, where his and Mary's foot- and handprints in the fore-court cement had begun a tradition, was no longer the site of spotlight premieres. Most of his contemporaries had stopped making films. For the first time since United Artists was formed, the announced list of releases for the 1931–1932 season had no contributions from Fairbanks, Pickford, or Chaplin. *Reaching for the Moon*, working its way to minor markets, was shaking out to be a disappointment.

Partially this was due to internal policies at United Artists. At this time United Artists and Schenck were in a war with the Fox West Coast theater chain over what Schenck perceived as monopolistic behavior and unfavorable terms. Schenck staged all his stars for a public "Declaration of Independence" from the chain, refusing to distribute UA films to them. They, in turn, banned UA films, meaning a significant portion of the country was not being covered by UA's distribution network.

United Artists had a Theatre Circuit business, which developed plans to build theaters in twenty-four key West Coast cities. Ten of these theaters were already under construction before Fox and Schenck finally reached a truce. Fox took over the operation of the new theaters and agreed to show UA films.

But the war had taken its toll. Art Cinema, Schenck's production unit, curtailed production in 1933 and liquidated. While Schenck bore the financial burden of the particular failure of *Reaching for the Moon* due to Fairbanks's refusal to bankroll the project, Doug found little satisfaction in being right. It was an embarrassment—and not merely a financial one. He had always represented not only success but wholesome success. One editorial columnist wrote, "In . . . *Reaching for the Moon*, there is much that is worthless and salacious." Another, under the disheartening headline of EXIT THE HERO, wrote: "The talking motion picture has claimed another victim."

He tried to resume his old life. He filmed studio shots to knit the travel footage into a reasonable narrative. He hosted the Prince of Siam and served as master of ceremonies for the pre-Olympic festivities at the L.A. Coliseum. He added a new wing and guest quarters to Pickfair to accommodate the anticipated influx of guests for the 1932 Los Angeles Olympics. He played back-lot football at the studio almost daily with the likes of Johnny Weissmuller and Johnny Mack Brown. The season would last, he told a reporter wryly, until they all got hurt or "somebody is lucky enough to get a job." He even found time to perform a rescue after witnessing an automobile collision on Holloway Drive, dropping through the shattered window of a flipped sedan to extract Mr. and Mrs. Melville Van Duerson of Hillside, New Jersey, presumably giving them a good tale to tell the folks back home.

He announced trips. He would go to Norway to fish. Or Scotland for grouse hunting. Then England for golf. No, no, he would go to the Amazon (as had his hero, Teddy Roosevelt) and search for gold. He would bring Victor Fleming along to film events. Scratch that—it would be Howard Hawks.

In the end, he went to New York City to premiere *Around the World in Eighty Minutes* at the Rivoli on November 19, 1931.

The big-city critics were not kind. The film was padded, they pointed out, and not all that interesting as a travelogue. Rural critics largely gave it positive reviews, but *Variety's* prediction turned out to be accurate: it was the sort of film that "will slide instead of climb on word of mouth in full week stands." The possibility that the Depression audience might not wish to watch the travels of a rich movie star had not occurred to Doug.

That he no longer had his finger on the public pulse was evident. On arriving in New York, he declared to reporters that the idea of the economic depression disgusted him. "Conditions are not worse than in 1929 when things were over-inflated," he said. "Being gloomy just undermines things." Mary, wearing a lovely suit with a fox collar, applauded him with what the reporter termed "a Pickfordian laugh." She loyally agreed that "depression talkers" only helped the depression.

One editor, perhaps in possession of a strong sense of irony, placed this article directly next to an account of a young mother, desperate over her husband's inability to find work, who killed her three small children, then herself.

Doug probably never read the story. He announced that he was off to the Orient to film another travelogue; he sailed in mid-November, 1931.

He got no farther than Europe, and skiing in the mountains of St. Moritz with Charlie Chaplin. Whether it was due to the political situation in China, the disappointing reports on *Around the World*, or his capricious nature is unclear, but he canceled his planned trip to the Far East by mid-December. A mad dash followed, and he was home at Pickfair in time for Christmas dinner.

18

Castaway

Fairbanks made it home for Christmas, but he was not to stay for long. He wanted to travel, but the anemic returns of *Around the World in Eighty Minutes* made another travelogue out of the question.* Still, he was desperate to get away. Perhaps it was not merely his restlessness.

An example serves to illustrate: A columnist came to visit Pickfair on a night when Mary was dining at home alone, as Doug was expected to remain at the studio until ten. At six thirty, Mary left the house. Fairbanks, calling from the studio, was informed that Mary was out. No, the butler did not know where. He rushed home and the columnist watched the actor phone every friend and relative he could think of. Doug's anxiety rose as he paced the floor and started imagining the worst. She had been in an accident! She had been kidnapped!

By the time Mary returned, her husband was on the verge of summoning the authorities. This scene, in the writer's mind, was clear evidence that the rumors of trouble in the marriage were false. Look at that devotion! Was this not the behavior of a man in passionate love?

---

* Some theaters would not take the film; others put it as the bottom bill of a double feature. Ultimately the film would turn a profit due to its very low costs, resulting essentially in a tax-deductible world tour for its star. But this was not yet evident in January 1932.

The scribe might better have considered whether this was the behavior of a man dealing with an alcoholic.

Mary had been drinking, drinking certainly since her mother's death, possibly before. Jack, Lottie, and Charlotte had never scorned the bottle, but Mary, breadwinner for all, had been as abstemious as her husband. Or almost. Doug Jr. noted, "She was something of a secret drinker when she was married to my father, but it was nothing serious at all; a glass of sherry sneaked at dinner, something like that." The more roguish element knew better. Eddie Sutherland, who was to direct *Mr. Robinson Crusoe*, recalled Jack Pickford bringing him to Mary's bathroom when they had run out of alcohol while on a bender. "Gin or whiskey?" he recalled Jack asking. "The hydrogen peroxide bottle's gin, the Listerine bottle's scotch."

Doug tried, ineffectually, to keep control over her drinking. May McAvoy recalled with astonishment an episode when the Pickfair butler refused to bring Mary and her guests drinks by the pool. "He said," she recalled, "that Mr. Fairbanks gave express orders that no drinks were to be served. Mary was so embarrassed," she added. "What right had that man to treat her so? Did he think she was a drunk?"

In fact, he was beginning to fear just that. And McAvoy did little to support her own indignation in her description of dinners at Pickfair. "After dinner . . . Mary would take us up to her room. She'd go in the bathroom and take a big slug of something, then rinse her mouth out with mouthwash."

There were other instances of her drinking—some in public settings. "If the truth were known," Fairbanks Jr. said, "the Pickford family was the reverse of the genie that comes out of the bottle; they all disappeared into it."

Doug's solution came in the form of a story of his own devising. He did not know it at the time, but *Mr. Robinson Crusoe* was to be the last film that he would personally produce. It was a simple tale of a wealthy yachtsman who, on a bet, spends time on a desert island to see if he can survive. Survive he does, with the aid of his faithful dog (played by Fairbanks's own mutt Rooney) and a beautiful girl Friday (or, in this case, Saturday).

Tom Geraghty worked up a script from Doug's ideas. His original treatment is revealing of Fairbanks's state of mind:

> Steve Drexel had grown suddenly tired of bluebloods, of conventions and formalities. Polite society bored him, debutantes annoyed him, and dinner parties distressed him. Steve was a bundle of nervous energy, handicapped by a fortune and a name, stifled by a life of inactivity. Occasionally he had kicked over the traces to become society's bad boy, but this time he had rebelled, once and for all.

A team was quickly assembled. Fairbanks chartered Joseph Schenck's yacht *Invader* and sent it ahead, animals and technicians aboard, to meet him in Tahiti.* Fairbanks sailed on February 27, 1932, from San Francisco aboard the *Makura*, accompanied by Eddie Sutherland, the director; silent film veteran William Farnum; trainer Chuck Lewis; and Maria Alba. The last of these was a Barcelonan beauty contest winner who had been brought to the United States to act in Spanish-language versions of American films.† She learned that she had won the role only a day before departing. She recalled that Pickford, whom she met for the first time on the boat, treated her coolly. Her youth and beauty seemed to threaten Mary, though the young actress did not understand why.

The press of Doug and Mary's mutual fame interfered with their parting. "They would retire to the main salon, and instantly be surrounded by tourists with autograph books," one observer noted. "They would flee to an upper deck, only to have cameramen pointing at

---

* The crew had a brief scare when Ga-Ga, a trained monkey brought for the filming, left a ship's bathtub faucet running, draining most of the freshwater for the trip. A timely tropical storm saved the day, and technicians and translators arrived in Tahiti safely.

† Dubbing had not yet been developed, and studios were obliged to film alternate-language versions of their major films.

their good-bye kiss. Finally they went into Doug's stateroom and bolted the door while the captain kindly kept the ship fifteen minutes beyond sailing time to give them a few moments together. When they came out Mary was crying. 'W-write to me, Doug—you know you've p-promised,' she said."

There is little evidence that he did so. They telegraphed each other liberally throughout their separation but largely on operational issues related to travel or business.

Alba recalled the trip on the *Makura*. The cast and crew would dine together every evening, discussing the film well into the night. Fairbanks was "a larger than life personality," she said. "Everybody gravitated to him." He was full of energy and never seemed to sleep. He was already on the deck when she arrived in the morning and stayed there past her retiring at night. "His brain," she said, making spiraling gestures over her ears, "was in constant motion." Their arrival at Papeete was remarkable only for the avidity of the local celebrations on their arrival. Fairbanks, as was his dapper wont, arrived with forty pieces of luggage.* He and Tom Geraghty bunked together at the house built by the recently deceased director F. W. Murnau, despite—or perhaps because—they had been warned by the locals that the place was haunted. After the first night, they discovered various objects had been moved or were missing. Each thought the other was playing tricks. On the second night, both were watchful. "I had a pair of white linen knickers on a chair near my bed," Fairbanks recalled. "First thing I knew, I heard a slight sound and saw the knickers move. I turned on my flash and the knickers were absolutely quiet. I turned the light off and waited. The knickers made a forward leap and landed on the floor [and] dashed almost to the door."

---

* Still, when he learned that local Chinese tailors would produce a linen suit for only three dollars, he could not resist. He gave the tailor one of his most expensive Savile Row outfits, with instructions to reproduce it exactly. This the man did, right down to duplicating a cigarette burn in the sleeve.

They moved out the next day ("because we had to get some sleep"). Ultimately they discovered the cause: rats were coming down from the thatched roofs and scurrying off with items to line their nests.

Rats were not the only natural challenges. An octopus almost killed poor Rooney, and a softball-size spider dropped on Tom Geraghty's neck and ran down his arm one evening. "I never saw a dinner table deserted so quickly," remembered one observer. Ever the practical joker, Doug rigged a replica spider out of lamp wicks and peanuts, and lowered it over Geraghty's bed with a string. Alba, recalling the pranks said, "These men are like children!"

There were other trials. Sound equipment failed. A tropical storm nearly foundered the yacht on a coral reef, also wreaking havoc on the sets. A native drowned soon after eating a hearty meal provided by the company. Fairbanks himself encountered difficulties. In one shot, he was to scamper up a palm tree. He fell, and the company laughed good-naturedly. He tried repeatedly but kept falling. In the words of Maria Alba, he became "so furious!" The crew, normally encouraged to mirth and good humor, was reduced to stifling their smiles not to frustrate him further.

His body had never failed him before. It was failing him now.

His reputation took another hit the day he was to film a high dive from the mast of the yacht. The natives had taken to calling him "the Man the Devil Fears," by virtue of not only his movie escapades (the Papeete theater had yet to be wired for sound) but because mosquitoes did not bite him. Hundreds turned out to see him take the dive, lining the shore and surrounding the yacht in their canoes. The activity attracted a number of sharks, however, and Fairbanks, spying the dorsal fins, started to descend the rigging. This disappointed the crowd, who let up a howl for him to jump. He was the Man the Devil Fears, they exclaimed. No shark would hurt him!

He was forced to demur. The devil might fear him, true, but there was a strong possibility that no one had thought to inform the sharks. The sequence was delayed to another day.

Still, most of the shoot was a delight. Alba recalled Fairbanks as "very gracious, very patient during filming." The company enjoyed two days' festivities when the chief of Fairbanks's technical staff married a Tahitian princess. Alba remembered Fairbanks pulling her out into the group and charming her into joining the dancers. Never, she said, had she laughed so hard in her life. Her private photos show a bare-chested Fairbanks, a wreath of flowers jauntily askew on his head, dancing with the natives as cheerfully and enthusiastically as he had done during the filming of *The Mollycoddle* with the Hopi, a dozen years before.

Others have suggested that Fairbanks and Alba had a "discreet affair" during the shoot. She adamantly denied this on direct questioning. He was married; she was heavily chaperoned. Further, charisma aside, he was "very full of himself." The evidence supports her story: they had never met before her audition; she only saw him upon their return for studio shoots and sound dubbing and at the film's premiere. Of the Polynesian beauties and their conquests, director Eddie Sutherland said, "That wasn't Doug, that was me. The girls there were very friendly, which meant most of them had the clap. I made friends with the doctor, and he told me which ones didn't. All Doug did was walk on the beach and look at the sunset with them. Doug was too square to fool around."

The film is a minor charmer, very close in situations to the other stranded-on-a-desert-island film Fairbanks made, *Down to Earth*. The problem, of course, was the intervening years. He was not making films every six weeks now but every year or two. Audiences had come to expect major films from Fairbanks the producer, and there was no going back. It did not do well.

This also applied to the journey. The trip home to San Francisco was, to Maria Alba's mind, not nearly as much fun as the journey out. There seemed to be tension coming from Fairbanks. Perhaps, she thought, he and William Farnum were not getting along. Since Doug served as best man at Farnum's wedding shortly after their return, this may not have been the case. More likely, the strain rose from the mere fact that he was *going* home.

Upon his arrival in early May at San Francisco, he met Mary with the misbehaving monkey on his shoulder by way of a gift.* He returned to life at Pickfair. Sound dubbing and studio shoots (about 30 percent of *Robinson Crusoe* was produced in Hollywood) distracted him for May, and the Los Angeles Olympics kept him busy in June. The expansion of Pickfair provided room to host guests for the games, among them Amelia Earhart, the Prince of Wales, and the king of Siam.

Doug seemed to need busyness, noise, to keep him diverted. He frightened the locals on the Fourth of July by firing a thousand blank rounds from a Thompson machine gun with George M. Cohan. Mary and others joined in the cacophony with sawed-off shotguns and Doug's vintage .45s.

The antique guns may have been what put him in mind of his western memorabilia collection. By the end of the month he and Mary parted ways again, she to New York City to confer on a story (she was always conferring on stories around this time, but not filming any), he to New Mexico to look for artifacts of the West. His attempt to buy an old western bar failed, but he conceived a plan to purchase a store where Billy the Kid had staged a gun battle. Further, he announced to the press his plans to start a movement to preserve such relics. "If something isn't done," he announced, "all these famous landmarks will go to looters like myself, and I wouldn't think of buying them if they were not being allowed to go to ruin."

He never bought the store. He never started the movement. Mary was the one to follow through, purchasing enough western relics to furnish a full bar in the basement of Pickfair. She had it assembled, complete with brass spittoons and a Wooton desk, as a Christmas surprise.

---

* Ga-Ga the monkey lived at the Pickford-Fairbanks Studios, until he shinnied up the side of the administration building and burst in on Samuel Goldwyn in the midst of a story conference. Goldwyn was not amused. Ga-Ga was donated to an Albuquerque zoo shortly thereafter.

But Christmas was four months away when he announced he would be off on another adventure. This time his motive for escape may have included jealousy. Magazine articles were getting bold, noting "rumors were current that linked Mary's name with Buddy Rogers, Johnny Mack Brown and a number of others." Never mind that in the same paragraph, Doug's name was associated with Lupe Vélez, a Hawaiian princess, a British peeress. A man could not stand to be cuckolded, regardless of his own sins.

And by this point, it was clear indeed that this is what was happening. Shortly after his return from filming *Crusoe*, Paul O'Brien (Cap's son) reluctantly told Fairbanks of an incident made public during his absence. Mary and Buddy had been boating on the Hudson River. They were alone. This quiet indiscretion would never have been noted but for the failure of the boat's engine and the embarrassing need to be towed to shore.* O'Brien stated that Doug simply "laughed like hell." Knowing his jealousy, one suspects that the laugh was hollow. Or, perhaps, brave.

He appeared to have kept his own counsel on the subject. Upon departing, he left behind fifty handwritten notecards to accompany flowers that he had arranged to greet her each morning. As with his other correspondence, she kept every scrap, and there is poignancy in reading them with the benefit of hindsight. Was he desperate to keep the marriage whole? Or placating a wife from whom he was escaping?

One can only guess. His words remain for more intuitive minds to interpret: "For my sweetheart," "I want my Frin," "A thought in every petal," "To the boss," "Birdeens on the neck," "Look at your picture 100 times a day dear."

And so the wandering hero wandered again. His claimed intent was to go to Tibet to hunt longhaired tigers, but he had departed in such

---

* In Booton Herndon's 1977 biography, O'Brien claims this event occurred before Fairbanks left to film *Around the World in Eighty Minutes*. O'Brien's memory was understandably imperfect, given the passage of years. Contemporary news accounts place it shortly after *Mr. Robinson Crusoe*.

a rush that he forgot to pack his gun. He spent more time on Asian golf courses. It was from Shanghai that he wired advice on Mary's next (and ultimate) film. She had posed the question: should she take another try at *Secrets*? He replied: LIKE IDEA SHANTY TOWN OR IRISH STORY STILL STRONG FOR SECRETS UPSETS SOMETIME BEST THING WORK MORE INTENSIVELY YOUR BACK AGAINST WALL STOP IF YOU REALLY FEEL COULD HELP WILL RETURN PRESENT CONDITION HISTORY OF MANY YOUR BEST PICTURES ALL LOVE.

Her reply is lost, but in any event he did not return. He golfed, then traveled again: Hong Kong, Saigon, Singapore, Bali, Ceylon, Cairo, Venice. By December he had decided his next destination: London. He would go there to buy clothes, he wired her.

Perhaps that was his intent. He was an inveterate clotheshorse, after all. He was routinely listed on the top-ten best-dressed lists with such contemporaries as the Prince of Wales.* Ten years earlier his valet had defined his wardrobe:

> He possesses 60 to 70 suits of clothes, 35 overcoats (he has a special fondness for this garment and anyone can sell him any sort of new one),† 50 pairs of shoes, to say nothing of outside footgear such as sneakers, slippers and boots, 8 to 10 dozen shirts, 19 dozen hand-kerchiefs, 300 neckties and many dozens of garments of even more intimate character which it is not necessary to fully describe here.

His wardrobe had only grown since then. But clothing may not have been the only temptation. Sylvia, after all, was in London. Whatever

---

* In 1930 Edward Knoblock provided him a reference to one of the top Savile Row tailors, Anderson and Sheppard. There his records are still kept, along with the notations ("double pleats, high") that characterized his taste. He in turn passed on the favor for friends such as Victor Fleming. His son ultimately ended up getting his bespoke suits from the same source, although not on his father's referral but on that of Noël Coward.

† According to a former managing director at Anderson and Sheppard, he "had a fetish for overcoats: we made him so many that we had to keep a large book with cloth cuttings so he did not duplicate them."

the cause, he lingered there so long that he ended up having to make another hasty scramble to be at Pickfair in time for Christmas. There he was met with a door decorated like a Christmas package. Behind it was the western bar that Mary had had so carefully assembled and installed in his absence. One cannot imagine that he could have been anything but pleased—perhaps even touched.

But it would be the last Christmas they would spend together.

19

"Felt Terribly Blue . . . Although I Was Laughing"

T HE YEAR 1933 BODED ill for Doug and Mary both, but she received the first blow—literally. Shortly before New Year's Eve, a falling studio light struck her on the head. Doug was on the set at the time, and she came back to consciousness in his arms, badly bruised but otherwise none the worse for wear.

Far more serious was the figurative blow she was dealt a few days later. Jack had been in a Paris hospital since the prior October, in the final stages of neurosyphilis (or, as the papers more politely termed his condition, "progressive multiple neuritis"). Doug had visited him during his return from Asia, but Mary had not seen her dying brother in months. A New Year's Day telegram brought the news that Jack was in a delirium.

Mary was the consummate professional. No one would have known her worries the next day, when she served as the first female grand marshal of the Tournament of Roses Parade. She rode in a coach drawn by two white horses, leading a four-mile procession that carried the theme "fairy tale in flowers." Doug at her side, she smiled through her time in the reviewing stand and at the luncheon in her honor.

Her brother died the following day.

Doug stayed in Southern California long enough for Jack's body to arrive and, grim faced, to escort the grieving Mary and Lottie at the

Forest Lawn cemetery in Glendale. But before the month was over, he was on a train to New York City. His wire to Mary from the first stop was to define his remaining years: GOOD NIGHT DEAR FELT TERRIBLY BLUE WHEN I LEFT ALTHOUGH I WAS LAUGHING.

He had reason to be blue, but so did she. It is not clear exactly when she learned that another woman had tempted her husband. It was said that a bracelet intended for Sylvia was mis-delivered to Mary. Some accounts claim that she gave him an ultimatum during his Christmas visit.

There is indirect evidence that the issue of Sylvia erupted during this time. Telegrams between Doug and Mary had always, by necessity, been coded; in later years Sylvia Ashley was referred to as "McLaren." In their telegraphic exchange as he traveled east in 1933, Sylvia may have been assigned the name of Fairbanks's mongrel dog, Rooney, while Mary retained her nicknames "Frin" and "Hipper" and Doug was once again "Duber." In the first of several messages, Fairbanks (referring to himself, as he often did, in the third person) gives a clue to their parting scene:

GOT MAD AT HIM IN THE STATION FRIT* DUBER.

The second was more specific:

FEEL TERRIBLY ABOUT ROONEY MUCH WORSE ABOUT FRIN HURRY O [*sic*] LOVE YOU.

Mary's response demonstrated her fury:

JEALOUS ROONEY AND MAD AT THE DUBER FRIT† ON ALL DOGS TWELVE FOOT STREAM ON ROONEY LOVE HIPPER.

---

* It does not require a rhyming dictionary to deduce the expletive Fairbanks was going for here.

† Ditto Pickford.

But her answers softened as he continued to cross the country. As he boarded a ship in New York City in early February, he spoke to reporters about his hopes that Mary would join him abroad. "She's got to come along," he said. "I couldn't get anywhere without her to make the plans. . . . She has the head and I have the feet." Indeed, she did plan on joining him, embarking on a train east later that week. He wired her from St. Moritz: BON VOYAGE DEAR COME ON AND PLAY DUBER.

He was in a mood to conciliate. He wired Chuck Lewis's wife, traveling with Mary aboard the Italian-bound SS *Rex*, that he was going to board the ship at an earlier stop to surprise her. Surprised she may have been, but it is clear that on this reunion they were to ultimately to be disappointed. If he had fostered expectations that they would return to their pattern of travel together or that she would suddenly find sobriety, or if she had nursed the illusion that he would give up this new woman and return to Pickfair, they were to find their hopes mutually dashed. She wrote in later years that it was on this trip that she learned about Sylvia, although the telegrams suggest otherwise. Perhaps it was here that the misdirected bracelet brought the message home. In any event, she was steaming home on the *Rex* in a matter of weeks. Upon arriving in New York, she headed straight to Chicago, where actor/musician Buddy Rogers's orchestra was playing.

Douglas spent March and April in Biarritz, Monte Carlo, Paris— golfing in tournaments and wiring Mary about his travels as blithely as if there had been no strain at all between them. Her replies were more somber. In early April she wired him: ADVISE YOUR CURBING YOUR EXPENSES AS MUCH AS POSSIBLE LOVE. His reply came from the most expensive hotel in Biarritz: DON'T WORRY REASONABLE CURBING EXPENSES CAN WEATHER PRESENT CONDITIONS . . . OUTLOOK CHEERFUL LOVE. He then left for Spain to see a bullfight.

No wonder, one is tempted to say, that the poor woman drank.

He returned briefly in early May, being photographed leaping over the railing of the *Aquitania* before rushing home to celebrate his fiftieth birthday with Mary. She asked if he planned to stay. He assured her he did. But she found steamer tickets that told another tale, and without warning she departed the night before his birthday on a train to New York City.

He was left opening gifts in strained silence as Kenneth Davenport, Chuck Lewis, and friend Earle Browne stoutly attempted to keep up the celebratory chatter. By the time Robert arrived at the house, the chauffeur was loading the car for a trip to the airport. Doug asked him to come along. Robert's recollection of the conversation was distinct. "Mary didn't tell me she was leaving," Doug said to him. "She's never acted like this before."

Robert pointed out the obvious cause, adding, "One trouble, Douglas, everybody's been talking too damn much."

"You're right," was the reply. "If they'd all shut up and just leave it to Mary and me! Well this time we'll talk everything out. That's all we need, just a good talk." He demonstrated a dogged inability to assume accountability for his own actions. "*That* woman doesn't mean a thing to me," he continued. "And I'm not going to stand in the corner with a dunce's cap on my head because of a simple emotional binge. I've got it out of my system and that's that."

But he hadn't. He caught up with Mary in Albuquerque, as he planned, and managed to charm his way into her compartment on the train for the remainder of the trip east. Mary claimed that he continued to vehemently deny the rumors about Sylvia. Before sailing on the *Queen Mary*, he asked Mary her intentions. Would she wait for him to return? "I replied that I would do nothing and that, while he was hurting me cruelly, he was like a man with a high temperature and even if he struck me in his delirium I would not blame him, knowing he was not responsible."

High-sounding words. Her recollections are colored, of course, by her need to preserve and craft her own image. Given the fact that she was herself conducting an affair with Buddy Rogers at the time, this reply is a little too calculated, too saintly, perhaps. One suspects that she said something far more to the point.

He boarded the ship with Tom Geraghty and Doug Jr., and by June he was back in London with Sylvia. He remained, he wired Mary, to see the Ryder Cup matches. He wanted to buy some suits. He was up to his neck, he claimed, in tailors.

He was up to his neck in other troubles as well. Sylvia, it seems, required a medical procedure. That she was pregnant is conjecture, true, but it is not an unreasonable one. She was young; he was fertile. A showgirl in that era could have multiple "appendectomies"—a medical anomaly that disappeared with the advent of reliable birth control. And in Fairbanks's next action there is a hint of—what? Panic? Obligation toward Sylvia? It is hard to say. But whatever the motive, he wired Mary stating that he was staying in England and that if she wished to remain at Pickfair, she would have to assume full financial responsibility for it.

This was hitting her where she lived: in the heart *and* the purse. She showed the telegram to Frances Marion. Frances, in turn, convinced her to show it to columnist Louella Parsons.

And so an inky explosion ensued. Every newspaper carried the story on the front page. Doug and Mary were separating!

Sympathy was universally with Mary. "I love my husband—divorce from someone you love as dearly and tenderly as I have loved Douglas for sixteen years is an almost unbearable thought," Louella quoted her as saying—adding for effect that Mary spent hours at home weeping.

In the first days of the scandal, Sylvia's existence was only hinted at. "Mary is said to have been displeased by Doug's liking for the English nobility, by whom he has been extensively entertained," Louella hinted slyly. But soon the word was out, and Sylvia's seedy origins were recounted at length. She belonged to a London society composed "principally of ex-actresses [whom] hotheaded young lords had wedded into the English nobility." She was of the sort that would go anywhere for free food and drink. Unlike our dear Mary, Sylvia had hair that was *dirty* blonde. And she was a *terrible* smiler. She had a lithographic smile, it was written. "A prop smile sterilized of all real mirth. The smile of the blonde in the second row end."

The press—particularly the Hearst press, happy publishers of Louella Parsons's delicious scoop—was even harder on Doug. The gloves were off, and the schadenfreude was gleeful. He was a jolly old bounder who was tremendously flattered by royal names, the only short man anyone had seen Mary Pickford dance with. He wasn't really as large and powerful as he had appeared to be in films; he had merely surrounded himself with shorter men. He was going to give up his citizenship and become a British subject. He was so unpopular that United Artists had to remove his name from all UA publicity material, including the stationery.* He was rumored to have acquired a monocle, "which Mary Pickford now can put first among her reasons for wanting a divorce."

Mary, on the other hand, the scribes wrote, "has met her problems with a dignity that has made those who know her marvel at her courage."

It was a public relations disaster. Robert attempted to stifle the flames. It was "all a tempest in a teapot," he said, "and will blow over." Doug avoided the press but was finally caught at a London hospital, visiting the recuperating Sylvia. Exclaiming, "I don't want to say anything," he beat an ignominious retreat down a fire escape. He did not aid his cause by going to Italy when Sylvia went there to convalesce.

Fairly or not, he was exasperated. The press had taken Mary's side, and he had no retort. He could not even imply his wife's infidelity or her alcoholism without being an unbearable cad and scoundrel. His moral code may have been remarkably elastic, but it did not stretch that far.

This was never better demonstrated than in the "exclusive" that *Motion Picture Magazine* ran in March 1934, a putative provision of both Mary's and Doug's sides of the story. Mary provided a personal interview. She was philosophic, and she couched her words carefully. "I believe that a great deal of love, so-called, is selfishness. Mere possessiveness," she said—perhaps remembering the incident on her honeymoon when her husband abandoned her in their German quarters. "It is the ME and not the YOU that matters. I think we do not learn this philosophy—this acceptance of life as it is and not as we would like to have it, childishly petulant, while we are very young. . . . All of which means that Douglas is a child-spirit. He is perpetually young, you know. His eager enthusiasms, his abounding vitality, his interests

---

* There is no evidence that this was true.

that fly the world around are *young*. The very pictures he makes are indicative of the boy in him." Mary, in her version of events, was an old soul. Douglas was not. "I took the final step between Douglas and myself because I believe it to be for the good of both of us," she continued. "I wanted to set him free, not only for myself, but for him. It will define our positions clearly."

It was tidy and dignified, and it was an adept portrayal of her generosity of spirit. How was one to counter this?

He could not, *would* not, speak directly. Not only would it be ungentlemanly, but it would only make him look worse. Instead, he sent a friend to tell his side of the tale. It was likely Tom Geraghty. Whomever the anonymous interview subject was, he handled the case as deftly as could be done. First, he told the reporter, Fairbanks would never speak on the subject. "His parting words to me were, 'Don't defend me! I must keep silent!'" But, the source said, he must deliberately break this promise. His regard for Fairbanks was too deep to "stand idly by while Hollywood and the whole world viciously attack him."

First, he planted the hint of Buddy. "The trouble between Mary and Doug started in the latter part of 1927 when she was making *My Best Girl* with Buddy Rogers. Vaguely, Doug and Mary suddenly realized that their perfect accord was slipping in spots because her interests had suddenly turned away from Douglas."

He covered Charlotte's death, and the bobbing of Mary's curls. "She had new ambitions—new plans for a greater fame than had ever before been hers. But Douglas was tired of their monotonous life—circumscribed, as it was, almost entirely by work. He pleaded with Mary that now was their time to play. . . . Mary refused to entertain—even for a moment—the suggestion of retirement."

It was subtle but potentially effective. Mary had developed an interest in another man, and her ambitions were thwarting the simple boyish desires of her husband to play. Now he moved in closer to the issue at hand. He hinted at her drinking.

"Then, very suddenly, Mary became the center of a lively bunch of youngsters who were beginning to make their mark in pictures," he continued. "She entertained frequently and gaily. It was like a second youth to her." The source did not note the apparent contradiction: mere moments before, the complaint had been that Mary only wanted to work and did not play. Now, it seems, she was playing too much—and with the wrong crowd. "Doug tried desperately to enter into the fun of Mary's new friends. Always keeping in superb physical condition, he had never taken a drink before. But now, so that he might not feel an outsider, he drank with the rest of them. And he hated it."

Then, according to the confidant, a deal was struck. Doug would stick around Hollywood for six months of the year, doing as Mary wished, as long as the other six months she would travel with him, "doing the thing closest to *his* heart!" The first half of 1929 was thus devoted to *The Taming of the Shrew*. Here, the informant said, it was apparent to everyone that something was wrong. The tension on the film set was evident throughout the entire shooting schedule. Then came the second half of the deal: a half year of travel. "I don't believe that either one of them doubted for a moment that the trip would set aright whatever was amiss with them."

But again, according to the source, the problem lay with Mary. She was a poor traveler. She got seasick often. It was Doug who was invited everywhere, while Mary remained in her suite at the hotel. Then came Doug's first solo trip to the golf tournament. The source made no whisper of any possible infidelity on Fairbanks's part. There was no English lady leading him astray. Instead, the narrative took us directly to Doug's "jaunt to the Orient" and Mary's refusal to go along. Fairbanks made *Around the World in Eighty Minutes*, claimed the source, to stem the tide of gossip and protect his wife's pride. His solo trip was clothed as a location shoot.

By the time he was filming *Mr. Robinson Crusoe*, the informant said "both of them now knew definitely that their romance was over. . . . He hated Hollywood society; and she hated his restless feet."

Now, he went in for the kill. While Doug was manfully making his tropical comedy, Mary was "favoring Buddy Rogers' constant attentions." This "hurt Doug frightfully. Doug was not a man to be brought back to a woman's side by jealousy. He was like a little boy who had been slapped. He was too bewildered to think coherently. Doug," the source said, "was fed up!"

He tried to win her back. She tried to win him back. "But a divine spark can never be rekindled," the source said resignedly. "Mary made gestures to prove to him that her life could go on without him. She entertained lavishly. She became a familiar figure at the popular restaurants. At premières she was escorted by Buddy Rogers. . . . Don't blame Doug entirely for this smash-up."

It was a valiant effort, but it failed. The world saw Mary as the victim, and their hero became their former hero.

With the public relations detritus coming down around his ears, Doug tried to turn back to work. Issuing a flat denial ("all nonsense!") that he intended to become a British subject, he toured an English film studio with the Prince of Wales. He had seen *The Private Life of Henry VIII* before its release and had been so impressed with Alexander Korda's film that he wired UA, suggesting the film be distributed in the United States. By mid-August, a joint deal between UA and London Films was announced for a production unit in London, with Fairbanks at its head. Doug would become a shareholder in London Films and star in a film about Don Juan. (One can only wonder what went through his wife's mind at the latter news.) Other stars, he claimed, would be brought into the company: Leslie Howard, Herbert Marshall, Colin Clive, Boris Karloff—possibly even Charlie Chaplin and Charles Laughton.

The plan made sense, from a business perspective. The British market represented nearly 80 percent of UA's foreign profits. In the late 1920s the British government had passed the so called Quota Act, which required that 5 percent of exhibitors' films and 7.5 percent of distributors' films in Great Britain be of British origin. UA had signed a contract with Herbert Wilcox in 1932 to produce twelve pictures a year for the following three years. In 1933 the company signed Alexander Korda to a sixteen-picture contract. The success of *Henry VIII* contributed to Korda's joining UA as a partner in September 1935.

To Mary, he sent mixed messages, to which she responded with the sensitivity of a tuning fork. Signals were negative: he gallivanted publicly with Sylvia and booked a suite at the London hotel where she stayed; she put Pickfair on the market. Then signals were positive: he telephoned, claiming that he did *not* want a divorce; she took the house off the market.

They would seesaw thus for the next two years.

Having waited five months to file for divorce, she sent a letter to one of her lawyers making her frustrations clear:

> You are probably wondering why we have all taken so long in going through with the legal proceedings but, in self-protection, I wanted to leave no stone unturned. I can honestly say I have done everything that anyone could expect of me and now I am ready next Monday to start proceedings.
>
> . . . Once before we started to negotiate for the house and told Robert Fairbanks our intentions of filing suit, which information he transmitted to Douglas. Five hours after Robert had sent the wire, Douglas called me long distance. He said he had heard a report from several sources which he hoped was not true. I replied that it was true and he asked if I would reconsider. That evening I received a telegram from him saying that he, personally, did not desire a divorce and unless I had a special reason for wishing one he hoped I would not go through with it. Having heard nothing from him since although I answered his wire very fully, setting forth my reasons and more or less leaving the door open to him to reply and tell me what his plans for the future were and what he expected of me. I did not hear from him; however, I did receive a cable from Tom Geraghty who, as you know, has been with him ever since he left New York, stating that Douglas was crushed and terribly upset about the continued attacks of W.R.* upon the ridiculous question of his becoming a British subject and that he would never love anyone but me.

---

* William Randolph Hearst.

To me the whole affair continues to grow more puzzling. Up to the time I heard from him on the telephone I was convinced he wanted his freedom. Now I don't know what to think. Robert assures me that Douglas will return after the completion of his next picture but that seems an eternity away and, in the meantime, Mr. Wright* fears something might happen that might prove injurious to me.

Knowing Douglas' temperament as I do, I realize that he would not fail to come to me or at least communicate with me if I were of any importance to his future happiness or if he included me in his plans. It is quite possible that those close to him have convinced him that a divorce at this time would not be to the interests of his picture; however, I may be doing him an injustice.

The "next picture" to which she referred was to be his last. But there were miles to go before *The Private Life of Don Juan* would be screened. Mary officially filed suit on December 8, 1933, citing what Fairbanks Jr. described as his father's "gypsy foot" and his public pro-nouncements "that he had no interest in life except travel." This, Mary's filing pointed out, "destroyed the legitimate ends of matrimony." As of 1930, she stated, he "disregarded her wishes and assumed an attitude of indifference toward their marital status." When the press asked her attorney what Miss Pickford meant in the claim that Mr. Fairbanks "lacked consideration for her feelings and sensibilities," he was forced to hedge politely, finally claiming that Doug "stole the show" in *The Taming of the Shrew*. What could be more thoughtless, he implied, than upstaging your wife?

It was a sad, absurd claim in a sad, absurd drama. And once Mary actually filed for divorce, the ever-variable Doug let it be known through back channels that he was open to reconciliation. Thus began a series of communications that were conducted not only by letter and telegram but also by headline. Mary, smiling to reporters, stated, "I cannot affirm

---

* Likely Lloyd Wright, one of Mary's divorce attorneys.

or deny any reports that, well, that there may be stockings above the mantel-piece at Pickfair on Christmas Day." Stopping in Chicago en route to New York, she preached, "Women ought to learn that kindness is sometimes the most devastating and weakening influence. Wives especially make this mistake. There ought to be a school where women are taught how to be reasonably selfish. It is the unselfish ones who ruin themselves and everyone depending on them." They cabled each other at Christmas. She wired him at New Year's that columnist Karl Kitchen would carry a letter for him across the Atlantic. He wired back that this was an excellent idea. She sent him his 1934 horoscope. He sent Joseph Schenck from London to Los Angeles with the message: "Kiss Mary and tell her that I am coming to America just to see her." (Schenck reported with some poignancy that Mary's "face lighted up and while she made no reply . . . I felt that she was drinking in every word and that in her heart she still loves Douglas.")

The delicate long-distance dance was brought up short when Lord Ashley, he of the drooping Sandhurst mustache and the missing chin, suddenly appeared on the scene. Initially he claimed no knowledge of "Miss Pickford's husband" having any acquaintance with his wife. But less than two months later, in February 1934, he filed suit for divorce, naming Fairbanks as the correspondent.

Doug received notice of the papers at quarter to three in the morning, while escorting Lady Ashley to her home in the Mayfair district of London. The press was in wait. He beat a retreat on foot to his own hotel suite, his only recorded words being "Very embarrassing." The next morning he was to be seen, his face hidden by an old hat and a turned-up collar, dodging a phalanx of journalists and driving his Rolls-Royce to the home of his solicitor. There he was observed through a front window frantically pacing back and forth for the next three hours. "Frequently," one journalist wrote, "he put his hands to his head in a gesture of distraction and appeared greatly distressed." He wired Mary: HIPPER DEAR PASSING THROUGH WORST PERIOD I HAVE EVER KNOWN TRYING TO PULL MYSELF TOGETHER TO START PICTURE LOVE DUBER.

Yet still, he stood a chance. Mary told the ever-paternal Schenck that, "if Doug would woo her all over again there was every possibility their difficulties could be patched up and their marriage resumed without a divorce."

Schenck was not alone in his efforts. Tom Geraghty scuttled back and forth with messages. And Doug began a series of transatlantic calls. He was near Barcelona, scouting exteriors for *Don Juan*, when he visited boxer Max Schmeling's training camp. Schmeling's manager, Joe Jacobs, showed no hesitation in giving the press his opinion:

> It's in the bag. How do I know? Say, Doug come over from London to Schmeling's training camp near Barcelona, and spent three days with us. Didn't I see him dashing for a phone to call her up? Twice he calls her in New York and once in Detroit and when he'd get her, boy, how he would talk. The rate to New York was $34.50 for 3 minutes and it was $32 to Detroit, but he didn't watch the clock. When a fellow spends that much dough to talk to a woman he just has to be in love with her. At first, Mary was going to go over there, but Doug said "no." He said that people would think she was chasing him. So he's going to come back in June—just as soon as he finishes with his picture work over there.

He was described as happy and cheerful as he returned to England for studio shooting—"a new man [who] apparently has forgotten about the Lady Ashley affair." Said another insider: "It is just a matter of time now. . . . The Ashley incident only caused strained relations for two days. The first fury quickly subsided and now the situation is even better than it was then." Doug, it was said, had given up plans to stop working. Mary would withdraw her divorce petition.

But he would not have been Doug if he had been stable. As he got closer to reconciliation, he undercut himself. For the filming of *Don Juan*, he rented an enormous estate on over a thousand acres in North Mimms Park in Hertfordshire. There were eighty-two bedrooms—so many that Tom Geraghty got lost one night trying to find his and was reduced to changing clothes in the hall. With this many sleeping chambers, one might have hoped that Fairbanks would have had the discretion to place that of Lady Ashley, when she visited—and she visited continuously—a little farther away from his own. Their chambers, however, were adjoining—a point Lord Ashley was happy to make in a supplemental petition to the court in July.

Mary responded in kind. She started having frequent—and public— dinner dates with Buddy. Still, her signals were positive. "Men are like naughty little boys," she told a reporter (presumably for her husband's consumption). "When they are tired of being naughty they are glad to come home."

Perhaps he was tired of being naughty. Filming finished, he gave up North Mimm's Park, as well as his Alford Street town house. He went to the south of France with Sylvia, but still kept up his calls to Mary. It was from there that he abruptly boarded the SS *Rex* half an hour before sailing, leaving Sylvia without so much as a by-your-leave. Informed by reporters of his departure, she could only speculate that her errant lover might disembark at Gibraltar.

He did not. He arrived in New York City in mid-August, temples and mustache a little grayer after his fourteen-month absence but grinning broadly. The smile continued as he crossed the country, disappearing only for his appearance at the Colorado funeral of his sister-in-law Margaret, John's widow, who died while he was en route. A private train car brought him to Los Angeles, where Robert's daughters met him. With them were reporters. He refused, they said, to discuss his marital affairs. But he was smiling the Fairbanks smile.

He wasted no time. He met Mary in Beverly Hills, getting into her car and driving her for hours, with his own car and driver trailing behind. They were reported to be joking and laughing. They dined together at Pickfair that night and then went for another long drive in the moonlight. He was there bright and early the next morning, and the pattern repeated. By the weekend, they had retired to their respective corners—Mary at Pickfair and Doug at Rancho Zorro—to think things over. He brought her there on Monday, and they inspected the gardens and discussed locations for the proposed ranch house. He had, the newspapers reported, "his old-time zest."

When Mary reconstructed this period for her autobiography, twenty years later, she portrayed herself as resolute. Her heart wept for him, she said, but her mind was made up. She was adamant. But memory and pride are tricky things, and the evidence is that she wavered mightily. When in late August 1934 reporters were asking her about a reconciliation, she replied coyly, "I won't deny it." A matter of weeks later, things were different. She shortened her hair—Doug hated her hair short—and announced that she was not going to be "rushed into any decision." And by the time of the UA directors' meeting in late September, things seemed worse. They smiled distantly at each other but only spoke perfunctorily. The photographer asked for a picture of the two, but Doug shook his head and motioned for Schenck to sit between them. In the photo, they looked strained and glum.

By October, things had warmed up again. They telegraphed frequently when apart: he was her "Darling Duber"; she was his "Darling Hipper." He would send her gardenias and call her from distant airstrips, stuffing coin after coin into the payphone, before making yet another of his dashes to Pickfair for dinners with Mary and the likes of Kay Francis and the Countess Di Frasso. They may even have resumed sexual relations. In one telegram Doug wrote: HIPPER DARLING I MISSED YOU SO MUCH DEAR CERTAINLY MISSED THE LITTLE FRIEND LOVE DOUGLAS. In fact, he missed the little friend so much that he proposed following her to New York. She wired back: DUBER DARLING THINK IT WOULD BE IN VERY QUESTIONABLE TASTE . . . UNPLEASANT AND GRUELING ENOUGH AS IT IS LOVE YOU HIPPER.

He announced that he was selling his holdings in London Films and would make movies only in the States. At a Kansas train stop, Mary reportedly told a friend that she and Douglas "were reconciled—happily reconciled." By the time she arrived in Chicago, she denied the story as a rumor. The laconic Robert was asked his opinion and could only offer: "Well, they've been running around together a lot."

Still, there were strains. Sylvia's divorce was coming up, and it was uncontested. Sylvia herself seemed to have lost no time and was reported to be hobnobbing with a young, wealthy Warwickshire peer.

Fairbanks was conspicuous by his absence at the *Don Juan* premiere in Hollywood in late November.

The film, a failure at the time, is little short of a painful revelation. Either Fairbanks had a strong sense of irony or Korda had a brilliant sense of casting. Perhaps both. But no stronger statement had been made to date on the effects of age and the thousand petty stings that come with a fall from celebrity. Substitute "movie star" for "famed lover" and the tale is that *of* Fairbanks, enacted *by* Fairbanks. It is subtly played and rueful, both superbly entertaining and heartbreaking to watch.

His introduction in the film is gradual: first we see him only by shadows, throwing roses to lovely women on their balconies. We progress to just his shapely leg, having its reflexes tested by a doctor. The doctor wishes to know his age. He won't give it. His problem? "When I sit down to a quiet game with a lady, I'm no longer sure of holding the cards."

At one point Korda holds the camera in for a close-up of Fairbanks, looking handsome yet world weary, his face showing the early sagging indignity of the years. He delivers his speech with none of the pressure or fist-waving urgency of his earlier sound performances. He speaks simply, with subdued pain. "I want to rest," he says. "To lead a simple life with simple people. Not to be a celebrity for a while. To be unknown. No women, and alone. To eat what I like, to do what I like." It is either a brilliant performance or a man stating an actual belief.

The film is relentless. At one point a jealous husband kills a Don Juan imitator, and Don Juan's adviser urges him to let well enough alone. "Leave off while they still think of you as you were . . . ten years ago. Before these wrinkles, these lines, these gray hairs." Don Juan tries to convince the mob that he still lives. He interrupts a biographical stage performance. *He* is Don Juan!

The crowd hoots him down—painful documentation that no man can live up to the illusion he has created. The illusion outstrips him, and the audience, worshipping the fantasy, destroys the frail form behind it. Better to be a large, grand shadow casting roses than a mere man upon the stage, too short, and perhaps not as broad in the shoulders as everyone thought.

The world was not ready for such irony. Viewers still wanted their protagonists triumphant and not stumbling into old age. Or perhaps they did not wish to see the hero of their childhood tales in a story so amusingly jaded and ironic. Alistair Cooke, one of the many who, as a child, adored Fairbanks, wrote indignantly of the film, "There is hardly a clue to the undoubted fact that Fairbanks is a truer artist than any of the more pretentious ones who surrounded him."

It mattered not. The film was a failure.

And in the life-imitating-art category, the details on the Ashley divorce did nothing to help. The entire hearing lasted only eight minutes, but that was long enough for such salacious testimony as that of Lady Ashley entering Fairbanks's bedroom at the Hyde Park Hotel, with instructions from Doug that they were not to be disturbed, or that they were both living in the Dorchester Hotel the prior September, with Doug leaving the bedroom in his dressing gown and pajamas and the good lady being noted therein "bareheaded." The divorce was quickly granted, and Fairbanks was ordered to pay the $10,000 expenses.

This brought out the Hearst press, and for Doug it was the equivalent of poking a bear. He wired Mary: HIPPER DEAR LOUELLA IS AT IT AGAIN THINK IT IS TERRIBLE ABSOLUTELY UNFOUNDED.

Some exchange of words—likely never to be known—followed, and the situation worsened. HIPPER DARLING POOR DUBER FRIT FRIT, he wired. Her response: DARLING WAS SORRY TO HAVE UPSET YOU BUT AM WARNING YOU BECAUSE I LOVE YOU.

By Christmas week it all came to a head. He was in New York City, running from reporters and autograph seekers by hiding in restaurant kitchens. She was at Pickfair, her second Christmas alone. It was Christmas Eve. They spoke on the phone. It did not go well.

After he had hung up on her, she sat down with a pencil and two pieces of thin, cream-colored paper. Her handwriting was steady, although her use of pronouns was not. She wrote:

> In case in after years you may seek to blame me—make me unhappy and miserable because of what has happened I want to write down while it is still fresh in my mind some of Duber's remarks on the telephone tonight. He was unfortunate in being found* and threatened Frin that things would be different <u>when</u> it was known what Frin was doing—that she was alright since she had good publicity being such a good friend of Hearst's—he couldn't see why he shouldn't go to London since Hipper saw that fellow†—what did I expect him to do—he <u>wanted</u> to go—he was surprised and annoyed with Allen.‡ He was going mad not having anything to do—although he had just spent that evening with a nineteen year old "flirt". He could see no harm in his going over there and said I was taking it much too seriously—when I asked him please not to go he said I had no right to—that he had made no demands upon me for seven years, which is a plain damned lie—I can't remember the exact words he used about the publicity and Hearst, but it was very insulting and made me cry—He ended our conversation by hanging up. Although I told him it was the last time I would ever speak to him—had he been willing to talk things over with me and plan our joint future things might have been so different—I was willing to forgive and forget—I know I've been far from perfect and not entirely blameless but the Duber preferred to discuss our personal affairs with all our friends but never with me. The innuendos about all the young girls, what transpired in the living room after he had put me in the car and sent me to work should prove (if any further proof is necessary) that our future together was absolutely hopeless—I simply could not pick up and go with

---

* Found out in his infidelity, as opposed to Mary, who was not.
† Buddy Rogers.
‡ Likely Allen Boone, a family friend who dined with them at Pickfair during the reconciliation attempt.

him on a boat for a year—leave Gwynne, a young girl just emerging into life, my business also needs my attention—besides I know that [I] could never have stood the sea sickness and misery of living and travelling on that small boat.

Well! Hawkes* (and believe me she's well named) is welcome to it—I shall be interested to watch their union—they should be able to vie with one another in seeing who will be the most inconstant. Will she be willing to undergo the hardships of travel that I have suffered? Be as self-effacing and considerate of his every whim? Well, I pray God he won't be too unhappy. I love him and probably will as long as I live—and I certainly don't want him punished. God give me strength to go through these next few weeks and wipe all bitterness and condemnation out of my heart—make me grateful for the good that has been ours, and forget all else.

She sealed the note in an envelope and wrote on the outside:

Private and Personal
Written December 24, 1934

She placed it in a small cardboard box that contained every love letter, note, and card that Douglas had sent her since 1917. The note was torn open, roughly, at some later date. One wonders: by whom? Mary herself in later days, when drinking and age had trapped her in her own bedroom for months, years? A curious Buddy, or his last wife? Or was it an employee of the auction house that ended up with the little cardboard box seventy years later, leaving the letter open to the coarse hands of dealers looking to buy for resale?

We shall never know. But we do know what Mary did that night. She wired Douglas Fairbanks at the Waldorf Astoria. His Christmas gift was a telegram: DARLING I UNDERSTAND IT IS TOO BAD THE WHOLE SORRY BUSINESS LOVE YOU HIPPER.

---

* Lady Ashley's maiden name.

20

A Living Death

DOUG BOOKED PASSAGE ON the *Isle de France* just before sailing, and boarded, in the words of one reporter, "deaf to all queries." He drank little and exercised compulsively on the voyage. He appeared worn upon arrival at Le Havre, France. Sylvia Ashley was waiting. They went to Paris, then St. Moritz, Fairbanks steadily refusing to make any personal statements. They were dancing until four in the morning the day his divorce was filed.

Mary went to court on January 11, 1935. Two days before, she had sent him a telegram: DEAR DUBER AM NOTIFYING YOU PERSONALLY HAVE DEFINITELY DECIDED AGAINST CANCELLING OUR CONTRACT IN JANUARY HAVE INSTRUCTED OUR RESPECTIVE ATTORNEYS TO THIS EFFECT KINDEST REGARDS HIPPER. It was over in a matter of minutes, and she was only required to say the word *yes* a few times. Still, her voice faltered and broke. When the judge granted the decree, she gave a small start and her eyes filled with tears. The divorce would be final in a year.

The Hearst press practically crowed. Louella Parsons trumpeted, "Mary Pickford's decision to go through with her divorce suit is no surprise to those close to her. Mary never had any intention of returning to Douglas Fairbanks as his wife."

He kept up his front as best he could. He was photographed in St. Moritz, sleigh riding, skiing, and ice skating with Sylvia. His smile in the photographs fails to convince. He wired his son in London: I AM VERY HAPPY MORE THAN I HAVE BEEN IN YEARS.

He wasn't.

In fairness, there was one thing he did have to be happy about: his improved relationship with his son. After "Jayar"—as he called him now, short for Junior (the son returning the favor by calling him "Pete," a name Fairbanks himself suggested)—reached adulthood, the two men discovered each other. Further, they found, to their mutual surprise, that they enjoyed each other. They golfed and traveled together, and the father found himself taking his son into his confidence. "I feel like his papa. He seems much younger than I," Jayar said at the time. "He is always coming to me for advice. He's sort of Peter-Pan, you know, irresponsible. I try to make him do the sensible thing as often as possible."

His success was, admittedly, mixed. Doug and Sylvia became the 1935 precursors of jet-setters. From Switzerland to Rome, from Rome to London, from there to the Bahamas, from whence to St. Thomas to pick up a yacht—the 160 foot *Caroline*, with a crew of thirty-two. Then to Miami, where he nodded approval as Sylvia spent his money on beach togs and evening clothes. Along the way, he experienced a decaying relationship with the press. At one point he offered to "sock" reporters "in the nose" if they annoyed him. "For all I care," wrote one, "Douglas Fairbanks can swing from British chandeliers for the remainder of his career."

They arrived in Nassau with the yacht's windows closed and curtains drawn. His only comment to journalists: "The press has treated me rotten." The feeling was mutual. The London *Daily Express* held an unpopularity contest. Doug was ninth on the list of ten. His sole consolation: he was three slots below Hitler.

They went through the Panama Canal. In the party by this point were Fred Astaire and Benita Hume. All stayed below decks as the ship locked through. Doug, "severe in his denunciations of the Fourth Estate," refused interviews but let it be known that they were aiming for the South Seas and Tahiti. From there? Who knew—Japan, India, the Suez Canal?

They got as far as Fiji, when word came of a business crisis. Joseph Schenck, who was not only head of United Artists but also a provider of much-needed films for distribution, was leaving the company for Fox. With him went young producer Darryl Zanuck's production unit, 20th Century Pictures. With the founders no longer making content, this created a critical shortage of product.

Schenck had been chairman of the board of UA since 1924 and had been seminal in its success, shepherding his flock of quarrelsome and creative sheep through product deficits, technical innovations such as sound, and exhibitor wars. One of his brilliant strokes was in mid-1933, when he founded 20th Century Pictures, putting Zanuck in charge of production. Film executive Al Lichtman said of Zanuck at the time, "he personifies youth, brilliance, smartness and timeliness"—true words, indeed, and the sort that had been applied to Fairbanks twenty years before. To start, 20th Century signed a one-year distribution deal with United Artists, giving UA critical product in the 1933–1934 season, with nine out of the twelve films being solid hits. Still, at the end of the year, the owners declined to give Zanuck any stock in the company, which put Schenck on the spot. It took all his considerable charm and persuasion to convince Zanuck to give UA a second year's distribution contract. During that time, he proposed a scheme that he thought would serve the best interests of all parties—the nonproducing partners (Fairbanks and Pickford and, partially, Chaplin) as well as the producing partners (Schenck, Goldwyn, and Zanuck). UA would issue two classes of stock: Preferred, with a 7 percent return and a par value of $2.4 million, and Common, with no par value. All six partners would get one-sixth shares of the Preferred shares. The nonproducing partners would each get one-sixth of 40 percent of the Common shares. The producing partners would get the same one-sixth share of the 40 percent, as well as splitting the remaining 60 percent of the Common stock. For its part, 20th Century would sign a ten-year distribution deal with UA, would guarantee dividends on *both* types of stock, and would purchase the Preferred stock from the founders on request, at $400,000 for each one-sixth share.

It was an eminently fair proposal and would give each nonproducing member a slightly smaller share of what would be a far more successful company. Robert Fairbanks, on behalf of Doug, had enthusiastically agreed to the plan. Initially Sam Goldwyn also agreed, but neither Mary nor Charlie would go along. Then Goldwyn reversed his position.

Schenck had had it. "It is clear to me that Sam Goldwyn, Mary Pickford and Charlie Chaplin are determined to dominate and run the United Artists Distribution Corporation," he wrote. "Why they should at this time decide to do so is inexplicable to me as the company has been run by me very successfully and very fairly. They never showed any desire to manage and run the company when the company was $1,200,000 in the red." He took 20th Century over to Fox, the merger creating 20th Century-Fox. More important, at least as far as Fairbanks was concerned, Schenck sold his Art Cinema and UA stock back to the company and sold Sam Goldwyn the portion of 20th Century stock that owned the properties on the Pickford-Fairbanks Studios. Now only Goldwyn and Disney were still releasing through UA, and Goldwyn was the sole owner of the stages, the equipment, and all physical property of the studio. Doug and Mary owned only the land it stood upon.

Mary wired Doug in Singapore to return for an emergency board meeting. He arrived in British Columbia in early July and, depositing Sylvia on Vancouver Island, made his way to Hollywood.

Fairbanks and Pickford were brisk and efficient with each other publicly: a nod, a quick handshake. A prolonged ten-day stockholders' meeting resulted in many changes. Al Lichtman was appointed president, with Mary as first vice president. The board of directors was reconstituted to include stockholders, and the bylaws were amended to weaken management and strengthen the board.

Lichtman's reign was to be short: three months. Except for signing David O. Selznick to an eight-picture contract, he had little time to do anything. Mary then took the reins, lasting long enough to lose the Disney contract to RKO (Radio-Keith-Orpheum) Pictures. Given that Disney was in the midst of producing *Snow White*, the full-length feature that would become one of the decade's sensations, this was an unfortunate loss.

Mary was not alone in making bad financial decisions. During his brief stay in Hollywood, Doug was corralled by his brother-manager to look at the books. Upon seeing the cost of the March-to-July cruise—$100,000, by Robert's recollection—Doug was staggered. "I spent a fortune on that damned trip and didn't get a nickel's worth of fun out of it," he said.

Robert remained a man of few words, replying, "You paid the piper, all right."

Doug's response spoke to his frame of mind. "Apparently that's all I'm good for," he said. "And the worst of it is, I've got to keep on doing it."

And so he did. Soon he was flying to New York City, with a thousand pounds of luggage, to reconnect with Sylvia. They sailed on the *Empress of Britain* for England, there to get back on the tiresome merry-go-round that was to constitute the rest of his days. Photographers seemed never to tire of documenting his weary face at nightclub tables. Sylvia would be dancing or smoking or drinking, while in the words of one observer, Fairbanks "might have been a tired businessman from Milwaukee seeing the town under protest." Another described him as "a world-weary man, his eyes strange, far away and almost filmy with ennui, his shoulders slumping." *Thief of Bagdad* director Raoul Walsh was more succinct in his cruelty: "Finally, the jowls dropped, and he didn't look good at all. And he died."

But not right away. And, perhaps, only internally. He had four more years of a living death to go.

They spent months abroad. Sylvia sported a platinum ring on the third finger of her left hand. When asked about it, she simply laughed. "How can I be engaged to a man who is already married? Would you want me to get him jailed for bigamy?" Her divorce had been finalized in the spring, but his would not be final until the following January.

Doug made noises about producing films in England. He would remake *The Thief of Bagdad*, he said. Or *The Black Pirate*. This did not sit well with Mary from a business perspective. In December 1935 she wired him repeatedly on the subject:

WORRIED YOU HAVE CHOSEN BAGDAD AND PIRATE FOR FIRST PRO-
DUCTIONS NEED AMERICAN PICTURES ENGLISH FILMS DIFFICULT
TO SELL EVERYWHERE BUT ENGLAND BELIEVE YOU WOULD HAVE
MORE ENTHUSIASM FOR ENTIRELY NEW STORY LIKE CUSTER REDOING
OLD SUCCESSES RARELY PROVES SUCCESSFUL AND SHOULD ONLY BE
ATTEMPTED AFTER REESTABLISHING YOURSELF.

In fact, she was dogged in her attempts to get him to abandon
filmmaking in Great Britain:

YOU MUST LEAVE THERE IMMEDIATELY AND REESTABLISH YOURSELF
IN UNITED STATES WHAT FEELING IF ANY MAY EXIST WOULD BE MORE
THAN OFFSET BY SUCCESSFUL PICTURE I KNOW YOU CAN MAKE BE
COURAGEOUS TAKE YOUR FUTURE IN YOUR OWN HANDS DON'T LISTEN
TO OTHERS WHICH ONLY RESULTS IN CONFUSION THE COMPANY
NEEDS YOU THE INDUSTRY NEEDS YOU SO COME BACK IF HOLLYWOOD
DISTASTEFUL MAKE YOUR HEADQUARTERS IN NEW YORK BUT I FEEL
YOU NEED THE STIMULATION OF THE SPIRIT OF HOLLYWOOD TODAY
HOWEVER ALL IS WITHIN YOU THEREFORE LEAN UPON YOUR OWN
EXCELLENT INSTINCTS AND JUDGMENT.

Perhaps her words had their intended effect. For he did return
to the States—significantly, without Sylvia—in the first week of
January 1936. As with Mary, he had a prearranged code with Robert for their telegraphic communication. Upon receipt of the coded
signal from London, Robert would "build up a business pretext that
would necessitate [his] sudden return to Hollywood." Doug sent the
coded message in late December, and Robert came through. Soon the
press was announcing that Douglas Fairbanks had sent word ahead to
refurbish his dressing room and to fill his private pool at the studio.
He was going to begin preproduction, he announced, on a film about
Marco Polo.

Except to speak about it with reporters, there is no evidence that
he did any work on the film. In fact, Robert's recollection was that

he had already convinced Douglas the November before to shelve the project. Still, it would serve as a handy stalking horse for the next several months. He was frequently announcing that he was on his way to the Orient, to get footage for his latest epic.

In fact, he hoped against all reason to stop the divorce. During the five months he had been overseas, he continued to send feelers back to Mary. In an act of gall that spoke clearly to his desperation, he wired a two-hundred-word plea to his first wife, Beth, asking her to intercede. It was the highest—or should one say lowest?—example of that characteristic of his nature that would occasionally send a woman out to do what he could not. He had sent Beth to get him out of his contract with William Brady in 1907, and now, almost thirty years later, he asked her to plead his case to the woman who had broken up their marriage. She stoutly did her duty: Mary claimed that she said, "I know and the whole world knows that you are the great love of Douglas' life. Douglas was more like a brother to me than a husband."

Who is to say? Those words may actually have passed her lips. And, if said, she might even have meant them. Still, it was a squalid thing to ask—probably his least heroic act.

His direct plea to Mary, once he was back in California, was little more effective. "Let's put ourselves on the shelf" was the (admittedly secondhand) version of the pitch. "We're no longer important to the world and I don't think anyone really cares about us anymore. . . . Why don't we go away together and live in peace, perhaps in Switzerland, or if you like we can build on the ranch as we've always planned."

It was, in the dry words of Robert, the wrong approach. At any rate, it had no effect—at least according to Mary. Fairbanks Jr. had a different tale to tell, a last tragic twist to the story.

Doug stayed in Hollywood, attempting to convince Mary, until business forced a brief trip to New York City. He asked his son to join him on the train trip east. Jayar recalled that at every stop, "Pete sent long, long telegrams to Mary, written in intensely romantic desperately poetic language." When they reached Chicago, he stopped at the local UA office to see if Mary had left him a message. She hadn't.

He was glum, and he became glummer as they reached New York and he checked into the Waldorf Towers. An evening at a Bert Lahr musical cheered him briefly, but the next night he and Jayar saw Richard Barthelmess in *The Postman Always Rings Twice*. He was, in the words of his son, "terribly distraught, anxious and quite unreceptive to the public's cheers and waves." Dinner at the Persian Room was no better. He returned to the Waldorf, but not before scheduling a lunch the next day with his son and a number of his friends, including Tom Geraghty and Frank Case.

When Jayar arrived at the hotel the next morning, his father was gone. He had departed during the night for Europe. The clerk did not know what ship but handed Jayar a telegram that had arrived before Fairbanks had checked out, but which had been overlooked in the flurry.

Although it was addressed to his father, he opened it. It might have been important.

It was. It was from Mary. "The exact wording of the message is lost, but I could never, ever forget its gist," he wrote. "It was, in effect; 'All is forgiven . . . I want us to be together again too . . . forever . . . come back . . .'"

It took some mad scrambling to learn the details: ten minutes before the vessel sailed, between three and four in the morning, Fairbanks had boarded the *Aquitania* via the crew's gangplank. He traveled under a pseudonym. Jayar placed a radio call to the ship with the news of the telegram. His father's reaction was, paradoxically, anger. He accused his son of lying. Junior had never approved of Sylvia; he had always been on Mary's side, not his. He hung up and accepted no further calls from New York. He wired Jayar from the ship: THIS DECISION MADE IN PERSIAN ROOM LAST NIGHT WHEN WE WERE TALKING.

He did, however, take a call from Mary. She confirmed that, indeed, she had sent the telegram. Fairbanks paused long before replying. "It's too late," he reportedly said. "It's just too late." He had already proposed marriage to Sylvia.

He arrived at Cherbourg on March 3. As soon as he was ashore, he called Sylvia in London. She rushed to meet him in France, leaving behind such necessities as her birth certificate and divorce papers. He spent the following days playing a part in a sort of comic opera, scuttling about between lawyer and government offices, trying to get the residence and marriage banns requirements waived. His fame, or persistence, finally did the trick: on the sixth the state's attorney delivered papers suspending the French marriage laws. But now Sylvia's missing papers became an issue. These were flown to Paris, translated and attested to, but by the time this was done, city hall had closed for the day.

He became yet more frantic. He tried the American embassy, but the attachés had to tell him that no matter his fervor, or fame, they lacked the proper authority to marry him. It scarcely mattered: he also was without his divorce papers. He had to swear a special affidavit to one of the most famous facts of the past twenty years—that he had been married to, and divorced from, Mary Pickford.

Finally, on the next day, under a ceiling of floating fleshy cupids in the offices of the 8th arrondissement, the deed was done. The bride's roadster had hit a taxicab on the way to the ceremony—a bad omen, to the locals. She seemed unconcerned, appearing in a rose-colored coat with a large corsage of orchids pinned to her fur collar. The groom was in a black suit, tie, and hat, his wedding costume indistinguishable from mourning clothes.

The news was buried in the back pages of the papers. Still, some saw it, prompting one wag to produce the following doggerel:

> Douglas Fairbanks, Junior's pa,
> Looks for a new cine-ma
> Having canned his Lady Mary
> For that English Ashley fairy

It did not take long for the first marital spat. As they walked down the steps from the mayor's office, Sylvia chided Doug for not holding her arm. He bit back a retort and took her hand, with the reported words: "Now dearie, please!" Theirs was not the only local quarrel: Germany invaded the Rhineland the same day. Perhaps this knowledge soothed Douglas for the scant attention his final honeymoon received.

Which was just as well, as it did not go swimmingly. They flew to Spain on a private plane. In Seville, their unattended car was looted; stolen were two of his precious overcoats, a camera, luggage, and the fur wraps he had bought Sylvia in Paris as a wedding gift. ("It cost me 10,000 francs," Doug huffed indignantly to a world largely indifferent to the problems of the rich and formerly famous.)

And so he settled into the life as, in the words of niece Letitia, "a has-been." In early May, he brought his bride to America. As they arrived in the morning hours on the *Washington* in the Port of New York, they were still in their evening clothes. He shushed Sylvia repeatedly when she tried to speak while he was expounding to reporters. "Tell them you enjoyed the skyline," he instructed her. Skylines, evidently, didn't interest her. More important was the nation's perception of her hair color. "I am not a dirty blonde," she declared. She wished the press to refer to her hair color as "English mouse."

This critical issue put to bed, they moved into the Santa Monica beach house. He had elective surgery (likely a hernia repair necessitated by years of vigorous stunting) and settled uneasily into the uncharacteristic role of the man *not* in the arena: hitting the nightspots and charity circuits, occupying the first-class suites of transatlantic liners, making increasingly feeble claims of travel plans to China, and pledging—always pledging—to make another movie. But his actions belied his words. By October 1936 it was announced that Sam Goldwyn would coproduce *Marco Polo*. In the words of Goldwyn biographer A. Scott Berg: "Three meetings later, Fairbanks found Goldwyn taking over every aspect of the production." He pleaded with old friend (and Goldwyn's manager) David Rose "to get him out of the deal." He did so. By April 1937, Fairbanks had sold the rights to the *Marco Polo* project outright to his fellow producer. Goldwyn, who had provided a young Gary Cooper with his first important opportunity ten years earlier, now hijacked the star from his Paramount contract to take the lead in the film. The casting announcement was tantamount to announcing Doug's retirement from acting. "I'll let the young fellows carry on my swashbuckling roles," Fairbanks told a reporter. "There are twenty or twenty-five of 'em out there capable of carrying on."

He meant it. Perhaps the strongest declaration of this was when he sold the rights to *The Mark of Zorro* to Darryl Zanuck at Fox in early 1936. The rumored price was $50,000—almost a third of the film's original production costs. The gossips murmured that he made the sale reluctantly. He had always expected, it was said, to return again to the *Zorro* saga.

In truth, it was a surrender to economic realities. There were those who would claim that Sylvia Ashley was cheap (lawyer Cap O'Brien referred to her as "Lady Ashcan"), but none would say that she was inexpensive. Mary had made her own money—a shocking amount of money—and she and Doug had always kept their accounts separate. But now he was maintaining an establishment in London (at 99 Park Lane) and the Santa Monica beach house at a time when his income had plummeted. In 1930 his earnings from films and investments were over $450,000. Five years later this number had been reduced by 75 percent and would keep going down. And still the money went out: to the Ritz, to Harrods, to buy jewels, to buy cars. He had to pay the piper, and he would keep paying until his death, which occurred at the end of a tax year in which, for the first time, he showed a net loss.

Yet even in this, he was a fortunate man. It could have been worse, and for many a fallen silent screen star, subsisting in poverty, or something very much like it, it was. For the last ten years of his life he lived off the cushions built in the 1910s and '20s by his conservative brothers and advisers. They knew their generous, improvident, impulsive man well and constructed a web of bonds, trusts, and other investments that would protect him from himself and yet permit him to live as he had lived almost his whole adult life: in ease and luxury. Still, he was eating away his principal, and each year saw him selling assets that he had never imagined he would give up. The last year of his life he sold one of his Remingtons.

Other parts of his history were disappearing. A fire swept through Kenneth Ridge, taking the last vestiges of his life with Beth Sully. Sam Goldwyn, now with control of the Pickford-Fairbanks lot at Santa Monica and Formosa, announced plans to tear down the last few sets from *Robin Hood*, *The Thief of Bagdad*, and Mary's second version of *Tess of the Storm Country*. D. W. Griffith, perhaps still remembering the pain of seeing the *Intolerance* sets deteriorate a score of years before, raised a public outcry. But Doug said nothing as another bit of his past crumbled and vanished.

He could ignore Goldwyn's annexation of his studio, but the head-in-the-sand approach did not serve for another aspect of his past: Mary.

It is not that he didn't try. Mary and Buddy were openly seeing each other now, and marriage rumors were rampant. Doug was breakfasting at a Kansas City train station in the course of one of his frequent national crisscrossings in early 1936 when a newspaperman pointed out that they were very near the Olathe, Kansas, hometown of Rogers. "He shook his head and his face was blank," the reporter wrote, "as if he had never heard of Buddy." Privately, he voiced his disbelief to his brother. Mary would never marry that fellow, he told him. She had money, position. She was just "pretending" to make him jealous.

If that had ever been her motive early in her relationship with Buddy, it did not appear to be the case now. They married in June 1937. Still, at some level, he could not believe it. Around this time, one of the UA board meetings was held in Mary's bedroom, to accommodate the fact that she was under the weather. During the course of a heated debate one partner—very likely Goldwyn—actually shook his fist at her. Doug's response was immediate. "How dare you talk to my wife like that?" he was reputed to have said to the offender, before pitching him out of the room.

Before dismissing the story as apocryphal, consider the words of one of the UA presidents during this period. Goldwyn biographer A. Scott Berg quotes Dr. Attilio Henry Giannini:

"All my life I've been an adventurer, and have been in a lot of tough situations. . . . But let me tell you, I never saw fights like the ones at U.A. board meetings in my life." He said that "criminations, recriminations, cusswords"—even physical violence—became standard boardroom procedure.

On one level, one can scarcely blame Fairbanks. Mary may have no longer been his wife, but if ever there was a man, in Doug's mind, asking for a punch in the kisser, it was Sam Goldwyn. He had always been abrasive, but in a May 1937 directors' meeting, he advanced to toxic. He accused Pickford, Fairbanks, and Chaplin of contributing nothing to United Artists. They should have, he stated directly, the decency to sell out. He offered $500,000 for their shares.

They rebuffed this offer but retired privately to confer. They returned with a counteroffer: $2 million *each*. It was decided that Goldwyn and Korda could have until December 21 to try to get the money.

This would have been a godsend for Fairbanks. Clarence Erickson, who, with Robert, managed his finances, wrote, "If the deal can be concluded, I feel it is the greatest break Douglas has had in years. . . . Under the present income tax laws, Douglas can realize a net of about $1,450,000.00 after paying income taxes."

It was not to be. Korda was not in a strong position. His UA releases had, for the most part, not been successful. Further, the construction of Denham Film Studios in Great Britain for London Films was taxing his purse. The pair could only raise $4 million, and Chaplin was adamant: he would take $2 million or nothing. Various compromises were attempted, but none worked.

WE SHOULD NEVER HAVE GIVEN LENGTHY OPTION AND EXPOSED OURSELVES AND UNITED TO THIS PUBLICITY, Doug groused in a telegram to Cap O'Brien. The deal was dead.

Other reminders of mortality hovered near. The most pointed came after the February 1938 visit of Lord and Lady Plunkett. Lady Plunkett, a thirty-eight-year-old mother of three sons, was the daughter of silent film actress Fannie Ward, and a friend of Sylvia's. The couple vacationed at the Santa Monica beach house as guests of the Fairbankses and then flew from Burbank on William Randolph Hearst's private plane to the Hearst Ranch up north. Fog intervened, and the plane crashed in flames while attempting to land, killing the young couple. Understandably shocked, a somber and grave Fairbanks arranged the funeral services and took their ashes to London later that spring.

"For a man my age it would have been a blessing," he told his brother. "There's nothing that I haven't done at least twice before and I now look upon death as the only challenge, the only adventure left before me."

Dramatic words, true, from a man in a self-pitying mood. But he started to act as if he felt his days were numbered. He donated all the films in his legal and physical possession to the Museum of Modern Art. It was the largest film donation to date in the history of the museum.*

He continued the weary rounds, looking either bored and distracted or smiling a strained smile at such events as Elsa Maxwell's "Barn Party" at the Waldorf Astoria, complete with a hog caller and a dozen hogs. His extravagances, small and large, continued. He still topped the best-dressed lists and was described as the most extravagant patron of New York's Pajama Parlor, where the wealthy paid up to eighty dollars for a pair of custom-fitted pajamas. He was found on the slopes of St. Moritz and the *sestieri* of Venice in season. But he almost never looked happy.

He perked up briefly in April 1939 when Jayar, who had divorced Joan Crawford in 1933, married Mary Lee Epling, a beautiful young divorcee of independent means. Doug's son, deciding he had no close male friends, asked his father to be his best man. Jayar's recollection of

---

* Unhappily the organization did not prove to be responsible custodians of the gift, and many of the films he donated are, as of this writing, considered lost, among them *He Comes Up Smiling, The Knickerbocker Buckaroo, Bound in Morocco, Arizona, Headin' South,* and *Say! Young Fellow.* Others exist only because they—or portions of them—have been found in other archives.

the circumstance was colored by that ambivalence toward his father that remained decades after the older man's death. His father *seemed* pleased, he said. He "at least behaved as if he was happy at the prospect."

In point of fact, he was delighted, and when, months later, it was discovered that his first grandchild was on the way, he was over the moon. Jayar had been anxious on both accounts, fearing that the best man request and the news of his pending grandparenthood would somehow trigger an angry response. It was an understandable anxiety: his announcement in 1923 that he was going into motion pictures had caused a firestorm of misunderstandings and overreactions.

In fact, once Jayar was of age and Fairbanks did not think his son was being used for his name alone, he was enthusiastically supportive of his career and proud of his accomplishments.* He wired him frequently on the status of his current films† and was critical in influencing him to play the villain part in *The Prisoner of Zenda*. "He listened attentively," Jayar recalled, when recounting how he sought his father's advice about taking a supporting role. "When I finished, he burst out with the conviction that I *had* to accept." His father declared, "Nobody has played Rupert and failed to steal the show, on either stage or screen! It is *so* actor-proof, in fact, that Rin Tin Tin could play the part and walk away with it!"

Still, Jayar's mixed feelings were justified. For a brief period in the mid-1930s, he had lived in the guesthouse adjacent to the Santa Monica

---

* After Fairbanks's death, one young fan of the son wrote to him of his father: "When I think of him I always think of that day in 1932, in the forecourt of Grauman's Chinese Theatre. He was in golfing knickers, and standing in the sun with Mr. Grauman and others. He positively shone! He had that way of shining in the sun. Everyone was looking at him. . . . Mother hated me to stand and gape at the stars, so she said to me, 'Come, Betty. Don't stand and stare.' And I replied, 'No. I want to see Douglas' father.' Everybody within hearing distance laughed. Mr. Fairbanks looked at me and grinned from ear to here—that divine smile that he so nicely and generously lavished on everyone—and he said to me, 'That's one of the nicest things I've ever heard. Hello, there. How are you?'"

† A sample: JUST HEARD FROM SILVERSTONE SUCCESS OF YOUR PICTURE STOP. YOU GIVE ME ONE OF THE BIG THRILLS OF MY LIFE STOP. I WON'T BE PATERNAL AND SAY I AM PROUD OF YOU BUT AS MY FRIEND AND ASSOCIATE I HAVE NEVER BEEN SO HAPPY HURRAH FOR US.

beach house where Doug and Sylvia lived. This put the son in a bit of an awkward spot: he resented Sylvia as "the instrument that finally broke up my father's celebrated marriage . . . and also dislodged him from the pedestal on which he stood as a universally adored figure." More to the point: "What I resented was what I took to be her schemes to get another jewel or expensive present." (Sylvia preferred Rolls-Royces and got them.) In order to hide his dislike, he went out of his way to treat her warmly.

This, given Senior's pathologic jealousy, was a strategic mistake. Fairbanks decided that his son was flirting with his wife, and with his characteristic inability to face conflict or perform an unpleasant task himself, he sent an embarrassed Kenneth Davenport to deliver the eviction notice. He wanted Jayar out of the house, and he wanted him out of the house immediately.

It was not a wise move, on many levels. He could use every friend he could get, and there were few left. Old friends, including the beloved Tom Geraghty, were no longer in the inner circle, replaced by Sylvia's fast, late-night crowd. Even his old trappings were gone: as his son wrote, "He no longer had a large studio with a great suite of offices, a gymnasium, a Turkish bath, and a lounge-dressing room; there were no more luxuriously uncultivated foothills, gardens, panoramic views, and creature comforts of Pickfair; gone too were the private screenings of new films after dinner and a domestic staff that catered to his many whims. There was no Albert as Major Domo, and even Rocher had left very soon after Pete's marriage to Sylvia."

This last was indeed a blow to both men. Rocher wrote Jayar "to think of the past years at his service is to live again the happiest time of my life." It is likely the converse was also true.

Douglas's new acquaintances were not always worthy creatures. Perhaps he can be forgiven for being at a house party on the French Riviera with the Duke and Duchess of Windsor. Why, he was queried, didn't he go back into the movies? "I got out just before the public got wise to me," he replied. The Duchess of Windsor jerked her thumb over her shoulder at her husband and said, "You mean just as he did."

Less understandable, although perhaps more useful, was an instance in August 1939 when he was pictured in conversation with the occupant of the adjoining cabana at his beach retreat in Venice—none other than Joseph Goebbels, Nazi Minister of Public Enlightenment and Propaganda. Goebbels told him, enigmatically, that Germany would "go ahead with its program." What this program was he evidently failed to clarify. Publicly, Fairbanks stated that he doubted there would be a European war because "Britain is so ready, and [the Nazis] know it." (His timing was particularly bad, given the Labor Day weekend invasion of Poland that immediately followed.) Privately, he scrambled to get Sylvia, her sister, and her sister's children on an already-overcrowded ship to the United States. Unable to find passage for himself with his family, he remained behind, only to catch a boat to the Caribbean. A quick run on the *Dixie Clipper* brought him to Long Island ahead of Sylvia, and he was there to greet them as they arrived. He would never return to Europe again.

But if he missed the European conflict, Sam Goldwyn's private war against United Artists served as a substitute.

Shortly after Mary lost the distribution rights to Walt Disney's films to RKO, Dr. Attilio Henry Giannini replaced her as chairman of the board. There were advantages to this appointment: the good doctor had a track record of loaning money to the film industry through his brother's bank, the Bank of America. But Goldwyn wanted someone more favorable to his interests at the helm. When his attempt to buy out the partners failed, he moved in March 1938 to have Murray Silverstone put in charge of distribution.

This did not bode well for the founding partners. Neil McCarthy (formerly Howard Hughes's lawyer when he released through UA) wrote to Doug, "Silverstone will be subservient to Sam. . . . If Sam gets control of the company he will use it for his own selfish interests, regardless of the returns to the company. . . . He resents the fact that you and Mary and Charlie receive earnings from the distribution of his pictures."

Despite these (and other) warnings, the board approved the change, as well as others demanded by Goldwyn. Distribution fees were decreased from 30 percent to 25 percent. The Los Angeles office was closed. A fund was established to permit the producing partners to share in company profits.*

And still, Sam Goldwyn was not content. At the January 1939 meeting, he demanded full and sole voting rights for the company. Anything less and he would veto any proposals. One of these proposals (which he promptly vetoed) was made by Fairbanks, for a new production company. Goldwyn's stance was that Fairbanks's company's "pictures would not be good enough to give them the privilege of sharing in profits." The minutes reflect Doug's astonishment and despair. "Sam," he said. "I've been your friend for many years, and now that I ask this thing, you attach this condition? Surely you don't mean it?"

Goldwyn's reply: "Yes I do."

Fairbanks, it is reported, left the room in silence.

In March, Goldwyn went to court to attempt to win a judgment that would get him out of his distribution contract with United Artists. It bounced from court to court until December 27, when the US District Court in Delaware dismissed the suit. There was jubilation in the offices of United Artists. But Doug was not there to share it.

On Saturday, December 9, he and Sylvia attended the USC-UCLA football game. A photographer snapped a picture of him leaving the game with friend Kay Francis by his side. It was to be his last photograph. No newspapers picked it up for publication.

That night, he and Sylvia dined with the then-pregnant Mary Lee and Jayar to celebrate his son's thirtieth birthday. He had sent Jayar a telegram that afternoon wishing him many happy returns of the day.† "We played games and were frightfully gay," Mary Lee wrote two weeks later. Jayar's recollections of the dinner conversation were more

---

* This was established by what became known as the Silverstone Plan. The first $250,000 of profits was paid as dividends to the stockholders. The second $250,000 went into a producer bonus fund, a sliding scale rebate based on grosses during the year. All profits after the initial $500,000 were assigned fifty-fifty between the two groups.

† The telegram, which Jr. kept until his death, read simply: MANY MANY MANY MANY.

elegiac. "A good hour or more of which time he devoted to recalling 'the old days' in New York, and his experiences in the [Lambs] Club," he recalled. "He was particularly pleased that I had joined."

Not all of the evening involved reminiscing. Doug was planning to see a Lunt and Fontanne play on Tuesday. The war in Europe was also on his mind. "We talked of you both," Jayar wrote to Lord and Lady Mountbatten, "and the conversation led us to discussing plans to come to England next summer to produce a film which might help the allied cause."

Then came the toasts. "When my turn came," Jayar recalled, "I impulsively broke my lifelong habit of manly undemonstrativeness toward my father. This time, after a few light quips, I directed a brief, but affectionate toast 'to Dad.' Everyone appeared to be rather touched, but he most of all."

But warning signs were on the horizon. One of Douglas's nieces, Margaret Mary, noticed him close his eyes and rest his head against the back of his chair. Was he all right?

"I'm tired," she reported him replying. "So tired."

The next morning, he woke at his usual time:* 6 AM. But the day brought a new sensation—a feeling of tightness in his chest. Worse yet, he was short of breath. Lying or even sitting worsened his breathlessness, and he found himself standing repeatedly in front of an open window, trying to relieve the air hunger. He did not know it, but he had an occluded coronary artery, and the left ventricle of his heart—the part that pumps blood through the aorta to the rest of the body—had begun to fail. Fluid was backing up in his lungs. He was experiencing congestive heart failure.

Assistant Arthur Fenn arrived two hours later to work in the back bedroom that served as the vestige of the once-mighty Douglas Fairbanks

---

* Accounts vary in different sources as to which day Fairbanks suffered the attack. The physician's notations on the death certificate make it clear. Fairbanks incurred the infarct on the tenth, lived through that night and the day of the eleventh, and died shortly after midnight the morning of the twelfth.

Pictures Corporation. Doug complained to him of indigestion, but Fenn sensed something more serious was afoot. He called Robert. Robert was already concerned. He usually spoke with Doug shortly after six, and this morning had brought no call. A drive to Santa Monica and a quick look at his dyspneic brother was all it took to call in a cardiologist.

Dr. J. P. Sampson came, and with him came an electrocardiogram. The diagnosis was not hard to make: an acute occlusion of a coronary artery had resulted in what is now called a myocardial infarction, or as it was known at the time, a "coronary," or a heart attack. He was given a narcotic, likely morphine, which served to not only ease his pain but also dilate his blood vessels and relieve the symptoms of heart failure. He was put in bed and instructed that he was to remain at bed rest for weeks—possibly months.

The troops rallied. Chuck Lewis arrived, as did friend Clarence Erickson, Robert's and John's daughters, and Sylvia's sister. Erickson claimed, "They put him to bed, but he was the same old Doug, laughing and joking as usual." But by Monday, his mood was darkening. Jayar came to visit him that afternoon and found his father in a dimly lit room, grousing angrily ("Can you *imagine?*" and "*Dammit to hell!*" were his son's exact recollections) about not being allowed to follow the war news. Nothing must excite him, the doctor ordered. Nothing could aggravate him more. Jayar read to him from the poetry of Byron and Shakespeare until he fell asleep. The son stared at his father for a bit and then impulsively kissed him on the forehead before slipping down the stairs.

Later that night, Douglas awoke and spoke alone with Robert. He dreaded invalidism, he said, more than death. If anything should happen to him, he wanted Robert to call Mary for him. He was simply to say, "By the clock." She would understand. Robert agreed.

A male nurse was brought in to attend to him, but in the days before defibrillators and cardiac monitors, there was little that could have been done to prevent what happened next.

At midnight, Doug asked the nurse to open the casement windows that faced the ocean. How was he feeling? "I've never felt better!" he barked, and grinned, as of old. Across the distant stretch of beach, where in former days he had sat in the sun with Mary and Zorro, the Airedale terrier, the ocean murmured. Was he still thinking of Mary? Had his mind turned to Sylvia? She had been called home from the hairdresser's when his heart attack was diagnosed. She had spent much of Monday at a Red Cross meeting. But she was home now, in another bedroom.

Whatever his thoughts, he was not alone. Marco Polo, his immense Great Dane, slept at the foot of his bed, and the nurse came and went. As he dozed, the catastrophic happened. Medically, the most likely scenario is that his body dissolved the clot in his coronary artery. If the heart tissue beyond the blockage is already dead, this is of no consequence. But it was too soon. The heart muscle was dying, ischemic, irritable. The fresh influx of oxygenated blood caused the tissues of the heart to wiggle erratically, and he suffered a deadly heart rhythm known as ventricular fibrillation.

It is a quick, painless way to die. Even if he had been awake, he would never have known what hit him. The blood supply to his brain stopped and he lost consciousness in seconds.

The dog sensed something and growled. The nurse returned to the room and found that his patient had, in the words of the poet, slipped the surly bonds of earth. It was 12:45 AM on the morning of Tuesday, December 12, 1939.

Dr. Sampson was called and confirmed the evident. Sylvia devolved into hysterics, and Jayar was awakened by the sound of her voice over the phone shrieking, "He's dead! He's *dead*!" He and Mary Lee rushed to the house, where he found his father looking much as he had left him. "Except that this time," he wrote, "when I leaned down I whispered a loving good-bye, and then gently kissed his forehead for the second and last time."

In the end, it was Gwynne who called Mary. She and Buddy were at the Drake Hotel in Chicago. The call came at 4 AM, local time, barely an hour after Fairbanks had died. Gwynne had only to identify herself. The hour and the tone of her voice told Mary all she needed to know.

"Don't say it, Gwynne!" she recalled saying. "He's gone, isn't he?"

He was. She refrained from tears "out of respect for Buddy" until the following night, when she was alone on a train to New York City. Then she wept. His imprint never left her. In her final years, whether from alcohol or age, she would cry out in the night for him. Often, she would claim to have seen his ghost. Spectral or not, it was clear that Douglas Fairbanks was to haunt her for the rest of her life.

Back at the Santa Monica beach house, the tears were flowing freely. It was good that the doctor was present: Sylvia required heavy sedation. The body was embalmed at the house and remained there while Jayar and Robert made funeral arrangements.

They settled on services at the Wee Kirk o' the Heather chapel at the Forest Lawn cemetery. Sylvia's prostration delayed the event until Friday the fifteenth. Thousands lined the driveway leading to the chapel, which had a capacity of only 140 seats. The official claim was that there were no invitations, as the family did not wish to offend any of the "old timers who worked with Fairbanks." But with Joseph Schenck in charge of security, the family, the powerful, and the occasional intimates were able to pass through the filter. Those in the chapel included Murray Silverstone, Darryl Zanuck, Louis B. Mayer, Jack Warner, Mack Sennett, Tom Mix (in his best black cowboy outfit, suitable for mourning), Harold Lloyd, Kay Francis, Elsa Maxwell, Eileen Percy (his costar in most of the Artcraft films of 1917), Cap O'Brien, Lewis Milestone, Fred Astaire, Ted Reed, Norma Shearer, Walter Wanger, Allan Dwan, Gwynne Pickford, Raoul Walsh, D. W. Griffith, Ronald Colman, Cecil B. DeMille, George Fitzmaurice, Samuel Goldwyn, Raymond Griffith, William Cameron Menzies, Marlene Dietrich, Myron Selznick, and Arthur Hornblow Jr. and his wife, Myrna Loy. Victor Fleming skipped the world premiere of *Gone with the Wind* to attend.

Standing silent on the lawn, after a three-hundred-mile drive in from the desert, were Bear Valley Charlie, "a full-blooded Indian"; Jim Bell, a cowhand; and the faithful, grieving, cauliflower-eared Bull Montana.

Rev. Neal Dodd read the short service. There was no eulogy. Chico De Verdi, violinist, conducted the old Fairbanks studio quartet—piano, violins, and bass cello—in a medley of "La Violetera," "Te Quiero Mucho," "La Paloma," "Brahms's Lullaby," "Andante Cantabile," "Ave Maria," and, of course, Doug's favorite, "Cielito Lindo." To an outsider, it must have seemed a strange musical choice for a funeral, but for many there, the strains of *Ay, ay, ay, ay* . . . must have evoked a sudden, potent memory. The smiling, climbing, leaping Doug was, to this crowd of insiders, irrevocably linked to that humble little song. None could help but see him in their mind's eye as the music filled the church: youthful, brimming with enthusiasm, smile ever flashing, body ever young, and never, ever still.

It was still now. Douglas Fairbanks, "the symbol of romance and eternal youth, who set out to learn what Fear was and never found it," would embark on no more adventures. He was clad in a frock cutaway coat, morning trousers, white waistcoat, and white tie. Carrying his coffin were Joseph Schenck, Charlie Chaplin, Sid Grauman, Tom Geraghty, Clarence Erickson, and Chuck Lewis. Chaplin arrived and departed alone, looking as though he had lost his best friend.

The United Artists office in New York City closed for the afternoon. Business was suspended at the UA exchange in Los Angeles for the duration of the service. At the studio—now the Goldwyn Studio—the flag was at half-mast. A private memorial service was held in Doug's old dressing room and gymnasium. At least three hundred took part. Here he was mourned—genuinely mourned by the unsung: the plant superintendents, the construction men, the property men, the painters, the hairdressers, the dining room servers, the laborers.

Afterward the floral tributes were all carefully listed by a secretary, in order that acknowledgments and thanks could be sent. William Randolph Hearst sent a wreath of gardenias and orchids. Mr. and Mrs. Irving Berlin sent yellow roses, gardenias, and carnations. Fred and Phyllis Astaire sent a spray of gardenias and roses on an easel. There were 149 deliveries in all. Doug Jr.'s card had the quote from *Hamlet*, act 1, scene 2: "He was a man, take him all in all. I shall not look upon his like again." Sylvia provided a spray of pink roses, with the words "Love. Sylvia."

There was one, however, that the secretary couldn't place. Possibly, it was never acknowledged. It was a large wreath of gardenias and lilies of the valley. The card had one word: FRIN.

Acknowledgments

W HEN ONE IS IN the midst of writing a book, it feels like a very solitary project. But in pausing to contemplate the formidable list of those who have helped along the way, one discovers that one was never alone.

My greatest thanks must go to Kevin Brownlow. In the summer of 2009, he patiently gave me three days of uninterrupted time in his flat, fishing out every single index card, interview, or reference to Fairbanks from his lifetime of study and firsthand interviews. A wealth of never-before-published material comes from his years of hard work. Any other scholar would have kept that good stuff to himself; Brownlow instead shared it all, gladly.

Generous help from archives and libraries was provided by Ned Comstock at USC; Jenny Romero and Barbara Hall of the Margaret Herrick Library; John Johnson of the Gottlieb Center at Boston University; James Layton at the George Eastman House; and Karen Pedersen, Library Director, Writers Guild Foundation Library.

Dave Del Prete, head of security at the Lot, the site of the Pickford-Fairbanks Studios, spent a full day with me, generously letting me cover every nook and cranny of the offices and the studio lot. It is one thing to say that Fairbanks had a steam room; it is quite another to go into the present-day incarnation (where it seems to be a storage space for outdated computer equipment) and sit on the mint-green tiles where Doug and Charlie once sat.

I owe a debt to Dick Nelson, president of Alumni and Friends at East High School in Denver. Doug's grades are still missing (the search continues), but the story of the cut piano wires, which has been part of the oral history of the organization for over a hundred years, is now preserved in print. Karl Thiede is also deserving of thanks, for sharing with me his extensive collection of trade magazines of the era and patiently explaining just *how* one should report the financial return of a film in the 1910s and '20s.

I also owe thanks to Melissa Schaefer, who generously shared photos and interviews with her grandmother, Maria Alba; and Bob Birchard, who let me scan many of his fabulous Fairbanks photographs.

Elaina Archer and Jeffrey Vance, both of the Mary Pickford Foundation, were tremendously helpful. Elaina provided me with never-seen footage of Doug and Mary's travels, and the worth-a-thousand-words footage of the costume test from *The Taming of the Shrew*. Jeffrey, himself the author of a Fairbanks biography, shared press books and generously and patiently answered questions. "Look harder into those early years," he urged me, and he was right. There was undiscovered gold there.

Another Fairbanks author who has demonstrated tremendous generosity is John Tibbetts, of the University of Kansas. He shared the manuscript of *Douglas Fairbanks and the American Century* when it was still in galleys, and was even so generous as to dedicate the book to me and the future generation of Fairbanks scholars. Along the same lines, Allan Dwan biographer Fred Lombardi sent me his Fairbanks chapters while still in the manuscript stage and was available to answer questions about the specifics of his research at every step of the way. Michelle Vogel, Lupe Vélez's biographer, shared many details about the filming of *The Gaucho* and clearly defined all the reasons that Doug and Lupe's relationship was a flirtation, and nothing more. Michael Sragow, at the time a fellow Baltimorean, gave me cost information on *Around the World in Eighty Minutes*, obtained while writing his wonderful Victor Fleming biography. Hugh Munro Neely shared Pickford telegrams with me, and Marc Wanamaker spent hours with me at the old Clune studio.

Help also came uninvited, and from unexpected quarters. Les Hammer heard me speak at the ninetieth-anniversary screening of *The Thief of Bagdad* and later that week mailed me a 1924 *Picture Play* article by fencing master Ralph Faulkner about a visit to the *Thief* set. Patrick Musone found the music box Fairbanks gave to Pickford for their tenth wedding anniversary at the Rose Bowl flea market. Not only did he provide this treasure, but he later turned up the silver vanity set Doug gave Mary for her birthday in 1929.

Rob Byrne of the Film Preservation Society and the San Francisco Silent Film Festival, Serge Bromberg of Lobster Films, and Céline Ruivo of Cinémathèque française were integral in the restoration of *The Half Breed* and *The Good Bad Man*, permitting me to write about those films in more detail than has been available before.

Some were brave enough to read the manuscript in its rawest form. Donna Hill and Bill Ndini merit my grateful thanks for the time and patience it must have taken to read Doug's story as I produced it—in jumbled order. Melissa Fairbanks read portions as well and, though she never knew her famous grandfather, was able to provide insights about the family and her equally famous father.

J. B. Kaufman was tremendously helpful in sorting out the Civil War record of Fairbanks's father; Russell Merritt provided equally valuable insight in interpreting the D. W. Griffith period at Triangle, and beyond.

Leonard and Alice Maltin gave me calm and informed advice on seeking an agent and a publisher. Of immeasurable help in this capacity was Scott Eyman. One would expect a major author, preoccupied with his book riding the top of the *New York Times* bestseller list, would have little time for a fellow film scholar—especially one with no track record. Instead he guided me on my agent search, recommended the irreplaceable Eric Myers, read generous portions of the book, and provided an incalculable amount of support and encouragement. Speaking of Eric, he got this book placed in a matter of weeks and communicated with me every step of the way. Any author would be extremely fortunate to have an agent such as he. Or an editor such as Yuval Taylor, who demonstrated impeccable taste and judgment every step of the way.

So too did Cari Beauchamp, another author familiar with fame and biographic success. Twenty and more years ago, I read her article in the

New York Times about Italy's annual silent film festival in Pordenone. It led me to Pordenone, and a family of scholars as dear to me as my own kin. Never did I imagine that, decades later, she would also read my manuscript and provide invaluable advice about Frances Marion, Mary Pickford, and even Frank Case's daughter, Margaret. Until *she* called and told me the book was good, I didn't really believe it.

I am in debt to my dear friend Patty Tobias, whose suggestion it was that I write the book in the first place. It has been a ten-year journey and it was all her doing.

I owe a debt to my children, Molly and Sam Doyle, who had to put up with their mother periodically disappearing over the past ten years to spend time in yet another library or archive. But since they grew up not realizing that talking films existed until they were old enough to be taken to a movie theater, I know that they will forgive me.

Finally, I owe a debt to my husband, Robert Bader. When he saw that I was unhappy with my research to date on Fairbanks's antecedents, he dove into genealogy records with such verve that shortly I had more data than I had dreamed of getting. He made the book better in many ways: from finding Dorothy Parker's poem in *The Nonsense of Censorship* to providing me with a 1903 book full of firsthand accounts of the Iroquois Theatre fire. He even knew the term "those Moe Levy tickets" referred to the seller of cheap suits (since 1896!) in New York City. (He claims that his grandfather had a closet full of them.)

I have never met Richard Schickel, but I owe him a debt. I was so taken with his *American Heritage* article on Douglas Fairbanks in 1971 that I checked it out of the library and typed it up, every word, in order that I could retain a copy. If any of my phrasing mimics his, it was not intentional. He opened my eyes to this remarkable personality and stimulated an adolescent desire to learn more.

Douglas Fairbanks was a larger-than-life figure. So epic were his proportions, it seems, that it takes not a single biographer to write his story but a community of the generous and the intelligent. If I have left anyone out (and I have a horror that I have forgotten to name many), know that you are thanked, and loved.

Filmography

NOTE: Early film credits are consistent largely in their inconsistency. Actors' names may change spelling between films, and the spelling on the actual film may differ from that of the press book. Wherever available, the names and spellings of the characters and performers have been drawn from the actual films or the original press books. There will be variation from online sources and other resources accordingly. All attempts have been made to use the actual spellings as defined at the time of the original release.

1913

November 1913
Kinemacolor actuality (title unknown)
Depicts the cast of the Broadway play *The New Henrietta*, "in their social hours." It features Douglas Fairbanks and William H. Crane, the play's stars.
The film is currently considered lost.

1914

November 1914
Our Mutual Girl Sees the Yale-Princeton Game
Stage star Fairbanks makes a cameo appearance in the forty-seventh edition of the weekly *Our Mutual Girl* series, driving the titular heroine to the football game "in his racing runabout."
The film is currently considered lost.

I. Triangle

Each of these thirteen films was produced by the Fine Arts studio and distributed by the Triangle Film Corporation

1915

September 23, 1915 (premiere)
The Lamb
Working Title: *Blood Will Tell*
Director: W. Christy Cabanne (supervised by D. W. Griffith)
Camera: William E. Fildew
Scenario: W. Christy Cabanne
Titles: Anita Loos
Cast: Douglas Fairbanks (Son of the Idle Rich), Seena Owen (the American Girl), Alfred Paget (Her Model Type of Man), Monroe Salisbury (the Wealthy Miner), Kate Toncray (His Mother), Edward Warren (His Valet), Eagle Eye (Himself), William E. Lowery (Another Indian Chief), Lillian Langdon (Girl's Mother)

October 31, 1915 (premiere)
Double Trouble
Director: W. Christy Cabanne (supervised by D. W. Griffith)
Camera: William E. Fildew
Story: Herbert Quick (novel *Double Trouble*)
Scenario: W. Christy Cabanne
Titles: Anita Loos
Cast: Douglas Fairbanks (Florian Amidon/Eugene Brassfield), Richard Cummings (Judge Blodgett), Olga Grey (Madame Leclaire), Margery Wilson (Elizabeth Waldron), Gladys Brockwell (Daisy Scarlett)

1916

February 10, 1916 (premiere); February 13, 1916 (general release)
His Picture in the Papers
Director: John Emerson (supervised by D. W. Griffith)
Camera: George W. Hill
Scenario: John Emerson, Anita Loos
Cast: Douglas Fairbanks (Pete Prindle), Clarence Handyside (Proteus Prindle), Rene Boucicault (Pansy Prindle), Jean Temple (Pearl Prindle), Charles Butler (Cassius Cadwalader), Homer Hunt (Melville), Loretta Blake (Christine Cadwalader), Helena Rapport (Olga), Erich von Stroheim (Gangster, uncredited)

March 12, 1916 (premiere); April 7, 1916 (general release)
The Habit of Happiness
Director: Allan Dwan
Camera: Unknown
Scenario: Shannon Fife
Cast: Douglas Fairbanks (Sunny Wiggins), George Backus (His Father), Grace Rankin (His Sister Clarice), George Fawcett (Jonathan Pepper), Dorothy West (Elsie Pepper), Macey Harlam (Foster), William Jefferson (Jones)

April 21, 1916 (premiere); May 7, 1916 (general release)
The Good Bad Man
Director: Allan Dwan
Camera: Victor Fleming
Scenario: Douglas Fairbanks
Cast: Douglas Fairbanks (Passin' Through), Sam De Grasse (Bud Frazer), Doc Cannon (Bob Evans), Joseph Singleton ("the Weasel"), Bessie Love (Amy), Mary Alden (Jane Stuart), George Beranger (Thomas Stuart), Fred Burns (Sheriff)

May 28, 1916 (premiere); June 11, 1916 (general release)
Reggie Mixes In
Working Title: *The Bouncer*
Director: W. Christy Cabanne
Camera: Victor Fleming
Story: Roy Somerville
Cast: Douglas Fairbanks (Reggie Van Deuzen), Joseph Singleton (Old Pickleface), Alma Rubens (Lemona Reighley), A. D. Sears (Sylvester Ringrose), Bessie Love (Agnes), Alberta Lee (Her Mother), Tom Wilson (the Bouncer), W. A. Lowery (the Leader of the Gas-House Gang), Frank Bennett (Sammy, the Dude), Wilbur Higby (Gallagher)

May 28, 1916 (premiere); June 11, 1916 (general release)
The Mystery of the Leaping Fish
Director: John Emerson
Camera: Unknown
Story: Tod Browning
Scenario: Anita Loos
Cast: Douglas Fairbanks (Coke Ennyday), Tom Wilson (I. M. Keene), A. D. Sears (Gentleman Rolling in Wealth), Bessie Love (Inane), Alma Rubens (Female Confederate, uncredited)

June 25, 1916 (premiere); July 9, 1916 (general release)
Flirting with Fate

Director: W. Christy Cabanne
Camera: Unknown
Story: Robert M. Baker
Scenario: Anita Loos
Cast: Douglas Fairbanks (Augy Holliday), W. E. Laurence (Harry Hansum), Jewel Carmen (Gladys, the Girl), Dorothy Haydel (Phyllis, Her Chum), George Beranger (Automatic Joe), J. P. McCarty (the Detective)

July 9, 1916 (premiere); July 30, 1916 (general release)
The Half Breed
Director: Allan Dwan
Camera: Victor Fleming
Story: Bret Harte (novella "In the Carquinez Woods")
Scenario: Anita Loos
Cast: Douglas Fairbanks (Lo Dorman), Alma Rubens (Teresa), Sam De Grasse (Sheriff Dunn), Tom Wilson (Curson), Frank Brownlee (Winslow Wynn), Jewel Carmen (Nellie), George Beranger (Jack Brace)

September 10, 1916 (premiere); October 1, 1916 (general release)
Manhattan Madness
Director: Allan Dwan
Camera: Victor Fleming
Story: Charles T. Dazey, Frank Dazey, E. V. Durling
Scenario: Charles T. Dazey
Cast: Douglas Fairbanks (Steve O'Dare), Jewel Carmen (the Girl), George Beranger (the Butler), Ruth Darling (the Maid), Eugene Ormonde (Count Marinoff), Macey Harlam (the Villain), W. P. Richmond (Jack Osborne)

November 5, 1916 (premiere); November 12, 1916 (general release)
American Aristocracy
Director: Lloyd Ingraham
Camera: Unknown
Scenario: Anita Loos
Cast: Douglas Fairbanks (Cassius Lee), Jewel Carmen (Geraldine Hicks), Charles DeLima (Leander Hicks), Albert Parker (Percy Peck), Arthur Ortego (Delgado)

December 3, 1916 (premiere); December 16, 1916 (general release)
The Matrimaniac
Director: Paul Powell
Camera: Unknown

Scenario: Octavus Roy Cohen, Anita Loos

Cast: Douglas Fairbanks (Jimmie Conroy), Constance Talmadge (Marna Lewis), Wilbur Higby (Marna's Father), Clyde Hopkins (Wally Henderson), Fred Warren (Reverend Tubbs), Winifred Westover (the Maid)

December 24, 1916 (premiere)

The Americano

Director: John Emerson

Camera: Victor Fleming

Story: Eugene P. Lyle Jr. (novel *Blaze Derringer*)

Scenario: Anita Loos, John Emerson

Cast: Douglas Fairbanks (the Americano), Spottiswoode Aitken (Hernando de Valdez), Tote Du Crow (Alberto de Castille), Carl Stockdale (Salsa Espada), Charles Stevens (Colonel Gargaras), Tom Wilson (Harold Armitage White), Alma Rubens (Juana de Valdez), Lillian Langdon (Signora de Castille), Mildred Harris (Stenographer)

II. Artcraft

Each of these films was produced by the Douglas Fairbanks Pictures Corporation and distributed by the Artcraft Pictures Corporation, unless otherwise noted

1917

April 22, 1917 (premiere); April 30, 1917 (general release)

In Again, Out Again

Director: John Emerson

Camera: Victor Fleming

Scenario: Anita Loos

Art Direction: Erich von Stroheim

Cast: Douglas Fairbanks (Teddy Rutherford), Arline Pretty (Janie Dubb), Walter Walker (Sheriff Dubb), Arnold Lucy (Amos Jennings), Helen Greene (Pacifica Jennings), Homer Hunt (Henry Pinchit), Albert Parker (Jerry), Bull Montana (Quenton Auburn, the Burglar), Ada Gilman (Teddy's Mother), Frank Lalor (Pinkie, the Druggist), Betty Tyrel (the Nurse), Spike Robinson (the Trustee)

June 24, 1917 (premiere)

Wild and Woolly

Working Title: *A Regular Guy*

Director: John Emerson

Camera: Victor Fleming

Story: H. B. Carpenter

Scenario: Anita Loos

Cast: Douglas Fairbanks (Jeff Hillington), Eileen Percy (Nell Larrabee), Walter Bytell (His Father), Joseph Singleton (Hillington's Butler), Calvin Carter (Hotel Keeper, Bitter Creek), Forest Seabury (Banker), J. W. Jones (Lawyer), Charles Stevens (Pedro, Hotel Clerk), Sam De Grasse (Steve, Indian Agent), Tom Wilson (Engineer)

August 5, 1917 (premiere); August 16, 1917 (general release)
Down to Earth
Director: John Emerson
Camera: Victor Fleming
Story: Douglas Fairbanks
Scenario: Anita Loos, John Emerson
Cast: Douglas Fairbanks (Bill Gaynor), Eileen Percy (Ethel, the Girl), Gustav von Seyffertitz (Dr. Jollyem), Charles P. McHugh (Dr. Small), Charles Gerrard (Ethel's Lover), William H. Keith (Mr. Carter), Ruth Allen (Mrs. Fuller Jermes), Fred Goodwine (Jordon Jimmy), Florence Mayon (Mrs. Phattson Oiles), Herbert Standing (Mr. A. D. Dyspeptic), David Porter (Mr. Coffin), Bull Montana (Wild Man)

October 1, 1917 (premiere)
The Man from Painted Post
Director: Joseph Henabery
Camera: Victor Fleming
Story: Jackson Gregory (short story "Silver Slippers")
Scenario: Joseph Henabery
Cast: Douglas Fairbanks (Fancy Jim Sherwood), Eileen Percy (Jane Forbes), Frank Campeau (Bull Madden), Frank Clark (Toby Madden), Herbert Standing (Warren Bronson), Rhea Haines (Wah-na Madden), Charles Stevens (Tony Lopez), Monte Blue (Slim Carter)

October 1917
War Relief (half-reel promotional film)
Also Known As: *The All Star Production of Patriotic Episodes for the Second Liberty Loan*
Director: Marshall Neilan
Camera: Unknown
Scenario: Unknown
Cast: Douglas Fairbanks, Mary Pickford, William S. Hart, Julian Eltinge
Distributed by the US government; currently considered lost.

November 18, 1917 (premiere)
Reaching for the Moon
Director: John Emerson

Camera: Victor Fleming, Sam Landers
Story: Anita Loos
Scenario: Anita Loos, John Emerson
Settings: Wilfred Buckland
Cast: Douglas Fairbanks (Alexis Caesar Napoleon Brown), Eileen Percy (Elsie Merrill), Richard Cummings (Old Man Bingham), Eugene Ormonde (Prince Badinoff of Contraria), Frank Campeau (Black Boris)

December 28, 1917 (premiere); December 30, 1917 (general release)
A Modern Musketeer
Director: Allan Dwan
Camera: Hugh McClung, Harry Thorpe
Story: Eugene P. Lyle Jr. (short story "D'Artagnan of Kansas")
Scenario: Unknown
Cast: Douglas Fairbanks (Ned Thacker), Marjorie Daw (Elsie Dodge), Kathleen Kirkham (Mrs. Dodge), Eugene Ormonde (Forrest Vandeteer), Edythe Chapman (Mrs. Thacker), Frank Campeau (Chin-de-dah), Tully Marshall (James Brown), ZaSu Pitts (uncredited)

1918

March 10, 1918 (premiere)
Headin' South
Director: Arthur Rosson (supervised by Allan Dwan)
Camera: Hugh McClung, Harry Thorpe
Story: Allan Dwan
Scenario: Unknown
Cast: Douglas Fairbanks (Headin' South), Frank Campeau (Spanish Joe), Katherine Mac-Donald (the Girl), Jim Mason (His Aide)
The film is currently considered lost.

April 1918
Swat the Kaiser
Director: Joseph Henabery
Camera: Unknown
Scenario: Unknown
Cast: Douglas Fairbanks (Democracy), Bull Montana (Prussianism), Tully Marshall (Death), Helen MacKern (Justice), Frank Campeau (the Devil), Gustav von Seyffertitz (Uncle Sam)
Distributed by the US government; currently considered lost.

April 21, 1918 (premiere)
Mr. Fixit

Director: Allan Dwan
Camera: Hugh McClung
Story: Ernest Butterworth
Scenario: Allan Dwan
Cast: Douglas Fairbanks (Mr. Fixit), Wanda Hawley (Mary McCollough), Marjorie Daw (Marjorie Threadwell), Leslie Stuart (Reginald Burroughs), Ida Waterman (Aunt Agatha Burroughs), Alice Smith (Aunt Priscilla Burroughs), Mrs. H. R. Hancock (Aunt Laura Burroughs), Frank Campeau (Uncle Henry Burroughs), Fred Goodwin (Gideon Van Tassell), Mr. Russell (Butler Jarvis), Margaret Landis (Olive Van Tassell), Katherine MacDonald (Georgiana Burroughs)

June 16, 1918 (premiere)
Say! Young Fellow
Director: Joseph Henabery
Camera: Glen MacWilliams, Hugh McClung
Story: Joseph Henabery
Scenario: Joseph Henabery, Ted Reed
Cast: Douglas Fairbanks (the Young Fellow), Marjorie Daw (the Girl), Frank Campeau (the Villain), Edythe Chapman (a Sweet Spinster), James Neill (a Kindly Bachelor)
The film is currently considered lost.

July 28, 1918 (premiere)
Bound in Morocco
Director: Allan Dwan
Camera: Hugh McClung
Story: Allan Dwan
Scenario: Allan Dwan, Elton Thomas
Cast: Douglas Fairbanks (the Boy), Pauline Curley (the Girl), Edythe Chapman (Her Mother), Tully Marshall (Ali Pah Shush, Their Faithful Servant), Frank Campeau (Basha El Harib, Governor of the Province of Harib), Jay Dwiggins (Kaid Mahedi El Menebhi, Lord High Ambassador to the Court of El Harib), Fred Burns (Chief of the Bandits)
The film is currently considered lost.

September 8, 1918 (premiere)
He Comes Up Smiling
Director: Allan Dwan
Camera: Hugh McClung, Glen MacWilliams
Story: Byron Ongley & Emil Mytray (play)
Scenario: Frances Marion

Cast: Douglas Fairbanks (the Watermelon, Jerry Martin), Herbert Standing (Mike, a Hobo), Bull Montana (Baron Bean, a Tramp), Albert MacQuarrie (Batchelor, a Stock Broker), Marjorie Daw (Billie), Frank Campeau (John Bartlett, Her Father), Jay Dwiggins (the General), Kathleen Kirkham (Louise, Her Daughter)
The film is currently considered partially lost.

September 14, 1918
Sic 'em Sam
Director: Albert Parker
Camera: Unknown
Scenario: Unknown
Cast: Douglas Fairbanks (Democracy), Bull Montana (Prussianism), Tully Marshall (Death), Helen MacKern (Justice), Frank Campeau (the Devil), Gustav von Seyffertitz (Uncle Sam)
Distributed by the US government; currently considered lost.

December 15, 1918 (premiere)
Arizona
Director: Unlisted (partially directed by Allan Dwan; partially directed by Albert Parker)
Camera: Hugh Carlyle, Glen MacWilliams, Hugh McClung
Story: Augustus Thomas (play)
Scenario: Ted Reed
Cast: Douglas Fairbanks (Lieutenant Denton), Theodore Roberts (Canby), Kate Price (Mrs. Canby), Frederick Burton (Col. Benham), Harry Northrup (Captain Hodgeman), Frank Campeau (Kellar), Kathleen Kirkham (Estrella), Marjorie Daw (Bonita), Marguerite De La Motte (Lena), Raymond Hatton (Tony), Robert Boulder (Doctor), Albert MacQuarrie (Lieut. Hatton)
The film is currently considered lost.

1919

Premiere date unknown
Knocking Knockers
Director: Unknown
Camera: Unknown
Scenario: Unknown
Cast: Douglas Fairbanks (Democracy), Bull Montana (Prussianism), Tully Marshall (Death), Helen MacKern (Justice), Frank Campeau (the Devil), Gustav von Seyffertitz (Uncle Sam)
Distributed by the US government; currently considered lost.

May 25, 1919 (premiere)
The Knickerbocker Buckaroo

Director: Albert Parker
Camera: Glen MacWilliams, Hugh McClung
Story: Joseph Henabery, Douglas Fairbanks, Frank Condon, Ted Reed
Scenario: Ted Reed
Cast: Douglas Fairbanks (Teddy Drake), Marjorie Daw (Mercedes, the Girl), William Wellman (Henry, Her Brother), Frank Campeau (Sheriff, a Crook), Edythe Chapman (Teddy's Mother), Albert MacQuarrie (Manuel Lopez, the Bandit), Ted Reed (a New York Clubman)
The film is currently considered lost.

III. United Artists

Each of these films was produced by the Douglas Fairbanks Pictures Corporation and distributed by United Artists, unless otherwise noted

September 1, 1919 (general release)
His Majesty the American
Director: Joseph Henabery
Camera: Victor Fleming
Story: Joseph Henabery
Scenario: Joseph Henabery, Elton Thomas
Cast: Douglas Fairbanks (William Brooks), Marjorie Daw (Felice, Countess of Montenac), Frank Campeau (Grand Duke Sarzeau, Minister of War), Sam Sothern (Phillipe the Fourth, King of Alaine), Jay Dwiggins (Emile Meitz, Emissary from Brizac), Lillian Langdon (Marguerite, Princess of Alaine)

December 28, 1919 (premiere)
When the Clouds Roll By
Director: Victor Fleming
Camera: William McGann, Harry Thorpe
Story: Douglas Fairbanks
Scenario: Tom Geraghty
Art Direction: Edward M. Langley
Art Titles: Henry Clive
Cast: Douglas Fairbanks (Daniel Boone Brown), Albert MacQuarrie (Hobson, His Man-Servant), Ralph Lewis (Curtis Brown, His Uncle), Frank Campeau (Mark Drake), Herbert Grimwood (Dr. Ulrich Metz), Daisy Robinson (Bobby De Vere), Kathleen Clifford (Lucette Bancroft)

1920

June 13, 1920 (premiere)
The Mollycoddle

Director: Victor Fleming
Assistant Director: Ted Reed
Camera: Harry Thorpe, William McGann
Story: Harold MacGrath (short story)
Scenario: Tom Geraghty
Art Direction: Edward M. Langley
Technical Effects: Robert Fairbanks
Cast: Douglas Fairbanks (Richard Marshall III; Richard Marshall IV; Richard Marshall V); Wallace Beery (Henry Van Holkar); Morris Hughes, George Stewart, Paul Burns (American College Boys); Ruth Renick (Virginia Hale); Adele Farrington (Mrs. Warren); Betty Bouton (Molly Warren)

November 29, 1920 (premiere)
The Mark of Zorro
Working Titles: *The Curse of Capistrano*; *The Black Fox*
Director: Fred Niblo
Camera: William McGann, Harry Thorpe
Story: Johnston McCulley (*The Curse of Capistrano*, All-Story Weekly)
Scenario: Eugene Mullin, Douglas Fairbanks
Art Direction: Edward M. Langley
Cast: Douglas Fairbanks (Don Diego Vega/Zorro), Marguerite De La Motte (Lolita Pulido), Robert McKim (Capitán Juan Ramon), Noah Beery Sr. (Sgt. Pedro Gonzales), Charles Hill Mailes (Don Carlos Pulido), Claire McDowell (Doña Catalina Pulido), Snitz Edwards (Barkeep), Sydney De Grey (Don Alejandro), George Periolat (Governor Alvarado), Walt Whitman (Fray Felipe), Tote Du Crow (Bernardo)

1921

March 1, 1921 (premiere)
The Nut
Director: Ted Reed
Camera: William McGann, Harry Thorpe, Charles Warrington
Story: Elton Thomas, Kenneth Davenport
Scenario: William Parker, Lotta Woods
Art Direction: Edward M. Langley
Cast: Douglas Fairbanks (Charlie Jackson), Marguerite De La Motte (Estrell Wynn), William Lowery (Philip Feeny), Gerald Pring (Gentleman George), Morris Hughes (Pernelius Vanderbrook Jr.), Barbara La Marr (Claudine Dupree)

Premiere date unknown
The Non-sense of Censorship

Anti-censorship film featuring Douglas Fairbanks, Rupert Hughes, Edward Knoblock, Samuel Merwin, Thompson Buchanan, Rita Welman, and Montague Glass as themselves. *The film is currently considered lost.*

August 28, 1921 (premiere)
The Three Musketeers
Director: Fred Niblo
Camera: Arthur Edeson
Story: Alexander Dumas (novel)
Scenario: Lotta Woods, Edward Knoblock
Cast: Douglas Fairbanks (D'Artagnan), Adolphe Menjou (Louis XIII), Mary MacLaren (Anne of Austria), Nigel de Brulier (Cardinal Richelieu), Thomas Holding (Duke of Buckingham), Marguerite De La Motte (Constance), Willis Robards (De Treville), Boyd Irwin (Rochefort), Barbara La Marr (Milady), Lon Poff (Father Joseph), Walt Whitman (D'Artagnan's Father), Sydney Franklin (Bonacieux), Charles Belcher (Bernajoux), Charles Stevens (Planchet), Léon Bary (Athos), George Siegmann (Porthos), Eugene Pallette (Aramis)

1922

October 22, 1922 (Chicago premiere)
Robin Hood
Director: Allan Dwan
Camera: Arthur Edeson
Story: Elton Thomas
Scenario: Lotta Woods
Research: Dr. Arthur Woods
Art Direction: Wilfred Buckland, Irvin J. Martin, Edward M. Langley, Mitchell Leisen
Production and Construction: Robert Fairbanks
Cast: Douglas Fairbanks (Robin Hood), Wallace Beery (King Richard I), Sam De Grasse (Prince John), Enid Bennett (Lady Marian Fitzwalter), Paul Dickey (Sir Guy of Gisbourne), William Lowery (the Sheriff of Nottingham), Alan Hale (Little John), Willard Louis (Friar Tuck), Dick Rosson (Alan-a-Dale), Roy Coulson (the King's Jester)

1923

August 19, 1923
Hollywood
Director: James Cruze
Fairbanks plays himself among a host of stars doing cameo sequences.
Produced by Paramount; the film is currently considered lost.

1924

March 15, 1924
Dorothy Vernon of Haddon Hall
Director: Marshall Neilan
Starring Mary Pickford, this film features Fairbanks in an unbilled cameo, serving as a body double for leading man Allen Forrest.
Produced by Mary Pickford and distributed by United Artists.

March 18, 1924 (premiere)
The Thief of Bagdad
Director: Raoul Walsh
Assistant Director: James O'Donohoe
Camera: Arthur Edeson
Associate Photographers: Richard Holahan, P. H. Whitman, Kenneth MacLean
Story: Elton Thomas
Scenario: Lotta Woods
Research: Dr. Arthur Woods
Consultant: Edward Knoblock
Art Direction: William Cameron Menzies
Consulting Art Director: Irvin J. Martin
Associate Artists: Anton E. Grot, Paul Youngblood, H. R. Hopps, Harold W. Grieve, William Utwich, Edward M. Langley
Musical Score: Mortimer Wilson
Production and Construction: Ted Reed
Master of Wardrobe and Properties: Paul Burns
Costume Design: Mitchell Leisen
Technical Director: Robert Fairbanks
Master Electrician: Albert Wayne
Still Photographer: Charles Warrington
Technicians: Howard MacChesney, Clinton Newman, Walter Pallman, J. C. Watson
Directors of Mechanical Effects: Hampton Del Ruth, Coy Watson Sr.
Editor: William Nolan
Cast: Douglas Fairbanks (the Thief of Bagdad); Snitz Edwards (His Evil Associate); Charles Belcher (the Holy Man); Julanne Johnston (the Princess); Anna May Wong (the Mongol Slave); Winter-Blossom (the Slave of the Lute); Etta Lee (the Slave of the Sand Board); Brandon Hurst (the Caliph); Tote Du Crow (His Soothsayer); Sôjin Kamiyama (the Mongol Prince); K. Nambu (His Counselor); Noble Johnson (the Indian Prince); Mathilde Comant (the Persian Prince); Charles Stevens (His Awaker); Sam Baker (the Sworder); Charles Sylvester, Scott Mattraw, Jess Weldon (the Eunuchs)

1925

June 15, 1925 (premiere); August 30, 1925 (general release)
Don Q, Son of Zorro
Director: Donald Crisp
Assistant Director: Frank Richardson
Camera: Henry Sharp
Associate Photographer: E. J. Vallejo
Story: K. & Hesketh Prichard (novel *Don Q's Love Story*)
Scenario: Jack Cunningham
Art Direction: Edward M. Langley
General Manager: Robert Fairbanks
Editor: William Nolan
Cast: Douglas Fairbanks (Don Cesar de Vega; Zorro, His Father), Mary Astor (Dolores del Muro), Jack McDonald (General de Muro), Donald Crisp (Don Sebastian), Stella De Lanti (the Queen), Warner Oland (the Archduke), Jean Hersholt (Don Fabrique), Albert MacQuarrie (Colonel Matsado), Lottie Pickford Forrest (Lola), Charles Stevens (Robledo), Tote Du Crow (Bernardo), Martha Franklin (the Duenna), Juliette Belanger (the Dancer), Roy Coulson (Her Admirer), Enrique Acosta (Ramon)

1926

March 8, 1926 (premiere)
The Black Pirate
Director: Albert Parker
Camera: Henry Sharp
Story: Elton Thomas, adaptation by Jack Cunningham
Scenario: Lotta Woods
Research: Dr. Arthur Woods
Consultants: Dwight Franklin, Robert Nichols
Art Direction: Carl Oscar Borg
Associate Artists: Edward M. Langley, Jack Holden
Musical Score: Mortimer Wilson
General Manager: Robert Fairbanks
Production Manager: Ted Reed
Marine Technician: P. H. L. Wilson
Technicolor Staff: Arthur Ball, George Cave
Editor: William Nolan
Cast: Douglas Fairbanks (the Duke of Arnoldo/the Black Pirate), Billie Dove (Princess Isobel), Tempe Pigott (Duenna), Donald Crisp (MacTavish), Sam De Grasse (Pirate Lieutenant), Anders Randolf (Pirate Captain), Charles Stevens (Powder Man; assorted pirates

and victims), John Wallace (Peg-Leg Pirate), Fred Becker (Pirate), Charles Belcher (Chief Passenger), E. J. Ratcliffe (the Governor)

1927

September 9, 1927
A Kiss from Mary Pickford (*Поцелуй Мэри Пикфорд*)
This Russian comedy features footage from Doug and Mary's 1926 visit to Russia and was produced and distributed without their knowledge.

November 4, 1927 (Los Angeles premiere)
The Gaucho
Director: F. Richard Jones
Assistant Directors: William J. Cowan, Lewis R. Foster
Camera: Tony Gaudio
Story: Elton Thomas
Scenario: Lotta Woods
Art Direction: Carl Oscar Borg
Production Manager: Ted Reed
Costumes: Paul Burns
Editor: William Nolan
Cast: Douglas Fairbanks (the Gaucho), Lupe Vélez (the Mountain Girl), Geraine Greear (the Girl of the Shrine as a Child), Eve Southern (the Girl of the Shrine as an Adult), Gustav von Seyffertitz (Ruiz, the Usurper), Michael Vavitch (the Usurper's First Lieutenant), Charles Stevens (the Gaucho's First Lieutenant), Nigel de Brulier (the Padre), Albert MacQuarrie (Victim of the Black Doom), Mary Pickford (Virgin Mary, uncredited)

November 21, 1927
Carter de Haven's Character Studies
Carter de Haven filmed this short, split-reel film late in 1925 for inclusion in his vaudeville act at the Music Box Theater in 1926. The film featured the comic doing what were purported to be impressions, appearing as Harold Lloyd, Roscoe Arbuckle, Buster Keaton, Rudolph Valentino, Douglas Fairbanks (in Robin Hood costume), and Jackie Coogan, who, by use of editing, appeared as themselves. The film was later released for general booking as a short subject.

1928

November 20, 1928
Show People
Director: King Vidor

In this film starring Marion Davies, Fairbanks plays himself among a host of stars during a banquet scene.
Produced by MGM.

1929

February 21, 1929 (premiere)
The Iron Mask
Director: Allan Dwan
Assistant Director: Bruce Humberstone
Camera: Henry Sharp
Story: Elton Thomas, Alexander Dumas (novels *The Three Musketeers* and *The Man in the Iron Mask*), also based on the memoirs of D'Artagnan, Richelieu, and De Rochefort
Scenario: Lotta Woods
Research: Dr. Arthur Woods
Consultants: Jack Cunningham, Earle Browne
Art Direction: Maurice Leloir
Artists: Laurence Irving, Carl Oscar Borg, Ben Carré, Harold Miles, David S. Hall, Edward M. Langley, Wilfred Buckland, Jack Holden
General Manager: Robert Fairbanks
Master of Wardrobe and Properties: Paul Burns
Costume Design: Maurice Leloir
Costumes: Gilbert Clark, May Hallett, Western Costume Company
Editor: William Nolan
Cast: Douglas Fairbanks (D'Artagnan), Belle Bennett (the Queen Mother), Marguerite De La Motte (Constance), Dorothy Revier (Milady de Winter), Vera Lewis (Madame Peronne), Rolfe Sedan (Louis XIII), William Bakewell (Louis XIV; His Twin Brother), Gordon Thorpe (Young Prince; Twin Brother), Nigel de Brulier (Cardinal Richelieu), Ullrich Haupt (De Rochefort), Lon Poff (Father Joseph), Charles Stevens (Planchet, D'Artagnan's Servant), Henry Otto (the King's Valet), Léon Bary (Athos), Stanley Sandford (Porthos), Gino Corrado (Aramis)

November 14, 1929 (premiere)
The Taming of the Shrew
Director: Sam Taylor
Camera: Karl Struss
Story: William Shakespeare (play)
Scenario: Sam Taylor
Art Direction: William Cameron Menzies, Lawrence Irving
Production Staff: Earle Browne, "Lucky" Humberstone, Walter Mayo
Editor: Allen McNeil

Cast: Mary Pickford (Katherine), Douglas Fairbanks (Petruchio), Edwin Maxwell (Baptista), Joseph Cawthorn (Gremio), Clyde Cook (Grumio), Geoffrey Wardell (Hortensio), Dorothy Jordon (Bianca)

1930

December 29, 1930 (New York premiere); February 21, 1931 (general release)
Reaching for the Moon
Working Title: *Love in a Cottage*
Director: Edmund Goulding
Assistant Director: Lonnie D'Orsa
Camera: Ray June, Robert Planck
Story: Irving Berlin
Scenario: Irving Berlin, Edmund Goulding, Elsie Janis (additional dialogue)
Musical Director: Alfred Newman
Costumes: David Cox
Set Decoration: Julia Heron, William Cameron Menzies
Editor: Hal C. Kern, Lloyd Nosler
Cast: Douglas Fairbanks (Larry Day), Bebe Daniels (Vivien Benton), Edward Everett Horton (Roger, the Valet), Claud Allister (Sir Horace Partington Chelmsford), Jack Mulhall (Jimmy Carrington), Walter Walker (James Benton), June MacCloy (Kitty), Helen Jerome Eddy (Larry's Secretary), Bing Crosby (uncredited)
Produced by Joseph Schenck and distributed by United Artists.

1931

November 19, 1931 (premiere); December 12, 1931 (general release)
Around the World in Eighty Minutes
Also Known As: *Around the World with Douglas Fairbanks*
Director: Victor Fleming
Camera: Harry Sharp, Victor Fleming
Dialogue: Robert Sherwood
Production Manager: Chuck Lewis
Cast: Douglas Fairbanks (Himself), Victor Fleming (Himself), Duke Kahanamoku (Himself), Sôjin Kamiyama (Himself), Emilio Aguinaldo (Himself), Sessue Hayakawa (Himself)
NOTE: The title on the film proper is Around the World with Douglas Fairbanks, *but all advertising, reviews, and administrative documentation lists the film as* Around the World in Eighty Minutes.

1932

September 21, 1932 (premiere)
Mr. Robinson Crusoe
Director: Edward Sutherland
Camera: Max Dupont
Story: Elton Thomas
Scenario: Tom Geraghty
Music: Alfred Newman
Production Managers: Chuck Lewis, Harry Ham
Technical Effects: Walter Pahlman
Editor: Robert Kern
Cast: Douglas Fairbanks (Steve Drexel), William Farnum (William Belmont), Earle Browne (Professor Carmichale), Maria Alba (Saturday)

1934

September 5, 1934 (premiere)
The Private Life of Don Juan
Director: Alexander Korda
Assistant Director: G. Boothby
Camera: Osmond Borrodaile
Story: Frederick Lonsdale, Lajos Biro, Henry Bataille (play *L'Homme à la Rose*)
Scenario: Frederick Lonsdale, Lajos Biro
Music: Ernest Toch
Lyrics: Arthur Wimperis
Musical Director: Muir Mathieson
Don Juan Serenade: Michael Spolianski
Serenade Sung by: John Brownlee
Sound Director: A. W. Watkins
Production Manager: David B. Cunynghame
Architect: F. Hallam
Costumes: B. J. Simmons & Company
Settings: Vincent Korda
Technical Director: Marques de Portago
Special Effects: Ned Mann
Supervising Editor: Harold Young
Editor: Stephen Harrison
Cast: Douglas Fairbanks (Don Juan), Merle Oberon (Antonita, a Dancer of Passionate Temperament), Bruce Winston (Her Manager), Gina Malo (Pepitta, Another Dancer of Equal Temperament), Benita Hume (Dona Delores, a Lady of Mystery), Binnie Barnes (Rosita,

a Maid Pure and Simple), Melville Cooper (Leporello), Owen Nares (an Actor as Actors Go), Heather Thatcher (an Actress as Actresses Go), Diana Napier (a Lady of Sentiment), Joan Gardner (a Young Lady of Romance), Gibson Gowland (Her Poor Husband), Barry MacKay (a Young Man of Romance), Claude Allister (the Duke, as Dukes Go), Athene Seyler (a Middle Aged Lady of Youthful Sentiment), Hindle Edgar (a Jealous Husband), Natalie Paley (His Poor Wife), Patricia Hilliard (a Young Girl in Love), Lawrence Grossmith (Her Uncle, Who Knows Better), Clifford Heatherly (Don Juan's Masseur), Morland Graham (His Doctor), Edmund Breon (a Playwright, as Playwrights Go), Betty Hamilton (the Wife of a Tired Businessman), Rosita Garcia (Another Wife of Another Tired Businessman) *Produced by Alexander Korda and distributed by United Artists.*

1937

October 29, 1937
Ali Baba Goes to Town
Director: David Butler
Stars Eddie Cantor; Fairbanks plays himself among other stars, including Shirley Temple, Tyrone Power, and Dolores del Rio.
Produced by 20th Century-Fox.

Notes

Introduction

"Gatsby on a jungle gym": Michael Sragow, *Victor Fleming: An American Movie Master* (New York: Pantheon Books, 2008), 41.

"the Yankee Doodle Boy": Edward Wagenknecht, *The Movies in the Age of Innocence* (New York: Ballantine Books, 1962), 172.

1. The Father of the Man

"You fell off the roof, darling!": Letitia Fairbanks and Ralph Hancock, *Doug Fairbanks: The Fourth Musketeer* (New York: Henry Holt, 1953), 28.

"A smile at the right time": *Photoplay*, April 1918.

"I was three years old": *Rochester Democrat and Chronicle*, September 23, 1924.

His occupation was listed variably: US Federal Census Collection, Ancestry.com.

an 1873 passport application: US Passport Applications, Ancestry.com.

by 1876, he was the first president: *Atlanta Constitution*, May 13, 1876; *Janesville Gazette*, June 20, 1876.

They lived at 494 Jackson Avenue: New Orleans City Directory, 1872, Online Historical Directories Website, https://sites.google.com/site/onlinedirectorysite/Home/usa/la/orleans.

"The most distinguished looking man": *Macon Telegraph*, April 1, 1928.

he "was probably abusive": Fairbanks and Hancock, *Doug Fairbanks*, 41.

"I was the blackest baby you ever saw": Richard Schickel, *His Picture in the Papers: A Speculation on Celebrity in America Based on the Life of Douglas Fairbanks, Sr.* (New York: Charterhouse, 1974), 13.

"Almost anyone who begins to take up his past": Douglas Fairbanks, "Seriously Speaking" (unsourced article), Mary Pickford Papers, folder 1355, Margaret Herrick Library, Academy of Motion Picture Arts and Sciences, Beverly Hills, CA.

"Mr. Fairbanks was a splendid Shakespearean scholar": *Tampa Tribune*, April 23, 1916.

"even then as close as peas": Fairbanks and Hancock, *Doug Fairbanks*, 24.

"he had never known one yet": Ibid., 25.

he "would recite you as fine and florid an Antony's speech": Ibid., 40.

"Schooling as such didn't appeal to me": Ibid., 41.

"They were my first glimpses": Ibid., 27.

"That old biddy acts as if": Ibid., 32.

"with customary—but dramatic—solemnity": Ibid., 42.

The earliest evidence of this theatrical passion: *Photoplay*, May 1917.

"I braced him": Fairbanks and Hancock, *Doug Fairbanks*, 51.

he danced both a gavotte and a hornpipe: *Denver Rocky Mountain News*, January 13, 1896.

January 1897 saw him at the Masonic temple: *Denver Post*, January 20, 1897.

"Mother had a time getting Douglas": Fairbanks and Hancock, *Doug Fairbanks*, 53.

"Don't you remember when your mother used to say": *Mansfield News*, January 23, 1909.

"Get off that sofa!": Douglas Fairbanks Papers, scrapbook 1: condolence letters, Margaret Herrick Library.

"Yours, Lovingly": Ibid.

After the "dainty refreshments": *Denver Rocky Mountain News*, May 9, 1897.

an evening of "literary and musical entertainment": *Denver Post*, March 12, 1898.

"I had known him long": Douglas Fairbanks Papers, scrapbook 1: condolence letters, Margaret Herrick Library.

the Wolhurst Fete, an open-air fundraiser: *Denver Post*, August 26, 1898; *Denver Sunday Post*, August 28, 1898.

he was to appear with Hobart Bosworth: *Denver Evening Post*, September 3, 1898.

In October 1898 he was seen at Windsor Hall: Ibid., October 18, 1898.

part of a program of special attractions: *Denver Rocky Mountain News*, November 19, 1898.

he performed his comic dialect speeches: *Denver Evening Post*, November 20, 1898.

"A remarkable thing about the entertainments": *New York Dramatic Mirror*, December 10, 1898.

"Master Douglas Fairbanks has a part": *Denver Post*, November 20, 1898.

"One day happened to meet an actor man": *Chicago Daily Tribune*, April 28, 1912.

"The simple hurdles in this case": Fairbanks and Hancock, *Doug Fairbanks*, 60.

"America's greatest forgotten tragedian": Alan Woods, "Frederick B. Warde: America's Greatest Forgotten Tragedian," *Educational Theatre Journal* 29, no. 3 (October 1977): 333.

"the touring tragedian, a star actor": Ibid., 333–334.

The voice itself had a wealth: Allen Griffith, *Lessons in Elocution* (Chicago: Adams, Blackmer & Lyon, 1871), 14.

"Mr. Warde himself as Romeo": *Washington Post*, May 5, 1900.

"While in Denver, Colorado, I made an address": Frederick Warde, *Fifty Years of Make Believe* (New York: International Press Syndicate, 1920), 273.

"Here it is, teacher!": Booton Herndon, *Mary Pickford and Douglas Fairbanks: The Most Popular Couple the World Has Ever Known* (New York: Norton, 1977), 17.

He continued with temperate fibs: Fairbanks and Hancock, *Doug Fairbanks*, 76.

"His English teacher there": Ibid., 56.

The company consisted of twenty-five people: *San Diego Union*, December 1, 1899.

The production traveled with a sixty-foot baggage car: *Atlanta Constitution*, September 28, 1899.

He made thirty dollars a week: *Repository* (Canton, OH), March 2, 1923.

"The school boy Douglas was no more": *Chicago Daily Tribune*, April 28, 1912.

"to make a long story short": *Photoplay*, December 1917.

"Mr. Warde's company was bad": Schickel, *His Picture in the Papers*, 20.

"I probably wore the most astonishing costumes": *Theatre Magazine*, April 1917.

giving him progressively larger roles: Eric L. Flom, *Silent Film Stars on the Stages of Seattle: A History of Performances by Hollywood Notables* (Jefferson, NC: McFarland, 2009), 57.

a "laughing face, a curly head of hair": *San Diego Union*, May 24, 1923.

"Douglas saved him much money": *Riverside Daily Press*, April 5, 1923.

"He is one of the men whom fortune": *Omaha World Herald*, November 18, 1924.

Fairbanks claimed that he headed up the funeral procession: *San Diego Union*, May 24, 1923.

"If he says it was so, it must be true": Unsourced clipping, Douglas Fairbanks Papers, Margaret Herrick Library.

"Miss May Warde, as Benetta": *Fort Worth Morning Register*, November 10, 1900.

"Some actors draw a rapier": *Los Angeles Times*, December 13, 1900.

a sheriff deputy crawling over his box: *New York Times*, March 15, 1900.

"When I played at the old Willis Wood": *Amarillo News Globe*, May 21, 1933.

"Hockey scores will be given": *Manitoba Morning Free Press*, January 31, 1901.

2. The Heroine's Likable Younger Brother

More than forty "legitimate" theaters: Daniel Blum, *A Pictorial History of the American Theatre, 1860–1970* (New York: Crown, 1969), 54.

He was paid forty dollars per week: *Springfield Republican*, October 28, 1923.

"The most poorly drawn character": *Syracuse Post Standard*, March 16, 1902.

"capital as an impulsive, unsophisticated and not very discreet youth": *New York Dramatic Mirror*, February 8, 1902.

"naturalness and refreshing spontaneity": *New York Clipper*, January 18, 1902.

"boyish audacity": Ibid.

"The name Coppet appealed to me": George Creel, "A 'Close-Up' of Douglas Fairbanks," *Everybody's Magazine*, 1916.

"he is still remembered in that office": Ibid.

"For five days in the week I would say": Ibid.

"I shall never forget the day": Douglas Fairbanks Papers, scrapbook 1: condolence letters, Margaret Herrick Library, Academy of Motion Picture Arts and Sciences, Beverly Hills, CA.

"I was seized with a restless spirit": *Boys' Life*, June 1928.

"I walked from Liverpool to London": Chapter 4 in *From Hollywood to Paris* (draft copy) by Mary Pickford, Mary Pickford Papers, Margaret Herrick Library.

"I worked with street gangs": *Boys' Life*, March 1924.

Robert Florey claims: Robert Florey, *Filmland: Los Angeles et Hollywood les capitales du cinema* (Paris: Editions de Cinemagazine, 1923), 135.

"I think," she famously said: Letitia Fairbanks and Ralph Hancock, *Doug Fairbanks: The Fourth Musketeer* (New York: Henry Holt, 1953), 80.

"boyish, natural and interesting": *New York Dramatic Mirror*, October 11, 1902.

"with a good deal of judgment": *Jersey Journal*, January 20, 1903.

"feeling quite at home": Fairbanks and Hancock, *Doug Fairbanks*, 81.

He joined a group of young actors: *Boston Herald*, March 30, 1924.

role in *Mrs. Jack* for "a whole year": "How 'Doug' Fairbanks Made His First Thousand," *Three Musketeers* press book, 1922, private collection.

Nineteen years later, at the height: *San Antonio Express*, May 21, 1922.

"it would not be possible to become a brilliant attorney": Kenneth Davenport, Fairbanks studio biography, n.d., Thomas J. Geraghty Papers, file 22: miscellaneous, Margaret Herrick Library.

"No orchestra ever played loudly enough": Ibid.

"more charm than was right": Richard F. Snow, "William A. Brady," *American Heritage Magazine* 31, no. 3 (April/May 1980).

"The 'conductor' stood on the back platform": Edward Wagenknecht, *The Movies in the Age of Innocence* (New York: Ballantine Books, 1962), 9.

"Porter distinguished the movies": Lewis Jacobs, *The Rise of the American Film* (New York: Harcourt, Brace, 1939).

"500 men of good appearance": *Chicago Daily Tribune*, December 13, 1903.

It was being burlesqued in a sketch: *New York Times*, February 14, 1904.

"This was Landry Court": Frank Norris, *The Pit: A Story of Chicago* (New York: Doubleday, 1903), 15.

Doug played "with refreshing spirit": *New York Dramatic Mirror*, February 20, 1904.

"After a season of what I thought": "How 'Doug' Fairbanks Made His First Thousand."

"There were some stormy aspects": William A. Brady, *Showman* (New York: E. P. Dutton, 1937), 267.

"boyish, roistering, likable": *New York Clipper*, May 7, 1904.

"Discouragement isn't the word": "How 'Doug' Fairbanks Made His First Thousand."

the "cattle boat" was a passenger ship: Incoming Passenger Lists, 1878–1960, record for "Ella Fairbanks," National Archives, London, England; Douglas was misrecorded in the passenger list as "David."

He returned to New York late in August: Incoming Passenger Lists, 1878–1960, record for "DE Fairbanks" and "Mrs. Ella Fairbanks."

"In the first act the entire dramatis personae": Fairbanks and Hancock, *Doug Fairbanks*, 86.

noted not only for an unusually fine voice: *New York Dramatic Mirror*, January 21, 1905.

he sang a solo, "Just My Style": *Tampa Tribune*, May 4, 1924.

"He's not good-looking": Brady, *Showman*, 272.

"reigning craze for watering stocks": *Chicago Daily Tribune*, March 12, 1905.

"made up his mind to be a power": *New York Times*, April 4, 1905.

"When there were no natural obstacles": *Boys' Life*, November 1923.

"pleasing when he was not spouting platitudes": *New York Times*, April 4, 1905.

"fervor and enthusiasm": *New York Clipper*, April 8, 1905.

"shows the hurried pitchfork": *New York Dramatic Mirror*, April 15, 1905.

"I think the play is one of the best": *New York Morning Telegraph*, April 7, 1905.

four pages from a young theatergoer's album: Author's collection.

"Douglas Fairbanks . . . did excellently": *New York Morning Telegraph*, April 4, 1905.

"The general public will not be admitted": *Chicago Daily Tribune*, September 14, 1905.

"Robust fun of the usual huckleberry flavor": *New York Times*, December 26, 1905.

"If the minister portrayed in the play": *New York Dramatic Mirror*, January 6, 1906.

The crowds at the Garden were the largest in five years: *Middleton Daily Press*, January 9, 1906.

"In my home town I played": *Theatre Magazine*, April 1917.

Kenneth Davenport was able to step in: *Oakland Tribune*, October 31, 1906.

"Douglas Fairbanks gave his customarily truthful picture": *New York Dramatic Mirror*, September 22, 1906.

"Douglas Fairbanks . . . played an unimportant part": *New York Clipper*, September 22, 1906.

"During rehearsals, which always wore everybody else": Brady, *Showman*, 262.

"the simplest way": *New York Times*, October 28, 1906.

Fairbanks "had the audience with him": *Galveston Daily News*, February 24, 1907.

"Douglas Fairbanks played his now familiar ": *New York Times*, December 5, 1906.

"She epitomized that upper-class world": Douglas Fairbanks Jr., *The Salad Days* (New York: Doubleday, 1988), 17.

"Opposition to the suit aroused the fighting blood": *Trenton Evening News*, January 18, 1907.

"At the conclusion of the conference": Ibid.

The sun parlor at Kenneth Ridge: *Washington Post*, July 12, 1907.

"I think you are making a great mistake": Fairbanks and Hancock, *Doug Fairbanks*, 91.

"he will be launched as a full-fledged star": *Washington Post*, August 29, 1907.

3. Stage Stardom

the self-described "Captain of the Good Ship Take-it-Easy": Richard Schickel, *D. W. Griffith: An American Life* (New York: Simon & Schuster, 1984), 107.

rehearsals for *All for a Girl* began: *Anaconda Standard*, July 19, 1908.

"Another star burst forth": *New York Clipper*, August 29, 1908.

Fairbanks "is extremely clever": *Washington Post*, August 30, 1908.

"Mr. Fairbanks is not beautiful": *New York Times*, August 23, 1908.

"I played the part of a speedy young chap": *Theatre Magazine*, April 1917.

He had lunch with a friend: *Collier's Magazine,* June 18, 1921.

"Bully!" and "A corker!": Souvenir program for *A Gentleman from Mississippi*, author's collection.

Roosevelt was "energetic, stubborn, opinionated": Richard Zacks, *Island of Vice: Theodore Roosevelt's Quest to Clean Up Sin-Loving New York* (New York: Anchor, 2012), 4.

"He was tremendously excitable": Ibid.

"because it was the best [background] to demonstrate": Alistair Cooke, *Douglas Fairbanks: The Making of a Screen Character*, Museum of Modern Art Film Library Series 2 (New York: Museum of Modern Art, 1940), 19.

Sully "loves Roosevelt about as much": *Green Book*, October 1914.

"I expected he'd howdy do me": Ibid.

The success of the play was assured: *New York Dramatic Mirror*, October 10, 1908.

Doug's "fresh, breezy, wholesome way": *New York Times*, September 30, 1908.

Her father had advanced the young couple: Douglas Fairbanks Jr., *The Salad Days* (New York: Doubleday, 1988), 19.

"equally extravagant actor-husband": Ibid.

"the student body compelled Mr. Fairbanks": *Syracuse Post Standard*, April 19, 1910.

arriving in Great Britain in late May: Fairbanks Jr., *Salad Days*, 19; Incoming Passenger Lists, 1878–1960, record for "Douglas Fairbanks," Ancestry.com.

relaxation of official mourning for King Edward VII: *New York Times*, June 5, 1910.

"Douglas Fairbanks, the actor, chased a 'bookie'": *Washington Post*, June 3, 1910.

the family returned to the States: *New York Times*, August 8, 1910.

The Cub, which previewed in Boston in mid-September: *Boston Globe*, September 25, 1910.

a quarrel about a pig: *New York Clipper*, November 12, 1910.

a cub reporter, "fresh from college": *Washington Post*, January 26, 1911.

"The further progress of the ass": Ibid.

"In one scene he had to run upstairs": William A. Brady, *Showman* (New York: E. P. Dutton, 1937), 265.

until "my lawyers had made sure of him": Ibid., 267.

"Put him in a death scene": George Creel, "A 'Close-Up' of Douglas Fairbanks," *Everybody's Magazine*, 1916.

"It requires the physical endurance of a trained athlete": *Washington Post*, January 26, 1911.

"The audience was kept almost continually in laughter": *New York Clipper*, November 12, 1910.

a limited-run revival of *The Lights o' London*: *New York Times*, April 6, 1911.

a tremendous hit when it premiered in 1881: *New York Times*, April 15, 1911.

Brady himself played the policeman: Ibid., May 21, 1911.

"The prize melodrama of 30 years": *Washington Post*, May 7, 1911.

The opening curtain went up too early: Ibid.

the hapless uncle was murdered in bright light: *Chicago Daily Tribune*, May 7, 1911.

They threatened to quit: *Indianapolis Star*, May 14, 1911.

"one after another, sent a perfect shower of fish": *Los Angeles Times*, August 29, 1912.

"No doubt Fairbanks' temperament had a good deal to do": Brady, *Showman*, 266.

"a young man of medium height": P. G. Wodehouse. *A Gentleman of Leisure* (New York: Overlook Press, 2003), 15.

"the audience was treated to one of the most realistic fights": *New York Clipper*, September 2, 1911.

in order to make room for his production: *New York Times*, September 7, 1911.

featuring Grace George—his wife: Ibid., September 21, 1911.

"after the final curtain": Letitia Fairbanks and Ralph Hancock, *Doug Fairbanks: The Fourth Musketeer* (New York: Henry Holt, 1953), 94.

Mr. Fairbanks, from his dressing room at the Globe: *New York Times*, October 6, 1911.

He had a piece, *Jack Spurlock, Prodigal*: Ibid.

"Western capitalists" were planning to build a theater: *New York Times*, January 7, 1909.

"anxiously watching the till fill up": *Lowell Sun*, February 1, 1934.

"The public owes no more toward the theater": Frederic Lombardi, *Allan Dwan and the Rise and Decline of the Hollywood Studios* (Jefferson, NC: McFarland, 2013), 52.

"The typical young American": Fairbanks and Hancock, *Doug Fairbanks*, 95.

"I got the wanderlust so bad": Douglas Fairbanks, "Combining Play with Work," *American Magazine*, July 1917.

With him was friend and costar: New York Passenger Lists, 1820–1957, record for "Douglass Fairbank," Ancestry.com; the misspelling is correct: that is how he is listed and this is how one may find the reference.

From there he took a ship for the Yucatán Peninsula: Kenneth Davenport, Fairbanks studio biography, n.d., Thomas J. Geraghty Papers, file 22: miscellaneous, Margaret Herrick Library, Academy of Motion Picture Arts and Sciences, Beverly Hills, CA.

"I've got the young man in the drawing room": Fairbanks and Hancock, *Doug Fairbanks*, 96.

he signed with Arthur Klein: *Variety*, February 10, 1912.

"It was not uncommon to find": David Mayer, personal correspondence with author.

"first instance of record where two 'names'": *Variety*, February 19, 1912.

"a young lawyer, with nothing but debts": Ibid., February 24, 1912.

"He's the greatest kid in the world": Ibid.

the inaugural show for George M. Cohan's Grand Opera House: *New York Times*, March 4, 1912.

"who finds his money a nuisance": *Chicago Daily Tribune*, March 4, 1912.

"I was about three then": Fairbanks Jr., *Salad Days*, 20.

he assumed the part—second billed: *New York Times*, August 13, 1912.

only until his next play, *Hawthorne of the U.S.A.*, was ready: *Washington Post*, August 11, 1912.

"I made my first appearance by vaulting a wall": Douglas Fairbanks, "Let Me Say This for the Films," *Ladies' Home Journal*, September 1922.

"It went all right, but an actor can't put up": Fairbanks, "Combining Play with Work."

Out-of-town tryouts began in late September: *Washington Post*, September 22, 1912.

Preview audiences were not up to expectations: *Variety*, September 27, 1912.

the show was pulled for revisions: Ibid., October 11, 1912.

"most-ill-advisedly written in American slang": *Washington Post*, October 13, 1912.

buoyant, breezy, daring, agile: Ibid., October 22, 1912; *Variety*, November 8, 1912.

"one of the most skittenish and happy of our younger stars": *Chicago Daily Tribune*, November 7, 1912.

"a tumultuous greeting was accorded": *Anaconda Standard*, November 12, 1912.

"No matter who condemns the piece": *Variety*, November 8, 1912.

"to date the young star has been badly wounded": Ibid., January 10, 1913.

the house was still top-heavy: Ibid., February 21, 1913.

Fairbanks reportedly started making bets with the house manager: Ibid., February 7, 1913.

due to a quarrel with the star: Ibid., February 28, 1913.

"There is said to be a straining of the entente cordiale": Ibid., March 7, 1913.

a tale of a "popular chap": Ibid., May 12, 1913.

he was to enter rehearsals for *Cooper Hoyt, Inc.*: Ibid., July 18, 1913.

was now to be in a piece titled *Something for Nothing*: Ibid., August 1, 1913.

"unalterably opposed" to any of their stars: Ibid., November 15, 1912.

started the weary rounds of the New England variety circuit: Ibid., October 10 and 17 and November 14, 1913; *Portsmouth Herald*, October 15, 1938.

"jumping back and forth" to make his vaudeville appearances: *Variety*, November 14, 1913.

"his own very virile, positive personality": *New York Times*, December 23, 1913.

It "seemed almost a sacrilege": *Washington Post*, December 28, 1913.

He "surprised even his most intimate friends": *New York Clipper*, January 3, 1914.

"the best role the popular young actor has created": *Washington Post*, December 28, 1913.

The partnership, he declared, would run for at least five years: *Chicago Tribune*, December 9, 1913.

Mr. Fairbanks would return to vaudeville: *Chicago Tribune*, March 24, 1914.

He would premiere *He Comes Up Smiling*: *Washington Post*, May 13, 1914.

Fairbanks's "peppery maneuvers": *Variety*, May 22, 1914.

such towns as Atlantic City and Brighton Beach: Ibid., June 19 and August 21, 1914.

Rehearsals for *He Comes up Smiling* started in late June: *Washington Post*, June 14, 1914.

premiered on September 16 at Broadway's Liberty Theatre: *New York Times*, September 17, 1914.

the "whole-souled sunniness of a manner": Ibid.

"not true to the blithe spirit of the people": *New York Times*, September 20, 1914.

"with no end of money in his pocket": Ibid., September 17, 1914.

It did better than most new plays on Broadway: *Variety*, November 7, 1914.

Woods decided that the play did not have the legs: *Chicago Daily Tribune*, November 15, 1914.

The tour took him from Maryland to Pennsylvania to New York: *Variety*, November 21 and 28, 1914.

he "can easily go over the same route a second time": Ibid., December 4, 1914.

"Those Moe Levy tickets": Ibid., February 5, 1915.

"We are doing that awful thing": Fairbanks correspondence, author's collection.

the greater part of the floor seats could also be offered at the full fare: *Variety*, March 12, 1915.

"I guess I'll tackle the ten cent movies": James Forbes, *The Show Shop: A Farcical Satire in Four Acts* (New York: Samuel French, 1919), 129.

4. Triangle (as in Company)

"A short time later Fairbanks told me": Frank Case, *Tales of a Wayward Inn* (New York: Frederick A. Stokes, 1938), 82.

"The night that I saw *The Birth of a Nation*": Douglas Fairbanks, "Let Me Say This for the Films," *Ladies' Home Journal*, September 1922.

"It has grown to a fad almost": *Variety*, December 20, 1912.

"I went along [directing] as usual": Partial manuscript of autobiography, p. 4, Brenon Collection, box 3: correspondence 1951–55, Frances Howard Goldwyn Hollywood Regional Library, Los Angeles, CA.

By the fall of 1913, he had progressed: Grace Dawley, "J Searle Dawley, Director" (unpublished manuscript), pp. 78–79, private collection of Kevin Brownlow.

"I know nothing about business": Ibid.

"My many questions must have bored everyone": Douglas Fairbanks, "How I Got In" (unsourced article), Douglas Fairbanks Papers, scrapbook 5, Margaret Herrick Library, Academy of Motion Picture Arts and Sciences, Beverly Hills, CA.

His first public film appearance was in early November 1913: *Variety*, November 7, 1913.

"He agreed to come with Essanay": *Photoplay*, June 1924.

Jesse Lasky and Sam Goldwyn, of Famous Players, contemplated: Robert S. Birchard, *Cecil B. DeMille's Hollywood* (Lexington: University Press of Kentucky, 2004), 36.

Fairbanks "in his racing runabout": *Naugatuck Daily News*, January 11, 1915.

Stars from "the legitimate" were being signed: "Charge of Movie Brigade Lands Score of Legits as Film Stars," *Variety*, April 23, 1915.

"a quick mind and a ready tongue": Richard Schickel, *D. W. Griffith: An American Life* (New York: Simon & Schuster, 1984), 201.

Of note is the fact that D. W. Griffith: Ibid., 206.

"[His] financial affairs were sufficiently complicated": Kalton C. Lahue, *Dreams for Sale: The Rise and Fall of the Triangle Film Corporation* (New York: A. S. Barnes, 1971), 29.

Fairbanks's "talents and professional standing": Contract between Douglas Fairbanks and the Mutual Film Corporation, July 1915, author's collection.

"I don't want my reputation spoiled": Kevin Brownlow, notes on interview with Gilbert Seldes, n.d., private collection of Kevin Brownlow.

"We picked Douglas Fairbanks as a likely film star": Alistair Cooke, *Douglas Fairbanks: The Making of a Screen Character*, Museum of Modern Art Film Library Series 2 (New York: Museum of Modern Art, 1940), 13.

D. W. Griffith was not there to meet him: *Variety*, July 23, 1915.

"They call it the juvenile jump": Edna Ferber, *Roast Beef, Medium: The Business Adventure of Emma McChesney*, serialized in *Correctionville News*, December 24, 1914.

"It is an interesting question": *Variety*, September 24, 1915.

a two-story California-Japanese bungalow: Ibid., August 6, 1915.

A new open-air stage: *Moving Picture World*, September 11, 1915.

under his supervision: "The Meaning of 'Griffith-Supervised,'" *Motography*, January 15, 1916.

"Hollywood is a world being made": *Repository* (Canton, OH), April 26, 1924.

"I swear that during my first week here": *Film Players Herald*, February 1916.

photographs of Fairbanks: *Moving Picture World*, September 25, 1915.

He famously claimed, for example: Paolo Cherchi Usai, ed., *The Griffith Project*, vol. 6 (London: British Film Institute, 2002), 164.

Kevin Brownlow explains: Kevin Brownlow, personal correspondence with author.

"he rode and shot with the best of them": Triangle press sheet, September 1915, Margaret Herrick Library.

"brown as an Indian, lively as a grasshopper": Ibid.

"Probably there never will again be such a bunch": Ibid.

"No event of the season has been so fraught with interest": *Motion Picture News*, September 25, 1915.

"a good fast director": Joseph Henabery, interview with David Shepard, January 12, 1970, Directors Guild of America, Los Angeles, CA.

"a rollicking, typically American melodrama": *Photoplay*, December 1915.

"*The Lamb* . . . is by far the high spot": *Motion Picture News*, September 25, 1915.

"*The Lamb* was his first picture": Douglas Fairbanks Jr., interview with Kevin Brownlow, 1975, recorded for *Hollywood* (documentary TV series), 1980, private collection of Kevin Brownlow.

"One incident which is 'sure fire'": *Motion Picture News*, September 25, 1915.

No less an authority than Russell Merritt: Paolo Cherchi Usai, ed., *The Griffith Project*, vol. 8 (London: British Film Institute, 2004), 126.

"Columns of praise would not do justice to *The Lamb*": *Variety*, October 1, 1915.

his recently deceased friend Elmer Booth: *Moving Picture World*, July 3, 1915.

took over the small town of Santa Ana: *Twin Falls Times*, September 28, 1915.

cast and crew arrived at Triangle's studios: *Motography*, October 16, 1915.

A boxing match was filmed: Ibid., December 11, 1915.

"His personality is so all-pervading": *Moving Picture World*, February 12, 1916.

studio in Fort Lee and another facility: Richard Koszarski, *Fort Lee: The Film Town (1904–2004)* (Bloomington: Indiana University Press, 2004), 164.

Critics at the Knickerbocker premiere noted: *Motion Picture News*, February 12, 1916.

The script has such unsavory references: Private collection of Kevin Brownlow.

"He had a varied assortment of friends": Charlie Chaplin, *My Autobiography* (Brooklyn: Melville House, 2012), 199.

"low-slung foreign car with a half top": Mary Pickford, *Sunshine and Shadow* (New York: Doubleday, 1955), 116.

"Miss Pickford thinks Mr. Fairbanks will do wonderful things": Elsie Janis, *So Far, So Good!* (New York: E. P. Dutton, 1932), 167.

"Women are just about as companionable": Mary Pickford, Daily Talks (syndicated column), July 23, 1916.

5. Mary and Charlie

"the focal point of an entire industry": Edward Wagenknecht, *The Movies in the Age of Innocence* (New York: Ballantine Books, 1962), 121.

Mary, "whose face seemed to move": Eileen Whitfield, *Pickford: The Woman Who Made Hollywood* (Lexington: University Press of Kentucky, 1997), 75.

"Now there's a young fellow": Mary Pickford, Daily Talks (syndicated column), July 16, 1916.

"and I'm quite certain Douglas didn't either": Mary Pickford, *Sunshine and Shadow* (New York: Doubleday, 1955), 118.

"He was just about the best morale booster": Margery Wilson, *Douglas Fairbanks*, Thumb Prints of the Famous (Los Angeles: Chimes Press, 1928), Douglas Fairbanks Papers, Margaret Herrick Library, Academy of Motion Picture Arts and Sciences, Beverly Hills, CA.

"People of attainment fascinated him": Pickford, *Sunshine and Shadow*, 119.

"He told me to observe cultured people": Bessie Love, *From Hollywood with Love* (London: Elm Tree Books, 1977), 58.

"I found him disarmingly honest": Charlie Chaplin, *My Autobiography* (Brooklyn: Melville House, 2012), 199.

reportedly he showed up the next morning: Letitia Fairbanks and Ralph Hancock, *Doug Fairbanks: The Fourth Musketeer* (New York: Henry Holt, 1953), 126–128.

"He didn't smoke or drink much": Gary Carey, *Doug & Mary: A Biography of Douglas Fairbanks & Mary Pickford* (New York: E. P. Dutton, 1977), 38.

the numbers of his "extracurricular fancies": Douglas Fairbanks Jr., *The Salad Days* (New York: Doubleday, 1988), 24.

He next invited Mary to the Netherland Hotel to "meet the family": Ibid., 35.

"Mary had made another conquest": Ibid.

"a man with a strong dramatic sense": Kevin Brownlow, *The Parade's Gone By* (New York: Knopf, 1968), 96.

"I was a little bit like that myself": Peter Bogdanovich, *Who the Devil Made It* (New York: Knopf, 1997), 75.

Dwan (he himself claims) and Fairbanks are sitting on the Triangle lot: Ibid., 72.

"We had to call the picture back": Ibid., 75.

"My criticism is leveled": *Photoplay*, June 1916.

"Douglas Fairbanks, Senior employed a number of directors": Kevin Brownlow, transcript of recorded interview with Douglas Fairbanks Jr., May 31, 1962, private collection of Kevin Brownlow.

"My father had great respect": Ibid.

"When Doug did any of his stunts": Allan Dwan, interview with Kevin Brownlow, slate 319, take 1, recorded for *Hollywood* (documentary TV series), 1980, private collection of Kevin Brownlow.

Fairbanks's screen character was such a close fusion: Alistair Cooke, *Douglas Fairbanks: The Making of a Screen Character*, Museum of Modern Art Film Library Series 2 (New York: Museum of Modern Art, 1940), 20.

"He was once in a Chicago hotel": Wilson, *Douglas Fairbanks*.

a "breezy American mining engineer": Three-sheet poster for the film, 1916, private collection.

"riding a mountain trail": Sinclair Lewis, *Dodsworth* (New York: P. F. Collier, 1929), 5.

"I'm going to have a bungolaoh [sic]": Leslie-Judge Company, *Film Flashes* (New York: Leslie-Judge Company, 1916), 102.

"What the actor didn't know": *Moving Picture World*, February 12, 1916.

Buried deep in the ledgers: US Majestic Motion Picture Co. ledger, January 1915–June 1917, reel 8, Wisconsin Center for Film and Theater Research, Madison, WI.

"In his writing for the screen": *New York Times*, April 22, 1916.

"*The Good Bad Man* might have been designed": Ibid.

"a motion picture house, pure and simple": Ibid.

"persistent phone calls and telegrams": Fairbanks and Hancock, *Doug Fairbanks*, 140.

"she should learn that panting in a close-up": *New York Times*, May 29, 1916.

"So next to me Mr. Fairbanks looked six foot tall": Love, *From Hollywood with Love*, 58.

"a trip to Balboa, during which the ever-agile Doug": Alma Rubens, *Alma Rubens, Silent Snowbird*, ed. Gary Don Rhodes and Alexander Webb (Jefferson, NC: McFarland, 2006), 76.

"who but Mr. Fairbanks could mix in": *New York Times*, May 29, 1916.

"It is quite probable that if there were many more": Ibid.

Released on the same bill as Reggie: *Triangle Magazine* 2, no. 11 (July 1, 1916).

"Patrons complained of undiluted Keystone shorts": Russell Merritt, "The Griffith Third: D. W. Griffith at Triangle," in *Sulla via di Hollywood, 1911–1920*, ed. Paolo Cherchi Usai and Lorenzo Codelli (Le Giornate del Cinema Muto, 1988), 264.

"Mr. Fairbanks was a perfectionist": Love, *From Hollywood with Love*, 58.

Fairbanks appealed up to the Supreme Court of New York: Fairbanks v. Winik, 206 App. Div. 449 (N.Y. App. Div. 1923); Fairbanks v. Winik, 198 N.Y.S. 299 (Sup. Ct. 1922).

"refreshing nonsense, farcical to the last degree": *Motion Picture News*, July 15, 1916.

"John Emerson staged the travesty": *Variety*, May 26, 1916.

the film "didn't quite come off": Love, *From Hollywood with Love*, 58.

"to see Doug at bay and fighting": Richard Schickel, *His Picture in the Papers: A Speculation on Celebrity in America Based on the Life of Douglas Fairbanks, Sr.* (New York: Charterhouse, 1974), 47.

"melodramas decorated by acrobatics": Cooke, *Douglas Fairbanks*, 16.

"pictorially ravishing": Michael Sragow, *Victor Fleming: An American Movie Master* (New York: Pantheon Books, 2008), 47.

"We, who had a hand in its making": *Photoplay*, March 1918.

"There is also less than the usual": *Motion Picture News* 14, no. 3: 452.

"Douglas Fairbanks in a heavy dramatic role!": *Photoplay*, February 1918.

Doug "apparently had liked me": Rubens, *Alma Rubens*, 76.

"Up, above the ordinary level": *Photoplay*, October 1916.

"looks rather more like Peter Pan": *New York Times*, July 10, 1916.

"It didn't look good at all": *Photoplay*, March 1918.

Originally Fairbanks was slated to play Octavius: Ibid., April 1916.

he appeared in the smaller role of young Cato: *Los Angeles Times*, May 20, 1916.

ARRIVE AT 9:40A.M.: *Triangle Magazine* 2, no. 9 (June 17, 1916).

"A pleasant surprise took us quite off our feet": Mary Pickford, Daily Talks, *Duluth News Tribune*, July 23, 1916.

"Let's hope the mermaids enjoy it": Mary Pickford, Daily Talks, *Anaconda Standard*, September 22, 1916.

"with a twinkle in his eyes": Ibid.

"The man of him has never lost sight": Mary Pickford, Daily Talks, *Flint Daily Journal*, October 11, 1916.

"It is a good sign, a healthful sign": *Everybody's Magazine*, 1916, 729–738.

"that as an all-around athlete": *Motion Picture News* 14, no 13: 2058.

"The set was ready": Ben Carré, unpublished memoirs, 196, private collection of Kevin Brownlow.

"if Mr. Fairbanks had not swung quickly": Mary Pickford, Daily Talks, *Flint Daily Journal*, July 30, 1916.

"with hands in trouser pockets": *New York Times*, September 11, 1916.

"rather fancied the dashing look": Fairbanks Jr., *Salad Days*, 22.

"no real newsboy ever looked": Ibid., 43–44.

"Dad was absent so often": Ibid., 30–31.

"Senior was perfectly tender": Schickel, *His Picture in the Papers*, 58.

"Fairbanks and his lasso": Leslie-Judge Company, *Film Flashes*, 55.

"loved Eunice, then only six": Douglas Fairbanks Papers, scrapbook 1: condolence letters, Margaret Herrick Library.

"jolly and vigorous but infrequent": Fairbanks Jr., *Salad Days*, 30.

"Then our ears caught a suspicious sound": Jesse L. Lasky Jr., *Whatever Happened to Hollywood?* (New York: Funk & Wagnalls, 1975), 11.

"I'm so—goll-darned tough": Fairbanks Jr., *Salad Days*, 31.

Senior was "sport enough": Ibid., 43–44.

"Satire is an advanced form": *Photoplay*, March 1917.

"It drivels out into a mere vehicle": *Moving Picture World*, November 4, 1917.

"Mr. Fairbanks is being completely eaten up": *Photoplay*, February 1917.

"He vaults a dozen walls and fences": *New York Times*, November 6, 1916.

she was paid $500: Anita Loos Papers, folder 26, Margaret Herrick Library.

a "nondescript vehicle": *Moving Picture World*, November 18, 1916.

the highest weekly take: *Variety*, November 17, 1916.

Hundreds milled outside: *New York Times*, November 6, 1916.

"that he craved two boons": *Moving Picture World*, November 4, 1916.

"Now make me laugh": Ibid., December 9, 1916.

"From Constance I had heard": Chaplin, *My Autobiography*, 199.

"Doug Fairbanks was my only real friend": Schickel, *His Picture in the Papers*, 89.

"Sweet Douglas": Ibid., 221.

"an incredible cowardice in Doug": Anita Loos, *Cast of Thousands* (New York: Grosset & Dunlap, 1977), 244–245.

"It would have made a whopper": *Variety*, December 8, 1916.

"Fairbanks represents physical agility": *Moving Picture World*, December 16, 1916.

"Douglas Fairbanks is a tonic": Alfred Cheri, "Reflexions sur l'art de Douglas Fairbanks," *Cinéa-Ciné pour tous*, November 1, 1927.

"saying that these were the money-making things": *Exhibitors Trade Review*, March 3, 1917.

"All the actors and actresses who had been selected": Ibid.

"No modern millionaire would do that!": Ibid.

"There's a lot of opportunity ahead": *Moving Picture World*, October 7, 1916.

"Time and again I have sat through plays": Ibid., December 12, 1916.

"He left New York in a hurry": Ibid., December 28, 1916.

And, on January 2, 1917: *Variety*, February 9, 1917.

$3,250 a week: Ibid., February 12, 1917.

"No self-respecting actor can afford": *Photoplay*, May 1917.

"One story," wrote *Variety*: *Variety*, January 12, 1917.

"ensure against any judgment": Ibid., February 2, 1917.

when it came time for the legal filings: *Exhibitors Trade Review*, March 3, 1917.

"deponent is familiar with the earnings": Deposition with Walter E. Green, President of the Artcraft Pictures Corporation, May 8, 1923, Douglas Fairbanks Papers, Tax Dispute Files, Margaret Herrick Library.

"Mr. Daniel Sully, the father": Ibid.

"enjoy a profit of $2500 a week thereby": Ibid.

"Sully then sought to influence": Ibid.

"Douglas Fairbanks Indemnity a/c": US Majestic Motion Picture Co. ledger.

they had already lost over $8,000: Paolo Cherchi Usai and Lorenzo Codelli, *L'Eredita DeMille* (Pordenone, Italy: Edizioni Biblioteca dell'Immagine, 1991).

"Nobody has ever thought": Triangle Film Corp. v. Artcraft Pictures Corp., 250 F. 981, 982 (2d Cir. 1918).

6. Triangle (as in Love)

Fairbanks stopped by Charlie Chaplin's studio: *Photoplay*, March 1917.

"Ella's natural instinct": Letitia Fairbanks and Ralph Hancock, *Doug Fairbanks: The Fourth Musketeer* (New York: Henry Holt, 1953), 143.

"he wasn't a mother's boy": Ibid., 144.

"I can get along without you, Mother": Ibid., 144.

Douglas "paced up and down": Ibid., 145.

"Don't be blue": Douglas Fairbanks correspondence, private collection.

he reportedly pulled Mary out: *Fresno Bee Republican*, August 11, 1934.

"Just a few lines in a hurry": Mary Pickford correspondence from unknown lover, private collection.

"Mary I was so stuck on you": Marshall Neilan, letter to Mary Pickford, September 13, 1958, Mary Pickford Papers, Margaret Herrick Library, Academy of Motion Picture Arts and Sciences, Beverly Hills, CA.

Charlotte paid him to go to Denver: *Greely Daily Tribune*, August 11, 1934.

Fairbanks escaped by sprinting: *Fresno Bee*, August 11, 1934.

"his great patriotic picture": *Moving Picture World*, May 12, 1917.

"The single stunt": Ibid.

"I was discharged on account": Arthur Lennig, *Stroheim* (Lexington: University Press of Kentucky, 2000), 45.

He "went to New York": Ibid., 46.

Rutherford, New Jersey ultimately provided: *Moving Picture World*, May 19, 1917.

Fairbanks needed an "outstanding pug-ugly": *Oakland Tribune*, September 10, 1922.

"He was a huge fellow": Adolphe Menjou, *It Took Nine Tailors* (New York: McGraw-Hill, 1948), 91.

"Douglas, like royalty": Frank Case, *Do Not Disturb* (New York: Frederick A. Stokes, 1940), 211.

"I disliked the idea of drawing": Edward Knoblock, *Round the Room* (London: Chapman and Hall, 1939), 317.

"Fairbanks was, as my father described him": Helen Reed Lehman, correspondence with Kevin Brownlow, June 2, 1991, private collection of Kevin Brownlow.

at the 81st Street Theatre: *Variety*, May 18, 1917.

"when Fate edged up and nudged me": Anita Loos, *Cast of Thousands* (New York: Grosset & Dunlap, 1977), 73.

The Rialto alone grossed $17,880: *Variety*, May 4, 1917.

"One is easily able to understand": *Motion Picture News* 15, no 26: 4110.

He even would stand still for the *Photoplay* photographer: *Photoplay*, October 1919.

"I could see that it was being written": Joseph Henabery, *Before, In and After Hollywood: The Autobiography of Joseph E. Henabery* (Lanham, MD: Scarecrow, 1997), 157.

"The judge was amused": *Moving Picture World*, September 7, 1918.

"You might hang on": *Warren Evening Mirror*, August 6, 1917.

"I know that D'Artagnan's name": Charles Russell, *Good Medicine: The Illustrated Letters of Charles M. Russell* (New York: Doubleday, 1966), 90.

"The wily Douglas": *Moving Picture World*, June 9, 1917.

Bull Montana declared it: *Photoplay*, August 1917.

"Did you ever see a self respecting autograph stamp": Douglas Fairbanks letter, private collection.

"We . . . saw Douglas Fairbanks in his little Mercer Raceabout": Chick Larsen, letter, September 28, 1916, private collection.

He was one of the few stars: *Photoplay*, September 1918.

"the golden triplets": Ibid., August 1917.

"Taking it by and large": *Moving Picture World*, June 9, 1917.

"Charlotte surveyed the suite": Scott Eyman, *Mary Pickford, America's Sweetheart* (New York: Donald I. Fine, 1990), 80.

Photoplay featured a photo spread: *Photoplay*, October, 1917.

"I'm going to kill that climbing monkey": Mary Pickford, *Sunshine and Shadow* (New York: Doubleday, 1955), 121.

"My Darling—Just two million thoughts": Fairbanks correspondence, private collection.

the player in question was a small spotted dog: *New York Dramatic Mirror*, July 14, 1917.

"But the producers have looked": Ibid., August 18, 1917.

"Book it, Mr. Exhibitor": *Variety*, August 17, 1917.

"If we are to look closely": *Motion Picture News*, August 25, 1917.

Fairbanks is a peppermint-eating product: Anita Loos, *Anita Loos Rediscovered: Film Treatments and Fiction*, ed. by Cari Beauchamp and Mary Loos (Berkeley: University of California Press, 2003), 66–75.

an especially egregious example of Loos's casual racism: Anita Loos Papers, Margaret Herrick Library.

"the leader was of utmost value": *Moving Picture World*, May 19, 1917.

"Miss Anita Loos, who appears to believe": Ibid.

"Emerson and Doug were a little bit": Kevin Brownlow, transcript of recorded interview with Joseph Henabery, December 19, 1964, private collection of Kevin Brownlow.

"Anytime that Douglas and Mary wanted": Anita Loos, recorded interview, n.d., private collection of Kevin Brownlow.

"I was surprised to be asked": Henabery, *Before, In and After Hollywood*, 161.

"I had to write them myself": Ibid., 166.

"It's the sort of square Western": Michael Sragow, *Victor Fleming: An American Movie Master* (New York: Pantheon Books, 2008), 54.

"What we get is a ranch": Unsourced clipping, Douglas Fairbanks Papers, scrapbook 5, Margaret Herrick Library.

"It was made in a hurry": *Photoplay*, March 1918.

"worldwide acclaim had made Doug touchy": Anita Loos, *The Talmadge Girls: A Memoir* (New York: Viking, 1978), 33.

"Then it was decided to let Emerson and Loos": Henabery, *Before, In and After Hollywood*, 167.

"The first conference concerning *Reaching for the Moon*": John Emerson and Anita Loos, "Photoplay Writing," *Photoplay*, April 1918.

"One thing you can't reproduce with scenery": "Douglas Fairbanks Crosses Country for a Few Scenes" (unsourced article), Douglas Fairbanks Papers, scrapbook 5, Margaret Herrick Library.

"Just as the Czar of Russia": Ibid.

"One 'close-up' which he did yesterday": Ibid.

"a series of fist fights": *Variety*, November 23, 1917.

A young woman watching the action fainted: *Photoplay*, February 1918.

"When John asked for a cancellation": Loos, *Talmadge Girls*, 33.

John Emerson ("a pimp"): Anita Loos, *A Girl Like I* (New York: Viking, 1966), 275.

"We made Douglas Fairbanks": Anita Loos, personal communication with Kevin Brownlow.

the hall "fairly rocked with laughter": Bernard Rosenberg and Harry Silverstein, *The Real Tinsel* (New York: Macmillan, 1970), 406.

"One always dislikes giving up": *Motion Picture Magazine*, March 1918.

"Of course we liked Mr. Fairbanks": Ibid.

"to get away from Los Angeles": Ibid.

A full scenario exists: Joseph Henabery Papers, folder 132, Margaret Herrick Library.

"Fairbanks makes the Dumas swashbuckler": *Photoplay*, March 1918.

he gave Dwan a Twin Six Packard: *Motography*, January 5, 1918.

A review of the *Musketeer* script reveals: Anita Loos Papers, Margaret Herrick Library.

"Leaving here for the Painted Desert": Fairbanks correspondence, private collection.

"Dad's once or twice leading lady": Douglas Fairbanks Jr., *The Salad Days* (New York: Doubleday, 1988), 29.

"really the only intimate [woman] friend": *Lowell Sun*, September 16, 1921.

astride a horse in the Canyon de Chelly: *Photoplay*, February 1918.

Daw spent three years of her adolescence: Ibid., July 1918.

Eagle Eye was, at the time of the injury: *Moving Picture World*, March 23, 1918.

"He said 'Go down and look'": Kevin Brownlow, transcript of recorded interview with Joseph Henabery, December 19, 1964, private collection of Kevin Brownlow.

"The Fairbanks smile is carrying a load": *Photoplay*, May 1918.

"Whereas *A Modern Musketeer* was the perfectly balanced combination": *Motion Picture News*, March 16, 1918.

"Mr. Fairbanks is prodigal": *Variety*, May 3, 1918.

all shots involving Fairbanks: *Motography*, March 30, 1918.

7. Citizen Doug

"Five dollars a foot": *Photoplay*, September 1917.

He spent a day in San Diego: *Motography*, January 19, 1918.

It was an elaborate event: *Moving Picture World*, January 12, 1918.

Doug then paid to move the entire enterprise: Ibid., February 23, 1918.

Fairbanks contemplated touring nationally: *Capital Times*, April 19, 1918.

He raised a million dollars: *Motion Picture Magazine*, June 1918.

$100,000 of which was his personal subscription: *Moving Picture World*, June 23, 1917.

he and Doug invented a game: *Photoplay*, February 1929.

"His million-dollar grin": *Nevada State Journal*, May 2, 1918.

they were there for the crowds at Fort Wayne: *Gettysburg Times*, April 1, 1918; *Fort Wayne News and Sentinel*, April 5, 1918; *Moving Picture World*, May 4, 1918.

They sold bonds on the Capitol plaza: *Oakland Tribune*, April 7, 1918; *La Crosse Tribune and Leader-Press*, April 7, 1918.

It was Roosevelt who bought the first bond: *Washington Post*, May 5, 1918.

Upon arrival each was served in a lawsuit: *Variety*, April 19, 1918; *Motography*, May 11, 1918.

WIRED YOU AFFAIR WAS OFF: Scrapbook, Douglas Fairbanks Jr. Papers, Howard Gotlieb Archival Research Center, Mugar Memorial Library, Boston University, Boston, MA.

RATHER BLUE SPLENDID MOON TONIGHT: Pickford telegrams, Mary Pickford Foundation.

"Mary Pickford sold one of her famous gold curls": *Logansport Press*, July 8, 1933.

"I think the three of us all got stage fright": *Film Fun*, June 1918.

The *New York Times* published a photo: *New York Times* photo archives.

the "one big love": *Bridgeport Telegram*, April 15, 1918.

the work of "German propagandists": *Oakland Tribune*, April 21, 1918.

"I have not the remotest idea": Ibid., April 12, 1918.

"I am sorry the woman who has caused": Ibid.

"I deeply sympathize with Mrs. Fairbanks": *Oakland Tribune*, April 12, 1918.

"It was like him to add this": Ibid.

"Then, too, comes the lingering suspicion": *Moving Picture World*, May 25, 1918.

her husband's denial "had the opposite effect": *Variety*, April 19, 1918.

Fairbanks's image was hissed: Ibid., May 3, 1918.

"Of the country, I see nothing": *Motion Picture Magazine*, August 1918.

Fairbanks was in Detroit, Flint, and Saginaw: *Variety*, April 19, 1918.

"he rushed about the city like mad": *Moving Picture World*, May 4, 1918.

By the next day he was in Ohio: *Evening State Journal and Lincoln Daily News*, April 12, 1918.

"The only thing left for him": *Moving Picture World*, May 4, 1918.

"Mr. Fairbanks also talked at Macaulay's Theater": Ibid.

"When here he was on the verge": *Mansfield News*, May 21, 1918.

All visits were canceled: *Racine Journal-News*, April 15, 1918; *La Crosse Tribune and Leader-Press*, April 15, 1918.

"a nervous wreck": *Mansfield News*, May 21, 1918.

"Mr. Pickford Moore": *Clearfield Progress*, April 20, 1918.

Moore "hadn't proved anything": Ibid.

"If anyone thinks I am about to retire": *Oakland Tribune*, May 12, 1918.

"Of that I have absolutely nothing to say": Ibid.

a mass meeting at Clune's Theatre: *Moving Picture World*, June 15, 1918.

He competed in a "drinking bout": Ibid., June 29, 1918.

He promoted the "Smileage" campaign: *Motion Picture Magazine*, August 1918.

"Our amusements here are limited": Ibid.

"There was a lot of 'trick stuff'": *American Classic Screen* 3, no. 3 (January–February 1979).

"Hunch" was prone to such pearls: *Say! Young Fellow* title sheet, Joseph Henabery Papers, Margaret Herrick Library, Academy of Motion Picture Arts and Sciences, Beverly Hills, CA.

visualized "in a kind of allegorical way": Unsourced clippings, Joseph Henabery Papers, Margaret Herrick Library.

"Doug was as happy": Joseph Henabery, *Before, In and After Hollywood: The Autobiography of Joseph E. Henabery* (Lanham, MD: Scarecrow, 1997), 178.

on a set adjacent to the Lasky pool: Ibid.

it was the ending that caused comment: Joseph Henabery, interview with Kevin Brownlow, n.d., private collection of Kevin Brownlow.

A stray firecracker thrown onto the roof: *Moving Picture World*, July 27, 1918.

He asked all seventeen thousand theaters: *Motography*, April 13, 1918.

a new four-minute film every three days: *Washington Post*, September 17, 1918.

Fairbanks's contribution to the spring drive: Unsourced clippings, Douglas Fairbanks Papers, scrapbooks, Margaret Herrick Library.

"clean living and physical fitness": Ibid.

"morale pictures" in the early postwar months: *Moving Picture World*, January 25, 1919.

"The good-bad loveable chap": *Photoplay*, March 1917.

"He is what every American might be": *Motography*, March 23, 1918.

"He was the Yankee Doodle Boy": Edward Wagenknecht, *The Movies in the Age of Innocence* (New York: Ballantine Books, 1962), 172.

He brought on his brother Robert: *Variety*, July 12, 1918.

"He was more spit than fire": Frances Marion, interview with Kevin Brownlow, n.d., private collection of Kevin Brownlow.

"My father, though not in the least religious": Douglas Fairbanks Jr., *The Salad Days* (New York: Doubleday, 1988), 49.

He paid $10,000 for the rights: *Motography*, May 25, 1918.

four rooms and two hallways simultaneously: *Wid's Daily*, September 10, 1918.

Marion, who trained birds as a hobby: *Photoplay*, December 1918.

"A knockout—and then some": *Motion Picture News*, September 21, 1918.

"the fastest and funniest thing": *Wid's Daily*, September 15, 1918.

Arizona first made its appearance: *New York Times*, September 9, 1900.

how they were "getting on with his drama": *Moving Picture World*, November 23, 1918.

"When he was not 'kidding'": Unsourced article, Douglas Fairbanks Papers, scrapbook 3, Margaret Herrick Library.

"The parting of star and director": *Photoplay*, March 1919.

on July 2 he sent a telegram: Joseph Henabery Papers, folder 267, Margaret Herrick Library.

"Believe me, it is a tough job": Ibid.

Fairbanks was avid to stop playacting: Frances Marion, *Off With Their Heads! A Serio-Comic Tale of Hollywood* (New York: Macmillan, 1972), 54.

"Dad's efforts to enlist": Fairbanks Jr., *Salad Days*, 48.

Ten thousand movie theaters: *Photoplay*, January 1919.

The trip was made with scant notice: *Wid's*, October 9, 1918.

issuing a press release upon his discharge: *Variety*, November 1, 1918.

"I am positively sure": Fairbanks correspondence, author's collection.

"Why shouldn't I divorce?": Anita Loos, interview with Kevin Brownlow, slate 592, take 1, recorded for *Hollywood* (documentary TV series), 1980, private collection of Kevin Brownlow.

tagged as mail, Third Class: *Wid's*, October 17, 1918.

"Mr. McAdoo then instructed the crowd": *Moving Picture World*, November 2, 1918.

"Fifth Avenue, the great highway": Ibid.

He took this heady show on the road: *Wid's*, November 13, 1918.

Albert Parker had appeared as the villain: *Variety*, August 30, 1918.

"That Mr. Fairbanks is alone": *Motion Picture News*, December 28, 1918.

"His performance of Lieutenant Denton": *Moving Picture World*, December 28, 1918.

"The truth about 'Arizona' is so bad": Virginia Tracy, "The Dazzling Sameness of Douglas Fairbanks" (unsourced article), Douglas Fairbanks Papers, scrapbook 3, Margaret Herrick Library.

"Success, particularly if easily won": *Boys' Life*, December 1923.

"Teddy decided to go out and do something": *Knickerbocker Buckaroo* press book, 1919, private collection.

"Hell, I would have committed murder": Frank T. Thompson, *William A. Wellman*, Filmmakers Series, no. 4 (Metuchen, NJ: Scarecrow, 1983), 29.

Fairbanks met him on the third Liberty Loan drive: Michael Sragow, personal correspondence with author.

He built an "idealized Mexican village": *Knickerbocker Buckaroo* press book, 1919.

8. United

Harry Schwalbe of Philadelphia: *Moving Picture World*, January 18, 1919.

The meeting, it was said: Ibid.

"full of rumors": *Moving Picture World*, January 25, 1919.

"Let her go to First National": Mary Pickford, *Sunshine and Shadow* (New York: Doubleday, 1955), 112.

"I am really very happy about Zukor": Fairbanks correspondence, private collection.

"A dozen different representatives": *Moving Picture World*, January 18, 1919.

"Exhibitors were rugged merchants": Charlie Chaplin, *My Autobiography* (Brooklyn: Melville House, 2012), 221.

"a very clever girl, smart and attractive-looking": Ibid.

with full access to the actor's papers: David Robinson, *Chaplin: His Life and Art* (New York: McGraw-Hill, 1985), 35.

"[Zukor] and his associates were forming": Chaplin, *My Autobiography*, 222.

"From the first, the aggressive Abrams": Will Irwin, *The House That Shadows Built: The Story of Adolph Zukor and the Rise of the Motion Picture Industry* (New York: Doubleday, Doran & Company, 1927), 253.

"How vast and grand it seemed": Budd Schulberg, *Moving Pictures: Memories of a Hollywood Prince* (New York: Open Road, 2012; orig. publ. 1981), e-book.

"We decided that the night before": Chaplin, *My Autobiography*, 224.

"Doug was sizzling around": Tino Balio, *United Artists: The Company Built by the Stars* (Madison: University of Wisconsin Press, 1976), 13.

"While our lawyers haggled out legal technicalities": Chaplin, *My Autobiography*, 224.

"One night I was up against Zukor": Irwin, *House That Shadows Built*.

but by April he had resigned: *Variety*, April 4, 1919.

hearing that the former secretary was fond: *Moving Picture World*, February 15, 1919.

"The railroads and the treasury were at best": *Photoplay*, May 1919.

"Schulberg has the tendency of writing": Dennis O'Brien, letter to Morris Greenhill, August 20, 1920, United Artists Papers, US MSS 99AN, series 1A, box 211, folder 3, Wisconsin Center for Film and Theater Research, Madison, WI.

he was to send Woodrow Wilson: *Cumberland Evening Times*, January 10, 1920.

"McAdoo's reported connection": *Wid's Daily*, February 6, 1919.

"The air is filled with bombs": *Variety*, January 24, 1919.

"We believe this step necessary": *Moving Picture World*, January 25, 1919.

"There is certain to be tremendous jealousy": *Variety*, January 31, 1919.

"The star is the cause of more trouble": *Moving Picture World*, March 15, 1919.

Others speculated that the stars' existing contracts: *Wid's Daily*, January 28, 1919.

Hearst telegrammed each of the owners: Ibid., January 23, 1919.

"legalizing their emotions": *Moving Picture World*, March 1, 1919.

He sold out his share: *Oelwein Daily Register*, September 20, 1920.

"Movie producers are liars": *Boston Daily Globe*, May 25, 1919.

the Artcraft films continued to push the envelope: *Variety*, September 9, 1919.

by the time *A Modern Musketeer* hit the screens: *Motography*, February 23, 1918.

The norm for other films in 1919: *Motion Picture Magazine*, July 1919.

"[The War Department] laid down": *Moving Picture World*, January 25, 1919.

"We open with Democracy, a young tree": *Film Fun*, January 1919.

"Doug promised to include in his next release": Joseph Henabery, *Before, In and After Hollywood: The Autobiography of Joseph E. Henabery* (Lanham, MD: Scarecrow, 1997), 183.

"As soon as he finishes with one bunch": *Wid's Daily*, July 21, 1919.

"Hard work and money went into making it": Henabery, *Before, In and After Hollywood*, 184.

"another routine Douglas Fairbanks celluline cyclone": *Motion Picture News*, January 20, 1920.

"My feeling about that thing": Kevin Brownlow, transcript of recorded interview with Joseph Henabery, December 19, 1964, private collection of Kevin Brownlow.

Even a month before its release: *Wid's Daily*, August 15, 1919.

The Capitol Theatre in New York paid a record price: Ibid., June 27, 1919.

the "wild and delirious nightmare": *His Majesty the American* press book, private collection.

"The revolving room—that was my idea": Joseph Henabery, recorded interview with Kevin Brownlow, 1964, private collection of Kevin Brownlow.

"rather incensed over the fact": *Variety*, January 16, 1920.

"The story was the original idea": Ibid., February 6, 1920.

Four enormous electric pumps: *Winnipeg Free Press*, January 3, 1920.

"If he had begun his United Artists' career": *Photoplay*, March 1920.

He took out a quarter-page ad in the trade papers: *Wid's Daily*, June 16, 1920.

He also brought Geraghty out to New York: Ibid., June 10, 1920.

"There just wasn't anyone in the world": Allan Dwan, interview with Kevin Brownlow, slate 318, take 1, recorded for *Hollywood* (documentary TV series), 1980, private collection of Kevin Brownlow.

"He did almost all of his own stunts": Mary Astor, *A Life on Film* (New York: Bantam Doubleday Dell, 1967), 30–31.

In late April, the avalanche special effect was triggered: *Wid's Daily*, April 30, 1920.

dragged on "an unconscionably long time": *Motion Picture Classic*, September 1920.

"If a horse which Mr. Fairbanks was riding": Legal correspondence, Douglas Fairbanks Papers, Tax Dispute Files, Margaret Herrick Library, Academy of Motion Picture Arts and Sciences, Beverly Hills, CA.

Fairbanks standing on a cabinet phonograph player: *Akron Register-Tribune*, July 1, 1920.

Several Remington paintings, as well as a piano: *Democrat Tribune* (Mineral Point, WI), February 13, 1920.

9. Love and Marriage

Mary had traveled to New York City: *Renwick Times*, January 8, 1920.

"My own darling beautiful": Fairbanks correspondence, private collection.

Mary swore before a judge in Minden County: *Reno Evening Gazette*, March 31, 1920.

"Then I shall never be excommunicated": *Photoplay*, June 1920.

It was beautiful weather but bad for outdoor work: *Syracuse Herald*, March 10, 1920.

"I had a hunch": *Morning World Herald* (Omaha, NE), March 31, 1920.

she wanted to be married on a Sunday: *Buffalo Enquirer*, March 31, 1920.

"far from the way a man usually looks": Ibid.

having his name withdrawn from nomination: *Winnipeg Free Press*, June 29, 1920.

He survived censure: *Oneonta Daily Star*, June 30, 1920.

Certainly the attorney general of the State of Nevada: *Chronicle Telegram* (Elyria, OH), April 5, 1920.

The governor of Nevada found his office deluged: *Reno Evening Gazette*, April 6, 1920.

without his aid, the Nevada officials could prove nothing: *Eau Claire Leader*, April 8, 1920.

a reported "nervous collapse": *Oakland Tribune*, April 9, 1920.

"Her state of health forbids the slightest worry": *Lincoln Daily News* (Lincoln, Il.), April 10, 1920.

the attorney general filed a complaint: *Reno Evening Gazette*, April 16, 1920.

Mary, no fool, hired Gavin McNab: *Modesto Evening Journal*, April 16, 1920.

"I can't honestly say I was completely surprised": Joseph Henabery, *Before, In and After Hollywood: The Autobiography of Joseph E. Henabery* (Lanham, MD: Scarecrow, 1997), 184.

The attorney filed suit against Moore: *Modesto Evening News*, July 24, 1920.

"I don't think what Doug would say to me": Joseph Henabery, recorded interview with Kevin Brownlow, 1964, private collection of Kevin Brownlow.

a "White List" of motion picture actors: *Variety*, April 22, 1921.

Variety wrote a long and indignant editorial: Ibid., April 16, 1920.

Thousands of telegrams of congratulation poured in: *Olean Times*, April 1, 1920.

"They're married now—let 'em alone!": *Photoplay*, August 1920.

"Except for a small coterie": *World Magazine* (*New York World Newspaper Sunday Magazine*), August 1, 1920.

"A positive bellow of savage and strident sound": Ibid.

"They have only been married a few weeks": *Chicago Herald and Examiner*, June 1, 1920.

"Somebody asked me if the baby was mine": *Evening State Journal and Lincoln Daily News*, May 31, 1920.

"Keb, sir? Taxi-any-part-of-the-city?": Clipping from *Sunday Gazette* (Atlantic City), n.d., Douglas Fairbanks Papers, scrapbook 6, Margaret Herrick Library, Academy of Motion Picture Arts and Sciences, Beverly Hills, CA.

"It's great, simply *great*": *Syracuse Herald*, June 4, 1920.

They popped down to Washington for a day: *Oxnard Daily Courier*, June 8, 1920.

"Men with cameras seemed to appear": Unsourced clipping, Douglas Fairbanks Papers, honeymoon scrapbook, Margaret Herrick Library.

"Door opens. Mary appears": *Billings Gazette*, August 22, 1920.

"Immediately I felt it lock": Mary Pickford, *Sunshine and Shadow* (New York: Doubleday, 1955), 127.

"At first, when I saw the 'entire British nation'": *Des Moines Daily News*, July 14, 1920.

"As the motor-car turned out into Piccadilly": Unsourced clipping, Mary Pickford Papers, scrapbook of Pickford-Fairbanks honeymoon, Margaret Herrick Library.

"They were a living proof": Alistair Cooke, *Douglas Fairbanks: The Making of a Screen Character*, Museum of Modern Art Film Library Series 2 (New York: Museum of Modern Art, 1940), 21.

"the ten foot brick wall": Pickford, *Sunshine and Shadow*, 126.

"A welcoming committee met us": Ibid., 129.

"After a day of shopping and sight-seeing": Ibid.

"I don't expect any 'twosing'": Ibid., 130.

"Douglas doesn't like it": *Washington Herald*, June 6, 1920.

"Our tickets for Basle": Chapter 4 in *From Hollywood to Paris* (draft copy), Mary Pickford Papers, Margaret Herrick Library.

He returned, according to Mary, "in a brand-new car": Ibid.

their guide made such a fuss over Fairbanks: Pickford, *Sunshine and Shadow*, 132.

"'Ully gee! Douglas and Mary!'": *Chicago News*, July 29, 1920.

"Some of the things women wear abroad": *Hardin County Ledger*, September 9, 1920.

Mary was obliged to be rescued: *Galveston Daily News*, August 1, 1920.

"Those marvelous memories": Douglas Fairbanks Papers, scrapbook 1: condolence letters, Margaret Herrick Library.

10. "Having Made Sure I Was Wrong, I Went Ahead"

"Douglas Fairbanks was a man": Margaret Case Harriman, *The Vicious Circle: The Story of the Algonquin Round Table* (New York: Rinehart, 1951), 222.

a letter from Cap O'Brien: Booton Herndon, *Mary Pickford and Douglas Fairbanks: The Most Popular Couple the World Has Ever Known* (New York: Norton, 1977), 208.

"He had 'that thing'": *Oakland Tribune*, October 11, 1936.

"Since parting company from Miss Loos": *Photoplay*, October 1918.

"Doug was timid about doing": Enid Bennett, phone interview with Kevin Brownlow, April 1967, private collection of Kevin Brownlow.

"Douglas Fairbanks has not 'slipped'": *Photoplay*, November 1919.

"Now some of the critics are beginning": *Motion Picture Magazine*, May 1919.

"I admitted freely that when it came": *Colliers*, June 18, 1921.

"I was a little timid": Douglas Fairbanks, "Let Me Say This for the Films," *Ladies' Home Journal*, September 1922.

hiring Belgian world fencing champion M. Harry Uttenhover: *Las Vegas Optic*, January 5, 1921.

Orphaned at sixteen: *Seattle Daily Times*, August 5, 1923.

In its first week, *Zorro* broke all attendance records: *Wid's Daily*, December 8, 1920.

"UA's product could not be sold": Tino Balio, *United Artists: The Company Built by the Stars* (Madison: University of Wisconsin Press, 1976), 38.

Michigan exhibitors organized: *Wid's*, December 9, 1922.

delayed the film's release from February 22 to March 1: *Variety*, February 4, 1921.

"one of his few commercial failures": Richard Schickel, *His Picture in the Papers: A Speculation on Celebrity in America Based on the Life of Douglas Fairbanks, Sr.* (New York: Charterhouse, 1974), 73.

the "relative failure" of *The Nut*: Jeffrey Vance, *Douglas Fairbanks* (Berkeley: University of California Press, 2008), 86.

Publicity for the film trumpeted: *Variety*, May 13, 1921.

He purchased the rights from Famous Players–Lasky: *Wid's Daily*, February 8, 1921; agreement between Famous Players–Lasky Corporation, Mazie LaShelle Hunt (individually and as executrix under the last will and testament of Kirk LaShelle) and Owen Wister (of Philadelphia) and Douglas Fairbanks re: *The Virginian*, Douglas Fairbanks Papers,

Margaret Herrick Library, Academy of Motion Picture Arts and Sciences, Beverly Hills, CA.

"There is a shortage of money": *Variety*, January 21, 1921.

"You know as much about the high cost": Lillian Gish and Ann Pinchot, *Lillian Gish: The Movies, Mr. Griffith, and Me* (Englewood Cliffs, NJ: Prentice-Hall, 1969), 247.

"Right now the studio is as much": *Variety*, April 22, 1921.

"The Ince plant issues a statement": Ibid., July 29, 1921.

"I had always wanted to do *The Three Musketeers*": Douglas Fairbanks, *Douglas Fairbanks: In His Own Words* (New York: iUniverse, 2006), 102.

"Nothing could have exceeded": Edward Knoblock, *Round the Room* (London: Chapman and Hall, 1939), 299.

"Pickfair was about—certainly, the most": Lord Mountbatten, interview with Kevin Brownlow, slate 340, recorded for *Hollywood* (documentary TV series), 1980, private collection of Kevin Brownlow.

he had found himself surrounded: *Film Fun*, December 1919.

When they finally located the misplaced manservant: *Photoplay*, August 1920.

"He's old-fashioned enough": *Bridgeport Telegram*, January 23, 1922.

"Although D'Artagnan figured throughout": Knoblock, *Round the Room*, 303.

"Working in a Fairbanks picture": Adolphe Menjou, *It Took Nine Tailors* (New York: McGraw-Hill, 1948), 89.

"Doug invariably got the very best": Ibid., 92.

"Sometimes we worked so late": Mary Pickford, *From Hollywood to Paris* (New York: Press Publishing Company, 1922), Mary Pickford Papers, Margaret Herrick Library.

"Thus Douglas had learned to know": Robert Florey, *Filmland: Los Angeles et Hollywood les capitales du cinema* (Paris: Editions de Cinemagazine, 1923), 135.

"We had to resort to the good old glycerine": *Motion Picture Magazine*, November 1922.

Fairbanks "went completely unorthodox": Menjou, *It Took Nine Tailors*, 91.

"Untrue, perhaps, but why unkind?" *News Sentinel* (Uniontown, PA), June 9, 1921.

"Her mother made her": Author interview with Tom Moore, nephew of Owen Moore, to whom Mary confided this story in the mid-1960s, December 2013.

"Not less than four babies": *Oakland Tribune*, July 29, 1921.

"An old age without children": *Reno Evening Gazette*, December 24, 1921.

"darling little baby girl": Fairbanks correspondence, author's collection.

Mary had won the first round: *San Antonio Light*, June 26, 1921.

his bride "was very much gratified": *Independent* (Helena, MT), June 26, 1921.

He did, and the following June: *Oelwein Daily Register*, June 1, 1922.

Fairbanks optimistically leased the Lyric Theatre: *Variety*, August 5, 1921.

Alexander filed suit in federal court: *Nebraska State Journal*, September 1, 1921.

Cap O'Brien brought the case: *Variety*, August 12, 1921.

The issue hinged on the failure: Ibid., September 16, 1921.

The commission ruled in Fairbanks's favor: *Lima News*, September 29, 1922.

"The crowds were gathered": Charlie Chaplin, *My Trip Abroad* (New York: Harper and Brothers, 1922), e-book.

"Charlie found at least five places": Pickford, *From Hollywood to Paris*.

"I suggested a few changes": Chaplin, *My Trip Abroad*.

"*The Three Musketeers* with Douglas Fairbanks is not only a great picture": *Exhibitors Trade Review*, December 3, 1921.

"Search high and low": *Exhibitors Trade Review*, December 3, 1921.

"Liberties have been taken": *Motion Picture Magazine*, December 1921.

"There was one whole phase": *New York Times*, November 6, 1922.

"His excuse was safety": Kevin Brownlow, *Behind the Mask of Innocence* (New York: Knopf, 1990), 5.

"acted as an enlightened censor": Ibid.

"The movies are patronized by thousands": *Photoplay*, March 1916.

"A sure money-getter": *Motography*, March 30, 1918.

"In the early June pea": *Variety*, December 28, 1917.

"There are the Movie Censors": Dorothy Parker, "Reformers: A Hymn of Hate," in *Non-senseorship* (New York: G. P. Putnam's Sons, 1922), 95.

"Douglas Fairbanks walks in on a cue": *Variety*, April 15, 1921.

"burst like depth charges": Brownlow, *Behind the Mask of Innocence*, 13.

Republicans in Congress fronted a proposal: *Variety*, September 23, 1921.

"For several years now the name": Ibid., September 16, 1921.

"by restricting subject matter": Brownlow, *Behind the Mask of Innocence*, 17.

"I have always believed that censorship should be worked out": Douglas Fairbanks, "A Huge Responsibility," *Ladies' Home Journal*, May 1924.

looking like a "startled mouse": Brownlow, *Behind the Mask of Innocence*, 15.

he had "teeth like mixed nuts": Greg Merritt, *Room 1219* (Chicago: Chicago Review Press, 2013), 276.

"From some mysterious and unknown place": All quotes from Fairbanks and Pickford regarding their trip to Europe are from *From Hollywood to Paris* by Mary Pickford.

Fairbanks later confessed that watching Robert's face: *Nebraska State Journal*, January 8, 1922.

11. Prince of Thieves

he was still considering *The Virginian*: Robert Florey, "How Douglas Fairbanks Made Robin Hood," *Le Film Montreal*, October 1922; all Florey quotes in this chapter derive from this source.

reports at the time of preproduction: *Wid's*, January 18, 1921.

"The spectacle of a lot of flat-footed outlaws": Robert E. Sherwood, *The Best Moving Pictures of 1922–23* (New York: Revisionist, 1974), 42.

"He couldn't see any agility": Allan Dwan, interview with Kevin Brownlow, slate 318, take 1, recorded for *Hollywood* (documentary TV series), 1980, private collection of Kevin Brownlow.

Doug "was tremendously interested": Ibid.

"I came by chance upon some old manuscripts": Sherwood, *Best Moving Pictures*, 42.

he wanted to play Richard the Lion-Hearted: Notes from a talk to photoplay students at Columbia University, Douglas Fairbanks Papers, folder 177, Margaret Herrick Library, Academy of Motion Picture Arts and Sciences, Beverly Hills, CA.

"if, instead of sentencing him": Sherwood, *Best Moving Pictures*, 43.

"We had nothing real": Douglas Fairbanks, "Why Big Pictures," *Ladies' Home Journal*, March 1924.

"There were just tales": Allan Dwan, interview with Kevin Brownlow, slate 319, take 1, transcript p. 2, recorded for *Hollywood*.

an operatic version of Robin Hood: *New York Times*, August 11, 1912.

"If these critics know what book": Kevin Brownlow, *The Parade's Gone By* (New York: Knopf, 1968), 254.

When they purchased the Hampton Studio: *Variety*, February 3, 1922.

"Mary had a complete bungalow": Bruce Humberstone, oral history files, T2B/P61, Directors Guild of America, Los Angeles, CA.

Workmen built a concrete-lined trench: *Warner Hollywood News* (studio newsletter) May/June 1993; as of 2010, at least, the trench was still there.

"I never cross the yard": *Bismarck Tribune*, September 30, 1922.

"heavy velvets and rich cloths": Brownlow, *Parade's Gone By*, 251.

"This suit's been going on": *Fresno Bee*, February 17, 1922.

Both Mary and Mama Charlotte testified: *Newark Advocate*, March 2, 1922; *Ogden Standard-Examiner*, February 22, 1922.

"I can't compete with that": Brownlow, *Parade's Gone By*, 251.

While present and accounted for: *Oakland Tribune*, March 1, 1922.

"He got as far as the gate": Allan Dwan, interview with Kevin Brownlow, slate 319, take 1, recorded for *Hollywood*.

"I purposely engineered it": Notes from a talk to photoplay students at Columbia University, Allan Dwan Papers, folder 177, Margaret Herrick Library.

O'Brien suggested that the film, upon release, be titled: *Variety*, June 9, 1922.

"If he is going through his daily workout": Adolphe Menjou, *It Took Nine Tailors* (New York: McGraw-Hill, 1948), 92.

"Doug slapped him on the back": Ibid.

"One of the tough things": Kevin Brownlow, interview with Mitchell Leisen, n.d., private collection of Kevin Brownlow.

"He is delighted when they beat": *Picture Play*, April 1924.

"The war made *Robin Hood* easy": *Motion Picture Magazine*, February 1923.

"Doug would hold up the work": Frank Case, *Tales of a Wayward Inn* (New York: Frederick A. Stokes, 1938), 98.

"He played all the time": Ibid.

He opened the studio to the public: *Oakland Tribune*, June 18, 1922.

A trained falcon was purchased: *Washington Post*, May 20, 1922.

It arrived with a list of instructions: *Oakland Tribune*, July 23, 1922.

Originally named War Bond, the pooch: *Motion Picture Magazine*, May 1921.

When this was pointed out: *New Castle News*, August 17, 1933.

"had neither interest nor ability": Letitia Fairbanks and Ralph Hancock, *Doug Fairbanks: The Fourth Musketeer* (New York: Henry Holt, 1953), 198.

They went by way of Vancouver: *Lethbridge Herald*, October 21, 1922.

The Chicago premiere was on October 22: *Wid's*, October 16, 1922.

Doug, jauntily perched on a tractor: *Oakland Tribune*, October 8, 1922.

The trend caught on, and soon other stores: Hat advertisements for Young's Hats can be readily seen in multiple issues of the *New York Times* in October 1922.

"The telephone in his suite rings constantly": *Christian Science Monitor*, October 17, 1922.

"some deviltry within him": Richard Schickel, *The Fairbanks Album* (New York Graphic Society, 1975), 123.

it hit him in the chest: *Oxnard Daily Courier*, October 18, 1922.

"Conversation and laughter ceased": Frank Case, *Do Not Disturb* (New York: Frederick A. Stokes, 1940), 163.

"It isn't safe to admit": *Photoplay*, May 1922.

"We don't know anything a-tall": *Fresno Bee*, February 17, 1922.

"The whole motion picture industry should not be condemned": *Oakland Tribune*, February 14, 1922.

"'What,' we asked, 'should the industry do'": *Nebraska State Journal*, March 19, 1922.

"Eliminate actual choking by Robin Hood": *Robin Hood* censorship records, October 11, 1922, Motion Picture Division, New York State Education Department.

"These atrocities of King John": *New York Times*, November 26, 1922.

A second showing was staged at midnight: *Photoplay*, January 1923.

Some surly few suggested that the first half: *Film Daily*, November 5, 1922; *Variety*, November 3, 1922.

"Douglas Fairbanks in *Robin Hood* out-spectacles": *Film Daily*, November 1, 1922.

Doug and Mary returned to Hollywood by way of Chicago: Ibid., November 18, 1922.

the discovery of a suicide victim: *Oakland Tribune*, December 1, 1922.

12. The Fairy Tale

"But Douglas," the portrait artist recalled: *Seattle Daily Times*, October 21, 1923.

"That he is very deeply in love": Ibid.

"I've just bought a hill": *Indianapolis Star*, September 10, 1922.

"In the case of Douglas and Mary": *Motion Picture Magazine*, April 1923.

"I'll tell you about me": *Plain Dealer*, March 4, 1923.

"The motion picture has sustained an irreparable loss": *Daily Register-Gazette* (Rockford, IL), January 19, 1923.

Robert's daughter related an anecdote: Letitia Fairbanks and Ralph Hancock, *Doug Fairbanks: The Fourth Musketeer* (New York: Henry Holt, 1953), 203.

"When I keep moving I'm in harmony": *Repository* (Canton, OH), April 6, 1924.

"There hasn't been a good picture showing ancient Rome": *Cinea*, July 1924.

"Let's do an *Arabian Nights* story": Fairbanks and Hancock, *Doug Fairbanks*, 202.

"a graduate engineer who charged fifteen cents": Letitia Fairbanks and Ralph Hancock, *Doug Fairbanks: The Fourth Musketeer*, 203.

"Doug never heard any complaints": Ibid.

Kenneth Davenport had warned Florey: *Cinea*, July 1924.

Even the press reflected this confusion: *Variety*, June 14, 1923.

"I had to find a picture to fit my hair": *Oregonian*, June 11, 1923.

"A special problem that faced us": Douglas Fairbanks, "Films for the Fifty Million," *Ladies' Home Journal*, April 1924.

"The whole scene immediately lifts us": *Pictures and Picturegoer*, September 1924.

"It isn't easy to work with Doug": *Cinea*, March 9, 1923.

"While he was dressing": *Picture Play*, April 1924.

"Of course, breakdown boards and sheets": *American Cinematographer*, April 1992.

"a perfect type of screen beauty": *Seattle Daily Times*, May 13, 1923.

"I just didn't like the part": John Kobal, *People Will Talk* (New York: Knopf, 1986).

"There seems to be a difference of opinion": *Screenland*, October 1923.

"One morning I went out horseback riding": Kobal, *People Will Talk*.

They notified Cap O'Brien to file suit: *Variety*, November 1, 1923.

"And what started it I don't know": Kobal, *People Will Talk*.

"He had to get past Wong Sam Sing": Graham Russell Hodges, *Anna May Wong: From Laundryman's Daughter to Hollywood Legend* (New York: Palgrave Macmillan, 2004), 48.

Fairbanks was looking for unconventional casting: *Springfield Republican*, June 24, 1923.

"You have the eyes of a saint": *Camera! The Digest of the Motion Picture Industry*, February 2, 1924.

"I did not fancy it": Ibid.

"Sadakichi Hartmann was not very cooperative": Julanne Johnston, phone interview with Kevin Brownlow, March 26, 1985, private collection of Kevin Brownlow.

He "seemed to have a strange predilection": *Camera! The Digest of the Motion Picture Industry*, February 2, 1924.

"such as some Chinese Pavlova": Ibid.

Sôjin and other Japanese members of the cast: *Evansville Courier and Press*, September 23, 1923.

"My father adored Douglas Fairbanks": Kevin Brownlow, transcript of recorded interview
    with Marion Shaw, November 1987, private collection of Kevin Brownlow.

"Mephisto must have humor": *Motion Picture Magazine*, July 1923.

but "he always countered with 'Can you imagine'": *Oregonian*, February 25, 1923.

"He threw back his head": Jesse L. Lasky Jr., *Whatever Happened to Hollywood?* (New York:
    Funk & Wagnalls, 1975), 14.

"I think Mother saw": Douglas Fairbanks Jr., *The Salad Days* (New York: Doubleday,
    1988), 86.

"sort of a minor revenge": Ibid.

"be bound to be embarrassed": Ibid.

"I often thought back on that idea": Ibid., 90.

Doug sent Beth a telegram: *San Diego Union*, April 26, 1923.

The early headlines: Lasky Jr., *Whatever Happened to Hollywood?*, 14.

"The picture was terrible": Harry T. Brundidge, *Twinkle, Twinkle Movie Star* (New York:
    E. P. Dutton, 1930).

"I asked him to withdraw any opposition": Ibid.

Cameraman Arthur Edeson: Robert Florey, *Deux ans dans les studios Americains* (Paris:
    Editions d'Aujourd'hui, 1984), 132.

managers of all the major local hotels: *Exhibitors Trade Review*, September 8, 1923.

gave them forty-two-minute tours: *Variety*, January 31, 1924.

over twenty-three thousand spectators: *Exhibitors Trade Review*, September 8, 1923.

"I did not encourage outsiders": Raoul Walsh, *Each Man in His Time: The Life Story of a
    Director* (New York: Farrar, Straus and Giroux, 1974), 176.

"appeared to put more snap": Ibid.

Mary requested "Roses of Picardy": Safford Chamberlain, *The Unsung Cat: The Life and
    Music of Warne Marsh* (Lanham, MD: Scarecrow, 2000).

Other sources claim it was a quartet: *Thief of Bagdad* souvenir program, Grauman's Egyptian
    Theatre, 1924, private collection.

"the new grace which has crept": *Pictures and Picturegoer*, November 1924.

"Fairbanks' stage straining never counted": Alistair Cooke, *Douglas Fairbanks: The Mak-
    ing of a Screen Character*, Museum of Modern Art Film Library Series 2 (New York:
    Museum of Modern Art, 1940), 28.

Doug and Mary arrived on February 15: *Wid's*, February 17, 1924.

Mary's mother, maid, and secretary; little Gwynne: *Riverside Daily Press*, February 11, 1924.

Throngs blocked Forty-Second Street: *Boston Herald*, March 19, 1924.

historians as early as 1931 were claiming: Benjamin Hampton, *A History of the Movies*
    (1931), quoted in *Douglas Fairbanks* by Jeffrey Vance (Berkeley: University of Cali-
    fornia Press, 2008), 178.

Pickford and Fairbanks departed for London: *Oregonian*, April 13, 1924.

"When I get on the other side": Ibid.

They were hosted by Lord Mountbatten: *Omaha World Herald*, April 20, 1924.

"From the first we decided": *Film Daily*, July 23, 1924.

Paris, where the now-familiar drama: *Seattle Daily Times*, April 30, 1924.

a case of *la grippe*: *Seattle Daily Times*, May 3, 1924.

they contemplated a visit to Copenhagen: *Bellingham Herald*, May 8, 1924.

"Quite sufficient cause for war": *Daily Register-Gazette* (Rockford, IL), May 9, 1924.

before Denmark, they stopped in Berlin: *Rockford Republic*, June 17, 1924.

The king and queen of Spain, upon arriving: *Trenton Evening Times*, August 24, 1924.

The idea of bullfights intrigued him: *Exhibitors Trade Review*, July 5, 1924.

these weeks in San Sebastián: *Richmond Times-Dispatch*, July 6, 1924.

They went next to Copenhagen, where the mobs that greeted them: *Repository* (Canton, OH), June 19, 1924.

Then it was back to Paris: *Idaho Statesman*, July 6, 1924.

There Doug was awarded a medal: Ibid., June 22, 1924.

"Tell that to Sweeny": *Seattle Daily Times*, June 30, 1924.

Pranksters both, they disguised themselves: Gloria Swanson, *Swanson on Swanson* (New York: Random House, 1980), 217.

"had it in for Paramount": Ibid.

their return to New York City on July 20: *Wid's*, July 10, 1924.

THIS RECENT ACTION OF YOURS: Richard Schickel, *D. W. Griffith: An American Life* (New York: Simon & Schuster, 1984), 445.

"unanimously decided to not only carry out": Tino Balio, *United Artists: The Company Built by the Stars* (Madison: University of Wisconsin Press, 1976), 49.

Deeming Doug's wire "antagonistic": Ibid.

Stern words were exchanged: *Wid's*, July 24, 1924.

a public statement was released: *Exhibitors Trade Review*, August 9, 1924.

UA had been trying to woo Schenck: Balio, *United Artists*, 52.

"Mr. Hayes has nothing whatever to do with the art": *Wid's*, January 27, 1923.

"Perhaps the younger man had an unconscious desire": Schickel, *D. W. Griffith*, 504–505.

13. Buckling Down

Don Q, Son of Zorro, the forgotten blockbuster, was announced: *Richmond Times-Dispatch*, January 18, 1925.

"*The Thief of Bagdad* is one of the biggest things": *State Times Advocate* (Baton Rouge, LA), February 5, 1926.

"I looked forward to meeting this man": Mary Astor, *My Story: An Autobiography* (New York: Doubleday, 1959), 33.

Valentino signed a three-picture deal: *Exhibitors Trade Review*, March 21, 1925; *Variety*, November 11, 1925.

"It was all fun for him": Mary Astor, interview with Kevin Brownlow, slate 518, take 1, recorded for *Hollywood* (documentary TV series), 1980, private collection of Kevin Brownlow.

He would delight to show his hand calluses: *Springfield Republican*, September 20, 1925.

"Snowy was hired to wield the whip": Astor, *My Story*, 83–84.

Filming began on January 26: *Exhibitors Trade Review*, February 7, 1925.

Donald Crisp's broken foot: *Evansville Courier and Press*, May 3, 1925.

delayed by a day when a nearby wildfire: *Miami Herald*, February 24, 1926.

a large cake sculpted to look: *Exhibitors Trade Review*, October 10, 1925.

reported that he took he took tango lessons: Ibid., May 9, 1925.

"For years the pioneers held the claims": *Photoplay*, May 1925.

"From the standpoint of costly production": *Exhibitors Trade Weekly*, February 21, 1925.

"Without doubt one of the best": *Variety*, June 17, 1925.

"It is guaranteed to drive little boys into frenzies": *Photoplay*, August 1925.

"I ruined a beautiful grape arbor": Scott Eyman, *John Wayne: The Life and Legend* (New York: Simon & Schuster, 2014), 26.

"If *Don Q, Son of Zorro* is not as good": *Evansville Courier and Press*, March 15, 1926.

"As the years pass and age begins its inroads": *Plain Dealer*, October 19, 1925.

"Doug has never leaped so high": Ibid.

Historically, summer was the worst time: *Variety*, June 10, 1925.

But *Don Q* packed the house: Ibid., July 1, 1925.

The run was intentionally short: *Exhibitors Trade Review*, May 16, 1925.

"a stiff fight": *Variety*, June 10, 1925.

"If I had five pictures opening there": *Springfield Republican*, June 28, 1925.

Mary remembered being alone at Pickfair: Mary Pickford, *Sunshine and Shadow* (New York: Doubleday, 1955), 158.

The detectives actually used a stethoscope: *Evening Tribune* (Hornell, NY), July 28, 1925.

considered nabbing little Jackie Coogan: *Daily Illinois State Journal*, May 31, 1925.

"the last word in daintiness": Pickford, *Sunshine and Shadow*, 160.

One evening in late May: Ibid., 161.

Fairbanks testified before a grand jury: *Riverside Daily Press*, June 5, 1925.

The trial began on July 22, and he attended: Ibid., July 22, 1925.

When finally his turn came: *Morning Star* (Wilmington, NC), July 29, 1925.

"I think in sentencing them": Pickford, *Sunshine and Shadow*, 163.

"The public has no idea": *Riverside Daily Press*, August 14, 1925.

reporters were obliged to acknowledge: Ibid.

an ex-convict now wanted: *Riverside Daily Press*, November 19, 1923.

"Mary and I have decided": *Miami Herald*, January 15, 1926.

even staged a rodeo for their conventioneers: *Variety*, June 10, 1925.

Doug, gripping his .45 revolver: Ibid., September 30, 1925.

Doug's contribution to the kerfuffle: *Seattle Daily Times*, October 11, 1925.

There, on the bottom of his pool: *Oregonian*, June 7, 1925.

Kinemacolor was the first truly photographic color process: Fred Basten, *Glorious Technicolor: The Movies' Magic Rainbow* (Easton Studio Press, 2005), xii.

"etch, print or hand block": Ibid.

"a puzzling situation": Ibid.

"to take the color out of color": *Motion Picture Classic*, May 1926.

The Glorious Adventure, filmed in Prizma Color: Catalog of the 33rd Le Giornate del Cinema Muto, Pordenone, Italy, 2014.

"We were afraid that the public might at first": R. J. B. Denby, interview, 1926, reprinted in *Liberty Then and Now*, Spring 1975.

Pickford replaced Dove in one of the final shots: *Picture Play*, February 1928.

an opportunity to dip into the deep pool: *Photoplay*, June 1926.

Jack Dempsey's former sparring partner: *Oregonian*, November 15, 1925.

Multiple camera tests were taken: *State Times Advocate* (Baton Rouge, LA), November 16, 1926.

Fairbanks reviewed Dove's color tests: *American Cinematographer* April 1992.

Dove was being touted: *Seattle Daily Times*, November 1, 1925.

Fairbanks himself cornered a traffic cop: Ibid., September 10, 1925.

"You don't know—nobody can know": *Picture Play*, June 1926.

One scholar argues that Fairbanks's annoyance: Jeffrey Vance, *Douglas Fairbanks* (Berkeley: University of California Press, 2008), 198.

Hugo Ballin claimed: *Motion Picture Classic*, July 1926.

"There's only *one* Fairbanks": Letitia Fairbanks and Ralph Hancock, *Doug Fairbanks: The Fourth Musketeer* (New York: Henry Holt, 1953), 244.

"He was always striving": Booton Herndon, *Mary Pickford and Douglas Fairbanks: The Most Popular Couple the World Has Ever Known* (New York: Norton, 1977), 237.

"We had a place on the lot": Ibid., 238.

he proceeded to dislocate a finger: *Omaha World Herald*, September 13, 1926.

Anders Randolf, who shaved his head: Ibid., October 11, 1925.

Fairbanks himself separated a rib: *Morning Star* (Wilmington, NC), October 14, 1925.

fencing master Fred Cavens: *Plain Dealer*, October 11, 1925.

"Pirates always were a bloody lot": *Oregonian*, October 24, 1925.

filming took only nine weeks, five of which: *State Times Advocate* (Baton Rouge, LA), November 12, 1926.

Fairbanks purchased and had restored: *Oregonian*, October 8, 1925.

a reproduction Spanish galleon was built: Ibid., December 1, 1925.

Doug's "particular brain child": *Richmond Times-Dispatch*, December 6, 1925.

Mary came along for three weeks: *Springfield Republican*, December 13, 1925.

The ship snapped her hawsers: *Richmond Times-Dispatch*, November 15, 1925.

A miniature of the *Morse*: *Picture Play*, July 1926.

a stranded lumber schooner, the *Muriel*: Clipping from *Motion Picture Director*, 1925 (no month), Margaret Herrick Library, Academy of Motion Picture Arts and Sciences, Beverly Hills, CA.

He named the galley the *Yo-Ho*: *Seattle Daily Times*, December 20, 1925.

Two tugboats served as supply ships: Ibid., December 27, 1925.

Evenings and lunch breaks were spent: *Times-Picayune*, November 29, 1925.

They returned in time for the company: *Oregonian*, December 24, 1925.

"Right here at Christmas time": *Motion Picture Magazine*, February 1926.

"I love my home": *Screenland*, May 1926.

They leased their studio to Joseph Schenck: *Motion Picture News*, February 20, 1926.

Norma and Constance Talmadge moved into: *Variety*, February 17, 1926.

They would travel through Europe: *Riverside Daily Press*, November 27, 1925.

Schenck formed a business entity: *Times-Picayune*, February 28, 1926.

shortly after Christmas, she consented: *Rockford Republic*, December 30, 1925.

The princess briefly made headlines: *Seattle Daily Times*, January 18, 1926.

Mr. and Mrs. Fairbanks were excluded: *Oregonian*, October 21, 1925.

He would be seen playing tennis: Ibid., March 14, 1926.

dining at the Park Avenue apartment: *Lexington Herald*, March 31, 1926.

"He drew successful people to him": Pickford, *Sunshine and Shadow*, 135.

Charlotte's surgery did not take place: *Variety*, February 24, 1926.

Fairbanks stayed by her side: *Omaha World Herald*, March 1, 1926.

He and Mary departed for New York: *Wid's*, March 3, 1926.

just in time to attend the premiere of *The Black Pirate*: *Wid's*, March 8, 1926.

"*The Black Pirate* is everything one has come to expect": *Plain Dealer*, March 14, 1926.

"Up to now, the Technicolor process": *Springfield Republican*, March 21, 1926.

Doug Gets Away With It: Unsourced clipping, Douglas Fairbanks Papers, scrapbook 4, Margaret Herrick Library.

"He can have nothing of boyhood": *Motion Picture News*, April 17, 1926.

"I never saw a movie that taxed the intelligence": *Plain Dealer*, March 21, 1926.

she "never went anywhere": *Seattle Daily Times*, March 19, 1926.

Charlotte, unwell from her cross-country train trip: *Bellingham Herald*, April 3, 1926.

"Sunlight in films makes one look so old": *Omaha World Herald*, April 4, 1926.

both posed for the cameras: *Springfield Republican*, April 14, 1926.

They attended the premiere of *Little Annie Rooney*: *Rockford Republic*, April 29, 1926.

"We met Mussolini at every corner": *Oregonian*, October 3, 1926.

"I would like to see the Prime Minister": *Prensa*, April 30, 1926.

They met Mussolini: *Tampa Tribune*, May 11, 1926.

Mary was suitably cowed: *Springfield Republican*, May 16, 1926; *Oregonian*, October 3, 1926.

"He's a great man": *Repository* (Canton, OH), October 17, 1926.

"When Douglas Fairbanks met Premier Mussolini": *Aberdeen Daily News*, May 24, 1926.

The orchestra played "The Star-Spangled Banner": *Seattle Daily Times*, May 23, 1926.

"Tonight I am not Douglas Fairbanks": *Plain Dealer*, June 13, 1926.

There was general objection, it seemed: *Winston-Salem Journal*, June 12, 1926.

"surely had no intention": *Omaha World Herald*, April 25, 1926.

the main character wore a black shirt: *Motion Picture Magazine*, July 1926.

"nothing short of a national hero": *Wid's*, July 20, 1926.

Motorcyclists raced across Moscow: *Seattle Daily Times*, July 18, 1926.

"At last accounts, the movies taken": *Macon Telegraph*, April 4, 1926.

"He typifies not only physical prowess": *Wid's*, January 10, 1926.

"The finest pictures I have seen": *Wid's*, August 26, 1926.

"I used to think I knew something": *Morning Star* (Wilmington, NC), September 4, 1926.

"If you are taken ill in a foreign country": *Motion Picture Magazine*, June 1927.

"In Russia, the moving picture": *Trenton Evening Times*, August 26, 1926.

"Does Mr. Fairbanks hold the opinion": *Richmond Times-Dispatch*, August 30, 1926.

"One day Rudolph Valentino": Pickford, *Sunshine and Shadow*, 185.

They canceled their trip to the Far East: *Educational Screen*, November 1926.

Negotiations with Cecil B. DeMille stalled: *Omaha World Herald*, January 14, 1925.

he even conferred with Erich von Stroheim: *Variety*, May 27, 1925.

the affiliation with Samuel Goldwyn: *Oregonian*, May 6, 1925.

"It is almost certain to go through": *Wid's*, November 15, 1925.

UA historian Tino Balio argues: Tino Balio, *United Artists: The Company Built by the Stars* (Madison: University of Wisconsin Press, 1976), 62.

called Charlie a "kicker": Ibid.

"He was always welcome to come": Pickford, *Sunshine and Shadow*, 138.

"Charlie was always so proud": David Robinson, *Chaplin: His Life and Art* (New York: McGraw-Hill, 1985), 168.

"But Charlie, you know Schenck": Pickford, *Sunshine and Shadow*, 143.

14. Death . . .

John suffered a second stroke: *Wid's*, November 28, 1926.

"behind which life will drowse": *Miami Herald*, October 18, 1925.

they had shooed a hot dog vendor away: *Photoplay*, June 1927.

"I like the colorful life": *Miami Herald*, October 18, 1925.

"The whole place will have a Spanish tang": *Evening Tribune* (Hornell, NY), January 20, 1927.

The nine-thousand-acre Rancho Santa Fe: Ibid., October 15, 1927.

He bought 847 acres: Ibid., January 20, 1927.

then, for $125,000, another 2,700: *San Diego Union*, May 20, 1927.

he owned Black Mountain: Ibid., March 23, 1927.

A pump house was constructed at the base: *Evening Tribune* (Hornell, NY), April 13, 1927.

Fifteen thousand Valencia orange seedlings: Ibid., July 16, 1927, and August 13, 1927.

the largest installation of its kind: Ibid., September 10, 1927.

improvements on the property were reported: Ibid., September 24, 1927.

"It has been planned to have the house": *San Diego Union*, January 20, 1927.

"He didn't have to draw on his regular account": Ibid., December 31, 1927.

In 1927 his cost for improvements: Schedule F, 1927–1930, income tax schedules, Fairbanks
    Papers, Margaret Herrick Library, Academy of Motion Picture Arts and Sciences,
    Beverly Hills, CA.

A front facade for a ranch house: *Architectural Digest*, September 1982.

The organization was not his brainchild: Robert Osborne, *65 Years of Oscar* (New York:
    Abbeville Press, 1989), 8.

$100 subscriptions: *Wid's*, May 13, 1927.

"dishonorable or unethical conduct": *Bellingham Herald*, May 12, 1927.

the industry had "been making pictures": Ibid., July 19, 1927.

"The Academy . . . has been organized": *Motion Picture News*, July 29, 1927.

"button-hole makers": *Riverside Daily Press*, July 29, 1927.

a standard contract for freelancing workers: *Wid's*, October 26, 1927.

Actors wished to be paid: *Exhibitors Herald and Moving Picture World*, February 25, 1928.

He even gave the inaugural lecture: *Educational Screen*, March 1928.

"Courses in acting for the screen": *St. Albans Daily Messenger*, August 23, 1927.

night courses were set up at USC: *Riverside Daily Press*, October 11, 1927.

"Those of us who get our names in electric lights": *Transactions of the Society of Motion
    Picture Engineers* 12, no. 33 (1928).

a film about the progress of civilization: *Wid's*, November 24, 1926.

It would be called *The Brotherhood of Man*: Ibid., December 29, 1926.

"First mention to me of Martian idea": Lotta Woods, diary for 1927, private collection.

"Disappointed to find there was no story": Ibid.

a modern-day version of *A Houseboat on the Styx*: *Winston-Salem Journal*, January 15, 1927.

explore the history of the Children's Crusade: *Boston Herald*, January 19, 1927.

"a devil-may-care Mohammedan": *Picture Play*, March 1927.

he would film a version of *Captain Cavalier*: *Oregonian*, March 17, 1927.

Reinhardt came to California at Fairbanks's invitation: Unsourced clipping, Mary Pickford
    Papers, folder 1760, Margaret Herrick Library.

"stronger character and bolder relief": *Motion Picture News*, May 6, 1927.

Fairbanks invited director Edwin Carewe: *Seattle Daily Times*, July 10, 1927.

claiming Southern was "lunched" to fame: *Springfield Republican*, May 15, 1927.

originally intended for Dolores del Rio: *Oregonian*, March 27, 1927.

he now worked to master the bola: *Seattle Daily Times*, May 15, 1927.

His job was to run across the lot: *Daily Register-Gazette* (Rockford, IL), March 8, 1928.

six hundred longhorns were shipped: *Oregonian*, September 4, 1927.

Exhibitor complaints poured in: *Exhibitors Herald and Moving Picture World*, September 8, 1928.

"It is not always easy to distinguish": *Plain Dealer*, May 22, 1927.

Fairbanks took his dancing lessons: *Seattle Daily Times*, March 28, 1927.

"symbolize the wild life": *Plain Dealer*, May 22, 1927.

"Already the famous agile star": Jan and Cora Gordon, *Star-Dust in Hollywood* (London: George G. Harrap, 1930), 154.

He was slashed on the leg: *Oregonian*, June 4, 1927.

an ailment variably described as peritonitis: *Wid's*, August 11, 1927.

or malarial fever: *Oregonian*, August 22, 1927.

"If Mary did have or was inclined to like Buddy": Bruce Humberstone, oral history files, T2B/P61, Directors Guild of America, Los Angeles, CA.

"I have never known a man to read": Mary Pickford, *Sunshine and Shadow* (New York: Doubleday, 1955), 185.

All sources are adamant: Booton Herndon, *Mary Pickford and Douglas Fairbanks: The Most Popular Couple the World Has Ever Known* (New York: Norton, 1977), 283.

"My own darling little baby": Fairbanks correspondence, private collection.

"If there was an affair going on": Bruce Humberstone, oral history files.

"that he had made no demands": Pickford note to self, December 24, 1934, private collection.

"He was not thrilled": Lotta Woods, diary for 1927.

the film had a "favorable prognosis": Ibid.

"A queer combination of pictorial heights": *Wid's*, November 30, 1927.

"It is a tale partly barbaric": Ibid.

"Maybe Douglas Fairbanks' ardent fans": *Picture Play*, February 1928.

the "paradigmatic American man": Scott Eyman, personal correspondence with author.

"Talkies were not an evolution": Scott Eyman, *The Speed of Sound: Hollywood and the Talkie Revolution, 1926–1930* (Baltimore: Johns Hopkins University Press, 1999), 22.

"In the course of a decade or so": "Doug Shoots Tomorrow's Perfect Film," *Liberty Magazine*, 1926, reprinted in *Liberty Then and Now*, n.d., Douglas Fairbanks Papers, Margaret Herrick Library.

"There I remained for eighteen weeks": Pickford, *Sunshine and Shadow*, 180.

"The report is idle street talk": *San Diego Union*, April 20, 1928.

hustled her off to Europe: *Idaho Statesman*, April 19, 1928.

In such a hurry was he that he left town: *Seattle Daily Times*, April 19, 1928.

They visited Geneva: *Evening Tribune* (Hornell, NY), May 11, 1928.

travel to visit friends in Surrey: *Boston Herald*, May 29, 1928.

Mary, Winchell reported, "was brooding": *Evansville Courier and Press*, November 8, 1928.

"Dialog may and may not be the ultimate result": *Motion Picture Magazine*, May 1927.

The court let him off: *Evening Tribune* (Hornell, NY), April 25, 1928.

"When I removed my hat": Pickford, *Sunshine and Shadow*, 176.

"was and is witheringly bad": Eyman, *Speed of Sound*, 275.

"Why not D'Artagnan": Maurice Leloir, *Cinq mois a Hollywood avec Douglas Fairbanks* (Paris: J. Peyronnet, 1929), 11.

"It wasn't unusual for Doug": Bruce Humberstone, oral history files.

Lady de Winter dislocated Constance's pretty jaw: *Sunday Repository* (Canton, OH), January 6, 1929.

a nationwide radio broadcast in late March: *Oregonian*, March 30, 1928.

They gathered in front of a six-foot microphone: Ibid., March 28, 1928.

"the transmission of the program": Ibid., March 30, 1928.

Preview prints also had Fairbanks: *Plain Dealer*, April 10, 1929.

"And thus it was in France of old": Application for reexamination, *The Iron Mask* censorship records, February 29, 1929, Motion Picture Division, New York State Education Department.

"Finally, we got a complete take": Eyman, *Speed of Sound*, 272.

"And gosh, we stopped it quick": Allan Dwan, interview with Kevin Brownlow, slate 324, take 1, transcript p. 5, recorded for *Hollywood* (documentary TV series), 1980, private collection of Kevin Brownlow.

"While we were about halfway through": Laurence Irving, interview with Kevin Brownlow, slate 672, take 1, recorded for *Hollywood*.

While there were tests of sound recordings: *San Diego Union*, May 19, 1929.

15. . . . and Taxes

Handwritten schedules of his deductions: Tax records, Douglas Fairbanks Papers, Margaret Herrick Library, Academy of Motion Picture Arts and Sciences, Beverly Hills, CA.

"It is the desire and intention of the parties": Notarized document, April 20, 1922, Mary Pickford Papers, Margaret Herrick Library.

It was not as if he were a tax scofflaw: *Motion Picture Magazine*, February 1925.

At least that nice Mr. Coolidge: *Photoplay*, January 1929.

fourteen-seat trimotored Ford monoplane: *Daily Illinois State Journal*, March 24, 1929.

for $175 per hour: *Screenland*, July 1929.

green and airsick: *Oregonian*, March 25, 1929.

They gave up after Phoenix: *Riverside Daily Press*, March 26, 1929.

smashed all box office records: *Motion Picture News*, March 9, 1929.

"Doug has always managed to feed it": Ibid., March 2, 1929.

"It was a better picture [than *Robin Hood*]": Allan Dwan, oral history files, Directors Guild of America, Los Angeles, CA.

"He spoke distinctly": *Evansville Courier and Press*, February 10, 1929.

"We have not heard many Shakespearian actors": *Movie Makers*, May 1929.

"registered like warm dish water": *Times-Picayune*, June 30, 1929.

Doug Must Make Actions Speak: *Daily Illinois State Journal*, March 30, 1929.

"It was absolutely charming": Douglas Fairbanks Jr., *The Salad Days* (New York: Doubleday, 1988), 144.

"He could not have enjoyed": Ibid., 151.

reports circulated that Ernst Lubitsch would direct: *Plain Dealer*, August 11, 1923.

"It would be very unwise": *Repository* (Canton, OH), August 17, 1924.

They were considering a play by Karl Vollmöller: *Trenton Evening Times*, July 4, 1926.

he "could do King Lear or Lady Macbeth": *Plain Dealer*, April 7, 1929.

"Mary has made good in the all-talkies": *Greensboro Record*, May 1, 1929.

"It will be the greatest thing": *Morning Olympian*, April 13, 1929.

"Right now my biggest worry": *Daily Illinois State Journal*, May 5, 1929.

Initial production on the film was delayed: *Dallas Morning News*, April 28, 1929.

Black Pirate and *Gaucho* had grossed: *Variety*, April 3, 1929.

a quiet run to New York City: *Motion Picture News*, May 4, 1929.

"There is no chance of the deal going through": *San Francisco Chronicle*, May 17, 1929.

"Now [Doug and Mary are] not talking": Bruce Humberstone, oral history files, T2B/P61,
Directors Guild of America, Los Angeles, CA.

"Believe it or not," Fairbanks declared: *Times-Picayune*, August 11, 1929.

"That is exactly what I do—read them": *Evening Tribune* (Hornell, NY), June 19, 1930.

"I am going to be Douglas' leading lady": *Daily Illinois State Journal*, May 5, 1929.

"Mary, in real life": Bruce Humberstone, oral history files.

"There were undoubtedly cross-currents": Edward Bernds, *Mr. Bernds Goes to Hollywood:
My Early Life and Career in Sound Recording at Columbia with Frank Capra and Others*
(Lanham, MD: Scarecrow, 1999), 87.

"Fairbanks is truly capital": *Motion Picture News*, October 12 and 19, 1929.

"Doug walks away with the whole show": *Oregonian*, November 14, 1929.

"I have always thought that he and Mary": Kevin Brownlow, handwritten notes on interview
with Herbert Brenon, n.d., private collection of Kevin Brownlow.

One surly wit suggested: *Macon Telegraph*, October 13, 1929.

the condensation was expert: Sam Taylor, telegram to Lawrence Irving, Mary Pickford
Papers, Margaret Herrick Library.

"The studio later became convinced": *San Francisco Chronicle*, September 29, 1929.

A fire and explosion: *Daily Illinois State Journal*, October 25, 1929.

They were in London that October: The narrative for the 1929 world trip is derived from
"Our Trip Around the World", New York World Syndicate, 1930.

16. Mischief and Music

"Four months is long enough": *Evening Tribune* (Hornell, NY), January 18, 1930.

"the original, Simon-pure": *Bluefield Daily Telegraph*, December 1, 1931.

"Golf is great fun": *Aberdeen Daily News*, March 27, 1927.

"His pace is too much for me": *Syracuse Herald*, May 18, 1931.

one of entertainment's "link bugs": *Variety*, May 12, 1916.

Jack Pickford, suffering from tertiary syphilis: *Tampa Tribune*, January 25, 1930.

Fairbanks joined D. W. Griffith: *Morning Star* (Wilmington, NC), March 6, 1930.

A special celebration was held for them: *Tampa Tribune*, April 2, 1930.

the customization of an antique music box: Author's collection.

he planned to remake *The Mark of Zorro* in sound: *Variety*, February 5, 1930.

He would play Murrieta: *Dallas Morning News*, March 23, 1930.

releasing his production and office staff: Ibid., August 27, 1930.

rumors that he intended to retire: *Daily Register-Gazette* (Rockford, IL), March 27, 1930.

"Mary and I looked at a silent picture": *Tampa Tribune*, April 13, 1930.

"I find in talkies I can't be active": *Morning Star* (Wilmington, NC), July 11, 1930.

They had slept apart only once: *Motion Picture Magazine*, August 1930.

The first time they dined apart: *Fresno Bee Republican*, June 30, 1933.

"One thing I don't believe in is marital vacations": *Plain Dealer*, February 5, 1928.

"just for the purpose of telling them": *Motion Picture Magazine*, August 1930.

"I can't let her get more than one picture ahead": *Rochester Democrat and Chronicle*, May 4, 1930, Mary Pickford Papers, folder 429, Margaret Herrick Library, Academy of Motion Picture Arts and Sciences, Beverly Hills, CA.

"I just live from one telegram": Fairbanks correspondence, private collection.

He rose early every morning: *Daily Mail*, May 6, 1930.

"Our conversations probably": *Riverside Daily Press*, May 30, 1930.

He went with the American golfers: *Western Daily Press* (Bristol, England), May 8, 1930.

a dinner party studded with lords and ladies: *Bath Chronicle and Weekly Gazette*, May 17, 1930.

Jones attributed his general state of fitness: *Omaha World Herald*, April 3, 1930.

DON'T HAVE TOO GOOD A TIME: Pickford telegrams, Mary Pickford Papers, Margaret Herrick Library.

Her father had been a stable hand: *Evening Independent* (St. Petersburg, FL), July 10, 1933.

"a garment so sketchy": *Daily Oklahoman*, February 17, 1934.

at the Strand: *Lethbridge Herald*, March 3, 1934.

"Such an alliance is unthinkable": *Daily Oklahoman*, February 17, 1934.

"You have an intensely emotional nature": "Delineation of the Horoscope: Douglas Fairbanks" (booklet), Mary Pickford Papers, folder 1249, Margaret Herrick Library.

"But it's no use trying": *Advocate* (Baton Rouge, LA), May 29, 1930.

"Mary got about as far as the thirties": *Plain Dealer*, May 31, 1930.

Fairbanks faced down a trio of burglars: *Springfield Republican*, August 5, 1930.

Fans wrote in to movie magazines: *Motion Picture Magazine*, November 1930.

"So Doug burgled Mary": *Omaha World Herald*, August 6, 1930.

the week before, their publicist had resigned: *Times-Picayune*, August 6, 1930.

"I have heard talk about this woman": *Omaha World Herald*, July 10, 1930.

Fairbanks was reluctant to invest: *Variety*, July 16, 1930.

Then over the course of nine months: *Richmond Times Dispatch*, October 12, 1930.

He struck a deal with Schenck: *Variety*, December 10, 1930.

"He actually takes direction": *Motion Picture Magazine*, February 1931.

his "lethargic indifference to anything": Ibid.

he recalled it as Fairbanks; his biographer states: Gary Giddens, *Bing Crosby: A Pocketful of Dreams; The Early Years, 1903–1940* (Boston: Little, Brown, 2001), 233.

17. Around the World in Eighty Minutes

"He has such little ideas of catching a boat": *Variety*, February 7, 1913.

"Mr. Fairbanks had the idea of making films": Bessie Love, *From Hollywood with Love* (London: Elm Tree Books, 1977), 61.

"It is quite possible": *Wid's*, November 23, 1918.

announced to the press their plans to visit: *Lethbridge Herald*, January 17, 1931.

Two dozen singers in flowered kimonos: Telegram, Douglas Fairbanks Papers, Margaret Herrick Library, Academy of Motion Picture Arts and Sciences, Beverly Hills, CA.

in New York, she claimed, on "a rampage": *Daily News* (Huntingdon, PA), January 19, 1931.

"My Goddess": Fairbanks correspondence, Douglas Fairbanks Papers, Margaret Herrick Library.

THREE HUNDRED FEET EXCELLENT STUFF: Telegram, Douglas Fairbanks Papers, Margaret Herrick Library.

"it was an interesting experience": *Syracuse Herald*, August 21, 1934.

Mary, taking care to have the media present: *San Antonio Light*, May 8, 1931.

The ship docked at Southampton: *Edwardsville Intelligencer*, May 18, 1931.

he "marked himself a generous sportsman": *Titusville Herald*, May 19, 1931.

husband and wife posed for a joint picture: *Ames Daily Tribune*, June 1, 1931.

On midnight of the eighth day: *Lethbridge Herald*, May 27, 1931.

twenty-one steamer trunks: *Van Wert Daily Bulletin*, June 2, 1931.

Sid Grauman's Egyptian Theatre: *Capital Times*, June 23, 1931.

"In . . . *Reaching for the Moon*, there is much": *Hayward Daily Review*, August 27, 1931.

"The talking motion picture has claimed": *Kingsport Times*, August 2, 1931.

"somebody is lucky enough to get a job": *San Mateo Times and Daily News Leader*, October 15, 1931.

He would go to Norway to fish: Ibid., July 2, 1931.

he would go to the Amazon: *Oakland Tribune*, September 28, 1931.

"will slide instead of climb": *Variety*, November 24, 1931.

"Conditions are not worse": *Coshocton Tribune*, November 3, 1931.

One editor, perhaps in possession of a strong sense: Ibid.

He got no farther than Europe: *Galveston Daily News*, January 3, 1932.

A mad dash followed: *Daily Northwestern* (WI), December 29, 1931.

18. Castaway

A columnist came to visit Pickfair: *Motion Picture Magazine*, May 1932.

"She was something of a secret drinker": Douglas Fairbanks Jr., personal communication with Kevin Brownlow.

"Gin or whiskey?" he recalled Jack asking: Eileen Whitfield, *Pickford: The Woman Who Made Hollywood* (Lexington: University Press of Kentucky, 1997), 266.

"He said," she recalled, "that Mr. Fairbanks gave express orders": Booton Herndon, *Mary Pickford and Douglas Fairbanks: The Most Popular Couple the World Has Ever Known* (New York: Norton, 1977), 277.

"If the truth were known": Scott Eyman, *Mary Pickford, America's Sweetheart* (New York: Donald I. Fine, 1990), 230.

"Steve Drexel had grown suddenly tired": Thomas J. Geraghty Papers, Margaret Herrick Library, Academy of Motion Picture Arts and Sciences, Beverly Hills, CA.

"They would retire to the main salon": *Moving Picture World*, May 1932.

"a larger than life personality": Melissa Schaefer, interview with author, 2012.

Fairbanks, as was his dapper wont: *San Antonio Light*, May 15, 1932.

"I had a pair of white linen knickers": *Oakland Tribune*, August 21, 1932.

He gave the tailor one of his most expensive: *San Antonio Light*, May 15, 1932.

"I never saw a dinner table deserted": *Oakland Tribune*, May 19, 1912.

A native drowned soon after eating: *Zanesville Signal*, July 31, 1932.

suggested that Fairbanks and Alba had a "discreet affair": Jeffrey Vance, *Douglas Fairbanks* (Berkeley: University of California Press, 2008), 293.

"That wasn't Doug, that was me": Herndon, *Mary Pickford and Douglas Fairbanks*, 288.

as best man at Farnum's wedding: *Evening Independent* (St. Petersburg, FL), June 9, 1932.

He frightened the locals on the Fourth of July: *San Mateo Times*, July 19, 1932.

he and Mary parted ways again: *Edwardsville Intelligencer*, July 21, 1932.

"If something isn't done": *Circleville Herald*, July 30, 1932.

he shinnied up the side: *San Mateo Times*, June 1, 1932.

"rumors were current that linked Mary's name": *Syracuse Herald*, July 31, 1932.

Doug simply "laughed like hell": Herndon, *Mary Pickford and Douglas Fairbanks*, 285.

"For my sweetheart": Fairbanks correspondence, private collection.

he forgot to pack his gun: *Tyrone Daily Herald*, October 19, 1931.

LIKE IDEA SHANTY TOWN: Fairbanks telegrams, Mary Pickford Papers, Margaret Herrick Library.

"He possesses 60 to 70 suits of clothes": *Photoplay*, November 1921.

There his records are still kept: Anderson and Sheppard, 17 Clifford Street, London W1S 3RQ.

he "had a fetish for overcoats": David Kamp, "A Style Is Born," *Vanity Fair*, November 2011.

There he was met with a door: *San Antonio Light*, December 28, 1932.

19. "Felt Terribly Blue . . . Although I Was Laughing"

a falling studio light struck her: *Fresno Bee Republican*, December 29, 1932.

Jack had been in a Paris hospital: *Modesto News Herald*, January 3, 1933.

"progressive multiple neuritis": Ibid.

she served as the first female grand marshal: *Daily News* (PA), January 2, 1933.

GOOD NIGHT DEAR FELT TERRIBLY BLUE: Mary Pickford Papers, Margaret Herrick Library.

"She's got to come along": *Syracuse Herald*, February 5, 1933.

"Mary didn't tell me she was leaving": Letitia Fairbanks and Ralph Hancock, *Doug Fairbanks: The Fourth Musketeer* (New York: Henry Holt, 1953), 235.

He caught up with Mary in Albuquerque: *Oakland Tribune*, July 25, 1933.

"I replied that I would do nothing": Mary Pickford, *Sunshine and Shadow* (New York: Doubleday, 1955), 188.

"I love my husband": *Fresno Bee Republican*, July 30, 1933.

"Mary is said to have been displeased": *Brainerd Daily Dispatch*, June 30, 1933.

"principally of ex-actresses": *Fresno Bee Republican*, October 18, 1933.

She was of the sort that would go anywhere: *Waterloo Daily Courier*, August 6, 1933.

Sylvia had hair that was *dirty* blonde: *Syracuse Herald*, May 1, 1936.

"A prop smile sterilized": *Fresno Bee Republican*, April 18, 1936.

He was a jolly old bounder: Ibid., August 11, 1933.

who was tremendously flattered by royal names: *Waterloo Daily Courier*, August 6, 1933.

the only short man anyone had seen: *Evening Independent* (OH), June 30, 1933.

He wasn't really as large and powerful: *Hayward Daily Review*, July 11, 1933.

He was going to give up his citizenship: *Fresno Bee Republican*, August 11, 1933.

He was so unpopular that United Artists: *Port Arthur News*, October 3, 1933.

"which Mary Pickford now can put first": *Bismarck Tribune*, June 11, 1934.

"has met her problems with a dignity": *San Antonio Light*, July 5, 1933.

"all a tempest in a teapot": *Ogden Standard-Examiner*, July 3, 1933.

finally caught at a London hospital: *Daily News* (PA), July 7, 1933.

"I don't want to say anything": *San Mateo Times*, July 6, 1933.

going to Italy when Sylvia went there: *Modesto News Herald*, July 8, 1933.

"I believe that a great deal of love": *Motion Picture Magazine*, March 1934.

a flat denial ("all nonsense!"): *Vidette Messenger* (Valparaiso, IN), August 14, 1933.

a joint deal between UA and London Films: *Daily Gleaner*, September 4 and 8, 1933.

he gallivanted publicly with Sylvia: *Syracuse Herald*, October 12, 1933.

she put Pickfair on the market: *Daily News* (PA), July 10, 1933.

she took the house off the market: *Dunkirk Evening Observer*, August 15, 1933.

"You are probably wondering why": Mary Pickford, letter to Nathan Burkan, November 17, 1933, Mary Pickford Papers, academy correspondence B, Margaret Herrick Library, Academy of Motion Picture Arts and Sciences, Beverly Hills, CA.

Mary officially filed suit: *Modesto Bee*, December 9, 1933.

"That destroyed the legitimate ends": *Daily Northwestern* (WI), November 9, 1933.

claiming that Doug "stole the show": Ibid.

"I cannot affirm or deny any reports": *Lowell Sun*, November 18, 1933.

"Women ought to learn that kindness": Ibid., January 5, 1934.

They cabled each other at Christmas: *Gleaner*, January 18, 1934.

"Kiss Mary and tell her": *Lincoln Star*, February 6, 1934.

no knowledge of "Miss Pickford's husband": *Oakland Tribune*, February 10, 1933.

Doug received notice of the papers: *Edwardsville Intelligencer*, February 6, 1934.

"Very embarrassing": Ibid.

"Frequently," one journalist wrote: *Nevada State Journal*, February 7, 1934.

"if Doug would woo her": *Syracuse Herald*, February 27, 1934.

Tom Geraghty scuttled back and forth: *Times Evening Herald* (New York, NY), February 13, 1934.

"It's in the bag": *Edwardsville Intelligencer*, March 27, 1934.

"a new man [who] apparently has forgotten": *Helena Daily Independent*, March 4, 1934.

"It is just a matter of time now": *Ogden Standard-Examiner*, March 12, 1934.

he rented an enormous estate: *San Mateo Times*, June 25, 1934; *Daily Gleaner*, March 23, 1935.

Tom Geraghty got lost one night: *Edwardsville Intelligencer*, August 13, 1934.

Their chambers, however, were adjoining: *New Castle News*, July 20, 1934.

She started having frequent—and public—dinner dates: *Daily Times-News* (Burlington, NC), June 18, 1934.

"Men are like naughty little boys": *Fresno Bee*, April 13, 1934.

he gave up North Mimm's Park: Ibid., July 23, 1934.

he abruptly boarded the SS *Rex*: *San Mateo Times and Daily News Leader*, August 8, 1934.

she could only speculate that her errant lover: Ibid., August 8, 1934.

He arrived in New York City in mid-August: *Syracuse Herald*, August 16, 1934.

the Colorado funeral of his sister-in-law: *Greely Daily Tribune*, August 16, 1934.

A private train car brought him: *Vidette Messenger* (IN), August 25, 1934.

But he was smiling the Fairbanks smile: *Lincoln Star*, August 21, 1934.

He met Mary in Beverly Hills: *Modesto Bee and News-Herald*, August 22, 1934.

They dined together at Pickfair that night: *Lima News*, August 22, 1934.

He was there bright and early the next morning: *Helena Daily Independent*, August 22, 1934.

they had retired to their respective corners: *Ogden-Standard Examiner*, August 24, 1934.

they inspected the gardens and discussed locations: *Nevada State Journal*, August 27, 1934.

"his old-time zest": *Galveston Daily News*, August 23, 1934.

"I won't deny it": *Oneonta Daily Star*, August 29, 1934.

She shortened her hair: *Modesto Bee and News-Herald*, September 12, 1934.

"rushed into any decision": Ibid.

They smiled distantly at each other: *Nevada State Journal*, September 19, 1934.

she and Douglas "were reconciled": *Syracuse Herald*, November 3, 1934.

"Well, they've been running around": Ibid.

Sylvia's divorce was coming up: *Daily Chronicle* (Centralia, WA), October 2, 1934.

Fairbanks was conspicuous by his absence: *Modesto Bee and News-Herald*, November 20, 1934.

"There is hardly a clue": Alistair Cooke, *Douglas Fairbanks: The Making of a Screen Character*, Museum of Modern Art Film Library Series 2 (New York: Museum of Modern Art, 1940), 30.

they were not to be disturbed: *Hayward Daily Review*, November 23, 1934.

Doug leaving the bedroom in his dressing gown: *Fresno Bee*, November 28, 1934.

"In case in after years": Pickford note to self, December 24, 1934, private collection.

20. A Living Death

"deaf to all queries": *San Mateo Times*, December 29, 1934.

He drank little: *Gleaner*, January 8, 1935.

They went to Paris: *Mansfield News*, January 8, 1935.

They were dancing until four in the morning: *Lincoln Star*, January 11, 1935.

DEAR DUBER AM NOTIFYING YOU PERSONALLY: Mary Pickford Papers, Margaret Herrick Library, Academy of Motion Picture Arts and Sciences, Beverly Hills, CA.

her voice faltered and broke: *Evening Tribune* (Albert Lea, MN), January 11, 1935.

When the judge granted the decree: *Lincoln Star*, January 11, 1935.

"Mary Pickford's decision to go through with her divorce": *Modesto Bee and News Herald*, January 1, 1935.

He was photographed in St. Moritz: *Fresno Bee Republican*, January 13, 1935; *Syracuse Herald*, January 19, 1935.

"I feel like his papa": *Hammond Times*, March 5, 1936.

From Switzerland to Rome: *Ogden Standard-Examiner*, January 29, 1935.

from Rome to London: *Gleaner*, February 8, 1935.

from there to the Bahamas: *Syracuse Herald*, February 14, 1935.

he nodded approval as Sylvia spent: *Nevada State Journal*, March 13, 1935.

he offered to "sock" reporters "in the nose": *Greely Daily Tribune*, February 20, 1935.

"For all I care": *Lowell Sun*, March 5, 1935.

"The press has treated me rotten": *Nevada State Journal*, March 10, 1935.

The London *Daily Express* held an unpopularity contest: *San Mateo Times*, March 14, 1935.

All stayed below decks: *Gleaner*, March 28, 1935.

"severe in his denunciations of the Fourth Estate": Ibid.

was leaving the company for Fox: *Ogden Standard-Examiner*, May 29, 1935.

"he personifies youth": Tino Balio, *United Artists: The Company Built by the Stars* (Madison: University of Wisconsin Press, 1976), 120.

"It is clear to me that Sam Goldwyn": Ibid., 122.

Mary wired Doug in Singapore: *Gleaner*, June 8, 1935.

a nod, a quick handshake: *Hammond Times*, July 8, 1935.

"I spent a fortune on that damned trip": Letitia Fairbanks and Ralph Hancock, *Doug Fairbanks: The Fourth Musketeer* (New York: Henry Holt, 1953), 256.

a thousand pounds of luggage: *Oakland Tribune*, July 10, 1935.

They sailed on the *Empress of Britain*: *Port Arthur News*, July 13, 1935.

Fairbanks "might have been a tired businessman": *Evening State Journal*, June 1, 1937.

"a world-weary man": *Reno Evening Gazette*, September 4, 1936.

"Finally, the jowls dropped": Peter Bogdanovich, *Who the Devil Made It* (New York: Knopf, 1997), 166.

"How can I be engaged to a man": *Kingsport Times*, July 18, 1935.

Robert would "build up a business pretext": Fairbanks and Hancock, *Doug Fairbanks*, 259.

Fairbanks had sent word ahead to refurbish: *Reno Evening Gazette*, January 4, 1936.

and to fill his private pool at the studio: *Nevada State Journal*, January 5, 1936.

"I know and the whole world knows": Mary Pickford, *Sunshine and Shadow* (New York: Doubleday, 1955), 193.

"Let's put ourselves on the shelf": Fairbanks and Hancock, *Doug Fairbanks*, 259.

"Pete sent long, long telegrams to Mary": Douglas Fairbanks Jr., *The Salad Days* (New York: Doubleday, 1988), 252.

"terribly distraught, anxious and quite unreceptive": Ibid., 254.

"The exact wording of the message is lost": Ibid., 254.

Fairbanks had boarded the *Aquitania*: *Lethbridge Herald*, February 27, 1936.

He traveled under a pseudonym: *Hayward Daily Review*, March 4, 1936.

"It's too late," he reportedly said: Fairbanks and Hancock, *Doug Fairbanks*, 261.

He arrived at Cherbourg on March 3: *Middletown Times Herald*, March 3, 1936.

leaving behind such necessities as her birth certificate: *Syracuse Herald*, March 6, 1936.

scuttling about between lawyer and government offices: *Lima News*, March 5, 1936.

trying to get the residence and marriage banns requirements waived: *Helena Independent*, March 5, 1936.

the state's attorney delivered papers: *Port Arthur News*, March 6, 1936.

city hall had closed for the day: *Ironwood Daily Globe*, March 6, 1936.

he also was without his divorce papers: *Daily Gleaner*, March 16, 1936.

under a ceiling of floating fleshy cupids: *Gettysburg Times*, March 7, 1936.

a rose-colored coat with a large corsage: *Hammond Times*, March 7, 1936.

"Douglas Fairbanks, Junior's pa": *Headline Parade*, March 7, 1936.

"Now dearie, please!": *Fresno Bee*, March 8, 1936.

They flew to Spain on a private plane: *Evening Tribune* (MN), March 9, 1936.

"It cost me 10,000 francs": *Vidette Messenger* (IN), March 17, 1936.

"a has-been": Fairbanks and Hancock, *Doug Fairbanks*, 263.

they were still in their evening clothes: *Syracuse Herald*, May 1, 1936.

"Tell them you enjoyed the skyline": Ibid.

Sam Goldwyn would coproduce *Marco Polo*: *Syracuse Herald*, October 27, 1936.

"Three meetings later, Fairbanks found Goldwyn": A. Scott Berg, *Goldwyn: A Biography* (New York: Knopf, 1989), 317.

"I'll let the young fellows carry on": *Arcadia Tribune*, July 24, 1936.

The rumored price was $50,000: *Charleston Gazette*, January 28, 1936.

O'Brien referred to her as "Lady Ashcan": Booton Herndon, *Mary Pickford and Douglas Fairbanks: The Most Popular Couple the World Has Ever Known* (New York: Norton, 1977), 292.

he was maintaining an establishment in London: *Evening State Journal* (Lincoln, NE), January 7, 1938.

A fire swept through Kenneth Ridge: *Seattle Daily Times*, May 16, 1939.

Sam Goldwyn, now with control: *Edwardsville Intelligencer*, August 19, 1938.

Doug was breakfasting: *Kansas City Journal-Post*, February 3, 1936.

"He shook his head": Ibid.

During the course of a heated debate: Robert Windeler, *Sweetheart: The Story of Mary Pickford* (New York: Praeger, 1973), 181.

"How dare you talk to my wife like that?": Fairbanks and Hancock, *Doug Fairbanks*, 264.

"'All my life I've been an adventurer:'" Berg, *Goldwyn*, 317.

"If the deal can be concluded": Balio, *United Artists*, 146.

WE SHOULD NEVER HAVE GIVEN LENGTHY OPTION: Ibid., 147–148.

The most pointed came after the February 1938 visit: *Nevada State Journal*, February 21, 1938; *Daily Herald* (Circleville, OH), February 25, 1938; *Fresno Bee Republican*, March 2, 1938.

"For a man my age": Fairbanks and Hancock, *Doug Fairbanks*, 265.

He donated all the films: *Springfield Republican*, April 30, 1939.

Elsa Maxwell's "Barn Party": *Portsmouth Times*, January 19, 1937.

He still topped the best-dressed lists: *Vidette Messenger* (IN), May 12, 1938.

the most extravagant patron: *Times Herald* (New York, NY), November 24, 1936.

He was found on the slopes of St. Moritz: *Fitchburg Sentinel*, December 12, 1936.

He "at least behaved as if he was happy": Fairbanks Jr., *Salad Days*, 325.

"When I think of him I always think": Douglas Fairbanks Papers, scrapbook 1: condolence letters, Margaret Herrick Library.

JUST HEARD FROM SILVERSTONE: Douglas Fairbanks Jr. Papers, Howard Gotlieb Archival Research Center, Mugar Memorial Library, Boston University, Boston, MA.

"to think of the past years at his service": Douglas Fairbanks Papers, scrapbook 1: condolence letters, Margaret Herrick Library.

"I got out just before the public got wise": *Times-Picayune*, May 12, 1939.

Germany would "go ahead with its program": *Fitchburg Sentinel*, September 2, 1939.

"Britain is so ready, and [the Nazis] know it": Ibid.

A quick run on the *Dixie Clipper*: *Marietta Journal*, September 6, 1939.

"Silverstone will be subservient to Sam": Balio, *United Artists*, 151.

"pictures would not be good enough": Ibid., 155.

"I've been your friend for many years": Berg, *Goldwyn*, 337.

There was jubilation in the offices of United Artists: *Variety*, December 28, 1939.

He had sent Jayar a telegram that afternoon: Douglas Fairbanks Jr. Papers, box 157, Howard Gotlieb Archival Research Center.

"We played games and were frightfully gay": Unless otherwise indicated, quotes from this section are from carbon copies of responses to condolence letters in Douglas Fairbanks Papers, scrapbook 1: condolence letters, Margaret Herrick Library.

"When my turn came": Fairbanks Jr., *Salad Days*, 347.

"I'm tired," she reported him replying: Herndon, *Mary Pickford and Douglas Fairbanks*, 299.

"They put him to bed": *Variety*, December 13, 1939.

impulsively kissed him on the forehead: Fairbanks Jr., *Salad Days*, 3.

"Don't say it, Gwynne!": Pickford, *Sunshine and Shadow*, 207.

she would cry out in the night for him: Windeler, *Sweetheart*, 4.

"old timers who worked with Fairbanks": *Variety*, December 13, 1939.

Standing silent on the lawn: Unmarked clippings in Douglas Fairbanks Papers, scrapbook 1: condolence letters, Margaret Herrick Library.

Chico De Verdi, violinist, conducted: *Variety*, December 16, 1939.

"the symbol of romance and eternal youth": *Educational Screen*, April, 1928.

He was clad in a frock cutaway coat: *Los Angeles Examiner*, Dec 16, 1939.

The card had one word: Douglas Fairbanks Papers, scrapbook 1: condolence letters, Margaret Herrick Library.

Bibliography

Amid, John. *With the Movie Makers*. Boston: Lothrop, Lee & Shepard, 1923.

Astor, Mary. *A Life on Film*. New York: Bantam Doubleday Dell, 1967.

Balio, Tino. *United Artists: The Company Built by the Stars*. Madison: University of Wisconsin Press, 1976.

Basten, Fred. *Glorious Technicolor: The Movies' Magic Rainbow*. Easton Studio Press, 2005.

Beauchamp, Cari. *Without Lying Down: Frances Marion and the Powerful Women of Early Hollywood*. Berkeley: University of California Press, 1997.

Berg, A. Scott. *Goldwyn: A Biography*. New York: Knopf, 1989.

Bernds, Edward. *Mr. Bernds Goes to Hollywood: My Early Life and Career in Sound Recording at Columbia with Frank Capra and Others*. Lanham, MD: Scarecrow, 1999.

Birchard, Robert S. *Cecil B. DeMille's Hollywood*. Lexington: University Press of Kentucky, 2004.

Bitzer, G. W. *Billy Bitzer: His Story*. New York: Farrar, Straus and Giroux, 1973.

Bogdanovich, Peter. *Who the Devil Made It*. New York: Knopf, 1997.

Brownlow, Kevin. *Behind the Mask of Innocence*. New York: Knopf, 1990.

———. *Hollywood: The Pioneers*. New York: Knopf, 1979.

———. *Mary Pickford Rediscovered: Rare Pictures of a Hollywood Legend*. New York: Harry N. Abrams, 1999.

———. *The Parade's Gone By*. New York: Knopf, 1968.

———. *The War, the West, and the Wilderness*. New York: Knopf, 1979.

Card, James. *Seductive Cinema: The Art of Silent Film*. New York: Knopf, 1994.

Carey, Gary. *Anita Loos: A Biography*. New York: Knopf, 1988.

———. *Doug & Mary: A Biography of Douglas Fairbanks & Mary Pickford*. New York: E. P. Dutton, 1977.

Case, Frank. *Do Not Disturb*. New York: Frederick A. Stokes, 1940.

———. *Tales of a Wayward Inn*. New York: Frederick A. Stokes, 1938.

Chaplin, Charlie. *My Autobiography*. Brooklyn: Melville House, 2012.

Cherchi Usai, Paolo, ed. *The Griffith Project*. Vol. 6. London: British Film Institute, 2002.

——. *The Griffith Project*. Vol. 8. London: British Film Institute, 2004.

——. *The Griffith Project*. Vol. 9. London: British Film Institute, 2005.

Cohan, George M. *Twenty Years on Broadway, and the Years It Took to Get There*. New York: Harper & Brothers, 1924.

Cooke, Alistair. *Douglas Fairbanks: The Making of a Screen Character*. Museum of Modern Art Film Library Series 2. New York: Museum of Modern Art, 1940.

DeMille, Cecil. *The Autobiography of Cecil B. DeMille*. Edited by Donald Hayne. Englewood Cliffs, NJ: Prentice-Hall, 1959.

Dumas, Alexandre. *The Three Musketeers*. Translated by Richard Pevear. New York: Viking, 2006.

Everett, Marshall. *The Great Chicago Theater Disaster*. Publishers Union of America, 1904.

Eyman, Scott. *John Wayne: The Life and Legend*. New York: Simon & Schuster, 2014.

——. *Mary Pickford, America's Sweetheart*. New York: Donald I. Fine, 1990.

——. *The Speed of Sound: Hollywood and the Talkie Revolution, 1926–1930*. Baltimore: Johns Hopkins University Press, 1999.

Fairbanks, Douglas. *Douglas Fairbanks: In His Own Words*. New York: iUniverse, 2006.

——. *Youth Points the Way*. New York: D. Appleton, 1924.

Fairbanks, Douglas, Jr. *The Salad Days*. New York: Doubleday, 1988.

Fairbanks, Letitia, and Ralph Hancock. *Doug Fairbanks: The Fourth Musketeer*. New York: Henry Holt, 1953.

Fenin, George N., and William K. Everson. *The Western: From Silents to the Seventies*. New York: Grossman, 1973.

Fleming, E. J. *Wallace Reid: The Life and Death of a Hollywood Idol*. Jefferson, NC: McFarland, 2007.

Flom, Eric L. *Silent Film Stars on the Stages of Seattle: A History of Performances by Hollywood Notables*. Jefferson, NC: McFarland, 2009.

Florey, Robert. Florey, Robert. *Deux ans dans les studios Americains*. Paris: Editions d'Aujourd'hui, 1984.

——. *Filmland: Los Angeles et Hollywood les capitales du cinema*. Paris: Editions de Cinemagazine, 1923.

Giddens, Gary. *Bing Crosby: A Pocketful of Dreams; The Early Years, 1903–1940*. Boston: Little, Brown, 2001.

Gish, Lillian, and Ann Pinchot. *Lillian Gish: The Movies, Mr. Griffith, and Me*. Englewood Cliffs, NJ: Prentice-Hall, 1969.

Gordon, Jan, and Cora Gordon. *Star-Dust in Hollywood*. London: George G. Harrap, 1930.

Graham, Cooper C., Steven Higgins, Elaine Mancini, and Joao Luiz Viera. *D. W. Griffith and the Biograph Company*. Filmmakers Series, no. 10. Metuchen, NJ: Scarecrow, 1985.

Griffith, Allen. *Lessons in Elocution*. Chicago: Adams, Blackmer & Lyon, 1871.

Haines, Richard W. *Technicolor Movies: The History of Dye Transfer Printing*. Jefferson, NC: McFarland, 2003.

Henabery, Joseph. *Before, In and After Hollywood: The Autobiography of Joseph E. Henabery*. Lanham, MD: Scarecrow, 1997.

Henderson, Robert M. *D. W. Griffith: The Years at Biograph*. New York: Farrar, Straus and Giroux, 1970.

Herndon, Booton. *Mary Pickford and Douglas Fairbanks: The Most Popular Couple the World Has Ever Known*. New York: Norton, 1977.

Hodges, Graham Russell. *Anna May Wong: From Laundryman's Daughter to Hollywood Legend*. New York: Palgrave Macmillan, 2004.

Irwin, Will. *The House That Shadows Built: The Story of Adolph Zukor and the Rise of the Motion Picture Industry*. New York: Doubleday, Doran & Company, 1929.

Kirkpatrick, Sidney. *A Cast of Killers*. New York: E. P. Dutton, 1986.

Knoblock, Edward. *Round the Room*. London: Chapman and Hall, 1939.

Kobal, John. *People Will Talk*. New York: Knopf, 1986.

Koszarski, Richard. *Fort Lee: The Film Town (1904–2004)*. Bloomington: Indiana University Press, 2004.

———. *Hollywood on the Hudson: Film and Television in New York from Griffith to Sarnoff*. New Brunswick, NJ: Rutgers University Press, 2008.

Lahue, Kalton C. *Dreams for Sale: The Rise and Fall of the Triangle Film Corporation*. New York: A. S. Barnes, 1971.

Lasky, Jesse L., Jr. *Whatever Happened to Hollywood?* New York: Funk & Wagnalls, 1975.

Leider, Emily Wortis. *Dark Lover: The Life and Death of Rudolph Valentino*. New York: Farrar, Straus and Giroux, 2003.

Leloir, Maurice. *Cinq mois a Hollywood avec Douglas Fairbanks*. Paris: J. Peyronnet, 1929.

Lennig, Arthur. *Stroheim*. Lexington: University Press of Kentucky, 2000.

Lombardi, Frederic. *Allan Dwan and the Rise and Decline of the Hollywood Studios*. Jefferson, NC: McFarland, 2013.

Loos, Anita. *Anita Loos Rediscovered: Film Treatments and Fiction*. Edited by Cari Beauchamp and Mary Loos. Berkeley: University of California Press, 2003.

———. *Cast of Thousands*. New York: Grosset & Dunlap, 1977.

———. *A Girl Like I*. New York: Viking, 1966.

———. *The Talmadge Girls: A Memoir*. New York: Viking, 1978.

Love, Bessie. *From Hollywood with Love*. London: Elm Tree Books, 1977.

Lyle, Eugene P., Jr. *Blaze Derringer*. New York: Doubleday, Page, 1910.

Marion, Frances. *Off With Their Heads! A Serio-Comic Tale of Hollywood*. New York: Macmillan, 1972.

McKinley, Cameron Curtis. "California Dream Realized: The Former Ranch of Douglas Fairbanks." *Architectural Digest*, September 1982.

Menjou, Adolphe. *It Took Nine Tailors*. New York: McGraw-Hill, 1948.

Milne, Peter. *Motion Picture Directing: The Facts and Theories of the Newest Art.* New York: Falk, 1922.

Moss, Marilyn Ann. *Raoul Walsh: The True Adventures of Hollywood's Legendary Director.* Lexington: University Press of Kentucky, 2011.

Nelson, Al P. "Roy E. Aitkin: Movie Mogul." *Northliner Magazine*, Autumn 1975.

Parker, Dorothy. "Reformers: A Hymn of Hate." In *Nonsenseorship*, 95–98. New York: G. P. Putnam's Sons, 1922.

Parrish, Robert. *Growing Up in Hollywood.* Boston: Little, Brown, 1988.

Pickford, Mary. *Sunshine and Shadow.* New York: Doubleday, 1955.

Prichard, K., and Hesketh Prichard. *Don Q's Love Story.* New York: Grosset & Dunlap, 1925.

Richards, Jeffrey. *Swordsmen of the Screen, from Douglas Fairbanks to Michael York.* Boston: Routledge and Kegan Paul, 1977.

Robinson, David. *Chaplin: His Life and Art.* New York: McGraw-Hill, 1985.

Rosenberg, Bernard, and Harry Silverstein. *The Real Tinsel.* New York: Macmillan, 1970.

Rubens, Alma. *Alma Rubens, Silent Snowbird.* Edited by Gary Don Rhodes and Alexander Webb. Jefferson, NC: McFarland, 2006.

Russell, Charles. *Good Medicine: The Illustrated Letters of Charles M. Russell.* New York: Doubleday, 1966.

Schickel, Richard. *D. W. Griffith: An American Life.* New York: Simon & Schuster, 1984.

———. *The Fairbanks Album.* New York Graphic Society, 1975.

———. *His Picture in the Papers: A Speculation on Celebrity in America Based on the Life of Douglas Fairbanks, Sr.* New York: Charterhouse, 1974.

Sennett, Mack. *King of Comedy.* The Lively Arts. San Francisco: Mercury House, 1954.

Sherwood, Robert E. *The Best Moving Pictures of 1922–23.* New York: Revisionist, 1974.

Sragow, Michael. *Victor Fleming: An American Movie Master.* New York: Pantheon Books, 2008.

Swanson, Gloria. *Swanson on Swanson.* New York: Random House, 1980.

Talmey, Allene. *Doug and Mary and Others.* New York: Macy-Masius, 1927.

Taves, Brian. *Robert Florey, the French Expressionist.* Filmmakers Series, no. 14. Metuchen, NJ: Scarecrow, 1987.

Thomas, Augustus. *Arizona: A Romance of the Great Southwest.* New York: Grosset & Dunlap, 1914.

Thompson, Frank T. *William A. Wellman.* Filmmakers Series, no. 4. Metuchen, NJ: Scarecrow, 1983.

Tibbetts, John C. *Douglas Fairbanks and the American Century.* Jackson: University Press of Mississippi, 2014.

Tibbetts, John C., and James Michael Welsh. *His Majesty the American: The Cinema of Douglas Fairbanks, Sr.* South Brunswick, NJ: A. S. Barnes, 1977.

Vance, Jeffrey. *Douglas Fairbanks.* Berkeley: University of California Press, 2008.

Vogel, Michelle. *Olive Thomas: The Life and Death of a Silent Film Beauty.* Jefferson, NC: McFarland, 2007.

Wagenknecht, Edward. *The Movies in the Age of Innocence.* New York: Ballantine Books, 1962.

Walsh, Raoul. *Each Man in His Time: The Life Story of a Director.* New York: Farrar, Straus and Giroux, 1974.

Warde, Frederick. *Fifty Years of Make Believe.* New York: International Press Syndicate, 1920. Reprint, Miami: HardPress, 2013.

Westmore, Frank, and Muriel Davidson. *The Westmores of Hollywood.* Philadelphia: Lippincott, 1976.

Whitfield, Eileen. *Pickford: The Woman Who Made Hollywood.* Lexington: University Press of Kentucky, 1997.

Windeler, Robert. *Sweetheart: The Story of Mary Pickford.* New York: Praeger, 1973.

Wise, Thomas A. *A Gentleman from Mississippi.* New York: J. S. Ogilvie, 1908.

Young, James. *Making Up.* New York: M. Witmark & Sons, 1905.

Zierold, Norman. *The Moguls.* New York: Coward-McCann, 1969.

Index